D0456890

THE EMPATHIC CIVILIZATION

ALSO BY JEREMY RIFKIN

Common Sense II

Own Your Own Job

Who Should Play God?
(WITH TED HOWARD)

The Emerging Order

The North Will Rise Again
(WITH RANDY BARBER)

Entropy
(WITH TED HOWARD)

Algeny

Declaration of a Heretic

Time Wars

Biosphere Politics

Beyond Beef

Voting Green
(WITH CAROL GRUNEWALD)

The End of Work

The Biotech Century

The Age of Access

The Hydrogen Economy

The European Dream

THE EMPATHIC CIVILIZATION

THE RACE TO GLOBAL CONSCIOUSNESS IN A WORLD IN CRISIS

JEREMY RIFKIN

JEREMY P. TARCHER/PENGUIN

A MEMBER OF PENGUIN GROUP (USA) INC.

New York

JEREMY P. TARCHER/PENGUIN
Published by the Penguin Group
Penguin Group (USA) Inc., 375 Hudson Street, New York, New York 10014, USA • Penguin
Group (Canada), 90 Eglinton Avenue East, Suite 700, Toronto, Ontario M4P 2Y3, Canada
(a division of Pearson Penguin Canada Inc.) • Penguin Books Ltd, 80 Strand, London WC2R 0RL,
England • Penguin Ireland, 25 St Stephen's Green, Dublin 2, Ireland (a division of Penguin Books Ltd)
• Penguin Group (Australia), 250 Camberwell Road, Camberwell, Victoria 3124, Australia (a division
of Pearson Australia Group Pty Ltd) • Penguin Books India Pvt Ltd, 11 Community Centre, Panchsheel
Park, New Delhi–110 017, India • Penguin Group (NZ), 67 Apollo Drive, Rosedale, North Shore
0632, New Zealand (a division of Pearson New Zealand Ltd) • Penguin Books (South Africa)
(Pty) Ltd, 24 Sturdee Avenue, Rosebank, Johannesburg 2196, South Africa

Penguin Books Ltd, Registered Offices: 80 Strand, London WC2R 0RL, England

Copyright © 2009 by Jeremy Rifkin
All rights reserved. No part of this book may be reproduced, scanned, or distributed
in any printed or electronic form without permission. Please do not participate in or
encourage piracy of copyrighted materials in violation of the author's rights. Purchase
only authorized editions. Published simultaneously in Canada

Most Tarcher/Penguin books are available at special quantity discounts for bulk
purchase for sales promotions, premiums, fund-raising, and educational needs. Special
books or book excerpts also can be created to fit specific needs. For details, write
Penguin Group (USA) Inc. Special Markets, 375 Hudson Street, New York, NY 10014.

Library of Congress Cataloging-in-Publication Data

Rifkin, Jeremy.
The empathic civilization: the race to global consciousness in a world in crisis / Jeremy Rifkin.
p.   cm.
ISBN 978-1-58542-765-9
1. Empathy.   2. Conduct of life.   3. Civilization, Modern—21st century—Forecasting.
4. Twenty-first century—Forecasts.   5. Social prediction.   I. Title.
BJ1475.R54   2009   2009036616
901—dc22

Printed in the United States of America
1   3   5   7   9   10   8   6   4   2

Book design by Marysarah Quinn

While the author has made every effort to provide accurate telephone numbers
and Internet addresses at the time of publication, neither the publisher nor the
author assumes any responsibility for errors, or for changes that occur after
publication. Further, the publisher does not have any control over and does not
assume any responsibility for author or third-party websites or their content.

January 27, 1945

To all those who survived.
To all those who perished.
To all those yet to come.

To Carol Grunewald

Acknowledgments

I WOULD LIKE to thank Lisa Friedberg for her outstanding work directing the research for the book. The research extended for more than a four-year period and involved thousands of source materials across every major academic discipline and professional field. Lisa's extraordinary ability to locate vital information and coordinate and categorize the sheer volume of research at hand was instrumental in moving the project forward.

Thanks to Dr. Sally Wengrover for coordinating the final preparation of the book. Her keen eye for detail and extensive knowledge of many of the areas covered in the book were invaluable. Thanks also to the following research interns who contributed to the book: Deanna Cho, Juli Diamond, Kristina Dunphy, Daniel Frawley, Ashley Goldwasser, Eric Hammerschmidt, Kara Horton, Adriane Javier, Jin-Young Kang, Alex Jue, Anirudh Khandelwal, Siddi Khara, Andrew Linowes, Georg Loefflmann, Vijay Ramakrishnan, Cjay Roughgarden, Richard Savage, Erica Shapiro, Shivani Softa, Jenna Trebs, Marc Vincent, Miriam Weiss, and Comly Wilson.

I'd like to extend my appreciation to Clara Mack for her help in preparing the resource material. Clara's penchant for perfection helped facilitate the entire research process. I would like to thank Jennifer Lawrence and Nicholas Easley for their meticulous editorial assistance during the last several weeks of the project. Thanks to Drew Johnston and Angelo Consoli for their many contributions at various stages of the project. Thanks as well to Leda Scheintaub for her expert copyediting of the final manuscript. I'd also like to thank my agent, Robert Barnett.

I'd like to extend my warm gratitude to my old friend Jeremy Tarcher for making a place for me in his publishing fold over these many years, and to Joel Fotinos, my publisher, for his unswerving support, as well as to Lance Fitzgerald for ensuring a wide reading audience for my books around the world.

A very special thanks to my longtime editor, Mitch Horowitz, for his critical help in shaping the direction of the book. Our many fruitful—and enjoyable—conversations over nearly half a decade were instrumental in honing the final manuscript.

Thanks to Tarcher/Penguin for generously allowing me to cite material from my previous books that were particularly apropos in advancing the themes in *The Empathic Civilization.*

Finally, thanks to my wife, Carol Grunewald, for the many spirited discussions of the critical themes and ideas that make up the heart of the book.

CONTENTS

INTRODUCTION

This book presents a new interpretation of the history of civilization by looking at the empathic evolution of the human race and the profound ways it has shaped our development and will likely decide our fate as a species.

A radical new view of human nature is emerging in the biological and cognitive sciences and creating controversy in intellectual circles, the business community, and government. Recent discoveries in brain science and child development are forcing us to rethink the long-held belief that human beings are, by nature, aggressive, materialistic, utilitarian, and self-interested. The dawning realization that we are a fundamentally empathic species has profound and far-reaching consequences for society.

These new understandings of human nature open the door to a never-before-told journey. The pages that follow reveal the dramatic story of the development of human empathy from the rise of the great theological civilizations, to the ideological age that dominated the eighteenth and nineteenth centuries, the psychological era that characterized much of the twentieth century, and the emerging dramaturgical period of the twenty-first century.

Viewing economic history from an empathic lens allows us to uncover rich new strands of the human narrative that lay previously hidden. The result is a new social tapestry—The Empathic Civilization—woven from a wide range of fields, including literature and the arts, theology, philosophy, anthropology, sociology, political science, psychology, and communications theory.

At the very core of the human story is the paradoxical relationship between empathy and entropy. Throughout history new energy regimes have converged with new communication revolutions, creating ever more complex societies. More technologically advanced civilizations, in turn, have brought diverse people together, heightened empathic sensitivity, and expanded human consciousness. But these increasingly more complicated milieus require more extensive energy use and speed us toward resource depletion.

The irony is that our growing empathic awareness has been made possible by an ever-greater consumption of the Earth's energy and other resources, resulting in a dramatic deterioration of the health of the planet.

We now face the haunting prospect of approaching global empathy in a highly energy-intensive, interconnected world, riding on the back of an escalating entropy bill that now threatens catastrophic climate change and our very existence. Resolving the empathy/entropy paradox will likely be the critical test of our species' ability to survive and flourish on Earth in the future. This will necessitate a fundamental rethinking of our philosophical, economic, and social models.

Toward this end, the book begins with an analysis of the empathy/ entropy conundrum and the central role this unlikely dynamic has played in determining the direction of human history. Part I is given over to an examination of the new view of human nature that is emerging in the natural and social sciences and in the humanities, with the discovery of *Homo empathicus*. Part II is devoted to exploring the empathic surges and the great transformations in consciousness that have accompanied each more complex energy-consuming civilization, with the aim of providing a new rendering of human history and the meaning of human existence. Part III reports on the current race to global peak empathy against the backdrop of an ever-quickening entropic destruction of the Earth's biosphere. Finally, we turn our attention to the fledgling Third Industrial Revolution that is ushering in a new era of "distributed capitalism" and the beginning of biosphere consciousness. We are on the cusp, I believe, of an epic shift into a "climax" global economy and a fundamental repositioning of human life on the planet. The Age of Reason is being eclipsed by the Age of Empathy.

The most important question facing humanity is this: Can we reach global empathy in time to avoid the collapse of civilization and save the Earth?

ONE

THE HIDDEN PARADOX
OF HUMAN HISTORY

THE EVENING of December 24, 1914, Flanders. The first world war in history was entering into its fifth month. Millions of soldiers were bedded down in makeshift trenches latticed across the European countryside. In many places the opposing armies were dug in within thirty to fifty yards of each other and within shouting distance. The conditions were hellish. The bitter-cold winter air chilled to the bone. The trenches were waterlogged. Soldiers shared their quarters with rats and vermin. Lacking adequate latrines, the stench of human excrement was everywhere. The men slept upright to avoid the muck and sludge of their makeshift arrangements. Dead soldiers littered the no-man's-land between opposing forces, the bodies left to rot and decompose within yards of their still-living comrades who were unable to collect them for burial.

As dusk fell over the battlefields, something extraordinary happened. The Germans began lighting candles on the thousands of small Christmas trees that had been sent to the front to lend some comfort to the men. The German soldiers then began to sing Christmas carols—first "Silent Night," then a stream of other songs followed. The English soldiers were stunned. One soldier, gazing in disbelief at the enemy lines, said the blazed trenches looked "like the footlights of a theater."[1] The English soldiers responded with applause, at first tentatively, then with exuberance. They began to sing Christmas carols back to their German foes to equally robust applause.

A few men from both sides crawled out of their trenches and began to walk across the no-man's-land toward each other. Soon hundreds followed. As word spread across the front, thousands of men poured out of their trenches. They shook hands, exchanged cigarettes and cakes and showed photos of their families. They talked about where they hailed from, reminisced about Christmases past, and joked about the absurdity of war.

The next morning, as the Christmas sun rose over the battlefield of Europe, tens of thousands of men—some estimates put the number as high as 100,000 soldiers—talked quietly with one another.[2] Enemies just twenty-four hours earlier, they found themselves helping each other bury their dead comrades. More than a few pickup soccer matches were reported. Even officers at the front participated, although when the news filtered back to the high command in the rear, the generals took a less enthusiastic view of the affair. Worried that the truce might undermine military morale, the generals quickly took measures to rein in their troops.

The surreal "Christmas truce" ended as abruptly as it began—all in all, a small blip in a war that would end in November 1918 with 8.5 million military deaths in the greatest episode of human carnage in the annals of history until that time.[3] For a few short hours, no more than a day, tens of thousands of human beings broke ranks, not only from their commands but from their allegiances to country, to show their common humanity. Thrown together to maim and kill, they courageously stepped outside of their institutional duties to commiserate with one another and to celebrate each other's lives.

While the battlefield is supposed to be a place where heroism is measured in one's willingness to kill and die for a noble cause that transcends one's everyday life, these men chose a different type of courage. They reached out to each other's very private suffering and sought solace in each other's plight. Walking across no-man's-land, they found themselves in one another. The strength to comfort each other flowed from a deep unspoken sense of their individual vulnerability and their unrequited desire for the companionship of their fellows.

It was, without reserve, a very human moment. Still, it was reported as a strange lapse at the time. A century later, we commemorate the episode as a nostalgic interlude in a world we have come to define in very different terms.

For nearly seventeen hundred years in the West, we were led to believe that human beings are sinners in a fallen world. If we were to hope for a respite, we would have to settle for salvation in the next world. At the cusp of the modern era, the British philosopher Thomas Hobbes quipped that "the life of man [is] solitary, poor, nasty, brutish, and short."[4] His only answer to the nightmare of human existence was to call for the tight hand of government authority to keep people from killing each other in a war of "each against all."

Enlightenment philosophers tempered Hobbes's less-than-kind view of the human condition with a number of new narratives to explain human nature. John Locke, the English philosopher, argued that human beings are born tabula rasa—our minds are a blank slate—and then molded by society. But to what end? Here Locke compromised his blank slate theory just enough to suggest that we come into life with a predisposition. We are, he proclaimed, an acquisitive animal by nature. We use our hands and tools to expropriate nature's resources, transforming the Earth's vast wasteland into productive property. To be productive, declared Locke, is man's ultimate mission, the reason for his very existence on Earth. He wrote,

> Land that is left wholly to nature, that hath no improvement
> of pasturage, tillage, or planting, is called, as indeed it is,
> waste. . . .[5] Let any one consider what the difference is
> between an acre of land planted with tobacco or sugar, sown
> with wheat or barley, and an acre of the same land lying in
> common, without any husbandry upon it, and he will find,
> that the improvement of labour makes the far greater part of
> the value.[6]

Locke believed that "[t]he negation of nature is the way toward happiness."[7]

A century later, the English philosopher Jeremy Bentham qualified the idea of happiness by suggesting that the universal human condition boiled down to the avoidance of pain and the optimizing of pleasure. His utilitarian spin was later sexualized by Sigmund Freud at the turn of the twentieth century in the form of the pleasure principle. Each newborn, Freud reasoned, is predisposed to seek pleasure, and by this he meant eroticized pleasure. The mother's breast is more than a mere source of nourishment—it is also a source of sexual gratification that serves the infant's insatiable libido.

Yet what transpired in the battlefields of Flanders on Christmas Eve 1914 between tens of thousands of young men had nothing to do with original sin or productive labor. And the pleasure those men sought in each other's company bore little resemblance to the superficial rendering of pleasure offered up by nineteenth-century utilitarians and even less to Freud's rather pathological account of a human race preoccupied by the erotic impulse.

The men at Flanders expressed a far deeper human sensibility—one that emanates from the very marrow of human existence and that transcends the portals of time and the exigencies of whatever contemporary orthodoxy happens to rule. We need only ask ourselves why we feel so heartened at what these men did. They chose to be human. And the central human quality they expressed was empathy for one another.

Empathic distress is as old as our species and is traceable far back into our ancestral past, to our link with our primate relatives and, before them, our mammalian ancestors. It is only very recently, however, that biologists and cognitive scientists have begun to discover primitive behavioral manifestations of empathy throughout the mammalian kingdom, among animals that nurture their young. They report that primates, and especially humans, with our more developed neocortex, are particularly wired for empathy.

Without a well-developed concept of selfhood, however, mature empathic expression would be impossible. Child development researchers have long noted that infants as young as one or two days old are able to identify the cries of other newborns and will cry in return, in what is called rudimentary empathetic distress.[8] That's because the empathic predisposition is embedded into our biology. But the real sense of empathic extension doesn't begin to appear until the age of eighteen months to two and a half years, when the infant begins to develop a sense of self and other.[9] In other words, it is only when the infant is able to understand that someone else exists as a separate being from himself that he is able to experience the others' condition as if it were his own and respond with the appropriate comfort.

In studies, two-year-old children will often wince in discomfort at the sight of another child's suffering and come over to him to share a toy, or cuddle, or bring him over to their own mother for assistance. The extent to which empathetic consciousness develops, broadens, and deepens during childhood, adolescence, and adulthood, depends on early parenting behavior—which psychologists call attachment—as well as the values and worldview of the culture one is embedded in and the potential exposure to others.

THE HUMAN STORY THAT'S NEVER BEEN TOLD

It has become fashionable in recent times to question the notion that there may be an underlying meaning to the human saga that permeates and transcends all of the various cultural narratives that make up the diverse history of our species and that provides the social glue for each of our odysseys. Such thoughts would most likely elicit a collective grimace from many postmodern scholars. The evidence suggests, however, that there may be an overarching theme to the human journey.

Our official chroniclers—the historians—have given short shrift to empathy as a driving force in the unfolding of human history. Historians, by and large, write about social conflict and wars, great heroes and evil wrongdoers, technological progress and the exercise of power, economic injustices and the redress of social grievances. When historians touch on philosophy, it is usually in relationship to the disposition of power. Rarely do we hear of the other side of the human experience that speaks to our deeply social nature and the evolution and extension of human affection and its impact on culture and society.

The German philosopher Georg Wilhelm Fredrich Hegel once remarked that happiness is "the blank pages of history" because they are "periods of harmony." Happy people generally live out their existence in the "microworld" of close familial relations and extended social affiliations.

History, on the other hand, is more often than not made by the disgruntled and discontented, the angry and rebellious—those interested in exercising authority and exploiting others and their victims, interested in righting wrongs and restoring justice. By this reckoning, much of the history that is written is about the pathology of power.

Perhaps that is why, when we come to think about human nature, we have such a bleak analysis. Our collective memory is measured in terms of crises and calamities, harrowing injustices, and terrifying episodes of brutality inflicted on each other and our fellow creatures. But if these were the defining elements of human experience, we would have perished as a species long ago.

All of which raises the question "Why have we come to think of life in such dire terms?" The answer is that tales of misdeeds and woe surprise us. They are unexpected and, therefore, trigger alarm and heighten our interest. That is because such events are novel and not the norm, but they are newsworthy and for that reason they are the stuff of history.

The everyday world is quite different. Although life as it's lived on the ground, close to home, is peppered with suffering, stresses, injustices, and foul play, it is, for the most part, lived out in hundreds of small acts of kindness and generosity. Comfort and compassion between people creates goodwill, establishes the bonds of sociality, and gives joy to people's lives. Much of our daily interaction with our fellow human beings is empathic because that is our core nature. Empathy is the very means by which we create social life and advance civilization. In short, it is the extraordinary evolution of empathic consciousness that is the quintessential underlying story of human history, even if it has not been given the serious attention it deserves by our historians.

There is still another reason why empathy has yet to be seriously examined in all of its anthropological and historical detail. The difficulty lies in the evolutionary process itself. Empathic consciousness has grown slowly over the 175,000 years of human history. It has sometimes flourished, only to recede for long periods of time. Its progress has been irregular, but its trajectory is clear. Empathic development and the development of selfhood go hand in hand and accompany the increasingly complex energy-consuming social structures that make up the human journey. (We will examine this relationship throughout the book.)

Because the development of selfhood is so completely intertwined with the development of empathic consciousness, the very term "empathy" didn't become part of the human vocabulary until 1909—about the same time that modern psychology began to explore the internal dynamics of the unconscious and consciousness itself. In other words, it wasn't until human beings were developed enough in human selfhood that they could begin thinking about the nature of their innermost feelings and thoughts in relation to other people's innermost feelings and thoughts that they were able to recognize the existence of empathy, find the appropriate metaphors to discuss it, and probe the deep recesses of its multiple meanings.

We have to remember that as recently as six generations ago, our great-great-grandparents—living circa mid-to-late 1880s—were not encultured to think therapeutically. My own grandparents were unable to probe their feelings and thinking in order to analyze how their past emotional experiences and relationships affected their behavior toward others and their sense of self. They were untutored in the notion of unconscious drives and terms like transference and projection. Today, a hundred years after the coming of the age of psychology, young people are thoroughly immersed in therapeutic consciousness and comfortable with thinking about, getting in touch with and analyzing their own innermost feelings, emotions, and thoughts—as well as those of their fellows.

The precursor to empathy was the word "sympathy"—a term that came into vogue during the European Enlightenment. The Scottish economist Adam Smith wrote a book on moral sentiments in 1759. Although far better known for his theory of the marketplace, Smith devoted considerable attention to the question of human emotions. Sympathy, for Smith, Hume, other philosophers, and literary figures of the time, meant feeling sorry for another's plight. Empathy shares emotional territory with sympathy but is markedly different.

The term "empathy" is derived from the German word *Einfühlung*, coined by Robert Vischer in 1872 and used in German aesthetics. *Einfühlung* relates to how observers project their own sensibilities onto an object of adoration or contemplation and is a way of explaining how one comes to appreciate and enjoy the beauty of, for example, a work of art. The German philosopher and historian Wilhelm Dilthey borrowed the term from aesthetics and began to use it to describe the mental process by which one person enters into another's being and comes to know how they feel and think.[10]

In 1909, the American psychologist E. B. Titchener translated *Einfühlung* into a new word, "empathy."[11] Titchener had studied with Wilhelm Wundt, the father of modern psychology, while in Europe. Like many young psychologists in the field, Titchener was primarily interested in the key concept of introspection, the process by which a person examines his or her own inner feelings and drives, emotions, and thoughts to gain a sense of personal understanding about the formation of his or her identity and selfhood. The "pathy" in empathy suggests that we enter into the emotional state of another's suffering and feel his or her pain as if it were our own.

Variations of empathy soon emerged, including "empathic" and "to empathize," as the term became part of the popular psychological culture emerging in cosmopolitan centers in Vienna, London, New York, and elsewhere. Unlike sympathy, which is more passive, empathy conjures up active engagement—the willingness of an observer to become part of another's experience, to share the feeling of that experience.

Empathy was a powerful new conceptual term and quickly became the subject of controversy among scholars. Those wedded to a more rational Enlightenment approach quickly attempted to strip the term of its affective content, suggesting that empathy is a cognitive function wired into the brain but requires cultural attunement. American philosopher and psychologist George Herbert Mead argued that every human being takes on the role of another in order to assess that person's thoughts, behavior, and intentions, and thus create an appropriate response. Jean Piaget, the child development psychologist, concurred. In the child developmental process, according to Piaget, the youngster becomes increasingly adept at "reading" others in order to establish social relations. The cognitive proponents, in their theories, came close to suggesting—although not overtly—that empathy is an instrumental value, a taking of measure of the other to advance one's own social interest and maintain appropriate social relations.

Others in the field of psychology more inclined to the Romantic bent viewed empathy as essentially an affective or emotional state with a cognitive component. The empathic observer doesn't lose his sense of self and fuse into the other's experience, nor does he coolly and objectively read the experience of the other as a way of gathering information that could be used to foster his own self interest. Rather, as psychology professor Martin L. Hoffman suggests, empathy runs deeper. He defines empathy as "the involvement of psychological processes that make a person have feelings that are more congruent with another's situation than with his own situation."[12] Hoffman and others don't discount the role cognition plays—what psychologists call "empathic accuracy." But they are more likely to perceive empathy as a total response to the plight of another person, sparked by a deep emotional sharing of that other person's state, accompanied by a cognitive assessment of the others' present condition and followed by an affective and engaged response to attend to their needs and help ameliorate their suffering.

Although most people probably would view empathy as both an emotional and cognitive response to another's plight, empathy is not just reserved for the notion that "I feel your pain," a phrase popularized by former president Bill Clinton and later caricatured in pop culture. One can also empathize with another's joy.

Ofttimes empathizing with another person's joy comes from a deep personal knowledge of their past struggles, making their joy all the more valued and vicariously felt. Another person's empathic embrace can even transform one's own suffering to joy. Carl Rogers put it poignantly:

> [W]hen a person realizes he has been deeply heard, his eyes
> moisten. I think in some real sense, he is weeping for joy. It is
> as though he were saying, "Thank God, somebody heard me.
> Someone knows what it's like to be me."[13]

There has been a steady rise in interest in the import and impact of empathy on consciousness and social development over the past century. That interest has mushroomed in the past decade as empathy has become a hot-button topic in professional fields ranging from medical care to human resources management.

Biologists talk excitedly about the discovery of mirror neurons, the so-called empathy neurons that establish the genetic predisposition for empathetic response across some of the mammalian kingdom. The existence of mirror neurons has touched off a wide-ranging debate in the academic community over long-held assumptions about the nature of biological evolution and especially the nature of human evolution.

Edward O. Wilson, the Harvard biologist, turned upside down centuries of thinking about the nature of human beings' relationship to other animals with his essay on biophilia. Christian theologians had always taken a utilitarian view of our fellow creatures, arguing that God had given humankind dominion over the other animals to dispose of them as we chose. For the most part, with the exception of Saint Francis of Assisi, the Church's perspective was that animals, like human beings, were fallen creatures, useful but of little intrinsic value. Even the Enlightenment philosophers showed little regard for the other animals that populate the Earth. Most shared René Descartes's view of living creatures as "soulless automatons" whose movements were little different from those of the automated puppetry that danced upon the Strasbourg Clock.[14]

Wilson argues to the contrary, that human beings have a genetic predisposition—an innate hankering—to seek empathic affiliation and companionship with other creatures and the wild, and dared to suggest that increasing isolation from the rest of nature results in psychological and even physical deprivation, with profound consequences for our species.[15]

Educators have picked up the banner of empathic attunement in the burgeoning field of "emotional intelligence," suggesting that empathic extension and engagement is an important marker by which to judge the psychological and social development of children. Some schools in the United States have begun to revolutionize curricula to emphasize empathetic pedagogy alongside the more traditional intellectual and vocational programs.

New teaching models designed to transform education from a competitive contest to a collaborative learning experience are emerging as schools attempt to catch up to a generation that has grown up on the Internet and is used to interacting and learning in open social networks where they share information rather than hoard it. Meanwhile, service learning has revolutionized the school experience. Millions of youngsters are now required to perform public service in neighborhood organizations where they assist others in need and advance the quality of life of the community.

All of those educational innovations are helping to nurture a more mature empathic sensibility. The traditional assumption that "knowledge is power" and is used for personal gain is being subsumed by the notion that knowledge is an expression of the shared responsibilities for the collective well-being of humanity and the planet as a whole.

Early evaluations of student performance in the few places where the new empathic approach to education has been implemented show a marked improvement in mindfulness, communications skills, and critical thinking as youngsters become more introspective, emotionally attuned, and cognitively adept at comprehending and responding intelligently and compassionately to others. Because empathic skills emphasize a non-judgmental orientation and tolerance of other perspectives, they accustom young people to think in terms of layers of complexity and force them to live within the context of ambiguous realities where there are no simple formulas or answers, but only a constant search for shared meanings and common understandings. The new empathic teaching experience, though still nascent, is designed to prepare students to plumb the mysteries of an existential universe where the ultimate questions are not just "how to" but also "why"?

In the law, the traditional concept of meting out justice has been broadened to include the idea of reconciliation—a radically new approach to addressing wrongdoing on the basis of restoring relationships between perpetrators of crimes and their victims, rather than merely imposing punishment on the guilty party.

The Truth and Reconciliation Commission instituted in South Africa in the 1990s after the end of apartheid was the first of several such bodies established in the aftermath of mass violence in various countries. Similar commissions have been established in Ireland, Argentina, and East Timor.

Reconciliation commissions bring together those who have committed the crimes and their victims. The victims bear public witness to the atrocities committed and talk openly about the physical and emotional suffering they experienced at the hands of the perpetrators. The perpetrators, in turn, are given the opportunity to make a full and truthful disclosure of their crimes in front of their victims and, if they choose, to ask for forgiveness. The experience is designed to provide a "safe environment" to allow for an empathic catharsis, reconciliation and healing among the parties.

A similar process called restorative justice is being implemented in court jurisdictions in several countries. Imprisoned felons and their victims are encouraged to come together in carefully choreographed therapeutic settings to talk face-to-face and share their feelings about the crime. The hope is that the perpetrator, after hearing the victim recount the experience and the suffering and anguish that resulted, might feel guilt, thereby activating an empathic response, remorse and an effort to seek forgiveness.

The reconciliation commissions and restorative justice programs are a formal recognition that the question of morality extends beyond the issue of fairness to include the equally important issue of caring and that righting a wrong includes emotional reparations as well as criminal convictions. These novel legal entities are a new way of dealing with conflict resolution that puts as much emphasis on empathy as on equity. Such bodies would have been unheard of in previous periods of history. Their success in mitigating future abuses and criminal behavior, while mixed, is nonetheless encouraging and suggests a broadening of the vision of criminal justice and the role of law in addressing wrongdoing in society.

Even economics, the dismal science, has undergone a partial makeover. For two centuries Adam Smith's observation that nature inclines each individual to pursue his or her own individual self-interest in the marketplace seemed the undisputable last word on the nature of human nature. In his *Inquiry into the Nature and Causes of the Wealth of Nations* (1776), Smith contended that

> [e]very individual is continually exerting himself to find out
> the most advantageous employment for whatever capital he
> can command. It is his own advantage, indeed, and not that
> of society, which he has in view. But the study of his own
> advantage naturally, or rather necessarily, leads him to prefer
> that employment which is most advantageous to the society.[16]

Smith's characterization of human nature, while still gospel, is no longer sacrosanct. The IT (Information Technology) and Internet revolutions have begun to change the nature of the economic game. Network ways of doing business challenge orthodox market assumptions about self-interest. Caveat emptor—let the buyer beware—has been replaced with the belief that all exchanges should be, above all, completely transparent. The conventional notion that views market transactions as adversarial has been undermined by network collaboration based on win-win strategies. In networks, optimizing the interest of others increases one's own assets and value. Cooperation bests competition. Sharing risks and open-source collaboration, rather than Machiavellian-inspired intrigues and manipulations, become the norm. Think Linux—a business model that simply would have been unimaginable twenty years ago.

The idea behind this global software business is to encourage thousands of people to empathize with the plight of others who are experiencing glitches with their software programming and codes and freely give time and expertise to help solve their problems. The notion of economic altruism no longer seems like an oxymoron. Adam Smith would, no doubt, be incredulous. Nonetheless, Linux works and has become a competitor with Microsoft on the world stage.

The new insights into human beings' empathic nature has even caught the attention of human resources management who are beginning to put as much emphasis on social intelligence as professional skills. The ability of employees to empathize across traditional ethnic, racial, cultural, and gender boundaries is increasingly regarded as essential to corporate performance, both within the workplace and in external market relations. Learning how to work together in a thoughtful and compassionate manner is becoming standard operating procedure in a complex, interdependent world. (We will examine the powerful paradigmatic impact the new empathic surge is having across the global society in Part III: The Age of Empathy.)

What does this tell us about human nature? Is it possible that human beings are not inherently evil or intrinsically self-interested and materialistic, but are of a very different nature—an empathic one—and that all of the other drives that we have considered to be primary—aggression, violence, selfish behavior, acquisitiveness—are in fact secondary drives that flow from repression or denial of our most basic instinct?

The first hint that such might be the case—at least in scientific literature—occurred in an obscure laboratory study by psychologist Harry Harlow in 1958 at the University of Wisconsin. Harlow and his team conducted an experiment on infant monkeys to observe their affectional responses. What they found shook the world of biology, with ripple effects that spread into the social sciences and other fields.

Harlow and his team erected two artificial surrogate mothers. The first was a wood block with sponge rubber around it and draped in cotton terry cloth. A lightbulb radiating heat was placed behind the surrogate. The second surrogate mother was far less comfortable. It was made of wire mesh, warmed by radiant heat. Both surrogates lactated milk.

The infants all preferred to nestle up to the cloth surrogate. However, even when the cloth mother stopped lactating, the infants clung, refusing to take the few necessary steps over to the wire-mesh surrogate for nourishment. They persisted, to the point of starvation and death.

Writing in *American Psychologist,* Harlow reported that even

> [w]ith age and opportunity to learn, subjects with the lactating wire mother showed decreasing responsiveness to her and increasing responsiveness to the nonlactating cloth mother.[17]

Astounded by what they observed, Harlow and his fellow researchers concluded with the suggestion that

> the primary function of nursing as an affectional variable is that of insuring frequent and intimate body contact of the infant with the mother. Certainly, man cannot live by milk alone.[18]

Researchers need not have torn the infant monkeys from their mothers and subjected them to such a cruel experiment. Evidence was already well in hand by then, showing that human infants exhibited similar behavior in foundling hospitals earlier in the century. These public institutions were built and administered during the great waves of immigration to America—between the 1880s and 1930s—to house and care for orphaned and abandoned infants or infants taken from indigent families that could not take care of them. Influenced by the progressive-era dogma that emphasized a combination of modern hygiene and strict detached care designed to transform a child quickly into an independent and autonomous being—touching was looked on as potentially unhygienic and a way to spread germs and infection—hospital administrators frowned on nurses caressing or stroking infants. It was thought that affection would retard children's moral development, make them more dependent, and impede their speedy maturation into self-possessed little human beings. The infants were, for the most part, well-fed, well-supervised, and kept in germ-free environments.

Although attended to, thousands of these children languished. They exhibited high degrees of depression and stereotypical behavior of the kind that occurs in extreme isolation. Despite ample food, adequate medical attention, and reasonably comfortable surroundings, the mortality rate was far above the norm for children raised with biological parents or even foster or adoptive parents.

It wasn't until the 1930s that psychologists began to urge a change in infant care. Nurses were instructed to pick up and caress the infants, rock them, soothe and comfort them, and develop a sense of intimate contact. Infants responded almost immediately. They came to life and became engaged, affectionate, and vital.

What had been missing in the foundling homes was one of the most important factors in infant development—empathy. We are learning, against all of the prevailing wisdom, that human nature is not to seek autonomy—to become an island to oneself—but, rather, to seek companionship, affection, and intimacy. The conventional belief that equates self-development and self-consciousness with increasing autonomy has begun to lose its intellectual cachet. A growing number of child development psychologists now argue the contrary—that a sense of selfhood and self-awareness depends on and feeds off of deepening relationships to other people. Empathy, in turn, is the means by which companionate bonds are forged.

Were the seeking of companionship not so basic to our nature, we wouldn't so fear isolation or ostracization. To be shunned and exiled is to become a nonperson, to cease to exist as far as others are concerned. Empathy is the psychological means by which we become part of other people's lives and share meaningful experiences. The very notion of transcendence means to reach beyond oneself, to participate with and belong to larger communities, to be embedded in more complex webs of meaning.

William Fairbairn, Heinz Kohut, Ian Suttie, Donald Winnicott, John Bowlby, Mary Ainsworth, and others—whom we will hear from shortly—were among a growing number of psychiatrists and pediatricians who broke with Freud in the late 1930s and 1940s, taking umbrage with his notion of the reality principle. Recall that Freud believed that every newborn seeks to satisfy his or her libidinal drive—the pleasure principle. It is only later—at around the age of eighteen months to two years—that parents introduce their children to the reality principle. For Freud, reality is imposing restraints and constraints, first in the form of toilet training and scheduled feedings. The baby, says Freud, needs to be taught to delay gratification, to repress his or her instinctual drives in order to conform with the norms that make social life possible. Socialization for Freud meant repression of basic drives, which he viewed as ultimately self-destructive and antisocial.

Many of the renegade psychologists of the 1930s and 1940s thought differently. They argued that children are born with a reality principle, and that principle is to seek affection, companionship, intimacy, and a sense of belonging. The search to belong, they suggested, is the most primary of all drives. Society often tempers or represses the drive for affection and intimacy to serve socially constructive ends, but it remains the essential nature of human beings. (We will turn our attention to the new scientific understandings about human beings' empathic nature in Part I: Homo Empathicus.)

If in fact human beings are, at the get-go, social animals who seek companionship and use empathetic extension to transcend themselves and find meaning in relationship with others, how do we account for the incredible violence our species has inflicted on each other, our fellow creatures, and the Earth we inhabit? No other creature has left such a destructive footprint on the Earth. Cultural historian Elias Canetti once remarked that "[e]ach of us is a king in a field of corpses."[19] Canetti said that if we reflected on the vast number of creatures and Earth's resources each of us has expropriated and consumed in the course of our lifetime to perpetuate our own existence, we would likely be appalled by the carnage. Yet there may be an explanation for this perplexing duality. There is, I believe, a grand paradox to human history. At the heart of the human saga is a catch-22—a contradiction of extraordinary significance—that has accompanied our species, if not from the very beginning, then at least from the time our ancestors began their slow metamorphosis from archaic to civilized beings thousands of years before Christ.

First, we must understand that widespread wanton violence has not been the norm in human history but, rather, the exception, that is, if one considers the entire span that anatomically modern human beings have existed on Earth. Granted, some expropriation of other animals and manipulation of our environment is essential to maintain human sustenance, as is the case with every other mammalian species. For 93 percent of our species' existence we lived as foragers/hunters in small tribal groups of between 30 and 150 people. Archaic men and women were nomadic and communal. While aggression and violence existed among our Paleolithic ancestors, it generally was limited in scale and confined to maintaining territorial migratory grounds against intrusion or conflicts over mate selection. Like our closest chimpanzee relatives, far more time was spent on grooming, play, and other pro-social behavior.

Even in the early European garden/agricultural societies of the Neolithic Age, archeologists find virtually no weapons or remains of military fortifications and little evidence of violent warfare or occupation.[20] Archeologist Marija Gimbutas notes that the early European agriculturalists lived a relatively peaceful existence. Their societies were largely egalitarian and matrilineal. Craft technology was advanced and the archeological findings of the period reveal a highly artistic culture.

Beginning around 4400 BC, however, Europe was rocked by a wave of invasions from the East.[21] Nomadic horsemen of the Eurasian steppes swept into southern and eastern Europe, destroying the tranquil agricultural life that had existed for several thousand years. Known as the Kurgan people, the invaders bred horses that could carry human mounts. The mounted horse gave them a superior military advantage, allowing them to surprise, overrun, and occupy village communities across much of Eurasia in the ensuing centuries.

These ancient cowboys brought with them a new warrior sensibility. Equally important, they learned to domesticate the bovine and herd large numbers of animals. The herds were forms of capital. In fact, the very word "cattle" comes from the same etymological root as the word "capital."[22] Cattle meant property. Cattle were regarded as movable wealth, an asset that could be used as a standard medium of exchange and a tool for exerting power over people and territory.

It wasn't long before the lessons of how to transform animals into capital and a source of health and power were applied to human beings. In the Middle East, around the fourth millennium BC, we see the beginnings of societies based on the herding of thousands of human beings into giant work groups to build canals, erect dikes, and create the first large-scale hydraulic agricultural civilizations.

The creation of what Lewis Mumford called the human "mega-machine" ushered in a radical restructuring of human society. Matriarchal forms of familial relations gave way to new patriarchal forms of power. Governance, which traditionally had been structured around cohort groups, marking the passage of life from infancy to old age, made way for abstract rule in the hands of a single ruler who exercised absolute power. That power was administered by centralized bureaucratic authority designed to rein in and regiment the lives of tens of thousands of people to the task of exploiting the Earth's largesse and creating ever-greater surpluses to extend the bounds of human empire. It is at this juncture—the dawn of civilization—that our story begins. It is a hopeful yet discouraging tale built on what is surely the strangest contradiction in history.

The reality is that each new, more complex energy-consuming civilization in history increases the pace, flow, and density of human exchange and creates more connectivity between people. Increased energy flow-through also creates surpluses and allows for growing populations and more expanded commercial relations and trade with near and faraway communities. The very complexity of more advanced civilizations—the hydraulic agricultural societies based on large-scale irrigation systems, and the industrial societies based on fossil fuel utilization—require greater differentiation and individuation in the form of specialized talents, roles, and responsibilities, in ever more interdependent social milieus. The differentiation process pulls individuals away from the collective tribal "we" to an ever more individual "I." Role differentiation, in turn, becomes the path to selfhood.

Small family and extended kinship units of 30 to 150 people, which are so characteristic of forager/hunter–based oral cultures, exhibit only minimal role differentiation and thus little to distinguish the individual as a unique self. Archaic man and woman lived collectively, but not as a collection of self-aware individuals. Their life contrasts sharply with the setting in midtown Manhattan in 2010, where an individual is exposed to potentially 220,000 or more people within a ten-minute radius of their home or office, and each of these thousands of people have their own unique roles, responsibilities, and identities that set them apart from the group. Yet they function together in a highly interdependent and integrated economic and social organism.

The awakening sense of selfhood, brought on by the differenti-ation process, is crucial to the development and extension of empathy. The more individualized and developed the self is, the greater is our sense of our own unique, mortal existence, as well as our existential aloneness and the many challenges we face in the struggle to be and to flourish. It is these very feelings in ourselves that allow us to empa-thize with similar existential feelings in others. A heightened empathic sentiment also allows an increasingly individualized population to affiliate with one another in more interdependent, expanded, and inte-grated social organisms. This is the process that characterizes what we call civilization. Civilization is the detribalization of blood ties and the resocialization of distinct individuals based on associational ties. Empathic extension is the psychological mechanism that makes the conversion and the transition possible. When we say to civilize, we mean to empathize.

Today, in what is fast becoming a globally connected civilization, empathic consciousness is just beginning to extend to the far reaches of the biosphere and to every living creature. Unfortunately this comes right at the very moment in history when the same economic struc-tures that are connecting us are sucking up vast reserves of the Earth's remaining resources to maintain a highly complex and interdependent urban civilization and destroying the biosphere in the process. We have come to empathize with the polar bears and penguins at the far cor-ners of the Earth, as the ice beneath them begins to melt away from industrially induced global warming. The poles have been encased in ice for million of years, but now our scientists say that by 2030, "we may have no ice at all in the Arctic Ocean in summer."[23] And everywhere people are beginning to ask a question never before entertained in history: Can we continue to sustain our species?

The thought of extinction, first raised with the dropping of atomic bombs on Hiroshima and Nagasaki, Japan, in 1945 by the U.S. government, now takes on an even more dramatic urgency with the report by James Hansen, the head of the NASA Goddard Institute for Space Studies, that human-induced climate change, brought on by a voracious global economy, might lead to a six-degree rise in the Earth's temperature by the end of the century, or shortly thereafter, and the demise of civilization as we've come to know it. He warns that

> if humanity wishes to preserve a planet similar to that on which civilization developed and to which life on Earth is adapted, paleoclimate evidence and ongoing climate change suggest that CO_2 will need to be reduced from its current 385 ppm to at most 350 ppm, but likely less than that.[24]

This would require a reduction beyond any current benchmark being discussed by the nations of the world.

If there were any lingering doubt as to how close our species is coming to the very limits of its sustainability on Earth, a single statistic is revealing of our current state of affairs: Our scientists tell us that the nearly seven billion human beings now inhabiting the Earth make up less than 1 percent of the total biomass of all the Earth's consumers.[25] Yet with our complex global economic and social infrastructure, we are currently consuming nearly 24 percent of the net primary production on Earth—"the net amount of solar energy converted to plant organic matter through photosynthesis."[26] (We will investigate the extent of the global environmental crisis in Chapter 12, The Planetary Entropic Abyss.)

The irony is that just as we are beginning to glimpse the prospect of global empathic consciousness we find ourselves close to our own extinction. We rushed to universalize empathy in the last half of the twentieth century. In the aftermath of the Holocaust in World War II, humanity said "never again." We extended empathy to large numbers of our fellow human beings previously considered to be less than human—including women, homosexuals, the disabled, people of color, and ethnic and religious minorities—and encoded our sensitivity in the form of social rights and policies, human rights laws, and now even statutes to protect animals. We are in the long end game of including "the other," "the alien," "the unrecognized." And even though the first light of this new biosphere consciousness is only barely becoming visible—traditional xenophobic biases and prejudices continue to be the norm—the simple fact that our empathic extension is now exploring previously unexplorable domains is a triumph of the human evolutionary journey.

Yet the early light of global empathic consciousness is dimmed by the growing recognition that it may come too late to address the specter of climate change and the possible extinction of the human species—a demise brought on by the evolution of ever more complex energy-consuming economic and social arrangements that allow us to deepen our sense of selfhood, bring more diverse people together, extend our empathic embrace, and expand human consciousness.

We are in a race to biosphere consciousness in a world facing the threat of extinction. Understanding the contradiction that lies at the heart of the human saga is critical if our species is to renegotiate a sustainable relationship to the planet in time to step back from the abyss.

The essential task at hand is to examine the depths of the conundrum of human history, to fully explore its workings and pathways and twists and turns so that we might find a way out of our predicament. Our journey begins at the crossroads where the laws of energy that govern the universe come up against the human inclination to continually transcend our sense of isolation by seeking the companionship of others in ever more complex energy-consuming social arrangements. The underlying dialectic of human history is the continuous feedback loop between expanding empathy and increasing entropy.

THE LAWS OF THERMODYNAMICS
AND HUMAN DEVELOPMENT

Albert Einstein once mused about which laws of science were most likely to withstand the test of time and not be subject to deconstruction, irrelevance, or abandonment by future generations. He chose the first and second laws of thermodynamics. Einstein noted that

> [a] theory is more impressive the greater is the simplicity of its
> premises, the more different are the kinds of things it relates
> and the more extended its range of applicability. Therefore,
> the deep impression which classical thermodynamics made on
> me. It is the only physical theory of universal content which I
> am convinced, that within the framework of applicability of its
> basic concepts, will never be overthrown.[27]

The first and second laws of thermodynamics state that the "total energy content of the universe is constant, and the total entropy is continually increasing."[28] The first law, the conservation law, posits that energy can neither be created nor destroyed. The amount of total energy in the whole universe has been fixed since the beginning of time and will remain so until the end of time.

Although the energy in the universe remains constant, it is continually changing form but always in one direction, from available to unavailable. This is where the second law of thermodynamics comes into play. According to the second law, energy always flows in one direction—from hot to cold, concentrated to dispersed, ordered to disordered. Consider the burning of a piece of coal. The energy remains but is transformed into sulfur dioxide, carbon dioxide, and other gases that spread into space. While no energy has been lost in the conversion process, we can never reburn the original piece of coal again and get useful work out of it. The second law states that whenever energy is transformed, some amount of available energy is lost in the process: that is, it is no longer able to perform useful work. This loss of usable energy is called "entropy," a term coined by the German physicist Rudolf Clausius in 1868.

Clausius observed that in order for energy to be converted into work, there must be a difference in energy concentration (namely a difference in temperature) in different parts of the system. Work occurs when energy moves from a high level of concentration to a lower level (or a higher temperature to a lower temperature). For example, a steam engine does work because part of the system is very cold and the other is very hot.

It is important to emphasize that when energy goes from one level to another, less energy is available to perform the work the next time. When, for example, a red-hot poker is removed from the fire, it cools, because heat always flows from the hotter to the colder body. Eventually the poker is the same temperature as the surrounding air. This is the "equilibrium state," in which there is no longer any difference in energy levels and therefore no more ability to perform work. The once-useful energy is no longer concentrated in the red-hot poker but is now randomly dispersed in the air and unavailable.

But can't we recycle energy and therefore reverse entropy? Yes, but always at the expense of using additional energy in the recycling. The additional energy, when used, increases the overall entropy.

While the sun's energy is not expected to burn out for billions of years, and will continue to bathe the Earth with new energy for as long as we can imagine, it must be understood that energy concentrated in material form here on Earth, whether it be in metallic ore or fossil fuels, is relatively fixed in the geological time frame of importance to society. That is because in thermodynamic terms, Earth is a partially closed system in relation to the solar system and the universe. There are three kinds of thermodynamic systems: open, partially closed, and isolated. Open systems exchange both energy and matter. Partially closed systems exchange energy but do not exchange any significant matter. Isolated systems exchange neither energy nor matter. The Earth is a partially closed system; that is, it exchanges energy with the solar system, but, except for an occasional meteorite and cosmic dust, it does not exchange appreciable matter with the outside universe. The point that needs to be emphasized is that the solar inflow of energy does not by itself produce matter. The sun can flow into an empty jar forever without producing matter of any kind. The Earth has a fixed endowment of terrestrial matter that can be converted into other useful forms, including life, with the help of solar energy. For example, the sun's energy interacted with terrestrial matter during the Jurassic era, helping transform matter into life. That life, now decomposed, comprises the carbon deposits that we burn today in the form of coal, oil, and natural gas. The spent energy, in the form of gases, is no longer available to do work. While similar carbon deposits might conceivably accumulate in some future period of geological history, for all intents and purposes, that time is so distant as to be irrelevant to human needs. That is why we call fossil fuels "nonrenewable sources of energy."

To summarize, the first law of thermodynamics states that all energy in the universe is constant, that it cannot be created or destroyed. Only its form can change. The second law states that energy can only be changed in one direction, that is, from usable to unusable, from available to unavailable, or from ordered to disordered. Everything in the universe, according to the second law, began as available concentrated energy and is being transformed over time to unavailable, dispersed energy. Entropy is the measure of the extent to which available energy in any subsystem of the universe is transformed into an unavailable form.

Societies are organized and maintained by converting the available energy from the environment into energy to sustain human existence. Nobel laureate chemist Frederick Soddy made the very perceptive observation that the laws of thermodynamics

> control, in the last resort, the rise and fall of political systems,
> the freedom or bondage of nations, the movements of
> commerce and industry, the origin of wealth and poverty,
> and the general physical welfare of the race.[29]

But if energy is continually being transformed from an available to an unavailable state, or from order to disorder, or from concentrated to dispersed, how do we reconcile the fact that life and social systems seem to maintain a high level of concentrated energy and order, in apparent contradiction to the thermodynamic imperative?

Early on biologists weren't quite sure how to explain what appeared to be an anomaly when it came to life and social structures. The eminent biologist Harold Blum stepped in to explain how biology fit within the overarching frame of the thermodynamic laws.

In his book *Time's Arrow and Evolution*, Blum points out that life is just a special case of how the laws of energy work. All living beings, Blum points out, live far away from equilibrium, by continually feeding on available energy from the environment but at the expense of increasing the overall entropy in the environment. Blum explains that "the small local decrease in entropy represented in the building of the organism is coupled with a much larger increase in the entropy of the universe."[30]

Here's how the process works. The source of free energy is the sun. Plants take up the sun's energy in photosynthesis and provide a source of concentrated energy that animals can then consume directly by eating plants, or indirectly by eating other animals. The Nobel laureate physicist Erwin Schrödinger observed that "by continually drawing from its environment negative entropy . . . what an organism feeds upon is negative entropy; it continues to suck orderliness from its environment."[31]

We stay alive by continually processing energy through our bodies. If the energy flow were to stop, or our bodies were unable to process the energy properly because of disease, we would quickly move to death, or an equilibrium state. At death, the body begins to decompose rapidly, and our physical being dissipates and disperses into the surrounding environment. Life, therefore, is an example of nonequilibrium thermodynamics; that is, life maintains order and remains far removed from equilibrium or death by continuous processing of free or available energy from the larger environment.

The process of maintaining a nonequilibrium state, away from death, is costly in energy terms. Even the plants, our most efficient "power plants" on Earth, absorb only a tiny fraction of the Earth's incoming energy through photosynthesis. The rest is dissipated. Thus, the tiny entropy decrease in the plant is secured at the expense of a far greater entropy increase in the overall environment.

The twentieth-century philosopher and mathematician Bertrand Russell noted that "[e]very living thing is a sort of imperialist, seeking to transfer as much as possible of its environment into itself and its seed."[32] The more evolved a species is in nature's hierarchy, the more energy is required to maintain it in a nonequilibrium state and the more entropy is created in the process of keeping it alive.

Consider the case of a simple food chain consisting of grass, grasshoppers, frogs, trout, and humans. According to the first law, energy is never lost. But according to the second law, available energy is turned into unavailable energy at each step of the food chain process, increasing the overall entropy in the environment. Chemist G. Tyler Miller reminds us that in devouring prey, "about 80 percent to 90 percent of the energy is simply wasted and lost as heat to the environment."[33] In other words, only 10 to 20 percent of the energy of the prey is absorbed by the predator. That is because the act of transforming energy from one life-form to another requires the expenditure of energy and therefore results in the loss of energy.

The amount of free energy needed to keep each more complex species alive is staggering. Miller calculates that

> three hundred trout are required to support one man for a year. The trout, in turn, must consume 90,000 frogs, which must consume 27 million grasshoppers, which live off of 1,000 tons of grass.[34]

Every life-form on the evolutionary ladder, then, maintains itself in a nonequilibrium ordered state at the expense of creating greater disorder (dissipated energy) in the overall environment. Energy is continually flowing through every living organism, entering the system at a high level and leaving the system in a more degraded state in the form of waste. Again, the more complex the organism, the more energy it requires to sustain itself against equilibrium.

This means that as we travel up the evolutionary ladder, each succeeding species has to be better equipped physiologically to capture available energy. Biologist Alfred Lotka says that we can think of living beings as "transformers" of energy. "The close association of the principal sense organs, eyes, ears, nose, taste buds, tactile papillas of the fingertips, with the anterior (head) end of the body, the mouth end, all point [to] the same lesson," notes Lotka.[35] Natural selection favors those organisms that are able to

> increase the total mass of the system, rate of circulation of
> mass through the system, and the total energy flux through the
> system[36] . . . so long as there is present an unutilized residue of
> matter and available energy.[37]

Anthropologist Leslie A. White observes that in the evolution of culture, human beings' first "power plants" were their own bodies. For most of human history, *Homo sapiens* lived a forager/hunter existence and captured the energy stored in wild plants and animals. By acting collectively and cooperatively on their environments, they could increase their critical mass and use their human power plants to secure what they needed to sustain small kinship communities. Later, as our species made the transition from foragers/hunters to farmers and pastoralists, human beings were able to sequester more energy from their environment. By domesticating plants and animals, they secured a continuous and reliable supply and surplus of readily available energy and, by so doing, increased the amount of energy that could flow through their bodies and communities.

Plant cultivation—aided by irrigation systems—greatly increased the yield per unit of human energy or labor expended. Agricultural surpluses also freed at least some people from toil on the land. Freeing people from labor created the beginnings of a social hierarchy and the differentiation of tasks. Priest and warrior classes slowly emerged, as did an artisan class somewhat later on. The differentiation and specialization of tasks spawned new, more complex institutional arrangements, which in turn helped to facilitate an even greater energy flow-through.

The cultivation of cereals some ten thousand years ago in North Africa, the Middle East, India, and China, marked a turning point for human society. The cereals have been called "the great moving power of civilization."[38] The food surpluses provided an energy endowment to sustain growing populations and the establishment of kingdoms, and later of empires. The great civilizations of Mesopotamia and Egypt rose from cereal cultivation. Large engineering projects were undertaken, including the establishment of elaborate hydraulic systems to irrigate fields. Women invented pottery, providing containers to store surplus grain for inventory and/or trade. The metallurgical arts aided in the development of more sophisticated weaponry for conquest and capture of additional land and slaves.

The shift from agriculture to an industrial way of life once again increased the amount of energy that could be captured, stored, and utilized—this time in the form of fossil fuels harnessed and processed by machines. The new mechanical energy acts as a substitute slave, multiplying the amount of energy and power available per capita and for society as a whole.

American anthropologist George Grant MacCurdy, in *Human Origins*, writes of the human experience as an evolutionary journey in the increasing use of available energy: "The degree of civilization of any epoch, people, or group of peoples is measured by the ability to utilize energy for human advancement or needs."[39] Many anthropologists agree. Leslie White, for example, uses energy as a yardstick for measuring the success of all human cultures. He argues that whether a culture is low or high in achievement is directly correlated to the amount of energy consumed per capita. The very function of culture, argue White and other anthropologists, is to "harness and control energy so that it may be put to work in man's service."[40] Howard Odum, one of the pioneers in the field of natural energy systems, cautions that in the coming together of "man, mind, and energy," one must bear in mind that it is the source of the energy, not human inspiration, that ultimately sets limits on human progress. Odum writes:

All progress is due to special power subsidies, and progress
evaporates whenever and wherever they are removed.
Knowledge and ingenuity are the means for applying power
subsidies when they are available, and the development
and retention of knowledge are also dependent on power
delivery.[41]

The most important constraint for every society in history, says
Odum, is the availability of energy. All the human creativity in the
world will inevitably come up short in advancing the well-being of the
race absent sufficient energy reserves to be captured and harnessed.

White offers a shorthand for measuring the relationship between
energy use and cultural evolution. There are, he says, three critical
factors in assessing the "progress" of any culture: first, "the amount of
energy harnessed per capita per year"; second, "the efficiency of the
technological means with which energy is harnessed and put to work";
and third, "the magnitude of human need-serving goods and services
produced."[42] Putting these factors together, White concludes that "culture evolves as the amount of energy harnessed per capita per year is
increased, or as the efficiency of the instrumental means of putting the
energy to work is increased."[43] Very much in the materialist tradition
of the European Enlightenment, White is unequivocal in his belief
that energy is the ruling factor, both in biological and cultural systems.
"Thus we trace the development of culture from anthropoid levels to
the present time," says White, "as a consequence of periodic increases
in the amount of energy harnessed per capita per year effected by tap-
ping new sources of power."[44]

White has captured part of the human journey. Energy is critical,
but it doesn't stand alone. The great economic revolutions in history
occur when new energy regimes converge with new communications
revolutions. The convergence of energy and communications revolutions is what changes the human condition for long periods of time.
New communications revolutions become the command-and-control
mechanisms, the means of structuring, organizing, and maintaining
the energy flow-through of civilization.

For example, consider the Sumerians in ancient Mesopotamia, who were the first to establish a sophisticated hydraulic system of agriculture.[45] Digging canals and building dikes to provide irrigation, establishing transport systems for routing the grain to storage facilities, and managing the distribution of grain required a new level of organization and more complex management than was the case in small rain-fed horticultural societies. The Sumerians had to sequester and manage thousands of workers to erect and maintain the hydraulic system. They had to develop specialized craft skills to build and operate the hydraulic technologies. Labor became highly differentiated and tasks more specialized. The hydraulic agricultural system in Mesopotamia spawned the first urban settlements.

Managing an increasingly complex energy regime necessitated a concomitant communications revolution. The Sumerians' invention of cuneiform—the first written script—was equally important to the invention of hydraulic technology in the production, storage, and distribution of grain. Cuneiform made it possible to oversee and supervise the vast complex operations required to maintain the whole hydraulic enterprise. Record keeping allowed the Sumerians to track all of the operations, including monitoring the day-to-day storing and distributing of the grain.

Wherever large-scale hydraulic agricultural systems were established, societies independently created writing to manage them—in the Middle East, India, China, and Mexico.

In the early modern age, the print-press-communications revolution converged with coal, steam, and rail to create the First Industrial Revolution. The German craftsman Johannes Gutenberg invented the first print press with movable type in 1436—although it should be noted that both the Chinese and Koreans already had put into use earlier versions of the print press in their respective kingdoms.[46]

The print-press revolution played an important role in the unfolding of the Protestant Reformation. Indeed, scholars suggest it made the revolt possible. Martin Luther, and the reformers who followed, encouraged the mass production of bibles in vernacular so that each Christian convert could be versed in God's word and be prepared to stand alone before his or her maker, without having to rely on the Church's emissaries—the priesthood—to interpret God's will. The Great Schism of Christianity, beginning with the Reformation and followed by the Counter-Reformation, the Thirty Years' War, and the Peace of Westphalia—which helped establish the modern notion of national sovereignty—changed the social and political face of Europe.[47]

But the full economic impact of the print revolution had to await the invention of the steam engine by James Watt in 1769.[48] The print revolution converged with the coal, steam, and rail revolution to create the First Industrial Revolution.

Between 1830 and 1890, in both Europe and North America, print communications underwent a revolution. Efficient steam-powered print presses made the print production process both quick and cheap.[49] Public schooling and mass literacy were introduced on both continents, and within two generations produced the first nearly fully literate populations in history. The communications revolution became the means to organize and manage the vast complex operations and infrastructure of the coal, steam, and rail revolution. Within a sixty-year span in the nineteenth century, the First Industrial Revolution infrastructure was put in place. It would have been impossible to organize the dramatic increase in the pace, speed, flow, density, and connectivity of economic activity, made possible by the coal-fired steam engine, using the older codex and oral forms of communications.

In the late nineteenth century and throughout the twentieth century, first-generation electrical forms of communications—the telephone, movies, radio, television, electric typewriters, and calculators—converged with the introduction of oil, the automobile, and the mass-production of manufactured goods, becoming the communications vehicle for organizing and marketing the Second Industrial Revolution.

The convergence of energy and communications revolutions not only reconfigure society and social roles and relationships but also human consciousness itself. Communications revolutions change the temporal and spatial orientation of human beings and, by so doing, change the way the human brain comprehends reality. Oral cultures are steeped in mythological consciousness. Script cultures give rise to theological consciousness. Print cultures are accompanied by ideological consciousness, while early electricity cultures spawn psychological consciousness.

Each more sophisticated communications revolution brings together more diverse people in increasingly more expansive and dense social networks. By extending the central nervous system of each individual and the society as a whole, communications revolutions provide an ever more inclusive playing field for empathy to mature and consciousness to expand.

If there is an "invisible hand" at work it is that empathy matures and consciousness expands to fill the temporal/spatial boundaries set by the new energy regime. Empathy becomes the thread that weaves an increasingly differentiated and individualized population into an integrated social tapestry, allowing the social organism to function as a whole. Each new stage of consciousness represents an enlarged central nervous system encompassing broader and deeper realms of reality, made possible by more complex energy-consuming civilizations. The question is this: Is consciousness merely a critical management tool at the disposal of complex societies to organize survival far away from equilibrium and an entropic state? Or are new energy/communications regimes the vehicles that consciousness uses to expand its horizons? (We will look at the relationship between changes in energy, communications, and consciousness and the empathy/entropy dialectic in greater depth in Part II: Empathy and Civilization.)

Most scientists would argue that new energy/communications/ consciousness structures are simply the means by which human beings thrive in a state far away from equilibrium. Each successive social complex requires greater amounts of energy flow-through to maintain populations and ensure continuity between generations, with the result that their perpetuation increases the overall entropy in the environment.

The late Belgian physical chemist and Nobel laureate Ilya Prigogine observed that many nonliving systems and all living systems are dissipative structures. They maintain their organization by the continuous flow of energy throughout the system.

The flow of energy keeps the system in a constant state of flux. For the most part, the fluctuations generally are small and can be adjusted to by negative feedback. However, occasionally, according to Prigogine, the fluctuations become so great that the system is unable to adjust, and positive feedback takes over. The fluctuations feed off themselves and amplification can easily overwhelm the whole system. That's exactly what's occurring today as civilization heads to global peak oil production and into the early stages of real-time climate change impacts. When the fluctuations overwhelm the system, it either collapses or reorganizes itself. If it's able to reorganize itself, the new dissipative structure will often exhibit a higher order of complexity and integration and a greater flow-through than its predecessor. Each successive ordering, because it's more complex than the one preceding it, is even more vulnerable to fluctuations, collapse, and reordering. Prigogine believed that increased complexity creates the conditions for evolutionary development.[50]

Human beings, of all the millions of creatures that have inhabited the Earth in the 3.8 billion years of life on this planet, have created the most complex systems, and each succeeding qualitative shift in social structure, up to now, enjoyed greater energy through-put and produced more entropy than the social structures that preceded it.[51] It should be noted that the progression of complex energy/communications/consciousness structures have not always followed in a linear pattern. In the West, for example, 1,300 years separate the fall of Rome from the onset of the First Industrial Revolution. The collapse of the Roman Empire led to a fractured, decentralized, and subsistence culture and economy across Europe during the Dark Ages and early medieval era.

Now our complex social arrangements are beginning to embrace the whole of the Earth, our energy through-put is without precedent, and the entropy bill—climate change brought on by the spent fossil-fuel energies of the First and Second Industrial Revolutions—has brought us to a tipping point in the very chemistry of the biosphere, with incalculable consequences for our species and planet.

There are new voices, however, in the academic community who argue that there is more to life's journey than merely surviving and reproducing. They begin their quest by asking an important question. Why do we human beings engage in ever more elaborate, interdependent, and complex social structures as a way of life?

FINDING MEANING BEYOND SURVIVAL

A growing number of scholars suggest that it is not just our need to survive and reproduce that has driven this dynamic of ever greater complexity and extension. If it were only about survival, we would have maintained ourselves in far smaller numbers in a Paleolithic mode.

Rather, they believe, there is something deeper at work. If we are by nature an affectionate species that continuously seeks to broaden and deepen our relationships and connections to others, in effect to transcend ourselves by participating in more expansive communities of meaning, then our increasingly complex social structures provide the vehicles for our journey. More complex energy-consuming civilizations allow human beings to compress time and space. As mentioned, we extend our collective central nervous systems to encompass greater swaths of existence. We do so in order to find meaning in belonging to ever richer and deeper realms of reality. Hungarian polymath Michael Polanyi sees man as "the innovator and explorer, passionately pouring himself into an existence closer to reality."[52]

Author Edith Cobb agrees with Polanyi and goes a step further by suggesting that

> [i]f man is evolution become conscious, surely this is due to his own consciousness striving to join forces with the universe in

this passionate pursuit of the realities of temporal and spatial relations.[53]

Cobb believes that there is a force inherent in the human biology itself that is even more powerful than the classic Darwinian idea of self-reproduction. She writes that

> [t]he need to extend the self in time and space—the need to create in order to live, to breathe, and to be—precedes, indeed, of necessity exceeds, the need for self-reproduction as a personal survival function.[54]

We begin to sense the possibility that there may be a purpose after all to the human journey: that the deepening sense of selfhood, the extension of empathy to broader and more inclusive domains of reality and the expansion of human consciousness, is the transcendent process by which we explore the mystery of existence and discover new realms of meaning.

Strict Darwinists might be aghast at such heresy. They would argue that the human compulsion to create more complex living arrangements and social structures is simply a manifestation of our innate biological need to assure our own individual survival and reproduction potential. Suffice it to say that critics have pointed out that the Darwinian assumption that any and every social innovation and construction that allows life to proliferate is ultimately traceable back to the need to perpetuate our genes becomes a bit tautological if not tiresome.

However, if we look closely at the historical evidence that chronicles the human journey, and especially the dialectical feedback between extended empathy and greater entropy, whole new possibilities for imagining human nature and the human quest open up for our consideration.

The recognition of another's finite existence is what connects empathic consciousness to entropic awareness. When we identify with another's plight, it's their will to live that we empathize with and seek to support. The laws of thermodynamics, and especially the entropy law, tells us that every living moment is unique, unrepeatable, and irreversible—we grow older, not younger—and for that reason we owe our very existence to the borrowed available energy of the Earth that makes up our physical being and that keeps us far away from an equilibrium state of death and decomposition. When we empathize with another being, there is an unconscious understanding that their very existence, like our own, is a fragile affair, which is made possible by the continuous flow of energy through their being. Only recently, however, have we become consciously aware that we each owe our well-being, in part, to the buildup of our own personal entropic debt in the surrounding environment.

The second law of thermodynamics and entropy is a constant reminder of the nature of the struggle that animates each of our lives and that joins us together in fellowship and solidarity. Empathetic extension is the awareness of the vulnerability we all share, and when expressed it becomes a celebration of our common yearning to live.

At the same time, ever more complex energy-consuming civilizations provide an opportunity for greater exposure to and contact with other unique selves. The richer the diversity of exposure, the greater the likelihood that an individual will come to see facets of themselves in the struggle of others and extend empathic awareness.

What is so interesting about the process is that empathic extension not only allows an individual to experience another's plight or condition "as if" it were one's own, but the engagement itself also loops back to reinforce and deepen one's own sense of selfhood because he's been there himself. Sociology professor Chan Kwok-bun sums up the feedback process:

> The authenticity of what I have discovered about myself is
> strengthened because I have found affirmation of a bit of
> myself in you, and you, in me . . .[55]

The constant empathic feedback is the social glue that makes possible increasingly complex societies. Without empathy it would be impossible to even imagine a social life and the organization of society. Try to conjure up a society of narcissists, sociopaths, or autistically challenged individuals. Society requires being social and being social requires empathic extension.

More complex social structures, then, promote greater selfhood, greater exposure to diverse others, and a greater likelihood of extended empathy. Village life is traditionally more closed and xenophobic. Its tight-knit communities are far more likely to view strangers as alien and other. On the other hand, urban life, with daily exposure to more social and commercial intercourse with diverse others, generally encourages a more cosmopolitan sensibility, although that is not always the case. But here again is the contradiction. The price we pay is greater entropy to the environment. Or we could turn the proposition around and say that, up to now, more complex social structures that require greater energy through puts and produce higher levels of entropy also create the conditions for extending empathy to more diverse others.

The tragic flaw of history is that our increased empathic concern and sensitivity grows in direct proportion to the wreaking of greater entropic damage to the world we all cohabit and rely on for our existence and perpetuation.

We are at a decisive moment in the human journey where the race to global empathic consciousness is running up against global entropic collapse. While our empathic gains are impressive, our entropic losses are equally foreboding.

If human nature is materialist to the core—self-serving, utilitarian, and pleasure-seeking—then there is little hope of resolving the empathy/entropy paradox. But if human nature is, rather, at a more basic level, predisposed to affection, companionship, sociability, and empathic extension, then there is the posssibility, at least, that we might yet escape the empathy/entropy dilemma and find an accommodation that will allow us to restore a sustainable balance with the biosphere.

A radical new view of human nature has been slowly emerging and gaining momentum, with revolutionary implications for the way we understand and organize our economic, social and environmental relations in the centuries to come. We have discovered *Homo empathicus.*

PART I

HOMO EMPATHICUS

TWO

THE NEW VIEW OF HUMAN NATURE

WHAT ARE WE MADE of? In an age obsessed with material interests, it's not surprising that biologists—not to mention chemists and
physicists—have looked to material explanations in their efforts to capture the essence of life. Most of our philosophers, till late, have been no
less unequivocal in their belief that our essential nature is materialist to
the core. To wit: Every individual seeks to secure his or her material
well-being and to incorporate the world into themselves. The pop star
Madonna captured the spirit of the age when she proclaimed to be a
"material girl" in a "material world."

As we noted in Chapter 1, Hobbes viewed human nature as aggressive and self-interested. We are born to fight and compete and are
engaged in a relentless struggle with one another to dominate and prevail and secure our material well-being at the expense of our fellows.
John Locke took a gentler, even benign approach, arguing that in a
pure state of nature human beings are sociable and kindly disposed to
one another. Nonetheless we are, according to Locke, acquisitive by
nature and use our mental and physical labor to expropriate the material world and reshape it into productive property. Jeremy Bentham and
the utilitarians agreed with Locke that we are by nature materialists
and, as such, seek to optimize pleasure and mitigate pain.

In the late nineteenth century, the burgeoning interest in the workings of the human mind gave rise to the new field of psychology.

Scholars turned their attention to what drives the human psyche itself. Although less interested in abstract philosophical musings on the nature of man and more concerned with clinical scientific observation of how the human mind actually works, many—but not all—of the early psychologists retained their material biases and preconceptions about the nature of human nature. Like Adam Smith, they assumed that each individual is born to pursue his or her naked economic self-interest. And following Darwin's lead, they presumed that each human being's primary concern is his or her own physical survival and perpetuation.

FREUD: THE LAST GREAT UTILITARIAN

Although Sigmund Freud is often regarded as a seminal thinker, responsible for reshaping the human conversation regarding the nature of human nature, in many of the most important aspects of his theoretical speculations, he scrupulously followed the materialists' script. Freud managed to combine in his thesis a secular version of the earlier, medieval church notion of man's fallen and depraved nature with the materialist narrative of the eighteenth-century Enlightenment. His terrifying and devastating portrait of human nature was so evocative and powerful that it has continued to frame the public perception of the human story all the way to the present day, with consequences that reverberate across every aspect of society, from the way we parent children to the conduct of social life, the workings of commerce, and the enactment of public policy.

Freud's great legacy is that he eroticized material self-interest. It wasn't long before the new eroticized version of human nature was hijacked by a contemporary of Freud, John B. Watson, another early pioneer in the field of psychology, who left the fold to apply the new psychological insights in the new realm of mass advertising. Much of the success of consumer capitalism over the course of the past century is due, in no small part, to the eroticization of desires and the sexualization of consumption. Our advertising appeals are permeated with erotic references.

Freud begins by asking what men "demand of life and wish to achieve in it." Here he lines up squarely with nineteenth-century utilitarian theory, suggesting that the human endeavor has two sides, a positive and a negative one. It aims, on the one hand, at an absence of pain and unpleasure and, on the other, at the experiencing of strong feelings of pleasure.[1]

Freud takes his thesis a step further, arguing that

> [i]f we assume quite generally that the motive force of all
> human activities is a striving towards the two confluent goals
> of utility and a yield of pleasure, we must suppose that this is
> also true of the manifestations of civilization. . . .[2]

Freud then asks rhetorically what afforded man the "strongest experience of satisfaction, and in fact provided him with the prototype of all happiness." He concludes that it is "sexual relations" and, that being the case, man decided that "he should make genital eroticism the central point of his life."[3]

The drive for sexual satisfaction is so powerful, says Freud, that all external reality becomes merely instrumental to achieving sexual release. If unrestrained, man allows nothing to impede his quest for sexual climax. He is, therefore, driven by libido and is aggressive by nature, seeking only to satisfy his unquenchable sexual appetite. He is, in fact, a monster. Freud writes:

> The element of truth behind all of this, which people are so
> ready to disavow, is that men are not gentle creatures who
> want to be loved, and who at the most can defend themselves
> if they are attacked; they are, on the contrary, creatures among
> whose instinctual endowments is to be reckoned a powerful
> share of aggressiveness. As a result, their neighbour is for them
> not only a potential helper or sexual object, but also someone
> who tempts them to satisfy their aggressiveness on him, to
> exploit his capacity for work without compensation, to use
> him sexually without his consent, to seize his possessions, to

humiliate him, to cause him pain, to torture and to kill him.
Homo homini lupus.[4]

Man is revealed as "a savage beast to whom consideration towards
his own kind is something alien."[5]

Civilization, in turn, is little more than an elaborate psycho-cultural
prison set up to restrain man's aggressive sexual drive, lest it lead to a perpetual war of all against all and mutual destruction. Freud goes so far as
to explain away love as an "aim inhibited" method designed to curb the
more primitive sexual drive and aggression. As for the Golden Rule that
one should "love one's neighbor as oneself," Freud is dismissive, saying
"nothing else runs so strongly counter to the original nature of man."[6]

Society, in Freud's schema, is merely an expedient compromise man
has begrudgingly accepted, in which he has "exchanged a portion of
his possibilities of happiness for a portion of security."[7]

If man's nature is to destroy and kill one another, as Freud suggests,
then how do we account for the fact that life itself appears to seek more
order, complexity, and integration? Freud, like many of his contemporaries, was forced to wrestle with the new scientific field of thermodynamics and the laws of conservation of energy, which observe that
biological organisms and living communities are caught in a relentless
struggle to create greater order and complexity against the inevitable
pull of entropy, equilibrium, and death. If the drive to destruction and
death were all that man was about at his biological core, then it would
appear that human nature was at odds with both Darwin's theory of
biological evolution and the newly emerging laws of thermodynamics.
Freud found his way out of the dilemma by positing what he called the
"death instinct." It was to become the centerpiece of his view of human
nature. Freud says that the notion of the death instinct came to him
when he wrote *Beyond the Pleasure Principle* in 1920,

> Starting from speculations on the beginning of life and from
> biological parallels, I drew the conclusion that, besides the
> instinct to preserve living substance and to join into ever larger
> units, there must exist another, contrary instinct seeking to

dissolve those units and to bring them back to their primeval, inorganic state. That is to say, as well as Eros there was an instinct of death. The phenomena of life could be explained from the concurrent or mutually opposing action of these two instincts.[8]

Freud viewed the death instinct—the drive to aggressiveness and destruction—as a force that could be

pressed into the service of Eros, in that the organism was destroying some other thing, whether animate or inanimate, instead of destroying its own self. Conversely, any restriction of this aggressiveness directed outwards would be bound to increase the self-destruction, which is in any case proceeding.[9]

In the first instance, the death instinct manifests itself in the form of sadism and in the second instance, masochism, both of which are expressions of the instinctual sexual drive. That sexual drive seeks release in omnipotence and power over others in the case of sadism and in humiliation and self-destruction in the case of masochism.[10]

Freud ultimately concluded that all of life was at the service of the death instinct. His deeply pessimistic view of human nature was embraced by many of the leading thinkers of the day. Freudian psychoanalyst Géza Róheim referred to the death instinct as the "pillar of metapsychology."[11] Not everyone, however, was won over to Freud's dark assessment of the human spirit. Ian D. Suttie was one of a number of psychologists who broke away from Freud's analysis in the 1920s and 1930s, referring to his theory as

the supreme expression of hatred, elevating this, as it does, to the status of a primal, independent purpose in life—a separate appetite which like hunger requires no external provocation and is an end-in-itself.[12]

Every other human emotion, in Freud's world, is but a residual repression of the sexual drive and the death instinct. Even love and tenderness are viewed as repressed or weakened expressions of the erotic impulse.[13] Civilization has only one purpose: to become the means by which human beings satisfy their libidinal needs by pursuing mastery over others and advancing their material self-interest.

Strangely absent from Freud's analysis is any deep consideration of motherly love, a powerful and undeniable force found among animals that nurse their young. Herein lies a clue to Freud's own personal psychology and even pathology. In *Civilization and Its Discontents*, Freud makes a revealing admission that speaks volumes. Regarding the infant's feeling of oneness with the mother, Freud writes, "I cannot discover this oceanic feeling in myself."[14] While he acknowledges that others might have such a feeling, it eludes him. Freud regards the infant, as the later adult he will become, as libido driven from the outset. The mother is not an object of love and affection but, rather, an object of sexual and material utility, whose sole purpose is to fulfill the infant's internal drive for sexual satisfaction and pleasure. Attachment, love, affection, and companionship are illusions. The entire parenting relationship, from beginning to end, is utilitarian and designed to optimize the child's pleasure. Freud writes that *"[i]f the nurseling longs to behold the mother, it is only because it knows from experience that she satisfies all its requirements without delay."*[15] As Suttie points out:

> This dictum definitely denies the possibility of the inheritance
> of a craving for companionship apart from that affording
> satisfaction to the bodily appetites. According to Freud then
> the infant *learns* to value the mother as a *utility to itself.*[16]

Freud raises the interesting question as to whether the oceanic feeling of oneness so often talked about in infancy might play itself out later in life in terms of the need for religion and attachment to God but dismisses it as unlikely, at least in regard to a substitute for a mother's care. Far more likely, says Freud, is that the source of the religious impulse is found in "the child's feeling of helplessness and the longing it evokes for a father." Here's where Freud reveals his own emotional blind spot and that of the age in which he grew up.

> I could not point to any need in childhood as strong as the
> need for a father's protection. Thus the part played by the
> "oceanic" feeling, which I suppose seeks to reinstate limitless
> narcissism . . . cannot possibly take the first place. The
> derivation of the religious attitude can be followed back in
> clear outline as far as the child's feeling of helplessness. . . .
> There may be something else behind this, but for the present it
> is wrapped in obscurity.[17]

The religious impulse then, for Freud, is utterly utilitarian and directed to a father figure, who can guarantee a sense of security. Maternal love and care and the sense of mutual affection and companionship are figments of the imagination masking a deeper, narcissistic drive.

Nearly a quarter of a century after Freud laid out his thesis, the distinguished twentieth-century anthropologist Ashley Montagu would write that the psychological foundation of Freud's belief was deeply mired in a masculine mystique in which the feminine plays only a marginal role, if at all. Freud's psychoanalysis, wrote Montagu,

> is a patriarchal psychology—the nature of women seems
> utterly to have escaped Freud, and he virtually confessed as
> much, and for this reason . . . he never quite grasped the true
> meaning of the relationship between mother and child or the
> meaning of love.[18]

Freud was the last of the old guard. A master storyteller, he gave a brilliant secular defense of the ancient patriarchal narrative, whose roots lay in the great hydraulic civilizations of the Near and Far East, and that flowered with the Abrahamic religions and Confucianism. In a grand last stand, Freud brought the full force of the newly discovered unconscious to bear, arguing that male dominance is the natural order of things. The story of the Oedipus complex was an imaginative bit of theater designed to lock in the male protagonist as the central figure in human history. As to the role of the female, Freud was, by his own admission, perplexed about what endowed her character, aside from bearing children and nursing them with her milk. Whatever other mental and emotional makeup she might possess and express, Freud reasoned, was forever a pale shadow of the male. It's no wonder, then, that Freud explained away the female psyche, arguing that the sum total of her behavior is ultimately a reflection of "penis envy," which she brings with her from the womb.

But even Freud's spirited and ingenious defense of male dominance couldn't hold the line against the forces of history that were beginning to chip away at the patriarchal foundation of civilization that had stood the test of time for more than five thousand years. The new communications/energy complexes of the First and Second Industrial Revolutions broke down the patriarchal walls, freeing women from centuries of slavery, serfdom, and servanthood. Print, especially the romance novel, allowed women to put a mirror to their relationships and to themselves and begin the arduous journey of discovering their selfhood. At the same time, the telephone provided a new source of communication that allowed millions of women to escape the confines of their homes and begin to share their lives with one another across electrical wires, creating a powerful new networking tool for exploring their mutual gender interests. (When we think of the early telephone, the picture that comes to mind is women conversing with one another on party lines.) While the novel provided a tool for self-reflection, the telephone provided a tool for gossip and helped create a sense of gender solidarity.

Both forms of communications would play a role in liberating women from the watchful eye of men, allowing them to find their identity and their voice. Before mass literacy and print and the telephone, women's ability to think on their own and join in solidarity beyond the narrow range of sequestered conversation among female members of an extended family was limited. The overwhelming male presence ensured their docility. The print and electrical communications revolutions gave women the tools they needed to extend their minds and their horizons and find their womanhood. The cinema, radio, and TV gave women additional communications outlets to explore and expand their identities.

Public schooling and mass literacy began to put women on an even communications playing field with men. The introduction of the automobile, the electrification of homes and the advent of mass-produced home appliances and other household goods freed women, at least partially, from the backbreaking tasks of providing all of the necessities of life for kin. Steam power and later electricity also shifted manufacturing, logistics, and services from physical to mental and emotional labor, allowing women to take their place in the factories and front offices of modern commerce. While their talents and skills were less fully employed than men's and they were paid only a fraction of the compensation, the emergence of the semi-independent female wage earner cannot be exaggerated in the historical shift in gender relations.

Freud wrote his stories during the very decades that Europe and America and other enclaves of the world were transitioning from a First to a Second industrial revolution. His most eloquent tracts were written in the 1920s, when the factories were shifting over from steam power to electrification, women were taking the wheel in Henry Ford's Model T car, and female liberation was becoming all the rage. The writer F. Scott Fitzgerald branded the new women the flappers and their image of defiance of male domination became the signature for what would be called the Roaring Twenties.

WHAT BABIES REALLY WANT

All of this was not lost on a younger generation of psychologists who began to question the central tenets of Freud's vision of human nature. Fittingly, the first psychologist of standing to challenge Freud's thesis, although quite unintentionally, was a woman, Melanie Klein. Her theory of "object relations" opened the door a crack, but it was just enough to allow others to crash through the Freudian fortress and herald to the world a new story about the nature of human nature—one more compatible with the new technological, commercial, and social forces that were reshaping civilization.

Klein restored the mother to a primary role in the human story, although again, it should be emphasized that she had no thought of doing so, and she regarded herself as a staunch disciple of Freud to the end of her life.

Freud was the first to use the term "object" in his discussion of the sexualization of relationships. In his 1905 work titled *Three Essays on the Theory of Sexuality*, Freud categorized "the person from whom sexual attraction proceeds the *sexual object* and the act towards which the instinct tends the *sexual aim*."[19] Each individual, according to Freud, is aggressively moving from one object to another in search of satisfying his or her sexual desire, with the goal of "temporary extinction of the libido."[20]

Klein, who is credited with pioneering the British school of object relations, stayed true to Freud's script, with a single exception. While she agreed with Freud that both libido and aggression are the primary drives, she put more emphasis on the latter. The aggression is first directed at the mother's breast. The infant splits the primary object, the breast, into the good breast that satisfies his libidinal drive and the bad breast that frustrates and persecutes him, denying him satisfaction.

Klein departs from Freud in still another important respect, arguing that the ego is at play in a primitive form from birth, allowing the infant the ability to create internalized object relations. By asserting that some form of consciousness is present from early infancy, Klein inferred that the baby's first internalized object is the mother, not the father.

In the early stages of infancy, then, the baby's natural aggression is directed toward the mother, not the father. But because the breast is split into a good breast and a bad breast, the infant comes to have ambiguous feelings toward the object. As the infant matures and begins to recognize the mother as more than breasts and as a caring being, the ambivalence leads to the fear that his aggression could harm the good object, and he begins to feel a sense of remorse and guilt and the desire to make reparation, lest he destroy the relationship he depends on to satisfy his libido.

Although Klein continued to believe that an infant's primary drive is libidinal and aggressive, she opened up the possibility, at least, that human relationships could be tempered by sociability.[21] Yet because she believed, like Freud, that the destructive urge and the death instinct were wired into the human psyche, she was unable to turn the corner and believe that sociability was a primary drive and not just a compensatory one.[22]

Others, however, took advantage of the small bit of hope Klein introduced and mounted an all-out assault on the Freudian premise that the baby is born to expropriate and destroy in the pursuit of libido. Unlike Klein, who believed that sociability was a secondary response to a more primary aggressive drive, psychologists like William Fairbairn, Heinz Kohut, Donald Winnicott, and Ian Suttie suggested that sociability is the primary drive and that a preoccupation with libido, aggression, and destruction is a compensatory response to the thwarting of that most basic of all human needs. For those psychologists, relationships with objects are not driven by expediency and the need to satisfy libido but, rather, by the need for human connection, love, affection, and companionship.

Fairbairn launched the rebellion with a simple question: "Why does a baby suck his thumb?" Fairbairn suggested that "[u]pon the answer to this simple question depends the whole validity of the conception of erotogenic zones and the form of libido theory based upon it."[23]

Freud would have us believe that the baby sucks its thumb "because his mouth is an erotogenic zone and sucking provides him with erotic pleasure." While it might at first glance seem convincing, Fairbairn asks a second question: "Why his thumb?" Fairbairn says that "the answer to this question is—'Because there is no breast to suck.'" Fairbairn posits that thumb sucking "represents a technique for dealing with an unsatisfactory object-relationship. . . ."[24] In other words, the infant is providing a substitute object-relationship to satisfy himself because he is being denied what he really desires, which is a relationship with the mother's breast and the mother herself. Here Fairbairn parts company with Freud and Klein, creating a schism in psychoanalytical theory. He writes:

It must always be borne in mind, however, that it is not the
libidinal attitude which determines the object-relationship, but
the object-relationship which determines the libidinal attitude.[25]

All of the forms of infantile sexuality that Freud was so obsessed
with, says Fairbairn, are compensatory actions to alleviate the infant's
anxiety over what he really desires but is partially or mostly denied.
And what does every child desire above all else and fear he may be
denied? Fairbairn is unequivocal on this matter.

Frustration of his desire to be loved as a person and to have
his love accepted is the greatest trauma that a child can
experience; and it is this trauma above all that creates fixations
in the various forms of infantile sexuality to which a child is
driven to resort in an attempt to compensate by substitutive
satisfactions for the failure of his emotional relationships with
his outer objects.[26]

When a child feels he is not loved as a person or that his love is
not accepted, his maturation stalls, and he begins to develop aberrant
relationships and express pathological symptoms, including aggression,
obsession, paranoia, and hysterical and phobic behavior.[27] All of these
behaviors stem from a deep feeling of isolation and abandonment.

Fairbairn reaches the inescapable conclusion that Freud's view of
human nature was dead wrong in two essential respects—the primary
importance of the libidinal drive and gratification.

Amongst the conclusions formulated . . . are the following:
(1) that libidinal "aims" are of secondary importance
in comparison with object relationships, and (2) that a
relationship with the object, and not gratification of impulse,
is the ultimate aim of libidinal striving.[28]

The implications of these two observations are enormous, as they
challenge the very bedrock assumptions of Freud's story about the

nature of human nature. Freud, recall, believed that the libido is an intrinsic and primary force. The infant seeks unlimited pleasure in various eroticized forms from the very start of life—the pleasure principle. Even before there is an ego there is an id, a primal force in search of libidinal satisfaction. But, eventually, the pleasure principle must be reined in by society if orderly social intercourse is to take place. Therefore, the "reality principle" is superimposed by society in the form of parental restraints, beginning with toilet training and other conditioning agents. These restraints help form the ego, which is little more than a mechanism to repress libidinal drives and control the id in the name of socialization.

Fairbairn turns Freud's thesis on its heels, arguing that the ego structure begins to develop at birth and that impulses are means by which the ego seeks relationships with others. In other words, the reality principle exists from the get-go. Every infant seeks the other and is forming strands, if not bonds, of socialization from birth. Fairbairn makes the point that "[u]ltimately 'impulses' must be simply regarded as constituting the forms of activity in which the life of the ego structures consists," and that activity is directed toward creating relationships.[29]

The reality principle, in Fairbairn's schema, is primary. The infant is continuously engaged in making connections with the other—to the end of affecting relationships. This is what the reality principle is all about. To the extent that the primary aim of sociability is thwarted and the ego is not allowed to mature properly, the pleasure principle becomes a poor substitute. Fairbairn is unsparing in his critique of Freud's central thesis. He explains his differences with Freud this way:

> In accordance with this point of view, the pleasure principle
> will cease to be regarded as the primary principle of behaviour
> and will come to be regarded as a subsidiary principle of
> behavior involving an impoverishment of object-relationships
> and coming into operation in proportion as the reality
> principle fails to operate, whether this be on account of the
> immaturity of the ego structure or on account of a failure of
> development on its part.[30]

Others joined Fairbairn in criticizing Freud's thesis and rounding out a counter-theory of human nature centered on the importance of social relationships to the development of the psyche and selfhood. Heinz Kohut agreed with Fairbairn that the destructive drive is not intrinsic to man's makeup but, rather, an expression of the failure to build trusting relationships. He added, however, an important caveat to Fairbairn's analysis, the important role that empathy plays in the development of a mature self and the dire consequences to the formation of the ego if it is absent.

In *The Restoration of the Self*, Kohut argues, like Fairbairn, that the destructive drive—whether aimed at others or oneself—occurs when the infant experiences repeated failures in connecting emotionally with a self object. He writes:

> Man's destructiveness . . . arises originally as the result of the failure of the self-object environment to meet the child's need for optimal—not maximal, it should be stressed—empathic responses. Aggression . . . as a psychological phenomenon, is not elemental.[31]

Although Kohut acknowledges that infants are born with a drive to be assertive, he distinguishes that from overt aggression, rage, and destructiveness. The former is instrumental to ego formation and the development of a mature self, while the latter represents a failure of the self-object relationship to blossom because of an empathic deficit on the part of the parent or parents.[32]

Kohut's own clinical observations of patients over the years convinced him that it is not the drives themselves but "the threat to the organization of the self" that is so critical to development.[33] If the empathic response of the parents is weak or nonexistent, the child's development is arrested. It's in these circumstances that the drives "become powerful constellations in their own right" and destructive rage sets in.[34]

Kohut takes a swipe at Freud's preoccupation with the sexual anatomy, saying that "a child is much more significantly influenced by the empathic attitude of the grownups around him or her than by the givens of organic equipment." When a small boy "discovers that his penis is very small as compared with the penis of a grown man," it is of little importance and hardly relevant to the adult he will become. But the importance of having admiring and empathic parents is critical to the kind of person he eventually will be. Kohut concludes that "the importance of the matrix of empathy in which we grow up cannot be overestimated."[35]

Kohut makes a final observation that is worth noting. He found that it makes little difference who the early parental provider is, as long as she or he provides the appropriate empathic response for the child's development. He referenced an example, reported by Anna Freud and Sophie Dann, to emphasize the point that a biological mother is not essential to providing the necessary empathic environment to nourish the child's developmental process. Freud and Dann related the story of six children who had survived a German concentration camp in World War II. Over the course of their three years of imprisonment, they were taken care of by an ever-changing set of mothers. As each set of mother surrogates was exterminated, others took their place, until their own deaths. Although the children were justifiably disturbed by the experience, they had a reasonably cohesive self, which can only be attributed to the empathic regard and affection they were given by the many women who took care of them.[36]

While Fairbairn and Kohut mounted a full frontal assault on Freud's theory of human nature, another of their contemporaries, Donald Winnicott, a pediatrician by background, launched a more subtle but no less effective attack based on his decades of work with infants. Winnicott challenged the very notion of the self-absorbed little individual who views the world as so much bounty to feed its insatiable appetites. Winnicott argued that the idea of an individual baby, per se, is a misnomer. Babies don't exist on their own. They don't even have a coherent sense of self. "At this very early stage," says Winnicott, "it is not logical to think in terms of an individual . . . because there is not yet an individual self there."[37] Although considered counterintuitive at the time—but rather obvious with hindsight—Winnicott was making an insightful point; that while a baby is formed in the womb, an individual is formed in a relationship.

> If you show me a baby you certainly show me also someone
> caring for a baby, or at least a pram with someone's eyes and
> ears glued to it. One sees a "nursing couple."[38]

What Winnicott is saying is that a relationship precedes an individual, not the other way around. In other words, individuals don't create society. Rather, society creates individuals. This simple observation challenged the very core of modernity, with its emphasis on the self-contained, autonomous individual exerting its will on the world.

Winnicott drove his thesis home with a telling account of a baby's first glimmer of self-consciousness. He asks us to consider the overriding importance of the baby's first act . . . finding his mother's nipple. From his years of pediatric experience, Winnicott observed that the way the baby is introduced to his mother's nipple sets the course for the child's future development as an individual being. Because this initial act is also the baby's very first initiation into a relationship with another being, the way the relationship is entered into is determinative of the kind of expectations—or lack of expectations—a child develops regarding others.

In the very first feed, says Winnicott, the mother must allow the baby to find the nipple, making the experience a playful present and, more important, giving the baby the sense—although dimly perceived—that he has created the nipple and, by doing so is "creating the world."[39] What is going on here, observes Winnicott, is that "[t]he mother is waiting to be discovered."[40] This marks the beginning of the baby's first relationship and guides his development to selfhood. It is through this creative act that the sense of "I" and "thou" later develops. Winnicott sums up the importance of the first feed.

> Memories are built up from innumerable sense-impressions
> associated with the activity of feeding and of finding the object.
> In the course of time there comes a state in which the infant

feels confident that the object of desire can be found, and this means that the infant gradually tolerates the absence of the object. Thus starts the infant's concept of external reality. . . . Through the magic of desire one can say that the baby has the illusion of magical creative power, and omnipotence is a fact through the sensitive adaptation of the mother. The basis for the infant's gradual recognition of a lack of magical control over external reality lies in the initial omnipotence that is made a fact by the mother's adaptive technique.[41]

If the mother, for example, does not allow the child to playfully discover and magically create the nipple but, rather, places the baby's mouth onto her breast, the child is denied the opportunity of building up the sensory memories that will allow him to eventually perceive himself as a separate individual who acts on and with separate others. By the way the mother enters into this first relationship with the baby, then, she is helping him become an individual being. From the very beginning, the relationship creates the individual.

The failure to allow the infant to "contribute" thwarts the relationship—it takes two to tango—and arrests his development of selfhood. Winnicott cautions that

> [i]t is very easy to be deceived and to see a baby responding to skillful feeding, and to fail to notice that this infant who takes in an entirely passive way has never created the world, and has no capacity for external relationships, and has no future as an individual.[42]

Winnicott concludes that

> [t]here is perhaps no one detail which the psychologist can teach which if accepted would have a more profound effect on the mental health of the individuals of the community than this matter of the need for the infant to be the creator of the nipple of the breast of the mother.[43]

Fairbairn, Kohut, and Winnicott, each in their own fashion, chipped away at the assumptions of Freudian psychoanalysis, creating a counter-theory of human nature that emphasized the importance of social relationships over libidinal drives in the development of the individual psyche and selfhood. Ian Suttie took the process one step further, positing an alternative explanation of the nature of human nature that, in every respect, is the mirror opposite of Freud's views on the subject.

Suttie recalls that his journey to an alternate view of human nature began when he

> saw the possibility that the *biological* need for nurture *might*
> *be psychologically presented in the infant mind*, not as a bundle of
> practical organic necessities and potential privations, but as
> a pleasure in *responsive* companionship and as a correlative
> discomfort in loneliness and isolation.[44]

Suttie came to see "the innate need-for-companionship" as the infant's primary means of assuring self-preservation and argued that it is the core of human nature.[45]

Suttie, like Fairbairn, Kohut, and Winnicott, viewed Freud's notion that libido governs human nature as unfounded, in both theory and practice. The idea that an unformed infant's desires for his mother are all sexualized from the very outset of life and then spread to every other relationship an individual is engaged in later on in life seemed at odds with common sense and the emotional experience of the vast majority of people. Rather, Suttie opined that all of a person's later interests—the way we play, cooperate, compete, and seek out cultural and political interests, are a substitute for the first relationship, the bond between infant and mother. Suttie says that "*[b]y these substitutes we put the whole social environment in the place once occupied by mother.*"[46]

Suttie is at odds with Thomas Hobbes and the later Enlightenment thinkers, who argued that material self-interest is the guiding motivation of human beings. Instead, Suttie argues, like Johan Huizinga and others, that play is the most important social activity because it is where we create companionship, engender trust, and exercise human imagination and individual creativity. Play is where we overcome our sense of existential loneliness and recapture the feeling of companionship we first discovered with our primordial playmates, our mothers.[47] Suttie bolsters his claim that companionship and play are essential to becoming a human being by pointing out that

> the period between infancy and adulthood . . . [is] . . .
> dominated by an almost insatiable social need, which
> uses the plastic energy of human interest for its satisfaction in
> play.[48]

Unlike Freud, who viewed tenderness as a weak sublimation of sexual arousal, Suttie saw it as a primary force that manifests itself from the very beginning of life. His notion of "tenderness" overlaps with Kohut's ideas on the importance of the empathic bond in the creation of social relations.

Suttie dismisses the idea that all human relations—even among infants—are driven by the quest to assert power over one another. While such behavior exists as some infants mature into childhood, it represents a secondary impulse arising from a deficit in tender reciprocity in the very first social relationship with a mother. Suttie says that to believe that a very young infant is aware of a sense of gain or loss of power in his or her relationship with the mother before he has even developed a rudimentary consciousness of self is absurd. This is because

> [t]he primal state is not one of omnipotence, for omnipotence
> implies the consciousness of self as distinct from mother,
> which differentiation (as is known) cannot exist in early
> infancy. Prior to this differentiation of the self from the not
> self, as I have shown, there can be no question of power, nor a
> conflict of interest or wish nor any awareness of the distinction
> between gain or loss. The interactions between mother and
> infant are entirely pleasurable or unpleasurable and convey no
> sense of advantage or defeat to either side.[49]

It is only when the mother refuses to give herself to the infant or rejects gestures of affection or gifts from the baby that "anxiety, hate, aggression (which Freud mistakes for a primary instinct), and the quest for power" begin to manifest themselves.[50]

The infant begins life, then, according to Suttie, with an inchoate but nonetheless instinctual need to receive as well as give gifts, which is the basis of all affection. Reciprocity is the heart of sociality and what relationships are built on. If reciprocity is blocked, the development of selfhood and sociability is stunted and psychopathology emerges.[51]

THE MOST SOCIAL ANIMAL

While object relationship theorists like Fairbairn, Kohut, Winnicott, and Suttie were raising the hackles of traditional Freudian analysts with their belief that babies are prewired for companionship and sociability rather than driven by sexual libido, other researchers, often working independently of one another, were coming to the same conclusion. In a series of controlled studies of infants raised in orphanages and/or adopted out to foster parents, psychologists were reporting disturbing findings that bolstered the sociability thesis.

Psychoanalyst David Levy was interested in infants raised by overprotective mothers. He established a control group made up of children who had never had maternal care as infants and who subsequently were unable to establish attachment bonds with adoptive parents. Most of these children had spent their early years in orphanages and later boarding homes before being placed with a family. His attention soon turned to the control group, however, as he began to notice a frightening pattern. The children who lacked early bonding with a mother figure, although often affectionate on the surface, showed little or no real emotional warmth underneath. They were often sexually aggressive and engaged in antisocial behavior, including consummate lying and stealing. Virtually all of them were unable to make meaningful friendships. Levy categorized those children as suffering from "primary affect hunger." They were unable to express the full range of human feelings that grow out of a meaningful relationship with a mother figure. Levy asked the rather chilling question of whether it is possible "that there results a deficiency disease of the emotional life, comparable to a deficiency of vital nutritional elements within the developing organism."[52]

Other researchers were noticing equally disquieting behavior among infants confined to orphanages and other public institutions. Loretta Bender, the head of the child psychiatry ward at Bellevue Hospital in New York City, observed that such children are eerily antihuman. She wrote:

> They have no play pattern . . . cannot enter into group play but abuse other children, and cling to adults and exhibit a temper tantrum when cooperation is expected. They are hyperkinetic and distractible; they are completely confused about human relationships, and . . . lose themselves in a destructive fantasy life directed both against the world and themselves.[53]

Deprived of maternal care, these children developed psychopathic personalities.

The lack of maternal care in these institutions was exacerbated by the hygienic standards imposed, ironically to safeguard the physical health of the children. Recall in Chapter 1 the mention of the almost obsessive preoccupation with maintaining a sterile living environment in orphanages and foundling hospitals so as not to spread disease. Toward this end, personnel were discouraged from ever touching babies or picking them up and cuddling them for fear of spreading germs and disease. Most infants were prop-fed so that the attendant would not need to come into physical contact at all with the infant. The infants languished. Shockingly, death rates in some of the orphanages ranged from 32 percent to 75 percent in the first two years of infancy. Although well fed and raised in clean environments, these children were dying in droves. The infants were often misdiagnosed as malnourished or were categorized as suffering from "hospitalism," all of which masked the underlying problem.[54] Denied affection and maternal companionship, the infants lost the will to live.

Those governing protocols remained the norm for orphanages from before World War I to the 1930s, despite the mounting evidence that something was very wrong in the management of those institutions. It wasn't until 1931, when a pediatrician, Harry Bakwin, became head of the pediatric unit at Bellevue Hospital, that conditions on the infant wards began to change. Bakwin published a paper, titled "Loneliness in Infants," in which he connected the dots between infant death and emotional starvation. In a particularly telling and sad passage of the paper, he observed that the obsession with isolating infants had reached tragic proportions in the hospital. He noted that the management had gone so far as to devise

> a box equipped with inlet and outlet valves and sleeve
> arrangements for the attendants. The infant is placed in this
> box and can be taken care of almost untouched by human
> hands.[55]

Bakwin ordered new signs be put up across the pediatric unit that read: "Do not enter this nursery without picking up a baby."[56] Infection rates declined, and infants began to thrive.

At the same time, other researchers were finding a correlation between intelligence and language skills and emotional deprivation. Children raised in orphanages often tested with low and even retarded IQs, while those in foster care tested normally.[57] Those studies flew in the face of the orthodox thinking of the time that IQ was inherited.

In a landmark study conducted by Harold Skeels of the Iowa Child Research Welfare Station, thirteen children from orphanages, all below two-and-a-half years of age, were each placed in the care of a feeble-minded older girl in a public institution. During a nineteen-month period, the average IQ of the infants under the care of the older girls shot up from 64 to 92, demonstrating that emotional bonds play a far more crucial role in the development of human intelligence than previously suspected.[58] The long-held conventional wisdom that individual human intelligence is preordained by one's biology no longer seemed convincing. Was it possible that a child's mental intelligence flowed from the innate emotional need for affection and companionship?

The mounting number of studies on infant care and lack thereof in the 1930s and 1940s began to slowly shift opinions within the psychiatric profession regarding the nature of human nature. But it was the visceral, emotional impact of a single film that shook the very foundations of the field and changed forever the ideas about proper professional care of children, and parenting as well.

In 1947, a short amateur film was shown to a small group of physicians and psychoanalysts at the New York Academy of Medicine. The film, made by René Spitz, a psychoanalyst, was entitled *Grief: A Peril in Infancy*. It was a silent film, shot in black and white, showing a number of infants who had been previously attended by mothers, but forced by various circumstances to be placed in a foundling home, where there was only a single nurse and five assistant nurses for forty-five babies.

The first little baby is shown just after her mother had dropped her off for a three-month stay. The baby is smiling, giggling, and playing with an adult supervisor. Seven days later, the same child has turned into another person. She looks forlorn and is unresponsive. She sobs uncontrollably, sometimes kicking the adult supervisor. Her expression is one of utter terror. The film scans other babies who appear dazed, depressed, and lifeless. Many of the babies are emaciated and exhibit stereotypical behaviors, including gnawing at their hands. A number of the babies cannot even sit or stand. They remain expressionless and motionless, devoid of spirit. They are empty shells. A title card appears on the screen saying, "The cure: Give mother back to baby."[59]

The impact of the film on the psychologists, doctors, and nurses was overwhelming. Some openly wept. In the coming years, thousands of professional psychologists, psychiatrists, social workers, doctors, and nurses would view the film. Many more read Spitz's book on the subject, *The First Year of Life*. It transformed the debate over infant care, but it would be two more decades before a solid majority of the pediatric profession would embrace the underlying findings and the implications that flowed from the Spitz film.

The man most responsible for advancing a coherent theory to explain what Spitz and the other researchers were chronicling was an English psychiatrist, John Bowlby. His Attachment Theory was articulated in a series of three scientific papers delivered at the British Psychoanalytic Society in London between 1958 and 1960. The first paper, titled "The Nature of the Child's Tie to His Mother," rattled the psychoanalytic community and eventually helped lay to rest Freud's view of human nature.

Building on object relations theory, and especially the pioneering insights of Fairbairn, Bowlby argued that a child's first relationship with a mother shapes the individual's emotional and mental life for a lifetime. Like Fairbairn, Bowlby believed that a child's primary drive is to seek relationships with others. He wrote:

> When a baby is born he cannot tell one person from another and indeed can hardly tell person from thing. Yet, by his first birthday he is likely to have become a connoisseur of people. Not only does he come quickly to distinguish familiars from strangers but amongst his familiars he chooses one or more favorites. They are greeted with delight; they are followed when they depart; and they are sought when absent. Their loss causes anxiety and distress; their recovery, relief and a sense of security. On this foundation, it seems, the rest of his emotional life is built—without this foundation there is risk for his future happiness and health.[60]

Like other object relations theorists, Bowlby disagreed with the still-dominant Freudian theory that the craving for food is the primary human motivation and that personal relationships are mainly secondary and sought after to satiate libidinal drives.[61] But Bowlby went a giant step beyond his colleagues by grounding object relations in evolutionary biology, giving it the necessary scientific gravitas to challenge and overturn the Freudian orthodoxy.

Bowlby's theory was greatly influenced by the work of the Austrian ethologist Konrad Lorenz. Back in 1935, Lorenz published an important work on imprinting in birds. His observations became the foundation for Bowlby's own theory on human attachment. In an article titled "The Companion in the Bird's World," Lorenz reported that in some species of bird, like ducks and geese, the ducklings and goslings bond quickly to the first adult with whom they come in contact. Bowlby was impressed that

> [a]t least in some species of bird, [Lorenz] had found, strong
> bonds to a mother figure develop during the early days of life
> without any reference to food and simply through the young
> being exposed to and becoming familiar with the figure in
> question.[62]

Bowlby had hit upon a body of work coming from the field of ethology that validated his own observations of how human infants develop. He would later recount his epiphany:

> I mean talk about *eureka*. They were brilliant, first-class
> scientists, brilliant observers, and studying family relationships
> in other species—relationships which were obviously
> analogous with that of human beings—and doing it so
> frightfully well. We were fumbling around in the dark; they
> were already in brilliant sunshine.[63]

In his 1979 book, *The Making and Breaking of Affectional Bonds*, Bowlby would acknowledge the great debt he owed to Lorenz and his fellow ethologists. He wrote:

> I outlined a theory of attachment in a paper published in
> 1958 . . . [a]rguing that the empirical data on the development

of a human child's tie to his mother can be understood better
in terms of a model derived from ethology. . . .[64]

Bowlby observed that attachment behavior exists in almost all species of mammals. An immature animal will bond to a mature adult,
almost always a mother, generally for protection, and such behavior is
different from feeding and sexual behavior.[65]

While all of this appears incontrovertible, Bowlby took the ethologists' insights a step further, noting that among mammals, attachment
behavior is only part of the unfolding relationship with the mother.
A seemingly antithetical behavior is also at work. He noted that in all
mammals, "exploratory activity is of great importance in its own right,
enabling a person or an animal to build up a coherent picture of environmental features which may at any time become of importance for
survival." Bowlby points out that

> [c]hildren and other young creatures are notoriously curious
> and inquiring, which commonly leads them to move away
> from their attachment figure. In this sense exploratory
> behaviour is antithetical to attachment behaviour. In healthy
> individuals the two kinds of behaviour normally alternate.[66]

The critical question is what connects the two forms of behavior
that are so widely observed among mothers and their infants in the
animal world? It is here that Bowlby found the dialectic relationship
that exists between attachment and independence that would shape his
own theory about human nature. The just good enough parent, says
Bowlby, provides a child "with a secure base" and "encourage[s] him
to explore from it."[67]

Unless a parent provides a baby with a secure sense of protection,
care, and affection, he or she will not be able to develop to the point
of engaging the world and becoming an independent being. Yet, at
the same time, a parent needs to encourage the baby's innate desire to
explore and engage the world that surrounds. It is the success or failure
of this delicate process that determines the future emotional life and

sociability of every child. Bowlby concludes that a just good enough parent needs to have

> an intuitive and sympathetic understanding of the child's
> attachment behaviour and a willingness to meet it and
> thereby terminate it, and, second, recognition that one of
> the commonest sources of a child's anger is the frustration of
> his desire for love and care, and that his anxiety commonly
> reflects uncertainty whether parents will continue to be
> available. Complementary in importance to a parent's respect
> for a child's attachment desires is respect for his desire to
> explore and gradually to extend his relationships both with
> peers and with other adults.[68]

If the parent is able to create the right balance between maintaining secure attachment and at the same time encouraging independent exploration, the child will develop a healthy sense of self and acquire the appropriate emotional maturity to engage others and develop meaningful relationships. If, however, the parent is not able to provide a sense of warmth and security and allow the infant to explore the world, the child will grow up with an arrested sense of self and be unable to enter into more than superficial relationships with others.

Bowlby did not devote a lot of attention to the question of why one parent might be better attuned than another to make the process work. Subsequent research into the parent/child dynamic, however, clearly shows that the more empathic the mother or father figure, the more able they are to identify emotionally and cognitively and to read their child's needs. A parent with immature, inadequate, or deficient empathic sensitivity is not going to be as successful in producing a well-adjusted, trusting, and caring child, who feels both secure and independent and able to enter into meaningful relationships with others. And a child without a consistent parent figure or who is without one altogether is unable to establish meaningful social relationships from the get-go.

Bowlby's own research suggested that in the United States and

Britain more than half the children were growing up with the proper parenting to allow them to thrive, while more than one third were not.[69] The latter grew up with parents who were unresponsive to the child's care-eliciting behavior or disparaged the child or rejected the child outright. Any of those parental behaviors can lead the child to live in a constant state of anxiety—what Bowlby calls anxious attachment—for fear of losing an attachment figure and result in a range of pathogenic behavior, from neurotic and phobic in nature to psychotic and sociopathic.[70]

A child can also exhibit what Bowlby calls a compulsive self-reliant behavior, just the opposite of anxious attachment. Instead of seeking a love that is elusive, he or she keeps a stiff upper lip and attempts to be completely autonomous and without need of the warmth and affection of others. This behavior is often referred to as avoidant. These children are distrustful of close relationships and often crack under stress and experience a high rate of depression.

Bowlby emphasized that

> whatever representational models of attachment figures and of self an individual builds during his childhood and adolescence, tend to persist relatively unchanged into and throughout adult life.[71]

In other words, he or she will tend to attach to new people in his life—friends, a spouse, an employer—in the same manner and expressing the same behavioral repertoire as he or she did with their first adult attachment figure in infancy.

Bowlby's analysis seems rather commonplace today. Yet we need to understand that it wasn't until the 1960s that pediatricians in the United States and the UK began to take notice and change the way they counseled parents on relating to their infants and not until the late 1970s that pediatricians in continental Europe caught up to the change in infant care.

Bowlby's theory wasn't accepted overnight. The opposition was fierce. The Freudians were reluctant to give up their materialist and utilitarian ideas about human nature and clung to the notion that the body is biologically driven to satiate material and sexual desires. Others argued that attachment theory put far too much emphasis on the relationship with the parent in how the child develops and not enough on the inborn temperament of the child.

The behavioralists were equally unimpressed, arguing that there is no evidence to suggest that infants are biologically wired for companionship. Rather, they are born tabula rasa, and because they seek pleasure and attempt to avoid pain, their behavior is infinitely malleable by proper conditioning. The behavioralists were particularly dismissive of Bowlby's attachment theory. After all, they adhered to the notion, advanced by the psychologist John B. Watson in the 1920s, that too much affection and "coddling" of babies spoiled them and made them less malleable to molding later on. Watson counseled young mothers to

> [t]reat them [the babies] as though they were young adults. Dress them, bathe them with care and circumspection. Let your behavior always be objective and kindly firm. Never hug and kiss them, never let them sit on your lap. If you must, kiss them once on the forehead when they say goodnight. Shake hands with them in the morning. Give them a pat on the head if they have made an extraordinary good job of a difficult task.[72]

Even some early feminists and professional career women were miffed, arguing that Bowlby was attempting to imprison women in the traditional role of sole caretaker of children. It should be pointed out that Bowlby had no such intention in mind. Although he was quick to emphasize that a baby needs a consistent parent figure until the age of three, the attachment figure could be the biological mother or father or other relative or even a nanny. Still, his caveats did little to quell the uproar.

All of the critics were like-minded in one respect. If attachment behavior is biologically wired, as Bowlby suggested, they demanded the scientific findings that could validate his theory. They got what they were looking for from Mary Ainsworth, a Canadian psychologist who had enjoyed a long working relationship with Bowlby. In the 1960s, Ainsworth initiated a series of studies at Johns Hopkins University in Baltimore, Maryland, that would provide Bowlby with the rigorous research data that he needed to show that his theory matched reality. Ainsworth developed four scales to rate a mother's way of being with her baby and then compared her behavior with the reaction of her baby. Was the mother sensitive to the baby's signals? Did she express acceptance or rejection of the baby? Did she accommodate the baby's desires and synchronize with his rhythms, or did she interfere, forcing the child to accept her pace when handling, playing, or feeding? And how available was she to the baby? Conversely, how often did she ignore the infant?

Ainsworth then concocted a brilliantly simple protocol, which she called "The Strange Situation," to assess Bowlby's thesis. She explained that the idea was to place the mother and her baby in a "strange environment" with toys to encourage exploration. A stranger would be introduced so that researchers could observe the baby's response. At a certain point, the mother would leave the baby with the stranger. The researcher would then observe how the baby responded to the departure and subsequently to her mother's return. They would then create a second situation with the baby by itself in the room, to observe whether the baby's stress would ease when the stranger returned. Finally, they would make room for another reunion with the mother. Ainsworth said that she and her colleagues devised the whole idea in less than an hour.[73]

The studies backed up Bowlby's thesis that the securely attached baby is able to reach out on his or her own to explore the world, while the insecurely attached baby has difficulty doing so. Ainsworth observed three distinct behavioral sets among the children: the securely attached, who were upset when their moms left but greeted them eagerly upon their return and who were comforted by their mother's embrace; the avoidantly attached, who seemed more aloof from their mothers but who sometimes attacked them—even though these children were also upset when their mothers left the room, they showed no interest in her upon her return, and the ambivalently attached, who were the most anxious, and who, unlike the avoidant children, were clingy and demanding at home, and who, like the other children, were upset when their mothers left the room but were inconsolable in their grief upon the mothers' return.

The mothers of "securely attached children" were far more likely to hold them longer and attend to their needs. They were more emotionally engaged and more consistently attentive. In contrast, the mothers of the ambivalent children were more arbitrary and unpredictable in their responsiveness, while the mothers of the avoidant children were more rejecting in their behavior.[74]

Ainsworth's studies poured cold water over the long-dominant belief that babies should not be overly cuddled or picked up and given too much attention, lest they become too clingy and dependent and fail to develop a sense of independence and autonomy. Quite the contrary. The children who were the most securely attached and who had been provided an ample amount of care, attention, and affection were the most likely to separate from their mothers and play and explore the world around them, while the least securely attached were the most likely to cling or avoid others altogether, isolate themselves, and fail to develop a sense of independence. Ainsworth emphasized that it was not the amount of time mothers held their babies that made them more secure but, rather, the way they held them. They showed much more tenderness and affection and were careful never to be rough in handling their child. And, equally important, they held their babies when the infants wanted to be held, demonstrating that they perceived the infants' intentions as a separate being.

Ainsworth later went on to hone her studies, adding several subgroup categories to further refine the notion of secure, ambivalent, and avoidant children. She provided a scientifically valid method of identifying the how and why of the parental/child relationship and bond.

Ainsworth's strange situation protocol was taken up by other researchers in the field and their studies confirmed and reinforced her original findings. L. Alan Sroufe and Byron Egeland, at the University of Minnesota, followed up with children who had been assessed in the strange situation protocol as infants and found that their subsequent behavior at various stages of life, all the way into adulthood, tracked almost seamlessly with their initial assessment as toddlers, just as Bowlby had theorized and Ainsworth had later predicted in her first tests of the attachment behavior years earlier. The studies showed that the more securely attached infants grew up to be the more sociable adults. They were more sensitive to others, shared higher levels of cooperation with peers, and developed more intimate relationships. What those children all shared in common was a highly developed, empathic consciousness. And why is this the case? Sroufe said to understand this, one needs to start with the observation that "[i]f you're in a relationship, the relationship is part of you." Sroufe then asks rhetorically:

> How do you get an empathic child? You get an empathic child
> not by trying to teach the child and admonish the child to be
> empathic, you get an empathic child by being empathic with
> the child. The child's understanding of relationships can only
> be from the relationships he's experienced.[75]

Yet despite the consistency of findings in the studies, there were still some who remained unconvinced. The emerging field of behavioral genetics provided fodder for the critics. Studies conducted at the University of Minnesota of identical twins separated at birth and reared in different homes and environments seemed to add weight to the idea that one's genes are a more decisive determiner of one's emotional development than environmental factors. A spate of studies of identical twins reared apart reported on the uncanny mirror likeness in mood and behavior, casting some doubt on the Bowlby thesis. But it should be pointed out that Bowlby and Ainsworth were quite aware that each baby is born with inborn rhythms and behavioral predispositions and that they affected their subsequent attachment behavior. Bowlby commented

> An easy newborn may assist an uncertain mother to develop a
> favorable pattern of care. Conversely, a difficult unpredictable
> newborn may tip the balance the other way. Yet all the
> evidence shows that a potentially easy baby is still likely
> to develop unfavorably if given unfavorable care and also,
> more fortunately, that with only few exceptions a potentially
> difficult baby can develop favorably if given sensitive care.
> The capacity of a sensitive mother to adapt to even a difficult
> unpredictable baby and thereby enable him to develop
> favorably is perhaps the most heartening of all recent findings
> in the field.[76]

The question then was this: Acknowledging that both nature and nurture come into play in the establishment of the attachment bond, is one likely to play a more important role than the other? Dymph van den Boom, professor of general pedagogy at the University of Amsterdam, conducted an elegant study to assess the importance of nature versus nurture in attachment behavior.

Critics have long argued that babies who exhibit irritability from birth are less likely to create secure bonds and more likely to be anxious at the end of their first year. To test the assumption, van den Boom studied one hundred babies who had been diagnosed as highly irritable at birth. These infants were not only far more difficult than smiling babies, but they also were born to low-income families whose parents were uneducated and stressed by their dire circumstances and less likely to exhibit the patience and calm attentiveness required for their newborn to become securely attached.

The hundred pairs of children and mothers were divided in half. One group of mothers received three counseling sessions of two hours each between their babies' sixth and ninth months to deepen their sensitivity to their babies and the efficacy of their care. The other mothers received no counseling assistance. The results of the counseling were dramatic. Of the mothers who received counseling, 68 percent of their children were categorized as "securely attached" at one year old, while in the control group only 28 percent of the babies were categorized as secure. So while critics are right that irritable babies are less likely to become securely attached as suggested by the low rate of success in the control group, counseling of mothers upped the success ratio to nearly 70 percent.[77]

Robert Karen, the author of *Becoming Attached: First Relationships and How They Shape Our Capacity to Love,* observes that babies' brains are largely unformed at birth but become organized in the first months of life. The brain circuitry becomes wired as the result of the baby's interaction with the mother, which is the child's primary environmental world. This being the case, it's reasonable to conclude, says Karen, that

> [t]he baby's ability to regulate itself, especially in all those areas related to emotion, depends on parental attunement and empathy; and if the mother fails to attune to the baby emotionally, the baby's brain may exhibit lasting physiological deficits.[78]

Object relations theorists put a new mirror to human nature, and what they saw reflected a view of our species as an affectionate, highly social animal who craves companionship, abhors isolation, and is biologically predisposed to express empathy to other beings.

BUT ARE WE UNIQUE among the social animals in our ability to empathize with one another and our fellow creatures? New scientific discoveries over the past decade have forced a wholesale reappraisal in our thinking about the very nature of biological evolution. The conventional notion of evolution, with the emphasis on the competitive struggle to secure resources and reproduce offspring, is being tempered, at least at the mammalian level, with new findings suggesting that survival of the fittest may be as much about pro-social behavior and cooperation as physical brawn and competition. Moreover, at least some other species express empathic distress. The new insights into the biological roots of social behavior are beginning to have a paradigmatic effect on the way we perceive the living world around us as well as our own role in the unfolding story of life on Earth.

The message is we are not alone in our ability to empathize. This simple but profound realization can't help but change the way we perceive our fellow creatures as well as strengthen our sense of responsibility to steward the Earth we cohabit.

THREE

A Sentient Interpretation
of Biological Evolution

IN THE EARLY 1990s, scientists in Parma, Italy, took note of a curious phenomenon. A team led by Giacomo Rizzolatti was exploring the part of the brain in macaque monkeys that is involved in planning movements. The monkeys had wires implanted in the area of the brain that sends a command control for the primates' movements. They observed that neurons in the F5 region of the frontal cortex of a macaque's brain became activated before he grabbed a peanut. One day they were taken by utter surprise when the same F5 neurons also became active when the monkey saw a researcher grab for a peanut, even though the monkey hadn't moved a muscle. "We didn't believe it," Rizzolatti said afterward.[1] On subsequent experiments they observed that certain cells would fire when the monkey pried open a peanut or heard someone else do it.

Rizzolatti and his team followed up with functional magnetic resonance imaging (fMRI) on human beings who were observing other people's hand movements and facial expressions and found that, like the macaque monkey, a part of the brain, including the frontal cortex—which is homologous to the F5—would also activate in the same area as if they were making the hand movements or facial gestures.

It would be several more years before the Italian team finally understood the significance of what they had discovered.

WHAT MIRROR NEURONS TELL US ABOUT
NATURE VERSUS NURTURE

In 1996, Rizzolatti's team published the results of their research, setting off a scientific tsunami in the academic community. They called their discovery "mirror neurons." Since then, scientists have extended Rizzolatti's findings, discovering mirror neurons in other primates as well.

Mirror neurons allow humans—and other animals—to grasp the minds of others "as if" their thoughts and behavior were their own. The popular-science press has begun to refer to mirror neurons as "empathy neurons." What is most striking, says Rizzolatti, is that "[m]irror neurons allow us to grasp the minds of others not through conceptual reasoning but through direct simulation. By feeling, not by thinking."[2]

The discovery of mirror neurons has forced biologists, philosophers, linguists, psychologists, and others to rethink the Cartesian mind/body split that sealed reason away from bodily sensation, feelings, and emotions, making it an autonomous disembodied force.

The new discoveries, writes University of Wisconsin psychology professor Arthur M. Glenberg, "provide an alternative to Cartesian dualism." The implications for rethinking the nature of the mind are enormous. Glenberg observes that

> [t]he discovery of mirror neurons helps to bridge the gap
> between cognition and biology by providing a neural
> mechanism that reaches up to psychological theory and
> suggests solutions to a range of problems in cognitive science.[3]

We've long known that human beings and other mammalian species are "social animals." The discovery of mirror neurons, however, opens the door to exploring the biological mechanisms that make sociability possible.

Dr. Daniel J. Siegel, director of the Mindsight Institute, suggests that "the mirror neuron system . . . along with other areas such as the insula, superior temporal cortex, and middle prefrontal regions, form the interconnected 'resonance circuitry.' "[4] The resonance circuits, notes Siegel,

> have been shown to not only encode intention, but also to be fundamentally involved in human empathy, and also in emotional resonance, the outcome of attunement of minds.[5]

Dr. Marco Iacoboni, a neuroscientist at the University of California at Los Angeles and one of the leading researchers of mirror neurons, explains their importance in cueing into and reading other minds.

> [I]f you see me choke up, in emotional distress from striking out at home plate, mirror neurons in your brain simulate my distress. You automatically have empathy for me. You know how I feel because you literally feel what I am feeling.[6]

The point that Iacoboni and other scientists are making is that we are wired for empathy—it is our nature and what makes us social beings.

The growing body of experimental research into the role mirror neurons play in empathic development is impressive and is already rewriting the script on the evolution of human development.

While scientists have noted that visual gestures and expressions, as well as auditory resonances, activate mirror neurons, they are also finding that touch does so as well, creating still another sensory path for empathic extension. We've all had the experience of watching a spider or snake crawling up on another person and feeling the same shiver of repulsion as if it were crawling on us. In a series of experiments, researchers hooked up participants to fMRI and "found that the secondary somatosensory cortex is activated both when the participants were touched and when they observed someone or something else getting touched."[7]

Other studies show that when people react to a foul smell with a feeling of disgust, it activates some of the same cortical regions, especially the insula, that are activated when we observe an expression of disgust on another person's face as they sniff a fowl odor.[8]

Likewise, when we say "I feel your pain," the reality is that specific mirror neurons allow us to do just that. A study published in the journal *Science* reports on sixteen couples. In the study, the women were hooked up to an MRI machine while their romantic partners remained nearby. Then the researchers gave a brief electric shock either to the back of the woman's hand or her partner's. While she could not see her partner, an indicator informed her of who would be shocked next and how intense it would be. The same pain areas of the limbic system, including the anterior cingulate cortex, the thalamus and the insula, were activated in the women, causing pain both when it was directly administered to them or simply imagined, when administered to their partner.[9] This experiment demonstrated, in an unusual way, how very real empathic response to another's feelings can be.

Even more complex social emotions like shame, embarrassment, guilt, and pride are attached to mirror neuron systems found in the insula of the brain. Dr. Christian Keysers, of the University of Groningen in the Netherlands, conducted a study in which people viewed a hand reaching out to caress someone and then saw another hand aggressively push it away. Interestingly, the insula in the observers fired the neurons that activate the feeling of rejection.[10]

In virtually all of the studies of mirror neuron activation, researchers find that participants who score high on empathic profile tests show more active and elevated mirror neuron responses. This distinction is important because it suggests that while children with normal brain activity are prewired for empathy, the extent to which their mirror neurons activate depends as much upon nurture as nature.

Conversely, researchers find that the mirror neuron circuitry in autistic children is either nonfunctioning or partly functioning. Scientists at UCLA published research demonstrating a breakdown in the mirror neuron system among autistic individuals. Autistic children are characterized by the inability to read other people's intentions, express emotions, learn languages, and exhibit pro-social behavior. They are unable to empathize. The UCLA brain imaging studies showed a "clear link between a child's inability to imitate expressions on the faces of other people and a lack of activity in the mirror-neuron system."[11] Mirella Dapretto, associate professor of Psychiatry and Biobehavioral Sciences at UCLA, suggests, on the basis of her teams' findings, that "a dysfunctional mirror-neuron system may underlie the impairments in imitation and in empathizing with other people's emotions typically seen in autism."[12]

Researchers at the cutting edge of cognitive science are justifiably excited about the discovery of mirror neurons and resonance circuitry, and the potential implications. Still, they caution that the new findings are just the beginning of a journey to map the pathways of cognition. What they are finding is that the biological circuitry becomes activated by social exercise. In other words, parental and community nurture of infants is essential to trigger mirror neurons' circuitry and establish empathic pathways in the brain. These findings are reopening the age-old question of the relationship between biology and culture and sparking a rigorous debate across the natural and social sciences disciplines.

It's long been assumed that biology and culture operate on different tracks, despite efforts over the years by scholars like C. P. Snow to find a connection and an accommodation. Just as the discovery of mirror neurons breaks the hold of Cartesian dualism, it also suggests that the split between biology and culture is equally erroneous. Mirror neurons, says Patricia Greenfield, a psychologist at the University of California at Los Angeles,

> provide a powerful biological foundation for the evolution of culture. . . . [N]ow we see that mirror neurons absorb culture directly, with each generation teaching the next by social sharing, imitation and observation.[13]

We used to believe that only human beings evolve by creating culture and that all other creatures are imprisoned by their biological design. It was fashionable, as late as the 1960s, for most biologists to believe that while human beings pass cultural capital on by teaching their young, other creatures operate by a rigid preprogrammed behavior—popularly referred to as instinct. The idea of animals teaching their young would have seemed far-fetched among most biologists until recently.

Now we know that for many species, behavior is as much learned as inherited. For example, we used to believe that geese migrate south each year to specific destinations because it's wired into their biology. We now know that geese have to teach their young by showing them the route.

Researchers at Emory University in Atlanta and the University of St Andrews in Scotland report on an experiment with chimpanzees that showed the passing of newly learned skills to other chimpanzees—in effect creating a new, acquired skill set by way of cultural transmission. Two chimps were taught two different techniques for freeing a piece of food from a container. After the chimps returned to their respective groups, they began to use the new techniques. The other chimps observed what the chimps had learned and began to use the new techniques as well. Two months later, the chimps in both groups were still using the new techniques.[14]

Biologists have discovered a whole range of learned behavior in the animal kingdom, especially among mammals that are social and that nurse their offspring, which means that at least a rudimentary form of culture exists within many species. The point is that with many species, ways of acting and behaving in the world are passed down from one generation to the next.

A case in point. Several years ago, zoologists noted a bizarre change in behavior among adolescent elephants in an animal park in South Africa. They began to taunt rhinos and other animals and even began to kill them, something never before seen. Scientists were puzzled by the strange behavior and unable to find a satisfying explanation. Then one of the zoologists recollected that years earlier they had culled out the older male elephants in order to ease crowding. They reasoned that there might be a correlation but were not sure what it could be. Nonetheless, they airlifted two older male adults back into the park and within just a few weeks the teenagers had stopped exhibiting what amounted to antisocial behavior and began to fall in line with the behavior of the older male elephants. What the zoologists observed is that young elephants learn from their elders, just like human children, and when the role models are absent they have no guide to teach them what appropriate social behavior should be.[15]

The discovery of the mirror neuron system in human beings and primates is precipitating a fundamental shift in the way we think about the nature–nurture relationship. These neural circuits are giving us a window into the very complex way that biology connects with psychology. Vilayanur Ramachandran, a neuroscientist at the University of California at San Diego, says that the discovery of the biological mechanisms that make empathic consciousness possible and the cultural catalysts that activate them allow us to begin to understand how nature and nurture interact to create human nature. Ramachandran suggests that the study of the mirror neurons will change our way of thinking about psychology as significantly as DNA has for biology.[16]

Scientists studying animal behavior believe that many animal species besides primates probably have rudimentary mirror neuron systems. Elephants, dolphins, dogs, and other "social animals" are high up on the list of suspected species that might have the biological mechanisms for at least primitive empathic response. Elephants—and perhaps dolphins—are particularly good candidates because, like chimpanzees, they are able to grasp the notion of their selfhood. Many cognitive scientists believe that in order to read another creature's feelings and intentions, some kind of self-awareness is required.

We've long known that chimpanzees are aware of the self as a separate identity. In the mirror test used by scientists to see if an animal has self-awareness, chimps pass with flying colors. If a lipstick mark, for example, is put on the forehead of a chimp and the chimp is then put in front of a mirror, he will examine the mark and even touch it or try to erase it, showing that he knows that the reflection in the mirror is his.

Recent experiments conducted by researchers at the Yerkes Primate Center in Atlanta and the Wildlife Conservation Society show that elephants also pass the lipstick test in the mirror. Researchers painted a white X on the left cheek of an elephant named Happy. She stood before the mirror and repeatedly touched her trunk to the mark, a feat that requires an understanding that the mark is not in the mirror but on her body. Another elephant, Maxine, used the mirror to examine the inside of her mouth and her ear—a kind of self-directed behavior that zookeepers had never witnessed before.[17]

Elephants also exhibit behavior that can only be described as empathic. In his book *When Elephants Weep*, Jeffrey Masson recounts the story of an elephant attempting to rescue a rhino calf who had become stuck in the mud at a salt lick. An adult elephant approached the young rhino, running its trunk gently over it. The elephant then knelt, placed its tusks underneath the calf's belly, and attempted to lift it from the mud. The mother rhino, spotting the elephant, charged over to it, forcing the elephant to retreat. After repeated attempts by the elephant to dislodge the calf, only to be rebuffed by a charging rhino mother, the elephant left. The most plausible explanation for the elephant's behavior is its sense of empathy for the plight of the calf and its determination to come to the calf's aid.[18]

Scientists suspect that dolphins might also self-identify. Other species, as far as we know, don't self-identify. When they see themselves in the mirror, there is no sense whatsoever of self-reflection. They simply don't know that the image in the mirror is their own.

While only a few species pass the mirror test for self-identity and despite the fact that mirror neuron systems, to date, have been found in only a few species—most species have not yet been studied— experiments show that many species demonstrate in their behavior that they possess theory of mind.[19]

Experiments conducted by Brian Hare of Harvard University and Michael Tomasello of the Max Planck Institute for Evolutionary Anthropology in Leipzig showed that "domestic dogs understand what is meant when a human being points at something (as in 'the food's under this one!')."[20] While we take for granted that when one person points to an object, another knows how to look over at it, for a dog to do the same, he needs to know that "your movements aren't about your arm and hand but about the mind that drives them."[21] That recognition requires that the dog be able to read the person's mind and understand their intention in making the gesture. In other words, he must have a theory of mind.

Some animal species even understand the idea of fairness, which requires a sophisticated awareness of oneself in relationship to another. Anthropologist Sarah Brosnan at Emory University coordinated several experiments in which monkeys were taught to exchange a "token" with a trainer in return for food. If the monkeys saw a cagemate exchange a token for a highly coveted grape, while they were only offered a lowly cucumber for a token, they would more often than not refuse to give over the token because of the unfair nature of the exchange.[22]

THE DARWIN WE NEVER KNEW

Charles Darwin anticipated the recent breakthroughs in cognitive science—especially the importance of sociability in evolution—in his own keen observation of animals. In his later works, *The Descent of Man* and *Expression of the Emotions in Man and Animals*, Darwin noted the social nature of most animals and even their emotions and moral responsibilities. Of their social nature, he wrote:

> Every one must have noticed how miserable horses, dogs, and
> sheep are when separated from their companions, and what
> strong mutual affection horses and dogs, at least, show on their
> reunion.[23]

Darwin also took note of the grooming behavior of animals. He said he was intrigued with how "social animals . . . perform many little services for each other. Horses nibble, and cows lick each other on any spot that itches. Monkeys search each other for external parasites."[24]

Darwin was particularly taken by other creatures' sense of humor. He observed that

[d]ogs show what may be fairly called a sense of humor, as distinct from mere play. If a bit of stick or other such object is thrown to one, he will often carry it away for a short distance and then squatting down with it on the ground close before him, will wait until his master comes quite close to take it away. The dog will then seize it and rush away in triumph, repeating the same maneuver and evidently enjoying the practical joke.[25]

Although Darwin is unduly portrayed as a fierce believer in the idea that nature is red in tooth and claw and a battleground where only the fit survive, his views were actually far more tempered and nuanced. He observed that, "[m]ost of the more complex emotions are common to the higher animals and ourselves" and, "animals not only love, but desire to be loved."[26] (The mischaracterization of his views is largely the fault of Herbert Spencer, who widely distorted his theory to fit his own social agenda. Historians would refer to the misconception of Darwin's hypotheses as "social Darwinism.")

In his later years, Darwin saw evolution from a far different perspective from what was laid out in his master work *The Origin of Species*. He viewed many of the higher animals as social beings, full of emotions and endowed with a capacity to care for the plight of their fellows. Perhaps most striking is Darwin's remarks about animals extending sympathy for other animals in trouble. He remembered his own experience with a dog "who never passed a cat who lay sick in a basket, and was a great friend of his, without giving her a few licks with his tongue, the surest sign of kind feeling in a dog."[27] He wrote that "[m]any animals certainly sympathize with each other's distress or danger."[28]

Near the end of his life Darwin spent far more time describing the social nature and even affectionate bonds among creatures, all of which might come as quite a surprise to orthodox Darwinians. Nonetheless, Darwin came to believe that survival of the fittest is as much about cooperation, symbiosis, and reciprocity as it is about individual competition and that the most fit are just as likely to enter into cooperative bonds with their fellows.

Despite the fact that Darwin's theory of the survival of the fittest, articulated in *The Origin of Species*, seems to provide a biological justification of the self-interested utilitarian ethos of the period, in his last writings he challenged John Stuart Mill and other utilitarian thinkers of the day, arguing that human "impulses do not always arise from anticipated pleasure."[29] To illustrate his point, Darwin uses the example of a person rushing to the rescue of a stranger in a fire at great personal peril without the least thought of a utilitarian reward. Darwin says that such behavior comes from a more deeply ingrained human impulse than the drive for pleasure—the social instinct.[30]

Darwin lived before the heyday of psychological consciousness, in a world where the very word "empathy" had yet to be invented. Still, he gleaned the importance of the empathic bond. In the case of the man saving a victim from the fire, the rescuer instinctually senses the victim's struggle as if it were his own and comes to his aid and comfort. This is what Darwin meant by "the social instinct."

In a remarkable passage, Darwin writes presciently of a coming age when humanity will stretch its social instincts and sympathetic impulses, "becoming more tender and more widely diffused until they are extended to all sentient beings." As to how this might come about, Darwin muses that

> [a]s soon as this virtue is honored and practiced by some few
> of us it spreads through instruction and example to the young
> and eventually becomes incorporated in public opinion.[31]

DEEP PLAY AND DEVELOPMENT

Today cognitive scientists are putting flesh on Darwin's intuitions about nature and, in the process, changing the way we view human evolution. What they are finding is that when it comes to the most important aspects of social life, many of the other mammalian species exhibit behavior that is remarkably similar to human beings. Social species—especially mammals—have to be able to read the feelings and intentions of their offspring and peers and have some basic empathic sensibility if they are to nurture their progeny and create social bonds with their fellows.

Many zoologists now believe that "play" performs a powerful role in the development of empathy and the establishment of pro-social behavior among animals, just as it does with humans. Play is the means for creating attachment, mindfulness, trust, affection, and social bonds when growing up and a way to maintain sociability in adulthood.

When denied play opportunities, young animals often fail to develop the social skills that allow them to behave appropriately later on in life in an adult community. Horse breeders, for example, have observed that when a foal is raised without play experience with other foals, he or she often exhibits inappropriate social skills and antisocial behavior as an adult and is never fully accepted into the herd. Dr. Karen Hayes, an equine reproduction specialist, observes that like human infants, after bonding with their mothers, foals begin to play with other horses. "If foals don't learn social skills," says Hayes, "they're in for a life of confusion and certain stress . . . they'll learn to survive but they'll always be stressed."[32]

Neural scientist Jaak Panksepp observes that all young animals are biologically wired to engage in play. In his book *Affective Neuroscience*, Panksepp points out that the same brain circuitry that prompts play also stimulates joy and is found in all mammals.[33]

For humans, play becomes a defining feature of development. American physician and neuroscientist Paul MacLean writes that "[f]rom the standpoint of human evolution, no behavioral developments could have been more fundamental" than the brain's potential for play. MacLean believes that play "set[s] the stage for a family way of life with its evolving responsibilities and affiliations that has led to worldwide acculturation."[34] The social bonding that comes from play, says MacLean, "favored the evolution of the human sense of empathy. . . ."[35]

To understand the importance of play in the development of empathic potential, we need to step back and examine its essential features. To begin with, play is deeply participatory in nature. It is an embodied experience. We generally don't think of play as something we do in our mind by ourself—that would be fantasy. Rather, play is activity we engage in with others. It is more often a shared enjoyment rather than a solitary pleasure. Play is rarely instrumental but an end in and of itself.

Openness and acceptance are inherent parts of a playful environment. Although there are consequences that flow from one's actions, all of the players feel free to express themselves, to be vulnerable, because forgiveness permeates play. "I was just pretending" is a standard retort that every child in history has understood and used when engaged in play.

Play tends to be open-ended. The world of play is often a timeless realm, as anyone who has ever been caught up in play and lost all sense of the passage of time knows. Play also takes place in a space that is symbolically marked off from instrumental space. "Playgrounds" are safe havens, independent of the "real world." A "playground" is not something one owns or possesses but, rather, a pretend setting that people temporarily share.

Play, then, takes place in a temporal and spatial dimension but is often experienced as timeless and spaceless. The experience itself is "pretense," giving it a transcendent quality. It has both a worldly and otherworldly feel to it.

The play environment is the classroom by which we learn to be empathic with our fellow human beings. It is where we exercise our imagination by placing ourselves in other personas, roles, and contexts and try to feel, think, and behave as we believe they would. When little girls and boys play house or pretend to be a mommy, daddy, or older sibling, or their teacher at school or President of the United States, they are practicing empathic extension.

It's difficult to "imagine" how empathy could develop in the absence of play. Dutch historian Johan Huizinga even refers to human beings as *Homo ludens*—man the player. Huizinga suggests that all cultures arise in play. "It is through this playing," says Huizinga, "that society expresses its interpretation of life and the world."[36]

Lev S. Vygotsky, the great Russian psychologist of the early twentieth century, reminds us that "[f]rom the point of view of development, creating an imaginary situation can be regarded as a means of developing abstract thought."[37] For example, when a child imagines what it might be like to be riding on a horse, he might take hold of a piece of wood, put it in between his legs, and yelp and gallop down the street. The wood becomes an imaginary symbol of the horse and a way for the child to create a simulation of the experience and ride it out. Similarly, when children pretend to play doctor and nurse and turn a hollow can into a stethoscope to listen to each other's hearts, they are letting their imagination open the door to exploring another's state of being. The imagination, expressed through play, allows empathic consciousness to grow and develop. Vygotsky rightfully regards play as "the highest level of preschool development."[38]

What makes play such a powerful socializing tool, then, is that it is the means by which imagination is unleashed. We create alternative realities and delve into them for suspended amounts of time. We become explorers of the vast other—all of the infinite possible realms of existence that could be. Through play, we incorporate parts of these other imagined realities into our being. We become connected.

The imagination process allows us to bring together embodied experience, emotions, and abstract thoughts into a single ensemble, the empathic mind. In this sense, the human imagination is both emotional and cognitive. We express emotion and create abstract thought simultaneously.

Many philosophers regard play as the highest expression of human development. In his *On the Aesthetic Education of Man*, written in 1795, Friedrich Schiller observed that "man plays only when he is in the fullest sense of the word a human being, and he is fully a human being only when he plays."[39] That's because play in the cultural realm is the supreme expression of human bonding. We play with one another out of love of human communication. It is the deepest act of participation between people and is made possible by collective trust—the feeling that each player can let down his defenses and abandon himself, for the moment, to the care of others so he can experience the elation that comes from a communion.

Freedom and play also share common ground. True play is always entered into voluntarily. One can't be forced to play. The players give themselves freely "for the love of the game." The goal is joy and a reaffirmation of the life instinct. It is through the experience of play in the cultural sphere that one learns to participate equally and openly with one's fellow human beings. We revel in one another. Human beings can never be really free until we are able to fully enter into play. It was the French philosopher Jean-Paul Sartre who said, "As man apprehends himself as free and wishes to use his freedom . . . then his activity is to play."[40] Does anyone ever feel more free than when engaged in play?

Play, then, is far from a trivial pursuit. It is where we stretch our empathic consciousness and learn to become truly human.

THE EMPATHIC ROOTS OF LANGUAGE

New insights into the role of mirror neurons and play in social development have sparked interest in the question of the origin and development of language. The older disembodied notion that language is innate and an autonomous biological mechanism—most recently articulated by Noam Chomsky et al.—is now being challenged by a new generation of neurocognitive scientists.

The mirror neuron system hypothesis, put forth by Michael Arbib, traces language development back to our primate ancestors' neural mechanisms that support imitation of hand movements. He sees an evolutionary progression from hand movement to more complex pantomime in which one communicates rather than just manipulates an object and then to protosigns, all of which extend the repertoire of manual communication and provide a foundation for "protospeech."[41]

Animal behaviorists are beginning to study our closest relatives, the great apes and other primates, both in the wild and in laboratory environments, to try to understand how language might have evolved. What they suspect is that language is, in reality, a sophisticated mechanism for expressing empathic communication and may have evolved through the exercise of hand movements in play and grooming in primates.[42]

The lives of primates, in many ways, parallel our own, albeit on a more primitive scale. Chimpanzees are particularly interesting to observe because their behavior is remarkably similar to what one might expect of a two- or three-year-old child. Like humans and other social animals, chimpanzees organize their social lives in hierarchies. While they don't create grand conceptual narratives to rationalize their relationships to each other and the world around them, they do have rudimentary culture. They teach their young to use tools, engage in reciprocal activity, cooperate and compete in play, entertain one another, express a wide range of emotions, have a primitive self-awareness and, most important, express empathy toward one another. On this last point, based on decades of research, a growing number of primatologists suggest that a nascent form of empathy is at the root of chimpanzees' communicative nature. Dutch primatologist Frans de Waal goes so far as to suggest that

> empathy [in primates] is the original, pre-linguistic form of inter-individual linkage that only secondarily has come under the influence of language and culture.[43]

Dr. de Waal, like Jane Goodall, Dian Fossey, and other primatologists, argues that "communication among nonhuman primates is thought to be emotionally mediated."[44]

Dr. de Waal notes that natural selection must have favored mechanisms that allow individuals to read one another's feelings and intentions in order to respond accordingly and build cooperative links and social solidarity. This is, after all, the heart of what communication is all about. If that's the case, says de Waal, then "[e]mpathy is precisely such a mechanism."[45] In other words, the empathic impulse is the biological means of fostering communication, at least among the more evolved mammalian species.

Close observation of other species shows a steady progression of the empathic impulse in biological evolution. For example, in a classic study conducted more than half a century ago, researchers found "that rats that had learned to press a lever to obtain food would stop doing so if their response was paired with the delivery of an electric shock to a visible neighboring rat."[46] Subsequent experiments with rhesus monkeys yielded the same results—except, in the latter case, the emotional response was more long-lasting and had deeper consequences. One monkey stopped pulling the lever for five days, another for twelve days, after seeing the shocking effect on another monkey. The monkeys would rather starve than be responsible for meting out pain on a fellow.[47] The behavior of the rats and the rhesus monkeys would simply be unexplainable if the empathic impulses were not in play.

Most empathic responses are seen within a species. Still, researchers have recorded countless examples of animals extending the empathic bond beyond their kind, like the example cited earlier about the elephant coming to the assistance of a rhino calf.

Dr. de Waal recounts witnessing a bonobo named Kuni capturing a starling. The chimp gathered up the starling and proceeded to climb up a tree. She then delicately unfolded the bird's wings and threw the bird toward an outer wall. Although the bird fell in the moat, Kuni went over to it and guarded it. De Waal notes that Kuni could not have done what she did without somehow adopting the bird's viewpoint and plight. De Waal explains that

> [w]hat Kuni did would obviously have been inappropriate
> towards a member of her own species. Having seen birds in
> flight many times, she seemed to have a notion of what would
> be good for a bird, thus offering us an anthropoid version of
> the empathic capacity.[48]

Primatologists have also noted chimpanzees' ability to console—an emotional act that requires a fairly advanced empathic communication. It is not uncommon in chimpanzee communities for a third party to intercede after a conflict, and to attempt to console the victim of the aggression. This level of emotional sophistication is not seen in macaques and other monkeys. While researchers have recorded numerous examples of reconciliation in many different species, consolation is different. De Waal points out that reconciliation is driven more by self-interest and the desire to restore social harmony, whereas consolation is purely an empathetic act without any other intention but to acknowledge another's plight and comfort them. Scientists suggest that the reason they may be able to console is that chimpanzees, unlike macaques, exhibit a sense of self-awareness—they pass the mirror test for identity and are therefore better able to distinguish themselves from others, which enables them to console the other, aware that their feelings are directed solely to the other's condition.[49]

While consoling behavior plays a meaningful role in the life of chimpanzees, no less important is the experience of gratitude, an emotional quality we've long believed to be the exclusive preserve of human social relations. Gratitude is most often communicated in chimpanzee society by extending gifts of food to those who have performed grooming services. It can be rightfully argued that grooming is among the most important social activities in chimpanzee society and takes up a sizable portion of the chimpanzees' waking time. De Waal reports on an experiment in which researchers measured hundreds of spontaneous grooming events among chimpanzees during the morning hours. At noon, the chimpanzees were each given two bundles of leaves and branches to eat. Researchers then recorded nearly seven thousand interactions over food. They found that chimpanzees are more likely to share their rations with those who had provided grooming services.[50] De Waal emphasizes that substantial time elapsed between the grooming events and the sharing of food, meaning that the chimpanzees remembered the kindness extended and expressed their gratitude later by sharing their food. Gestures of gratitude link members of the community into more intimate social bonds.

Grooming is not only important in establishing gratitude. Animal behavioralists and a growing number of cognitive scientists believe that it may also be a key to the development of empathic pathways in the brain and even the evolution of communication from gestures, to protosigns, to protolanguage, and finally to human speech. The progression of communications, in turn, provides ever richer means of reading feelings, understanding intentions, and making empathic connections.

Like play, grooming creates bonds of sociability. In otherwise hierarchically stratified social arrangements—typical of social species—play and grooming often provide a time and place to relax distinctions and status barriers and allow individuals to connect on a "more intimate and egalitarian basis." In some species, more than 20 percent of each day is given over to grooming activity.[51]

Both play and grooming promote empathy and deeper communication. Play, however, is often a group exercise, while grooming is always a one-to-one affair. In the practice of grooming, the two participants use the full range of their senses to explore the other's physicality and mentality. Grooming another requires a mindfulness of their needs and feelings—what pains them and pleases them. The individual being groomed, in turn, has to be able to communicate his or her needs and feelings—cooing, snapping, nudging, snuggling, stroking—in a way that the groomer can understand. Grooming is the most intimate form of communication—far more so than sexual encounters—for other species, and it is also the most important way for animals to get to know each other's inner being. The grooming experience begins with nursing and parental care and, along with play, is the way animals learn to communicate with one another. Grooming stimulates the release of the body's natural opiates, the endorphins, and has a narcotic effect, relaxing the animal.[52] Equally important, however, is that grooming establishes trust and bonds of friendship, both essential to maintaining social life.

If grooming, along with play, is the most basic form of communication between social animals, what, if any, connection might it have to the development of human language—one of the great unsolved mysteries of biological evolution?

British anthropologist and evolutionary biologist Robin Dunbar, in his book *Grooming, Gossip and the Evolution of Language*, offers an interesting yet controversial thesis. He starts with the assumption that grooming is the essential mechanism by which animals create bonds of intimacy, trust, and sociability. He then notes an interesting biological phenomenon, namely that, in large part, the size of the neocortex in mammals' brains defines the social group size. The neocortex is the part of the brain where conscious thought occurs. He observes that in most mammals, the neocortex amounts to approximately 30 percent to 40 percent of the total brain volume, whereas among primates it ranges "from a low of 50 percent among some prosimians to 80 percent of total brain volume in humans."[53]

It turns out that the size of the neocortex correlates quite closely to the group size of a species. That is, the larger the size of the neocortex relative to the total volume of the brain, the larger the number of animals in a social group. The reason for this, Dunbar speculates, is that social animals need to continuously keep track of each other's feelings and interactions and adjust to each other's needs and moods in order to maintain the proper social cohesion of the group.

The larger the neocortex, the greater the capability of organizing complex social relationships among larger numbers of individuals. Human beings, with the largest neocortex among the primates, also live in the largest extended social groups. The primary group is the clan, which usually contains upward of 150 people or so. Clans organize in larger, more loosely affiliated groups called mega-bands, usually comprised of 500 or so people, and mega-bands affiliate in even larger groups called tribes, which are united by language or dialect and vary between 1,500 to 2,000 people.[54]

If we look to our closest primate relatives and further down the line to other mammals, we see that group size is directly related to the time devoted to social grooming because of the cultural function it performs in establishing and maintaining social relations and group cohesion. As mentioned earlier, the other primates spend up to 20 percent of their day in grooming activity and live in groups of only about 40 to 50 animals. Studies of existing forager/hunter societies show that men and women spend, on average, about 25 percent of their day socializing, which roughly corresponds to the time given over to social grooming among some of our primate relatives.[55] But for human beings that live in clans of up to 150 people or so, it would mean that at least 40 percent of the social time would need to be taken up in social grooming to maintain a measure of social cohesion. Thus, Dunbar speculates that when human groups become so large that they require more than 30 percent of their time be spent in social grooming—which would have compromised the time necessary to forage and hunt and perform other survival activities—some form of vocal as opposed to physical grooming came into play to facilitate more extended social bonds. Dunbar suggests that language started as gossip—which is a way of vocalizing grooming and establishing more extensive social relations.[56]

The development of oral language, then script, print, and now electronic connections, has allowed human beings to vastly extend their social networks and to live in more densely populated and complex social environments. At every stage of our social evolution, the primary task of communications has been to expand the empathic domain, whether it be grooming each other or gossiping over the Internet, so that we can express our social nature and our deep desire for companionship with our fellows.

Understanding the importance of play and grooming in the making of human culture is critical to rethinking the nature of human nature. It is important to note that animal behavioralists used to believe that play was a means to sharpen instinctual competitive skills useful in the hunt and in warfare in the case of males, and domestic skills useful in overseeing the brood in the case of females. The utilitarian functions were emphasized. Similarly, with grooming it was long suspected that the primary purpose was hygienic and designed to keep each other and the pack physically fit. Although animal behavioralists and cognitive scientists don't dismiss these strictly utilitarian functions, they are now more apt to regard the social bonding function as far more important. The growing awareness that play and grooming are, first and foremost, means of connecting feelings, emotions, intentions, and desires and establishing social bonds, has sparked a rich new debate around the origin of language. In both play and grooming, researchers note that communication between animals is experienced physically, which has led to the theorization that language might have developed from bodily gestures.

Arbib suggests that biological evolution provided human beings with a "'language-ready brain' able to master language as the child matures within a language-using community" but that the development of language itself is culturally driven. In other words, a child doesn't just begin to speak at two years of age because of an innate universal grammar but, rather, learns to speak by progressing through prior stages of gesturing tied to empathic extension. At each stage of infant development, more complex gestural communication patterns trigger mirror neurons and establish more elaborate resonance circuitry, laying the foundation for the most complex form of empathic communication—speech itself. The point is we aren't born with the ability to speak.[57] Rather, it is the final stage in the increasing complexity of gestural communications made possible via empathic extension and cultural transmission.

David McNeill, professor of linguistics and psychology at the University of Chicago, argues that gestures and language develop together. In his book on the subject, *Hand and Mind*, McNeill concludes that "gestures are an integral part of language as much as are words, phrases, and sentences—gesture and language are one system."[58]

The early gestural forms of communication remain with us and accompany speech throughout life. Communication by speech is virtually always accompanied by hand movements, facial expressions, and bodily gestures. They provide the visual nuances that amplify, qualify, and modify our utterances. They ground our communications in a spatial and temporal gestalt and help others interpret what we really mean and are as important as tone and inflection in conveying intent.

The notion that the evolution of language lies in hand movement would seem to add credence to the argument that communication began with play and social grooming among the primates. In the act of grooming, primates' hands become probes of, as well as responders to, another individual's feelings, emotions, needs, and desires. The hands become the intimate language of communication during the grooming process. The groomers' hands cue into the bodily reactions and facial gestures of the recipient and continually readjust to the felt presence of the other. That is to say, the hands become the organs and touch becomes the primary source for early empathic communication. It's not difficult to imagine how the grooming process might then evolve into more abstract pantomime and symbolic protosigns to express bodily feelings and intentions and extend the empathic bond.

Arbib and others claim that without a functioning mirror neuron system, language would be impossible. We simply would not be capable of learning how to read another's mind and be able to respond in kind—in other words, we would be unable to communicate. Severely autistic children who have an impoverished mirror neuron system are unable to learn language because they don't have the potential empathic building blocks—mirror neurons—and therefore are unable to learn about and from others.

The Arbib thesis on the evolution of human language and other recent biological discoveries and insights is giving us a much clearer picture of the emotional, cognitive, and even communicative biological origins of human evolution. What scientists are finding is that human beings share a much richer history with our fellow mammals than previously thought. We now know that mammals feel, play, teach their young, and show affection and, at least some species, have a rudimentary culture and express primitive empathic distress.

We are finding kindred spirits among our fellow creatures. Suddenly, our sense of existential aloneness in the universe is not so extreme. We have been sending out radio communications to the far reaches of the cosmos in the hopes of finding some form of intelligent and caring life, only to discover that what we were desperately seeking already exists and lives among us here on Earth. This discovery can't help but awaken a new sense of communion with our fellow beings and advance the journey toward biosphere consciousness.

With the recent discovery that many animals and humans are wired for empathic distress, researchers have the scientific grounding for a far more rigorous exploration of how nature and nurture interact to create a social being. What they are learning about the way children evolve changes our most basic thinking about what it means to be a human being.

FOUR

BECOMING HUMAN

PARENTS HAVE NOT always viewed their children the same way over history. A Christian parent at the close of the first millennium AD might look into the eyes of a newborn for clues as to whether the devil lurked somewhere deep inside, ready to possess them. Today, at the beginning of the third millennium AD, a parent is more likely to scrutinize a child's inner being for signs of his or her inherent good nature and sociability. That's not to say that parents expect their children to grow up to be a Mahatma Gandhi or a Nelson Mandela or a Martin Luther King, Jr. Only that they expect them to be more like them than, say, an Adolf Hitler or a Joseph Stalin. All of which points to the fact that while most human beings are neither saints nor monsters, we expect pro-social behavior rather than antisocial behavior of one another. That's because it is in our nature to be affectionate and caring and not remote and hateful. The misanthrope is always the exception and never the norm in any culture. We are born to nurture.

Today a new generation of psychologists, developmental biologists, cognitive scientists, and pediatric researchers are probing deeply into the complex pathways of human development and pinpointing the critical role that empathic expression plays in making us into fully formed human beings.

SIX LEVELS IN THE DEVELOPMENT
OF HUMAN CONSCIOUSNESS

Dr. Stanley Greenspan, clinical professor of psychiatry at George Washington University Medical School, takes us through the developmental stages of consciousness, while Dr. Martin L. Hoffman, professor of psychology at New York University, explains how empathic expression manifests itself in ever more complex and subtle ways at each leg in the journey to self-consciousness, selfhood, and social integration.

Greenspan identifies six levels in the development of human consciousness. At the first developmental level, the infant is busy organizing her sensations—touch, smell, sound, and sight—into organizable patterns. She also begins the difficult task of controlling her own movements so that she can begin to act on the world. In this earliest stage, the infant has no sense of self and world, no feeling of being an "I." She and the world are still undifferentiated . . . what Freud referred to as the oceanic sense of oneness. William James referred to this state as "one great blooming, buzzing confusion."[1] The infant's sole thrust is ordering her own sensations and controlling her bodily movement. In this stage, the infant is learning how to focus attention, which is the essential precursor to consciousness.

Once the infant has mastered the ability to be attentive, she is ready to notice "the tones, expressions, and actions of the people close to her [and react] to them with pleasure."[2] This is the entry point to stage two, which is the beginning of intimacy, generally with a primary adult caregiver. Although the infant is not yet able to differentiate herself from what is not herself, she is slowly learning to distinguish the living world of human relationships from the inanimate world around her. She is beginning to exist in relationship to others. She becomes aware of the pleasure of interaction with her primary caretaker and experiences despair if her overtures are not responded to. The infant begins to communicate with her caretaker by cooing, facial gestures, and the like. When the adult responds according to her wishes and desires, she begins to glimpse a sense of self and other. For example, if the infant purposely throws food from the table to express her dislike, the facial, auditory, and other gestural and emotional responses of the adult begin to create a marker between "who I am" and "this other I wish to influence," although at this stage the sense of self and other is only marginally felt.[3]

The ability to communicate a wish or need and get an appropriate response lays the groundwork for a sense of intentionality. The baby senses her own will and is reinforced by the appropriate responses to her intentions. This third level of development, when a baby begins to exercise a sense of intentionality toward others and receives feedback, is the true beginning of human relationships. The mother or father and the baby are now engaged with each other in a rich pre-verbal dialogue. The infant is beginning to experience the border between "me" and "you." She is also becoming dimly aware that others exist beyond her primary caretakers, with whom she can enter into relationships.

Greenspan cautions that at this stage, if the primary caretaker is arbitrary or unresponsive to the infant—for example, not picking up the child for a hug when she reaches out or ignoring the baby's cooing attempts to get mom's attention—the child's development can be seriously arrested and her ability to form intimate relationships later damaged.

At this third level, the baby becomes willful and begins to act "reciprocally and contingently." Greenspan says that

> [i]t is at this time that the baby begins to have a discrete
> sense of herself as a separate being—not, to be sure, a whole,
> integrated, or organized self, but one no longer incapable of
> distinguishing itself from others.[4]

What Greenspan and others are saying reinforces the theoretical and clinical observations of the object-relations trailblazers, that every individual is formed out of a relationship with others, rather than the long-held view that relationships are entered into by already formed individuals.

At about eighteen months, the infant is ready to advance to level four. The child is able to direct the mother by, for example, leading her to the refrigerator and pointing to a specific food item. The toddler's gestural repertoire grows. She begins to read faces and body language and to distinguish emotions like joy and distress. She is beginning to "size up situations on the basis of subtle behavioral cues."[5]

The toddler is now confident enough to be able to separate herself from her mother or father for brief periods to explore her surroundings, but always with the reassurance that they are close by. The child begins to imitate the expressions and gestures of others, for example, stirring a pot on a toy stove the way mom does. The child is experiencing herself as another, which is the essential training ground for developing empathic expression. Greenspan says that this period opens the door to a flood of more complex human feelings like "[a]nger, love, closeness, assertiveness, curiosity, [and] dependency. . . ."[6]

Between the second and third year, the child makes a leap forward, to the fifth level, and begins to form images and ideas. She develops the ability to abstract her emotions and feelings into symbols. She can engage in pretend play, like having her dolls cuddle each other. The child can express her feelings in words. For example, she can tell her mom she feels sad or happy or that she wants some milk, rather than just taking mom by the hand and directing her to the refrigerator.[7]

This is the age when the child begins to learn how to reflect on her actions and situations. For example, the toddler might express the desire to go in the car, to which a parent might respond by asking why, forcing the child to think about her intentions.[8] In pretend play, the child can now put herself in the place of another person and imitate what it would be like to be them. To do so, she has to be able to imagine what the other person is like. She has to form an idea of that person in her mind. Then she has to suspend her own identity for a brief time to take on another's identity. This kind of extremely complicated cognitive process is seen only spottily among mature chimpanzees—whose own consciousness equals that of a two-and-a-half-year-old human—when they mimic another being, but it is rare in the rest of the mammalian kingdom.

By the time the child is three, she is able to engage in rather elaborate forms of pretend play, taking on characters and roles and acting out dramatic sketches that involve rudimentary plots and changing locations.[9]

Between the third and fourth year, the child graduates to the sixth level and begins to connect ideas to emotions. Greenspan uses the example of the child who might say "I am sad because I can't see Grandma." The child begins to comprehend time and can distinguish concepts like past, present, and future. With this new time orientation, the child is able to plan ahead and create goals. She comes to understand how present actions have future consequences—for example, being naughty might mean being denied time to watch her favorite cartoons on TV. Spatial orientation also becomes comprehensible. The toddler begins to distinguish here from there. The child also begins to understand the difference between fantasy and reality.[10] She can also retain the idea of another person, both in real time and in her imagination. In a word, she is becoming self-conscious and taking on an individual identity.

Greenspan is quick to point out that the development of a self-conscious identity is totally dependent on the empathic relationship between parents and child.[11] It is only by the parents' consistent and continuous ability to accurately read the toddler's emotional state and respond effectively that the child comes to respond in kind. The empathic connection opens the child's mind to the emotional and social world around her, and gives her the warmth and affection she needs to become trusting, as well as the confidence that she can act on others and have her intentions positively responded to in a reciprocal manner.

Greenspan takes us beyond the nature/nurture dichotomy with a simple but important observation. While the baby's body takes in information from the senses, it is the intimate relationships and emotional experiences formed between adult caregivers and the infant that, in turn, become abstracted by the infant's nervous system into patterns that encode these experiences. In other words, "[c]onsciousness develops from this continuous interaction in which biology organizes experience and experience organizes biology."[12]

When we use the term *"developed consciousness,"* says Greenspan,

> [w]hat we mean is the ability to experience the most basic
> emotions in ourselves and others and to reflect on these in the
> context of our families, society, culture, and environment.[13]

This is just another way of saying that a developed consciousness
is the expression of a mature empathic sensibility. Greenspan, like the
object-relations theorists who preceded him, is clear that "the ability to
consider the feelings of others in a caring, compassionate way derives
from the child's sense of having been loved and cared for herself."[14]
Mental health, says Greenspan, "requires a feeling of connectedness
with humanity . . ." which, in turn, requires "a well-developed sense
of empathy. . . ."[15]

HOW EMPATHY DEVELOPS IN CHILDREN

While Greenspan provides a useful map for chronicling the child's
journey to self-consciousness and personhood, Martin L. Hoffman
explains how the child's innate predisposition for empathic engagement is manifested at each stage of the maturation process, providing
the individual with the emotional and cognitive foundation to become
a fully formed social being.

Hoffman identifies five modes of empathic arousal in the developmental process. The first three are preverbal, automatic, and for the
most part involuntary: "motor mimicry and afferent feedback; classical
conditioning; [and] direct association of cues from the victim or his
situation with one's own painful past experience."[16] Hoffman stresses
that those preverbal behaviors precede any real sense of self and are
all the more powerful because they demonstrate that human beings
are biologically predisposed from birth to express empathy and create
bonds of intimacy and sociality.

The two higher-order cognitive modes are mediated associations
and role-taking or perspective-taking. The first allows the observer

to associate the victim's distress with one's own painful past experience. The second allows the observer to imagine how the victim feels as if it were his own experience.[17] As the child climbs from one level to another, he becomes increasingly adept at empathic expression and the mastering of empathic sensibility, in turn, allows him to become increasingly self-aware and conscious.

Adam Smith, interestingly enough, was among the first to recognize the emotional importance of mimicry. The philosopher who, more than any other individual of the Enlightenment era, popularized the notion of man's innate drive to promote his own self-interest without regard to the interest of others, nonetheless sensed another side of human nature, although he never fully developed the insight or questioned its implications regarding his own theory of man's selfish nature. He wrote:

> When we see a stroke aimed, and just ready to fall upon the
> leg or arm of another person, we naturally shrink and draw
> back our own arm. . . . The mob, when they are gazing at
> a dancer on the slack rope, naturally writhe and twist and
> balance their own bodies as they see him do.[18]

Researchers note that infants just after birth begin trying to mimic facial gestures. One-month-old infants already "smile, stick out their tongues, and open their mouths when they observe someone else doing the same thing."[19] In fact, in the first three months of life, a baby's visual ability to recognize faces is greater than at any other time in its life. An infant can recognize a jumbled photograph of her mother as quickly as an intact photograph—older children are not as adept at this exercise. By nine months of age, they mimic the mother's expressions of joy and sorrow. Mothers and other adults similarly mimic the facial expressions of infants, often involuntarily.[20] Imitating facial expressions of others continues throughout life. Studies have shown that viewers of television programs unconsciously mimic the expressions of the people they're watching on the set.[21] Again, the mimicking is, for the most part, unconscious. In one experiment, researchers studied subtle facial movements of participants as they looked at pictures of happy and angry faces using electromyography (EMG) technology. They found that the subjects' muscles involved in smiling moved when they viewed photos of smiling faces, and the muscles involved in frowning moved when they viewed photos of people with angry expressions on their faces.[22]

Human beings also mimic accents, tones of voices, and speech rhythms.[23] For example, in a study observing twenty-minute conversations, partners not only matched the time each spoke so that it roughly coincided, but they also matched each other's rhythms of speech and even the duration of pauses and silences between utterances.[24] Again, this matching behavior is, for the most part, involuntary and automatic, suggesting the deep biological roots of sociality.

The posture of others is also often mimicked. A study found that students often mimic the posture of their teachers, and the more pronounced the mimicking, the greater the likelihood of rapport between students and their teacher. Similar studies of couples show that the more the partners' movements were in sync with each other, the higher their emotional rapport.[25]

Emotional mimicking is also commonplace, but we have a tendency not to realize it, both because it is involuntary and automatic and because we like to think that we have some control over the generation of our own feelings. When participants in a series of experiments listened to tape recordings of either happy or sad speakers, their own moods changed to reflect the mood of the speakers, without even consciously recognizing the causality.

In a chapter of *The New Unconscious*, Tanya Chartrand, William Maddux, and Jessica Lakin note that nonconscious mimicking is an automatic process. The primary adaptive function, from a biological perspective, say Chartrand et al., is "that it [mimicry] binds and bonds people together and fosters empathy. . . ."[26] The recent discovery of mirror neurons in the premotor cortex of monkeys and humans provides the neurological clues for how mimicry is activated.[27]

Psychologists Robert W. Levenson and Anna M. Ruef explain that physiological synchrony and emotional synchrony are bidirectional— that is, "emotional synchrony can produce physiological synchrony, and physiological synchrony can produce emotional synchrony."[28] While the bidirectional nature is duly noted, Hoffman believes that the physiological component is a more powerful driver than we previously thought. William James drew attention to the significance of the physiological trigger in inducing an emotional state. He observed that "[w]e feel sorry because we cry, angry because we strike, and afraid because we tremble."[29] We call this afferent feedback. (The term "feedback" was first popularized by Norbert Wiener, the father of cybernetics theory, in the 1950s.)

In an interesting study conducted in the 1970s, researchers were able to lend scientific credibility to James's theoretical musings. Electrodes were placed on the faces of subjects. The researcher then arranged the subjects' faces into emotional expressions—smiles and frowns—without their realizing it, simply by asking them to contract various muscles. The subjects in the smile condition felt happier than the control group, while the subjects in the frown condition reported feeling angrier than the control group. When shown cartoons, the subjects in the smiling mode rated them as being funnier than cartoons they viewed when frowning. Even more interesting, the subjects in the "smile" condition were better at remembering happy events in their lives than sad events, while subjects in the "frown" condition were better able to conjure up sad experiences from their past. One of the subjects in the study subsequently related her surprise over the effect that the facial gesture had on her emotions.

> When my jaw was clenched and my brows down, I tried not
> to be angry but it just fit the position. I'm not in any angry
> mood but I found my thoughts wandering to things that made
> me angry, which is sort of silly, I guess. I knew I was in an
> experiment and knew I had no reason to feel that way, but I
> just lost control.[30]

Afferent feedback suggests that a baby can begin to empathize with another's feelings before he has experienced that feeling himself. James D. Laird, professor of psychology at Clark University, who did the pioneering experiments on facial expressions and the conjuring up of moods, says that both afferent and cognitive inference exist. He notes that

> [s]ome people are happy because they smile, angry because they scowl, and sad because they pout; others define their emotional experience in terms of situational expectations.[31]

In other words, one can become more empathic both by internalizing another's emotional state as well as by comparing another's emotional states to one's own past emotional experiences.

For a long time, anthropologists and psychologists suspected that facial expressions and emotions were socially derived rather than biologically driven. We now know that there are certain facial expressions that conjure up the same feelings across all cultures and for every human being. Anthropologist E. Richard Sorenson and psychologists Paul Ekman and Wallace V. Friesen observed a preliterate New Guinea tribe and found that they identified the same facial expressions with the same feelings and emotions as people in the United States, Brazil, and Japan.[32] Different cultures, in turn, mold these common facial expressions and moods to the prevailing social ethic.[33]

The scientific evidence, says Hoffman, suggests that

> mimicry is probably a hard-wired neurologically based empathy-arousing mechanism whose two steps, imitation and feedback, are directed by commands from the central nervous system.[34]

Studies cited by Hoffman indicate that when people mimic one another they are expressing solidarity. By displaying a reaction that is appropriate to another's situation, the observer is conveying his awareness, regard, support, and comfort.[35] Mimicry requires that one be "mindful" to another and "attuned" to their state of mind, both necessary conditions to promoting empathic expression and bonds of sociality.

By the time an infant is one year old, she can begin to read the facial expressions of others and detect their emotional state. Psychology professor Andrew Meltzoff, at the University of Washington, has examined the gazes of thousands of babies. Dr. Meltzoff and his colleague Rechele Brooks found that if infants demonstrated poor gazing skills at 12 months of age, they were likely to exhibit less developed language skills at two years of age. Meltzoff argues that

> [y]ou can tell a lot about people, what they're interested in and what they intend to do next, by watching their eyes. It appears that even babies know that. . . . This is how they learn to become expert members of our culture.[36]

Classical conditioning is the next level of empathic arousal in the developmental process. For example, if a mother feels anxious and stiffens her body, her stress can be passed on and internalized by the baby in her arms. The mother's facial and verbal expressions that accompany the tension can even provoke distress in the infant when not being held. The infant then comes to feel similar distress whenever he observes similar facial and verbal expressions in others.

The third level of empathic arousal, direct association, occurs when another person's plight conjures up similar past experiences and accompanying emotions in the memory of the observer. Hoffman uses the example of a boy witnessing another child cut himself and cry, reminding him of his own past experiences of feeling pain. Unlike conditioning, in which one's distress is matched to the distress of others, in the case of direct association, the observer need only associate someone else's very specific painful experience with the feeling of pain one might have experienced in a similar but not exactly the same situation to trigger an empathic response.[37] For example, as mentioned in Chapter 1, it's not unusual for a toddler to try to comfort a tearful playmate by bringing him over to his mother, even if the other child's mother is present. This act demonstrates that the child is experiencing empathetic distress because of the other child's plight but is still unable to distinguish his own distress from the plight of the other child. That's because even though the child is aware of the other child as a separate being, he still doesn't realize that the other toddler has his own feelings. Instead, he attributes his own feelings to the distressed playmate and therefore takes him to be comforted by his own mother.

Mimicking, conditioning, and direct association are all involuntary and rather primitive forms of empathic arousal. But they demonstrate, very dramatically, the deep biological roots of empathic expression in the human animal. We are built to "forcefully experience another's emotion" as if it were our own.[38]

Still, for mature empathy to be expressed, it is necessary to add language and cognitive development into the emotional equation. When that happens, the child is prepared to graduate to levels four and five, mediated association and role-taking.

With mediated association, the victim's emotional situation is communicated via language. The observer takes in the words of the victim—for example, "I am frightened because my mother is dying." He then decodes the words by checking their meaning against his own past situations—a cognitive appraisal—and gives forth with an empathic response. Mediated association combines both the affective and cognitive functions to create an empathic response.

Role-taking is the fifth and final level of empathic arousal in the Hoffman developmental model. Role-taking requires a high level of cognitive processing. One needs to imagine what it might be like to be in another person's situation. The early studies on role-taking as an empathic arousal mechanism were conducted by Ezra Stotland in the late 1960s. Subjects were asked how they would feel if they were subjected to the same painful heat treatment being administered to someone they were viewing in a one-way mirror. These subjects showed more empathic distress than subjects who were only asked to closely observe the victim's movements. They also showed more empathic distress than subjects who were only asked to imagine how the victim felt. In other words, self-focused, as opposed to other-focused, role-taking elicited the most empathic distress.

Hoffman warns that empathic distress generated by self-focused role-taking can lead to what he calls "egoistic drift." While the empathic response might be more intense, there is the risk of the experience becoming more self-directed and less truly empathic.[39]

How, then, do children learn to take their innate biological drive for empathic expression and transform it into a mature empathic consciousness? Hoffman says the key to whether children develop a mature empathic sensibility is, in large part, traceable to the way parents discipline them. It is in the disciplining experience that children develop a keen sense of empathic expression.

While babies are rarely disciplined in their first year of life, they begin to be disciplined regularly thereafter—approximately every eleven minutes between the ages of twelve to fifteen months.[40] By the time the child has reached what parents call "the Terrible Twos," and the toddler is becoming increasingly willful, "two-thirds of all parent-child interactions are discipline encounters in which parents attempt to change children's behavior against their will."[41] Between the ages of two and ten years, parental attempts to change their children's behavior occur approximately every six to nine minutes, in what amounts to a war of wills.[42] A good percentage of the discipline episodes involve some kind of harm the child has inflicted—emotional or physical—on another.

Introducing a sense of morality into the child's experience isn't easy. Studies done by psychology professors William F. Arsenio and Anthony Lover in the 1990s found that when children under the age of eight years old were told about fictional kids who stole or refused to take turns, the children thought that the storybook characters would be happy about what they did and not concerned about the distress of the victims.[43] The key to transforming innate empathic impulses to mature empathic responses lies in the nature of the disciplining mode.

Obviously, inflicting corporal punishment on the child for a social transgression is likely to have the opposite effect and make the youngster less empathic in the future. Rather, the best way to bring out one's mature empathic potential is through induction, "in which parents highlight the other's perspective, point up the other's distress, and make it clear that the child's action caused it."[44] When the intervention is done with care, nurturance, and fairness, and the child becomes genuinely aware that he caused another's distress, it can lead to a sense of guilt and remorse and a sincere effort to want to make reparation. For example, if the child takes another child's toy away from him, the parent might sit him down and ask him how bad he would feel if someone did the same thing to him. Then the parent might ask him to imagine how bad the other child now feels.

So although inductions, like other forms of discipline, let the child know of the parents' disapproval, they are also social learning opportunities. By pointing out the victim's distress and asking the child how he might feel in the same circumstance, the parent is allowing the empathy-arousing mechanisms to trigger. For example, the parent might ask the child to go over and look at the other child in the eyes. The other child's sad face and streaming tears might then touch off an automatic mimicking response in the transgressor—and he too will begin to cry. Similarly, asking the child to imagine what the other kid is feeling might elicit a mediated association. The arousal of empathic distress then metamorphoses into a sense of guilt and the felt need to make compensation to the victim.

Induction discipline is a kind of script, says Hoffman, that follows a predictable plot line. First, the "child's transgression, followed by [the] parent's induction, followed by [the] child's feeling [of] empathic distress and guilt," and ending with the parent suggesting a reparative response—an apology, hug, or kiss for the victim—and the child experiencing a sense of relief and diminishing of guilt. These scripts build up in the memory and become part of the brain circuitry. Each scripted memory deepens the child's repertoire of empathic experiences and offers a mental library of experiences to call upon in future social encounters.[45]

Children generally are introduced to induction scripts in the third year, as parental discipline becomes more sophisticated and communication between parent and child becomes more rich, varied, and interactive.[46] Interestingly, this stage of empathic development generally occurs slightly after the toddler is able to identify himself in the mirror, signaling an awareness of self. Induction discipline works at this stage because the child is "becoming aware that others have inner states"—emotions, desires, thoughts—that often differ from his own.[47] This is the beginning of the reflective self. The growing sense of selfhood and recognition of others as separate beings with their own thoughts and feelings enables the child to learn, through inductive discipline, to be more empathic.

Induction discipline is a delicate balancing act. Hoffman reminds us that parents are powerful figures in the life of a child. They are the nurturing agents and the child's emotional and personal lifeline to the world. Their ability to command the child's attention and assert their will as well as withdraw their affection makes them a formidable force in the life of an infant. That said, if a parent is too lenient and fails to provide a predictable disciplinary framework, the toddler might end up ignoring their will when it is exercised. On the other hand, if parents are too controlling and overwhelm the infant with their assertive power, the child is likely to become either aggressive and angry or withdraw from emotional contact. The just good enough parent—as Winnicott might say—applies just enough pressure on the child during a disciplinary moment so that he will be open to listening to what they have to say about the distress he has caused another. If the child's behavior is approached in a nonjudgmental but concerned manner, it is likely to trigger the empathic distress and a sense of guilt and the consequent desire to make reparation to the victim.

What induction disciplining is really teaching the child is the substance of human morality—responsibility for one's actions, compassion for others, a willingness to come to another's aid and comfort, and a proper sense of fair play and justice. The maturation of empathy and the development of a moral sense are one and the same thing.

When we talk of guilt, we need to be clear not to confuse it with shame. Often the two terms are used interchangeably when, in fact, they are quite different. While guilt can trigger empathic distress and the desire to reach out and make amends to another whom one has harmed, shame denigrates a person's being, making them feel worthless and inhuman. To be shamed is to be rejected. Shame is a way of isolating a person from the collective we. He or she becomes an outsider and a nonperson. Shame has the effect of turning off the innate empathic impulse. If one feels like a nonbeing, socially ostracized and without self-worth, he is unable to draw upon his empathic reserves to feel for another's plight. Unable to emotionally connect with others, he either shrinks into withdrawal or acts out his sense of abandonment by exercising rage at others. Why rage? Because it is often the only way he has open to him to communicate and engage his fellow human beings. The idea of the "loner," isolated from society and full of rage toward his fellows, is a phenomenon in every society.

When one is made to feel guilty, it is one's humanity that is being called upon to do the right thing by another person. Unlike shaming someone, which isolates him from humanity, guilt is an internal mechanism that reminds one of his deep social connection to others and the need to repair the social bond.

Guilt needs to be handled carefully. If a parent's induction discipline creates too much of a sense of guilt in the child, he is likely to grow up feeling that nothing he can do will ever be adequate to amend a hurt or restore a social bond. If, on the other hand, a parent's induction discipline doesn't result in instilling at least a minimum of guilt in the child, he will grow up without being able to reflect on how his behavior affects others and unable to trigger sufficient empathic distress to re-heal the social bond. Just good enough parenting lets the child know that he did something wrong, but in a caring way that lets him know that he is still loved and regarded as a person. By explaining how the other person might feel and asking him how he would feel in the same situation, the parents are letting him know that they trust his innate goodness and desire to empathize with others and make amends. Equally important, the parents are teaching a child that their love for him is no less because of his wrongful behavior. No one is perfect. The best we can expect of each other is to learn from our indiscretions and try to do better next time.

By shaming a child, however, the parents are letting him know that he is not living up to their expectations and, therefore, not worthy of their consideration. Their expectations, rather than his humanity, become the focal point of the disciplinary exercise. The child is left with the impression that his very being is a disappointment and that he must conform to an "ideal image" of what his parents expect from him or suffer the consequence of rejection.

Guilt cultures create a very different human being from shaming cultures. The American philosopher Martha Nussbaum puts it this way:

> Moral guilt is so much better than shame, because it can be atoned for, it does not sully the entirety of one's being. It is a dignified emotion compatible with optimism about one's own prospects. . . . Rather than making a forbidding and stifling demand for perfection, [morality] holds the child in her imperfection, telling her that the world contains possibilities of forgiveness and mercy, and that she is loved as a person of interest and worth in her own right. She therefore need not fear that her human imperfection will cause the world's destruction. And because she is not stricken by annihilating shame at her imperfection, she will have less need for envy and jealousy, emotions that express her desire for omnipotent control of the sources of good.[48]

Ironically, while a shaming culture pretends to adhere to the highest standards of moral perfection, in reality it produces a culture of self-hate, envy, jealousy, and hatred toward others. Shaming cultures, throughout history, have been the most aggressive and violent because they lock up the empathic impulse, and with it the ability to experience another's plight and respond with acts of compassion. When a child grows up in a shaming culture believing that he must conform to an ideal of perfection or purity or suffer the wrath of the community, he is likely to judge everyone else by the same rigid, uncompromising standards. Lacking empathy, he is unable to experience other people's suffering as if it were his own and therefore is likely to judge their plight as their own fault because they failed to live up to the standards of perfection expected of them by society.

Shaming cultures still exist in traditional societies. It is not uncommon to hear about a woman who has been gang-raped and who is then stoned to death by her own family and neighbors, because she has brought shame on herself and her family. Rather than empathize with her suffering, the community inflicts even greater punishment on her by taking her life. In the eyes of the community, she bears the shame of the rape, despite the fact that she was the innocent victim. As far as her family and neighbors are concerned, she is forever defiled and impure and therefore an object of disgust to be blotted out. The power of shaming cultures to squelch empathy and transform human beings into monsters is terrifying to behold.

It should be emphasized that induction discipline is a relatively new learning tool and perhaps the most revolutionary change in parenting behavior in history. Previously, a child's misbehavior toward others was met generally with corporal punishment and shaming. Parents were not yet acculturated in therapeutic thinking and able to lead a child through the induction process. Getting a child to understand how his behavior affects another child and how he would feel were he the victim of the same misbehavior requires that a parent already have a well-developed psychological consciousness. Helping a child reflect on his own behavior, feel a sense of guilt and remorse, and make an effort at reparation is a deeply therapeutic process. In effect, the parent serves as the child's first therapist, enabling him to make the appropriate emotional connections to advance pro-social behavior. This kind of parenting would have been impossible to conceive of before the era of psychological consciousness.

Freud would have considered the notion of induction discipline wrongheaded. While he believed that guilt is critical to establishing a moral sense, his concept of guilt derives from the exact opposite premise of object-relations theorists and devotees of attachment theory. Freud believed that guilt was activated by fear of parental punishment, not another's distress. Infants are born narcissists and are continually engaged in a contest of will with their parents to advance their libidinal self-interests. On the one hand, they fear their parents' control and authority while, on the other hand, they need parental protection, Freud argued, to survive. The child's relationship with parents, then, is ambivalent and manipulative from the start, with the child continuously employing various means to get what he needs, but always anxious for fear of reprisal or abandonment. It is the fear of losing the parents' protection, Freud suggested, that triggers guilt and conditions a child to become moral.

> Thus we know of two origins of the sense of guilt: one arising
> from fear of an authority, and the other, later on, arising from
> the fear of the super-ego. The first insists upon a renunciation
> of instinctual satisfactions; the second, as well as doing this,
> presses for punishment, since the continuance of the forbidden
> wishes cannot be concealed from the super-ego.[49]

A sense of guilt, then, according to Freud, arises from fear of parental punishment, and that guilt is then internalized and conditions the child to be moral, for fear of punishment by parents and later by society. Morality in this context is negatively induced. Human beings are moral, despite their instinctual drive to advance their own self-centered will at the expense of their fellows, to avoid punishment. Freud, like Hobbes, believed that societies are concocted to restrain individual self-interests, lest human beings run amok, and that moral behavior is imposed in the form of laws to ensure a certain amount of social cohesion.

Freud's pessimistic view of human nature, however, did not go unchallenged at the time. In 1919, the British sociologist Wilfred Trotter advanced the thesis that human beings are herd animals whose instinctual drive is to protect one another and that such behavior promoted the survival of both the individual and the group. Altruism, according to Trotter, is the way human beings express their herd instinct and is built into the core of our biological being. Here was another view of natural selection at odds with the conventional wisdom in Freud's day. Humans feel responsible for one another and come to their assistance. The extent to which one feels responsible to individuals beyond extended kin is conditioned by the societal context in which one lives.

Trotter's theory was anathema to Freud, for, if he was right, then the carefully contrived story Freud set forth was pure fiction and without a sound biological foundation. Freud responded to Trotter with a counterthesis.

> Let us venture, then, to correct Trotter's pronouncement
> that man is a herd animal and assert that he is rather a horde
> animal, an individual creature in a horde led by a chief.[50]

In the horde, according to the Freudian story, the father is a powerful, dominating, and ruthless authority figure who commands complete allegiance. Filled with rage at their father, the sons are forever plotting to depose and kill him so they can enjoy incestuous pleasure with their mother and rule over the horde.

Research on infants' emotional and cognitive development in the past half-century has finally laid to rest Freud's rather bizarre explanation of human nature. Trotter was onto something, and the object relations theorists and child development researchers confirmed his suspicion. We now know that empathic distress is biologically inherited. When it is triggered as a result of exposure to another's plight, especially if one senses he might in some way be partially responsible for the other's condition, it can lead to guilt and the desire to make amends.

It's worth emphasizing a point made earlier that empathic distress, guilt, and the desire to make reparations is itself circumscribed by natural selection. There are both minimum thresholds and outer limits to empathic expression. There are countless situations in which another's plight is not sufficient to set off empathic distress—either because they are strangers, or members of groups one has been conditioned to regard unfavorably, or because their plight does not appear immediate, either in time or space. Individuals can also experience empathic over-arousal, which Hoffman defines as

> an involuntary process that occurs when an observer's
> empathic distress becomes so painful and intolerable that it is
> transformed into an intense feeling of personal distress, which
> may move the person out of the empathic mode entirely.[51]

Caregivers, especially nurses and doctors, are vulnerable to what is called "compassion fatigue." So are other people in the helping professions—social workers and people involved in emergency aid relief in war zones or in the aftermath of natural calamities are particularly prone. The continuous empathic over-arousal can lead to emotional exhaustion, the dulling of the empathic response, and emotional withdrawal.

If everyone were to experience empathic distress and altruistic behavior at every moment, they could not attend to their own needs sufficiently to assure their own emotional, cognitive, and physical well-being. Our physiology seems to understand this, and it establishes minimum thresholds and maximum limits to our empathic arousal.

The empathic maturation process quickens in the preschool period as children become emotionally skilled in using language to express emotions.[52] They also become adept at reading between the lines and understanding that another person's outward appearance and demeanor may mask very different feelings on the inside.[53]

By the age of four to five years, a child develops a sense of social reciprocity. He comes to understand what's expected of him in terms of appropriate social response to another child's overtures or actions aimed at him and is capable of experiencing a sense of guilt if he hurts the other child by failing to reciprocate in kind.[54] For example, if a friend shares his toys but the child refuses to reciprocate by sharing his own, leading the other child to break into tears, the sense of guilt can trigger an empathic response and lead to an effort to make some kind of reparation.

Around the time children are seven years old, they begin to realize when they are experiencing an empathic response to another's plight. A study involving children who were five, seven, eight, and thirteen years of age revealed that children seven years of age and up were aware of being empathic, while the younger children were not. The children were shown films of children in highly stressful situations—a child unjustly punished by a parent, a disabled child learning to climb stairs with a cane, and a child forcibly removed from the family. The seven-year-olds and the older children said they felt sad because of the children's situations in the film, suggesting that they were aware that their own sad feeling was in response to the other children's plight and that they were experiencing empathy. The younger children, however, were not able to comprehend that their own distressed feeling was causally related to their experience of the other child's condition. They did not realize that they were empathizing.[55]

Children between six and eight years of age add the sense of social obligation to their moral repertoire. They learn that keeping promises, for example, is essential to maintaining friendships and that failure to do so can result in a feeling of betrayal and hurt.[56] Again, if such behavior causes a feeling of guilt and the desire to make amends, then the child is learning how to become a moral being.

Eight- and nine-year-olds are able to pick up on levels of self-esteem in others.[57] They are also able to modify their empathic response to another's condition based on extenuating circumstances. For example, children were asked how mad they would feel if another child stole their cat. They were then informed that the perpetrator's own cat ran away and his parents wouldn't give him a new companion. When given additional information, children "who were eight years [and] older said they would be less mad" after hearing about what led the other child to commit the transgression than were kids in a control group that weren't told. Children seven years or younger, however, were unmoved by the additional information, suggesting that children don't begin to factor in another person's past experience in their emotional response until around eight years of age.[58]

Children between the ages of ten and twelve are also able to think in morally abstract ways about what their behavior should be in society writ large. They can experience a general sense of moral obligation and guilt beyond the immediate circumstance. They begin to reflect on what it means to be a good person and a morally upright human being and conduct their life's activity with an internal moral compass that keeps them on track. Their sense of guilt is now abstracted as well. They come to internalize a sense of social guilt by anguishing over their failure to live up to the moral standards of society.[59]

By the time children are ten or eleven years old, they are able to comprehend the notion of experiencing two contradictory feelings simultaneously—for example, that one might feel embarrassed about having a disabled sibling but at the same time feel empathy toward him or her.[60] Also around this age, children are able to realize that negative feelings come as much in response from memories of past experiences as from reactions to the immediate events around them.[61]

In early adolescence—twelve to thirteen years of age—youngsters are far more discerning in their emotional response to others. They are able to detect the various levels of emotional expression in others to the point of sensing when another's mood reflects more than just the circumstance at hand. For example, the other person's sadness might reflect a deeper sense of depression if it seems far too dark to be appropriate to the immediate situation.[62]

There comes a point in the journey to mature empathic consciousness when a young adult is able to emotionally and cognitively take notice of the whole of another person's existence and develop an empathic response to the totality of their experience and being. For example, one might empathize with another person's impoverished existence or their severe physical or mental disability. One might even empathize with another's condition in instances when the other person is unaware of their own plight. Hoffman relates the following account of a student's empathic response to a small child's plight to which even the child was unaware.

> My cousin's mother died. He was too young to understand
> and he just kept on playing with his toys. I tried to smile and
> play with him but I kept on thinking about how not having
> his mother would affect him. He wouldn't have the sweet hugs
> when he bumped his knee. . . . And all I could think of was
> that the softness of his mother was gone and he'd miss that. But
> he wasn't recognizing it. He thought everything was great.[63]

Finally, the most mature form of empathic response is the ability to experience an entire group of people or even other species as if their distress were one's own.[64] Often this happens when one empathizes with an individual's plight and that plight is indicative of what his or her whole group experiences; for example, abused women or certain religious minorities or gay men, who all suffer at the hands of the dominant culture. The universalizing of empathy to include whole groups and categories of beings approaches the notion of a universal consciousness.

The World Values Survey, which will be discussed in Chapter 11, shows a clear trend toward the universalizing of empathy among the younger generations, at least in the more developed nations of the world. Fundamental changes in parenting and attachment behavior, longer periods of adolescence, more exposure to diverse peoples, communities, and cultures, greater global connectivity, increasing economic interdependence, and more cosmopolitan lifestyles have all contributed to the universalization of empathic consciousness.

ALTRUISM VERSUS SELF-INTEREST

Shortly after Charles Darwin published his theory of natural selection, Herbert Spencer put his own political spin on the work, suggesting that it provided the scientific proof that life is a ruthless, competitive struggle in which self-interest rules and only the fittest survive. Others weren't so sure. The Russian scientist Pyotr Alexeyevich Kropotkin argued that survival in nature depends as much on cooperation and reciprocity. The debate over the nature of nature, and especially human nature, has flared ever since Darwin published his theory, with scientists, philosophers, and social theorists dividing up on the matter, arguing their respective opinions with a degree of intensity that suggests how important the resolution of this question is to our species. We are, in an existential sense, desperate to know who we are and what drives us. What does it mean to be human?

The new studies on child development—not to mention the wealth of new research data on the behavior of our fellow mammals—is finally giving us some tentative answers to this age-old question of the meaning of human nature.

We are both a cooperative and competitive animal. But it is the former sensibility that is wired to our biology and that sets the ground rules. We are, first and foremost, a social species. Within that context, we sometimes compete to advance our interests. If, however, our self-interest strays too far from the social bond, we risk ostracization.

The advocates of a self-interested view of human nature, however, counter that the human propensity to engage in reciprocal social behavior—cooperation—is more of a "tit for tat" negotiation than a deeply felt expression of comforting and assisting our fellow beings. Even in the case of altruism, the extreme manifestation of empathic regard for another, the cynics would argue that there are other more subtle egoistic aims involved in a decision to sacrifice for another. For example, we might engage in altruism to alleviate our own distress, or to experience personal pleasure and joy in helping another, or because we feel it will add a few points on our moral scorecard, or elevate our status in the broader community. So what appears to be altruism is really masking a more subtle egoism that feeds our libidinal drives and utilitarian goals.

The issue of whether altruism is really innate and unselfish has been difficult to assess. In the past, we've had to rely on anecdotal evidence of seemingly heroic examples of altruism—ordinary people making extraordinary sacrifices, sometimes even giving their lives to assist others in need. And certainly everyone who's ever lived could cite personal examples of such behavior. But how do we find out if altruism, in the purest form, is more commonplace than extraordinary?

In recent years, researchers have concocted some ingenious experimental studies to test the pure altruism thesis. Their findings provide a growing body of evidence that we are empathic by nature and that altruism is the most mature expression of our empathic regard for others.

A study conducted with six- and ten-month-old infants by researchers at Yale University and published in the journal *Nature* in 2007 tested the question of whether babies could distinguish between good Samaritans and unkind people and which they found more attractive.

The results were eye-opening. They showed that even infants at an early age, before they had developed the most rudimentary sense of self, preferred individuals who help rather than hinder others.

Researchers set up two experiments. In the first, the infants viewed a climber made up of wood, with glued-on eyes, motionless at the foot of a hill. On the first two attempts at climbing up the hill, the climber failed. On the third effort, the climber was "either aided by a helper who pushed it from behind or pushed down by a hinderer."[65] The infants were then encouraged to choose between the helper and hinderer by reaching for one of them. Fourteen of the sixteen ten-month-old infants and twelve of the twelve six-month-old babies chose the helper.[66]

In the second experiment, the climber first approached the helper, which is unsurprising, and then the hinderer, which is surprising, and the ten-month-old infants looked longer at the second event, "indicating surprise when the climber approached one who had previously hindered it." By contrast, "The six-month-olds looked equally at both, indicating they did not yet understand why the climber's attitude toward the two might differ, even though they still preferred the helper to the hinderer. According to the researchers, this second result might indicate that the "capacity for social evaluation may develop before the ability to infer others' evaluations."[67]

The researchers conclude that

> [t]he capacity to evaluate individuals by their social actions
> may also serve as a foundation for a developing system of
> moral cognition. Plainly, many aspects of a full-fledged moral
> system are beyond the grasp of the preverbal infant. Yet the
> ability to judge differentially those who perform positive and
> negative social acts may form an essential basis for any system
> that will eventually contain more abstract concepts of right
> and wrong.[68]

The Yale studies show that infants under the age of one are able to differentiate good Samaritan or kind behavior from antisocial or unkind behavior. Other new studies show that by eighteen months of age, toddlers are also able to perform altruistic acts themselves. Psychology researcher Felix Warneken, of Germany's Max Planck Institute for Evolutionary Anthropology, published the results of a study of toddlers exhibiting altruistic behavior far earlier than previously expected, again demonstrating the biological nature of human altruism.

Warneken carried out a series of tasks in full view of the infants—stacking books or hanging towels with clothespins. Occasionally he struggled with the task, dropping the clothespins or knocking over the books. Every one of the twenty-four toddlers crawled over to help him pick up the pins or books, but only in those instances where his facial and bodily gestures suggested he needed assistance. Warneken was careful not to ask for help or acknowledge the help with a thank you, in an effort not to bias the experiment by conditioning the toddlers to perform in return for heaping praise. Warneken emphasizes that the babies didn't offer their help when he purposely took a book from the stack or tossed a clothespin on the floor, but only in those cases when he clearly needed help, thus exhibiting a keen sensitivity to his plight and a willingness to come to his aid.[69] The toddlers expressed a pure sense of altruism—offering help with no expectation of getting something in return.

Despite the mounting research evidence that humans are wired for empathy and often express their empathic regard by engaging in altruistic activity, the naysayers cling to the defense that people act that way because they have learned, through past experience and conditioning, that helping another person mutes their empathic distress and provides them a sense of relief and, on occasion, even pleasure, because they have been morally accountable. Hoffman points out that just because one feels better because he or she was able to help another in distress doesn't mean that it is the sole or even a major reason for being altruistic. The pleasure might be an unexpected by-product, but not a prime motivating factor, for engaging in altruistic behavior in the first place. Hoffman says, "[T]here is no evidence that people help in order to feel good, and there is evidence to the contrary."[70]

The evidence Hoffman refers to is compelling. C. Daniel Batson conducted a series of experiments in the early 1990s, showing that empathic response to another's plight, in the form of pure altruism, is commonplace. In the first set of experiments, Batson tested the assumption that a bystander's primary motivation for helping someone in distress is to relieve his own empathic distress. Their assistance, in other words, is self-serving. Since the observer's empathic distress can only be relieved by either coming to the aid of the suffering person or by escaping from the scene, the experiment creates the conditions for easy and for difficult escape to assess the hypothesis that altruism, in the final analysis, is self-serving. Those expressing low empathy in the pre-study profiling are likely to choose to escape, if relatively easy, rather than to stay and help relieve the empathic distress. But high-empathy participants are likely to stay and assist even if escape is relatively easy, because their primary motivation is pure altruism—that is, caring for the other rather than alleviating their own empathic distress.

Some participants were informed that if they did not help, they would continue to have to witness a worker receive electrical shocks (difficult escape). Others were told they would be able to leave quickly without further need to witness the shocks (easy escape). The results show that only among the observers experiencing high levels of personal distress but low levels of empathy was the option of easy escape taken. Among those expressing high levels of empathy, however, the option of easy escape to alleviate distress was not exercised.

The second set of experiments tested the hypothesis that some individuals will engage in altruistic behavior for fear that if they don't they will be shamed in the eyes of others and be punished by losing moral standing in the community. Batson informed the participants of a victim, a younger woman, in need of assistance. To find out if one's decision to help another is dependent on worrying about what others might say or think if one didn't act, Batson introduced additional information to justify not helping.

The subjects of the study were told that other potential helpers had said no to a request to help the victim, reasoning that it would give the new participants justification for opting out as well. Individuals of low and high empathy were given the option of donating time to assist the woman in stress. The pledge form also recorded the pledge responses of previous subjects in the study. In one pledge form, the participants were told that five of seven previous participants had pledged to help (low justification for not helping), and on the other form, participants were told that only two of seven previous players had pledged to help (high justification for not helping). As expected, the low-empathy people were more likely to help the woman if they thought that a majority of previous participants had pledged to commit their time to assist her and less likely to help her if others had also refused. The high-empathy participants, however, pledged to help the woman regardless of whether a majority or minority of previous participants in the study had pledged to do so.[71]

The third set of experiments tested the hypothesis that altruistic behavior is motivated by the desire to experience empathic joy and that the relief of the victim's plight is merely instrumental to that self-serving end. The empathic-altruism hypothesis, in contrast, argues that the joy a helper feels is "a consequence, not the goal, of relieving the need."[72]

Subjects were briefed about a person in need and then presented with a choice of either getting an update on her condition or hearing about someone else. Before making the choice, participants were provided information from experts on the likelihood the victim's situation would be substantially improved by the time of the update. Some were told that the likelihood of improvement was only 20 percent, while others were told it was 50 percent, and some were told it was 80 percent. The speculation was that if the feeling of empathy for another person in dire straits is activated by the need to experience empathic joy, then there would be a linear relation between the likelihood that the victim would improve and the choice to hear again about her updated condition. In other words, few subjects would choose to hear about her condition if there was only a 20 percent chance of her improving, more subjects would choose to hear if there was a 50 percent chance of her improving, and even more if there was an 80 percent chance of her getting better.[73]

If, however, the prime concern of the subjects was the needy person's well-being, then the desire to get an update on her condition should be highest at the 50 percent level, where there is the most doubt about the outcome of her situation. In other words, the pattern should be curvilinear rather than linear. To the extent that subjects already know what her updated condition is likely to be at the 20 percent likelihood of improvement and the 80 percent likelihood of improvement, they should be less likely to need to hear an update.

The results of the experiment show that high-empathy individuals were interested in hearing about the woman in need, but their interest peaked at 50 percent, where the diagnosis was most uncertain—confirming that their motivation was concern for the person in need and not their own desire to experience joy. If it had been otherwise, the subjects would have shown less interest in hearing an update of her condition if there was only a 20 percent chance of her improving and more interest in learning about her condition if there was an 80 percent chance of an improvement in her condition. By contrast, low-empathy subjects did show a linear response pattern, expressing greater interest in hearing about the victim as the likelihood of an improvement in her condition went from 20 percent to 50 percent to 80 percent, thus confirming their greater interest in experiencing the joy of hearing good news rather than being attentive to the plight of the victim.[74]

Batson qualifies the empathy-altruism thesis with the observation that if the pain inflicted on the helper becomes too great, by assisting another—for example, having to accept extremely painful, although harmless, electric shocks—even those reporting high empathy for the person in need might put their own self-concern first.[75] Quite understandable. Still, there are many instances where people make significant sacrifices and even give their lives for others, sometimes complete strangers. During the Nazi reign of terror, thousands of people in occupied nations across Europe hid Jews or helped them escape, even though the consequence, if caught, would be their own execution.

CULTURAL VARIATIONS IN EMPATHY

Child development researchers have become increasingly skilled at identifying the stages of cognitive development and empathic maturation.

Still, they are quick to caution that although there appears to be a universal pattern at play in how the process unfolds that extends to all cultures, particular societies' attachment styles and cultural conditioning determine whether the process is arrested at various stages and/or set along divergent tracks. In other words, what they are saying is that under conditions that optimize the kind of post-Bowlby approach to attachment behavior, one can expect to see cognitive and empathic development proceed along the lines outlined.

That having been acknowledged, it's also important to note that while in virtually all of the developed nations—east and west—the post-Bowlby attachment style of parenting is becoming nearly universal, each culture is coming to the new child-rearing style with their own unique cultural traditions, meaning they are putting their own stamp on the process.

For example, in the American culture, with its long tradition of glorifying individualism and personal autonomy, the parenting emphasis might focus more on enhancing a child's personal self-esteem. Whereas in Asian cultures, especially in China, Korea, and Japan, where traditionally the focus in child-rearing is less on molding an autonomous individual and more on preparing a youngster to become a harmonious part of the complex relationships that comprise the larger society, the emphasis might be more on encouraging self-criticism rather than self-esteem in the creation of a mature empathic sensibility. In these cultures, argue Shinobu Kitayama et al., in an article published in the *Journal of Personality and Social Psychology*, where Buddhism emphasized compassion and Confucianism stressed role obligation, parents are far more likely to accentuate "fitting in" than "standing out" in the parenting styles.[76] The difference in cultural approaches influence the way parents and, later, teachers engage children in induction disciplining. For example, in American schools, self-esteem instruction abounds. If a child's behavior hurts another child, he might be asked by the teacher to reflect on how his actions might have affected the other child's self-esteem and how his own self-esteem might have been affected had the other child acted the same way toward him.

In a Japanese school, by contrast, where self-improvement is emphasized over self-enhancement, children are asked at the end of each school day to reflect—*hansei*—on "where their individual or group performance fell short of class goals."[77] Kitayama et al. point out that in the Japanese culture "self-improvement is a symbolic act of affirming the value of the relationship of which one is part, thereby fulfilling the sense of the self as a fully interdependent entity."[78] If, then, a Japanese child's behavior caused another student to suffer, the teacher might ask him to reflect on how his actions caused pain to both the other child and the group and undermined the harmonious relations in the classroom. Likewise, the child might be asked how he and the group would feel if the other student had treated him the same way and undermined the harmonious relations in the classroom. Either approach is likely to trigger empathic distress and guilt and a desire to make amends.

WHILE OUR CONCEPT of human nature and ideas about parenting have changed dramatically in recent years, our philosophical and political thinking has been woefully slow to catch up. We still live with the shibboleths inherited from the eighteenth-century Enlightenment. Rethinking human nature, however, calls for rethinking the very meaning of the human journey and, with it, our most cherished beliefs about what we hold important, how we define our aspirations, and how we choose to live our lives.

FIVE

RETHINKING THE MEANING OF THE HUMAN JOURNEY

In October 2006, a Harvard University task force responsible for reviewing the general education curriculum proposed that all undergraduate students be required to take a course on the theme "reason and faith." The proposal sent shockwaves through the academic world and became the subject of a national controversy. Suddenly a question that the intellectual establishment had long since passed judgment on was back in the headlines, dividing the scholarly and religious communities once again.

Religious leaders and a variety of scholars were happy to pounce on the proposal, suggesting that one of the nation's most venerable academic institutions had finally come to its senses and acknowledged the essential role faith plays in the lives of most people. A UCLA survey at the time found that 79 percent of college freshman believe in God and 69 percent pray and "find strength, support and guidance in their religious beliefs."[1]

The more secular professors at Harvard worried that requiring students to take such a course could open the door to a religious revival on campus and foster demands for the religionization of other parts of the curriculum. They were reluctant to reopen the ancient debate over faith and reason that had been so contentiously fought for nearly two centuries. More important, there were concerns that a Harvard imprimatur might set a precedent and lead to similar course requirements in universities across the country.

What started off as an innocent enough academic proposal escalated into a major rift, putting two dominant worldviews at loggerheads, once again. The curriculum committee tried to explain that their intention was not to introduce religious apologetics but to help students examine "the interplay between religion and various aspects of national and/or international culture and society."[2] Their aim, they said, was not to pit reason against faith but to apply reason to the examination of faith to better prepare students to engage in thoughtful religious discussion and reflection. Their attempt to calm the waters failed. Columnists, political pundits, and radio talk show hosts all weighed in on the matter, anxious to spur a deeper discussion on the relative merits of two very different approaches to human consciousness.

Several weeks after the curriculum proposal was made, it was summarily dropped. Instead, the task force suggested that religion and faith courses be substituted by courses on "what it means to be a human being."[3]

The Harvard tempest over faith versus reason, though short lived, is reminiscent of a stream of earlier efforts to reconcile reason and faith. In the late medieval Christian era, Saint Thomas Aquinas wrestled with the very same questions. In the thirteenth century, the carefully constructed Christian worldview that had been crafted by Saint Augustine at the very beginning of his Church's reign was starting to unravel. A market economy was beginning to emerge out of the dark recesses of feudal life. New technologies—especially watermills and windmills and new agricultural tools—were increasing agricultural production, yielding surpluses and spawning population growth and the beginning of urban life for the first time since the fall of the Roman Empire. The new technological progress stimulated interest in more rational approaches to organizing life. The rediscovery of Greek philosophy and science—the Moors reintroduced the ancient texts into Europe via Spain—spurred interest among Christian scholastics in logic and rational modes of thinking.

By the thirteenth century, the rational ordering of thought and action had taken on a life of its own and began to challenge the faith-based criteria of the Church. Here was a nascent approach to organizing life in this world that was practical and helped ameliorate the lot of humanity. It wasn't long before worldly rationalization came up against otherworldly grace and salvation.

Thomas Aquinas (1225–1274), the great thirteenth-century cleric and scholastic, took on the task of reconciling the two very different ways of understanding and ordering reality in the hopes of saving faith without condemning reason. In two works, *Summa Theologica* and *Summa Contra Gentiles*, Saint Thomas attempted to harmonize Aristotelian logic and philosophy with Christian theology in what scholars of a later period would refer to as "the delicate synthesis." Saint Thomas agreed with Aristotle that the universe is orderly and that reason can help man better understand the created world. But that is only possible, argued Saint Thomas, because God created this orderly and rational universe. Human reason, then, allows man a window to the divine. By understanding God's universe with the aid of reason, we get closer to God. As the medieval historian R. S. Hoyt observes, "In harmonizing Aristotle's philosophy with Christian doctrine it is the Aristotelian element that must be fitted into the Christian system, not the other way around."[4] In other words, reason is a gift God bestowed on man to bolster his faith in a divinely inspired rational universe. But reason is only possible once "revelation" opens up to the vista of God's grand design. Thus, when it comes to the two kinds of truth that exist, revelation and reason, the latter is always relegated to a secondary role. If reason appears to conflict with revelation, then reason errs and must be corrected by additional reasoning until the error is resolved.[5]

The Enlightenment philosophers also attempted to reconcile faith and reason by paying homage to Saint Thomas's notion that God created a divinely rational universe. The French philosopher René Descartes never doubted for a moment that God created a rational universe— nor did most of his contemporaries. Descartes, however, attempted to discover the "laws of nature" by which God set up the cosmos. He wrote:

> As I considered the matter carefully, it gradually came to
> light that all those matters only are referred to mathematics
> in which order and measurement are investigated, and that it
> makes no difference whether it be in numbers, figures, stars,
> sounds, or any other object that the question of measurement
> arises. I saw, consequently, that there must be some general
> science to explain that element as a whole, which gives rise to
> problems about order and measurement. This, I perceived, was
> called universal mathematics. Such a science should contain
> the primary rudiments of human reason, and its province
> ought to extend to the eliciting of true results in every
> subject.[6]

Descartes looked into God's creation and saw a rational and calculable domain. "To speak freely, I am convinced that it [mathematics] is
a more powerful instrument of knowledge than any other that has been
bequeathed to us by human agency, as being the source of all things."[7]

It was left to Isaac Newton, a deeply religious man and the last of
the great medieval alchemists, to discover the mathematical methods
Descartes dreamed of for describing the mechanical motions that govern God's creation. His three laws of matter and motion were meant to
explain the workings of the divine blueprint.

God was praised for being the grand architect of a rationally and
mathematically orchestrated mechanical universe. It wasn't long, however, before the divine inspiration was reduced to a footnote as successive generations of scholars, merchants, and tradesmen became more
occupied with manipulating the cosmic gears for human ends than
paying homage to the divine engineer. The personal God of medieval
Christianity was transformed into the distant divine clockmaker who
wound up the universe and then stepped aside to let his human surrogates tend the machine.

In the fired-up Promethean world of coal mines, steel furnaces, and
steam locomotion that seemed to hold forth the promise of a cornuco-
pia on Earth, more and more people found the age-old idea of suffer-

ing in this lifetime in expectation of salvation through God's grace and faith in the next world far less appealing.

Still, both faith and reason have remained remarkably resilient despite the premature requiems that secularists and the faithful have periodically rendered on each other. And like Saint Thomas and, later, the Enlightenment philosophers who attempted to find a reconciliation of the two schools of thought, other more contemporary scholars have made their own valiant efforts to do the same.

Although such attempts seem admirable and no doubt most human beings would welcome a convincing case, the efforts keep coming up short. In large measure it's because both narratives fail to plumb the depths of what makes us human and therefore leave us with cosmologies that are incomplete stories—that is, they fail to touch the deepest realities of existence. That's not to dismiss the critical elements that make the stories of faith and reason so compelling. It's only that something essential is missing—and that something is "embodied experience."

Both the Abrahamic faiths—Judaism, Christianity, and Islam—as well as the Eastern religions of Buddhism, Hinduism, and Taoism either disparage bodily existence or deny its importance. So too does modern science and the rational philosophy of the Enlightenment. For the former, especially the Abrahamic faiths, the body is fallen and a source of evil. Its presence is a constant reminder of the depravity of human nature. For the latter, the body is mere scaffolding to maintain the mind, a necessary inconvenience to provide sensory perception, nutrients, and mobility. It is a machine the mind uses to impress its will on the world. It is even loathed because of its transient nature. At best it is something to tolerate and manipulate but not venerate. At worst it's a constant reminder of human weakness and our own mortality. The body is used as an "object" of lust in youth and regarded with disgust in old age as it withers and decays beneath us.

Most of all, the body is to be mistrusted, especially the emotions that flow from its continuous engagement with and reaction to the outside world. Neither the Bible nor Descartes's ruminations make much room for human emotions, except to depreciate them as untrustworthy and an impediment either to obedience to God in the first instance or to the rational will in the second instance.

The Bible drives the point home when God calls upon Abraham to slay his son, Isaac, to show his unswerving obedience to divine authority. Abraham's emotional anguish was of little concern to the wrathful God that governed the universe. The very foundation of the Abrahamic faiths is God's law. The Jews are the people of the book. Human feelings and emotions are often the source of being led astray. Even New Testament apostles and theologians, despite their emphasis on fraternal love, view the body as depraved and loathsome and a reminder of the temporary nature of a fallen earthly life. Bodily experience in this world, and the suffering and pain it inflicts, is viewed as a penance on the way to eternal salvation in the next world.

In the modern era, with its emphasis on rationality, objectivity, detachment, and calculability, human emotions are considered irrational, quixotic, impossible to objectify, not subject to detached evaluation, and difficult to quantify. Even today, it is common lore not to let one's emotions get in the way of sound reasoning and judgment. How many times have we heard someone say or have said to someone else, "Try not to be so emotional . . . try to behave more rationally." The clear message is that emotions are of a lesser ilk than reason. They are too carnal and close to our animal passions to be considered worthy of being taken seriously—and worse still, they pollute the reasoning process.

WRITING FEELINGS AND EMOTIONS
BACK INTO HISTORY

Faith-based consciousness and rational consciousness share a disembodied approach to existence. But it's the very feelings and emotions they discount that allow human beings to develop empathetic bonds and become fully mature social beings. Without feelings and emotions, empathy ceases to exist. A world without empathy is alien to the very notion of what a human being is.

New developments in psychology and cognitive science are laying the groundwork for a wholesale reappraisal of human consciousness. The premodern notion that faith and God's grace are the windows to reality and the Enlightenment idea that reason is at the apex of modern consciousness are giving way to a more sophisticated approach to a theory of mind.

Researchers in a diverse range of fields and disciplines are beginning to reprioritize some of the critical features of faith and reason within the context of a broader empathic consciousness. They argue that all of human activity is embodied experience—that is, participation with the other—and that the ability to read and respond to another person "as if" he or she were oneself is the key to how human beings engage the world, create individual identity, develop language, learn to reason, become social, establish cultural narratives, and define reality and existence.

The notion of embodied experience is a direct challenge to the older faith- and reason-based approaches to consciousness. While the new theory of mind makes room for both within a broader empathic framework, they no longer stand alone as autonomous constructs for framing reality. The idea of embodied experience takes us past the Age of Faith and the Age of Reason and into the Age of Empathy, without, however, abandoning the very special qualities of the previous world-views that continue to make them so attractive to millions of human beings.

"I think, therefore I am" is perhaps the most important philosophical utterance of the modern age. Descartes wrote those words in his *Discourse on the Method* in 1637. This scholarly work became the foundation for the way we have come to think about human consciousness ever since. Descartes explained how he came to this discovery by way of an observation:

> If I look out of the window and see men crossing the square,
> as I just happen to have done, I normally say that I see the
> men themselves. . . . Yet do I see any more than hats and coats
> which could conceal automatons? I *judge* that they are men.
> And so something which I thought I was seeing with my eyes

is in fact grasped solely by the faculty of judgment which is in my mind.[8]

Descartes viewed the human being as made up of a bodily machine that sends sensory signals to a mind that then uses rational thought to decipher the messages and form judgments. Descartes saw thinking as a separate domain that, while physically connected to the world, acted independently of it. He perceived thinking to be the essence of a human being and wrote that

> for its existence there is no need of any place, nor does it depend on any rational thing, nor does it depend on any material thing; so that this "me," that is to say, the soul by which I am what I am, is entirely distinct from body. . . .[9]

Descartes paints the picture of a disembodied mind, ruling over the body and, by extension, the body of nature. His ideas have continued to influence generations of philosophers and scientists up to the present day. When one listens to Descartes, one can't help but be struck with how similar his thought processes are to what psychologists and neuroscientists today might think of as a high-functioning Asperger's personality. Descartes wanted to eliminate what he regarded as the uncertainties of bodily experience—the messy, unpredictable, spontaneous feelings and emotions that continually erupt and disrupt thought and that characterize what it means to be an alive, sentient creature. He sought solace in the world of pure thought, convinced that mathematical proof provides the kind of certainty that allows the human mind to order, control, and manage the physical world.

Descartes's human being serves as an earthly overseer for God. Just as God is a nonmaterial essence who arranges the inanimate material world into an orderly machine and puts it into motion by a sheer act of mind—God is, after all, the mind head of the universe—man, equipped with reason and acting as his steward here on Earth, does the same by willing passive matter—including the human body—into motion and engagement.

The enemy of rational calculability is the emotions. If left free to roam, they can distract and even overwhelm the rational mind. By eliminating the emotions from the human "equation," Descartes leaves us with a non-feeling, rational, calculating being that in many ways is far more robotic and machine-like than the material world he categorized as mechanical in nature. His view of the ideal human being is caricatured and satirized in the popular television series *Star Trek*. Mr. Spock, the rational being from the planet Vulcan, resembles human beings on Earth in physical appearance but is devoid of the capacity to express human feeling and emotions. His continuous interplay with the very emotional Captain Kirk is one of the main motifs of the show. In crisis situations, his judgments, although completely rational, often lack the empathy necessary to appropriately address the social reality at hand. His cool, detached, and disembodied persona fails to grasp the underlying emotional drama being played out and, as a result, his suggestions are often overruled.

By discounting the physicality of embodied experience, Descartes and the philosophers and scientists who followed him eliminated, in one fell swoop, the very mortality of being. To be alive is to be physical, finite, and mortal. It is to be aware of the vulnerability of life and the inevitability of death. Being alive requires a continuous struggle to be and comes with pain, suffering, and anguish as well as moments of joy. How does one celebrate life or mourn the passing of a relative or friend or enter into an intimate relationship with another in a world devoid of feelings and emotions?

Neurologist Antonio Damasio, in his book *Descartes' Error*, reminds us of what we give up if we accept the disembodied approach to human nature. He writes:

> [P]erhaps the most indispensable thing we can do as human
> beings, every day of our lives, is remind ourselves and others
> of our complexity, fragility, finiteness, and uniqueness.[10]

If we repress the very corporeality of our existence and dismiss the emotions that tie us in a very physical way to the world, we lose the ability to empathize with others, which is the very essence of what it means to be a social being.

Damasio came to his insights about the crucial role that emotions play in structuring human thoughts and pro-social behavior in researching the effects that damage to parts of the brain have on human behavior and decision-making abilities. He reported on a patient with a neurological disease that had ravaged part of his brain. The patient continued to appear normal on the surface. He was articulate and attentive, and he retained his memory, was able to perform calculations, amd could master abstract problems. His disease, however, had damaged a part of the brain that allowed him to normally experience feelings.[11] As a result, his reasoning processes were flawed. He was unable to accurately read situations and respond in an appropriate manner. He lacked a social compass. Damasio concluded that "certain aspects of the process of emotion and feeling are indispensable for rationality."[12]

Damasio and other neurologists have observed some of the bizarre behavior that occurs in brain-damaged patients, especially as it relates to feelings, emotions, and reasoning. Consider for a moment a condition physicians refer to as anosognosia, which is clinically described as the inability to acknowledge disease. Victims of a catastrophic stroke, for example, when asked how they feel, report that they are "fine." Although aware that they are partially paralyzed, damage to a particular part of the brain renders them unable to express much emotion relative to their condition. When informed of their dire straits and the terrible possibilities that might lie ahead, their response is curiously blank. They never express sadness, anxiety, anger, or fear. Anosognosic patients show no emotions and feelings. The result is that their ability to make sound judgments regarding their treatment is absent—equally absent is their ability to plan their future and make socially appropriate decisions, all of which we associate with rational thought.[13]

Neurologists have zeroed in, of late, on regions of the brain where emotions and reasoning interact. Of particular interest is the anterior cingulate cortex.[14] Damasio notes that

[d]amage to this sector not only produces impairment in
movement, emotion, and attentiveness, but also causes a
virtual suspension of the animation of action and of thought
process such that reason is no longer viable.[15]

Scientists are quick to point out that there is no one single place that
is solely responsible for what we call the act of thought. Instead, they are
learning that a human being "interacts with the environment as an ensemble," to use Damasio's term.[16] What we call mind is a complex orches-
tration of biochemical and neural regulatory circuits that operate as a
whole. The inference is that "mental phenomena can be fully understood
only in the context of an organism's interacting in an environment."[17]

In other words, the act of thinking combines sensations, feelings,
emotions, and abstract reasoning in an embodied way. "I participate,
therefore I am"—a far cry from Descartes's detached autonomous mind
that thinks from above and afar and is not sullied by the physicality of
experience.

Neuroscientists are not alone in their reappraisal of disembodied rationality. A new generation of biologists, philosophers, linguists, psychologists, and sociologists are beginning to enter the fray as well, offering a
new embodied approach to understanding human nature that is rewriting the human story and laying the foundation for an emerging empathic
era. What unites the work across the disciplines is the belief that we each
exist only in relation to the other. Russian philosopher Mikhail Bakhtin
put it best when he observed

To *be* means *to communicate*. . . . To be means to be for another,
and through the other, for oneself. A person has no internal
sovereign territory, he is wholly and always on the boundary;
looking inside himself, he looks *into the eyes of another* or *with
the eyes of another*."[18]

How different from Descartes's world, where each mind operates
independently, is disembodied and, therefore, is in no need of entering

into a relationship with others in order to know oneself or experience one's existence. In the disembodied world of pure rationality, there are only a priori truths ready to be discovered independently by each person. The certainties of reality already exist in advance, in the form of truths, subject to mathematical proof, and require only a pure mind able to access them for the purpose of understanding, interpreting, categorizing, and passing judgments on events that unfold in the physical world.

Advocates of embodied experience eschew the idea that knowledge, reason, and thought itself are something that exist a priori, requiring only an inquiring mind to pluck them from the ether and store them in consciousness. They also take umbrage with the Newtonian assertion that reality is made up of discrete phenomena that can be measured in isolation, categorized and connected in a sterile causal way.

Rather, they assert that mental life is always relational because it's based on the idea that I know, that you know, that I know that you know—the very concept of a theory of mind. The development of thought itself, therefore, necessitates relationships to others. Indeed, we can only know ourselves in relationship to others. It is by the continuous process of engagement with others that we become who we are. In this sense, we are each an embodiment of that part of the other's experience with us that we have absorbed into ourselves. Our relationships form us and make us who we are. Language itself, the ability to form thoughts with words, only emerges in relationships with others. We can't imagine the possibility that a toddler cared for only by mechanical surrogates and without human contact would be able to create language for the simple reason that language is something that occurs among people. The point is, our individual identity and consciousness are formed by our unique experiences with countless others. There is no simple autonomous "I," but only a unique constellation of numerous "we."

Psychotherapists John Rowan and Mick Cooper observe that

> the contents of our "inner" lives are not radically hidden
> "inside" us as individuals; they are "in" our living of our lives,

"in" the responsive ways in which we relate our momentary
activities to all else occurring around us. . . .[19]

If this is in fact so, say Rowan and Cooper, then "all our truly mental
activity is primarily 'out there' in the world between us: that is where it
originates, and that is where it has its most meaningful expression."[20]

Immanuel Kant (1724–1804), the great German philosopher of the
eighteenth century, like René Descartes, would have considered the
idea of embodied knowledge wrongheaded. Kant believed that there
exists, a priori, innate categories that are the basis of knowing, not
unlike the Platonic idea of pure forms. They exist above and beyond
the chaos of a corporeal life in a kind of magisterial realm. Kant lauds
the sublime order of this fixed domain in contrast to the delusional
world of everyday experience. He muses,

> We have now not merely explored the territory of pure
> understanding [the a priori categories] and carefully surveyed
> every part of it, but have also measured its extent and assigned
> to everything in its rightful place. This domain is an island,
> enclosed by nature itself with unalterable limits. It is the land
> of truth—an enchanting name!—surrounded by a wide and
> stormy ocean, the native home of illusion, where many a fog
> bank and many a swiftly melting iceberg give the deceptive
> appearance of farther shores, deluding the adventurous seafarer
> ever anew with empty hopes. . . .[21]

Kant sought certainty in a troubled world and found it in the a priori categories of pure thought. Yet the real world is anything but fixed.
Everything is continually in flux, even our own bodies. Our very physicality is forever changing. What we think of as our physical self is more
like a pattern of activity that is continually taking from and giving back
to the world. In a very real sense, each of us is an extended being, living
off the entropic flow. The physical "I," then, is continually being remade
moment to moment, yet our identity somehow seems to remain intact.

Perhaps that's why most human beings buy into the disembodied schema, at least in part. When, for example, one loses a limb, one doesn't think of it as one's own identity but, rather, as an appendage. We have the sense that our identity is of a nonmaterial substance, a guiding will that governs our physical body. As the late neuroscientist Francisco Varela notes, "we do not say 'I am body' but 'I *have* a body.' "[22]

In 2008, a Polish doctor, Maria Siemionow, successfully grafted an entire new face on a severely disfigured woman. The public was fascinated by the controversial procedure and questioned whether the patient would experience the ultimate identity crisis when she finally looked in the mirror and saw another face. She subsequently reported that she was comfortable in the new face and did not feel it changed her sense of identity. Millions of people over the past half-century who have had organ transplants, cosmetic surgery, and gender reassignment and been fit with artificial hearts, limbs, and the like have had similar reactions.

Advocates of the embodied experience school of thought argue that while people sense that their self is independent of their physical body, it's not because their thought processes are in another extracorporeal realm. Rather, it's because who we come to think we are is bound up in the ebb and flow of experiences and relationships with others that gives each of us our own unique history. While the experiences are embodied and physical, the "communion" that comes with sharing a moment with the other, be it human, another sentient being, or nature, is of a nonmaterial nature and becomes part of the stored memory that makes up each of our unique histories and identities.

Professors of cognitive linguistics George Lakoff and Mark Johnson deftly summarize the differences between the disembodied and embodied approaches to the functioning of reason. In the disembodied view,

> the contents of mind, the actual concepts, are not crucially
> shaped or given any significant inferential content by the body.
> It is the view that concepts are formal in nature and arise from

the mind's capacity to generate formal structure in such a way
as to derive further, inferred, formal structures.[23]

The experiential approach, by contrast, claims that every species
comes equipped with its own unique sensory apparatus that sets the
limits of how it senses reality. For example, some animal species, like
dolphins and whales, only see in black and white and will never know
the rich world of colors available to the human eye. Seeing a world in
black and white shapes the mentality and reality of a species in a different way than a species whose view of the world is in color. Lakoff and
Johnson make the point

> that the very properties of concepts are created as a result of
> the way the brain and body are structured and the way they
> function in interpersonal relations and in the physical world.[24]

Eagles can see a rabbit from a height of a mile.[25] An eagle's bodily
experience from on high provides a very different embodied orientation than that of dolphins careening on and below the ocean surface.
Lakoff and Johnson write that

> [r]eason is not disembodied, as the tradition has largely held,
> but arises from the nature of our brains, bodies, and bodily
> experience. . . . The same neural and cognitive mechanisms
> that allow us to perceive and move around also create our
> conceptual systems and modes of reason. . . . [R]eason is
> not, in any way, a transcendent feature of the universe or
> of disembodied mind. Instead, it is shaped crucially by the
> peculiarities of our human bodies, by the remarkable details of
> the neural structure of our brains, and by the specifics of our
> everyday functioning in the world.[26]

Humans, for example, are the only completely bipedal species.
Standing and walking erect in the world provides a very different

spatial and temporal orientation and creates a unique sense of reality. As emotionally close and communicative as your companion dog might be, her four-legged frame of reference gives her a very different orientation about the nature of the world she must navigate and survive in. Sigmund Freud observed that man's deep sense of alienation from nature stems from the "adoption of erect posture and the lowering in value of the sense of smell."[27] A species that relies primarily on smell is going to know the world in a very different fashion than one to which sight is the primary sense.

REALITY IS WHAT WE MAKE OF IT

The fact that different species perceive reality very differently is quite evident. But it gets particularly interesting when it comes to human bodily experience. We are the only species able to transform our bodily perceptions into language that can then be used to create primary metaphors that then can be used to create more abstract metaphors.

When we stop to think about how much of our daily communications are based upon bodily metaphors, we begin to realize how important bodily experience is to the thinking process. We "grasp" an idea, are out of "touch" with reality, "stretch" our mind, "grab" onto a possibility, "walk" through a problem, "feel" someone's pain, "smell" a rat, "see" through what someone is telling us, "lose ground," "stand up" for our principles, "run" up a bill, "stumble" into a relationship, and on and on.

It is through use of metaphors, Lakoff reminds us, that we imagine and construct most of our reality. Using metaphors is a way of enriching our bodily experience and giving us a story-line that others can use to identify with us because they too base their experience on a common bodily, spatial, and temporal orientation that is the same for all human beings.

The use of metaphorical language provides a vehicle by which two people can share each other's inner world. The building up of more and more abstract metaphors from more simple primary metaphors that are common to the experience of every member of our species is the key to imagining each other's "reality." For example, when someone says to us that they have "fallen" head over heels in love, one inevitability "grasps" the feeling they are conveying of losing their sense of "grounding," of not being in complete control of their senses, of feeling the thrill and danger and vulnerability of giving their being over to another's trust.

The idea of embodied experience provides the rigorous intellectual framework for the Age of Empathy, just as Descartes's a priori disembodied truths provided the intellectual foundation for the Age of Reason and Saint Augustine's exegesis on Revelation and God's grace provided the castings for the Age of Faith.

The great transformation from "I think, therefore I am" to "I participate, therefore I am" places empathy at the very center of the human story—a place it has always inhabited but which society has never fully acknowledged or recognized. Polish philosopher Henryk Skolimowski writes, "*[t]o be a person in the participatory universe entails the recognition of the bond of participation. . . .* If we recognize this bond, then we ipso facto recognize empathy."[28]

If we do live in a participatory world and our very bodily experience is one of continuous engagement with others, then empathy becomes the means by which we enter deeply into each other's lives. It is also the means by which we understand and make our common reality. Still, many of us have difficulty accepting the idea of reality as the collective understandings we create about the world around us by dint of the relationships we enter. That's in large part because we were weaned on the "scientific method," which informed us that objective reality exists and human beings are capable of knowing it by becoming detached observers—the exact opposite of the embodied approach to reality.

Francis Bacon, the pre-Enlightenment English philosopher, wrote of a new way to understand and order reality in his master work, the *Novum Organum*. Bacon outlined what would later be called the scientific method. Impatient with the ancient Greek approach to science with its emphasis on the "why" of things, Bacon turned his attention to the "how" of things. The Greeks, he wrote, had not "adduced a single experiment which tends to relieve and benefit the condition of man."[29]

Bacon was far more interested in harnessing nature for productive ends than merely contemplating the reason for its existence.

Bacon's method, which was heavily influenced by the new ideas about "perspective" that were revolutionizing art, is based on the idea that the only way to know reality is to remove oneself and create a neutral barrier so that a disembodied mind can observe and make value-free judgments about its workings. Bacon was convinced that the scientific method was a powerful new mental tool that would allow the human mind to "conquer and subdue" nature and "shake her to her foundations." The goal of the new science, said Bacon, was to "establish and extend the power of dominion of the human race itself over the universe."[30]

Bacon and the rationalist philosophers who followed him believed that nature is little more than a storehouse of valuable resources and that the only relationship that counted was the exercise of power over it. Reality, for Bacon, was objective and manifest in expropriation. We come to know nature by the way we manipulate it.

The embodied experience philosophers, by contrast, suggest that understanding reality comes not from detachment and exercise of power but from participation and empathic communion. The more deeply we empathize with each other and our fellow creatures, the more intensive and extensive is our level of participation and the richer and more universal are the realms of reality in which we dwell. Our level of intimate participation defines our level of understanding of reality. Our experience becomes increasingly more global and universal in character. We become fully cosmopolitan and immersed in the affairs of the world. This is the beginning of biosphere consciousness.

A RADICAL REFORMULATION OF TRUTH, FREEDOM, AND EQUALITY

The participatory or embodied approach to understanding the nature of human nature forces us to rethink the most basic notions of human thought, including not only our perception of reality, but also our conception of what constitutes truth and how we define freedom and equality.

When we talk about what's "true," we generally mean what is "real" as opposed to "imaginary." Getting to the truth is often synonymous with reality. We often use the phrase "separating fact from fiction." Facts are what exist in reality. But what is "the real"? In the Cartesian scheme of things reality is made up of truths that exist a priori and are fixed and immutable. We discover truths but we don't create them.

In the embodied philosophical frame, truth lies elsewhere. The new philosophers would argue that if reality is something we make together out of our shared experiences, then truths are not objective autonomous phenomena but, rather, the explanations we make about the common experiences that we share with each other. When we say "we seek the ultimate truth," we are really saying that we seek to know the full extent of how all of our relationships fit together in the grand scheme. Our pursuit of the truth is the search for how we belong to the larger picture and why.

When people of faith say God is all-knowing, what they mean is that he is privy to all of the relationships that make up the participatory and interconnected world. Embodied human experience is the way human beings work their way toward making all of the connections that comprise what we call reality. Equally important, in the mere process of participation, we also partially create new reality as we go. The more expansive our bodily experiences and interrelationships, the more we make reality and the closer we get to an all-encompassing reality and the truths of existence—at least as those truths reflect a human frame of reference.

To sum up, if reality is experience and experience is always in relationship to the other, then the more extensive the relationships, the deeper we penetrate the various layers of reality and the closer we come to understanding the meaning of existence.

Truths, then, are explanations of how everything relates together. Truths are not objective or subjective, but rather are understandings that exist in the interstitial realm where the "I" and "thou" come together to create a common experiential ground. This is "reality making."

All of our truths are just a systemizing of our existing relationships and commonly shared understandings. The truth of our existence is that it is inseparable from our relationships. In this sense, an embodied philosophical approach is a radical departure from faith and reason, both of which discount our experiential existence.

When we begin to ponder the question of the meaning of existence, we are really attempting to know if there is some purpose or direction to life and, if so, how we each fit into it. The Scholastics would argue that the ultimate purpose is bound up in faith in God's grace and obedience to his will in order to secure a place in heaven. The rationalists would say it's to optimize pleasure via the pursuit of material progress. The Darwinians would say it's to survive and produce offspring. The embodied experience philosophers, however, would argue that the meaning of life is to enter into relationships with others in order to deeply experience, as much as one can, the reality of existence. The meaning of life is to celebrate it as fully and expansively as possible.

This very basic difference in how we think about the meaning of life changes our notions about freedom. Freedom was a core concept of the Age of Reason. To be free, argued the rationalists, is to be autonomous and not dependent on or beholden to others. Freedom in the modern age has been closely associated with the ability to control one's labor and to secure one's property, because that is the way to optimize pleasure and be happy. Freedom has also been closely aligned with representation in the political arena and choice in the marketplace. The French revolutionaries exclaimed that each person is a sovereign in the public sphere. The classical economists argued that every individual is free to the extent he or she can pursue their individual self-interest in the material world. Both are seen as means to secure one's autonomy. Freedom, in the rational mode, is a negative freedom—the freedom to exclude, to be independent of others, and to be an island to oneself. To be free is to be "self-possessed" and self-sufficient.

The embodied approach to freedom is based on the opposite premise. Freedom means being able to optimize the full potential of one's life, and the fulfilled life is one of companionship, affection, and belonging, made possible by ever deeper and more meaningful personal experiences and relationships with others. One is free, then, to the extent that one has been nurtured and raised in a society that allows for empathetic opportunities.

The litmus test for which definition of freedom is more salient is the deathbed judgment. When looking back on one's life, few would measure the meaning of their existence in terms of the money they amassed or the autonomy they achieved. In fact, as we've learned, greater wealth and autonomy tend to isolate one from meaningful relationships with others. Our lived reality becomes more insular and restricted, our lives more lonely. When near death, most people reminisce about the experiences of deep connections they had with others—family, friends, and colleagues. It is the empathetic moments in one's life that are the most powerful memories and the experiences that comfort and give a sense of connection, participation, and meaning to one's sojourn.

These two very distinct ideas about freedom are accompanied by two very different ideas about the nature of strength and what it means to be courageous. When we think of freedom, we generally associate it with being independent and brave. The U.S. national anthem, "The Star-Spangled Banner," ends with the phrase "the land of the free and the home of the brave." In an era in which we have come to regard freedom as something to fight for and claim as a possession, bravery becomes a sign of our fiercely independent determination to be "the captains of our fate and the masters of our soul." We think of freedom as liberation from bondage. Many "freedom fighters" go so far as to equate freedom with invulnerability—the totally self-contained and self-sufficient person glorified in the sagas of the American frontier. The pioneers, mountain men, and cowboys who set out alone to tame the wilderness are romanticized as truly free spirits.

Although the pioneering spirit is certainly laudable, the embodied school takes a different approach, asserting that real freedom requires that one exercise vulnerability rather than invulnerability. If freedom is the ability to live out the full potential of one's possibilities and if the measure of one's life is the intimacy, range, and diversity of one's relationships, then the more vulnerable one is, the more open he or she will be to creating meaningful and intimate relationships with others.

Vulnerable in this sense does not mean being weak or a victim or prey but, rather, being open to communication at the deepest level of human exchange.

Real courage, embodied advocates contend, is allowing oneself to be exposed—warts and all—to another person. It is the willingness to place the most intimate details of our lives in the hands of another. To be vulnerable is to trust one's fellow human beings. Trust is the belief that others will treat you as an end not as a means, that you will not be used or manipulated to serve the expedient motives of others but regarded as a valued being. When one is treated by others as an end, not as a means, one becomes truly free. One can't really be free in a world where everyone mistrusts each other. In such a world, freedom is immediately reduced to a negative, the ability to close oneself off from others and be an island unto oneself. Authoritarian societies that promote paranoia and mistrust and pit each against the other squash the spirit of freedom.

The very basis of freedom, then, is trust and openness among people. Freedom is never a solitary affair, as the rationalists contend—John Wayne alone in the frontier—but a deeply communal experience. We are only really free when we come to trust one another and allow ourselves to be open to sharing each other's struggle to be and flourish. Trust, in turn, opens up the possibility of extending empathetic consciousness into new more intimate domains.

Nelson Mandela is a good case study of the embodied sense of freedom. In the more than twenty-three years he was imprisoned, often in solitary confinement, he chose to befriend his jailers. He reached out to them as unique individuals with their own personal struggles. Rather than attempting to be invulnerable and stoic, he chose to be humane. His jailers began to experience him as a human being. Their preconceived biases melted away as they came to admire Mandela and finally trust him as a fellow human being whose struggles were not unlike their own.

Part of the reason the embodied notion of freedom resonates with most of us is that it draws on a deeper sense of what an individual is made of. The impregnable model—the lone wolf in complete control of his emotions—is a rare breed and not someone most of us have ever experienced. To be invulnerable is not to be in need of others and to be able to live one's life apart. Although there are ascetics and misanthropes able to live this way, their lives are less than complete. They have closed up the emotional channels that make human beings the most social of animals.

Invulnerability conjures up the idea of a super human being, unencumbered by the frailties and foibles that make us vulnerable, less than perfect, in need of each other and, therefore, human. Psychologists are quick to point out that a person feigning invulnerability and exhibiting an extreme libertarian sense of personal entitlement, devoid of emotions and compassion, is often someone so frightened by his own sense of vulnerability that his macho persona becomes a mask for hiding his fear.

One can't truly empathize with the vulnerability and struggle of another unless he is able to acknowledge the same vulnerabilities and struggles in himself. If a person locks up whole parts of his emotional make-up, he is truly unfree, imprisoning parts of his own psyche and closing off his unique being from meaningful expression and engagement with the world. He becomes the jailer of his own persona. No one ever gets to know the "real him" and establish a meaningful relationship. He is truly alone, as much as the individual who has been ostracized or banished.

The idea of freedom has also historically gone in tandem with the idea of equality. The American and French revolutionaries viewed the two ideas as inextricably linked. They became the alpha and omega of the New Order of the Ages. Equality, in the rationalist mode, is a calculable legal phenomenon. Laws are enacted to guarantee political sovereignty, individual civil rights, and market access.

The embodied philosophers define equality more in psychological terms. They ask how one comes to think of others as equal to themselves and vice versa. They view empathetic extension as the great leveler, the force that breaks down the myriad forms of status and distinctions that separate people into subjects and objects. They remind us that as long as equality is narrowly measured in material terms—the opportunity to succeed in the marketplace, even if it's by merit rather than by hereditary claims—the end result will always be defined in terms of "mine" versus "thine." Wealth and professional and academic distinctions will continue to create status distinctions and divide one from another.

Empathic extension is the only human expression that creates true equality between people. When one empathizes with another, distinctions begin to melt away. The very act of identifying with another's struggle as if it were one's own is the ultimate expression of a sense of equality. One can't really empathize unless one's being is on the same emotional plane as another. If someone feels superior or inferior in status to another and therefore different and alien, it becomes difficult to experience their plight or joy as one's own. One might feel sympathetic to others or feel sorry for them or take pity on them, but to experience real empathy for another requires feeling and responding "as if" you "are" that person. In an empathic moment, there is no "mine" and "thine," but only "I" and "thou." Empathy is a communion of kindred spirits, and it's elicited in a temporal and spatial zone that transcends distinctions based on social status.

That doesn't mean that empathetic moments erase status and distinctions. It only means that in the moment one extends the empathic embrace, the other social barriers—wealth, education, and professional status—are temporarily suspended in the act of experiencing, comforting, and supporting another's struggle as if their life were one's own. The feeling of equality being expressed is not about equal legal rights or economic entitlements but the idea that another being is just like us in being unique and mortal and deserving of the right to prosper.

Status hierarchies are, of course, designed to create inequalities. Status is about rankings and the claiming of authority over others. Every society establishes various boundaries of exclusion. A highly stratified society generally is low on empathetic consciousness because such societies are segmented between so many status categories that the ability to empathize beyond one's own group, both up and down the hierarchy, is limited.

On the other hand, in societies that are complex and where differentiation and selfhood are well developed, where most people live above the threshold of everyday comfort but the gap in incomes is narrow, people are generally happier, more tolerant, less envious and more empathetic to others—think Sweden, Norway, and Demark.

Both the philosophers of Enlightenment rationality and the enthusiasts of cosmopolitan embodied experience would agree that freedom is an essential prerequisite for establishing equality but would differ about which definition of freedom would best serve the cause after the threshold of comfort is reached. The modernists would continue to view freedom in terms of guaranteeing the political franchise, protecting property rights, and securing individual opportunities in the marketplace, while the cosmopolitans would go further and view freedom in terms of optimizing social rights and establishing a nurturing milieu that encourages empathetic extension, and with it the leveling of traditional hierarchies and the narrowing of social distinctions.

The ability to recognize oneself in the other and the other in oneself is a deeply democratizing experience. Empathy is the soul of democracy. It is an acknowledgment that each life is unique, unalienable, and deserving of equal consideration in the public square. The evolution of empathy and the evolution of democracy have gone hand in hand throughout history. The more empathic the culture, the more democratic its values and governing institutions. The less empathic the culture, the more totalitarian its values and governing institutions. While apparent, it's strange how little attention has been paid to the inextricable relationship between empathic extension and democratic expansion in the study of history and evolution of governance.

COMINGS TO TERMS WITH MORTALITY

If reality is in fact a reflection of embodied experience, why has civilization labored under the delusion of disembodied experience for so long? What is it about bodily experience that the world's great religions and the philosophers of the Age of Reason found so repellent? Embodied experience is a constant reminder of the fragility and mortality of life.

In prehistoric forager/hunter cultures and even in early horticultural societies, death didn't loom as large in people's psyche. While aware of death, the fear we associate with it in contemporary times did not exist. It wasn't until our ancient ancestors broke the cycle of nature and crawled their way into historical consciousness that the fear of the grim reaper began to shadow their lives.

In the long prehistory of human existence, people lived communally. The sense of self-awareness was dim and the idea of individuality only partially formed. Prehistoric consciousness was not unlike that of infants and young children up to the age of five or six for whom the concept of death and their own mortality is vague. Archaic men and women perceived time as cyclical. Its passage was marked by the changing seasons. And like the seasons, which were experienced as an annually reoccurring birth, death, and rebirth, human beings came to see their own lives in much the same way. Even death itself was perceived as just a passage to the netherworld. One went into a kind of hibernation or sleep.

We noted in Chapter 1 that self-awareness and a nascent individuality began to emerge in the age of the great hydraulic agricultural empires and were accompanied by the shift from primitive empathy to a more developed empathic sense. The empathetic projection and extension, however, was only possible because of a heightened sense of one's own unique being and mortal existence. Empathy is, after all, the ability to experience another's struggle as one's own and is only possible if one is aware of the fragility of their existence and the mortality of their being. While other mammals experience primitive empathy—akin to human infants—and show distress at another's struggle and even reach out to comfort them, a more mature empathy emerges with the awareness of death, one's own and that of others.

What's so interesting is that empathetic consciousness developed alongside disembodied beliefs. The great surges in empathetic consciousness during the Age of Faith and the Age of Reason were accompanied by cosmological narratives determined to blot out any acknowledgment of the finiteness of corporeal existence, either by faith in an afterworld or later by the rationalization of material progress and the creation of a future timeless earthly utopia.

Western culture has institutionalized its images of immortality by way of religion and politics. Gods and great leaders are looked to as our protectors against the ravages of time. In his main work *History, Time and Deity*, S.G.F. Brandon researched the great religions in world history and concluded that "the many and diverse beliefs and practices . . . are . . . found to have a common underlying motive—the defeat or avoidance of Time's inevitable process of decay and death."[31] Human beings have created religious images of the future in part as a refuge against the ultimate finality of earthly existence. Every religion holds forth the promise of either defeating time, escaping time, overcoming time, reissuing time, or denying time altogether. We use our religions as vehicles to enter the state of nirvana, the heavenly kingdom, or the promised land. We come to believe in reincarnation, rebirth, and resurrection as ways of avoiding the inevitability of biological death.

Our spiritual quest for immortality began to give way to a secular quest in the early modern era. The great intellectual thinkers of the Enlightenment espoused the radical idea of human progress, a wholly new vision of earthly immortality for Western civilization to rally around.

Progress was a revolutionary new idea for which there was little precedent. Time, in the new scheme of things, was no longer to be used in preparation for the Second Coming of Christ but rather as a means to advance the new temporal idea of progress. To believe in progress is to believe in a future that is always improving, enlarging, and, above all, enduring. There is no end to progress. It is unstoppable, relentless. It speeds us into a future where there are no boundaries or borders, a future that is infinitely expansive and "timeless." This new image of the future is steeped in materialism. Material progress is our ticket to immortality, our way of cheating death, of overcoming a fleeting existence.

Science and technology have become the new means of obtaining salvation. In times of crisis we look to science and to the technological products of science to rescue a fallen humanity from the forces of chaos that so often intrude on our efforts to eke out a safe domain. Modern science and technology are the secular messiahs in a materialist world.

They are the guarantors of our security and, ultimately, our immortality. Through science and technology we will extend our control over the future, the forces of nature, and our own bodily duration. We will live better, live longer, enjoy the good life, and enter into an earthly Eden of our own making where material abundance will provide a fortress against the ravages of time and the onslaught of death.

The new bourgeois image of the future seemed invincible. Human beings now believed that the more material possessions they could amass, the more invulnerable they would become. Everywhere they looked there were signs to confirm their new progressive vision.

At the beginning of the modern age, when the exuberance of the newfound future image of progress first impressed itself on European consciousness, the French aristocrat the Marquis de Condorcet captured the sense of euphoria that was sweeping over the intellectual community in words that have since become immortalized in history.

> No bounds have been fixed to the improvement of the
> human faculties . . . the perfectibility of Man is absolutely
> indefinite . . . the progress of this perfectibility, henceforth
> above the control of every power that would impede it, has no
> other limit than the duration of the globe upon which Nature
> has placed us.[32]

The disembodied cosmological narratives that make up the Age of Faith and the subsequent Age of Reason project an overwhelming fear of death and are the Janus side of the maturing phases of embodied empathic consciousness that celebrate life.

When one empathizes with another, the experience is an affirmation of her existence and a celebration of her life. Empathetic moments are the most intensively alive experiences we ever have. We feel super-alive because in the empathic act, which begins with being embodied, we "transcend" our physical confines and, for a brief period, live in a shared non-corporeal plane that is timeless and that connects us to the life that surrounds us. We are filled with life, our own and others, connected and embedded in the here and now reality that our relationships create.

The more mature our empathic consciousness, the more intimate and universal is our participation with life and the deeper our sense of the layers of reality. Celebrating life means living it robustly with others. Individuals whose empathy is shallow and experiences are limited live life less fully. A solitary life is always a life less lived.

Visions of eternal paradise and earthly utopias also share a common obsession with perfectibility. To be perfect is to transcend the spatial and temporal limits imposed on human corporeality. We are not talking about perfecting one's skills or craft but rather perfecting one's own being. When one conceptualizes the notion of a perfect human being, we think of someone who is impervious to the slings and arrows and stresses and sorrows that afflict most mortals. Perfect is someone without faults—someone frozen and cut off from the messiness of life—untouched by the ravages of decay and the loss of time. To seek perfection is to push away death.

In the religious scheme, perfection means leading a life of abstinence, unscathed by the blemishes of corporeal existence. To be celibate is the highest expression of disembodiment from the world. The obedient Christian is instructed to keep his or her gaze fixed on divine grace and deliverance to the heavenly world where the flesh is left behind and one's spirit dwells in a sublime state of perfection. Augustine cautioned the faithful that earthly existence is merely a way station to salvation: "Be in this world but not of this world."

In the Age of Reason, the notion of perfection takes on an earthly temporal dimension. Transcending one's physicality, a hallmark of religious consciousness, gives way to escaping one's duration. Efficiency substitutes for asceticism as the means to assure perfectibility and ward off death.

In the eighteenth century—before the dawn of the Industrial Revolution—the word "efficiency" had theological connotations. God is efficient. Genesis, the first book of the Old Testament, begins not with "once upon a time" but with God commanding the world into existence . . . making him the most efficient prime mover.

In the late nineteenth century, as the impact of the Industrial Revolution began to be felt across Europe and America, the word "efficiency" underwent a metamorphosis at the hands of the chemists and engineers. The introduction of the laws of thermodynamics spawned a keen interest in experimenting with energy flows in machines. Efficiency got a makeover. In the new industrial world, efficiency was redefined as maximizing output, with the minimum input of time, labor, energy, and capital. Engineers dreamed of the perfectly efficient state of perpetual motion in the hopes of overcoming the second law of thermodynamics. To be perfectly efficient is to produce the optimum output that could possibly exist, without having to expend any time, labor, energy, and capital. This is what occurred when God created the entire universe by simply thinking it into existence.

Efficiency becomes a temporal tool for securing immortality. The more efficient one becomes, the more productive one is, the more wealth one amasses, and the less time one loses, the closer one gets to a state that transcends the laws of thermodynamics and the dreaded entropy state. Efficiency has come to mean "buying time."

Efficiency was quickly taken up in industry and popularized in the factories and front offices by Frederick Taylor, who propounded his principles of scientific management. From there, it slipped into the schools, public life, and even family relations. To be efficient became the supreme virtue of modern man. Underneath the freneticism was the unconscious or at least unstated feeling that by being more efficient, one could somehow save time and cheat death.

Restructuring economic and social relations around the temporal value of efficiency has the effect of making all relations instrumental to productive outputs. Everything and the activity of every being becomes a means to optimize productive potential. But would we ever treat someone we really care for in an efficient manner? Would we express our love and affection and extend our warmth and attention by maximizing our output in the minimum amount of time, with the minimum expenditure of labor, energy, and personal capital? Can one experience true intimacy or joy efficiently? Is it possible to deeply empathize with another being in a highly efficient way? Turning relationships into efficient means to advance productive ends destroys the empathic spirit.

In the 1980s and 1990s psychologists and educators introduced the notion of "quality time" into family relations. The idea was for parents to set aside a few minutes in their otherwise over-burdened and busy day to get back "in touch" with their children. The forced efficiency of these structured intimate encounters often defeated the purpose of the exercise. Deep relationships require nurturing and suffer when yoked to the dictates of the clock.

The almost pathological obsession with efficiency in the modern era reflects an underlying fear of death and the hope that time can be saved and one's duration on Earth continually extended into the future. Anyone who has ever engaged a hyper-efficient personality can almost smell the fear. Getting close to such a person becomes nearly impossible.

Empathy, however, transcends death in a very different way—not by repressing the temporary nature of embodied experience but by acknowledging it, in all of its fragility, and then living life to its fullest. The drive for perfection gives way to the quest for self-realization. Instead of running away from life, one attempts to optimize it. The poet Rainer Maria Rilke wrote, "[w]hoever rightly understands and celebrates death, at the same time magnifies life."[33] Hegel reminds us that all living creatures "have the seed of passing away as their essential being: the hour of their birth is the hour of their death."[34] By accepting death, we affirm life.

We empathize with each other's struggles against death and for life. One acknowledges the whiff of death in another's frailties and vulnerabilities. No one ever empathizes with a perfect being. Supporting and comforting another and coming to her aid is an affirmation and celebration of her living being. The shared bond intensifies one's own sense of aliveness. Does one ever feel more alive than when in an empathetic embrace?

Mature empathy is a unique phenomenon that only living, mortal beings can experience. That's why it's possible to obey and serve God but impossible to empathize with his spirit because we cast it in perfection. God is immortal and not of the flesh and therefore can't feel the pain and struggle of a unique mortal being. We have no way to empathize with the divine, but one might add that God has no way to empathize with us either.

St. Paul and the early Christians tried to comprehend the divine by asserting that the man Jesus was God's only son, made carnate. Millions of human beings have come to empathize with his earthly struggle and premature death on the cross. Yet the idea of his resurrection to immortality—a point of controversy for more than two thousand years—tempers the powerful empathic bond one could have had with him, if his story was of a man like the rest of us. If in fact the historic Jesus was aware that he was the son of God sent here to save humankind and that God would inevitably resurrect him to heaven, then the story of his life and death on the cross becomes a bit less compelling for the very reason that he knows he's not really going to perish.

Empathetic consciousness would be strangely out of place in either heaven or utopia. Where there is no mortal suffering, there is no empathic bond.

It should also be noted that where empathic consciousness flourishes, fear of death withers and the compunction to seek otherworldly salvation or earthly utopias wanes. It's perhaps not coincidental that a younger postmaterial generation, while more empathic and spiritual, is less religious and less prone to otherworldly or utopian visions. If one is living an embodied full life of deep participation in the here and the now, there is less likelihood that he or she will dream of finding solace in a perfect state sometime in the distant future.

SALVAGING FAITH AND REASON
IN THE AGE OF EMPATHY

If empathic consciousness flows from embodied experience and is a celebration of life—our own and that of other beings—how do we square it with faith and reason, which are disembodied ways of looking at reality and steeped in the fear of death? Just as we relooked at the concepts of truth, freedom, courage, equality, democracy, and mortality from an empathic lens, and found very different ways of defining their meaning, the same holds true with faith and reason.

When we deconstruct the notion of faith, we find that at the core are three essential pillars: awe, trust, and transcendence. The religious impulse begins with the sense of awe, the feeling of the wonder of existence, both the mystery and majesty. Awe is the deepest celebration of life. We marvel at the overwhelming nature of existence, and sense that by our own aliveness, we somehow fit into the wonder we behold. We find clues to our relationship to the grand scheme of things in those moments when we reach out, in embodied experience, to embrace "the others" that make up the totality of existence. Empathy is the means by which we transcend ourselves, by exploring our relationships and connections with the awe of being. The transcendent impulse, say Arthur P. Ciaramicoli and Katherine Ketcham in their book *The Power of Empathy*, comes from "[f]eeling a craving for connection, a yearning for a relationship to something larger and more powerful than [ourselves]."[35] That larger something is the mystery of existence, which we hold in awe.

While awe can lead to transcendence, it can also lead to despair. If one is unable to discern any overall meaning to existence, awe can just as easily turn into angst. When that happens, we face a crisis of personal meaning, which is to say a crisis of faith . . . faith, after all, is the belief there is a meaning to existence.

The great Russian novelist Tolstoy experienced a crisis of faith not unlike what most of us experience at one time or another in our own lives. He wrote,

> I felt that something had broken within me on which my life
> had always rested, that I had nothing left to hold on to. . . . I
> did not know what I wanted. I was afraid of life; I was driven
> to leave it; and in spite of that I still hoped something from it.[36]

For two years Tolstoy anguished over his sense of utter existential aloneness and abandonment in the world. Then one day while walking in the forest, faith suddenly came to him. He realized that faith was the belief that one's life is worth living, and for that reason alone, it had meaning in the larger scheme of things and therefore needed to be lived fully in deep connection with others. Tolstoy concluded that,

> Faith is the sense of life, that sense by virtue of which man [sic] does not destroy himself, but continues to live on. It is the force whereby we live. If Man did not believe that he must live for something, he would not live at all.[37]

Although faith is set in motion by a feeling of awe and requires a belief that one's life has meaning in a larger, universal sense of things, it can be purloined and made into a social construct that exacts obedience, feeds on fear of death, is disembodied in its approach, and establishes rigid boundaries separating the saved from the damned. Institutional-ized religions, for the most part, do just that.

Salvaging a sense of awe as well as faith in the meaning of existence requires a nurturing milieu to allow embodied experience to grow and empathic consciousness to expand.

Empathic consciousness starts with awe. When we empathize with another, we are bearing witness to the strange incredible life force that is in us and that connects us with all other living beings. Empathy is, after all, the feeling of deep reverence we have for the nebulous term we call existence. Even though we're not sure what existence is, and would have a hard time explaining it, still "we know it when we expe-rience it." It inspires awe because it is so overwhelming and mysterious. Where did it really come from? How did it get there? Why are we part of it? What is its meaning? Does it have a purpose?

It is awe that inspires all human imagination. Without awe, we would be without wonder and without wonder we would have no way to exercise imagination and would therefore be unable to imag-ine another's life "as if" it were our own. We know that empathy is impossible without imagination. Imagination, however, is impossible without wonder, and wonder is impossible without awe. Empathy rep-resents the deepest expression of awe, and understandably is regarded as the most spiritual of human qualities.

But empathy also requires trust—the willingness to surrender our-selves to the mystery of existence at both the cosmic level and at the level of everyday life with our fellow beings. Trust becomes indispens-able to allowing empathy to grow, and empathy, in turn, allows us to plumb the divine presence that exists in all things. Empathy becomes the window to the divine. It is by empathic extension that we tran-scend ourselves and begin connecting with the mystery of existence. The deeper, more universalizing our empathic experience, the closer we come to experiencing the totality of being—that is, we become more all-participating, all-knowing, and all-belonging.

If one looks closely at the world's institutional religions, it is pos-sible to find snippets of this embodied approach to searching out the divine along the margins of the main texts. Theologians call this panentheism.

> Panentheism as a way of thinking about God affirms both
> the transcendence of God and the immanence of God. For
> panentheism, God is not a being "out there." The Greek roots
> of the word point to its meaning: *pan* means "everything,"
> *en* means "in," and *theos* means "God." God is more than
> everything (and thus transcendent), yet everything is in God
> (hence God is immanent). For panentheism, God is "right
> here," even as God is also more than "right here."[38]

Yet the central narratives of the world's great religions—Judaism, Christianity, Islam, Hinduism—remain, for the most part, disembod-ied and extraworldly, cutting off empathic extension and the search for connectivity and God's immanence.

In the Age of Empathy, spirituality invariably replaces religiosity. Spirituality is a deeply personal journey of discovery in which embod-ied experience—as a general rule—becomes the guide to making con-nections, and empathy becomes the means to foster transcendence. The World Values Survey and countless other polls show a generational shift in attitudes toward the divine, with the younger generation in the industrialized nations increasingly turning away from institutionalized religiosity and toward personal spiritual quests that are embodied in nature and empathic in expression.

Reason too can be salvaged from its disembodied Enlightenment roots and be recast within an embodied empathic frame. While reason is most often thought of in terms of rationalization, that is, abstracting and classifying phenomena, usually with the help of quantifiable tools of measurement, it is more than that. Reason includes mindfulness, reflection, introspection, contemplation, musing, and pondering, as well as rhetorical and literary ways of thinking. Reason is all of this and more. When we think of reason, we generally think of stepping back from the immediacy of an experience and probing our memories to see if there might be an analogous experience that could help us make the appropriate judgment or decisions about how best to respond.

The critical question is where does reason come from? The Cartesian and Kantian idea that reason exists independently of experience as an a priori phenomenon to be accessed does not conform to the way we reason in the real world. Reason is a way of organizing experience and relies on many mental tools. The point, however, is that reason is never disembodied from experience but rather a means of understanding and managing it.

Experience, as we learned earlier, begins with sensations and feelings that flow from engagement with others and quickly becomes bundled into emotions with the help of reason and then is transformed into purposeful behavioral responses, again with the aid of reason. Needless to say, experience is not always so neatly executed. One's feelings can remain raw and unformed. It is possible to not even know why one feels a certain way. Similarly, our emotions can run away with us, inflicting harm on ourselves and others.

Empathy brings together sensations, feelings, emotions, and reason in a structural way toward the goal of communion with the vast others that stretch beyond our physicality. If empathy did not exist, we could not understand why we feel the way we do, or conceptualize something called an emotion or think rationally. Many scholars have mistakenly associated empathy with just feelings and emotions. If that were all it was, empathic consciousness would be an impossibility.

We are beginning to learn that an empathic moment requires both intimate engagement and a measure of detachment. If our feelings completely spill over into another's feelings or their feelings overwhelm our psyche, we lose a sense of self and the ability to imagine the other as if they were us. Empathy is a delicate balancing act. One has to be open to experiencing another's plight as if it were one's own but not be engulfed by it, at the expense of drowning out the self's ability to be a unique and separate being. Empathy requires a porous boundary between I and thou that allows the identity of two beings to mingle in a shared mental space.

While one's sensations and feelings make possible the initial connection with the other, they are quickly filtered by way of past memories and organized by the various powers of reason at our disposal to establish an appropriate emotional, cognitive, and behavioral response. The entire process is what makes up empathetic consciousness. As mentioned in Chapter 1, empathy is both an affective and cognitive experience.

Reason, then, is the process by which we order the world of feelings in order to create what psychologists call pro-social behavior and sociologists call social intelligence. Empathy is the substance of the process. Reason becomes increasingly sophisticated as social constructs become more complex, human differentiation more pronounced, and human exchange more diverse. Greater exposure to others increases the volume of feelings that need to be organized. Reason becomes more adept at abstracting and managing the flood of embodied feelings. We get closer to a cosmopolitan mind. That's not to say that reason can't also be used to exploit others, for example, to advance narcissistic ends or create terror among people.

By reimagining faith and reason as intimate aspects of empathic consciousness, we create a new historical synthesis that incorporates many of the most powerful and compelling features of the Age of Faith and the Age of Reason, while leaving behind the disembodied story lines that shake the celebration out of life.

BRIDGING THE IS/OUGHT GAP

The inclusion of the core features of awe and reason into a broader, empathic consciousness takes us beyond the age-old schism between bodily experience and prescriptive behavior—the so-called is/ought gap—that has long plagued theology and philosophy.

Because both faith-based consciousness and rational consciousness largely denigrated bodily experience, perceiving human physicality and drives as depraved and contaminated in the case of religion, and pleasure seeking and utilitarian in the case of secular philosophy, there was always the need to impose moral codes from above to assure pro-social behavior. It was always assumed that physical feelings, emotions, and passions were evil, irrational, or potentially pathological and needed to be continually reined in by a higher authority. The Abrahamic religions relied on God's authority, coded in the Ten Commandments, to maintain a measure of morally appropriate behavior. While the Jews introduced the Golden Rule as a kind of super-morality, it is important to note that in its original guise it was often stated in negative terms: "Do not do unto others as you would not have them do unto you." The Asian religions, Hinduism, Buddhism, Confucianist philosophy, and Taoism, also introduced their own variations of the Golden Rule.

As we will see in Chapter 6, the widespread dissemination of the Golden Rule in ancient times represented a powerful empathetic surge and a qualitative shift in human consciousness, yet its impact on the human psyche was limited by the disembodied assumption that accompanied it. The faithful, especially among the Abrahamic religions, were expected to conform to the Golden Rule, not out of feeling for the other, but as a moral duty because it was the will of God, and God's laws needed to be obeyed, lest one experience divine wrath.

Even the story of the Good Samaritan in the tenth Book of Luke in the New Testament is tinged with the notion of one's duty to God rather than one's feeling of empathic identification with a stranger. In the parable, a legal scholar asks Jesus, "What must I do to inherit eternal life?" Jesus responds by saying, "You shall love the Lord, your God, with all your heart, with all your being, with all your strength, and with all your mind, and your neighbor as yourself."[39] If one shows compassion to a stranger and loves God, one will be assured eternal salvation. The act of comforting a stranger becomes inextricably linked with securing one's place in heaven and is, therefore, justifiably categorized as instrumental behavior.

Immanuel Kant made the rational case for the Golden Rule in the modern age in his famous categorical imperative. Kant's imperative is in two parts. First, "Act only on that maxim that can at the same time be willed to become a universal law."[40] Second, "Act in such a way that you treat humanity, whether in your own person or in the person of another, always at the same time as an end and never simply as a means."[41] Although Kant eliminated the self-interested aspect of doing good that was so much a part of most religious experiences, he also eliminated the "felt" experience that makes compassion so powerful and compelling.

As we learned earlier, Kant argued that the senses were not trustworthy guides to moral behavior—feelings, emotions, and passions are much too subjective and arbitrary to establish universal moral standards. Instead, he argued that his categorical imperative is an articulation of a universal moral code that is applicable at all times and under every conceivable circumstance, independent of the empirical situation. In other words, pure reason, detached from emotional subjectivity, dictates one's moral duty. The moral person is cool, detached, disinterested, and driven by reason and moral obligation rather than emotion and passion.

Even Freud in his masterful frontal assault on rational consciousness felt compelled to introduce a disembodied moral mechanism to oversee what he considered to be the irrational libidinal impulses. The introduction of the idea of "the unconscious" wreaked havoc on the older idea of a rational mind acting dispassionately as a governor of human agency. Human beings, he suggested, are ridden with primeval libidinal drives—this is the realm of the Id, where the pleasure principle rules.

Although Freud argued that the reality principle and ego formation are quickly introduced in early infancy to hold these powerful forces at bay, he nonetheless felt compelled to introduce a third structure, the superego, as a disembodied moral authority to govern social behavior. The Superego, the mind's moral authority, exists independently of the body's corporeal experience and acts as a universal moral compass, much like Kant's categorical imperative.

In all three stages of human consciousness—theological, ideological, and early psychological—moral authority is disembodied, at least in the mainstream orthodoxy. The reason is that bodily experience is considered either fallen, irrational, or pathological. The result is that throughout history, a schism exists between people's bodily experience on one hand and our moral prescription on the other hand. It's as if our bodily experience has to be forced, molded, and cajoled to adhere to our moral codes. In other words, the implied supposition is that human nature is at odds with morally correct behavior and needs to be "whipped into line" figuratively as well as literally. This is the is/ought gap our philosophers constantly allude to, the idea that it is impossible to bridge the divide between the way human behavior "is" and the way it "ought" to behave. As long as embodied experience is considered to be irrelevant or at odds with moral laws, there will always be a gap between what is and what ought to be human behavior.

Empathic consciousness overcomes the is/ought gap. Empathic behavior is embodied, is filled with a sense of awe, and relies on both feelings and reason. Equally important, empathic consciousness is both descriptive and prescriptive at the same time. There is no dividing line between what one is and what one ought to be. They are one and the same. When one identifies with another's struggle as if it were one's own and celebrates their life by comforting and supporting their quest, one is living authentically and fully. One's self is enlarged and expanded and spills over into broader, more inclusive communities of compassionate engagement. The process of being empathic extends the moral domain.

Anyone who's ever experienced empathy knows that it cannot be commanded into being felt or be pursued because it's one's moral duty and, therefore, a universal obligation. Empathy is felt and reasoned simultaneously. It is a quantum experience.

Empathic consciousness, then, does not rest on an externally imposed moral code but rather on a nurturing milieu. One develops a moral sensitivity to the extent one is embedded, from infancy, in a nurturing parental, familial, and neighborhood environment. Society can foster that environment by providing the appropriate social and public context. While primitive empathic potential is wired into the brain chemistry of some mammals, and especially the primates, its mature expression in humans requires learning and practice and a conducive environment. Moral codes, embedded in laws and social policies, are helpful as learning guides and standards. But the point is that one isn't authentically good because he or she is compelled to be so, with the threat of punishment hanging over them or a reward waiting for them, but, rather because it's in one's nature to empathize. We don't internalize morally appropriate behavior by fiat or promises, but externalize it by feelings of identification with the plight of others. To be truly human is to be universally empathic and, therefore, morally appropriate in one's embodied experience.

EMPATHY HAS become a buzzword recently in public discourse and a matter of debate in policy circles, the professional community, and civil society. Its newfound celebrity is in large part attributable to President Obama's championing of the term. The president has made empathy the core of his personal political philosophy and the centerpiece in his political decisions, from the conduct of foreign policy to the selection of Supreme Court Justices.

Yet without a proper understanding of the social evolution of the empathic impulse over the course of human history, we run the risk of trivializing the term in the public arena, even turning it into the subject of ridicule and caricature. As is often the case in a media-driven society, where attention-deficit/hyperactivity disorder has mutated from a childhood ailment to a social pandemic, it is possible that the opportunity to shoulder a responsible rethinking of our empathic nature could get spent in a momentary media frenzy, leaving the term a dead cliché. Nothing could be more important at this juncture in our history as a species than to have a meaningful cultural debate about the role empathy has played in the development and conduct of human affairs.

Such a debate is no longer an esoteric exercise but, rather, a life-or-death imperative for our species. Our ever more complex energy-consuming global civilization is careening the human race to the very brink of extinction. If our scientists are right, we may be within a century or so of our possible demise on this planet. While we are quickly evolving into *Homo empathicus,* our entropic debt is shadowing our steep climb as we approach the summit of global consciousness.

We need now, more than ever, to retrace our steps, to understand how we got here, so that we can find a new, more secure footing that can free us from the entropic shackle and allow us to thrive while living more lightly on Earth and in harmony with our fellow creatures and the ecosystems that nurture life. Our scientists tell us that we have but a few years to find a new economic road map for civilization—one that takes us into a new energy regime that is more sustainable and able to break the fever that is heating up the biosphere.

The task before the human race is daunting. For the first time, we have to defy our own history as a species and create a new, more interdependent civilization that consumes less rather than more energy, but in a way that allows empathy to continue to mature and global consciousness to expand until we have filled the Earth with our compassion and grace rather than our spent energy. To accomplish this undertaking requires that we know how human consciousness has developed over eons of history as we transitioned into a succession of ever more complex energy-consuming civilizations. By rediscovering our cognitive past, we find important clues to how we might redirect our conscious future. With our very survival at stake, we can no longer afford to remain unmindful about how empathic consciousness has evolved across history and at what expense to the Earth we inhabit.

A review of the great energy/communications complexes in history, the empathic surges and the forms of human consciousness that accompanied them, and the entropic impacts that they created will give us an anthropological map of where we have come from and hopefully a compass to correct our course and help us navigate our way into the Age of Empathy.

PART II

EMPATHY AND CIVILIZATION

SIX

The Ancient Theological Brain and Patriarchal Economy

No one would deny that human consciousness has changed over history. When we look closer, however, we see that shifts in consciousness accompany shifts in the way human beings organize their relationships to the natural world and, in particular, the way people harness the energies of the planet. Recall, people who live in foraging and hunting cultures think differently than those who live in hydraulic agricultural societies, just as people who live in industrial societies think differently than those in agricultural ones. That's because qualitative changes in energy regimes are accompanied by changes in the way people communicate with one another to manage energy flows. Those changes in communication reshape the way the human brain understands and organizes reality.

All forager/hunter societies are oral cultures. We know of no single example where a forager/hunter culture created writing. Similarly, virtually all of the great hydraulic agricultural societies created some form of writing and calculations to arrange the production, storage, and distribution of cereal grains. The First Industrial Revolution—coal, steam power, and rail—in the nineteenth century would have been impossible to arrange and manage without print communications. In the early twentieth century, first-generation electronic communications, especially the telephone and later mass radio and television, became the central command-and-control mechanisms for managing and marketing an oil-based Second Industrial Revolution organized around the internal-combustion engine and fossil-fuel-based technologies and goods.

Communications regimes, in turn, change human consciousness. Oral cultures are steeped in mythological consciousness. Script cultures give rise to theological consciousness. Print cultures are accompanied by ideological consciousness. First-generation centralized electronic cultures give rise to a full-blown psychological consciousness.

Of course, it's not all so neatly packaged. These various stages of consciousness don't magically appear just in the nick-of-time to organize new energy/communications regimes. Old forms of consciousness generally linger on, especially in the early stages of an emerging energy/communications revolution. But none of these distinct energy/communications constructs has ever ridden the crest of its own bell curve without the new form of consciousness running alongside.

Stages of consciousness are a mental repositioning of human perception, and they occur when new energy/communications revolutions give rise to new social arrangements. In extending our collective central nervous systems into new realms and terrains, we undergo what psychologists call a gestalt change. Our temporal and spatial orientation is recalibrated—to use a reductionist term from mechanics. We come to see things differently. Equally important, we undergo a process of reinterpreting our new environments and social context in an effort to locate our place and purpose in the new scheme of things. That process of reinterpretation is conditioned by the reality of the new relationships we fashion with the world around us. In other words, we come to see and interpret nature, the world, and the cosmos by the way we are currently interacting with them. Even the metaphors we use to describe our sense of selves and our sense of reality are borrowed from our organizing relationships. Hydraulic agricultural civilizations envision the world in hydraulic metaphors. The First Industrial Revolution cobbled together ideological consciousness using mechanical metaphors. The Second Industrial Revolution reenvisioned the cosmos in electrical terms.

Stages of consciousness set the outer boundaries of reality. They capture and reflect the present temporal and spatial reach and extension of the collective central nervous system of the civilization. The temporal/spatial social order represented by mythological consciousness, theological consciousness, ideological consciousness, and psychological consciousness are quite distinct. Each reflects a more complex social construct and a more extended temporal and spatial realm. And each opens up the possibility of extending the empathetic domain while simultaneously increasing the overall entropy of the biosphere.

Stages of consciousness also reset the boundary line between the "we" and the "others." Beyond the walls is no-man's-land, where the aliens reside. For mythological man, the alien is the nonhuman or demon or monster. For theological man, it is the heathen or infidel. For ideological man, it is the brute. For psychological man, it is the pathological.

At each stage of history, energy/communications revolutions have expanded the domain of the central nervous system, bringing more and more of the "other" into the realm of the familiar. Today global satellite television and the Internet, the IT revolution, and air travel are connecting nearly two-thirds of the human race in a 24/7 continuous-feedback loop. The alien domain is shrinking as globalization accelerates and the empathic impulse begins to encompass the totality of life that makes up the biosphere of the planet. Its quickening pace, however, is barely able to keep up with the quickening entropic bill.

Each of these stages of human consciousness is a chapter in the unfolding of the great drama that is at the center of the human journey—the evolution of empathic expression and the dark shadow of entropic debt that is its nemesis.

But how does one go about verifying something as seemingly amorphous as the evolution of empathic expression? Fortunately, we have a record that chronicles both the development of empathic expression and the evolution of human consciousness. The evidence is embedded deep in the conversations that make up the stories we've told about ourselves across history. It's in the narratives we've left behind.

FIRST THERE WAS THE WORD

The great German philosopher and scientist Johann Wolfgang von Goethe, who dedicated a lifetime to unlocking the mysteries of light and color, tells a story about what is the most important single thing in life. The golden king asks the snake, "What is more glorious than gold?" "Light," answers the snake. The king responds by asking, "What is more refreshing than light?" The snake replies, "Conversation."[1] To our knowledge, we are unique among the animal species in that we are the only ones who tell stories. We live by narrative. The narrative changes with each new stage of consciousness. But what remains constant is the central theme. We communicate with each other and listen to each other's stories because we seek each other's company and are predisposed to intimacy and affection, relationships, and sociability. Conversation, whether it be oral, script, print, or electronic, is our means of exposing ourselves to others and entering their realities, and by so doing, incorporating parts of their reality into our own. Louis Dupré, a professor of the philosophy of religion at Yale University, makes the point that:

> Dialogue requires that in some way one abandons one's own position to enter into that of the other. The more I give myself to the other, the better I know myself and the more I acquire a unique identity.[2]

Dialogue, then, becomes an essential tool for communicating our feelings with each other. It is through conversation that we create relationships, and these relationships shape our unique individual stories and identities.

University of Illinois psychology and communications professor Peggy J. Miller conducted an interesting set of experiments with young mothers and children in a blue-collar area of Baltimore to assess the role narratives play in the day-to-day socialization process. In the study, Miller recorded conversations between mothers and children and between adults with children within ear range, and found that in every hour of conversation, there are approximately 8.5 narratives, or one every 7 minutes, of which 75 percent were articulated by the mother.[3] These narratives start with a precipitating event and involve a protagonist, an agent, a victim, and an accomplice—all described in a linear fashion—and have a resolution. In other words, from the very beginning, children are introduced to the idea that life is an unfolding drama, told in the form of stories to one another. These stories are the means by which we organize our experiences and try to find meaning in them.

One of the most frequent means of encouraging language development and socialization is the telling of children's stories. Children hear their parents read a fairy tale or other story while looking at the pictures in the book and following the words on the page. Children's stories are all simply constructed dramatic narratives that introduce children into the world of social relationships. Because the story is always about a past experience as told in the present and is implicitly meant to provide some expression or guidance that might be helpful in the future, it is permeated with temporality. When parents read to their child a fictional story and ask them to reflect on it, or ask their child to reflect on an immediate personal past experience, the "reflection" is what creates the past, present, and future. To reflect is to think about something that has previously occurred in order to distill its importance for future action.

The induction scripts mentioned in Chapter 4 are examples of parents applying narratives to their children's experiences. The children, in turn, learn to become self-aware and self-conscious by internalizing stories and, later, through play, acting out their own dramatic narratives. The child in effect "grows into" the narratives.[4] Concepts like the past, present, future, and the resolution of conflict are all introduced to the child by way of narrative. On this last score, the American psychologist Jerome Bruner makes the telling observation that the "narrative gift" is "one of the principal forms of peacekeeping."[5] Presenting and dramatizing events allows people to step back and look on experience in its entirety. Telling the story requires reflection and a certain amount of distancing from the immediacy of the event. The distancing allows the storyteller to bring in mitigating circumstances and even to tell the story from multiple perspectives, all of which helps reduce potential conflict. It's not unusual after a conflict for an observer to ask the parties to slow down, relax and tell what happened. The very act of distancing oneself from the event and retelling what happened helps give the storyteller a feeling of regaining control by putting what occurred in context and framing it to gain some sense of meaning as to what transpired.

Often in daily conversation, the story of an event is told by several people, each with their own interpretation of what took place. Listening to multiple explanations of what occurred allows children to begin to understand that each person experiences a social interaction a bit differently. They come to realize that other's feelings may differ from their own. Equally important, in the act of listening to each other's interpretations of the same event, children not only discern the differences in perspectives, but they also search for any shared feelings. This is an essential learning experience on the way to developing self-consciousness—the ability to experience others as unique individuals, with their own feelings, perspectives, and stories, and to find some emotional common ground. Narrative is critical to transforming empathic distress to empathic engagement.

All of the stories we tell are ultimately designed to share our feelings with one another about how we experience life. Valerie Gray Hardcastle, dean of the University of Cincinnati's McMicken College, reminds us of the emotional importance of all human communication. She writes:

> Most of our life stories will be forgotten over time, but some
> will continue to be told and retold, forming a core around
> which we can hang our other life events. But at the heart
> of any story about self is the expression of some emotional
> reaction of the person talking . . . [Narrative] is a way of
> integrating and consolidating our affective reactions to the
> events around us, a way of making our life events meaningful,

to us and to others. It is a way of living a life as well as a way of understanding it.[6]

By retelling and reshaping our own life stories, we are continually honing our identities to accommodate each passage of life and the changing circles of relationships and experiences that accompany them. We are each a composite of the stories we tell about ourselves and the stories others tell about us.

Each successive communications revolution in history—oral language, script, print, and electronic—provides us with increasingly sophisticated ways of sharing our personal and collective stories and extending our emotional reach to diverse others over space and time. As communications revolutions connect more people, more quickly and over greater distances, they allow us to share our stories more broadly and facilitate the universalization of empathic expression.

By studying the great energy/communications paradigms, we can begin to spot important "empathic stages" in history and assess the contributions they have made toward universalizing the empathic drive.

MYTHOLOGICAL CONSCIOUSNESS

For more than 93 percent of human existence, people lived as foragers, and only occasionally as hunters. Like our closest relative, the chimpanzee, our ancient ancestors lived off the land, their daily and annual routines synchronized to the rhythms of the changing seasons.

Social units rarely extended beyond several dozen people in an extended kinship community. Life was lived collectively but not yet introspectively. The idea of selfhood had to await the dawn of civilization and far more complex social arrangements. In this early period of human existence there was little differentiation of skills. The idea of surplus did not exist and, for that reason, there were few ways to differentiate status distinctions between members of the commune. While a primitive pecking order existed, as with our chimpanzee relatives, usually consisting of alpha males and elders who were the depositories of the wisdom in the form of the collective memories of the group, life was far more egalitarian—not to be confused with democratic—than in any time since then.

From what we know from studying the few Paleolithic tribes still left on Earth, early human beings had to be adept at exploring their surroundings and maintaining an intimate memory of edible and inedible plants, insects and small animals, and the seasonal changes that conditioned their own hand-to-mouth survival. Darwin was taken aback by primitive people's keen senses of mimicking. They were constantly observing the behavior of other animals and mimicking their behavior as if to incorporate it into the making of their own. Lewis Mumford points out that mimicking was perhaps the most important invention of early man, allowing him to better expropriate his surroundings and secure his survival.

> Being imitative as well as curious, he may have learned
> trapping from the spider, basketry from the birds' nests, dam-
> building from beavers, burrowing from rabbits, and the art of
> using poisons from snakes. Unlike most species, man did not
> hesitate to learn from other creatures and copy their ways;
> by appropriating their diet[s] and methods of getting food he
> multiplied his own chances of survival.[7]

Like the chimps, archaic peoples' diets were overwhelmingly made up of fruits and vegetables. Infrequent hunting, however, gave them a smell for the death of another mammal and, no doubt, triggered their sense of primitive empathic distress—especially so because in these early times human beings did not clearly differentiate themselves from the rest of the animal world. Theirs was a diffuse and porous reality populated by animal, vegetable, and human spirits continually interacting and fusing with one another. It was commonplace in rituals to wear antlers, pelts, feathers, and other parts of their fellow creatures and to mimic their behavior in dance. When they killed a beast, they would mourn the passing and ask for understanding from the animal's spirit—pleading the case for their own families' care and survival, thus showing not only a sense of indebtedness but also primitive empathic distress.

Archaic man was not able to distinguish between the material and immaterial, the imaginary and the real, and the animate and inanimate worlds. The reality he experienced had only a limited past sense and virtually no future sense—he lived in the moment and was caught up in the sensations that bombarded him and required an immediate response. Every force that acted on him—wind, rain, falling rocks, the sun and the moon, and other creatures—represented spirits and demons who were regarded as friends or foes. If stones fell on him from a mountain cliff, he believed that an enemy sorcerer had slipped into the rocks to do him harm or that the stones were stone people attacking him.[8]

The great French philosopher-anthropologist Lucien Lévy-Bruhl called the primitive mind "a mist of unity."[9] Primitive man lived in a mystical and mythological world of deep involuntary participation. He would think of tigers or elephants as human beings who lived like him but took on the form of tigers and elephants.[10]

Most important of all, like a small child, primitive man did not possess a clear sense of his individual being—that is, he did not distinguish himself from everything else around him. Bruhl points out that "I" does not exist among primitive people—only "we." While there may exist a slight sense of "I," it is not clearly comprehended. This is most in evidence when a primitive man harms another being or kills an animal or cuts down a tree. Since even animals and trees are considered human, in other forms, and because they are not individualized any more than himself, he regards his assault as being aimed at the whole of their clan. Therefore, any retaliatory measure would be aimed at any or all of his clan. Since the notion of the individual doesn't exist, harm and counterharm are always collectively aimed. Vendettas and blood vengeance between clans and tribes have ancient roots in the "misty" past, where any given person merely stood for the collective to which he or she was attached.

Since empathic expression requires enough of a sense of selfhood that one can recognize another as a distinct being, not unlike oneself, it must be concluded that the empathic sense among primitive people is still at the entry level of empathic distress—much the same as it is with children until the age of six or seven.

If there is a silver lining in this undifferentiated "misty" existence, it is that archaic people do not have an existential sense of their own personal death because they do not conceive of themselves as finite, mortal beings. As previously mentioned, all primitive societies share the universal belief that people don't die but simply go to sleep and enter a netherworld—a parallel existence—which they inhabit, with occasional forays back to the land of the "living" as spirits.

Nor do primitive people have an understanding of birth. Rather, birth is considered a matter of immaculate conception. A spirit enters a girl's body and is then brought forth. Babies are not considered human beings as we know the term but, rather, hybrid beings, half spirits, half humans, who remain in contact with the world from which they came. The hybrid being becomes increasingly part of the community over a period of years by passing through various rites of passage. The human and spirit world is like a revolving door where the "dead" live for a time in the spirit world, only to be reincarnated back to the human form. The spirits might be former tigers or plants, rocks, or even stars. Their reincarnation in human form binds the world of the living and the dead in a seamless and perpetual web.

Lacking a sense of their own "unique" personal birth and death or that of others, they can't move beyond primitive empathic distress over another's suffering to an existential sense of identification with their unique existence. It's unlikely that anyone in a primitive society would ever perceive another's suffering in a mature empathic sense, any more than a young child today under the age of five or six, the point at which they become aware of the meaning of death, their own and that of others, as well as the origins of their own birth.

DOMESTICATING PLANTS, ANIMALS, AND OURSELVES

With the long shift out of the Paleolithic era and a foraging/hunting energy regime and into the Neolithic era and a gardening energy regime, we see a glimmer of selfhood emerging, and a taste of the kind of empathic consciousness that would develop and deepen in future millennia.

The Neolithic era dates back to around 8000 BC.[11] The new energy regime—garden agriculture and small-scale pastoralism—sharpened the nurturing instincts. This was the age of matriarchal dominance. Women, for the most part, were the inventors of agriculture. Men, for the most part, shepherded flocks and herds. Both tasks required an eye to nurture. Domesticating plants and gentling animals called for mindfulness and constant tendering. Small-scale agriculture and pastoralism also meant living a bounded existence. Habitats became more permanent and with more dependable supplies of food, population increased. The first village settlements began to emerge in the Middle East, the Indus Valley, China, and elsewhere.

In Chapter 1, we noted that neolithic life brought with it the pivotal invention of containers—pots, baskets, and bins—to store grain. With stored surplus, human beings created the possibility, for the first time, of planning ahead, establishing a bulwark against the vagaries of nature and gaining control over their environment. With surplus came economics, and the gnawing question that has plagued the human family ever since—who produces the surplus, who stores it, to whom is it distributed, and in what proportions.

Stored grain, as Lewis Mumford points out, is potential energy and, along with cattle, the oldest form of capital. He reminds us that premonetary commercial transactions were almost always in measures of grain.[12]

The analogy of containers with the human womb—both store potential energy—could not have been lost on our Neolithic ancestors. And like the womb, containers are protected spaces that require constant oversight. While in later periods of time, a more male dominated psyche tended to put greater emphasis on tools that dislodge, cut down, cut up, kill, or move things, it should be noted that without the invention of an artificial womb—in the form of sealable containers that can protect and preserve grain—civilization would have been an impossibility.

Our archaeologists tell us that the Neolithic era was the most peaceful in human history. The archeological evidence shows little record of weaponry. It may be the only period in human history to experience Immanuel Kant's vision of "perpetual peace." The "care and nurture of life" was the central dynamic of the Neolithic era.[13] Mumford writes:

> The protection of favored plants was an essential part of the whole effort to protect and foster and appreciate the forces of life. If hunting is by definition a predatory occupation, gardening is a symbiotic one; and in the loose ecological pattern of the early garden, the interdependence of living organisms became visible, and the direct involvement of man was the very condition for productivity and creativity.[14]

Aside from the more obvious ways that the care and nurture of plants and animals must have had on child-rearing practices, there were also collateral benefits that advanced empathic development. Surplus food and permanent residences increased survival rates of newborns, allowed for better care of babies, and created the physical conditions for more attentive parenting and attachment. Again Mumford observes,

> With protection and continuity ensured by the village itself, there was more time for the watchful guardianship and instruction of the young; and . . . a growing interest in children's needs . . . [Children] could now be enjoyed for their own sake, like puppies and kittens.[15]

THE DAWN OF HUMAN CIVILIZATION

There is good reason to believe that the empathic impulse picked up momentum during the long Neolithic era. It is with the dawn of civilization, however, that empathy began to reach beyond empathic distress, showing the first tentative signs of a self-aware empathic response.

In the fourth millennium BC, the first urban hydraulic agricultural societies began to form along the great river valleys in the Middle East and western and southwestern Asia.[16] The rivers' flood waters were harnessed with the erection of an elaborate system of canals and dikes to provide a dependable and manipulatable supply of water to irrigate land and raise cereal grains.

The first of the urban hydraulic societies was established by the Sumerians, along the Tigris and Euphrates rivers, in Mesopotamia. Hydraulic civilization was the first prototype of an urban industrial model to harness and employ energy. Thousands of laborers had to be indentured to build and maintain the canals and dikes. Specialized craft skills had to be developed to build the artifices and organize the production, storage, and distribution of grain. Architects, engineers, miners, metallurgists, bookkeepers, and the like made up the first specialized labor force in history. The Sumerians built magnificent city-states at Lagash, Nippur, Ur, Uruk, and Eridu and erected monumental temple structures to honor their gods.[17]

Most important, cuneiform, the first form of writing, was invented to manage the entire system. Virtually everywhere that large-scale complex hydraulic civilizations were created to capture solar energy in the form of photosynthesis in cereal plants, human beings independently invented some form of writing to organize the production, storage, and logistics operations—the Middle East, India, China, and Mexico.

The first written script in Sumer dates back to 3500 BC.[18] Writing was used not only to organize commercial and trade operations but also as an administrative tool for managing government bureaucracies and religious practices and as an artistic medium for literary works. Clay bricks, parchment, papyrus, and wax tablets were all used as writing surfaces. Goose quills—called pen knives and brushes—were used as styli, and inks from various vegetable sources were used to inscribe.

The early writing was in the forms of pictographic signs etched in clay. Phonetization followed suit. Special schools called "tablet-houses" were set up to teach scribes. Limited literacy ensured that at least skilled craftsmen, merchants, government officials, and palace priests could communicate among themselves. Later, the tablet-houses metamorphosized into schools, which became the center for learning in Sumer.[19] While it is estimated that less than 1 percent of the population in the Sumerian city-states was literate, the social, economic, and political impacts of living in the first even partially literate societies was immense and far-reaching.[20] School courses even included the study of mathematics, astronomy, magic, and philosophy.[21]

Writing led to the codification and public proclamation of laws, putting the administration of justice onto a more systematic footing. When the Akkadians, who were Semitic-speaking, conquered the Sumerians and consolidated the formerly semi-independent walled cities into a single empire, they further refined the justice system. Bringing together people of diverse cultural and linguistic backgrounds required a code of laws that would apply equally to all and ensure justice for every subject. The Hammurabi code—named after the ruler Hammurabi—was the first in history to ensure some limited rights of individuals, especially in regard to acquiring, holding, and inheriting private property. The Akkadians, who later founded the Babylonian empire, converted the Sumerian writing system to one that better suited their own language.[22] The Babylonian empire deserves a special place in the history of consciousness, for it was there that the "emergence of the individual in a literate society . . . occurs for the first time."[23]

By objectifying and codifying laws and ensuring a degree of individual legal rights, the justice codes had an effect on the development of individual self-consciousness. Establishing a common frame of reference for the administration of justice gave people an objective way to judge other's social behavior in relation to their own. The Hammurabi code meshed the varied experiences of injustice and the remedies prescribed to address wrongdoings across many different cultures and abstracted them into more generalized categories. This forced a certain amount of introspection and interpretation on the part of the observer to try to understand how his own experiences with injustice squared or was at odds with the prevailing norms, which were a composite of the experiences of many people that crossed a number of tribal boundaries and experiences. By contrast, in a single tribal culture, the taboos were clear and unambiguous and required little reflection and interpretation. One didn't have to think about how one felt. One simply had to conform one's behavior to what the ancestors said was appropriate to the situation. Formulaic oral cultures called for formulaic emotional and behavioral responses, while literate cultures required individual emotional and behavioral responses geared to the unique circumstances of each novel situation, measured against the abstract norms established in law.

An abstract legal code undermined the traditional tribal authority by creating a set of laws that applied equally to all and required individual compliance, thus partially severing each male from his former collective tribal affiliation. The Hammurabi Code formally recognized, in a small way, the individual self as a separate being, for the first time in history.

The quantitative leap in cereal grain production in Sumer vastly increased population and resulted in the first urban settlements— communities of upward of tens of thousands of inhabitants. Some of the production centers—the flour mills, ovens, and workshops—employed more than a thousand people, marking the introduction of the first urban workforces in history.[24]

Transforming entire river valleys into gigantic production facilities required a new form of highly centralized political control. The great hydraulic civilizations gave rise to the first government bureaucracies. Atop the bureaucracies all power was vested in a single ruler, a demigod with absolute discretion over the lives of his minions. The great pharaohs of Egypt were unsurpassed until the Roman Empire in the power they exercised over vast regions and diverse peoples. The bureaucracies oversaw every aspect of the productive life of the regions they administered, from mobilizing thousands of farmers during a part of the year to clean the canals, to transporting, storing, and distributing the grain, managing commerce with nearby regions, taxing the people, and maintaining armies to defend their borders.

Society was organized hierarchically with an autonomous ruler atop the government bureaucracy and thousands of specialized laborers, from palace priests and scribes to skilled craftsmen and foot soldiers on the various rungs of the political ladder, and finally common laborers and farmers tending the fields at the bottom.

While it is estimated that less than 10 percent of the populace—a fraction of the overall population—was engaged in specialized skills and callings, they represent the first inklings of civilized life.[25]

The price that humans beings paid for civilizing the species was a mixed one. On the one hand, people were subjected to ruthless regimentation and rigid control. Every aspect of one's life was orchestrated by powerful bureaucracies and a ruler who enjoyed complete power. On the other hand, the creation of specialized craft skills and labor tasks and the invention of limited forms of personal property and money exchanges, as well as wages, yanked individuals away from the collective "we" of prehistory, creating the first partial "selves."

The great Sumerian merchants enjoyed far more independence and freedom than any of the skilled craftspeople. While they were expected to do the bidding of the ruling family, they were also allowed to trade on their own accord. The merchants at Sumer became the first large-scale private entrepreneurs in history. Many of them amassed great fortunes.[26] The detached individual, unique and differentiated from the collectivity, breathed his first faint air of selfhood at Sumer.

SUMERIAN URBAN LIFE AND THE BIRTH OF SELFHOOD

All of the major hydraulic civilizations built elaborate road systems and waterways to transport workforces and animals and exchange grain and other goods in commerce and trade. King's highways, which were also used to maintain communications across the kingdoms, were among the other great inventions of the hydraulic civilizations, along with the wheeled chariots and sailing ships. The royal roads of Babylonia, Assyria, and Persia inspired the Greeks, and later the Romans, who copied and expanded their reach. Royal roads crossed all of India. A massive network of royal highways was constructed in China with the advent of the empire in 221 BC.[27] Royal highways made urban life possible.

The Sumerians, and other hydraulic civilizations that followed, developed rich urban cultures. Royal highways encouraged migration and facilitated city life. The urban centers became magnets for the mixing of cultures. The dense living arrangements invited cross-cultural exchange and the beginning of a cosmopolitan attitude. The new exposures often created conflict, but they also opened up the door to experiencing people who had heretofore been considered alien and other. The empathic impulse, which for all of previous history had been confined to small bands of close relatives and clans living largely in isolation, was suddenly presented with new opportunities and challenges. Finding the similar in alien others strengthened and deepened empathic expression, universalizing it beyond blood relationships for the first time.

The confluence of partial selfhood and exposure to diverse others previously regarded as alien and other was a breakthrough moment in human history. Just being exposed to individuals who were not part of their collective kinship group had the effect of sharpening their own sense of individuality, if only faintly. It is said that urban life creates isolation and aloneness. But it also creates a unique self able to identify with other unique selves by way of empathic extension. Partially weaned from the collectivity, one begins the process of reconnecting to others, this time as individual beings, and, by so doing, furthering one's own sense of selfhood. The awakening of a universal sense of empathy for other human beings only stirred slightly in the great hydraulic civilizations. It was enough, however, to mark the beginning of a new phase in the human journey.

Our ancestors began to walk down the road to becoming fully self-conscious human beings. But would we recognize anything in their behavior and way of thinking that would feel familiar? If we were to be transported back in time to 4,500 years ago on an urban street corner in Uruk, in the Sumerian Empire, and struck up a conversation with a literate resident, how likely is it that we could empathize with each other as two self-aware individual human beings? While we can never know for sure what such a conversation would be like, we have been left with a piece of archeological evidence that provides some tantalizing clues as to how the most literate minds of the day felt about themselves and their relationships with others, and the remarkable thing is how contemporary some of it sounds.

In 1844, an Englishman, Austen Henry Layard, was examining mounds in the city of Mosul—in what is now Iraq—and uncovered the ancient palaces of Nineveh. One of the rooms turned out to be the library of the last Assyrian king, Ashurbanipal (668–627 BC). There Layard discovered more than twenty thousand clay tablets inscribed in cuneiform. The tablets were transported to the British Museum and ignored. It wasn't until 1857 that archeologists realized that the tablets were written in Akkadian, the language of the Babylonian empire. In 1872, a curator found a tablet recounting the life, times, and adventures of an ancient Sumerian king, Gilgamesh, who ruled in Mesopotamia in the city of Uruk around 2750 BC.[28] He had discovered the oldest story in the world written down.

The epic of Gilgamesh ranks as one of the greatest literary works in all of history. The poet Rainer Maria Rilke captured its literary significance. He wrote,

> Gilgamesh is stupendous! I . . . consider it to be among the
> greatest things that can happen to a person. I have immersed
> myself in [it], and in these truly gigantic fragments I have
> experienced measures and forms that belong with the supreme
> works that the conjuring Word has ever produced.[29]

The story is about a powerful king who rules over a great city—Uruk. The hero, Gilgamesh, is portrayed as a complicated and troubled soul who has endured great hardship and experienced great sorrow. In the opening lines of the epic, the narrator says "[h]e had seen everything, had experienced all emotions."[30] His story is about the transformation of an arrogant tyrant who, after experiencing the depths of sorrow and despair, becomes a benevolent and kind ruler.

What is so extraordinary about Gilgamesh is that it provides a glimpse of the development of selfhood in the first partially urban civilization in history. While on the surface, Gilgamesh appears to possess superhuman attributes, underneath the veneer of invincibility is a deeply flawed and vulnerable human being consumed by the fear of death and in search of an immortality that continually eludes him.

Gilgamesh is also the first love story ever written down and, interestingly enough, it is a homoerotic one—a tale of two giants, Gilgamesh and his mirror opposite, Enkidu, who become intimate companions. (It's left to the reader to ponder whether they are in fact lovers.)

Gilgamesh convinces his new friend Enkidu that they must travel to the cedar forest, where he must slay the monster Humbaba, who is the protector and gatekeeper. While ostensibly the mission is to rid evil from the world, Gilgamesh confides in Enkidu that his real underlying motive is to gain fame by slaying the monster and be remembered forever.

Humbaba, as it turns out, is not an evil force. Quite the contrary: he is the guardian of the forest entrusted with the mission of protecting nature. At the critical moment of battle, when Gilgamesh is on top of the monster with a knife to his throat, he hesitates, as Humbaba pleads for mercy. But Enkidu will have none of it and urges his friend to finish the task. Enkidu's desire for Gilgamesh to succeed and gain fame and glory supersedes any empathic regard he might have for Humbaba.

By not showing mercy, the two were showing a lack of empathy for their victim. Although Gilgamesh was clearly troubled and felt a sense of guilt and remorse, his friend Enkidu did not. For his insensitivity and lack of compassion, the gods condemn him to death. Enkidu falls ill and dies. Gilgamesh is beside himself with grief.

Inconsolable, he abandons his throne, dons an animal skin, and leaves the great city of Uruk to roam the same wilderness Enkidu emerged from. His remorse, however, is more like the kind of empathic distress a small child experiences.

While his friend's death overwhelmed him, his grief now is mainly for himself. He becomes consumed with his own mortality and asks, "Must I die too?"[31] This then leads him on a search, first to overcome his own death and then to ask why do we all die, and finally to ponder the meaning of life. The once-bawdy, power-driven, self-aggrandizing king becomes the self-effacing, exposed individual—alone, scared, and without answers to the mysteries of life.

Gilgamesh travels the four corners of the Earth in search of answers. His far-flung adventures eventually lead to his own spiritual transformation. Realizing that he cannot escape his own death, he begins to embrace life. He comes to recognize, like Scrooge in *A Christmas Carol*, that life is to be lived in friendship with others. It is by acts of compassion that we feel most alive. Gilgamesh reenters the city of Uruk bearing gifts. He is a new man and now rules without violence and selfishness. He accepts his mortality and the finite nature of his existence that bonds him in solidarity with his fellow human being. He has become self-aware and human.

Although never fully able to understand or articulate his own innermost feelings or place himself in another's situation to experience their plight as his own, Gilgamesh nonetheless begins to glimpse his own selfhood and his proper relationships to his fellow human beings. His story is the beginnings of self-consciousness.

The Dawn of Theological Consciousness

The first stirring of universal empathy manifests itself in the form of theological consciousness. The great hydraulic civilizations of the Middle East, India, and China gave rise to polytheism and, later, to monotheism. The "spirit world" of the Paleolithic era and the "fertility goddesses" of the Neolithic era were challenged by a new pantheon of gods with more human characteristics.

It should be noted that the people of the Paleolithic era, and even the Neolithic era, did not feel superior to either other creatures or the forces of nature. Nor did they feel that they were somehow unique. Quite the contrary. They sometimes felt inferior and either paid homage to other creatures or entertained images of hybrid gods—half human, half animal—which became their gods. Mythological consciousness is steeped in the lore of the spirit world. Archaic man was driven by a sense of indebtedness to everything around him that affected his moment-to-moment existence. For this reason, every force and phenomenon is potentially spiritualized, reflecting a sense of utter dependency on the external world.

As human beings became more skilled at manipulating, expropriating, capturing, and redirecting the forces of nature for their own ends, they began to separate very slowly from their fellow creatures, creating the beginning of a boundary between themselves and other beings.

With the advent of the great hydraulic civilizations, human beings were able to bring the forces of nature under their direct control, on a massive scale. Over a long period of time, small, scattered hydraulic societies along river valleys—in the Middle East, India, China, and Mexico—were brought together by force of arms and conquests to create the first great kingdoms. As mentioned, power became centralized in the hands of ruling dynasties. At the top, a single human being ruled. His power was unrivaled and without precedent. He commanded the flood waters and determined the flow of water to fertilize crops. His palace priests learned to observe the movement of the planets and stars in the heavens and began plotting their course to better predict the changes in the seasons, so decisions could be made as to when to irrigate, when to sow, and when to reap. Armed with the new sciences of astronomy and mathematics and later meteorological prediction, they were able to create sophisticated calendars that could dictate, with near exactitude, when each activity needed to be rendered to ensure generativity and to secure a bounty. The ability to capture the secrets of nature and put them to practical use, to administer the economic and political functions of the kingdom, was a godlike quality.

During the transformation into hydraulic society, interest shifted from the gods of vegetation and animal fertility that characterized the Neolithic era to the sky gods—the sun, moon, and stars in the heavens. The former gods, notes Lewis Mumford, appeared fragile and vulnerable, while the gods of the sky appeared powerful, distant, and implacable, much like the kings who ruled over hydraulic society. Atum, Enlil, and Marduk were all "incarnations of cosmic power."[32] Understandably, the pharaohs of Egypt built great pyramids reaching up into the heavens and entombed their dead rulers inside, indicating the link they enjoyed to the cosmic kingdom.

In all of the great hydraulic civilizations, the kings increasingly took on divine attributes and eventually came to see themselves as sons of gods. The hydraulic societies in Egypt, Babylon, Assyria, and Persia were all theocracies. Mumford sums up the social history of the period. He writes:

> Space and time, power and order, became the main categories
> of a divinely regulated existence: the recurrent movements of
> the moon and the sun, or great expressions of natural power,
> such as flood and storm and earthquake, left a profound
> impression on the mind and awakened, it would appear, at
> least in the dominant minority, an interest in exerting their
> own physical power in imitation of the gods themselves.[33]

By identifying themselves with the impersonal and all-powerful order of the heavens, the divine kings assured their own power as well as the legitimacy they needed to rule over their kingdoms on Earth. The Sumerian king, it was said, was endowed with divine qualities in the womb and after birth was nurtured by the gods. His enthronement and coronation elevated him to the status of the divine.[34] He was, in essence, the adopted son of the gods, with divine authority on Earth.[35]

In Egypt, the pantheon of gods gave way to the all-powerful sun god, and the cult of Ra became the prevailing religion during the Fifth Dynasty.[36] The Sun God was declared the only god by the Pharaoh Akhenaten in the eighteenth century BC, a move that allowed him license to close the temples representing the other gods, abolish their priesthoods, and eliminate any challenges to his supreme authority. While his consolidation of power was short-lived, the notion of one god continued to gain sway. When Egypt succeeded in conquering and occupying foreign lands, the Sun God, the supreme god of Egypt, became "the Lord of the Universe."[37] American archaeologist and historian James H. Breasted makes the damning observation that "monotheism is but imperialism in religion."[38] In China, the emperors of the Chou Dynasty as well as emperors in subsequent dynasties used the term "Son of Heaven," and while they were considered to be humans, they were viewed as cosmic emissaries on Earth.[39] As power became more centralized on Earth with the consolidation of great hydraulic societies, so too did it become so in the heavens above. Not surprising. Every society and civilization in history has concocted an elaborate cosmological narrative that is a mirror image of its own labyrinthine social relationships as well as its relationships to the natural world. The cosmology comes to justify the established order while those in power legitimize their actions as conforming to the natural order of things.

The shift from mythological to theological consciousness and monotheism was a seminal turning point in the human journey. Cosmology became humanized, signaling humankind's new sense of its unique place in the grand scheme of things. Granted, in the great hydraulic civilizations, only one person—the God-King—becomes truly separate and distinct, an individual if you will. But the very idea of an individual was so shattering to the human psyche that it had to be locked up in divine robes. Subsequent generations, down through the millennia that followed, would gradually claim a similar status as they became more individualized, independent, and empowered. Selfhood, however, would not become a universal concept until the American and French revolutions of the modern era. But in ancient Sumer and the other great hydraulic civilizations, the journey to selfhood began with the rulers who staked their claims to autonomy and sovereignty on the cosmological narrative of divine conjugation or appointment.

THE DEVELOPMENT of an increasingly humanized universal God in Mesopotamia, Egypt, and the other great hydraulic civilizations to the east in India and China laid the groundwork for monotheism and the birth and spread of the world's great axial religions. Judaism and its offshoots, Christianity and Islam in the West and Buddhism in India, were weaned either in hydraulic civilizations or on their peripheries.

THE PEOPLE OF THE BOOK

Unlike the early mythological consciousness, which reflected the way of life of forager/hunter and garden agriculture societies and was transmitted orally, theological consciousness was the product of highly advanced agricultural civilizations and was transmitted by writing. The Jews are still referred to, even today, as the "People of the Book." Although literacy among the Jewish people was extremely high by the sixth or seventh century BC, the other axial powers enjoyed far smaller literacy levels until well into the modern era.[40] Still, theological consciousness is made up of stories that are written rather than told. The change in consciousness that accompanied the shift from an oral to a script state of mind is enormous.

To understand the full impact of the empathic surge brought on by monotheism and the world's axial movements, we need to understand how script cognition differs from oral cognition. Both forms of communication allow human beings to tell their story, but the narratives they tell have the unmistakable mark of the communication media being used. That's because modes of communication help create the very consciousness that they also manage. As the late Canadian philosopher Marshall McLuhan observed, "The medium is the message."

Oral consciousness relies on hearing, while script consciousness relies on sight. This difference alone accounts for the profound change in human consciousness that distinguishes a written culture from an oral one. Hearing is the most internalizing of the senses. While touch, smell, and taste also penetrate the interior of one's being, hearing is a more powerful experience as anyone who has ever enjoyed music knows so well. Hearing is a deeply participatory experience. It engulfs. One can immerse oneself in sound.

Vision, by comparison, is the least intimate and most abstract of all the senses. Sight isolates and dissects. As St. Louis University professor emeritus Walter Ong observes: "A typical visual ideal is clarity and distinctness, a taking apart. . . . The auditory ideal, by contrast, is harmony, a putting together."[41]

Oral cultures are deeply participatory. Often individuals from highly literate cultures are surprised and even put off by the nature of social discourse when they visit a country where the population is largely illiterate. In oral cultures, people huddle together when they speak and often seem to converse all at once as a group. There is little sense of personal boundaries. The "in-your-face," close-up conversation sometimes is regarded as a violation of one's personal boundary by guests. Visitors often are unable to make out who is saying what to whom, although the participants seem quite able to follow the flow of the conversation. For them, social cohesion overrides individual clarity. Sociality is not experienced in a linear way—he talks, she listens, she talks, he listens. Rather, the conversation is a communal one and often near simultaneous. What the individual has to say is not treated in isolation as an autonomous utterance but, rather, as an undifferentiated part of a community conversation. What counts is the ongoing collective meaning established by the group.

Sight, however, is always an individualized experience. One zeros in on another. With sight, it is very clear where the boundary is that separates the viewer from the seen. Sight creates a predisposition to think in terms of a subject and objects.

While sound surrounds, sight extends. The first leads to a cocooning sense of awareness and the second leads to an exploratory awareness. In oral cultures, life is lived publicly and the very notion of privacy, of being alone with one's thoughts or wandering off, would be regarded with suspicion. Historian Georges Duby points out that as late as the medieval era, when literacy was still low and consciousness was still overwhelmingly oral, "solitary wandering was a symptom of insanity. No one would run such a risk who was not deviant or possessed or mad."[42] Withdrawal from group activity was frowned upon and openly chastised.

Because in oral cultures life was lived publicly and privacy was considered bizarre, the notion of intimacy, which is so important to the development of empathic expression, was virtually nonexistent. In communal, oral cultures, everyone is always together. Even sexual activity was barely concealed, as people all slept huddled together through most of human history.

Writing introduces the idea of privacy. When composing a sentence, one is left alone with one's thoughts. Even though in early script cultures, people generally would read manuscripts aloud and together, eventually reading became more of a solitary activity. But even when reading alone, the individual would always speak the words aloud, again reinforcing the primacy of sound over sight.

During the long transition from oral to written cultures, the manuscript was seen as an adjunct to speech, as a less reliable medium of communications. Even account books were read aloud in the medieval era to assure everyone that what was written on the ledger could be trusted. The word "audit" has survived the transition into a literate culture and exists as a kind of historical reminder of the great store placed in oral communication in bygone times. In his commentary on the Gospel of Luke, Ambrose of Milan remarked that "sight is often deceived, hearing serves as a guarantee."[43]

Of the many thousands of languages that have been spoken in human history, only 106 have been put into writing sufficiently to produce literature. The late American linguist and anthropologist Munro S. Edmonson reminds us that of the three thousand languages that still exist today, only seventy-eight have literature.[44]

Whereas oral languages generally contain only a few thousand words, written languages often contain hundreds of thousands of words. English boasts more than one and a half million words in its arsenal.[45] This means that written languages offer a far more extensive menu of terms to describe every aspect of reality, including feelings, states of mind, and relationships. They contain a vast library of metaphors and terms by which people can explain themselves and understand the feelings and thoughts of others.

The ability to use language to describe one's feelings, tell one's story, and share experiences intensifies and deepens empathic expression. The more subtle the meaning of the words one can use to show one's feelings, the more able one is to communicate a deep sense of their situation and enlist an equally informed emotional response. Not being able to tell someone how one feels weakens the empathic impulse and response. That's why a written story of another's plight, if sufficiently nuanced and told in a compelling manner, can often elicit a more intense empathic response—even though the story might relate to a fictional person or someone one has never met—than a real-life, real-time encounter.

Oral cultures rely on formulaic means of expression in order to assure memory. Mnemonic speech patterns and the use of clichés were essential ways of maintaining the store of collective knowledge. Only by repeating standard lines of thought over and over could society guarantee predictable social intercourse. But formulaic responses are generalized utterances made to fit particular circumstances. They very often don't penetrate to the core of the unique situation at hand, and therefore don't adequately describe what's going on. Written language, however, allows communications between people to break out of the straitjacket of formulaic interaction. Every sentence is uniquely composed to communicate the particularity of the situation. Communication is individualized.

When children are raised in a writing culture, they come to use the same nonformulaic composition of sentences when they talk to others. The very act of becoming literate teaches people to treat every living sentence—whether orally or pictorially—as a unique construct uttered by a unique individual, tailored to a unique experience. The process of communication becomes increasingly individualized while the utterances become increasingly subtle so that one really knows how a unique other person feels and thinks. In other words, unlike a formulaic oral culture where people communicate in generalized clichés, talking at each other without deeply touching each other—communal talk— writing cultures encourage the individualization of language, both in writing and social discourse, and, by so doing, foster the creation of a growing selfhood. Since empathic extension deepens and universalizes to the extent that communication between people is increasingly individualized and expressive, writing cultures become a watershed in the evolution of empathic sensibility.

Soviet neuropsychologist Aleksandr R. Luria studied nonliterate people living in remote areas of Uzbekistan and Kirghizia from 1931 to 1932. His findings show the clear difference in consciousness that exists between oral and literate cultures, especially when it comes to emotional intelligence.

Luria attempted to get illiterate subjects to engage in self-analysis. Ong points out that to be self-analytical, one needs to isolate the self from the community in order to examine the self and describe it.[46] People living in an oral culture in which the collective "we" dominates and differentiation into a recognizable self is constrained are unable to think in self-analytical terms.

Luria reports on a middle-aged illiterate man who lived in a mountain pasture camp. Luria asked him, "What sort of person are you, what's your character like, what are your good qualities and shortcomings? How would you describe yourself?" The illiterate peasant responded, "I came here from Uch-Kurgan, I was very poor, and now I'm married and have children." Luria asked, "Are you satisfied with yourself or would you like to be different?" The subject responded, "It would be good if I had a little more land and could sow some wheat." Again Luria: "And what are your shortcomings?" "This year I sowed one pood of wheat, and we're gradually fixing the shortcomings."[47]

Luria found his illiterate subjects unable to analyze their feelings. They had no ability to articulate their own emotions. They lacked any sense of introspection. They could only describe themselves and their relations to others in the most concrete external ways.

His subjects were also unable to think abstractly and create symbols. For example, when shown geometric figures, they did not identify them as symbols but only as concrete things. When shown a circle, they would call it a plate, moon, or watch. They called a square a mirror or house.[48] Nor were they able to categorize things by group. For example, they were shown a hammer, saw, log, and hatchet, and asked to group together the items that were similar. The respondents consistently thought of the group in situational terms rather than categorical terms. Instead of putting the three tools together under tools, they put them together in the way they would use them. One respondent said, "They're all alike. The saw will saw the log and the hatchet will chop it into small pieces. If one of these has to go, I'd throw out the hatchet. It doesn't do as good a job as a saw."[49]

The point is that self-analytic thinking and categorical thinking are "text-formed thought," says Ong.[50] The very act of reading is a private experience. One is dislodged from the communal conversation and reads someone else's thought from a distance. While reading sacrifices the intimate participation characteristic of oral cultures, it allows one to be alone with someone else's thoughts as well with one's own thoughts as one ponders what he has read. Reading creates the conditions for introspection—that is, internalizing the meaning of a conversation alone.

Ong, echoing the analysis of Eric Havelock in his masterwork *Preface to Plato*, observes that:

> By separating the knower from the known, writing makes possible increasingly articulate introspectivity, opening the psyche as never before not only to the external objective world quite distinct from itself but also to the interior self against whom the objective world is set.[51]

The connection between the advent of writing, its facilitation of introspection, and the emergence of the world's great axial religions is not lost on Ong. He concludes,

> Writing makes possible the great introspective religious traditions such as Buddhism, Judaism, Christianity, and Islam. All these have sacred texts.[52]

"In the beginning was the Word and the Word was with God." And God instructed his chosen people through the word laid down on two tablets, marking a great change in human consciousness.

> And he gave unto Moses, when he had made an end of communing with him upon [M]ount Sinai, two tables of testimony, tables of stone, written with the finger of God.[53]

When Moses descended from Mt. Sinai with the Ten Commandments, he confronted a rebellious flock. In his absence, a dispirited people had turned their backs on the Lord God of Hosts, creating a golden calf, a graven image, to which they paid homage. Moses admonished his people and told them that henceforth they would obey the Ten Commandments.

Here we see, in a single narrative, the clash of cultures and consciousness. Some among the Hebrews had slipped back to an earlier mythological consciousness, preferring to cast their lot with the earth gods. Moses, however, prevailed. His people would forever be the People of the Book. The new universal God communicated by the written word via his prophetic and priestly scribes on Earth. Here was an abstract concept of God, an immaterial presence, both immanent and transcendent, who chose an abstract medium to convey his thoughts and carry on a conversation with his chosen people.

After millennia of paying homage to earthly spirits and cosmic forces, human beings began to communicate with a God that was so abstract that they were not allowed even to refer to him by name, lest they risk reducing his majesty to their anthropomorphic whims.

The story of the Hebrew people begins with the Patriarch Abraham, who left his father, Terah, in the city of Ur of the Chaldees in Mesopotamia. It is a story of a people who made the historical transition from tribal beginnings to a great nation, from polytheism to monotheism, and from a still largely oral culture to the first nearly universally literate people on Earth.

The Hebrews were the first to communicate their culture through the written word. They used the phonetic alphabet that was invented by the Semitic people who inhabited Canaan. The alphabet came into existence around the second millennium BC.[54] Before that time script was in the form of ideograms in all of the hydraulic civilizations. Using the written word, the Hebrews became the first people to record historical events on Earth. They invented the notion of history, where real people with real names engage in real events that can be located in the past. While other literate cultures—the Sumerians, Babylonians, Assyrians, and Hittites—had begun to record historical events, they generally were treated episodically and in isolation, with only a vague historical sense.

The written word allowed the Hebrews to chronicle their own history. The use of the phonetic alphabet gave them a versatile writing medium for storing much more varied information with far more interpretative capability.

The idea of history is a critical watershed in human consciousness. Indeed, historical awareness is, in many respects, the critical subtext of theological consciousness. Unlike mythological consciousness, in which the past exists not chronologically but, rather, cyclically, and where each story is ever-present and perpetually recyclable—as in "once upon a time"—historical awareness introduces the idea that every event and every individual story is unique, finite, and unrepeatable. Historical awareness raises the bar of consciousness relative to the importance of each person's life and times. Being able to grasp the notion of a unique personal history, with a past, present, and future, is one of the distinguishing marks in the development of self. As we learned in Chapter 4, children around the age of three to four begin to make sense of their own past and begin to both distinguish it from and connect it to their present and an as yet unlived personal future. It is only when one grasps the notion of his or her own unique unrepeatable personal history that a sense of self finally emerges. As mentioned earlier, in mythological cultures, people live in an endless now where personal histories don't exist and life is lived within a narrow temporal circle of birth, death, and rebirth—what the anthropologist Mircea Eliade called "the Eternal Return."

Selfhood and personal histories go together. Neither can exist without the other. The leap forward into historical awareness and personal histories quickened the empathic impulse. The shift from empathic distress to empathic expression requires a sense of one's unique finite existence—one's history—as well as a sense of another's.

We empathize with another's plight primarily because we sense their mortality and their desire to persevere. It is because we sense our own fragile existence—our one and only life—in the life of another that we come to their assistance. When we share a common history with a fellow human being we heighten our awareness of their struggle and come to feel it as our common struggle. That bond provides a frame of reference for an empathic response to another's state of mind.

If a sense of history brought out a more differentiated selfhood—that each of our lives is unique and special—the concept of a universal God that rules over all of existence served to further separate the individual from the collective.

In mythological consciousness, the connection to the divine was spatially constrained. The gods lived side by side and watched over specific territories where people lived. All gods were local. They looked after their people, not the lives of individual members of the community.

The great hydraulic civilizations consolidated control over diverse peoples stretching across many localities and, therefore, extended the territorial boundaries of their divinities. The shift from earth spirits and vegetation gods to cosmic divinities and even a single sun god broadened the geographic reach. But even the great sun god Aton only ruled over the far reaches of the Egyptian kingdom. Everything beyond was the void.

The Hebrews, who began as a nomadic, pastoral people, took their god with them. He was not a local god but a universal one. His domain was all of existence and his presence commanded all of history. More important, he was everyone's god. While Yahweh told the Hebrews that they were to be his "chosen people," he meant only that they were commissioned to spread the word of God among all people.

THE INVENTION OF THE INDIVIDUAL

The most significant change brought on by the Hebrews was the break from mythological consciousness, in which divinities spoke to a collective "we," to theological consciousness, where a single universal and powerful God carries on a dialogue with each individual human being. Every Hebrew male learned to read the Torah so that he could know God's thoughts and enter into a personal relationship with the Lord. It is said in Jewish lore that God created Adam and Eve because he sought companionship and dialogue. To be a Jew is to engage in an ongoing personal conversation with the Lord Almighty. But the conversation was never meant to be an exclusive affair between the Hebrews and the Lord. God's presence is equally available to everyone. He is everyone's confidant, teacher, and guide.

One has to imagine the power of this new story. For the very first time, individuals, not collectives, are told that there is only one universal God that reigns over the universe, but that this God seeks a relationship with every single human being.

Every individual, regardless of their stature in life, has access to the Lord of lords. No other previous cosmological story had ever elevated the individual in this manner. Each individual is now personally responsible—independently of the collective—for their life and is entitled by God to have a personal relationship with Him. Although the relationship was patriarchal, and the faithful were expected to be obedient, the Hebrew eschatology made room for an ongoing conversation, even argument and rebellion between individuals and the Lord.

The new Hebrew narrative was as much about the emergence of the self from the collective as it was about the advent of monotheism. And although the Torah is full of stories of God taking revenge on his people for the acts of a few—Yahweh was a jealous God—it is also equally replete with stories of individuals being comforted by their exalted relationship with the Lord. In a sense, writing, literacy and monotheism, the idea of an abstract, all-knowing, universal God, and the emergence of an accountable individual self in a full relationship with the Creator are inseparable parts of a single dynamic. The Hebrew cosmology is the story of the birth of the individual from the "mist" of the collective. This awakening self-consciousness ushered in the first truly empathic surge in human history.

While the Jews were the first of the great axial religions, they share a common context with the other axial movements in India and China. All emerged either within or on the periphery of hydraulic civilizations. They were the first societies to employ writing. Their frame of reference was urban.

The increase in populations, made possible by agricultural surpluses, extended commerce and trade, and the consolidation of diverse peoples into larger, more complex social units, threatened traditional tribal affiliations. Forced migrations and resettlements, the turmoil of religious and political wars, and imperialist expansion into kingdoms and empires all took a heavy toll on humanity. It was out of the depths of human suffering brought on by the birth pains of civilization that the first great empathic surge was born.

The Jewish identity was forged in oppression. Enslaved in Egypt under the Pharaoh, the Jews eventually fled into exile. For forty years they wandered in the desert in search of the promised land. Their search was as much a spiritual as a geographic journey. Alone and homeless, and without traditional landmarks to guide them, they began to despair and to ponder the very meaning of their existence. They found themselves at the foot of Mount Sinai, when their spiritual leader, Moses, descended the mountain, clutching God's Ten Commandments, written on two tablets.

The Ten Commandments were meant to apply not just to the Jews but to all human beings. The author and lecturer Erich Kahler reminds us that it was "the first truly moral code in history."[55] If there is a central, underlying theme to the Ten Commandments it is to "love thy neighbor as thyself" (Leviticus 19:18).[56] In the Talmud, there is a story of a nonbeliever who told the great Hebrew scholar Rabbi Hillel that he would become a Jew if the rabbi would teach him the whole Torah while he balanced on one leg. Hillel's response was quick and to the point. He told the man, "What is hateful to yourself, do not to your fellow man. That is the whole of the Torah and the remainder is but commentary. Go learn it."[57]

Lest some infer that the Golden Rule applies literally to only one's neighbors and blood kin, the Bible makes clear that it is to be regarded as a universal law. In Leviticus it is written:

> [T]he stranger that dwelleth with you shall be unto you as one
> born among you and thou shalt love him as thyself; for ye were
> strangers in the land of Egypt.[58]

Although the Hebrews were initially a warrior tribe, and despite the fact that they were continuously involved in military campaigns—some offensive, others defensive—at the root of the mature Jewish psyche is an acknowledgment of human travail, oppression and the need to transcend hatred and live fraternally with one's fellow human beings. The messianic spirit, which is the heart of Jewish theology, is embedded in the idea of a future state where every human being can live together in peace and harmony. The very mission of Judaism is to spread out across the world and bring humanity together in a shared covenant of brotherhood. That mission is made all the more challenging because it was left to every individual to consecrate the covenant with their Lord—to act as Yahweh's personal emissary to the world. The covenant was not fated but rather voluntary. Every person is free to make a choice to be accountable to God and be responsible for his fellow human beings. The covenant represents the first glimmer of individual moral responsibility and a benchmark in the development of self-consciousness.

The Bible is, more than anything else, a compendium of individual stories of common people attempting to live up to this new idea of personal moral accountability. The new moral accountability goes beyond individual efforts of kindness to others. The Book of Deuteronomy, thought to have been written in the seventh century BC, speaks to the social consciousness of every Jew. There are strict prohibitions against economic oppression. Land owners are required to donate a portion of their harvest to the poor. Debts are to be canceled every seven years and usury is outlawed.[59]

THE GOLDEN RULE SPREADS
THROUGHOUT THE WORLD

The Jews, with their long history of suffering, understood the fragility of the human condition, the vulnerabilities of life, and the tragedies that punctuate the individual and collective history of humanity. The Golden Rule, "Love thy neighbor as thyself," is an acknowledgment of the common struggle of humanity to flourish. In the halcyon days, as well as the dark days, when arrogance prevailed or desperation set in, Hebrew prophets would come to the fore and admonish or remind their people that to live as "a human being" is to extend the empathic embrace to as wide a circle of humanity as possible.

Nor were the Jews alone. The awakening of empathic consciousness appeared across the literate world, from the flood waters of the Jordan River to the Indus River Valley and the flood plains along the Yangtze. The Axial Age is the first budding of empathic consciousness. In every instance, the emergence of this new message arose out of the travails of social turmoil. British author Karen Armstrong reminds us that

> [i]n China, the Axial Age finally got under way after the collapse of the Zhou dynasty and came to an end when Qin unified the warring states. The Indian Axial Age occurred after the disintegration of the Harappan civilization and ended with the Mauryan empire;[60]

Armstrong takes us on a journey through the Axial Age, highlighting the empathic surges that changed human history. She begins with Confucius, who lived in China between 551 and 479 BC. Confucius took exception to the orthodox religious observances of the time, with the heavy reliance on ritual performances and sacrifices to secure the favors of the gods. He preferred a more down-to-home metaphysics that concentrated on the day-to-day ways that people related to one another. When once asked how a person should act toward the gods, Confucius is reported to have said, "Till you have learned to serve men, how can you serve spirits?"[61]

For Confucius, learning how to become a mature human being—a *junzi*—was the key to a full spiritual life. Like the Hebrews, he preferred to concentrate on this life rather than the afterlife. He believed that the real quest in life was not getting to heaven but, rather, knowing the way. By that he meant that man's task is transcendence and that it is found in leaving one's ego behind and entering into deep compassionate relationships with others. "[T]o enlarge oneself," he explained, "one should try to enlarge others."[62]

Confucius believed that the practice of *junzi* begins with one's immediate family and then extends beyond to neighbors and all of humanity. When asked what the single most important advice he might offer to others would be, Confucius answered: "Never do to others what you would not like them to do to you."[63] Here, 5,000 miles away from Israel, in a wholly different culture, a Chinese scholar was advancing a variation of the Golden Rule. While Confucius never made claims of being anything more than a mortal human being and saw his role as a simple teacher, much like Moses and the other Hebrew prophets, successive generations would come to elevate him to an almost god-like status. There is often a thin line between being "enlightened" and being treated as a God in the eyes of others.

A long line of distinguished sages and teachers followed in the footsteps of Confucius. Mencius (372 to 289 BC), considered among many Chinese historians to be second only to Confucius in his impact on Chinese culture, believed, like the Hebrews, that the empathic impulse was more than individual acts of kindness to others. It was the social glue that held society together. That being the case, Mencius argued that government too was accountable and needed to express a like-minded empathy and compassion, especially toward the downtrodden. More than 2,300 years before the term "empathy" had been coined and cognitive psychologists and developmental biologists even understood the physiological and psychological basis for the phenomenon, Mencius wrote,

> When I say that all men have a mind which cannot bear to see
> the suffering of others, my meaning may be illustrated thus:
> even nowadays, if men suddenly see a child about to fall into a
> well, they will without exception experience a feeling of alarm
> and distress. They will feel so, not as a ground on which they
> may gain the favor of the child's parents, nor as a ground on
> which they may seek the praise of their neighbors and friends,
> nor from a dislike to the reputation of having been unmoved
> by such a thing. From this case we may perceive that the
> feeling of commiseration is essential to man.[64]

In India, like the Middle East and China, empathic consciousness emerged in tandem with the introduction of hydraulic civilizations. In India, however, it took a different turn. By the fifth century BC, the doctrine of karma had become widely accepted. Unlike the Abrahamic religions, which viewed each life as a onetime experience, followed by death and, in the case of Christianity and Islam, passage to the other world for the rest of eternity, the Vedic religions in India emphasized reincarnation. Every living being is caught up in an endless cycle of eternal return. During each lifetime, one's karma, attitudes, and behavior determined what kind of being they would be reincarnated as to live out the next time around. One might, for example, be reincarnated as a blade of grass or a king depending on how one lived out the last incarnation and the lessons one learned.

Like the Middle East, by the sixth century BC parts of India were undergoing a massive change from small-time agriculture to hydraulic civilization. Populations were increasing, cities were emerging, and diverse peoples were thrown together and consolidated into larger social units. Tribal bonds were giving way to kingdoms, and labor was becoming differentiated. Craftsmen, manufacturers, shopkeepers, and merchants were becoming prominent, literacy was on the rise, and a sense of individualism was emerging, at least among a privileged few. While the old Vedic rituals, with their heavy emphasis on karma and fate, still found ready acceptance among the more traditional and static rural-based tribal communities, they were less appealing to a new, highly mobile urban class. The idea of being constrained by one's karma was particularly unappealing among tradesmen and merchants who, through personal initiative, were bettering their lives in this world and seemingly defying their fate.

Concerned over the loss of traditional values, the growing avarice of merchants, and the alarming debauchery and moral decay that seemed to accompany urban life, a new set of voices emerged calling for a third way. They were called the "renouncers," and they called upon people to mend their ways and take a new spiritual path that would liberate people from the dreary cycle of death and rebirth by way of "enlightenment." But unlike the Hebrew prophets, who called on the people to reform the institutionalized practices of society, the renouncers asked people to withdraw from the life of worldly desires and lead a life of asceticism and meditation. New spiritual leaders—gurus—sprung up, each with their own set of practices designed to free people from their karma.

One of the renouncers was a man named Gosala who lived between 497 and 425 BC. He was called Mahavira, or the "Great Hero," by his disciples. Mahavira traveled far and wide in the Ganges Valley, practicing an extreme form of asceticism. He went naked, lived outside in the elements, did not take shelter, and allowed himself only the minimum food to ensure survival. Mahavira believed that the road to enlightenment required renouncing bodily desires, treading lightly on the Earth, and living a life dedicated to harmlessness. He extolled the idea that every human being and every other creature, even inanimate things like water, rocks, fire, and air, had a divine soul and that they all had come back to the present state because of their karma from their past life. Because everything has a divine soul (*jiva*), all things needed to be treated with the same respect and sensibility that one would expect to receive in return. Mahavira taught his followers to befriend all beings and to never harm another, however lowly their state of being. If they followed these tenets and practices, they could become a *jina*, a spiritual leader. His followers were called Jains, and their spiritual community still exists in India and elsewhere today. The Jains were committed to nonviolence.

> All breathing, existing, living, sentient creatures should not be
> slain, nor treated with violence, nor abused, nor tormented,
> nor driven away. This is the pure, unchangeable, eternal law,
> which the enlightened ones who know have proclaimed.[65]

Practicing harmlessness required incredible vigilance. One had to be careful to ensure that every movement and activity in life took into consideration the well-being of another. Even walking had to be engaged in with caution, lest one inadvertently step on a small insect. Jains are encouraged to limit their activity to the bare minimum, to avoid doing harm to another being.

The Jains were committed to befriending the totality of living beings and showing compassion to all. Ironically, their empathic engagement and commitment to extending compassion was so extreme that to practice it they needed to curtail the living of their own lives. By pulling away from the living of life, however, one is less available to others and less able to extend empathy.

If compassion requires engaging fully in life with others, but if so much of life is bound up in self-gratification and the pursuit of desires, how does one transcend personal ego? In the fifth century, a twenty-nine-year-old named Siddhartha Gautama—later known as Buddha—left a young wife and child and a comfortable home behind to search for the meaning of life. Troubled by the pain and suffering he witnessed around him and plagued by the inevitable decay and death that stalked life, he was determined to find out if there was another side of the story that might justify existence and even exalt life.

One day, according to the popular lore, Gautama remembered an incident in his childhood. He was sitting under the shade of a tree, watching the field next to him being plowed. He noticed that the plow had mowed down and killed several insects. As he peered closer at the dead bodies, he became overwhelmed with a sense of grief, as if it had been his own family that had been killed. The empathy he felt for their deaths released a strange sensation of pure joy. He instinctively moved into a yoga position and entered into a trance.[66]

At the time, he was unaware of why these feelings were aroused. But as an adult he came to realize that what he was experiencing was a moment that transcended earthly desires. Although it would have to wait until the late nineteenth century before the proper words could be put together to explain the empathic state of mind, the young Gautama learned its importance. Perhaps this sense of disinterested compassion was the way toward human enlightenment.[67]

Before this time, traditional yoga was based on the principle of withdrawal from the suffering around one by renouncing life and becoming an ascetic. Gautama reasoned that the yoga tradition took humanity the wrong way and needed to be reversed. By becoming mindful and attuned to others people's suffering and developing a distinctive sense of compassion, one could find the way to enlightenment. Instead of fighting against life by repressing and renouncing it, one needed to engage life and find meaning by one's universal connection to and deep feelings for others.

His yoga meditations enfolded in four stages. In the first stage, one becomes attuned to extending friendship to every human being. In the second stage, one learns to experience other people's suffering and pain as if it were one's own. In the third stage, one experiences "sympathetic joy" in the happiness of others. In the final stage, one becomes so immersed in universal compassion toward all other living beings that he transcends the pleasures and pains of life and experiences a sense of equanimity toward others—this is the stage of universal, disinterested compassion.[68]

Like today's object-relations theorists and philosophers of embodied experience, Buddha taught that the idea of an autonomous self was an illusion that leads to desires that can never be met. Our identities, he believed, are always made up of the relationships we have with others. If we are the sum total of the relationships that make us up, then "loving thy neighbor as thy self" is tautological and descriptive rather than prescriptive. The key to enlightenment is putting away the misguided notion that there is an "I" and realizing that there are only many unique "we's." If one begins to change one's frame of reference regarding the nature of self-awareness and individual identity and sees it as being made up of empathic relationships, then ego-driven libidinal desires become less important and even irrelevant to a fully lived embodied existence.

THE ENTROPIC DECLINE OF HYDRAULIC CIVILIZATION

The vast hydraulic empires of the Middle East, India, and China gave rise to a great leap forward in human consciousness and the first bloom of universal empathic sentiment. But in the end, they were unable to escape the verity of the Second Law of Thermodynamics. A strong body of research into the rise and fall of hydraulic civilizations has shown that while there are many explanations that account for their eventual demise, at the very top of the list is the entropy bill brought on by the changes in soil salinity and sedimentation.

In Mesopotamia, the alluvial soils were carried inland by river and irrigation water. The irrigation waters contain calcium and magnesium as well as sodium. When the water evaporates and transpires, the calcium and magnesium precipitate as carbonates, leaving the sodium embedded in the earth. If not flushed down into the water tables, the sodium ions are absorbed by colloidal clay particles, resulting in the soil becoming virtually impermeable to water. Heavy concentrations of salt block the germination process and impede the absorption of water and nutrients by plants.

According to the archeological records, what is now southern Iraq experienced a serious problem with salinity between 2400 BC and 1700 BC, while central Iraq experienced a similar crisis between 1300 BC and 900 BC. An increase in the salinity of the soil forced a shift from wheat cultivation to the more salt tolerant barley crop. Whereas in 3500 BC the proportion of wheat and barley production was roughly equal, in less than one thousand years, the less salt-tolerant wheat crop made up less than one-sixth of the agricultural output. By 2100, wheat made up only 2 percent of the crops in the same regions and by 1700 BC, wheat cultivation had ceased in the southern alluvial plain.[69]

The salinization of the soil also led to a marked decline in fertility. In the city of Girsu, for example, the average agricultural yield, according to the records, was 2,537 liters per hectare in 2400 BC, but declined dramatically to 1,460 liters per hectare by 2100 BC. In the nearby city of Larsa, the yield had slipped to only 897 liters per hectare by 1700 BC.[70] The impact on the cities, whose populations of priests, government bureaucrats, merchants, craftspeople, and soldiers depended on agricultural surpluses to maintain an urban way of life, was devastating. Once powerful Sumerian city-states were wracked by political and economic turmoil, and their elaborate and majestic infrastructures were left in disrepair, while populations shriveled and neighborhoods were abandoned, reducing these city-states back to barely functioning villages. The same hydraulic technology that unleashed a vast increase in water energy flow, allowing the Sumerian people to build the world's first great urban civilization, extend the empathic bond, and advance human consciousness, led to an equally significant entropic impact on the surrounding environment that, in the end, canceled out much of the gains, leaving both the civilization and the environment impoverished. Thorkild Jacobsen and Robert M. Adams of the Oriental Institute of the University of Chicago, in their landmark paper on the subject, published in the journal *Science* more than a half-century ago, concluded that

> [p]robably there is no historical event of this magnitude for which a single explanation is adequate, but that growing soil salinity played an important part in the breakup of Sumerian civilization seems beyond question.[71]

It should be noted that increasing salinity of soil led to massive crop failures and a similar entropy crisis in the Indus Valley 4,000 years ago.[72] Likewise, archaeologists have found evidence of soil salinity leading to catastrophic crop failure and the abandonment of territory in the ancient Mayan hydraulic civilization in Central America.[73] In point of fact, salinization of soil and entropic buildup have been a precipitating factor in the weakening and collapse of complex hydraulic civilizations throughout history, reaffirming the inescapable relationship between increasing energy throughput and a rising entropy debt.[74]

ALL OF THE GREAT axial movements stressed the importance of the Golden Rule. But it was in Rome that the full impact of the new dictum came to the fore with the rise of a new urban religious sect that would be known as Christianity. The early Christian eschatology represented both the final flowering of the empathic surge of ancient theological times and the bridge to the modern era of humanism and the secularization of empathic consciousness.

SEVEN

COSMOPOLITAN ROME AND THE RISE OF URBAN CHRISTIANITY

THE ROMAN EMPIRE represents the "high watermark" for ancient hydraulic civilizations. Although Rome was situated at the divide between the East and the West, and was therefore on the periphery of the hydraulic world, the Imperium Romanum occupied and administered much of the hydraulic areas of the Mediterranean and Middle East and relied on the bounty of their agricultural surplus to provide a substantial proportion of the grain to feed Roman citizens as well as its slaves and men under arms.[1] Equally important, Roman rulers borrowed much of the administrative knowledge and governing expertise of the great hydraulic civilizations to the east to fashion their own despotic rule. In particular, the Romans relied on the well-advanced system of general taxation and a salaried officialdom, perfected over three millennia of history in the great hydraulic cultures, to consolidate their rule over an empire that stretched into the southern Mediterranean, the Middle East, western Asia, and northern Africa, and as far north as Britain. Between the second and third centuries, Rome had become a well-honed bureaucratic behemoth, operating mines, quarries, giant tracks of farmland, and merchant fleets all connected by the most sophisticated waterway and road system ever created. Rome was the quintessential centralized state governed by massive bureaucracies and legitimized by divine authority, with tentacles reaching into every facet of life across an empire.[2]

"All roads lead to Rome." To understand the majesty of the empire, one need look no further than to the masterful road system that connected every part of the empire to the Roman gates. The Roman highway system, unequaled until the laying down of the interstate highway system across the continental United States in the 1950s, was like an enormous central nervous system, connecting disparate peoples and cultures into a giant social organism.

The road systems were an administrative marvel. Augustus created a vast communications network—the Roman Imperial post—made up of runners to speed communications between Rome and its territories. Road stations, equipped with scribes, were set up at intervals across the road network. Troops were billeted at the postal service stations and all along the routes to assure the safety of travelers, protect against illegal contraband, and thwart criminal assaults. The royal roads also allowed for the quick dispatch of troops to oversee the colonies.

The safety and ease of travel across much of the Roman Empire encouraged mobility and brought individuals from diverse cultures together. Traffickers along the highways included government officials, merchants, craftsmen, seasonal farm workers, masons, artists and performers, teachers and students, pilgrims, priests, tourists, the sick seeking medical care, and countless others. Innkeepers, hostelries, blacksmiths, and vendors serviced the thousands of travelers alongside the roads.[3] One could travel between twenty-five and thirty miles a day by horse and up to twenty miles a day by foot.[4] The city of Rome itself was a microcosm of the known world. Thousands of immigrants flooded into Rome every month, making it the first cosmopolitan public square in history.

The Tiber River and other riverways became a central part of the transport system. Grain from around the empire was delivered by barges at the port of Ostia and then transported up the Tiber to feed a burgeoning Roman population. By the first century AD more than thirty million modii (one modus is approximately one quarter of a bushel) of grain was being delivered annually to the port from northern Africa. Egypt alone provided nearly one-third of the grain consumed in Rome.[5]

URBAN CHRISTIANITY AND THE
GREAT EMPATHIC SURGE

Rome became the center of one of the great empathic surges in human history. While Jesus was crucified in Jerusalem, it was urban Rome that became the spiritual cauldron for a new religion whose mission, in part, was to spread Jesus' teachings and universalize empathy across the world. The Apostle Paul traveled nearly 10,000 miles on Roman roads in his lifetime, visiting heavily populated cities where he spread the good word and converted masses of urban dwellers anxious to recast their lives and fortunes inside the Christian fold.[6] Rome and, to a lesser extent, the smaller cities, were ripe for the Christian story with its cosmopolitan emphasis on introspection, tolerance, compassion, universal brotherhood, and redemption.

The city of Rome boasted a population of more than a million inhabitants.[7] Rome was a great melting pot made up of foreign migrants from as far away as Asia Minor and Syria to the east, Africa to the south, and Gaul and Spain to the north. Much of the population was made up of slaves and freedmen (former slaves) from the colonies. In fact, slavery was essential to the creation of an urban, cosmopolitan way of life. Slaves and freedmen became the motive force—the human energy flow—that allowed Rome to be transformed from a small urban enclave to a giant metropolis, a complex social organism that supported increased differentiation of skills, a more literate population, and expanded commercial exchange.

From the very beginning, Rome wore two faces. There was the Rome that conquered the world, enslaved millions of people, occupied other lands, delighted in cruelty, and built a stadium—the Colosseum—that could seat 50,000 spectators, who cheered as Christians, criminals, and slaves were fed to the lions. It was also a place where self-awareness grew, individuality began to develop, and tolerance toward other religions became commonplace.[8]

Rome's policy in regard to slavery accounts for much of the contradiction. In AD 28 there were three million slaves and four million free people in Italy, an incredible ratio—and a powerful captive energy force upon which to build a great civilization.[9]

Slavery originally was confined to household tasks. But the need to fill the Roman legions with new recruits led to the forced enlistment of peasants and a steady abandonment of rural land. The land was then consolidated into giant plantations—latifundium—owned by large landowners who brought slaves in to work the fields and manage the herds and forests. The sheer magnitude of the slave trade was staggering. For example, after the conquest of Tarentum in 209 BC, 130,000 inhabitants of the city were sold into slavery. In the aftermath of the suppression of the revolt in Sardinia in 177 BC, 80,000 Sards were enslaved and sent to Rome. Ten thousand slaves a day came through the single port of Delos.[10]

The slave economy allowed urban society in Rome to flourish. But the increased cosmopolitan sensibility was purchased at the expense of an enormous human entropy bill. Millions of slaves were worked to exhaustion and death to provide the energy to run the empire. Listen to this description by Apuleius of shackled slaves being beaten by their overseers as they turned the millstones that ground corn.

> I began to study the internal discipline of this fatal factory
> with interest. God! What a rickety population of human
> beings, their skin livid and marked by the lashes of the whip!
> How miserable were the tatters which covered but did not
> hide their backs blackened by scars! All had been branded
> with a letter on their forehead and wore a shackle around
> their ankle. Nothing could be more hideous than to see these
> spectres, their eyelids eaten away by burning vapour and
> smoke, their eyes almost deprived of light.[11]

Slavery was brutal, especially in the countryside; yet the empire also supported a liberal policy in manumitting slaves and granting citizenship. Former slaves and their sons were employed across the crafts and trades and made up the majority of the plebian class during Cicero's lifetime.[12]

The advent of the empire and the consolidation of control over the provinces brought new commercial opportunities and the influx of a new immigrant class into Rome. Foreign merchants, teachers and tutors, physicians, and artists of all kinds swarmed into the capital city in search of business, government employment, and various private placements. They were both freemen and freedmen.

By the time of the empire, the old Roman aristocratic families had lost much of their influence. Meanwhile, prominent landowners from the provinces and wealthy merchants, bankers, and retail traders exerted increasing power over the political comings and goings of the city.

In the first half-century after Jesus' crucifixion, when Christian communities appeared on the scene, Rome was a thoroughly international city where cultures and races mixed freely.[13] The cosmopolitan nature of the city is reflected in the decision by Caesar to ensure that all popular festivals in the capital be translated not only into Latin and Greek but also a number of other languages, including Hebrew, Phoenician, and Syriac.[14]

At the same time that Rome accommodated native languages in its midst, it also undertook the task of translating the works of other languages into Latin. The intention, according to Cicero, was to discover norms and values of universal appeal and to find a common ground shared by all of humanity. Nothing could be more important philosophically or politically for an empire that needed to integrate diverse local cultures into a more unified body politic with a shared social reality.[15]

Rome extended the notion of a shared human universality into the political realm with the liberal granting of Roman citizenship to all freemen in its colonies. Extending citizenship to people from Gaul, Syria, Africa, and other colonies made foreigners equal human beings in the eyes of the law—a legal precedent largely unheard of in the other nations and empires that preceded Rome.

The extension of citizenship encouraged greater mobility across the empire and helped create an esprit de corps that served to break down the parochialism of local cultural affiliation. Citizenship is a political right extended to individuals. By becoming a citizen of the empire, a person's traditional loyalties to a clan or ethnic group are weakened, while his sense of individuality is strengthened by dint of enjoying a common legal status with millions of other individuals. To be a citizen is to be an individual among individuals, all of whom identify with a legal jurisdiction as opposed to a bloodline.

This new sense of personal freedom was the subject of much discussion in political circles. Rome was praised by foreigners and natives alike for its tolerance of others and its desire to expand the human horizon. A Greek observer in the third century opined:

> Cannot everyone go with complete freedom where he wishes? Are not all harbors everywhere in use? Are not the mountains as secure for travelers as the cities for inhabitants? Has not fear gone everywhere? What straits are closed? Now, all mankind seems to have found true felicity![16]

Rome's efforts to universalize the human story and individualize the human spirit, while impressive, were not sufficient in and of themselves to create a qualitative leap in human consciousness. Cast adrift from their tribal bonds and thrown together with people of different cultures from around the empire, large numbers of individuals suddenly found themselves alone in dense urban environments and without a sense of identity. It's fair to say that the Roman Empire spawned a mass identity crisis. What was missing was a powerful new narrative that could put every single individual at the very center of a compelling cosmic story of creation, tribulation, judgment, and redemption and, by so doing, recast the very meaning of human existence. While Rome created the conditions and context, it would be a young sect calling itself Christians that would take Rome and the empire by storm with their story and remake the world.

To understand how this came about, it is important to get a feel for the social dynamics in Rome at the time Christianity emerged and who exactly the people were that became Christians.

Although the rulers of the empire forbade the formation of political associations, they did allow the creation of trade associations and clubs where foreigners could practice their national cults and perform funerary rituals. The problem with the national cults was that the gods were all local vegetation and fertility gods tied to the territory from which the foreigners came. They therefore lost their potency in the cosmopolitan atmosphere of a vast urban metropolis. Caught between old loyalties and the new conditions of urban life they faced in Rome, many foreigners sought political refuge in the mystery cults that emphasized individual salvation. While the mystery cults provided an opportunity to break loose from the old cult moorings that had tied the individual to the collective and the collective to an agrarian way of life back home, foreigners' cults in Rome were reluctant to establish a universal claim for their beliefs that would then have forced them to open up their ranks to outsiders. "The mystery cults in Rome," noted the late Christian historian George La Piana, "lived and developed under the constant strain of this interior conflict between two opposite tendencies, that of keeping their national or racial character and that of becoming really and truly universal religions."[17]

The attempt to rejuvenate local cults by introducing the more universal message of individual salvation into them left practitioners with a fragmented cosmic story, a hodgepodge that failed to meet either their need to find security in a past-collective identity or the existential needs of a new highly mobile population of increasingly individualized foreigners living in Rome. The only way to overcome the problem was to abandon the local agrarian gods worshiped in their former homelands and take on a universal theology of individual salvation. Reluctant to take the final leap, the cults remained in limbo, trapped between an older mythological consciousness and a new theological consciousness.

The fact is that they had little room to maneuver. If they had laid claim to universality, it would have put them directly at odds with the official cults of Rome. La Piana describes the seeming impossibility of the task at hand.

In order to conquer the Roman world they had to come to
terms with, and eventually to supersede, the official cults
of Rome, and to acquire a control of political power to the
point where their cause should be identified with the cause of
the empire. It was here that they failed, and finally met their
doom.[18]

Rome was more than willing to allow conquered people to practice
their cults privately if they also gave public allegiance to the official
gods of Rome. After all, by conquering local peoples, Rome had demonstrated the superiority of their gods over local deities. As long as
the many foreign cults practicing in Rome understood that their gods
were of lesser importance in the divine pantheon, Rome was willing
to entertain a laissez-faire policy.

The one group that potentially could have broken out of the pact and
challenged Roman rule was the Jews. They made up a sizable portion of
the foreign population in the Roman Empire. More than fifty thousand
Jews lived in Rome, while another five to six million lived scattered
mostly in urban settlements across the Roman Empire.[19] More important, their God was universal, immaterial, immanent, and transcendent,
and, therefore, fully capable of absorbing the official Roman divinity
cults with a more cosmopolitan and universal cosmic story, in which
each individual had a unique existential relationship to the Lord.

But for all of their universalism, the Jews still regarded themselves
as the "chosen people," God's appointed emissaries on Earth. So, while
the inclusivity of their story would be appealing to an increasingly
individualized, urbanized, and cosmopolitan populace, their tribal
exclusion closed them off from their fellow Romans. Jews did not participate in the official cult activities required of other groups living in
the empire. Their special dietary practices and other codes governing
social activity kept them one step removed from the life of the city.
They offered a spiritual universalism, but only by becoming a part of
the Jewish nation. The Romans, by contrast, offered a political and
judicial universalism, but their civic gods were too cold and distant to

address the angst of an increasingly individualized Roman population in search of personal identification within a larger cosmic story.

Neither the Jews nor the cult of the Roman pantheon of gods could provide the new urban population of Rome the very personal spiritual succor they so desperately craved. Rome was ready for the Christian story. Erich Kahler eloquently sums up the historic significance of the rise of Christianity in Rome in the first three centuries of the AD era.

> The fundamental innovation of this whole epoch is that the individual stands forth, the lonely private individual, with all his ancestral, tribal bonds broken off, the earthly individual standing on his own feet, under the vast sky of universality. And this is the turning point of human history. From now on, from the beginning of the Christian era, the individual is the point of departure for all coming events, and the new developments are directed toward building up worldly communities of individuals, toward the formation of collectives in the true sense of the word.[20]

Who were the Christians? The archaeological evidence suggests that the early Christians came neither from the landed gentry nor the impoverished urban and rural poor. Rather, they were drawn from a heterogeneous group of upwardly mobile urbanites—freemen and freedmen—who enjoyed a modicum of status by dint of their skills, education, and newly acquired wealth but who were regarded with disdain and contempt by the traditional aristocracy. Although increasingly important in the commercial life of Rome, these upstarts were systematically barred from advancement into the upper reaches of political and social power by the traditional hereditary elite that that had long enjoyed a lock on Roman rule.

At least some of the early Christians were freedmen and the sons and daughters of freedmen. These former slaves had developed considerable skills in the crafts and trades and even in the arts and letters while in slavery and used their gifts to amass wealth and secure social positions as freedmen. It was not uncommon for persons of means to hand over the administration of their businesses to slaves and freedmen, who themselves became wealthy in the pursuit of their masters' business interests.

In the household of Caesar, slaves and freedmen who served a variety of bureaucratic functions often took freeborn women for wives, thus elevating their social status. It is estimated that two-thirds of the male members of the household of Caesar—both slaves and freedmen—married freeborn wives.[21] Conversely, slave-born women also married freemen, which elevated their status to freedwomen. One study of ancient records showed that 29 percent of slave women married their patrons.[22]

The early Christian movement—often referred to as Pauline Christianity after the apostle Paul—concentrated in major urban centers where large clusters of merchants and tradesmen lived. Besides Rome, early Christian associations grew in cities like Philippi, Petra, Gerasa, Beroea, Bostra, Philadelphia, Ephesus, and Corinth. While by modern standards these cities were small, their populations were packed together in dense living spaces, not unlike the urban tenements and slums characteristic of the nineteenth and twentieth centuries in London and New York City.[23]

The preponderance of evidence, then, shows that the early Christian converts came from a relatively small upwardly mobile middle class of free artisans and tradespeople—along with some former slaves—whose education level was high compared to the average Roman.[24] While men made up the leadership in the early Pauline Christian movement, women played a contributing role as compared to the Jewish community and other cults and associations.

If there is a single striking feature of the early urban Christian communities, it is the emotional intensity, affection, and goodwill among the members. Although on the one hand they were bound together in common longing for and expectation of a collective salvation in the next world with Christ's imminent second coming, on the other hand they were equally attached to each other in an intimate, almost familial way in their small communities. They looked on each other as brothers and sisters and children of Christ.

Pauline correspondence is laden with affectionate language. The faithful are referred to as "beloved." They talked of the apostles as "gentle among you, as a nurse would care for her own children." The outpouring of personal affection was unusual by the standards of the day and without historical precedent. Members were encouraged to approach local leaders "in love" and to "greet all the brothers with a holy kiss."[25] These new communities became tantamount to a reconstruction of family but, this time, one bound together by individuals committed to their personal salvation and the salvation of others among the faithful. Here was a new kind of family held together by theological beliefs rather than blood-ties and geography. Christian historian Wayne A. Meeks sums up the sociological significance of these new kinds of families.

> Whatever else is involved, the image of the initiate being adopted as God's child and thus receiving a new family of human brothers and sisters is a vivid way of portraying what a modern sociologist might call the resocialization of conversion. The natural kinship structure into which the person has been born and which previously defined his place and connections with the society is here supplanted by a new set of relationships.[26]

For freemen and former slaves who had suffered under the yolk of oppression, lost their traditional tribal moorings, and who faced this world and the next alone, Jesus' personal story resonated. Jesus' parents, Mary and Joseph, were common folks. Jesus was likely a carpenter. He mixed freely with people from all walks of life. He condemned the rich and powerful for oppressing the people. He said that everyone was equal in the eyes of the Lord. He stood up to tyrants and suffered a cruel and painful execution for his beliefs. But through it all, he preached love, even toward one's enemies. His strength came not from exerting brute force but from being vulnerable and open. In Jesus we are confronted with an individual who makes the conscious choice to empathize with his fellow human beings—not just immediate kin but every human being—even the lowest. The Christ story is first and foremost one of emotional equality.

> And [He] hath made of one blood all nations of men for to
> dwell on all the face of the earth. . . .[27] There is neither Jew
> nor Greek, there is neither bond nor free, there is neither male
> nor female: for ye are all one in Christ Jesus.[28]

Jesus' empathic impulse extended far beyond the accepted modes of the day. He reached out, even to those who would be his enemy, and offered up his vulnerability. In his sermon on the Mount, Jesus says to the faithful,

> Ye have heard that it hath been said, An eye for an eye, and a
> tooth for a tooth: But I say unto you, That ye resist not evil:
> but whosoever shall smite thee on thy right cheek, turn to him
> the other also.[29]

Jesus then asks his fellow human beings to do the unthinkable—to love their enemies—the ultimate expression of universal empathy and compassion. Christ says,

> Ye have heard that it hath been said, Thou shalt love thy
> neighbor, and hate thine enemy. But I say unto you, Love
> your enemies, bless them that curse you, do good to them that
> hate you, and pray for them which despitefully use you, and
> persecute you.[30]

In one of his last utterances, while bleeding to death on the cross, he pleads with God to forgive his executioners, "for they know not what they do."[31] And finally, for all those who suffered in silence and anguished over an unsure future, Jesus offered the ultimate reward, eternal salvation in the world to come.

By being part of an extraordinary story—the birth, life, death, and resurrection of the only son of God—thousands of upwardly mobile Roman middle-class individuals could leap beyond their ambivalent social status and become part of a cosmic narrative that transcended the power even of Caesar. At the same time, their individual, existential search for love, affection, intimacy, and companionship in a highly differentiated and estranged urban environment found an empathic friend in Jesus, who understood their vulnerability and the oppression they suffered and who "felt their pain." Jesus was also a role model whose own unselfish empathic behavior was universal and unconditional. Just as Jesus was vulnerable and oppressed but eventually triumphed by being resurrected to heaven, so too will everyone else be that walks in his path and accepts him as Christ.

The question of vulnerability is particularly important to the Christian story. Jesus' own vulnerable body—his corporeal existence—is put at the very center of the Christian narrative. *The Passion of the Christ* portrays a weak individual being, struggling to bear his cross on the long, winding trek to the hill where he'll be crucified. Along the route, he is beaten by his tormenters and stumbles and falls from the weight of the cross bearing down on him. His journey is torturous and conjures up an empathic response by all who hear about it and have had their own crosses to bear. Jesus' suffering becomes theirs just as their suffering becomes his. The journey to the cross awakens a universal sense of empathic extension. It's a recognition of the vulnerability and mortality of life and everyone's very private struggle against oppression, injustice, and intolerance. Vulnerability is the great equalizer.[32] Beyond status distinctions and the many other things that divide us from one another, we are all mortal—we each live and die. Awareness of our common vulnerability and mortality is the essential foundation for empathizing with our fellow beings.

Unfortunately, the universal empathic embrace extended to all human beings became increasingly conditional over the course of the next several centuries with the introduction of the devil into human affairs. The devil played virtually no role in Judaism. Satan came on the scene in the form of a demon, shortly after the crucifixion, among some Jewish groups. But the devil as a key player, pitted against Christ and the Lord, with vast power to deceive, sow seeds of chaos, and even challenge the power of God, was a Christian invention. Mark introduced "the devil" and his demonic kingdom. In the ensuing centuries the devil has been used as a device to demonize nonbelievers, the Jews, heretics, and others. Nonbelievers are accused of being "possessed" by Satan and recruited to help the forces of evil, in open rebellion to God. Satan, for all intents and purposes, has become the "other" in Christian eschatology—the alien in our midst, who lurks in the shadows, ready to seduce the faithful and turn them into agents of evil.

While the concept of us versus them has existed from the beginning of human existence, the Christian spin universalizes the distinction. Anyone who doesn't accept Christ is doomed to join Satan in the fires of hell for all of eternity. There are only the true believers, the unfaithful, and the nonbelievers. Princeton University professor of religion Elaine Pagels suggests that

> [w]hat may be new in Western Christian tradition . . . is how the use of Satan to represent one's enemies lends to conflict a specific kind of moral and religious interpretation, in which "we" are God's people and "they" are God's enemies, and ours as well. . . . Such moral interpretation of conflict has proven extraordinarily effective throughout Western history in consolidating the identity of Christian groups; the same history also shows that it can justify hatred, even mass slaughter.[33]

THE OTHER CHRISTIANS

It might have been otherwise. In the decades after the crucifixion and into the second century and beyond, there were other voices within the burgeoning Christian community who had a very different read on the Jesus story. In December 1945, an Egyptian peasant digging near a boulder uncovered a jar containing thirteen papyrus books bound in leather. Among the texts was the Gospel of Thomas. The first line of one of the texts reads: "These are the secret words which the living Jesus spoke, and which the twin, Judas Thomas, wrote down."[34] The writing contained some theological bombshells. Criticism was heaped on some key Christian beliefs at the time, including the idea of a virgin birth and the bodily resurrection of Christ. The jar also contained other gospels—the Gospel of Philip, the Gospel of Truth, and the Gospel to the Egyptians.

The documents date back to AD 350 to 400 and are translations of earlier manuscripts thought to be written around AD 140.[35] Some scholars date the original versions of these gospels to the "second half of the first century" (AD 50–100), making them contemporary with or even earlier than the Gospels of Mark, Mathew, Luke, and John, long considered the orthodox interpretations of the Jesus story.[36] These gospels represent the beliefs of early Christian communities who called themselves Gnostics. The term derives from the Greek language and means "knowledge." The Gnostics used the term in a more particular way, to mean "insight"—to know oneself. The Gnostics believed that "to know oneself . . . is to know human nature and human destiny."[37]

The Gnostics thought of Jesus not as a god but, rather, as an enlightened prophet and spiritual leader. Parts of the gospels read more like modern-day self-help books than theological tracts. Jesus is viewed almost in therapeutic terms as a mentor who has come to rid us of our illusions and help us achieve personal enlightenment.[38] The notion of original sin, repentance, and "bodily" salvation in the next world are looked on as naïve and misguided understandings of the meaning of the Jesus story propagated by the Pauline movement after Jesus' death.

Some scholars note the close parallel between Jesus' teachings as expressed in the Gospel of St. Thomas and Hindu and Buddhist teachings at the time. Edward Conze, the British historian, observes that "Buddhists were in contact with the Thomas Christians . . . in South India."[39] Buddhist missionaries were even proselytizing in Alexandria, where Gnosticism was being practiced in the period of AD 80 to 200.[40]

The evidence of a Buddhist connection is still speculative. Elaine

Pagels, in her book *The Gnostic Gospels,* says it's not unlikely that a similar strain of thought might have emerged independently in both India and the West.[41]

What we do know for sure is that in both the East and the West during this period, there was a deep sense of alienation as people struggled to find personal meaning in a world in the heaves of shifting from tribal bonds to individual self-awareness, from rural to urban ways of living and from oral to partially literate cultures. The search for meaning led some to embrace the Pauline story of original sin, repentance, and otherworldly salvation in Christ, while others were more attracted to the ideas of transcendence by way of personal enlightenment. The latter, according to the German philosopher Hans Jonas, were the first to experience the kind of existential crisis we normally associate with twentieth-century thinking.[42] Others, like the Dutch theologian Gilles Quispel, suggest that Gnosticism grew out of an awaking universal "experience of the self," grafted onto a religious framework.[43]

Clearly, the Gnostics viewed Jesus as a human being who had achieved enlightenment. There is no talk of him performing miracles or referring to himself as the Son of God or any recollection of Jesus dying for the sins of a fallen humanity.

On the question of salvation in heaven, the Thomasian Jesus is dismissive, even sarcastic.

> Jesus said, "If your leaders say to you, 'Look, the [Father's] imperial rule is in the sky,' then the birds of the sky will precede you. If they say to you, 'It is in the sea,' then the fish will precede you. Rather, the [Father's] imperial rule is inside you and outside you."[44]

The Gospel of Saint Thomas breaks ranks with the whole notion of an afterlife. When asked by his followers when the Kingdom will come, Jesus replies "the Father's imperial rule is spread out upon the earth, and people don't see it."[45]

Even the Pauline notion that Jesus came to Earth to sacrifice his life to save mankind is rejected by the Gnostic Christians. In the Gospel of

Saint Thomas, Jesus tells his followers to look to themselves, not him, if they are to save themselves.

> If you bring forth what is within you, what you have will save you. If you do not have that within you, what you do not have within you [will] kill you.[46]

The Gnostics believed that every individual has a spark of divine light within him that can reveal the "Kingdom of God" and the Kingdom is the totality of creation and of existence in all of its majesty into which they are inextricably connected.

Two thousand years before the transformation to "psychological consciousness," the Gnostics had an inkling of what was in store for the future of humanity down the road. Unlike the New Testament gospels, which exalted Jesus as the divine messiah who had come to rescue humanity, the Gnostics saw him as a fully developed and self-aware human being whose life was driven by empathy toward all others and whose compassion extended to every living being.

In the New Testament gospels, Jesus asks his disciples who they think he is and Peter answers, "You are the Messiah."[47] By contrast, in the Gospel of Thomas, Jesus says to his followers,

> "When you come to know yourselves" (and discover the
> divine within you), then "you will recognize that it is *you* who
> are the sons of the living Father"—just like Jesus.[48]

For the Gnostics, ignorance of one's true self, not sin, is the underlying cause of human suffering. Therefore, the key to unlocking the divine in each person is self-knowledge through introspection. The "Kingdom," for Gnostics, says Pagels, is a "transformed consciousness," or enlightenment.[49]

When certain Gnostic texts refer to evil, their frame of reference has less to do with moral evil and more to do with emotional harm. The Gnostics argued that "terror, pain, and confusion" lie at the heart of human suffering.[50] The process of self-discovery—of finding the divine light within—starts with experiencing the fear of death and destruction and ends with finding one's human nature. That journey of self-discovery, however, requires putting bodily concerns behind—including the fear of death—and concentrating on the nonmaterial and spiritual aspects of one's being. The journey to sparking the divine light is ultimately a solitary one. Each person must find "the way."

While the New Testament offers resurrection into eternal life, the Gnostic gospels offer a spiritual transformation through personal enlightenment. In both cases, however, bodily experience is shunned. The Paulines view the body as fallen and depraved. The Gnostics view the body as a cause of suffering and an impediment to true enlightenment. As Pagels points out, "the gnostic tended to mistrust the body, regarding it as the saboteur that inevitably engaged him [Jesus] in suffering."[51]

By not fully recognizing bodily experience as an essential part of the human experience, and by failing to acknowledge that it is the very vulnerability of corporeal existence that makes empathic extension more intense and universal, Gnostic Christians did not succeed in incorporating the breadth of Jesus' message into their own worldly behavior. The critical question is whether enlightenment comes from fully participating in the world around us in all of its vulnerability and corporeality or by withdrawing to an inner world removed from the vulnerability of corporeal existence. The historical Jesus was fully engaged in the world.

What we do know is that both the Pauline Christians and the Gnostic Christians were products of an awakening self-consciousness weaned in a highly differentiated urban environment. The converts to Christianity were among the first people in the world to feel the pain of an existential sense of aloneness and the need to find new meaning in their lives beyond blood ties and geography. They found it in the story of Jesus. The fact that the son of God—or simply a great teacher—could be vulnerable and empathic, express unconditional love toward all human beings, and even give up his own life for humanity touched a deep, personal emotional chord in others. His life encouraged and inspired others to express their own vulnerability, empathize with their fellows, and live a compassionate life.

A NEW KIND OF PARENT

The empathic surge that found such a powerful outlet with the Christ story raises an interesting question. Did the new empathic feeling affect parenting and child-rearing practices? In other words, did more empathic adults become more empathic parents and raise more empathic children? Since the parent/child attachment is so critical to self-development and the emergence of an empathic frame of mind, an empathic surge must have affected child rearing. Not surprising, the evidence shows it did. While the changes might appear minuscule by modern standards, they were significant at the time.

Recall that the hydraulic civilization sparked the rise of patriarchy. Abraham, the patriarch of the Jews, was born in the hydraulic city-state of Uruk. As mentioned in Chapter 5, in the very first test of his allegiance, Jehovah, the divine patriarch, summoned Abraham to lead his trusting son Isaac up the mountain, where he was to obey his command to slay him to show his obedience to the will of God. Abraham dutifully prepares to slit his own son's throat but is granted a reprieve by God at the very last moment. The point of the story is that obedience to the divine father is the starting point in a patriarchal chain of command that requires complete obedience of wife and children to the family patriarch—obedience to fathers is the very foundation of patriarchal social relations and stretches from the heavenly throne to the hearth in every home. And Moses said to his flock, "Thou shalt also consider in thine heart, that, as a man chasteneth his son, so the Lord thy God chasteneth thee."[52]

The Old Testament is full of advice on the proper rearing of children. Corporal punishment and teaching the child to bend to the rule of patriarchal authority is commonplace. The punishment for disobedience can be as extreme as death. In Deuteronomy, Moses tells the following grim story to his fellow Israelites as a cautionary tale:

> If a man [has] a stubborn and rebellious son, which will not
> obey the voice of his father, or the voice of his mother, and

that, when they have chastened him, will not hearken unto
them: Then shall his father and his mother lay hold on him,
and bring him out unto the elders of the city, and unto the
gate of his place; And they shall say unto the elders of his city,
This our son is stubborn and rebellious, he will not obey our
voice; he is a glutton, and a drunkard. And all the men of his
city shall stone him with stones, that he die: so shalt thou put
evil away from among you; and all Israel shall hear, and fear.[53]

Corporal punishment of children was common in all of the great
hydraulic civilizations and in societies on their peripheries. In Rome,
however, small but consequential changes in child-rearing practices
occurred. Before the Roman period, children were regarded as either
miniature adults or not yet formed adults. The notion of a child as a
unique being whose world was qualitatively different from the adult
world would have been impossible to grasp. In the more urban setting
of Rome, a number of forces and influences came together to change
the way parents related to their babies.

To begin with, for the more upwardly mobile and affluent, more
leisure meant more time to nurture their young, including more time
to play and enjoy their children. Awakening self-consciousness and
more exposure to diverse others also created a more tolerant attitude
in general. The children became beneficiaries of the empathic surge.
Although patriarchy still ruled and corporal punishment was the norm,
some subtle changes came into child rearing, reflecting the new sense of
self-awareness and introspection. Most early Christians, some Gnostic
groups aside, believed that babies came into the world depraved sinners
and, therefore, required a heavy hand to break their demonic will. Yet
there was also the dawning realization that physical punishment could
embitter a child and make him that much more rebellious. Augustine
took exception to the traditional wisdom that physical punishment is
necessary to rid babies of their demonic spirit. He wrote:

The custom of kicking a stone, as if it were a destroyer of
friendship, is less obnoxious than that of hitting an innocent

child with the fist if he runs between two people walking together.[54]

By the fourth century, a newly Christianized Rome began to pass legislation to prohibit child abuse. These laws were as revolutionary in their day as laws prohibiting animal abuse in the twenty-first century. For as long as anyone could remember, infanticide, the selling of babies, and widespread sexual abuse of children were commonplace. The Church fathers, however, argued that babies had souls and therefore were important. They were all God's children. Church authorities even began the practice of providing aid to abandoned children.

But it's when one reads the New Testament, especially Jesus' references to children, that it becomes clear that a change, however slight, in the perception of babies has occurred. When the disciples asked Jesus "who is the greatest in the Kingdom of Heaven," he responded by calling a child to sit with them. He then said to his followers,

> Verily I say unto you, Except ye be converted, and become
> as little children, ye shall not enter into the kingdom of
> heaven. . . . Take heed that ye despise not one of these little
> ones; for I say unto you, That in heaven their angels do always
> behold the face of my Father which is in heaven. . . . [I]t is not
> the will of your Father which is in heaven, that one of these
> little ones should perish.[55]

Unlike the Old Testament, with its emphasis on "tough love," there is not a single reference in any of Jesus' teachings in the New Testament in which he advocates physical punishment as a disciplinary tool for children.[56] Although Paul commanded children to "obey your parents in all things: for this is well pleasing unto the Lord," he was quick to clarify his remark by saying to the fathers, "provoke not your children to anger, lest they be discouraged."[57] Here was a remarkably contemporary psychoanalysis of the impact abusive parenting might have on the development of the child. For fathers to even understand the causal relationship between their behavior toward the child and their children's subsequent emotional development required a sense of self-awareness, an understanding of how one's behavior might affect the emotional life of another, an appreciation of the child as a being unto himself and an ability to feel a certain amount of guilt in inflicting emotional as well as physical harm on a defenseless child. Whether many fathers understood the full ramifications of what Paul was saying is unclear. Still, one would be hard-pressed to find similar psychological observations in writings before this time.

Although infanticide, the sale of children, and abandonment were still rampant in the Roman era, historian Richard B. Lyman, Jr. notes a "substantial change . . . in the nurturant role of the mother."[58] By the seventh century AD, Lyman observes, "parental love is often described as natural and forthcoming."[59]

The point Lyman and other scholars make is not that mothers (or fathers) didn't love their children before, but that the love was immature because it failed to see the child as a unique being but, rather, as a projection of their being, not unlike the kind of love still expressed today by some parents. Lyman is skeptical that a modern sense of empathy existed at the time, arguing that it was not "yet part of the psychological equipment of parents."[60]

Lloyd deMause, whose book *A History of Childhood: The Untold Story of Child Abuse* is a gruesome account of the inhumane treatment of children from the rise of the hydraulic civilizations up to the eighteenth century, still has some encouraging things to say about the progressive changes in parenting during the late Roman period. He concedes that the Romans were "an island of enlightenment in a sea of nations still in an earlier stage of sacrificing children to gods, a practice which the Romans tried in vain to stop."[61] What can't be denied is that Roman law began to recognize infanticide as murder in 374 AD.[62] Parenting, at least among a certain segment of the populace, became more nurturing. A small but demonstrable change in attitudes and behavior toward children had occurred by the fourth century AD in Rome.

Lyman sums up the effect that early Christianity had on parenting and child-rearing practices. He writes,

The coming of Christianity certainly did not signal the end of the "dark ages" for children, yet it may well have meant the beginning of a slightly less grim outlook.[63]

The Christian empathic surge lasted a mere three centuries; but in that time it made an incredible mark on history. By AD 250 the number of Christians in Rome alone had grown to fifty thousand people.[64] By the early fourth century upward of a third of the Roman population were Christians, making them a formidable force in the life of the empire.[65] Unable to bully and silence them and increasingly concerned over his own loss of legitimacy and political control in a disintegrating empire, Emperor Constantine converted to Christianity.

In a single stroke, Constantine transformed a religion that claimed universality into the universal religion of the Roman Empire, granting Christianity the spiritual legitimacy and protection its leaders craved and the government the universal spiritual energy it needed to keep the empire united and afloat, at least for a time.[66] In the process, Jesus was given a makeover.

> Christ was no longer . . . primarily the god of the humble, the miracle-worker and saviour. As Constantine viewed himself as God's vicar on earth, so God was viewed increasingly as the Emperor of Heaven.[67]

The heads of the Church declared themselves the direct successors to the apostles and God's emissaries on Earth. They also reserved the exclusive right of taking confessions and granting absolution from sins. The bishops were henceforth regarded as the mediators between laymen and God on all matters regarding one's salvation. They alone could bestow grace. The Church was considered infallible and the earthly vessel of the divine spirit.

The Catholic Church was born. The Emperor Constantine coroneted the church, and the bishops, in turn, coroneted themselves as God's voice in this world. The disparate Christian communities—especially the Gnostic Christians—were silenced. Any opposition to Church doctrine was considered heretical and dealt with by excommunication. The great empathic surge that began with Jesus' own life on Earth, and that was carried forward by the Christian communities until well into the early fourth century, was diminished by the imperialization of the Church and left to falter with the collapse of the Roman Empire and the deconstruction of urban life in the sixth century.

Nonetheless, that something extraordinary occurred in the development of human consciousness in the Roman/Christian era is indisputable. We see it up close in *The Confessions* of Saint Augustine, the leading intellectual light in the early Church's existence. He was the very first person we know of to write an in-depth narrative about his own awakening self-consciousness. Others would follow over the centuries. Their autobiographies would be increasingly introspective, self-revealing and self-conscious, reflecting the steady—albeit episodic—advance in self-awareness. Saint Augustine, however, was the first to articulate a self-conscious appraisal of his own life journey, which is less a testimonial to the man than to the age in which he lived.

The fact that Saint Augustine called his essay *Confessions* is notable. Public confession was a critical part of the life of the early Christian monastic communities. Public confession was supplemented with private confessions, a practice that "spread from the monastery to the lay world."[68] The faithful were encouraged not only to divulge misdeeds but also evil thoughts and intentions.[69] The practice of private confessions compelled individuals to examine their innermost feelings in order to discover their true self. The reward for introspection and revealing one's innermost evil feelings and thoughts to those in authority—the priests—is absolution and God's grace, which brings a sense of relief to the sufferer of a bad conscience. Many in the psychiatric profession in the twentieth century regard the ritual of confession as the earliest example of the kind of therapeutic practices that became so popular in the 1960s.

The Confessions is Saint Augustine's very public airing of his very private interior life, rife with impure thoughts, ambivalence, and confession. It is, from beginning to end, a work of penitence. The man whose master work *The City of God* became the centerpiece of Catholic theology for 1,500 years, felt compelled to examine his inner life and his relationship to the world in the light of his own conversion to Christianity. His story is one of a man becoming self-conscious.

The Confessions was written between AD 397 and 401, after Augustine became the Bishop of Hippo and nearly ten years after his conversion experience.[70] The book is written in a self-questioning style, with the clear intent of trying to comprehend what in his own life experience led him to conversion and, equally important, to understand how that conversion changed his sense of self.

Augustine longed for happiness and peace of mind. In one particularly revealing passage, he anguished over his own depraved being that he was reluctant to confront but from which he could no longer hide. He laments:

> Oh Lord, You were turning me around to look at myself. For I
> had placed myself behind my own back, refusing to see myself.
> You were setting me before my own eyes so that I could see
> how sordid I was, how deformed and squalid, how tainted
> with ulcers and sores. I saw it all and stood aghast, but there
> was no place where I could escape from myself.[71]

It is only when Augustine lets go of his ego needs and surrenders himself totally to a belief in a loving God that he becomes whole. Only then does he experience God's grace.

Augustine took seriously the Greek aphorism "know thy self," and, by so doing, set an example for other Christians who would follow. While there is little in *The Confessions* that speaks to the empathic impulse awakened by self-consciousness, Augustine nonetheless made introspection a vital part of what a Christian life ought to be about. The practice of introspection served the Church but, in a more important way, also served human consciousness by providing it with the "practice" of self-questioning that leads to the development of a fully mature sense of individuality and empathic extension.

THE THERMODYNAMICS OF ROME

Like the great hydraulic civilizations on its eastern periphery, the Roman Empire met its own demise at the nexus of a great empathic surge coming up against an even greater entropic deficit. The empire extended its imperial reach over vast terrains and the city of Rome and other satellite cities, in turn, grew in population and became opulent by sucking ever more energy from slave labor and from the soil. The urbanization of the empire created the conditions for an empathic surge that culminated in the advent of Christianity. But as the new consciousness took shape above the surface, the entropic bill resulting from increased energy flow from the environment to Rome continued to mount under the surface. In the end, even the great Roman Empire could not escape the realities imposed by the thermodynamics laws and the ensuing entropy bill.

Rome owed its greatness to its brilliant military conquests. Roman armies captured Macedonia in 167 BC, annexing the land and seizing the wealth of its king. The royal Roman treasury became so large that it allowed the government to stop taxing its own citizens. Shortly thereafter, Rome annexed the kingdom of Pergamon, and the bounty doubled the Roman state budget overnight. The conquests of Syria, in 63 BC, and then of Gaul, brought considerable gold and wealth to the empire.[72] The military conquests were so successful, from an economic point of view, that they paid for themselves and provided surpluses for continued military ventures. Slave labor, mineral resources, forestland, and cropland provided an ever-accelerating flow of available energy for the empire. The expansionary period ended with Augustus's conquest of Egypt. So much wealth accrued from the annexation that Augustus celebrated by distributing coins to the plebeians of Rome.[73]

After suffering a series of military defeats to the Germanic tribes, Rome retrenched and devoted its energy to building an infrastructure to maintain its empire. The shift from a conquest-based regime to a colonizing regime proved costly. With no new revenues coming in from captured lands, Rome found itself without sufficient funds to provide for basic services. Augustus instituted a 5 percent tax on

inheritances and legacies to pay for the retirement of military personnel. The imposition of the tax angered the Romans, who had not been
taxed at all during the period of the late republic.[74]

The expense of maintaining a military was particularly burden-
some. The standing army drained energy from the empire and took
away gains previously enjoyed by the Roman population. The cost of
salaries, rations, billeting of troops, and equipment continued to go
up. So too did the cost of maintaining public works and a bloated civil
service.

The public dole had also grown considerably during the heyday
of expansion and now had to be maintained with declining revenues.
During the reign of Julius Caesar, nearly a third of the citizens of Rome
were receiving some form of public assistance.[75]

The sheer logistical weight of maintaining a vast empire became
increasingly costly. Garrisoning troops throughout the Mediterranean and Europe, maintaining roads, and administering annexed
territories consumed more and more energy, while the net return in
energy secured from the territories steadily dropped. Marginal returns
had set in. In some instances, it cost Rome more money to manage
certain colonies—Spain and England, for example—than revenue
generated.[76]

No longer able to maintain its empire by new conquests and plun-
der, Rome was forced to look to the only other energy regime available
to it: agriculture. The story of Rome's gradual decline is intricately
bound up with the waning fortunes of its agriculture production.

The popular conception is that Rome collapsed because of the deca-
dence of its ruling class, the corruption of its leaders, the exploitation
of its servants and slaves, and the superior military tactics of invading
barbarian hordes. While there is merit to this argument, the deeper
cause of Rome's collapse lies in the declining fertility of its soil and
the decrease in agricultural yields. Its agricultural production could
not provide sufficient energy to maintain Rome's infrastructure and
the welfare of its citizens. The exhaustion of Rome's only available
energy regime is a cautionary tale for our own civilization as we begin

to exhaust the cheap available fossil fuels that have kept our industrial society afloat.

Italy was densely forested at the beginning of Roman rule. By the end of the Roman Imperium, Italy and much of the Mediterranean territories had been stripped of forest cover. The timber was sold on the open market and the soil converted to crops and pastureland. The cleared soil was rich in minerals and nutrients and provided substantial production yields. Unfortunately, the denudation of forest cover left the soil exposed to the elements. Wind blew across the barren landscapes and water ran down from the mountaintops and slopes, taking the soil with them. Overgrazing of livestock resulted in further deterioration of the soil.

The continuing decline of soil fertility came just at the time when Imperial Rome began to rely on its agriculture to provide an energy substitute for its failing foreign conquests. During the later period of the Roman Empire, agriculture provided more than 90 percent of the government's revenue.[77] Food production had become the critical linchpin in the survival of Rome.

Supporting a growing urban population of nonproducers put increasing strain on small farms. Agricultural production intensified to keep up with the food requirements of the urban population and the army.

The free distribution of corn was instituted in Rome in 58 BC. Under Caesar Augustus, more than 200,000 people were being provided with free grain.[78] Later, free bread, pork, and salt were also distributed. Successive regimes switched back and forth between distribution of grain and bread at a token price.[79]

The overworked land further diminished soil fertility, which in turn led to even more intense exploitation of an already exhausted soil base. Small farm holders could not produce sufficient yields on the eroded soil to pay the yearly taxes (the government imposed a fixed tax on the land irrespective of yield). Farmers borrowed to stay in business. Much of the debt they incurred went to pay taxes and little or none was left over with which to make improvements. Without any other source of revenue, farmers could not afford to let their soil lie fallow long enough to be rejuvenated. Instead, they continued to lay down seed on an ever more exhausted soil base, which left them with even lower yields and greater debt loads. Small farmers were forced to sell their holdings or give them up to the lending institutions. Throughout Italy and the Mediterranean, large landowners bought up smallholdings, creating great landed estates—the latifundia. Much of the land was no longer fit for growing food and had to be converted to pasture to raise livestock. Impoverished and uprooted, Italian farmers migrated to the cities, where they went on the public dole.

In the fourth century, more than 300,000 people in the city of Rome were receiving some form of public aid.[80] The growth in city expenditures to subsidize the lifestyles of the wealthy; provide for the welfare of the poor; finance public works and government bureaucracies; pay for the erection of monuments, public buildings, and amphitheaters; as well as the costs involved in financing public games and displays, all stressed the agricultural-energy regime beyond its limits. Depopulation of the countryside took place throughout the empire. In some of the provinces of northern Africa and throughout the Mediterranean, up to half of the arable land had been abandoned by the third century.[81]

Depopulation of the countryside also had other repercussions. Abandoned land was no longer being stewarded. The result was even greater erosion and loss of soil fertility. Lowlands were hit particularly hard by the massive depopulation of the countryside. Wet fields were no longer drained in the early spring and therefore were left swampy. The spreading swampland became a breeding ground for mosquitoes, which caused a spread of malaria. The disease weakened an already dispirited and hungry population, further sapping the human energy reserves.[82]

Plagues broke out in the second and third centuries, killing up to a third of the population in some regions of Italy.[83] The reduction in population meant fewer people available to farm and to fill the ranks of the civil service and military. The situation became so desperate that the government was forced to reintroduce conscription to raise its army. In 313, the Emperor Constantine issued an edict requiring some sons of soldiers to be routinely conscripted—establishing a hereditary military service. Similar statutes were enacted in the early fourth century, creating a hereditary civil service.[84] More controversially, around the same time, Constantine instituted the colonate, which in effect bound agricultural workers to the land they presently lived on—establishing the concept of serfdom.[85] This practice would outlive the Roman Empire and remain in place until the great Enclosure Acts were enacted in the 1500s in Tudor England, freeing serfs from bondage to the land.

The colonate was too little too late. By the fourth century, the rural population was so diminished that the remaining numbers, even when yoked by law to the land, were insufficient to rev up agricultural production in dying fields.

Even as agricultural yields were falling, Rome was expanding its military in a desperate effort to maintain a collapsing empire. In the fourth century, 650,000 men were permanently in uniform and under arms and stationed across the Roman Empire. They required huge amounts of rations. If far removed from Rome, troops had to rely on procuring local food supplies, which put an additional burden on food production.[86]

Rome was experiencing the harsh realities imposed by the laws of thermodynamics. Maintaining its infrastructure and population in a nonequilibrium state required large amounts of energy. Its energy regime, however, was becoming exhausted. With no other alternative sources of energy available, Rome put even more pressure on its dwindling energy legacy. By the fifth century, the size of the government and military bureaucracy had doubled. To pay for it, taxes were increased, further impoverishing the population, especially the dwindling farm population. The empire, writes anthropologist Joseph Tainter, began consuming its own capital in the form of "producing lands and peasant populations."[87]

Weakened by a depleted energy regime, the empire began to crumble. Basic services dwindled. The immense Roman infrastructure fell into disrepair. The military could no longer hold marauding invaders at bay. Barbarian hordes began to whittle away at the decaying Roman Empire in distant lands. By the fifth century, the invaders were at the gates of Rome. The great Roman Empire had collapsed. By the sixth century, the population of Rome, once numbering more than one million, had shrunk to under one hundred thousand inhabitants. The city itself was reduced nearly to rubble, a stark reminder of how unforgiving are the energy laws.[88] The other great cities of the empire were abandoned as well as people fled into the countryside. Here they languished in bondage under the yolk of feudal lords who ruled over the manorial estates. Europe descended into the Dark Ages. The urban environment that had provided the context and stimulus for cosmopolitanism, the rise of Christianity, and the great empathic surge of the first three centuries of the new era was now a giant footnote in human history.

The entropy bill was enormous. The available free energy of the Mediterranean, northern Africa, and large parts of continental Europe, reaching as far north as Spain and England, had been sucked into the Roman machine. Deforested land, eroded soil, and impoverished and diseased human populations lay scattered across the empire. Europe would not begin to recover for another five hundred years.

The rise and fall of the Roman Empire has generally been treated by historians as a great political phenomenon. But on a more fundamental level, it is a classic example of a recurring theme in history where the synergies created by a new energy and communications regime facilitate more complex social arrangements, which, in turn, provide the context for a qualitative change in human consciousness. The change in human consciousness is played out in a dialectic between a rising empathic surge and a growing entropy deficit. As that dialectic unfolds, the empathic surge generally peaks at the height of the energy flow-through of the society, only to wane as the energy flow-through declines and the entropic deficit mounts. When the entropic externalities eventually exceed the value of the energy flowing through the society's infrastructure, the civilization withers and even occasionally dies. The empathic gains slow and even reverse as economic conditions worsen, political stability erodes, and desperation sets in. Social trust weakens and individuals draw in their emotional reserves to a smaller circle.

While the unfolding interplay between an empathic surge and an entropic deficit often—but not always—leads to collapse, what remains is a residue of the new consciousness that carries forward, if however tenuously, and becomes a memory lifeline to draw upon when new energy/communications regimes emerge.

The empathic surge in ancient Rome, with the birth of Christianity, left a powerful residue that fed new streams of consciousness throughout the Dark and Medieval Ages. Those streams finally burst forth in the Renaissance, with another empathic surge and accompanying leap in human consciousness, setting the stage for the modern era.

EIGHT

THE SOFT INDUSTRIAL REVOLUTION OF THE LATE MEDIEVAL ERA AND THE BIRTH OF HUMANISM

ROME WAS an eerie sight in the seventh century. The once-bustling megalopolis was reduced to ruins. Her ports were empty. Roman roads were in disrepair and little traveled. Commerce and trade had been reduced to a trickle. The great centralized bureaucracies that had managed a far-flung empire were no more. While the Catholic Church still nominally presided over the remains of the Roman world, in reality all politics became local.

The new centers of power were scattered across thousands of feudal fiefdoms, while commerce gave way to subsistence agriculture. The life of Europe reverted back to its rural roots. Feudal landlords ruled over manor estates worked by serfs who were yoked to the land. The collapse of urban life led to a concomitant drop in literacy and learning.

The dumbing down of the European population reached a low-ebb in the ninth century. In many regions, only the monks in the monasteries retained even a rudimentary literacy. Latin, once the universal language of the Empire, gave way to local languages and idioms as whole populations slipped back into a purely oral culture and consciousness. Life was cloistered, lived behind closed walls in thousands of little valleys and mountain fortresses. Travel virtually ceased, except for roving bands of criminals and an occasional itinerant trader. For several centuries, virtually all communications to the outside world were cut off. Spatial reach was constricted to the nearby forest edge or mountain range. Mobility, both upward and outward, was nonexistent. Temporality became limited to the recurring daily rounds and changing seasons. The great events of history, of which urban life and empires are made of and that mark the passage of time in a linear world, no longer existed. No one bothered to ask "what's the news," because there was little to report and few strangers to report it.

Life was precarious, pleasures few, and opportunities to advance nonexistent. There was, however, a reprieve, of sorts, even in the darkest days of the Dark Ages. Every human being, regardless of how humble his station and meager his lot, was put under the overarching cloak of the Church and promised that in return for his unswerving fealty and allegiance to the feudal order to which he was assigned and his undying faith in Christ and obedience to the Church fathers, he could expect eternal salvation and a better life in the world to come. It was the Age of Faith, and devotion itself became the social glue that assured that everyone would assume their proper responsibilities and obligations along the Great Chain of Being, in what Voltaire would later satirize as the "best of all possible worlds."

If there was little mobility and even less history to record, there was also a marked decline in differentiation of labor. The feudal society had only three classes: those who ruled, those who prayed, and those who fought. Aside from the lords, the clergy, and the knights in arms, everyone else were serfs and villeins who worked the land on the feudal estates in return for protection by the local lord.

Christianity, which was initially a literate, urban, religious movement, changed its orientation to accommodate a largely illiterate rural peasantry. The introspective musings of the first urban Christians gave way to a rote catechism and blind faith, laced with magical rites and superstitions carried over from the pre-Christian era.

The empathic surge, born in the cosmopolitan crossroads of a great urban empire, dried up as the universality of an earlier time was replaced by the caprices of parochialism and place. Xenophobia became the new mantra. Every hamlet and valley became a fortress, and every mountain range a no-man's-land between the familiar and acceptable and the alien other.

The great malaise lasted for several hundred years. During that time, it could safely be said that there was "nothing new under the sun." The hiatus, however, was shorter in duration than some historians of the eighteenth and nineteenth centuries originally assumed. The era of decline lasted less than five hundred years—from the late fifth to the late tenth century AD.

THE LATE MEDIEVAL ECONOMIC REVOLUTION

Beginning in the tenth century, a new energy regime slowly began to take hold across Europe. The harnessing of horses, water, and wind power spawned a dramatic growth in population, the rebirth of urban life, the reintroduction of commerce and trade, and the resurgence of literacy and learning. The Italian Renaissance, in the thirteeth, fourteenth, and fifteenth centuries, which spread unevenly to other parts of Europe, signaled an official cultural awakening from centuries of European hibernation. In the fifteenth century, a new communications revolution—the print press—emerged and converged with the new energy regime, giving birth to a second Renaissance and the beginning of the humanist era. The new energy/communications revolution spawned new, more complex, urban environments, more dense living arrangements, greater differentiation, more diverse exposure to others, and a qualitative leap in self-consciousness and individualization.

Historian John Herman Randall, Jr., in his book *The Making of the Modern Mind*, notes that the reverse flow back from the countryside to the newly emerging towns, with their own unique "vows and obligations," was to have a profound impact on the whole future course of history. He writes:

> The rise of the urban civilization, first primarily commercial
> and later more and more industrial, was the outstanding social
> force in the later Middle Ages; from it can be traced practically
> everything that, beginning with the renaissance . . . created
> modern times.[1]

The new urban civilization brought with it an empathic surge that would take European consciousness to new heights. The late medieval empathic surge began with a technological revolution in agriculture and a novel harnessing of biological and inanimate energy.

The introduction of the horse into agriculture greatly increased agricultural productivity. While draught horses were used in a very limited way as far back as antiquity, it wasn't until the invention of the shoulder harness, iron horseshoes, and the harnessing of horses, one behind the other, that horses could be effectively utilized for plowing and other chores. Horses proved far superior to human labor or oxen. The invention of the moldboard plow, in turn, with its share and coulter, allowed farmers to plow the heavy soils of northern Europe, opening up vast new lands for cultivation. The shift from a two-field to three-field system of crop rotation greatly increased agricultural yields. Together, those inventions spawned a massive increase in agricultural yields in the thirteenth and fourteenth centuries that would go unrivaled for another five hundred years. Agricultural yields in many regions rose by one-third and human productivity by half.[2]

The new farming practices not only increased yields but also the diversity of crops under cultivation—especially legumes—which provided a more balanced diet. Lynn White, Jr., says that the importance of the agricultural revolution of the late Middle Ages can't be overemphasized.

> It was not merely the new quantity of food produced by
> improved agricultural methods, but the new type of food
> supply which goes far towards explaining, for northern Europe
> at least, the startling expansion of population, the growth
> and multiplication of cities, the rise in industrial production,
> the outreach of commerce, and the new exuberance of spirits
> which enlivened that age.[3]

The new agricultural innovations made up a vital part of the new energy regime. Equally important, however, was the harnessing of water and wind energies on a massive scale, beginning in the tenth century—what French historian Jean Gimpel describes as "the industrial revolution of the Middle Ages."[4] While watermills were employed as far back as Roman days—they were used in a very limited manner in Italy in the first century—the Romans preferred using slave power in "blood mills." The first water-driven grain mills were installed in the year 762.[5] By 1086, the number of watermills in England alone numbered more than 5,600, spread out over 3,000 communities.[6] By the late eleventh century, watermills were prevalent all over Europe.[7]

The use of watermills expanded from milling grain to laundering, tanning, sawing, crushing olives and ore, operating bellows for blast furnaces, polishing weapons, and reducing pigments for paint or pulp for paper.[8]

The great preponderance of watermills were built in cities along the rivers. By the eleventh century, France had more than 20,000 functioning mills, or one mill for every 250 people.[9] With watermills, one person could replace the labor of ten to twenty people, an incredible increase in productivity. The combined hydraulic power was equivalent to the labor power of 25 percent of the adult population.[10]

With watermills situated in virtually every available place along rivers and streams across much of Europe, attention turned to the idea of harnessing wind to perform similar functions. The first European windmill was installed in Yorkshire, England, in 1185.[11] Over the next several hundred years, windmills spread across the great plains of northern Europe, becoming a ubiquitous feature of the landscape. Windmills also spread to the Mediterranean, but in fewer numbers because of a still abundant reserve of rivers and streams for watermills.

Part of the appeal of windmill technology was its free access. Generally the lords' estates encompassed the best water resources. Windmills, however, could be erected anywhere, and the wind is essentially free and unencumbered by the property rights attached to water resources. Windmills were often erected in and near city jurisdictions, giving the local municipal governments a sphere of influence over power sources that remained outside the purview of the lords. The new power source was referred to as the "commoners' mills."[12]

Historians tend to overlook the technological innovations that ushered in a new energy revolution in the late Middle Ages and early modern era. The fact is, Europe by the end of the eighteenth century had ramped up a proto-industrial revolution of considerable magnitude, laying the foundation for the coal- and steam-power revolutions that would follow closely on its heels. In the 1790s, there were more than 500,000 watermills alone operating in Europe, with the equivalent of 2,250,000 horsepower, providing an inanimate source of energy in the production of most of the critical goods and products of an incipient capitalist economy. The average windmill provided upward of 30 horsepower, which by any previous standard marked a qualitative leap in productivity.[13]

This energy revolution would not have been possible without an accompanying technological revolution to harness it. Lynn White points out that not only did Europe create new diverse sources of inanimate energy, but it also invented the key engineering components to effectively harness and employ it in various industries. In the eleventh and twelfth centuries, the cam was first used in a number of operations. In the thirteenth century, craftsmen invented the spring and treadle. In the fourteenth century, Europeans honed gearing to higher levels of complexity. In the fifteenth century, improvements in cranks, connecting rods, and governors helped spur the transition from reciprocating into continuous rotary motion.[14]

White captured the historic significance of the new energy regime. He noted that as early as

the latter part of the fifteenth century, Europe was equipped
not only with sources of power far more diversified than
those known to any previous culture, but also with an arsenal
of technical means for grasping, guiding, and utilizing such
energies which was immeasurably more varied and skillful
than any people of the past had possessed, or than was
known to any contemporary society of the Old World or
the New. The expansion of Europe from 1492 onward was
based in great measure upon Europe's high consumption of
energy, with consequent productivity, economic weight and
military might.[15]

There is another aspect to the watermill and windmill energy revolution that's worthy of note. Unlike the great hydraulic empires and the Roman Empire, whose energy regimes were highly centralized and required either the indenture or enslavement of large numbers of people to operate them, windmill and watermill energies were, by nature, decentralized and more easily accessible, and they could be harnessed with relatively small amounts of labor and capital. While there was an ongoing struggle between feudal lords and an emerging bourgeois class of urban merchants and craftsmen for control over these new energies, the technology favored the latter group. For the first time in history, a qualitative leap in energy throughput could be harnessed by large numbers of urban skilled craftsmen and merchants, creating a new source of both commercial and political power.

The new, more decentralized energy technologies gave a boost to the economic and political fortunes of the thousands of towns and small cities emerging across the European continent and put an emerging burgher and bourgeois class at loggerheads with the entrenched feudal aristocracy—a conflict that would deepen and eventually spell the demise of the feudal order as protocapitalism metamorphosed into mercantilism and eventually industrial capitalism in the centuries that followed.

The new energy regime, because of its potential to democratize energy use while increasing the potential "power" of thousands of new entrants into the energy arena, gave new impetus to the notion of individual autonomy. It is perhaps no accident that the modern idea of the individual and the emerging sense of self-consciousness that accompanied the new bourgeois mentality developed in tandem with the democratization of energy and the "empowerment" of increasing numbers of urban craftsmen and merchants in the late Middle Ages and early modern era.

The convergence of the print revolution with the new democratizing energies after the mid–fifteenth century would create the context and framework for the maturing of selfhood in the ensuing centuries and lead to a great empathic surge whose force would pick up momentum throughout the whole of the modern era, affecting virtually every aspect of life.

THE PRINT REVOLUTION

A German, Johannes Gutenberg, is credited with inventing the print press in 1436. The new communications technology spread quickly. Within decades, printers' workshops were up and running in urban centers, mass-producing books in many of the languages of Europe.

The impact of the print revolution on the collection, storage, and distribution of knowledge was as important for the times as the information generated by the Internet today.

> A man born in 1453, the year of the fall of Constantinople, could look back from his fiftieth year on a lifetime in which about eight million books had been printed, more perhaps than all the scribes of Europe had produced since Constantine founded his city in AD 330.[16]

Literacy, which had been the prerogative of a small group of elites, had become partially democratized, along with the harnessing of energy. It is estimated that by the end of the sixteenth century, more than half the population of the cities was literate, less so in the rural and backward regions.[17]

The potential power of the new medium came to light in the Protestant Reformation. Martin Luther used the print press to great advantage in publicizing his breach with the Church and in enlisting recruits to the religious movement. The print press helped foment a revolution in Christianity. Between 1517 and 1520 alone, thirty publications written by Luther sold more than 300,000 copies, an enviable record even by today's standards.[18]

The mass production of bibles in vernacular became indispensable to the Reformation's religious emphasis on a "priesthood of all believers."

Luther argued that each man and woman must stand alone with their God. Armed with the Bible, it was the responsibility of every true believer to interpret the word of God without having to rely on Church emissaries—the priesthood—to serve as gatekeepers and go-betweens. In the new Protestant era, religious authority would come to be partially democratized, just like literacy and energy. The unexpected consequence, however, was that every Christian was expected to look deep into his soul and plumb the depths of his conscious being at all times to know if his feelings, intentions, and thoughts were in conformity with God's commands and biblical scriptures.

The Protestant home was transformed into a church and sanctuary. Mass-produced "self-help" religious books and pamphlets were taken up during household prayer sessions and became instruments for a sixteenth-century version of self-analysis—except the object was not to know thyself better but to know whether one's thoughts were pleasing to God or heretical. Print provided a new medium to carry on a searching, personal dialogue with the Lord.

> Through prayer and meditation, models for which they could
> find in scores of books, the draper, the butcher . . . soon
> learned to approach God without ecclesiastical assistance. . . .
> The London citizen learned to hold worship in his own
> household . . . the private citizen had become articulate in the
> presence of the Deity. . . .[19]

On a more subtle level, the emphasis on standing alone with one's God elevated the individual to a new status. He came to believe that his unique, individual soul mattered in the divine scheme of things. The Lord was interested in everyone's thoughts and stories and the lowliest human being enjoyed the same access to God as the pope himself.

The schism in Christianity also forced millions of Christians to make personal choices about their true religious feelings and convictions. For more than one thousand years there was only one Church, and the only choice was whether to be a believer or a heretic. With the Protestant movement, individuals were asked to decide between various interpretations of faith, especially as the Protestant movement itself splintered into many different groups and factions.

The Protestant movement not only forced people to question their faith but also to question their own salvation. For the Catholic Church, salvation was an uncomplicated idea. One had to accept Christ as one's savior, take confession, receive Holy Communion, and receive absolution before death to secure a place in the next world. Penance and doing good works helped pave the way to eternal life.

The Protestant route to salvation was more tortuous. Luther argued that every person is either elected to salvation or damned to hell at birth. One's fate was preordained by the Lord. Penance and good works could not reverse one's fate. But how does one know whether they are among the elect or damned? John Calvin argued that there are clues that can give one a hint as to one's status, including but not limited to whether one improved one's calling in life. Although personal achievements couldn't change one's fate, they could offer a sign of sorts as to whether one was among the elect.

Anxious to know whether they were among the saved or damned, Protestants spent endless hours searching their inner thoughts, moods, and behavior for any sign of their goodness or badness, faithfulness or impiety that might reveal their fate. While an earlier Christian in the feudal era would have little reason or inclination to entertain constant self-doubt and to mull over every thought to assess its meaning relative to one's salvation, the Protestant was embroiled in a constant state of self-analysis. As they probed deeper into their own psyches, they began to ask more subtle questions about their own thinking and especially their motivations. For example, when one performed an act of goodness, was it because one needed a sign of election—in which case the very act was merely self-deception.

The early Protestants used the new literary device of diaries to keep a daily account of all their actions—a kind of check-off list and tally they could refer back to in order to get "a read" on their behavior and actions and help them assess whether or not they were among the chosen.

The print revolution advanced the notion of individuality and selfhood in still other important ways. Print made important the idea of authorship. While individual authors previously had been recognized, they were few in number. Manuscript writing was often anonymous and the result of the collective contribution of many scribes over long periods of time. The notion of authorship elevated the individual to a unique status, separating him or her from the collective voice of the community.

Authorship conjures up the idea of the individual as a creative force. The very idea of personal creativity would not have occurred to people of an earlier era. Even in script cultures, while the writing process is solitary, the contributions are collective exercises—hundreds of scribes might take turns copying material from an earlier codex (a hand-inscribed book format that the ancient Romans invented to replace the scroll) into a newer copy. At best, an individual scribe might add some small amplification or slight revisions in the margins, but the work itself is meant to copy, not to create. Over a period of time, the idiosyncrasies of hundreds of scribes might find their way into the manuscript, changing the meaning of the context, but no one scribe saw himself as "an author." They were copiers. Of course, there was the occasional writer who might have felt inspired whose name we do recall—an Augustine or Aquinas—but there was always the feeling that the inspiration itself came from without. One was struck by an idea or thought. Personal creativity, however, is perceived to come from within, even if it is inspired by the muse's. Only in a culture where selfhood is advanced does the idea of personal creativity become part of the psychological landscape.

Individual creativity coincides with the notion of personal achievement. In an authorial culture, everyone becomes the author of their own achievements. One's life, which in feudal times was judged by fealty to one's local lord, the Church, and God Almighty, is increasingly judged in modern times by one's record of personal achievements. The Reformation theology of Martin Luther, and even more so John Calvin, with its emphasis on improving one's personal calling as a way of affirming one's election and salvation, metamorphosed over the following centuries into secular devotion to personal achievement in the marketplace. The great nineteenth-century sociologist Max Weber referred to the new Christian emphasis on personal achievement as the Protestant work ethic and credited it with laying the psychological foundation for the creation of the bourgeois men and women who propelled market capitalism onto the center stage of world history.

The idea of authorship facilitated the concept of owning one's own words. Copyright laws made communication among people a commodity. The notion that one could own thoughts and words and that others would have to pay to hear them marked an important change in the history of human relations.

Before print, people shared their thoughts together orally, in face-to-face dialogue and exchange. As mentioned earlier, even manuscripts were read aloud and were meant to be heard rather than seen. The print revolution helped nurture a more meditative environment. Books were read silently and alone, creating a new sense of personal privacy and, along with it, notions of self-reflection and introspection, eventually leading to the creation of a therapeutic way of thinking about oneself and the world.

Print also imprints the idea of completeness and enclosure on the psyche. In oral cultures, there are no firm boundaries of where one thought leaves off and another begins—only segues or pauses. Conversations and stories drift into one another. Speaking and listening is an open-ended process, often disjointed and fragmented, people floating onto other themes and topics only to drift back to previous subjects during conversation. Ideas and stories reduced to print are fixed. Each book is seen as autonomous and timeless in its own space. A book, after all, is temporally and spatially enclosed. It has a beginning, middle, and end to the story and is bound between the front and back jackets.

Walter Ong observes that ideas on a page are not subject to discussion. Readers can't talk back, argue the point, or take exception. They can however, write the author or publish their own rebuttal. Each counterpoint, however, is itself bounded and enclosed by the nature of the medium.[20] Every author knows all too well that the printed page is final copy. Once it goes to print and is mass-produced, it is untouchable. The text does not accommodate changes.[21]

In all of these particulars, print text creates the sense of autonomy and impenetrability. It's not difficult for one to imagine the idea of individual autonomy growing up in a literate print-oriented environment where so much of the communication itself is autonomous in nature. After all, reading is a solitary experience and requires great concentration. Interruption from others undermines one's attention. When one reads, one is usually engrossed and often loses the sense of passing time or where one is. When reading, one is in one's own world. The experience itself is enclosed and bounded. American historian Elizabeth Eisenstein remarks that a reading public is, by its very nature, more atomistic and individualistic than a hearing culture. She writes:

> The notion that society may be regarded as a bundle of
> discrete units or that the individual is prior to the social group
> seems to be more compatible with a reading public than a
> hearing one.[22]

Print communications strengthened the sense of individuality at the expense of loosening older communal ties. But, it also had the effect of connecting individuals in new kinds of affiliations and connections that stretched across broader swaths of space and time. Print became the vital command and control mechanism for managing the "energy throughput" of a new and increasingly complex urban commercial culture across Europe, America, and beyond. Consider the various contributions print made to the making of the modern world.

To begin with, the new print medium redefined the way human beings organize knowledge. The mnemonic redundancy of oral communication and the subjective eccentricities of medieval script were replaced by a more rational, calculating, analytical approach to knowledge. Print replaced human memory with tables of contents, pagination, footnotes, and indexes, freeing the human mind from continually recalling the past so that it might fix on the future. The shift in consciousness prepared the way for the new idea of human progress.

Print introduced charts, lists, graphs, and other visual aids that were to prove so important in creating more accurate descriptions of the world. Print made possible standardized, easily reproducible maps, making navigation and land travel more predictable and accessible. The opening up of oceans and land routes spread commercial markets and trade. Printed schedules, continually updated, mass-produced, and widely circulated, facilitated rail traffic and ocean voyages.

Print smoothed the way for a "contract" commercial culture by allowing merchants and capitalists to coordinate increasingly complex market activity and keep abreast of far-flung commercial transactions. Modern bookkeeping, schedules, bills of lading, invoicing, checks, and promissory notes were essential management tools in the organization of market capitalism. Print also made possible a uniform pricing system without which modern ideas of property exchange could not have developed.

Print also introduced the idea of assembly, a key component of the industrial way of life. Separating the alphabet into standardized units of type that were uniform, interchangeable, and reusable made print the first modern industrial process. With print, objects are uniformly spaced by positioning type on a chase and locking the chase onto a press. The composite type then can be reproduced over and over, each copy identical and indistinguishable from the original. Assembly, uniform and interchangeable parts, predictable positioning of objects in space, and mass production were the foundation stones of the industrial way of life.

Print organizes phenomena in an orderly, rational, and objective way, and in so doing encourages linear, sequential, and causal ways of thinking. The very notion of "composing" one's thoughts conjures up the idea of well-thought-out linear progression of ideas, one following the other in logical sequence, a mode of thought very different from that in oral cultures, where redundancy and discontinuity in thought often are the rules.

By eliminating the redundancy of oral language and making precise measurement and description possible, print laid the foundation for the modern scientific worldview. Phenomena could be rigorously examined, observed, and described, and experiments could be made repeatable with exacting standards and protocols, something that was far more difficult to achieve in a manuscript or oral culture.

Print made possible universal literacy, preparing successive generations with the communication tools they needed to manage the complexities of the modern market and new ways of working and socializing. In short, print created the appropriate mind-set and worldview for an "industrious" way of living and being in the world.

THE BIRTH OF HUMANISM

The convergence of print communications with inanimate sources of energy fundamentally altered human consciousness. The late Middle Ages and early modern era saw the birth of a new cosmopolitanism which, in turn, helped lay the groundwork for what historians call the humanist era. It was a period characterized by a great empathic surge whose influence is still being felt today.

The new consciousness manifests itself in a number of interesting ways. A fledgling urban bourgeoisie across Europe was beginning to experience daily life in a radically different manner than their ancestors.

Humanism begins in earnest in the sixteenth century. This was the century that opened with the scientific and artistic genius of Leonardo da Vinci and ended with the literary genius of Shakespeare. When we think of what it means to be a "Renaissance Man," it is the sixteenth-century flowering of the human spirit, in a multitude of brilliant forms, to which we refer. The period is often referred to as the late so-called Northern Renaissance.

We normally associate the Renaissance with the awakening of interest in the philosophical, political, and literary works of antiquity and the new realism and emotionalism found in art in Florence, Venice, and the other northern Italian cities in the late thirteenth century. More interesting, however, from a modern perspective, is the late

Renaissance period in northern Europe in the late sixteenth century, when the new energy/communication regime of the late Middle Ages was throttling up, and the new urban centers of an incipient capitalism were experiencing their first whiff of cosmopolitanism.

The sixteenth century was characterized by a break with the dogmatism of the medieval Christian worldview. While many of its leading lights still considered themselves good Catholics, they were far more willing to challenge stale orthodoxy and entertain new ideas. The literary and artistic elite were more curious and playful in their approaches to the world and even willing to expose the paradoxical and ironic aspects of the medieval world they had inherited.

Erasmus set the tone for the new openness by making fun of the rigid doctrine of traditional Church teaching—yet he remained firmly in the fold. Skeptical tolerance became the order of the day. It was a century punctuated by deep conversation, not only about the meaning of past intellectual and artistic accomplishments in ancient Greece and Rome, but also about the new world of possibilities that lay ahead. In this sense it was as much a birth as a rebirth. Above all, it was a century dedicated to the exploration and celebration of the richness and diversity of human life.

What made the period particularly unique is the willingness to peer behind the veneer of pious appearances, which put a premium on saintlike virtues, while castigating the ribald aspects of corporeal existence as venal. The literati of the Northern Renaissance delighted in the human condition—thus the Humanist Age—and were not afraid to explore the fragile underside of human existence, including the foibles and follies that make life both problematic and challenging. Their keen interest was in finding out what makes human life human.

While medieval clerics believed there was only one proper way to live life, the sixteenth-century humanists argued that there were multiple perspectives and that they should receive a fair hearing in the public arena.

A Shakespeare probably would have been burned at the stake just a few centuries earlier. Instead, the high and mighty and common folk flocked to the theatre and rocked with laughter and cried with abandon as Shakespeare's characters—Juliet, Hamlet, Shylock—came to life onstage, allowing audiences to empathize with their plights, applaud their triumphs, and even boo at their pettiness and nasty behavior.

The sixteenth century was, in many ways, a period of exploration. The great Spanish, Portuguese, and English explorers were navigating the globe, discovering new lands, and making contact with exotic cultures. While in the next century Church figures, mercantilists, and courtesans of European courts would characterize these new peoples as savage and less than human—in part to justify their enslavement and colonization—and urge their immediate conversion to Christianity, the humanists were far more interested in hearing their stories and comparing their experiences with their own. The humanists, says British philosopher Stephen Toulmin, chose to

> add these fresh and exotic discoveries to the pool of testimony
> about Humanity and human life, and so enlarge our sympathy
> to a point at which the accepted framework of understanding
> could accommodate the riches of ethnography.[23]

By the seventeenth century, the humanist insights were shunted aside amidst the growing clamor to imperialize the world.

Toulmin uses Montaigne as a good case study of the new humanist spirit let loose on the world. Although hardly rebellious—he was, after all, a practicing Catholic—Montaigne was human in the best sense of the word, and it came out in his writings. Toulmin points out that in his essays, Montaigne candidly discusses his own bad habits—for example, eating so greedily that he bites his tongue and fingers. But unlike Saint Augustine, in *The Confessions*, who is tortured by his human failings and who feels the wrenching need to confess his sins, Montaigne simply acknowledges that he is human and therefore imperfect.

Montaigne is at his best when he confronts the orthodox Christian attempt to disassociate the human mind from the human body. He writes sardonically,

> [The human mind] has such a tight brotherly bond with the
> body that it abandons me at every turn to follow the body
> in its need. I take it aside and flatter it, I work on it, all for
> nothing. In vain I try to turn it aside from this bond, I offer
> it Seneca and Catullus, and the ladies and the royal dances; if
> its companion has the colic, it seems to have it too. Even the
> activities that are peculiarly its own cannot then be aroused;
> they evidently smack of a cold in the head. There is no
> sprightliness in [the mind's] productions if there is none in the
> body at the same time.[24]

Montaigne is particularly harsh on the philosophers who seem consumed with hatred for the flesh. He quips,

> Philosophy is very childish, to my mind, when she gets up on
> her hind legs and preaches to us that it is a barbarous alliance
> to marry the divine with the earthly, the reasonable with the
> unreasonable, the severe with the indulgent, the honorable
> with the dishonorable; that sensual pleasure is a brutish thing
> unworthy of being enjoyed by the wise man.[25]

Montaigne ventured far beyond the early Christians of urban Rome
in his willingness to accept the totality of human experience and the
inseparability of body, mind, and spirit. For all of their talk of fraternal
affection for one another, the early Christians viewed man's corporeal
existence as fallen and, for that reason, they sought the ideal of an
ascetic existence while on Earth, for fear that the evil embedded in
their very physicality might contaminate their spiritual quest.

Montaigne, however, intuited that an ascetic life is a life less lived.
Hatred of the body could hardly endear one to another flesh-and-bones
human being. Embodied experience is the window to empathic expression. It's by experiencing another being's plight and struggle to be in
this world, as if it were our own, and by coming to their assistance so
they may live more fully, that we become more alive, more human,
more connected to deeper realities of existence and, by so doing, come

to learn about our place in the grand scheme of things. Empathy is a celebration of life, in all of its corporeality. Not paradoxically, it is also the means by which we transcend ourselves. Montaigne understood as much.

It was in the late sixteenth century that public life began to recede in importance and private life increasingly became a refuge. As one's personal life became more important, one's public persona became more ambiguous and vexing. Juggling the two created new sources of anxiety. Attitudes about marriage and raising children also underwent a profound change. These changes in consciousness both reflected the new empathic surge and helped facilitate it.

For the first time, human beings faced the question of their own identity. "Who am I?" became part of the interior conversation individuals had with themselves as well as a subject of public discussion.

Whereas earlier generations were far more concerned with the questions of personal piety and honor, reflecting the hold the Church and feudal order had over their lives, the emerging bourgeoisie began to focus much of its attention on the question of sincerity. Were others who they appeared to be or were they creating a public persona that hid their true self? By the sixteenth century, the emergence of selfhood brought with it a new sense of self-doubt, not only about one's own thinking and intentions but that of others as well. As people very tentatively began to create their own self-image and public image, although for the most part unconsciously, they began to question other people's public personas, wondering what inner self lay undisclosed and hidden away beneath the appearances.

The question of sincerity is a relatively new idea. The American literary critic Lionel Trilling makes the observation that we wouldn't ask whether Abraham, the Jewish patriarch, was sincere, or Achilles or Beowulf for that matter. "They neither have nor lack sincerity," notes Trilling.[26] But by the time Jane Austen was writing her books, her readers were preoccupied with the sincerity or lack thereof of her protagonists. In Shakespeare's *Hamlet*, Polonius turns to Laertes with a bit of paternal advice that barely raised an eyebrow among the theater-goers at the time but would have been considered nonsensical to people just a few centuries earlier.

Polonius cautions:

This above all: to thine own self be true
And it doth follow, as the night the day.
Thou canst not then be false to any man.[27]

It was at this time that people began signing their correspondences with the term "yours sincerely," a practice kept alive until today. The word "sincere" originally was used to communicate the idea of clean or pure or unadultered. Wines were referred to as sincere. When applied to people, the term "sincere" implied pure or virtuous. By the sixteenth century it was being used to contrast pretense from truth. Machiavelli's *The Prince* was a tutorial on how to create the public demeanor of appearing sincere as a powerful tool of political manipulation. The book became an overnight sensation.

Trilling reminds us that in 1550, London was a city of 60,000. But just a hundred years later it was the home to 350,000 people.[28] The shift from village life to urban life forced people to expand their sense of self and even to take on different personas in different circumstances and with different people. The homogeneity of village life, with its clear-cut social distinctions and relatively simple status levels, did not require various "public faces." You were simply who you were on all occasions. If you suddenly changed character, it would be immediately noticeable and the subject of concern for fear you were possessed.

City life not only called for plasticity in appearance but also encouraged it. Relative anonymity, amid the throng, allowed people to be different in different circumstances and with different people. With the appropriate change of attire, attitude, and demeanor, they could even escape their class backgrounds and hereditary stations in life, if just for a moment—something unheard of in previous times.

It's no wonder that increasing numbers of city dwellers began to question each other's true self. Urban dwellers in the sixteenth century, Trilling tells us, were "preoccupied to an extreme degree with dissimulation, feigning, and pretence."[29] Shakespeare's characters were caught up in a farcical parodying of the new sentiment as they wrapped themselves up in various disguises and got caught up in plots involving mistaken identities.

While we normally hold the notion of sincerity in high regard, it is also true that the ability to adjust one's persona to changing circumstances and diverse others can advance consciousness and extend empathy. While public masks can be used to deceive or hide from one's true self, they can also allow one to try on other personas, walk in others' shoes and be exposed to very different people than would be the case if still hemmed in by class and caste status.

The freedom to be someone else could allow one to experience another's plight "as if" it were one's own and deepen empathic extension. This is what cosmopolitan behavior is all about, at least in part—being comfortable in different roles in different places under different circumstances. If entered into with the notion of broadening one's exposure to and experiences with others, with the expectation of establishing new, meaningful relationships, the practice enriches one's identity and becomes transcendent rather than deceitful.

THE DISCOVERY OF SELF-CONSCIOUSNESS AND SEPARATENESS

The new emphasis on individuality, which became readily apparent by the sixteenth century, marked a significant change in how people perceived themselves. Family and kinship identity began to give way to personal identity made up of individual achievements, forged over one's lifetime.

The seismic shift in consciousness is evidenced in the spate of new terms introduced into the vernacular vocabularies of Europe. The word "self" emerged as a pronoun and meant "own" and "same." It wasn't until the Middle Ages—circa 1400—that it became a noun, but in its early use, it had a negative connotation, as in "[o]ure own self we sal deny, And folow oure lord god al-myghty."[30]

"Self" metamorphosed into a positive term in the sixteenth century and began to be used in compound words. Self-praise appeared in 1549, followed shortly thereafter by self-love, self-pride, and self-regard. By the early seventeenth century, self was being attached to so many words that it would have been difficult to pass a day without hearing it used in some new context. Self-interest, self-preservation, self-made, self-confidence, self-pity, and self-knowledge were all popular terms, liberally served up in normal discourse.

The modern definition of consciousness appeared in English in 1620. The noun "consciousness" appeared half a century later in 1678. In 1690, self was combined with consciousness and "self-consciousness" became the lynchpin to describe the mentality of the new man and woman of the modern era.

To be self-conscious is to be aware of one's separateness. The new-found interest in being self-possessed and autonomous was reflected in still another historic transformation in the way people lived. The communal, publicly lived life that characterized every previous era in history began to whither as people withdrew indoors and then to their own separate quarters. Privacy, a concept with little ontological meaning in the Middle Ages, began to be something to covet by the sixteenth century and became regarded as a birthright by the urban bourgeoisie of the eighteenth century.

The changing configuration of living arrangements between the late medieval era and the early modern era came to play a decisive role in fostering both privacy and the creation of the autonomous individual. The households of the feudal lords and burghers in the medieval era were very public places, with few boundaries separating family, kin, and neighbors. At any given time, the house might be inhabited by dozens of relatives and servants, not to mention friends and acquaintances. The rooms themselves were large and undifferentiated. Relatives and guests often socialized, ate, and slept in the same room.

The cottages of the poor were little more than "squalid hovels." It wasn't uncommon for twenty or more family members to share a one-room cottage that barely exceeded twenty square yards. Three generations might share the same bed. People went a lifetime never really having a moment alone. In pre-Napoleonic Europe, more than three-quarters of the population lived under these kinds of horrible conditions.[31]

By the eighteenth century, however, at least for the well-to-do, the notion of privacy had gained hold. The manor houses were divided into private spaces, each with a particular function. There was now a parlor, a formal dining room, private bedroom chambers, storage rooms, and quarters for the servants. In the new household, each person claimed his or her own private space and possessions, something unheard of in medieval times. The sectioning off of private space made each person that much more aware of his or her own individuality and autonomy. The notion of privacy was fast becoming the hallmark of the new autonomous individual. Privacy meant the ability to exclude others and was a mark of the new priority given to the individual life as opposed to extended-family relations, which had reigned as the dominant social unit from the very beginning of human experience.

The privatization of space encouraged greater intimacy and self-reflection, feelings that were barely exercised in the public life of the late medieval household. Even the poor gained a modicum of privacy. Between the mid–sixteenth and mid–seventeenth centuries, more than half of all laborers' homes had expanded to three or more rooms.[32]

The new emphasis on the self and personal autonomy was particularly notable in the changing style in furniture. The chair was introduced around 1490 at the Palazzo Strozzi in Florence.[33] Before that time, people sat on wooden benches that lined the walls or on three-legged stools, or they huddled together on cushions on the floor. The only chair in medieval palaces was the throne reserved for the sovereign, denoting his elevated status.

Uniform series of chairs came into vogue in France during the height of the Renaissance, reflecting the newly elevated status of the individual. The idea of the chair was truly revolutionary. It represented an emerging feeling among an incipient bourgeois class that each person was an autonomous and self-contained being, an island unto himself or herself. Historian John Lukacs observes that "the interior furniture of houses appeared together with the interior furniture of the mind."[34] With the widespread introduction of the chair in Europe, the autonomous individual of the modern era had arrived.

The transformation from public to private life and the growing emphasis on the individual was very much in evidence in the bedchamber. Medieval sleeping arrangements were communal, just like every other aspect of social life. Landlords and their mistresses, relatives, friends, and even valets and chambermaids slept alongside one another in makeshift beds. Members of the same sex often shared the same bed. Michelangelo slept with his workmen, four to a bed.

The permanent bed wasn't introduced until the sixteenth century. In the seventeenth century, four-poster beds with canopies were commonplace among the nobility and burgher class. Curtains were attached to the beds to provide some small bit of privacy. Still, it was often the case that a man and woman would be making love behind the curtains while relatives and friends were socializing just a few feet away.

Slowly, the practice of sleeping alone in a single bed behind closed doors became more common. The kind of indiscriminate bodily contact that was so frequent in the late medieval era became a source of embarrassment. Public exhibitions of lust and sexuality, so prominent a feature of the medieval era, became taboo in the better households. Sexual relations became increasingly a private act, consummated behind closed doors.[35]

The decline in kinship identification and the rise of self-identification affected every aspect of social life. For example, in the waning decades of the sixteenth century, the age-old practice of the vendetta all but died out in England. Other countries across Europe soon followed. In a society organized around kinship, a wrongdoing committed by an individual was subject to the punishment and even killing of any of his family members by the family of the victim. This ancient form of justice is in stark contrast to modern jurisprudence, which prescribes punishment only to the individual who commits the crime. The idea of limiting responsibility for a criminal act to the individual at fault makes sense in a society of individuals, but less so in a society of kinship relationships.

THE RADICAL IDEA OF COMPANIONATE MARRIAGE

Perhaps the biggest changes in this period were to be found in the altered notions of marriage and the raising of children. For most of history, marriages were prearranged by parents and kin relations. In some parts of the world, the practice still lingers on, even today. In the sixteenth century, the institution of arranged marriages began to unravel, in large part because kinship ties were slowly giving way to a society of individuals. Reformation theologians also began to emphasize the novel idea of conjugal affection as a way of maintaining the sanctity of holy matrimony. In England, in a prayer book published in 1549, Archbishop Cranmer suggested that marriage as an institution was to provide "mutual society, help and comfort, that the one ought to have of the other, both in prosperity and in adversity."[36] Toward this end, Protestant elders emphasized the need for affection between husband and wife. The new focus on the marriage bond as a special relationship further undermined kinship relations. Slowly the idea of a "nuclear family," held together by affection and intimacy, began to challenge extended kinship relationships and eventually led to their decline, at least among the emerging urban bourgeoisie.

The invention of companionate marriage and marriages based on love didn't take hold easily or quickly but, rather, emerged in stages. The slow pace of change was due, in part, to the mixed messages of Reformation theology. While on the one hand affection between husband and wife was encouraged, on the other hand the Reformation theology put an even heavier emphasis on patriarchal control over family relations than did the Catholic Church.

Since the idea of affection is a voluntary matter—one can't be forced to express affection—and because it requires a certain degree of equality between two people who enter into a relationship willingly and enthusiastically, it was often difficult, if not impossible, to achieve both objectives—that is, a strong patriarchal family orientation based on strict authority and obedience to the husband and "shared affection" between the spouses. Moreover, in a patriarchal environment, selfhood is thwarted in direct proportion to the exercise of authority. Strict obedience to another's dictates does not encourage the development of an independent will, which is essential to the development of selfhood. Women were expected to be weak and submissive. Listen to this passage from Matthew's Bible of 1537 instructing the male head of the household on how to manage conjugal relations. "[I]f his wife is 'not obedient and helpful to him, endeavoureth to beat the fear of God into her head, and that thereby she may be compelled to learn her duty and do it.' "[37] This kind of approach certainly was not conducive to nurturing a sense of selfhood in women—and without a mature sense of self, it is difficult to develop the kind of empathic sensibility required to express true affection to another, to comfort them and be a companion.

Still, love and affection won out in the long run. Economic and social forces helped the process along. Kinship marriage was from the start motivated by economic interest. The breakup of communal bonds and the increasing individualization of labor—first among craftsmen and merchants in the towns and then among serfs let loose from their collective bondage on the landed estates beginning with the great Enclosure Acts in the 1500s in Tudor England—put more and more people on their own. The Protestant emphasis on the patriarchal family, although still a formidable force until well into the nineteenth century and beyond, began to fray as early as the late 1500s with the rise of an urban population whose labor and personal identity was becoming increasingly individualized.

By 1600, the new emphasis on holy matrimony led to a giant crack in patriarchal family relationships. Young men and women were allowed to reject a potential marriage partner proposed by their parents—the only exception to this being in the ranks of the royal family and aristocracy, where arranged marriages continued to be the rule, with children having little say over their future matrimonial ties. Between the mid–seventeenth century and the beginning of the nineteenth century, according to British historian Lawrence Stone, children increasingly gained the power to choose their own spouses, while the parents retained veto power over economically and socially undesirable picks.[38] For the first time, at least in urban society and among the bourgeoisie, the idea that affection between prospective marriage partners ought to be the most important element in the decision to wed became acceptable and even preferable—although economic and social considerations still weighed heavily in the decision, as they do even today.

The changes going on in the family in England between 1560 and 1640 mirrored, to a great extent, the changes going on in the society at large. England was making the transition from a "lineage society" to a "civil society." The government was increasingly consolidating its hold over critical functions of society, including the administration of justice, military security, and the regulation of property relations and commercial activity. Human obligations, which traditionally had been centered in the family and local county and parish, became secondary to loyalty to one's country. Allegiance, in the new scheme of things, was exercised by "individual" subjects rather than by kinship groups. The slow breakup of kinship relations and the beginning of the nuclearization of family relations was a better social fit for the broader political and economic changes that were transforming Englishmen into individual subjects of the Crown and autonomous agents in the labor market. As Englishmen began to exercise a modicum of individual rights in the political and economic arena in the sixteenth and seventeenth centuries, they understandably felt entitled to exercise similar individual discretion in the choice of mates.

The economic, social, and political changes at the time emboldened a growing chorus of critics to take on the patriarchal family orientation championed by Protestant theologians. In 1634, the English political theorist Robert Filmer had put forth the argument in his *Patriarcha* that the authority of the Crown and the authority over the family both rested on the Ten Commandments, where it is written "Honor Thy Father." Unfortunately, Mr. Filmer conveniently forgot to mention that the same commandment also calls for honoring thy mother.[39] John Locke would have nothing of it. Tired of the sophomoric analogies connecting the father of one's country and the father of the family,

Locke bucked horns with Filmer. In his *Two Treatises of Government*, published in 1689, Locke explained that marriage is a contractual relationship regarding common interest and property but did not include the idea that a husband enjoyed a God-given right to exercise absolute control over his wife and children. As to children, Locke said that a father's responsibility is to assume temporary power over their lives, which included the obligation to nourish them, but that this limited power ceased when they came of age. Locke also reminded his countrymen that even the king did not enjoy unlimited authority over his subjects. Rather, adults voluntarily submit to monarchial rule in the form of a contractual arrangement as long as the monarch acts in a manner that represents their welfare.[40]

This new sense of "contractual obligation" permeated English thinking in the seventeenth and eighteenth centuries. When it came to family relations, the contractual foundation was meant to be as much about reciprocal love and affection as about property relations. In 1705, Bishop Fleetwood set forth the premise of the new "understanding" upon which family relations were to be based and judged. He pointed out that

> [t]here is no relation in the world, either natural or civil and
> agreed upon, but there is a reciprocal duty obliging each
> party. . . . I only mention this to make it very evident that the
> obligation of children to love, honour, respect and obey their
> parents is founded originally upon the parents' love and care of
> them.[41]

Similarly, while wives were still expected to be submissive and to obey their husbands, it was "the duty of the husbands to 'love their wives,' a duty which carried obligations of affection, fidelity and care."[42]

Although the question of what constitutes the appropriate measure of nurturing and affection is difficult to quantify, the laws in seventeenth-century England did begin to change, granting wives more legal control over their own property—signaling a shift, no matter how small, in the status of women.

By the late eighteenth century in England, companionate marriages, based on mutual affection, were the rule rather than the exception among the English middle and upper classes. It was estimated at the time that "three marriages out of four are based on affection."[43]

The sublime pleasures of compassionate marriage were extolled by men and women alike. In *A Letter of Genteel and Moral Advice to a Young Lady*, written in 1740, Wetenhall Wilkes contemplates the ideal marriage relationship.

> This state, with the affection suitable to it, is the completest
> image of heaven we can receive in this life; the greatest
> pleasures we can enjoy on earth are the freedoms of
> conversation with a bosom friend . . . When two have
> chosen each other, out of all the species, with a design to be
> each other's mutual comfort and entertainment . . . all the
> satisfactions of the one must be doubled because the other
> partakes in them.[44]

The little tell-tale signs of the shift in thinking about marriage speak volumes. Husbands and wives no longer referred to each other formally as "Madam" and "Sir" but, rather, used first names and even affectionate terms like "sweetie" and "honey," just as we do today.[45]

The new emphasis on companionship and mutual friendship also had an ancillary effect of encouraging greater education of women— among the middle and upper middle classes—so that they might be prepared to be true companions with their husbands after marriage. The *Ladies' Monthly Magazine* went so far as to claim that "many women have received a much better education than Shakespeare enjoyed."[46]

The new norms regarding marriage altered human relationships. The expectation of basing marriage on affection and companionship laid the groundwork for an empathic surge that changed the very nature of social relationships. Being an affectionate and caring companion is tautological with being an empathic mate. It is impossible to entertain the former without experiencing the latter. Today it's common for young people to say they are looking for their "soul mate," unmindful that their expectations are not age-old but a product of human self-development.

The changes in marriage vows in the seventeenth century were to have equally dramatic effects on the rearing of children.

THE CREATION OF CHILDHOOD

In the early sixteenth century, there was some evidence to suggest that parenting was beginning to undergo a slight change among the small numbers of upwardly mobile urban dwellers. The humanist Sir Thomas More, although deeply religious, did not regard his own children as evil creatures possessed by demonic forces—an all too familiar theme among parents during the early Middle Ages. More's deeply empathic parental embrace of his own children seems remarkably contemporary a half-millennium later. In a letter to his children, he reminds them that,

> I never could endure to hear you cry. You know, for example, how often I kissed you, how seldom I whipped you. My whip was invariably a peacock's tail. Even this I wielded hesitantly and gently, so that sorry welts might not disfigure your tender seats. Brutal and unworthy to be called father is he who does not himself weep at the tears of his child.[47]

Regrettably, this humanist interlude in the first half of the sixteenth century was limited and quickly forgotten in the Protestant rush to impose patriarchal rule in the home and "break the will" of the child, to ensure his or her piety. Part of the reason for the new and more severe treatment of children was the Protestant belief that each soul is worthy of saving and that the family patriarch had the responsibility to guide his child's development into adulthood. In other words, it wasn't from lack of regard but quite the contrary, from a sense of high moral purpose that Christian homes took on the task of preparing their children to stand alone with their Lord. The extension of schooling to large numbers of children also subjected youngsters to a merciless routine of flogging by teachers for the slightest violation of decorum or for underperformance. Lawrence Stone reports "that more children were being beaten in the sixteenth and early seventeenth centuries, over a longer age span, than ever before."[48]

The fear that children were vulnerable to being corrupted by the devil motivated even the most caring parents to revert to savage beatings, in the belief that the whippings, though painful, were necessary to rid their children's bodies of demonic forces. Parents saw corporal punishment as a way to save their children from the devil and an eternity in hell. Their behavior was in stark contrast to the sentiments of parents in the earlier Italian Renaissance, who came to look on their children as pure, innocent, and uncorrupted. Much of the reason for the new level of brutality, says Stone, is also attributable to the chaotic environment at the time. The Reformation and Counter-Reformation and the Thirty Years' War, pitting Protestant and Catholic neighbors against each other, often in deadly combat, heightened the sense of living in a fallen world. Restoring social order, many theologians believed, began with "the right disciplining and education of children."[49]

Stone sums up the complicated psychological relationship of Protestant parents with their children.

> Puritans in particular were profoundly concerned about their children, loved them, cherished them, prayed over them and subjected them to endless moral pressure. At the same time they feared and even hated them as agents of sin within the household, and therefore beat them mercilessly.[50]

In the 1660s, a slow change began to take place in child rearing, at the same time that changes were beginning to occur in the institution of marriage. John Locke's book *Some Thoughts Concerning Education*, published in 1692, was influential in changing the child-rearing practices of the day. Locke believed that infants were born tabula rasa—a clean slate—and told parents that they get out of children what they put into them. While he cautioned against being overly permissive, he was equally opposed to being overly strict and punitive. He urged a more "psychological" approach designed to help the child develop a sense of individual will and conscience. Locke's book enjoyed immediate success among the bourgeois class in England and, soon thereafter, on the continent.

A new literary genre—children's books—became popular in the eighteenth century. Unlike earlier reading materials aimed at children, the new books were not intended to teach children moral lessons so much as to entertain them, signaling the desire to amuse children and make their childhood a happy experience. Toy shops also sprouted up in towns and parents began buying their children dolls and doll houses, jigsaw puzzles, dice, and other games, a clear sign, notes Stone, that the "child-oriented" family was emerging for the first time in history.[51]

The reserved formality of parent/child relationships, so characteristic of the patriarchal Protestant families of the seventeenth century, gave way to a more intimate and affectionate relationship, more akin to what children experience today. Parents were no longer addressed as "Sir" or "Madam" but, rather, as Mama and Papa.[52]

Perhaps the most significant indication of the vast changes taking place in child rearing was the abandonment of the brutal practice of swaddling—an age-old convention that dated back to Roman times. In the seventeenth century, infants were still being tightly bound from neck to toe in bandages, at least for the first four months after birth, and even beyond. They were immobilized for long periods of time. They were often treated as tiny packages and moved from place to place, even hung on pegs on the walls, where they languished in limbo like little zombies.

Being severely bandaged for long periods of time, infants were rarely cuddled or kissed and thus denied the affection and attention of mothers and other adults during the critical months after birth. In the eighteenth century, the bandages started coming off. Rousseau helped ease the way by criticizing the practice. In keeping with the new spirit of individual freedom that was becoming in vogue at the time in philosophy and literature, as well as in governance and the marketplace, Rousseau lamented the fact that

> [t]he child has hardly left the mother's womb, it has hardly begun to move and stretch its limbs when it is deprived of its freedom. It is wrapped in swaddling bands, laid down with its head fixed, its legs stretched out, and its arms by its sides, it is wound round with linen and bandages of all sorts, so that it cannot move.[53]

By 1785, the practice of swaddling had been eliminated in England. It would take another half-century before swaddling was eliminated from most of the rest of western Europe.[54]

The new attentiveness to infants was evidenced in the renewed interest by well-off mothers in breast-feeding. Among the well-to-do, breast-feeding had long been frowned upon as an unappealing task, best left to wet nurses. Infants were farmed out immediately after birth, usually to poor women living in the countryside. There they were often abused and neglected. Many perished. Yet well-off women, anxious to maintain their youthful figures, please their husband's sexual appetites, and maintain an uninterrupted social life, were quite willing to outsource this most basic function of motherhood, with grave potential consequences to the infants' physical well-being and later psychological development.

Wet-nursing went out of favor in the latter half of the eighteenth century in England as new mothers sought to be more attentive and nurturing toward their young. In France, where wet-nursing was an even more common practice among all but the lowest classes, the practice didn't end until the late nineteenth century.[55]

The new expression of motherly affection ensured that the empathic impulse of the period would pass on to children, who would grow up loved and cared for and capable of empathizing with others, just as their parents had empathized with them.

The new nurturing approach to raising children spilled over into the education arena. Beating knowledge into little minds was increasingly looked on with horror among the urban upper and middle classes. In 1798, mothers were being lectured that "the first objective in the education of a child should be to acquire its affection, and the second to obtain its confidence. . . . The most likely thing to expand a youthful mind . . . is praise," all of which sounds remarkably similar to the self-esteem movement so popular in American schools in the 1980s and 1990s.[56]

In the English schoolroom, once a terror chamber, educators began to extol the virtue of affection over punishment as a means of educating the young. In 1769, Thomas Sheridan called for the abolition of corporal punishment in elite schools—a suggestion that would have been as horrifying for teachers a century earlier as the practice itself now was to the new teachers of the enlightened age. "Away with the rod," admonished Sheridan. "Let pleasure be their guide to allure the ingenious youth through the labyrinths of science, not pain their driver to goad them on."[57] Flogging died out altogether in England by the early nineteenth century.

All of these changes in human relationships were occurring within the context of tumultuous changes taking place in the economic and political life of Europeans. The harnessing of vast new stores of inanimate forms of energy, managed by the new print revolution, changed the economic and political landscape as much as it did the psychological and social environment in the late Middle Ages and early modern period. After the long sleep of the feudal era, an awakening world felt the birth pains of renewal at every turn. No part of human life was spared. From the deepest recesses of one's psychological being to the lofty corridors of monarchical power, the new opportunities opening up before people played out against the massive upheaval and turmoil caused by fundamental economic changes. The Great Chain of Being that had majestically arched over the slumbering Dark Ages, providing order and certainty for every person of faith, was torn asunder and began to look quite ridiculous, as people across Europe wrestled with new commercial and urban realities that the grand Christian cosmology was simply unprepared to address or even accommodate.

THE PUSH FOR FREE MARKETS

As mentioned earlier, a spate of new technologies in the early modern era in Europe shortened distances traveled, sped up exchanges, and decreased transaction times, making possible much bigger markets. Feudal governing institutions were too small and parochial to manage the new potential reach of commercial activity. In fact, these same institutions, for the most part, saw larger markets as a potential threat and acted to thwart them.

By the late medieval era, more than one thousand towns had sprung up throughout Europe. The towns had granaries, shops, and inns, and were served by local craftsmen. They produced a variety of goods and services requiring expertise not available on many manorial estates. Masons, fine weavers and dyers, metalworkers, and armorers, and later the broiderers and glovers, the scriveners, the upholsterers, and the hatters, clustered together in these prototype urban areas, establishing "free cities"—regions independent of the reach of the local lords. If a serf, for example, were to escape his lord and flee to a city and remain there for a year and a day, he was deemed to be free, having passed from the jurisdiction of his lord to the jurisdiction of the city burghers.[58]

Each craft industry established a guild to regulate the activity of its members. The guilds were responsible for maintaining quality standards for their industry, determining how much would be manufactured and sold, as well as the fair price for the sale of their goods and services. The guild economy operated by custom, not by market forces. The point was not to make a profit but, rather, to maintain a way of life. Guilds opposed an open market, free labor, the commercialization of land, and competitive prices—all of the essential hallmarks of a modern economy.

In the sixteenth century in England, an independent merchant class was beginning to challenge the guilds' control over the production of goods and services. Economic conditions in England, and later on the Continent, were making the guild system increasingly untenable.

The wave of land enclosures was freeing up peasants, providing a new exploitable workforce. Advances in transportation—the laying down of better roads and improvements in river navigation—were making it easier to move raw materials and finished goods between the country-side and towns. A burgeoning population was demanding more goods at cheaper prices.

The textile guilds were the first to be hurt by the new market forces being unleashed. Rogue merchants began to skirt guild con-trols and urban jurisdictions by dispersing work to cheaper labor in the countryside—called the "putting-out" system. New breakthroughs in technology and the organization of work led to a "division of labor," substantially reducing the costs of manufacturing goods and the time necessary to produce them. The new production model was better able to meet the upsurge in consumer demand.[59]

By providing the raw material and the tools necessary for produc-tion and by controlling the transport of supplies and finished products between country and town, the new merchants were able to exercise far greater control over labor costs. Already destitute, desperate, and without any other means to make a livelihood, peasant workers had little choice but to accept the conditions of employment imposed on them by a fledgling capitalist class. The guilds, for their part, could not compete with either the pace or the volume of production or the price of the finished products.

The introduction of the factory into Europe further eroded the power of the master craftsmen and their guilds. In the latter half of the sixteenth century, factory manufacture came to England. Paper mills, ironworks, cannon factories, and, later, textile factories introduced the idea of cen-tralizing all of the production tasks under one roof with a common energy source—first using watermills and windmills, and later using coal- and steam-powered machinery. Factory manufacture required large sums of capital—often several thousand pounds or more—well beyond the means of even the wealthiest master craftsmen. Only the new class of merchant capitalists could afford the cost of this new kind of manufacturing mod-el.[60] Historian Maurice Dobb argues that the subordination of production to capital, and the appearance of this class relationship between capitalist and the producer is, therefore, to be regarded as the crucial watershed between the old mode of production and the new.[61]

Europe found itself in the throes of a great struggle between a new commercial order and an old economic regime. New technologies were radically altering spatial and temporal realities. The old social economy, based on controlling production, fixing prices, and excluding competition from the outside, was too provincial to accommodate the range of new technologies that were making possible greater exchange of goods and services between more people over longer distances. The new technologies gave birth to a capitalist class hell-bent on exploiting their full potential. They found their commercial model in self-regulating free markets.

What was missing was a new, more expansive, and agile political framework that could impose its will on the thousands of local municipalities and force the elimination of local tolls and tariffs and countless other statutes and codes that maintained an aging medieval economy. In addition, there was a need to establish a common language, a unified educational system, a single police force, and other centralized mechanisms to make viable a nationwide internal commercial trading market. It was this need, says Karl Polanyi, "which forced the territorial state to the fore as the instrument of the 'nationalization' of the market and the creator of internal commerce."[62]

Although never intended, the emergence of the territorial nation state had a collateral effect that proved to be every bit as important as acclimating large populations of previously disparate people to national markets. Nationalism extended the empathic impulse to the new expansive borders of the nation itself.

THE EMERGENCE OF NATION-STATES

The nation-state is a relatively new institution for governing human society. Some scholars date its origins no further back than the American and French revolutions in the late eighteenth century, while others suggest that its roots extend even further back to England in the twelfth and thirteenth centuries. The popular conception of the nation-state is of an organic creation rooted in common culture, language, and customs that evolved over time into a modern state formation. Although there is a germ of truth to the notion, in reality the nation-state is more of an "imaginary community"—an artificial construct largely created by political and economic elites to foster more expansive national trading markets and to secure overseas colonies. That's not to say that there aren't exceptions to the rule. Certainly, some of the nationalists' ethnic struggles in the post-Communist era in Central and Eastern Europe have less to do with expanding markets than with preserving ethnic identities. Still, for the most part, the nation-state and national markets of the early modern era emerged together, each feeding off the other in a symbiotic relationship. National markets increased the pace, speed, flow, and density of exchange of property between people, while the territorial nation-state created and maintained the rules and regulations necessary to ensure an efficient flow of property over a unified and expansive geographic plane.

The genius of the nation-state lay in its ability to provide a new collective identity for the growing numbers of autonomous free agents who made up the world of private property relations in self-regulating markets. It did so by establishing itself as a near mirror image of the self-interested market maximizing individuals of the nascent capitalist economy. Like each of the autonomous individuals who claimed sovereignty over his own personal property domain, the nation-state claimed a similar right of sovereignty over the larger territory of which all the individual free agents were a part. And, like its citizens, the nation-state claimed its autonomy as an equal among nations and defended its right to protect the property under its control as well as to compete with other nation-states—through trade or war—for contested territory.

The difficult challenge for the budding nation-state was how to eliminate all the internal pockets of resistance to free trade in a national market while at the same time enlisting the emotional support of its subjects—later its citizens—in the collective tasks of society, including the collection of taxes and the conscription of armies to protect its national interests. This was no easy matter since, in many ways, the Enlightenment idea of the detached, self-interested, autonomous agent—operating only with his own material self-interest in mind and determined to optimize his own property holdings—seemed strangely at odds with an effort to forge a collective sense of common purpose and identity. How does the nation-state convince millions of newly emancipated individuals to give up some of their autonomy and freedom to the state?

The answer was to create a compelling story about a common past, one appealing enough to capture the imagination of the people and convince them of their shared identity and common destiny. The architects of the modern nation-state understood the magnitude of the task ahead of them. After Italian state unification in 1861, Massimo d'Azeglio, the former prime minister of Piedmont, was said to have remarked, "We have made Italy, now we have to make Italians."[63]

Every nation-state in the modern era has created a myth of origins complete with its own heroes and heroines and past moments of trials and tribulations, often memorialized in elaborate rituals. In an increasingly disenchanted secular world, the nation-state had to establish a powerful new image of a people who shared a noble past and were destined for future greatness. At the same time, the nation-state had to create a convincing enough utopian vision of what lay ahead to win over the loyalty of its subjects and, later, citizens. If the road to immortality no longer lay with accepting Christ as savior, then at least it could be found in the relentless pursuit of unlimited material wealth in the form of the accumulation and exchange of property. In return for giving one's allegiance to the state—the litmus test being whether the citizen would be willing to give his or her life for their country—the state would uphold its side of the covenant by protecting each person's right to own and exchange private property in a free marketplace.

Creating a shared identity was also essential to making viable an unobstructed national market. Before there was an England, France, Germany, and Italy, what existed was a thousand different stories and traditions being lived out in little hamlets, nestled in valleys and on mountainsides across the continent. Each story was passed on in a separate language or at least in a distinct dialect.

A myriad of local languages, customs, and regulations for conducting commerce kept the transaction costs high for producing and trading goods and services over a wide geographic terrain. Suppressing or even eliminating pockets of cultural diversity was an essential step in creating an efficient and seamless national market. Creating a single homogenized national myth required the often ruthless destruction or subordination of all the local stories and traditions that existed for centuries of European history.

The success of the nation-state model owes much to the adoption of rational processes for marshaling far-flung activities. To begin with, it was necessary to establish a single dominant language in each country so that people could communicate with one another and understand shared meanings. It's often thought that sharing a common language was indispensable to bringing people together under the aegis of the nation-state. However, that's not generally the case. Take France, for example. In 1789, on the eve of the French Revolution, less than 50 percent of the people spoke French, and only 12 to 13 percent spoke it correctly. In northern and southern France, it would have been virtually impossible to find anyone who spoke French. At the time Italy was unified in 1861, only 2.5 percent of the population used the Italian language for everyday communication. In eighteenth-century Germany, fewer than 500,000 people read and spoke in the vernacular that later came to be the official German language, and many of them were actors who performed new works onstage or scholars writing for a small intellectual elite.[64]

Much of the impetus for creating national languages had less to do with nation-state formation and more to do with the demographics facing the early print industry. Printers in the fifteenth and sixteenth centuries were anxious to expand the markets for the mass production of books. The problem was that while Latin was the official language of the Church and was used among European scholars and government officials in the palace courts, it represented too small a reading market for the new communications revolution. On the other hand, there were so many languages and dialects spoken across Europe that each one by itself would be too small a market to be commercially viable. The answer, in most countries, was to choose a single vernacular language, usually the most dominant in a region, and establish it as the language for reproduction—first in bibles and later for works of literature and science.

Even here, the languages that eventually became standard French, German, Spanish, Italian, and English were, in part, invented. They were usually the result of combining elements of all the various idioms spoken in a region and then standardizing the grammar.[65] However, once a common language became accepted, it created its own mystique of permanence. People came to think of it as their ancestral tongue and the cultural tie that bound them together.

Getting everyone to speak and read the new vernacular necessitated the creation of a national educational system in each country. A single educational system, in turn, created reliable and predictable standards of what was to be learned and how. Standardized national education was a wholly new phenomenon of the modern era and helped forge a national consciousness. With each generation of schoolchildren learning the same subjects, in the same way, in a common language, it wasn't long before people began to believe that they were part of a shared experience and a common destiny. A French minister of education, reflecting on the success of French public education, remarked that

> he could consult his watch at any moment of the day and say
> whether every child in France, of a given age, would be doing
> long division, reading Corneille, or conjugating . . . verbs.[66]

The nation-state's intervention into the affairs of its citizens merely began with the establishment of a common language and a universal educational system. The modern state's mission is to create a totally rationalized environment that can optimize the free play of property exchange in a market economy. Records have to be kept on every citizen. Birth certificates, school registrations, marriage licenses, death certificates, and passports all have to be issued. Taxes have to be collected, and government revenues need to be distributed. Full-time armies need to be trained, equipped, quartered, and sent into battle. Standards have to be set to regulate everything from the quality of food and medicine to the quality of the environment. Even reproducing the culture itself is no longer just left to chance or to the whims of local communities. Museums have to be built, memorials financed, historic dates recognized and celebrated, and parks set aside for recreation and entertainment. The list is nearly endless.

The formal recognition in international law of the sovereign rights of territorial states came in the form of a peace agreement in 1648 that ended the thirty-year war between Lutherans, Calvinists, and Catholics. The Peace of Westphalia recognized the irreconcilable differences between the various branches of Christianity and granted territorial rulers sovereign authority within their own domains to establish matters of religion, while restricting the rights of other countries to intervene in what was hereafter to be considered an internal matter within each respective country. The essential points laid out in the Peace of Westphalia, although modified over the course of the next three centuries, remained pretty much the same until the end of World War II.[67]

The treaty recognized that the world is made up of autonomous and independent states and that each state is sovereign over the internal affairs within its fixed territory. Moreover, each state is equal to every other state, and no superior authority exists over them. Finally, territorial states are each expected to preserve their own self-interests, and while free to enter into diplomatic relationships and bilateral or multilateral agreements with one another, they also have the right to use force to settle disputes if necessary.[68]

For a time, the interests of the new territory-based monarchical rulers and the emerging capitalist class and bourgeoisie coincided. The new state powers, anxious to consolidate their rule, needed to generate revenue. Armies had to be raised, ships had to be built, weapons had to be manufactured, and administrative bureaucracies had to be set up both to control their own territory and to colonize new territories abroad. It was, therefore, in the interest of the monarchies to stimulate domestic economic activity.

For their part, the merchants and manufacturers were desirous of reforms that would help speed the transition to free trade in national markets. They sought the elimination of legal and customary restrictions that hampered labor mobility, pushed for legal enforcement of commercial contracts backed by the police power of the monarchy, and pressed for improvements in roads, waterways, and communications to speed commerce and expand the geographic range of trade. They also wanted the centralized political authority to standardize weights and measures and create a single coinage to reduce transaction costs and expedite commercial activity. The monarchical authority was more than willing to facilitate the changes and back up the reforms with the full coercive force of the state because the state too had an interest in creating favorable conditions for the emergence of a national market.

Eventually, however, the mercantilist policies pursued by the new regimes threw an irreconcilable wedge between the nascent capitalist class and the government. The states were intent on accumulating precious metals—gold and silver—to finance their domestic spending and foreign adventures. They reasoned that the best way to increase their money holdings was to favor foreign over domestic trade. The strategy was to heavily regulate domestic production so they could secure high-quality goods at low prices and then sell the goods abroad for higher prices and be paid in precious metals.

Under the scheme, their overseas colonies would be restricted to producing only cheap raw materials for export back to the parent country and be forced to buy their finished manufactured goods from the home country at inflated prices. Any effort in the colonies to manufacture their own goods for domestic use or for trade abroad was forbidden, and any infractions were harshly punished.

The emphasis on foreign trade greatly benefited the export merchants, but at the expense of the domestic manufacturers. While the increase in foreign trade helped expand the home market for manufactured goods, the restrictions that governments like Britain eventually placed on the volume of domestic production that could be produced in order to keep export prices artificially high worked to the disadvantage of the manufacturers.[69]

The young capitalist class preferred open markets and free trade, believing that it was the best way to increase output, optimize their margins, and improve their profits. The peasantry, the urban working poor, and the rising middle class all felt the sting of higher prices on domestic products. They also suffered under the burden of increased taxes to finance government spending on armies, weaponry, and wars.

By the late eighteenth century, the breach between the emerging capitalist class and the monarchies was irreversible. On June 17, 1789, deputies of the third estate defied King Louis XVI by establishing their own National Assembly and demanding a French constitution. A few months later, the radicals issued the Declaration of the Rights of Man and the Citizen, which stated, among other things, that "the source of all sovereignty resides essentially in the nation: no body of man, no individual can exercise authority that does not emanate expressly from it."[70]

In a stroke of the pen, government ruled by divine authority and passed on by royal inheritance was dethroned. Henceforth, sovereignty was to lie with "the nation." Who comprised "the nation"? The citizens. And who were the citizens? Those who shared a common lived experience and were bound together by a collective past and future destiny. The citizen, the nation, and the state were conjoined as a single governing entity in France. From now on, government was to be of, by, and for the people.

The French Revolution was heavily influenced by the United States of America, which had already fought and won its own revolution to secure the rights of the people. The Americans and French were engaged in a radical new kind of political experiment, for which there was little precedent. Historian Anthony D. Smith writes,

> There was no question in earlier epochs of mobilizing the people to participate in politics at the center, nor of the need for men, let alone women, to become politically aware and active "citizens." Nor, as a result, was there any interest in providing an infrastructure and institutions, which would cater to all the needs and interests of the citizens.[71]

After the euphoria of declaring themselves sovereign died down, the French settled on a more restrictive definition of the citizen, "limiting political rights to men of property and education."[72] The Americans, the British, and most other new nation-states in the eighteenth and nineteenth centuries did so as well. Since it was assumed that the nation-state's raison d'être was to protect the property rights of its citizens, it made sense to extend the vote to only those "men" in society who owned property.

The great shift to modern nation-states, which began with England, the United States, and France, spread rapidly to other parts of Europe in the nineteenth and early twentieth centuries. By creating a shared narrative and a common identity stretching across a wide geographic expanse, the newly emerging nation-states provided the psychological reorientation to extend the empathic embrace far beyond local kinship affiliations to encompass multitudes of previously diverse peoples. Individuals came to think of themselves as Englishmen, Frenchmen, Americans, and so on, and began to find emotional common ground with their fellow countrymen. Englishmen empathized with Englishmen, Frenchmen with Frenchmen, and Americans with Americans. Nation-states, whatever their shortcomings, became, however unintentionally, breeding grounds for a vast expansion of empathic sensibility. While the call for patriotism drew a clear line between "we" and "they," it also extended empathic feelings inside national borders among "like-minded" citizens who now believed they shared a history and destiny.

THE CONSCIOUSNESS REVOLUTION OF THE EARLY MODERN ERA

In the great sweep of geological history and even in the minuscule history of the human journey on Earth, the half millennium that spanned the end of the Middle Ages and the dawn of the modern era is but a wisp of time. But in that period of less than twenty-five generations, human consciousness expanded more than at any other time that human beings have populated the Earth.[73]

A small part of humanity, a privileged few—mostly among the upwardly mobile, urban middle classes—began to think in a thoroughly modern way. The human spirit metamorphosed from obedient servants, undifferentiated from the collective will and embedded on preassigned rungs on a Great Chain of Being that descended from the gates of heaven to the fiery depths of hell, to sovereign and autonomous individuals, interacting on a linear playing field, affiliated by bonds of fraternity and committed to both the pursuit of individual happiness and unending human progress.

Although historians, until late, wrote little of the psychological changes that transformed human consciousness, preferring to concentrate on the deeds of great men, military conquests, economic advances, and political realignments, we are fortunate that the other aspect of human experience—the development of self-consciousness and the extension of empathic expression—has been carefully chronicled and preserved in the literary narratives.

The subtle, and not so subtle, changes in the writing of autobiographies provide a window into the changing conception of selfhood and the development of human consciousness during this critical period in human history. While Saint Augustine's *Confessions* was a singular event—the first real attempt at writing what one might consider an autobiography—the literary genre Saint Augustine pioneered was of little interest to other scholars. Between the years 500 and 1400 only about ten autobiographical works of note were written.[74] Autobiography thrives best in literate urban cultures. When urban society collapsed with the fall of the Roman Empire, the self-awareness and introspection that such environments spawn began to whither as well. Then too the Christian worldview of the Dark Ages and early medieval era, with its tight-knit cosmology—the Great Chain of Being—uniting feudal lords, the priesthood, knights, burghers, and serfs in a rigid hierarchically oriented collectivity, in which everyone had preordained roles and responsibilities, did not encourage the kind of self-expression that is the stuff of autobiography. What few autobiographies were written were glorified tales of religious figures leading a good Christian life. The figures were wooden caricatures made to fit an ideal image of God's faithful servants on Earth.

In the mid-eighteenth century, however, the autobiographical genre exploded. In his book *The Value of the Individual: Self and Circumstance in Autobiography,* historian and Columbia University professor Karl J. Weintraub shows in the autobiographies of Giambattista Vico, Edward Gibbon, Jean-Jacques Rousseau, and Johann Wolfgang von Goethe the line of progression in self-awareness and empathic expression that characterized the period leading up to the American and French revolutions and the opening of the modern age at the beginning of the nineteenth century.

The Italian scholar Giambattista Vico, in his autobiography, which was published in 1728, shared with his readers his belief that human nature is not preordained by God or determined by fate but, rather, an ever-evolving process in which human beings create their own realities and pass the lessons learned on to the next generation, who build upon it to fashion their own lives and stories. We have to remember that for his time, this was a remarkable contribution. In a sense, Vico's insights were the precursor to the notion of human evolutionary progress that would be so eloquently restated by the French aristocrat Condorcet at the time of the French Revolution at the end of the eighteenth century.

In his autobiography, Vico introduced the radical idea that the best way to understand the past and the unfolding human journey is to literally enter into the spirit of the great thinkers who came before and to try to identify with their individual lives, by imagining what they were feeling and thinking within the context of their times. Although he didn't use the term "empathy"—that would have to wait for nearly two more centuries—he grasped the notion that every life is lived within the context of others we interact with, either in real time or in our memories of past times. And it is by empathic identification that we understand the "autobiographies" of others and, therefore, better understand our own.[75]

In a like view, the historian Edward Gibbon, who wrote the magnum opus *The Decline and Fall of the Roman Empire,* saw history much the same as he saw his own life. When joined, personal histories are, after all, what makes up the collective history of our species. Like Vico,

Gibbon had little patience for the idea of fate and destiny and preferred to think that history is a much more personal affair made up of the individual idiosyncrasies, chance circumstances, and accidental encounters that interact with ever-changing environmental conditions and social contexts. People invent their way as they go—both in an autobiographical sense and a collective historical sense. We create our personal stories and our grand cosmological narratives and each interact with the other in an evolving process that is the very definition of human history.[76] A shocking thesis for the time.

It's only when we get to the brilliant Jean-Jacques Rousseau, the indefatigable French critic of the European Enlightenment, that we are exposed to the first thoroughly modern autobiography. His *Confessions*, written between 1764 and 1770, is in many respects the opposite of Saint Augustine's. While Saint Augustine's motivation was to come clean with God in order to secure redemption, Rousseau's motivation was entirely secular in nature. His intention was to bare his soul to men in the hopes that they would understand the core of his inner being and come to love him. Rousseau is unperturbed about his relationship to God. Believing himself to be ultimately good by nature because he remained true to his "natural self," he writes, rather unabashedly, "I who believe and always have believed that I am on the whole the best of men."[77]

Rousseau believed that all men and women were born equally good but were led astray by civilization.[78] Interestingly, Rousseau used this rule of thumb over and over again in his *Confessions* to absolve himself of any personal moral improprieties, arguing that his intentions had always remained faithful to his deepest natural instincts, so that fault for any injustice that others might attempt to attach to him must ultimately rest with the corrupt society in which he lived.

Rousseau made a point of emphasizing his motivation in writing the *Confessions*. "I resolved to make it a unique work by virtue of its unparalleled veracity so that in one instance at least one might see a man as he was inside."[79] He even boasted that he would disclose more about himself than anyone had ever previously done. Rousseau remained convinced that if others could know the real him—a man of natural goodness—they would come to love him.[80]

On the one hand, here was a man of great personal ego—of the kind that only the modern age, with its preoccupation with the self, could produce. His ego appeared to have no bounds, although he probably would have said that he was just trying to be honest about himself. He once remarked, "I am made unlike anyone I have ever met; I will even venture to say that I am like no one in the whole world. I may be no better but at least I am different."[81] He writes, "I would prefer being forgotten by the entire human race than being looked upon as an ordinary man."[82] In a letter to a confidant he laments, "Providence has erred; why did it decree that I should be born among men, yet made of different species from the rest of mankind?"[83] A contemporary analyst might psychoanalyze Rousseau as a narcissist, caught up in the delusions of his own grandeur.

On the other hand, when reading through his *Confessions*, one is also caught by the desperate sense of aloneness he feels and his yearning to experience intimacy and a deep sense of attachment to others. He tells his readers that "my strongest desire was to be loved by everyone who came near me."[84]

Perhaps the fact that his mother had died during his childbirth colored his sense that his life must add up to something special to make up for the loss. The very loss itself, however, might have contributed to his desperate need to find the love and affection denied to him by his mother's death at the very moment he drew his first breath of life.

Rousseau comes off as a brilliant, troubled, and complicated being. He is someone the reader truly comes to know and experience on an emotional level, something no other autobiography before that time succeeded in doing. The reader comes to dislike his pretentious nature and his sense of self-importance but feels a certain sense of compassion for the very troubling circumstances Rousseau found himself in during his life.

For example, in one of the more revealing passages in the *Confessions*, Rousseau reminisces about his "unbearable remorse" over an incident in his youth when he blamed an innocent servant girl for stealing a ribbon that he had in fact taken. Rousseau explains that he had stolen the ribbon to give to her, but at the very moment he was about to extend his gift of affection, he was asked to account for the theft and "threw the blame on the first person who occurred to me."[85]

What child hasn't found themselves in a similar circumstance? But then Rousseau tries to explain the incident away by claiming that his intentions were good—to share his affections in the form of a gift to another child. "Never was deliberate wickedness further from my intention than at that cruel moment."[86] Unwilling to bear the shame that went with confessing the naughty act, he preferred to shift the blame. Again, we've all been there. It's when he later reflected on the incident as an adult that the reader loses any sense of empathy and compassion for him. He tries to wiggle out of personal responsibility by suggesting that if the head of the household

> had taken me aside and said: "Do not ruin that poor girl. If you are guilty tell me so," I should immediately have thrown myself at his feet, I am perfectly sure. But all they did was to frighten me, when what I needed was encouragement.[87]

Perhaps. But to a contemporary reader, it sounds like the classic case of shifting the blame twice, first to the little girl, then to "society."

Where Rousseau finally loses credibility and the very empathy and affection he so desperately hopes to get from his readers is when he gives his account of a very secret part of his former life that few were aware of. Here was this man, whose book *Émile* electrified European audiences with its compassionate approach to educating youth, who confesses to having abandoned all five of his own children to orphanages immediately after their births. He explains away each case of abandonment with a glib excuse. With the first abandonment Rousseau says, rather implausibly, that

> the man who best helped to stock the Foundling Hospital was always the most applauded. . . . "Since it is the custom of the country," I told myself, "if one lives there, one must adopt it."[88]

Later on, as the abandonments heap up, Rousseau elevates his ratio-nale by suggesting that by allowing the state to educate his children, he was merely conforming with Plato's thoughts on the matter.[89] Feeling himself to be a moral man, the very epitome of a man driven by his heart and his natural instincts, he can't come to grips with the simple reality that even in a state of nature a parent doesn't normally abandon their offspring. If there was ever a "natural instinct," parental care and protection would most assuredly top the list. Yet Rousseau's sense of utter denial is chilling. He proclaims,

> I feel it and boldly declare, that it is not possible. Never, for
> a moment in his life, could Jean-Jacques have been a man
> without feelings or compassion [*sans entrailles*], an unnatural
> father. I may have been mistaken, but I could never be
> callous.[90]

Did he truly believe himself to be innocent? Or were his readers being conned, or was he deceiving himself, despite his protests that such was not the case? Yet with all of the self-justifying psychological backtracking, what cannot be denied is his almost obsessive need to love and be loved and to establish bonds of fraternity with humanity.

One comes away from Rousseau's *Confessions* with an overpowering impression that here was a man in search of an oceanic empathic expe-rience, despite the fact that many aspects of his own life fell wide of the mark. Weintraub's summation of Rousseau reads like the chronicle of a man both able to appreciate the importance of empathy and yet, at critical times in his life, unable to express it.

> He wishes to be able to read the hearts of his fellow human
> beings. In return he wants to make his soul transparent to
> the reader's eye. A man ought to "to show his heart upon his
> face." . . . He wanted to achieve that ecstasy of unmediated,
> immediate, unobstructed communing with men, and above
> all with women, which he, at times, was privileged to have
> with nature. . . . At such times he felt himself to be whole, to

be a harmonious part of a larger whole. At such moments he
needed nothing, not even words. . . . A simple exclamation
"Oh! Oh Nature! Oh Mother!" was the fully adequate
expression of his overflowing heart.[91]

Fittingly, the great German philosopher and scientist Johann Wolfgang von Goethe's autobiography *From My Life: Poetry and Truth*,
released in 1808 and continually updated until 1831, stands alone at the
beginning of modernity as the best attempt to reconcile the mechanistic
cosmology and rationalism of the Enlightenment extolled by Descartes
and Newton in the seventeenth century and the early Romantic reaction of Rousseau and his ilk in the eighteenth century. If one were to
have to choose a single individual who most embodied a cosmopolitan
view of the world and a universal empathic sensibility, Goethe would
be an easy pick. Goethe would have felt quite at home with the object
relations theorists, psychiatrists, and attachment theorists, as well as the
philosophers of embodied experience working at the cutting edge of
cognitive psychology research.

More than two hundred years ago he looked at the world, nature,
and the trajectory of human consciousness much the same way as the
millennial generation living in the highly cosmopolitan world of the
twenty-first century. He might well deserve the title of "man of all
ages."

Goethe believed that one's individuality emerged from the relationships that surround him, both in nature and in society. Each of us is
a unique individual, but that uniqueness should not be equated with
autonomy. Rather, what makes us unique is that each of us carries with
us the very particular relationships and encounters that fill us in as a
social being. Those relationships begin with our deep, inseparable affiliation with nature. We each emerge from nature and descend back into
nature. Between our birth and death, we are continually taking nature
into our being and releasing it back. He writes, "We are surrounded and
embraced by her [nature]—incapable of stepping out of her, incapable
of penetrating deeper into her."[92]

Goethe was struck by the fact that every creature is unique yet connected in a single unity. "Each one of her [nature's] creations has its own character [*Wesen*] . . . and yet all together make one. . . ."[93]

Goethe parted company with Descartes, Newton, and other Enlightenment thinkers whose cosmological models portrayed a world of pure being—orchestrated by fixed mathematical formulas and driven by strict mechanistic principles. He saw a nature continually in flux, always changing and evolving, creating new forms and realities. Goethe was awed not by nature's fixedness but by its novelty. His nature was full of surprises. It was a creative force. While constrained by physical and biological rules, life is not fated as if we were automatons, but exercises various levels of freedom. Reflecting on the nature he knows, Goethe muses that

> [f]or permanence she has no use, and puts her curse on all that
> stands still. . . . She spits forth her creatures out of the Nothing
> and does not tell them whence they come and whither they
> go. Let them run; she knows the course.[94]

Goethe felt that the purpose of living was to enrich life and that man is endowed with a special appreciation of life—a heightened consciousness—so that he might steward all that is alive. He saw his own life in that context.[95] Because of his deep love of nature and its rich diversity, Goethe engaged life from a nonjudgmental perspective. The nature he knew was not fallen and depraved, or simply utilitarian and exploitable, but a living, breathing community ruled by reciprocity. Breathing nature in and out was the way one takes in nature and remains connected to the larger whole.

Deepening those connections requires more than just toleration and acceptance of each other's unique individuality. It also requires an attentiveness to how others experience us and how we experience them. We learn about ourselves through the eyes of others.

> Our fellow men serve us best as they have the advantage of
> comparing us with the world from their perspective, thus
> being able to obtain closer knowledge of us than we can gain.

> In riper years I have therefore attended carefully to the manner
> in which others may see me, so that I might gain clarity about
> myself and my inner part through and in these others, as in so
> many mirrors.[96]

Goethe argued that taking account of oneself through the eyes of another was meant to be a reciprocal process. To "find my way into the condition of others, to sense the specific mode of any human existence and to partake of it with pleasure."[97] It is by this continuous empathic process that one informs and forms oneself and helps form the world of others. While "taking in the world" via introspection is important to the process, it is a mere means to the larger goal of connecting to the deeper realties that make up the unity of nature.

Goethe was, therefore, impatient with "navel gazing," or self-absorption, which leads not to transcendence but regression. He chose to live fully engaged in the world. He wrote "but if any one knows how to take in the world and then 'to speak to it' [*auszusprechen*], then he is a poet."[98]

Goethe summed up his own life and what he thought life was all about this way.

> [T]hat beautiful feeling that only mankind together is the true
> man, and that the single individual can be joyful and happy
> only when it has the courage to feel itself as a part of one.[99]

With Goethe, we see the secularization of the empathic impulse, embedded in embodied experience that includes not only human society but all of nature. His empathic view is truly universal in scope.

Autobiography gives us one important lens for viewing the changes in human consciousness between the late Middle Ages and the modern era. Other forms of literature, especially fiction, are even more revealing in depicting the deep changes in human cognition that gave rise to the modern mind and the growth in empathic expression.

The history of narrative, Erich Kahler rightfully notes, is a "process of internalization" and "consists in gradually bringing the narrated material down to earth and breathing into it a human soul."[100] The first great narratives were cosmogonies and theogonies and slowly descended into the chronicling of real earthly events.

Mythologies tell the story of tribal existence and are populated by spirits and the gods. The early epics—for example the *Odyssey*, *Iliad*, and *Aeneid*—are transitional stories and begin to introduce heroic humans with godlike attributes. They chronicle important events of the past in an idealized form and often still contain mythological references. Biblical stories are often real historical records but, again, laced with mythological themes.

The humanization of narrative is a very gradual process and provides a running account of the awakening of human consciousness from the fog of an undifferentiated collective consciousness. The early epics contain only scattered references to earthly historical events, usually lists recounting the names of battles or the listing of genealogies in the Bible or the cataloguing of ships in the *Iliad*. The Greek tragedies introduce human feelings and become vehicles for audiences to vent their emotions, empathize with the plight of the protagonists in the unfolding plot, and achieve an emotional catharsis with the actors in the final scenes. The Greek tragedies were the first literary form to provide a theatrical space for a collective empathic experience. The Christian era brought with it homilies designed to bring people into the fold or strengthen the beliefs of those already counted among the flock.

It wasn't until the invention of the chivalric romances of the latter Middle Ages, however, that we see in narrative the telling of a tale with the intention of stirring the emotions for purely personal entertainment. The moralizing tales, so prevalent in an era of theological consciousness, while still dominant, now had to compete with knightly adventure and romance. These romantic tales of knightly heroes came at a time when a newly urbanized Europe was leaving behind the agrarian ways of feudal society. The chivalric romances appealed to the emerging bourgeoisie of the cities, much the same way that cowboy stories did in the twentieth century, as the Wild West became a distant memory. Both genres spoke to the human yearning to break out of the confines of a new urban way of life and experience, if only vicariously, the daring and excitement of a wilder idealized past.

More important than the subject matter, notes Kahler, was the fact that "the narrative has become *symbolic*."[101] Through the lines of a particular story, the reader could contrast another period of time with their own and conjure up an emotional response that reflected the comparison. Moreover, the reader took away from the experience an appreciation that other people in other cultures in other times felt, thought, and acted differently—a revelation in the late Middle Ages that broadened one's sense of perspective regarding both the diversity and relative nature of human experience.[102]

The chivalric romances laid the psychological ground for the emergence of the great literary genre of the modern era—the novel. The first modern novel, most literary historians agree, was Cervantes's *Don Quixote*, published in 1605 in Spain. Interestingly, Cervantes's novel was meant to be a spoof or parody of the chivalric romances. But it goes far beyond that.

Alonso Quixano, a retired country gentleman and the protagonist, becomes obsessed with chivalric romances and decides to remake himself in the image of the feudal knights. He puts on a rusty suit of armor, rechristens himself Don Quixote de la Mancha, and sets out to save the world. His idealistic escapades, including his attack on windmills, thinking them to be monsters that need to be slain, are both meant to be hilariously funny and farcical. But in the telling, the reader comes to know Quixote not just as a bumbling do-gooder but also a sensitive soul who only wants his life to account for something.

Don Quixote was the first narrative to express universal human themes by the telling of an individual's own story. By doing so, it created the novel as a literary genre. What makes Don Quixote and the novels that followed over the centuries so fascinating is that the characters in the stories are fictional, yet the circumstances they find themselves in, the situations they confront, and the lives they live are so powerfully real in emotional content that they are able to create a reality and make the reader an intimate part of it.

Heroic characters are action-oriented but have little or no interior life. What they do is who they are. While their actions and deeds are meant to be courageous and, therefore, virtuous, we rarely get a read on what they are feeling. The characters are simple and uncomplicated and lack vulnerability and ambiguity. They think in black-and-white terms and are unable to pick up on the shades and nuances of other people's behaviors because they lack any introspection regarding their own.

By contrast, the characters that developed in the great era of fiction that extended into the twentieth century are increasingly full-bodied human beings whose lives and struggles mirror our own. The novel reorients the reader to the inner workings of the characters' psyches. The author asks us to journey into their world of emotions, thoughts, and behavior and to identify with them as if they were us. The novel is far more than sheer entertainment. It is the first learning tool ever designed to explore universal human sentiments in narrative form by the telling of "novel" stories.

The progression of the novel form over the past four centuries is one of ever-deeper probes into the human psyche, from the rather thin portrayal of Don Quixote to the nuanced psyche of Raskolnikov in Dostoevsky's *Crime and Punishment*. Characters became increasingly individualized, real, and complex, reflecting the growing sense of self-consciousness of each succeeding generation of readers. The novel, in turn, helped readers become more aware of their own selfhood by experiencing vicariously the lives of fictional characters.

By providing generation after generation of readers with more complex, ambiguous, and emotion-laden characters with which to identify, commiserate, and emulate, novels opened up the floodgates of human emotion so that millions of people could explore whole new realms of reality and universalize the empathic drive beyond anything experienced by previous generations.

The importance of the novel in the transformation of human consciousness is only recently getting the attention it deserves. Author and Duke University English professor Nancy Armstrong is one of a growing number of scholars who says that she seriously doubt[s] that individualism could have taken shape and spread throughout the West as fast and decisively as it did unless and until the novel had transformed the concept into narrative form.[103]

In the early novels the characters struggled with the very question of how to know another person's innermost feelings as well as how to articulate one's feelings toward them. It's as if the novels themselves were mirrors to the transformation going on in the nonfiction world as people engaged in a similar struggle to explore feelings, their own and that of others. The period was marked by an internal exploration of the psyche and was every bit as harrowing a journey as those of the great explorers of the time as they navigated the oceans and crossed the globe.

In Chamblain de Marivaux's *La Vie de Marianne*, published in sections beginning in 1731, Marianne, the protagonist, spends pages describing in minute details the emotional makeup of two important women in her life, Madame Dorsin and her benefactress, Madame de Miran. After doing so, she throws her hands up and admits that "[a]ll these portraits cause me trouble." Marianne feels a sense of deep inadequacy in not being able to penetrate to the core of how she truly feels about the ladies, at least in words. She laments,

A portrait can be sketched in a few words, but to draw in the exact details . . . is an endless task. . . . When I say that I am going to give you a portrait of these two ladies, I mean that I shall show you some of their traits. I would not know how to render what people are in their entirety; at least it does not seem to me possible to do this. I know the persons with whom I live much better than I could describe them; there are things in them that I cannot sufficiently single out in order to express them, and which I perceive only for myself and not for others. Or else, if I were to express them, I would express them badly; there are matters of feeling so complicated, so delicately precise, that they become all confused as soon as reflection intervenes. Then I no longer know where to take hold of them in order to express them; so that they are in me without my possessing them.[104]

The passages in *La Vie de Marianne* are revealing. This is the first time that a protagonist has so accurately described the nuances of other characters' emotional makeup yet despaired that she was not up to the task.

Marianne's very personal struggle to understand where her own feelings come from and how to capture and possess them in language and use them in social discourse reflects the angst of the modern age, as successive generations wrestled with the transformation of the human mind from theological consciousness to ideological and psychological consciousness.

Without an extraworldly divine presence to explain away the human condition, modern men and women were suddenly left on their own, with only their own minds to tell them who they are, why they are here, and what relevance their life has for them. The secularization of human consciousness accompanies the rise of the self-conscious individual. Henceforth human beings must rethink the meaning of "human nature" by engaging in an internal dialogue with their own consciousness and a social dialogue with the collective consciousness.

NINE

IDEOLOGICAL THINKING IN A MODERN MARKET ECONOMY

THERE WERE A NUMBER of "ideas" about the nature of human nature circulating at the beginning of the modern era, each vying for public attention and acceptance as the overarching framework for a new cosmology. This was the era of "ideological consciousness." Hobbes, recall, said that human nature was avaricious and needed to be constrained by a social contract. John Locke believed human beings are born a blank slate, except for their predisposition for acquisition of property, and needed to be educated into a virtuous life. Rousseau argued that human beings are born good in a state of nature but run the risk of being corrupted by society. Jeremy Bentham suggested that humans are utilitarian creatures who attempt to maximize pleasure and minimize pain and, therefore, create social constructs to advance their desires and mitigate their regrets. Thomas Jefferson introduced the idea that human beings are born with an unalienable predisposition to secure life, liberty, and happiness, establishing the notion that we are creatures in search of self-fulfillment.

All of these notions about human nature took for granted the idea of the individual as a cardinal reference point. By that time, there was widespread agreement that each person enjoyed his or her own unique self-consciousness.

When it comes to consciousness itself, one is struck by the fact that the human being is both a feeling and thinking animal. Therefore, one of the critical questions in the modern era has been which of the two—feeling or thinking—is the most relevant to understanding "human nature." How do the two modes interact? Is one a better measure of consciousness than the other? The era of ideological consciousness is all about the ideological struggle between two competing ideas of which mental activity is the authentic window to "the soul" and which is only auxiliary or, worse, a distraction or impediment.

Enlightenment philosophers were at odds on the question. John Locke, as we already noted, took the view that bodily sensations travel to the brain and there the mind organizes them into ideas and rational modes of action. In other words, our mind tells us how to feel. Hume disagreed. He argued that our feelings create our ideas.[1] We first feel things and then abstract them into categories—like, love, hate, desire—and then use the categories as metaphors for interpreting like-minded experiences.

The philosophers of the early modern era were, with but a few exceptions, inclined to the more rational approaches to defining human nature. The novelists, playwrights, and poets, however, were more interested in plumbing the emotional recesses of the human psyche and spirit. They found plenty of material for their stories, as a newly emerging bourgeoisie became enthralled with its own individuality and more curious about the workings of human emotions.

The growing interest in expressing one's feelings was, to some extent, a reaction to the strict asceticism of Calvinist theology and the detached rationalism of the Enlightenment philosophers. In many ways, the ascetic Calvinist reformers and the rational Enlightenment philosophers shared much in common. They both were dedicated to finding certainty in the universe. For the Protestant reformers, certainty was to be found in the theology of "election" and God's grace. For the Enlightenment philosophers, it was to be found in the certainty of the laws of physics that govern the movements of the universe. They were united in the repudiation of feelings and emotions, which the religious reformers viewed as depraved and the Enlightenment philosophers saw as irrational.

The ascetic Calvinists, dedicated to improving their calling, and the

Enlightenment philosophers, equally dedicated to the task of bringing rational principles of organization to a fledging capitalist marketplace and the growing bureaucracies of national governments helped create a new cosmological narrative that would govern Europe, America, and much of the world in the nineteenth century. The new "man" of the new age would be alone with his God, alone in the marketplace, and alone in the new urbanized culture, but armed with reason so that he might efficiently navigate a mechanistic universe operated by rational laws of physics, buoyed by faith that eternal salvation awaited him in the next world or, at least, that a material utopia lay just ahead on Earth.

SENSE AND SENSIBILITY

The severe asceticism and austere rationality did not go unchallenged. A powerful countermovement, first evidenced in what historians call the "Age of Sentimentalism" in the eighteenth century and later in the "Romantic Era" in the early nineteenth century, reared up, creating a countervailing narrative grounded in an outpouring of feelings and emotions. It was from the bowels of these countermovements that a second great empathic surge emerged in the early modern era, which would deepen and expand the empathic swell that began with the humanists in the sixteenth century at the tail end of the Middle Ages.

The newfound interest in emotions can be seen in the changing definition of the word "sensible," which originally referred to one's perceptiveness and the ability to reflect. By the eighteenth century, it was increasingly used in literary works to refer to feelings and one's ability to express refined emotions, as in the word "sensibility."

Although schoolchildren are instructed that the eighteenth century in Europe and America was the Age of Reason, that only describes part of the story. The century was far more than that. It became the playing field for a grand tug of war between reason and emotion as two very different social movements vied to become the new narrative for a secular age. The author Louis Bredvold makes the point that

> [w]e no longer accept . . . that the eighteenth century was an
> age of prose and reason; we are well aware that it was also
> an age of sentiment and that more tears were probably shed
> both in literature and in real life in that century than in the
> nineteenth.[2]

The late British barrister and philosopher Owen Barfield observed that the individual during this period lived an "imaginative double life," one caught up in "the order and reason of the moral and material universe" and the other in "sensibility in the little universe of himself."[3]

The disenchantment of the world brought on by the cold analytical logic of human reason was met head-on by what sociologist Colin Campbell calls "the re-enchantment of experience."[4] The author Eleanor Sickels defines sentimentalism as "the doctrine or practice of cultivating—and expressing—the emotions for their own sake."[5]

Though emotions cut a wide swath, the sentimentalists more narrowly viewed the emotions associated with tenderness, caring, and compassion as cardinal. Whereas the Calvinist stoics and the heroes of chivalric romances were admired for keeping a stiff upper lip, the new bourgeois sentimentalists were applauded and elevated in esteem for shedding a tear at a moment's notice and expressing their vulnerabilities in countless ways. The French dramatist Louis-Sébastien Mercier quipped that "[w]e must judge the soul of every man by the degree of emotion he displays in the theatre."[6]

The glorification of emotional vulnerability, to the point of public spectacle, was a phenomenon never before seen in any culture, at any previous time in human history. Sickels describes the over-the-top sensibility of the new Man of Feeling.

> He is exquisitely attuned to the slightest touch of joy or pain
> either in himself or in another. He is capable of swooning
> with joy or dying of a broken heart, or rejoicing in the
> good fortune of a rival or weeping over the sad tale from
> the antipodes or the death of a pet mouse. If poetically

inclined—as he usually is—he may write love elegies, not only about Negroes, whom he does not understand, but even about a turtle-dove who dies of a broken heart, or a nightingale who has lost her mate.[7]

While it's easy to poke fun at the specter of grown men weeping or jumping for joy at the drop of a hat, underneath the emotional excesses is the incredible change that was taking place in the human psyche, especially among males in the middle and upper middle classes. The very fact that the virtuous and admired male was increasingly judged by his vulnerability was an extraordinary turn of history. What's more important, the emotional outpouring, expressed both in social discourse and in the literature of the period, is geared primarily to the concern for the plight of others. The British academic Sir Brian Vickers described sensibility as

> an ideal sensitivity to—and spontaneous display of—virtuous feelings, especially those of pity, sympathy, benevolence, of the open heart as opposed to the prudent mind.[8]

To be sure, the new sensibility came with its own emotional baggage. As the movement became fashionable, many an individual became overly concerned that they were not expressing the appropriate level of emotional solidarity and would question their own emotional deficit or, worse, feign emotional exuberance for fear of social ostracization. Lady Louisa Stuart, after reading Henry Mackenzie's *The Man of Feeling*, confided that she was "secretly afraid lest she should not cry enough to gain the credit of proper sensibility."[9] Campbell points out that, for others, emotional catharsis became pleasurable in and of itself, making it more of a hedonistic experience.[10]

Still, it would be hard to exaggerate the importance of a public outpouring of sentiment. By legitimizing such feeling in the social arena, millions of individuals took a new cue on what it means to be a human being and ran with it. They began to dig deep into their own psyches to explore their feelings and, at the same time, became more attuned to the feelings of others. The consequence was an empathic surge of considerable weight.

By the last quarter of the eighteenth century, it was becoming apparent that a grand new narrative was under construction—one that would replace theological consciousness with ideological consciousness and lay the foundation for the American and French revolutions and the onset of the Industrial Age. The new narrative cobbled together reason and emotions in a tense dialectic that would continue to flare up over succeeding centuries. Even today Americans often divide along the classic lines of sense versus sensibility, with market conservatives accusing progressives of being "bleeding-heart liberals" and liberals shouting back, accusing conservatives of being cold, unfeeling rationalists interested only in personal material gain in the pursuit of utilitarian ends.

Jane Austen's book *Sense and Sensibility*, which was written in the 1790s but not published until 1811, at the very end of the era of sensibility and the beginning of the Romantic period, captured the spirit of the age. The novel is the story of the lifelong relationship between two sisters, Elinor and Marianne, each of whose personality epitomizes the two dominant currents of the time. Elinor is a woman of sense, while her sister, Marianne, is a woman of sensibility. Elinor is a woman with a deep sense of responsibility. She keeps her emotions in check, fulfills her social obligations, is reliable and predictable, and is nothing if not eminently reasonable. Her younger sister Marianne is emotional, spontaneous to the point of irresponsibility, and an incurable romantic. She lets her passion and feelings guide her.

Although the novel is meant to be a satire on the times, it deftly plumbs the strengths and weaknesses of each woman's personality and character as they go through life together. By the end of the story, the sisters have exchanged places. The sensible Elinor marries her true love after years of obstacles have blocked their union, while Marianne finds her own happiness with a man she did not initially love but who was sensible and ultimately proved to be a good match as a husband. Each finds happiness in the end, Elinor by finding her inner sensibility and acting on it and Marianne by exercising more sense and doing the same.

Austen's novel was about finding the proper balance between sense and sensibility and reason and feelings. Finding the balance also became the overarching challenge of modernity as the new ideological consciousness taking shape and form would have to accommodate both under a single tent. The first, the rational calculus, with its mathematical and mechanical assumptions about how the universe is organized, provided the intellectual scaffolding for managing an emerging industrial way of life. The second, the emotional largesse, allowed an increasingly differentiated and individualized populace to extend the empathic canopy to the very outer walls of the new cultural tent being raised, creating a new level of social integration.

The struggle to find an accommodation between sense and sensibility played itself out in both the American and French revolutions, but to different ends. The American Revolution and French Revolution are often talked about in the same breath, as if motivated by the same impulse. They were, nonetheless, distinct in some key respects. Both put a premium on ending monarchial power and establishing limited democracy. Both believed in the principle—if not the reality—of equality. But while the American Revolution emphasized individual opportunity in the marketplace and the right of every individual to pursue his or her own happiness, the French preferred to emphasize fraternity. The intellectual leaders in both countries were, for the most part, deists and committed to the Age of Reason. Yet the French departed from their American brethren on the question of man's essential human nature. They were much more disposed to the impassioned emotional writing of their fellow Frenchman Jean-Jacques Rousseau, while the Americans preferred the more tempered rationalism of the English philosopher John Locke, especially in regard to his belief that the desire to acquire private property is basic to human nature.

Reason and feelings continued to spar and vie for public acceptance in both England and France, and to a far less extent in the American colonies where the Puritan ethic remained a powerful conditioning force. The English however, tilted more to sense while the French tilted more to sensibility.

That is not to say that the French were only moved by sensibility.

If anything, they inflated both reason and feelings beyond their appropriate proportions, setting in motion the forces that would lead to the implosion of their revolution.

Nowhere was the French ambivalence over sense and sensibility more dramatically illustrated than in the reforms designed to reorder the temporality of French life.

The architects of the revolution were committed to ridding Western civilization of what they considered to be "religious superstition" and the cruelty, ignorance, and oppression of the Church and state reign of the previous era. They entertained a new image of the future in which both reason and natural emotions would reign as the cardinal virtues and provide the context for their utopian vision. To advance this revolutionary goal, the leaders of the new French Republic issued sweeping reforms in the social, economic, and political life of the society and then attempted to institutionalize these changes by transforming the entire temporal frame of reference of the French people.

On November 24, 1793, the National Convention of revolutionary France put into effect a radical new calendrical system, one that reflected the ideals and principles of the new revolutionary regime. Their motivation was clearly political. They realized that as long as the Christian calendar was allowed to remain the primary temporal reference, it would be impossible to rid French culture of the prerevolutionary influence of the Church.

The new French calendar was designed in part to de-Christianize time, that is, to eliminate the Church's influence over the time of the French people. It was also intended to inculcate a new temporal awareness in which the values of secularism, rationalism, naturalism, and nationalism would determine the sequencing, duration, scheduling, coordination, and temporal perspective of the new French man and woman. Eviatar Zerubavel sums up the revolutionary intent of the new calendrical decree:

> The abolition of the traditional temporal reference framework
> was deliberately meant to strip the Church once and for all of

one of its major mechanisms of exercising social control and regulating social life in France.[11]

The new calendar replaced the Christian era with the Republican era. Instead of using the birth date of Christ as the dividing point between ancient and modern history, they chose to substitute the birth date of the French Republic. Henceforth, 1792 was to be looked on as Year One in what the calendrical architects viewed as a new age in history.

In their zeal to be as rational and scientific as possible, the new government redesigned the entire year to conform with the decimal system. The revolutionary calendar was composed of twelve months, each containing thirty days. Each month, in turn, was divided into three ten-day cycles called decades. Each day was divided into ten hours, and each hour further divided into one hundred decimal minutes. Each minute contained one hundred decimal seconds.[12]

The days of the week were renamed using numbers only: Day One, Day Two, Day Three, and so forth. The designers were mindful of the long history of religious significance attached to the traditional names used to demarcate the week. In substituting pure numbers with mathematical references only, they believed they were advancing the interest of reason over religious superstition.[13]

The calendar represented the absolute extreme thinking of a rational state of mind, subjecting society to a temporal ordering that was mathematical, cold, and detached and designed to erase every vestige of human memory and experience. Yet the architects also attempted, at the same time, to infuse the new calendar with sensibility by reinvoking nature and social camaraderie back into the human experience. All of the saints' days and holy days in the old Christian calendar were abolished, and in their place were substituted natural phenomena. Instead of honoring a saint, the new French man and woman was expected to honor a particular tree, plant, animal, or flower. Even the names of the months were changed to reflect the interest in aligning the new era with the rhythms of nature. The new months were named Vintage, Mist, Frost, Snow, Rain, Wind, Seeds, Flowers, Meadows, Harvest, Heat, and Fruits.[14]

The French public did not take kindly to the elimination of holy days. Under the old Christian calendar, the Church laid aside fifty-two Sundays, ninety rest days, and thirty-eight holidays. The new calendar eliminated Sundays and all of the rest of the holidays, leaving the French citizen with nothing to look forward to but a regimen of never-ending work. To compensate, the calendar designers introduced a limited number of special rest days with names that suggested the Revolution's commitment to sensibility, like the Human Race Day, the French People Day, the Benefactors of Mankind Day, Freedom and Equality Day, Friendship Day, Conjugal Fidelity Day, and Filial Affection Day. By reducing the number of rest days from more than 180 to 36, the French Republic insured the animosity of the French people.[15]

The French revolutionary calendar lasted only thirteen years. In 1806, Napoleon reinstated the Gregorian calendar, in part to appease the French public, who had resisted the revolutionary calendar from the beginning and, in part, to placate the Pope in the hopes of entertaining a rapprochement with the Vatican. The new calendar had been doomed from the outset. By trying to obliterate every traditional benchmark in the life of the French people, the architects of the new calendar created the ideal condition for reaction, retrogression, and, inevitably, repudiation.

The attempt to accommodate both sense and sensibility under a single tent failed. The revolution became a caricature of both views of human nature. In the end, the frantic effort to be perfectly rational and detached, while remaining true to Rousseau's vision of natural innocence and the expression of pure unadulterated emotion, was too much to bear and too difficult to reconcile. The revolution turned in on itself, tilting wildly back and forth between extreme rational authority and impassioned emotional release, finally destroying itself from within.

The empathic surge—which began in the Italian Renaissance, picked up momentum in the late Northern Renaissance and the humanist period of the sixteenth century, and continued to gather strength in the Age of Sensibility in the eighteenth century—swept age-old conventions aside. While the surge ebbed and flowed as it made its twists and turns through the centuries, it never came to a halt or suddenly reversed itself as it did in the wake of the collapse of the Roman Empire. The institution of marriage, the rearing of children, the notion of God, and the concept of human nature were all affected by the metamorphosis of human consciousness that occurred in these pivotal centuries.

By the time American colonists issued their Declaration of Independence in 1776 and the French issued their Declaration of the Rights of Man and the Citizen in 1789, much of Europe had changed. Feudal life, at least in western Europe, had become a distant memory. The new man and woman of the bourgeoisie bore little resemblance to their medieval ancestors. The way the middle and upper classes felt about themselves and others and the way they conducted their lives was so completely different from what one might expect of a lord or burgher or serf in the thirteenth century that one might well have considered the difference a fork in the family tree.

THE LATE MEDIEVAL ENTROPY CRISIS

The last quarter of the eighteenth century saw not only the creation of the modern nation-states based on popular sovereignty but also the demise of the medieval energy regime and the beginning of a new energy regime and accompanying technology revolution that would catapult Europe, America, and the rest of the world into the throes of the First Industrial Revolution.

Recall that the energy revolution of the late Middle Ages and the early modern era ushered in the widespread use of inanimate forms of energy—watermills and, later, windmills. The coming together of the print press revolution with these new forms of energy led to a proto-industrial revolution and, with it, a quickening of population, greater urbanization, increasing individuation, and a deepening sense of self-consciousness. The first empathic surge of the modern era accompanied the new energy/communications revolution.

But as was the case with Rome and the earlier hydraulic civilizations, the dramatic rise of empathic consciousness occasioned by the new energy/communications complex was stalked, at every step of the way, by an equally dramatic increase in the entropic bill. That bill came due in the late eighteenth century.

Medieval Europe had long relied on wood as its primary fuel. The dense forest cover across western and northern Europe provided a seemingly inexhaustible thermal source. By the fourteenth century, however, wood was becoming increasingly scarce. Agricultural advances, including new drainage technologies, the cross plow, the introduction of three-field rotation, and the use of horse teams for plowing, helped boost the amount of land under cultivation and dramatically increased food production. Food surpluses led to an increase in the human population, which, in turn, put more pressure on farmers to overexploit existing farmland as well as deforest more marginal lands for cultivation. By the fourteenth century, Europe was facing an entropy problem not dissimilar to the one that faced Rome in the second, third, and fourth centuries. A growing population was using up its energy resources faster than nature could replenish them. Widespread deforestation and eroded soil created an energy crisis. Historian William McNeill writes:

> Many parts of Northwestern Europe had achieved a kind of
> saturation with humankind by the fourteenth century. The
> great frontier boom that began about 900 led to a replication
> of manors and fields across the face of the land until, at least
> in the most densely inhabited regions, scant forests remained.
> Since woodlands were vital for fuel and as a source of building
> materials, mounting shortages created severe problems for
> human occupancy.[16]

The depletion of wood was as serious a problem for late medieval society as the depletion of fossil fuels is for us today. Like oil, wood was an all-purpose energy resource, used for a hundred and one different things. Historian Lewis Mumford lists some of the many ways wood was used at the time.

The carpenters' tools were of wood but for the last cutting edge: the rake, the oxyoke, the cart, the wagon, were of wood; so was the wash tub in the bathhouse; so was the bucket and so was the broom; so in certain parts of Europe was the poor man's shoes. Wood served the farmer and the textile worker: the loom and the spinning wheel, the oil press and the wine presses, and even a hundred years after the printing press was invented, it was still made of wood. The very pipes that carried water in the cities were often treetrunks: so were the cylinders of pumps . . . the ships of course were made of wood and . . . the principal machines of industry were likewise made of wood.[17]

Mumford sums up the overriding importance of wood for medieval life, observing that "as raw material, as tool, as machine, as utensil and utility, as fuel and as final product wood was the dominant industrial resource."[18]

Much of the deforestation throughout the fifteenth century was undertaken to make room for expanding agricultural fields. In the sixteenth and seventeenth centuries, even more trees were felled to supply wood ash for cottage industries, including glassworks and soap. In England, the biggest strain on forests came from the increasing needs of the British navy. The building of ships required vast amounts of wood. Repeated attempts to regulate the cutting of forests proved futile. By 1630, wood was two and a half times more expensive than it had been in the late fifteenth century.[19]

In the eighteenth century the deforestation of Europe reached a crisis. Cities and industries were having to pay higher prices for scarcer thermal fuel to run their mills, factories, businesses, and homes.

The glass-works factories alone required the clearing of entire forests. Here's a prime example of the empathy/entropy conundrum. Medieval Europe pioneered the development of glass manufacture for the production of mirrors and optics, beginning in the thirteenth century. The mass production of mirrors focused attention on self-reflection, an idea that would have been impossible before mirrors came into

widespread use. The very term "self-reflection" suggests the importance of mirrors, which are reflective surfaces. Before the development
and mass-manufacture of mirrors, people were not able to see themselves clearly and were, therefore, less interested in the self as a unique,
identifiable object of contemplation. The mass-production of mirrors
certainly played a role in the evolution of the self-aware individual in
the late medieval era.

Similarly, optics became an indispensable tool, allowing artists the
visual means to zoom in on objects at a distance, reducing them to
flat surfaces so they could better hone the art of perspective. Optics—
telescopes and microscopes—also became a critical tool in the arsenal
of scientists like Galileo, Kepler, Newton, and so on, in their probing
of nature. Alan MacFarlane and Gerry Martin, in their book *Glass: A
World History*, observe that glass inventions were pivotal in advancing
the rational, scientific worldview that catapulted Western Europe into
the Modern era and the Industrial Age.

But while glass products helped deepen self-consciousness, extend
the central nervous system, and create a more complex civilization, the
entropy bill was staggering. Whole forests across Western and Northern
Europe were decimated to fuel the glassworks industry.

In the first half of the nineteenth century conflict over access to
diminishing forest reserves became even more acute as a growing population across much of Europe pressed the demand for wood products
for construction, heating, and proto-industrial manufacturing practices.
The burgeoning iron and leather manufacturing industries required
large amounts of wood for use as charcoal to forge pig iron and oak
bark for tanning. But even the wine-making industry was increasing
its demand for wood for stakes to hold up their vines and for barrels to
store their wine. In Prussia, both the government and its harshest critic,
a young Karl Marx, agreed that conflict over forest use was among the
more important political controversies of the period—often pitting traditional land uses, including foraging and hunting, against increasing
demand for wood for industrial purposes and for urban development.
The conflict put peasants against forest landlords, who still retained

seignorial privileges, villages against villages over disputes regarding common access, and rural against urban populations.[20]

Authors Jean-Claude Debeir, Jean-Paul Deléage, and Daniel Hémery observed that

> proto-industrialization appeared as a vast enterprise concerned with "de-stocking" forest reserves; for the first time, forests played the role that coal mines and oil wells would play later, that of a stock of energy perceived as inexhaustible, apparently so limitless that it could be wasted without restraint.[21]

The wood crisis was the entropy bill for an eight-hundred-year period of European expansion that began in the eleventh century with the clearing of forests to provide agricultural land and pasture for a growing population. The trees were used to build the farm equipment, erect the watermills and windmills, fire up the factory kilns, construct the ships, and provide the power for an increasingly urban civilization. Much of Europe's more dense forest cover had disappeared, leaving the landscape bare and bald. On the eve of the French Revolution, the English essayist Arthur Young wrote of his despair witnessing the scale of deforestation taking place in the Pyrenees, saying "I was shocked" at the wanton deforestation taking place.[22]

The Birth of the First Industrial Revolution

Unlike the entropy bill that helped hasten the collapse of the Roman Empire and threw Europe into a dark age for centuries, the disruptions caused by the wood crisis were minimized because Europe was able to convert to a new energy regime in time to avert a total collapse of European civilization. The continent found its salvation in coal and the steam engine. The new energy regime garnered and unleashed far more power than had been possible previously using watermill and windmill technology.

But it should be pointed out that the switch to coal was not exactly greeted with unrequited joy. Quite the contrary. Coal was considered an inferior energy resource: hard to mine, transport, and store, dirty to handle, and polluting when burned. Edmund Howes lamented that "inhabitants in general are constrained to make their fires of sea-coal or pit coal, even in the chambers of honorable personages."[23] Still, by 1700, coal had begun to replace wood as the primary energy resource for England. By the mid–nineteenth century, much of Europe had begun to convert to coal as well.

Mining coal was a difficult affair. After exhausting the more readily available supply near the surface, miners had to descend deeper into the ground. At a certain depth, water levels were reached, and drainage became a serious obstacle to bringing up the coal to the surface. In 1698, Thomas Savery patented the steam pump, providing miners with a tool to bring the water to the surface and thus remove coal from greater depths.

Coal was also much heavier and more bulky to transport than wood. It could not be easily moved by horse-drawn wagons over unsurfaced roads. The weight of the wagons, especially during rainy weather along rutted muddy roads, made transport all but impossible. Horse teams were also becoming increasingly expensive to use to pull the loads. With land for cultivation becoming more scarce, it was simply too costly to graze horses on precious agricultural soil. The answer to the transport problem came in the form of the steam locomotive set on iron wheels. The steam locomotive became one of the first energy machines of the fossil-fuel age and the forerunner of a new era.

The First Industrial Revolution quickened the pace, speed, flow, and density of human exchange. It also helped foster new agricultural technologies that led to unprecedented growth in human population, created an urban way of life on a scale not seen since the fall of Rome, and introduced the factory model for producing goods and services in quantities never before possible.

All of the economic and commercial developments furthered the process of individuation and deepened self-awareness, providing even more fertile ground for the extension of empathic consciousness in the nineteenth century.

Historians date the take-off of the Industrial Revolution to round about the 1780s. That's when the production of basic goods and services shot up in a demonstrable way in England, although it should be noted that no one at the time had much of an inkling that something extraordinary was afoot. After all, it wasn't until the 1830s that the term "Industrial Revolution" was even invented. Part of the reason its origins lie in ambiguity is that there was no epiphanic moment. While historians are fond of identifying coal as the defining energy and the steam engine as the defining technology of the Industrial Revolution, reality didn't conform quite so neatly to the official chronicle. Coal was already in widespread use as a thermal source in scattered parts of England by the 1760s, and it wasn't until 1776, at the dawn of the American Revolution, that James Watt invented and patented the modern steam engine. Even with the emergence of coal and steam power in the last quarter of the eighteenth century, most mills continued to operate by water and wind power. The textile industry, which was the first to be transformed into what we might consider a factory mode operated by men working with machinery, increased its output tenfold between 1760 and 1787, and it was powered by watermills.[24]

The first steam engines, using coal as an energy source, were employed in the British cotton industry in the late 1780s. The productivity gains were dramatic. Between 1787 and 1840, British cotton production "jumped from 22 million to 366 million pounds," while the cost of production plummeted.[25]

After 1830, coal-powered steam technology crossed the English Channel and began to be harnessed in earnest. Belgium doubled its steam engines in use between 1830 and 1838. By 1850, the country had become one of the most industrialized on the continent, with 2,300 engines producing 66,000 horsepower.[26] The Krupps introduced the steam engine into Germany in 1835.[27]

Even with these advances in coal-powered steam technology, the reality is that as late as 1848, the year of the great European Revolution, French hydraulic power "accounted for two and a half times more power than steam engines. . . ." Of the 784 firms in the French steel industry in 1845, 672 were still using watermills for their energy. Even in the French textile industry at the time, hydraulic energy powered more factories than coal-fired steam technology.[28]

In the next two decades, the advantage would turn to steam power in most European countries. The total steam power registered a four-and-a-half times rise, from 4 million horsepower in 1850 to 18.5 million horsepower just twenty years later.[29]

A country's coal reserves became a decisive factor in the speed of transition into a fully integrated industrial economy. Britain began with a distinct advantage, by being able to tap large amounts of readily accessible domestic coal reserves. Germany and the United States, however, with equally large coal reserves, quickly caught up.[30] By 1914, all three countries could claim superiority as industrial powers.

The steam locomotive was adopted across countries and continents even more quickly. The vehicle captured the attention of the public perhaps more forcefully than any technology in history. People were mesmerized by its speed. By the 1830s, steam locomotives were traveling up to 60 miles per hour.[31] The locomotive became the instant symbol of the new Age of Power. Countries scrambled together large sums of capital and harnessed thousands of workers to the task of laying down rail beds, to claim their place among industrial nations.

Steam locomotives transformed logistics and the supply chain, dramatically narrowing distances, delivery times, and costs between suppliers and producers and between producers and consumers. J. C. Debeir and others calculate that

> in 1850, a train of fourteen trucks pulled by a 100 HP
> locomotive could carry about 90 tons of merchandise, that is
> replace 18 stagecoaches, as many coach drivers and 144 horses.[32]

By 1845, forty-eight million British passengers were traveling on rails per year.[33] In the 1850s, more than 21,000 new miles of railroad were constructed in the United States, establishing an integrated rail network east of the Mississippi River.[34] Incredibly, a trip from New York to Chicago, which would have taken three weeks just a decade earlier, took only three days in 1857.[35]

Aside from speed, the steam locomotive had still another advantage—dependability in all kinds of weather. While canals were affected by droughts in the summertime, freezing over in the winter, and freshets in the spring, steam locomotives could run year round in almost any kind of weather. Moreover, a steam locomotive could make several back-and-forth trips in the time it took a canal barge to make one. Shipping costs were also dramatically cheaper. Steam locomotives could handle three times as much freight as barges for an equivalent price.

The coal-powered steamship also replaced the sailing ship in the nineteenth century. The steamship companies became operational in the 1830s, nearly the same time as the railways. Their operating costs were 15 to 20 percent lower than sailing ships. By 1900, steamships made up 75 percent of the world's tonnage.[36] Cheap fares on steamships allowed millions of Europeans to resettle in the Americas.

The nineteenth century might just as well have been called the acceleration revolution as the Industrial Revolution. Every aspect of life accelerated. While the steam locomotive was barreling across the countryside at lightning speeds, ferrying passengers and cargo to the far ends of continents, population was accelerating at a record pace as well. The new productivity was bringing with it new prosperity. The middle class bourgeoisie was living as well as kings had just a century earlier. And the new wealth, in turn, brought with it a steep rise in births. The UK doubled its population in the first fifty years of the nineteenth century.[37] At mid-century, England became the first country in which the urban population exceeded the rural population.[38] By the 1870s, there were four cities in Europe boasting a population of a million or more and an additional six with over a half million residents.[39] Prussia and Russia also experienced a doubling of population. Other European countries experienced similar population increases.[40]

By 1848, the year that revolutions shook virtually every capital of Europe, the complexion of society had radically changed. Bulging populations were filling in the last remaining wild spaces and spilling over borders. Millions left for the New World, in hopes of finding a little more room to breathe and maneuver. The railroads and steamships were connecting the world, creating the first truly global economy. Factories were churning out manufactured goods at a record pace. World trade nearly doubled in the first half of the century. In the twenty years following the revolutions of 1848, it would increase by 260 percent.[41]

The new coal-powered, steam-technology revolution promised greater conversion of raw resources into finished goods and greater connectivity between peoples, communities, and markets. Its ability to deliver, however, depended on the introduction of a comparable communications revolution to oversee and manage industrial life.

In 1814, Friedrich Koenig's steam printing machine with rollers began churning out news pages at *The Times* in London. The new presses could print 1,000 copies per hour compared to a meager 250 using the old-style presses.[42] A spate of technological innovations in printing over the course of the next seventy years, including the introduction of the rotary press in 1846 and linotype in 1886, dramatically reduced the cost and increased the speed of production, providing cheap print publications for the masses.[43]

Cheap print—in the form of newspapers, magazines, pamphlets, and books—encouraged literacy among the middle and working classes. Between 1830 and 1880, European nations, the United States, Canada, and other countries introduced public schools, making universal literacy possible for the first time in history.[44]

State-sponsored public education, at first a novelty, soon became a norm in much of Europe and North America. Schools doubled in France between 1833 and 1847, and school attendance tripled, reaching 3.6 million students.[45] The number of students attending secondary school increased from one in thirty-five in 1842 to one in twenty by 1864. Across Europe, the number of children attending primary school rose dramatically between 1840 and 1880. While the population rose by 33 percent, the number of children going to school rose by 145 percent.[46]

By the mid–nineteenth century, three-fourths of the adult population in Scandinavia and German states were literate, while in France, the Low Countries, and northern Italy literacy rates were between 40 and 60 percent. In the eastern and southern countries, literacy was much lower, with only 5 to 10 percent of adults able to read and write.[47]

A print-oriented literate workforce was indispensible to the supervision and operations of the First Industrial Revolution. As mentioned in Chapter 1, it would have been impossible to manage the technological and social complexity of the Industrial Age using codex or relying on an oral culture.

It's no accident that schools were set up to resemble factories. Children learned more than their ABCs. School life was structured around key temporal and spatial constraints. Students learned to be punctual and efficient and to sit at a desk for long periods of time concentrating on work. The new routines accustomed the children to the temporal expectations and physical conditions that awaited them in the new industrial factories and offices. They were also taught to think of learning as something one acquires and possesses. Knowledge was looked on as power and regarded as a tool or asset one could use to advance one's interest in the marketplace.

The mission of education was quite different from that of the humanist period where the focus was on philosophical and theological questions. In the modern era of public schooling, the goal set forth by the state educators was to produce batches of "productive citizens" for the emerging national economies.

The convergence of the new communications and energy revolutions made possible the construction of the most complex and efficient social structure for converting the Earth's raw resources into human utilities in history.

As the tempo of industrialization picked up speed, urbanization accelerated and national governments consolidated their political power, the "rationalization" of government, market, and social relations continued to keep pace. The period between 1790 and 1850 saw the increasing atomization of the individual in an ever more rationalized and integrated society. The utilitarian ethos became the operating norm of the day. But the growing estrangement of the individual, what the French call *anomie,* found a new voice in the Romantic movement, a successor to the age of sentimentality.

THE ROMANTIC ERA

The Romantic movement was a reaction to the Enlightenment fixation on reason. It became a powerful counterforce that deeply affected every convention and social institution, from marriage relations and the rearing of children to ideas about justice and governance. The Romantic movement reached its nadir in the Revolution of 1848 and the "Springtime of the Peoples." This period saw an empathic surge that would culminate in the first truly modern conceptualization of the meaning of empathic consciousness by Arthur Schopenhauer in his essay entitled "On the Basis of Morality," which was published in 1839.

No example better captures the opening of the Romantic era than the French image of an ideal citizen named "Marianne," who became the very symbol of compassion and empathic expression at the height of the French Revolution. Her body became the embodiment of the revolutionaries' hope for "nurturing a new kind of life."[48] Sociologist Richard Sennett, in his book *Flesh and Stone*, describes the importance Marianne took on in helping the French people articulate their newfound empathic sensibility.

Marianne was depicted as the archetype of a young French woman. The revolutionary artist Clément pictured the goddess in a 1792 rendering as the very epitome of a sensual—but not sexual—female with firm and full nipples and ample breasts. He titled his picture *Republican France, Opening Her Bosom to All the French*.[49]

In her openness, she expressed the ideal of "equal care for all." Sennett reminds us that, until the 1730s, French women who could afford to do so, outsourced their infants to wet nurses. The growing emphasis on the nuclear family and especially the new interest in nurturing children led to an abandonment of wet-nursing among mothers in the newly emerging urban middle class. Early feminist critics like Mary Wollstonecraft pointed out that Marianne was as much a caricature of the domesticated women of the time—a kind of secular version of the Virgin Mary, who performed a somewhat similar function in medieval times. She also bore a strong resemblance to Rousseau's literary portrait of Sophie in *Émile*, whose welcoming, flowing breasts depicted all that is kind and nurturing among human beings in their natural state. Marianne, like Sophie, was, in the words of Sennett, "at liberty to love her children . . . yet lacked the freedom of a citizen."[50]

In public festivals, Marianne statues became a rallying point. New rituals of public virtue took place in her presence. She was the freely giving empathic embodiment of the revolutionary order. Being in her presence solidified the feeling of both maternal nurturance and fraternity. Marianne expressed the deep-seated desire "to touch and be touched" by human warmth and, in that sense, notes Sennett, she "represents an emblem of compassion, of nurturing those who suffer."[51] For a newly urbanized and atomized French citizenry who no longer had theological certainty to hold on to, Marianne provided the symbol of fraternal bonds that would allow them to create a new sense of community based on empathic connection with one another.

Marianne also represented the new feeling of openness, mobility, ease of movement, and flow associated with liberty. French visionaries were determined to break down all of the confining barriers that had locked people up and constrained their freedom of movement, from swaddling babies to sequestered public spaces. Marianne was always placed in the center of a large open-air space to allow her devotees to breathe in the intoxication of open space and to enjoy the freedom of unconstrained movement and solidarity. She became the very symbol of liberation.

In the end, however, the revolutionary visionaries were unable to strike an accord between Marianne as a symbol of intimacy and Marianne as a symbol of liberation. The male-dominated regime's growing ambivalence about Marianne the symbol reflected their own ambivalence about the role women should play in the new order. While they were quite willing to see women as nurturing and selfless and even as intimate companions, they were not yet willing to support their liberation.

Sennett makes note of the fact that as the French Revolution "hardened," Marianne's own popularity waned, while Hercules, the Greek male warrior, became a more popular symbol. Marianne was even given a makeover. She softened, lost muscle tone, and became more passive and fragile in appearance. Her own misfortunes reflected those of French women, who early on had been among the leaders of the revolution but were increasingly suppressed by male radicals, who feared their growing power and prominence.[52]

The Marianne moment was just the opening scene in the Romantic era—a movement that would come to challenge virtually all of the assumptions of the Age of Reason. British historian Eric J. Hobsbawm captures the essence of the Romantic era—the period from 1789 to 1848—when he notes that the general trend was one of "empathic secularization."[53] Like the Renaissance, the Romantic movement was both a reaction to stultifying authority as well as a reaffirmation of the human spirit. The Renaissance, and especially the humanist period at the tail end of the sixteenth century, had tried to breathe a sensuous, earthy quality back into life by reawakening the human imagination and reinvigorating human passions and emotions, long repressed by a Church that glorified the ascetic life and looked to the next world for salvation. The Romantic era was similar in respect to goals, except its target was the cold, detached rationality of Enlightenment philosophy with its emphasis on materialism.

The Enlightenment philosophers viewed the world in mechanistic terms, believed that human beings were acquisitive by nature, and defined progress as material advance. The Romantics, by contrast, viewed the world in organic terms, believed human nature to be deeply affectionate and social, and defined progress as a creative force that unleashed the human imagination and fostered self-fulfillment and a sense of community. The British Isles, France, and Germany were the centers of the movement, although its tentacles stretched into central Europe and America. Its intellectual champions were philosophers, but also poets and novelists—men like Christoph Friedrich von Schiller, Friedrich Schelling, Johann Herder, Samuel Coleridge, William Wordsworth, Edgar Allan Poe, Arthur Schopenhauer, Nathaniel Hawthorne, Johann Wolfgang von Goethe, and William Blake.

The Romantic movement was as much a feeling as a philosophy. It found inspiration in nature rather than in mathematics and eschewed the Enlightenment philosophers' description of a distant watchmaker God who wound up the universe, set it in motion, and then remained aloof. The Romantics preferred to cast their lot with the sensuousness of the natural world, and, if anything, thought of themselves as pantheists. Many came to think of the divine light as immanent in all of nature.

In the Romantic cosmology, God was less the creator of nature than its soul. Like the philosopher Baruch Spinoza, they identified God and nature as one. John H. Randall, Jr., explains that for the Romantics "to live in closest harmony with it [nature], and develop in response to its development, is to know God and feel one's self a part of his spirit."[54]

The Romantics therefore reveled in a human nature that was deeply embedded in nature, and rather than repudiating nature, as the Protestant ascetics and Enlightenment philosophers chose to do, they embraced it with zeal. While the Protestant theologians thought of nature as fallen and the Enlightenment philosophers viewed it in utilitarian terms as useful resources, the Romantics viewed it as good and the basis of all creativity. Rather than elevating human beings from the bowels of nature, they chose to elevate nature, endowing it with supernatural qualities.

The Romantics believed that nature was not eternally fixed but an emerging creative force that was continually transcending itself. By going with the flow of nature, as Rousseau had advocated, each individual could find his or her own creative wave and ride along the crest of nature's transcendent force.

Like the Protestant reformers and Enlightenment philosophers, the Romantics emphasized individualism, but not so each person could stand alone with God in search of salvation or stand alone in the marketplace to pursue self-interest. For the Romantics, individuality was of a different kind. They believed that each person is a unique being endowed with creative potential and that the truly liberated life is the one that optimizes opportunities to be self-fulfilled.

If faith paved the way for Christian transcendence and reason for Enlightenment philosophers, imagination did so for the Romantics. For the very first time in history, human imagination became a topic of discussion and deep interest, signaling a change in human consciousness. Imagination allowed each person to tap into the creative force of nature and become a co-creator of the world and, by so doing, share in the divine process.

The new Romantic conception of self was nothing if not audacious. Nature was in the mind of man, just as the mind of man was in nature. By unleashing human imagination, each individual would rediscover his or her natural being and their place in the natural scheme of things.

The idea of becoming a co-creator of the world was a far cry from Christian belief in being God's humble servant or, for that matter, Enlightenment philosophy, which emphasized only material progress, subject to the verities of a preconceived mechanical universe.

How, then, do we liberate human imagination? Rousseau, the godfather of Romanticism, argued that each individual has within himself an infinite range of possibilities in a state of nature but that corrupt civilization acted as a deterrent, stamping out those natural inclinations and possibilities. The answer was to remake civilization so that its operating assumptions were compatible with the real nature of human beings. This is what the French Revolution attempted to do, but with disastrous consequences.

The problem, as Rousseau's own life and *Confessions* painfully show, is that the idea of being a unique being, endowed with special qualities and potentials, can as easily lead to egomaniacal selfishness as to selfless transcendence.

It all boiled down to how human beings chose to use their most important resource: imagination. It became popular at the time to talk about a new phenomenon, "the creative genius." While there were creative geniuses throughout history, previous generations had believed that inspiration "came to people" rather than emanated from them. By coming to believe that creative genius came from inside the individual and spilled out in the world, society began to look on such individuals as having godlike qualities, making them different and the subject of awe. And because the creative genius was so special, he or she was not subject to the same social norms and covenants that governed reciprocal relations between ordinary people. The "cult of genius" became a minor subtheme of the Romantic era and was picked up later in some of the edgier outer circles of the human potential movements of the 1960s—with talk of the "Aquarian conspiracy," and again at the millennium with the talk of "the new cultural creatives."

The mainstream Romantic thinkers, however, had something very different in mind when they conjured up the liberating spirit of human imagination. Believing that human nature is basically kind and good, affectionate, and social, the Romantics asked how we could recapture that primal state of being. By imagining the plight of other beings as if they were our own and acting on that imagination by coming to their aid and comfort, every individual would come to understand their deep affiliation and connectedness to all other living beings and their place as a co-creator in an evolving nature.

The British Romantic poet Percy Bysshe Shelley put it this way:

> A man, to be greatly good, must imagine intensely and comprehensively; the pains and pleasure of his species must become his own. The great instrument of the moral good is the imagination; and poetry administers to the effect by acting upon the cause.[55]

"Imaginative identification" with others was the Romantic way of describing empathy. If one lacked the ability to imagine the other, empathy would be impossible and the Romantic quest for earthly transcendence would be unattainable. John Ruskin captured the importance Romantics attached to imagination. He observed that "people would instantly care for others as well as for themselves if only they could *imagine* others as well as themselves."[56] With its emphasis on imagining the other as oneself, the Romantic movement secured its place in the historical evolution of empathic consciousness.

The poets of the period played a leading role in advancing the empathic spirit. They saw their poetry as a tool to spark the reader's imagination of the other and, by doing so, unleash the empathic impulse. Their poetry conjures up the awe and beauty of nature, the vulnerability of life, the pain of existence, the struggle to flourish, and the joy of communion more so than any poetry before or since in history.

The Romantic artists and composers of the day—Francisco Goya, Eugène Delacroix, Felix Mendelssohn, Frédéric Chopin—used their art and music to convey the same feelings and sensibilities.[57]

The Romantic movement, however, suffered from a glaring contradiction. Although largely an urban phenomena attracting alienated intellectuals, professionals, students, and dissidents among the bourgeois middle class, the movement tended to idealize Rousseau's primitive nature as the purest embodiment of the virtues they professed. The American Indian was a particularly favorite subject of adoration. There was also nostalgia for the simple folk practices of earlier rural society. Even Karl Marx, who was anything but naïve, was seduced by the misguided Romantic fervor that equated the good old days of Paleolithic, Neolithic, and even feudal life with a certain sensibility that needed to be recaptured. His referencing of an idealized past, like others at the time, reflected a growing sense of alienation felt by millions of Europeans caught up in the throes of a fast-industrializing society that was reducing all of life to self-serving material ends. Here's a passage from *The Communist Manifesto*, commenting on the raison d'être of capitalist society.

> It has drowned the most heavenly ecstasies of religious fervour, of chivalrous enthusiasm, of philistine sentimentalism, in the icy water of egotistical calculation. It has resolved personal worth into exchange value, and in place of the numberless indefeasible chartered freedoms, has set up that single, unconscionable freedom—Free Trade.[58]

The very idea of a highly urbanized and sophisticated public identifying with peasant folklore of an earlier time cast some doubt on the seriousness of the movement. The throwback also showed a lack of intellectual understanding of the evolution of the empathic process. Undifferentiated peasant cultures, lacking in self-awareness, might be able to exhibit primitive empathic distress but were hardly prepared to express the kind of mature empathic sensibility the Romantics championed. Quite simply, the ability of individuals to imagine diverse others as if they were oneself does not exist in such societies but does exist in the more complex urban environments from which the Romantics came and of which they were so critical.

Shortcomings aside, the Romantic movement offered a sophisticated countercosmology to the mathematical and mechanical universe of René Descartes and Isaac Newton. While Descartes found cosmic unity in mathematical laws and Newton in the laws governing gravitation, the Romantics saw it in the divine interconnectedness of all living beings. Their views anticipated the scientific vision of twentieth-century ecology. Alfred Tennyson wrote:

> FLOWER in the crannied wall,
> I pluck you out of the crannies,
> I hold you here, root and all, in my hand,
> Little flower—but *if* I could understand
> What you are, root and all, and all in all,
> I should know what God and man is.[59]

The Romantics, like the Enlightenment rationalists, believed in progress, but for them it had nothing to do with accumulation of wealth but, rather, the accumulation of natural wisdom.

Randall offers the best summation of the Romantic vision of nature, human nature, and man's role in the unfolding of history. The Romantics, wrote Randall, believed that

> [t]o live is to grow, to assimilate more and more of the riches of the world, to project upon the background of the setting of human life more and more of the infinite possibilities resident in human nature, and in so doing, to become more and more aware of the infinite ties binding all men to each other and to the great forces of the universe of which they are the noblest manifestation—in a word, to live is to bend all one's energies

toward the creation of a higher, better, and richer world, to realize God himself in the universe.[60]

The Romantics went beyond the French Revolution's notions of fraternity and solidarity that put man at the center of the universe and made human relationships the central orientation. For Romantics, human beings are embedded in even larger and more diverse communities with all of nature and thoroughly dependent on those relationships. The notion that human beings are inseparable parts of nature and indebted to the myriad relationships to which they are bound requires an enlargement of the notion of fraternity and solidarity to include all living beings. This notion was—and still is—far more radical than what the French revolutionaries had in mind when they hoisted the banner of liberty, fraternity, and equality. Their notion of solidarity stopped at the outer wall of the propertied male human domain.

The Romantics were committed to healing man's rift with nature by repositioning human beings back into nature. Where the theologians sought redemption in salvation in the next world through God's grace and the Enlightenment philosophers sought redemption in building a rational materialist utopia on Earth using reason, the Romantics, like Coleridge, sought redemption in a "Reconciliation from this Enmity with Nature" by universalizing empathic consciousness.[61]

The Romantic notion of progress sometimes takes on the breathy feel of a desperate search for immortality. Although nature is seen as a continuous striving and a never-ending becoming process, one reads some of the Romantic philosophers, poets, and novelists and comes away with the impression that somewhere between the lines is the unspoken desire to find some kind of immortality by dint of one's participation in the evolution of nature. The very idea of immortality however, contradicts the Romantic concept of each individual life being unique, finite, and with its own special creative possibilities. The notion of self-fulfillment, after all, conjures up completion and closure.

The desire for immortality also runs counter to the importance that the Romantics attach to human vulnerability. The empathic impulse is an acknowledgment that each life is unique and therefore precious, that all living creatures are vulnerable, subject to pain and suffering, and eager to be and thrive. Empathy smacks of mortality, is oriented by the smell of death and is directed to celebrating another's life. It is the very acceptance of death that allows one to empathize with another's struggle to live. As we noted earlier in Chapter 5, empathy does not exist in utopian worlds, where suffering and death are eliminated.

To the extent that some Romantics overidealized nature and attempted to "utopianize" it, they undercut the deeper nature of one's connectedness to the becoming process. We are all here for a moment, each a small tributary of consciousness feeding into the larger consciousness of nature itself. Our contribution adds to the journey but does not guarantee our own immortality.

Martha Nussbaum noticed the kink in the Romantic narrative in Walt Whitman's *Leaves of Grass*. The poem, published in 1855, is a brutally honest assessment of the human fear of sensuality—particularly the erotic side of human emotions. Whitman sees desire and longing as an expression of one's utter vulnerability and, therefore, also one's mortality. To be full of longing is to know that life is short. A sexual experience is nothing if it isn't surrender, a letting-go, a loss of control, a handing over of one's very being to another. There is nothing more corporeal and earthy than sex. It is a brief celebration of life between two people in all of their naked vulnerability.

While Whitman's poem is an urgent plea to accept our mortality and to love without fear and, by so doing, live life to its fullest, his own ambivalence about death and fear of mortality creeps into the poem. Nussbaum catches the contradiction. She writes that Whitman's effort

> is to at least some extent compromised by his constant emphasis on the mysterious unity of all things in nature, the continuity and therefore immortality of all life.[62]

Whitman, like other Romantics, seemed to believe that by becoming integrated into nature's flow, he somehow sheltered himself in some spiritual way from the finality of his own death. He writes,

I know I am deathless,

I know . . . I shall not pass like a child's carlacue cut with
     a burnt stick at night.[63]

Nussbaum makes the point that "to teach that death is not really a loss, or not really death, is to undercut the entire attitude toward eroticism and loss that the poetry, at its finest, has been promoting."[64]

SCHOPENHAUER'S TOUR DE FORCE

If there was an epiphany in the Romantic movement, a single moment that captured the tenor of the times, it was the publication of an essay on morality by Arthur Schopenhauer. The essay was written in response to a contest sponsored by the Royal Danish Society of Scientific Studies in 1837, offering a prize for the best essay on the question:

Are the source and foundation of morals to be looked for in
an idea of morality lying immediately in consciousness (or
conscience) and in the analysis of the other fundamental moral
concepts springing from that idea, or are they to be looked for
in a different ground of knowledge?[65]

Schopenhauer sent in his submission in 1839. His was the only entry. Nonetheless, he was denied the prize. The Royal Danish Society said he had failed to understand the question. But that was only a subterfuge. Their real reason for denying him the prize became clear later on in their explanation. Schopenhauer had dared to suggest, against all the prevailing wisdom of the time, that compassion, not pure reason, was the basis of morality and that emotions and feelings animated the compassionate instinct. Sheer heresy. In a last but telling rebuke, the jurors expressed their displeasure at the abusive manner in which Schopenhauer treated "several distinguished philosophers of recent times."[66] Although they didn't mention specific names, they had Immanuel Kant in mind. Schopenhauer savaged Kant, belittling his purely rational-based, prescriptive ethics as intellectual fantasy, out of touch with the way moral behavior unfolds in the real world. Like Hume, Schopenhauer believed that reason is the slave of the passions.

Recall Kant's categorical imperative mentioned in Chapter 5. First, "act only according to that maxim whereby you can at the same time will that it should become a universal law," and second, "act in such a way that you treat humanity whether in your own person or in the person of any other, always at the same time as an end and never really as a means to an end."[67] While at first glance, Kant's categorical imperative would seem to posit a secular version of the Golden Rule and be closely aligned with the empathic impulse, in reality it suffers from the same moral deficit as the earlier religiously and philosophically oriented maxims. Both view human emotions as an inadequate basis for morality and believe that people should treat others as they would be treated out of obedience to God's commands, in the first instance, and out of duty to reason in the second instance. Left behind is any heartfelt connection to another's plight as if it were one's own and the desire to comfort them because of a felt understanding of one's common humanity.

Schopenhauer finds Kant's idea that moral laws exist a priori and are knowable "independent of all inner and outer experience '*resting simply on concepts of pure reason*'" without any empirical basis.[68] He pointed out that Kant rejected the very idea that morality might be bound up in consciousness and connected to natural feelings "peculiar to human nature," which would give morality an empirical grounding. Kant is very clear on this point. In the *Foundation of the Metaphysics of Morals*, he writes that moral law

> must not be sought in man's nature (the subjective) or in the circumstances of the world (the objective) . . . *here nothing whatever can be borrowed from knowledge relating to man, i.e., from anthropology* . . . indeed we must not take it into our heads to try to derive the reality of our moral principle from the particular constitution of human nature.[69]

What we are left with, argued Schopenhauer, is an ethics that exists a priori of human experience and which is "entirely abstract, wholly insubstantial, and likewise floating about entirely in air."[70]

So, if morality is not found in human nature but, rather, exists a priori and independent of human nature, what compels someone to be moral? Kant says one acts in a morally responsible way because of "[t]he feeling that it is incumbent on man to obey the moral law . . . from a sense of *duty*, not from *voluntary inclination*." Kant specifically dismisses feelings as a basis for morality.

> Feelings of compassion and of tenderhearted sympathy
> would even be a nuisance to those thinking on the right
> lines, because they would throw into confusion their well-
> considered maxims and provoke the desire to be released from
> these, and to be subject only to legislative reason.[71]

Schopenhauer finds Kant's categorical imperative unpersuasive. Human beings simply don't act in a disinterested, moral way, because of a duty to uphold an a priori moral code. Unless, that is, there is some reward or punishment attached. On a closer examination of Kant's categorical imperative, Schopenhauer concluded that it sounded an awful lot like a theological ethics absent God's presence. After all, the Abrahamic religions are based on God's Ten Commandants, an a priori moral code handed down by God that exists independent of human nature but is expected to be obeyed because God wills it.

Schopenhauer argues that the moral code that accompanies theological consciousness is purely prescriptive. If human nature is "fallen," as the Abrahamic religions suggest, then there is no moral basis within an individual's being that would predispose him to do the morally right thing. God's commandments, therefore, are a prescriptive device telling human beings that this is the way they "ought" to behave if they are to be rewarded by God's grace and not punished by his wrath. But if there is nothing in the biological nature of a human being that would predispose him to be morally good, then why would he choose to do so out of pure duty to some a priori existing moral code, as Kant suggests, especially when there is no reward for doing so or punishment for not.

What Schopenhauer is really saying here is that Kant is attempting to offer a moral defense for the Age of Reason using a prescriptive device borrowed from the Age of Faith. In the end, concludes Schopenhauer, Kant fails to show how reason alone, as an abstract idea, can be the basis of a moral ethic.

The question then becomes whether there is any other source within the human animal itself that might be the basis of morality. Can we describe some quality of human behavior that predisposes people to be moral so that we don't run the risk of having to slip from what is to what ought to be—the famous is/ought gap? If we can't find such a predisposition burrowed deep in the nature of human beings, then the only way to save morality is to journey back to an earlier theological consciousness and view morality as always prescriptive and never descriptive.

After deconstructing Kant's categorical imperative, Schopenhauer offers a detailed description of moral behavior that he argues is embedded in the very sinew of human nature—with the qualification that it needs to be brought out and nurtured by society if it is to be fully realized. He argues that "compassion" is at the core of our human nature. Here's how he describes the phenomenon. In feeling compassion for another,

> I suffer directly with him, I feel *his* woe just as I ordinarily feel
> only my own; and, likewise, I directly desire his weal in the
> same way I otherwise desire my own. . . . At every moment we
> remain clearly conscious that *he* is the sufferer, not *we*; and it is
> precisely in *his* person, not in ours, that we feel the suffering,
> to our grief and sorrow. We suffer *with* him and hence *in* him;
> we feel his pain as *his*, and do not imagine that it is ours.[72]

In this single statement, Schopenhauer becomes the first person in history to clearly define the empathic process. All that is missing is the

term itself. But he goes further, describing not only the mental acrobat-
ics involved in an empathic extension but also the action that naturally
flows from it—in other words, the moral component. The compassionate predisposition, when fixed on someone's immediate plight, leads to

> the immediate *participation*, independent of all ulterior
> considerations, primarily in the *suffering* of another, and thus in
> the prevention or elimination of it; for all satisfaction and all
> well-being and happiness consist in this.[73]

Schopenhauer's description of compassion was broader than the
way the term was used at the time. What he really described is the
empathic process, within which compassion is the action component.
Schopenhauer viewed compassion as the basis of all morality, although
he admitted that he could not explain its psychological origins. He
referred to it as the "great mystery of ethics."[74] The physiological and
psychological basis would remain a mystery until the twentieth century
and the birth of psychological consciousness.

Although the origins of man's capacity for empathy was a mystery to
Schopenhauer, the teleology was clear. By feeling another's plight as if
it were our own and by extending a hand to comfort and support them
in their struggle to persevere and prosper, we recognize the unifying
thread that connects each of us to the other and to all of life on Earth.
Schopenhauer writes that

> [i]n the last resort, it is this knowledge to which every appeal
> to gentleness, leniency, loving-kindness, and mercy instead
> of justice, is directed. For such an appeal is a reminder of that
> respect in which we are all one and the same entity.[75]

THE ROMANTIC MOVEMENT was more than a philosophical, literary
and artistic movement. The ideas had consequences. The period from
1790 to 1848 was marked by social activism on a wide front. The new
activism went far beyond the traditional charitable activities associated

with religious practices, to include social engagement in a fledgling civil society.

By the time the Romantic era had peaked in the European revolutions of 1848, fundamental changes had taken place in the conventions of marriage, family relations, and the raising of children. The first civil society organizations to address the problems of the poor were created—the Friendly Societies. The cooperative movement was launched, providing an alternative business model based on cooperation rather than competition, and the first societies to prevent cruelty to animals were formed.

ROMANTIC RELATIONSHIPS

The Romantic movement's most enduring impact was on romance itself. The idea of companionate marriage based on affection, first popularized in the seventeenth century, was ratcheted up in intensity to include romantic love. Much of the impetus for this radical new approach to mate selection came from the widespread popularity of the new genre of romance novels, which dramatically changed expectations among young people of what they wanted out of a relationship. Marriage, which for eons of history was an economic enterprise, and which in the preceding two centuries had become a companion enterprise, was quickly becoming what British sociologist Anthony Giddens called an "emotional enterprise."[76]

The very idea of a man and woman entering into an "intimate" relationship was revolutionary. It is here at the most basic level of human relationships that the democratic spirit began to have its first real impact. Romance, after all, is entered into willingly, by choice. One cannot force another person's affection. In this sense, romance brings with it a certain sense of equality between the sexes. It's probably fair to say that the notion of gender equality began with the invention of romance. Equal participation in romantic courtship prepared the way for the demand for equal participation in the political arena in the second half of the nineteenth century.

Giddens points out that romantic love was essentially "feminised love."[77] While women still were denied the most basic legal and political rights, they were able, by dint of their more highly developed sense of nurturance, to claim an advantage over men. An article published in 1839 noted that

> the man bears rule over his wife's person and conduct. She
> bears the rule of his inclinations: he governs by law; she by
> persuasion. . . . The empire of the woman is an empire of
> softness . . . her commands are caresses, her menaces are tears.[78]

Women helped men learn how to love and express intimacy. Giddens makes note of the turnaround in male/female relationships. Traditionally, the male overwhelmed the female into submission. In the Romantic schema—visited repeatedly in romance novels—the conquest is reversed. The hardened and insensitive male is wooed by the nurturance and affection of the female. She senses the intimate qualities long buried inside her mate and by creating a sense of trust and affection is able to bring them out—to melt his heart.

Giddens observes that in romance novels, as in life,

> the capturing of the heart of the other is in fact a process of the
> creation of a mutual narrative biography. The heroine tames,
> softens and alters the seemingly intractable masculinity of her
> love object, making it possible for mutual affection to become
> the main guiding-line of their lives together.[79]

Romantic love became a vast training ground in empathic consciousness. Both female and male became mindful of the other's inner being, nature, and soul. They are continually asking each other, how do you feel, what are you thinking? At the same time, they are asking themselves, how do I feel about this person I'm with, and how does she feel about me? Through this practice of questioning, they become emotionally attuned to each other's feelings and are able to empathize with each other's plight as if it were their own—the very meaning of a "soul mate." To be able to weep with a mate and come to their aid and to be overjoyed by their triumphs and celebrate their successes with them is the very essence of romantic love.

Romance novels had the effect of introducing the love narrative into personal life. A writer in *The Lady's Magazine* in Britain in 1773 quipped that "[t]here is scarce a young lady in the kingdom who has not read with avidity a great number of romances and novels."[80] One's own life was also increasingly a "novel" story centering on love and intimacy rather than simply on religious obligations or family responsibilities. Love and intimacy with a mate became the centerpiece of each person's life story and has remained so until the present day.

Generations of individuals since the Romantic era have judged the worth of their life by the strength of the romantic ties and intimate connection they have with a mate. This is perhaps the most important legacy of the Romantic period.

IDEALIZING CHILDHOOD

The shift from companionate to romantic relationships spilled over into child rearing. Mary Ryan observes that relations in the home, which had already been undergoing a change in the past century, moved even further "from patriarchal authority to maternal affection."[81]

In 1808, a retired natural history teacher in Limoges reminisced about the kind of brutal childhood his generation experienced and the very different childhood that children experience now. He wrote that when he was a child,

> *Fear* was the principle on which upbringing was founded. Whoever taught the children to read would grab their shirts about the shoulders, then hold the book in one hand, the rod in the other, ready to flail away at the slightest oversight.[82]

He compared the terrifying specter of his own youth with the happy childhoods that he saw all around him in his old age.

> Cheeried up and embraced without end, [the children] will
> remain unknowing of ill will. Completely unconstrained in
> their clean sheets [swaddling had been eliminated] and well
> cared for, their beautiful little bodies develop rapidly. They
> need merely be of good humor and good health, and they'll
> draw the eyes of all who come near.[83]

The new concern for children was reflected in the proliferation of infant hygiene literature and the interest parents took in ensuring the health and well-being of their children. Suddenly doctors' offices were besieged by concerned parents, anxious to make sure that their child's slightest sniffle was properly attended to.[84]

Rousseau exerted an inordinate amount of influence on child-rearing practices during the Romantic era. His "self-help" book on proper parenting, Émile, was published in 1762 but became even more popular by the 1790s, at the dawn of the Romantic era. The book appealed to Romantics because of Rousseau's emphasis on nurturing the natural instincts of the child. Rousseau took exception to Locke's assertion that children are born into the world a blank slate—tabula rasa. Rousseau believed that infants came equipped with a natural predisposition to be good and that parents had the responsibility to let those instincts play out during childhood. He introduced the idea that a child should enjoy his or her childhood—that it was a special time that needed to be honored and nurtured so that children might mature their natural instincts. Rousseau cautioned parents to let the child be happy. It is the child's natural state of being.

Rousseau thought that child-care advice was too stuffy, too ready to prepare children to be "reasoned" little adults. He proclaimed that childhood "is the sleep of reason."[85] He urged parents to quit attempting to reason with their children and let them experience the sheer joy of childhood.

> Love childhood, indulge its sports, its pleasures, its delightful
> instincts. Who has not sometimes regretted that age when
> laughter was ever on the lips, and when the heart was ever

at peace? Why rob these innocents of the joys which pass so quickly, of that precious gift which they cannot abuse? Why fill with bitterness the fleeting days of early childhood, days which will no more return for them than for you.[86]

Rousseau's advice was radical and incendiary. He was saying that children are born naturally to be good and moral and if left to grow naturally, they will develop into moral beings. His thoughts on the nature of human nature didn't go down well with Protestant reformers who thought that children were born in sin and needed it beaten out of them, or with Enlightenment philosophers who believed that children needed to be made to put away their natural feelings and emotions—which were to be happy and affectionate—and quickly weaned into reasonable, responsible adults.

The Romantics elevated childhood to a higher status, transcending even their own. The new parents believed that the man is not in the child but, rather, that the child is in the man. William Wordsworth wrote the now famous line,

> *The Child is father of the man;*
> *I could wish my days to be*
> *Bound each to each by natural piety.*[87]

His ode to childhood influenced a generation to rethink their view of children and childhood. Some began to idealize their children as being closer to nature and more in sync with their true nature. They even hoped that their shared affection with their children would rub off on them and help them recapture the childlike innocence they once enjoyed. Wordsworth spoke eloquently to the new view of infants.

> *Not in entire forgetfulness,*
> *And not in utter nakedness,*
> *But trailing clouds of glory do we come*
> *From God who is our home:*
> *Heaven lies about us in our infancy!*[88]

Children, once regarded as possessed by the devil, came to be thought of as the living repositories of natural virtue from which parents could learn. Even some Catholic theologians were swayed. The future Cardinal Newman, writing in 1830, said of the child that he is "out of the hands of God, with all lessons and thoughts of Heaven freshly marked upon him."[89]

The impact of this change of heart and mind on how adults viewed childhood has remained with parents ever since, influencing child rearing in the most profound way. Who hasn't heard someone say, "We need to hold on to the childlike qualities within us"?

For a time, the new Romantic view of childhood even impacted the way little boys and girls were raised. The shared natural quality of goodness became a more important attribute to encourage than gender role differentiation. Traditionally parents saw it as part of their responsibility to raise little boys along male stereotypical lines and little girls the same. The Romantics believed that gender distinctions were far less important than the shared virtue that united all children—their innate goodness. That being the case, they put their emphasis on nourishing that natural instinct without discrimination by gender. For example, parenting books in the 1820s to 1840s emphasized "that both boys and girls should avoid anger." In the 1830s parents were encouraged to dress their little boys and girls in both knee-length dresses and long white trousers with short haircuts, with the aim of blurring sexual distinctions—a practice that wouldn't come back into vogue until the Roaring Twenties, when flappers cut and cropped their hair close to the head and donned long pants.[90]

Wordsworth summed up the incredible change the Romantic era had on the nature of childhood and, respectively, the nature of human nature when he wrote of children,

> *Mighty prophet! Seer blest,*
> *On whom those truths do rest*
> *Which we are toiling all our lives to find.*[91]

The Romantic movement's rethinking of childhood laid the foundation for the object relations and attachment theories of Fairbairn, Kohut, Suttie, Winnicott, Bowlby, Ainsworth, and others in the twentieth century. By making childhood a special time for expressing parental affection and bringing out a child's natural instinct for attachment, nurturing, and playful exploration, the Romantics were preparing the ground for the kind of child-rearing practices that foster an empathic consciousness across the generations.

If human nature is good and is only corrupted by a civilization gone astray, then it stood to reason that reforming society would allow its subjects and citizens to recapture the child within and their own natural goodness. Protecting the right of children to have a childhood quickly became a top priority.

Philanthropists were particularly incensed about children being forced into draconian work houses, where they slaved long hours under intolerable conditions to meet production quotas set by the new generation of factory bosses. These children were denied their childhood and robbed of their natural inheritance and innocence. Their affections sapped, they languished as empty shells, never knowing the lightness of being that goes with the playfulness of childhood.

EMPATHIC SOCIAL REFORMS

Coleridge and other Romantics began to push for child labor reform. The first child labor law was enacted in the 1830s in England, prohibiting children under nine years old from working in factories and limiting work hours of older children to eight hours a day until the age of fourteen.[92] France followed with its own child labor law reforms shortly thereafter.[93]

Elizabeth Barrett Browning captured the public sentiment at the time in her 1842 poem "The Cry of the Children."

> *The young lambs are bleating in the meadows,*
> *The young birds are chirping in the nest,*
> *The young fawns are playing with the shadows,*

The young flowers are blowing toward the west:
But the young, young children, O my brothers,
They are weeping bitterly!
They are weeping in the playtime of the others,
In the country of the free.[94]

The ardor for reform of society did not stop at the factory gates. The Romantic period saw the creation of the first antislavery societies and the beginning of the abolitionist movements in Europe and America. The Committee for the Abolition of the Slave Trade was founded in May 1787 in Britain. While religious denominations were among the earliest supporters of abolition—Methodists, Quakers, and Baptists—many in the general public, caught up in the throes of the Romantic movement, lent their voices to the opposition. Many were influenced by the brutal images of slavery portrayed by Romantic artists, including the artist and poet William Blake. His rendering of "A Negro Hung Alive by the Ribs to a Gallows" horrified the British public.

The Slave Trade Act, enacted by the British Parliament in 1807, banned the slave trade in the British Empire. In 1834, slaves were emancipated across the British Empire.[95] The slave trade was inimical to the Romantic vision, which emphasized the goodness of human nature and put high store on love of one's fellow human beings and living a compassionate life.

The British also pioneered in the creation of the first civil society organization—the Friendly Societies—dedicated to relieving the burdens of the poor. The Church had a long, if not spotted, history of providing alms to the poor. While the Crown administered various programs aimed at providing some relief for the destitute, the Friendly Societies marked the first truly civic activism to assist people in need. Inspired by notions of Christian charity, fraternal solidarity, and utopian socialism, the Friendly Societies' mission of compassion drew in thousands of members. By 1815, more than 925,000 people had joined its ranks.[96] The Friendly Societies were "Mutual Aid" organizations, made up largely of working people helping each other in times of need.

Some of the most important reforms to come out of the Romantic era dealt with the question of cruelty. Strangely, until this time cruelty was little considered in public discussions or public policy. It was so much a part of life that it was largely taken for granted. As late as the last half of the eighteenth century, public displays of judicial torture were common and "wrongdoers" were whipped, branded, broken on the wheel, drawn and quartered, and burned at the stake in front of their neighbors. Incredibly, such events were often the occasion of festive celebration, as the public vented its wrath against an individual thought to be possessed by the devil. Opposition to these barbaric, age old practices began to mount between the 1760s and the 1790s among the middle class, who were coming to see criminal behavior as a mark of individual weakness, rather than a sign of demonic possession.

The new emphasis on sentiment and the growing conviction that all human beings are alike in their bodily vulnerability, their aversion to suffering and pain, and their inherent predisposition to be good, spurred interest in reform and social rehabilitation as opposed to traditional retribution via judicially sanctioned torture. This was a radically new idea. The public began to experience criminals in their midst as individual human beings, not unlike themselves, with frailties not unlike their own, who by dint of personal misfortune or the fate of social circumstances went astray.

Increasing numbers within the middle class began to empathize, if only ever so slightly, with the plight of the criminal. Judicial torture was abolished in Prussia in 1754 and in Sweden in 1772. France followed suit in 1789 under the new revolutionary regime. Interestingly, Britain, often regarded as a trailblazer in individual rights, didn't abolish burning women at the stake until 1790.[97] Benjamin Rush, a physician and signer of the American Declaration of Independence, captured the growing public sentiment of the time, remarking that criminals, like everyone else, "possess souls and bodies composed of the same materials as those of our friends and relations."[98]

The movements to abolish public torture, prohibit cruelty toward children and ban slavery were not the only social reform efforts to draw the public's attention. Other forms of cruelty soon became the object of social abrogation.

The utilitarian philosopher Jeremy Bentham was the first to raise the question of compassion toward animals in a celebrated 1780 essay. Bentham suggested that "the question is not, can they reason? nor can they talk? but can they suffer?" Bentham compared the plight of domestic animals to that of slaves and said he hoped the day would come when "the rest of animal creation may acquire those rights which never could have been withholden from them but by the hand of tyranny."[99]

Bentham's words found a welcome audience among the early visionaries of the Romantic era. The Royal Society for the Prevention of Cruelty to Animals (RSPCA) was established in Britain in 1824. Other animal anticruelty organizations started to appear across Britain. These organizations began to educate the public on showing greater compassion for wild and domestic animals and lobbied for legislation to protect animals against human cruelty. The RSPCA and other groups also opened up the first veterinary hospitals and shelters to take care of abandoned and lost animals. In 1842, the term "vegetarian" was coined and the Vegetarian Society—the first of its kind—was founded in Britain in 1847.[100] Similar organizations began to pop up on the Continent and North America.

It's hard to exaggerate exactly how extraordinary the idea of animal compassion was at the time. Except for the kind utterances of Saint Francis of Assisi in the medieval era, never before had human beings coalesced around a movement on behalf of other species. Many of the early advocates of animal protection were active in the antislavery and early women's suffrage movements, as well as in child labor reforms. In the United States, Horace Greeley, a firebrand antislavery advocate, as well as prominent women's rights advocates like Lucy Stone, Susan B. Anthony, Amelia Bloomer, and Elizabeth Cady Stanton were vegetarians and outspoken in their defense of animals.[101] These men and women were the harbingers of a universalizing empathic process that would come of age in the late twentieth and early twenty-first centuries.

As increasing numbers of urban middle-class and working people began to feel the pain of a harsh new industrial order, they became more sensitive to the struggles of others, including other species. We have to remember that at the time these animal protection groups came on the scene, the abuse and torture of animals was quite common. Cats were routinely set on fire, dogs, roosters, and other animals were made to fight to their deaths in sporting arenas, and horses were savagely beaten.

Dick Martin's Act, named after a member of the British Parliament who introduced the first animal anticruelty statute, was passed by Parliament in 1822 and amended in 1833 and 1835. The legislation prohibited starving or beating cattle, baiting and fighting of dogs, bulls, bears, and cocks, and placed restrictions on the length of confinement in slaughterhouse yards. Similar legislation was passed in New York State in 1829 and in Massachusetts in 1836.[102]

The animal protection movement is a poignant example of the tremendous impact the Romantic movement had on changing the consciousness of the public. There is probably no other similar period in history when the empathic sensibility took such a giant leap forward in the human psyche and made such impressive inroads in transforming private life, social conventions, and public policies.

What made the Romantic era unique within the context of the evolutionary history of empathic consciousness is the great stress placed on what Rousseau, and later Wordsworth and Whitman, called the "Sentiment of Being." The Romantics argued that at the core of being there is an authentic self that is pure in nature, although corruptible by society. Lionel Trilling makes the point that authenticity is not to be confused with sincerity, which is being true to one's social self. Authenticity runs deeper—it is, in the words of Trilling, a "primitive" strength that is continually compromised by society. Maintaining one's core authenticity, for Rousseau and the Romantics, required a life of personal suffering and constant attention and sympathy to the plight of others. Only the alienated could enter into this world. Sartre, the French existential philosopher of the mid–twentieth century, defined the sentiment of being as the place where

> each of us finds himself as well as the others. The common place belongs to everybody and it belongs to me; in me, it

belongs to everybody; it is the presence of everybody in me. In its very essence it is generality; in order to appreciate it, an act is necessary, an act through which I shed my particularity in order to adhere to the general, in order to become generality. Not at all like everybody, but, to be exact, the incarnation of everybody.[103]

The Romantics believed that the enemy of being is having. Erich Fromm, the prolific twentieth-century psychologist, dedicated a book to the subject, entitled *To Have or to Be?* As we increasingly surround ourselves with possessions, they come to define us and we lose touch with our authentic being. It becomes diminished.

Karl Marx went to the heart of the alienation felt by increasing numbers of people caught up in the industrial onslaught. He wrote, "Everything which the economist takes from you in the way of life and humanity, he restores to you in the form of *money* and *wealth*."[104]

The Romantics were on a journey to discover the roots of human nature. They associated the sentiment of being as the key to that nature and defined it as the feeling of connectivity and solidarity with all of life. What they discovered was the empathic impulse. Where they erred, as mentioned earlier, was in believing that the less contact that impulse has with civilization, the more it will be preserved. Rousseau unequivocally stated that "[e]verything is good as it comes from the hands of the author of nature; but everything degenerates in the hands of man."[105] The Romantics failed to grasp the dialectical process through which empathic consciousness grows. Its very maturation requires embeddedness in increasingly complex social structures. While we are all born with a predisposition to experience empathic distress, this core aspect of our being only develops into true empathic consciousness by the continuous struggle of differentiation and integration in civilization. Far from squelching the empathic impulse, it is the dynamics of unfolding civilization that is the fertile ground for its development and for human transcendence. An undifferentiated human collectivity in a state of nature may be predisposed to empathy but is also unprepared to express it in the universalizing way Romantics had in mind. The Romantics were too close to their times to step back and reflect on how the very society they were justifiably critiquing also created the very conditions that allowed the empathic impulse to express itself so forcefully.

THE REVOLUTIONS OF 1848:
THE SPRINGTIME OF THE PEOPLES

The Romantic era peaked in the flush of revolutionary euphoria that swept over the capitals of Europe in the spring of 1848. In the early days of 1848, the French aristocrat and political philosopher Alexis de Tocqueville warned his political colleagues in the Chamber of Deputies that "[w]e are sleeping on a volcano."[106] Within weeks the volcano exploded in Paris and the white-hot flames of revolution spread quickly across the continent.

The revolution of 1848, which engulfed much of Europe in a matter of weeks, is sometimes referred to as the "Springtime of the Peoples." The insurrection came in the wake of several years of poor harvests, a continent-wide recession, and banking panic. But there were deeper reasons for the fissure. The year 1848 marked a transition of sorts between the proto-industrial period that had begun as far back as the eleventh century, with the shift to a water- and wind-power energy regime in Europe, and the takeoff of the coal-power steam-technology revolution that was quickly giving rise to the Industrial Age. Old political institutions and antiquated ideas about commerce and trade were increasingly unable to keep up with the new technological innovations and, more important, the economic and political aspirations of a newly minted capitalist class and its nemesis, a new labor proletariat.

While the revolution was precipitated by mounting economic woes, it attracted its fair share of utopian socialists whose sensibilities bridged the proletarian materialism of a Karl Marx with the Romantic vision of a Jean-Jacques Rousseau. The Revolution of 1848 was called the Springtime of the Peoples because of its youthful outpouring of Romantic feelings bound to the hoped-for birth of a new social order founded on man's natural goodness and sociability. The growing economic contradictions converged with the pent-up passion for spiritual renewal in the spring of 1848. The result was the political explosion that rocked the continent.

It was over almost as soon as it began. The epicenter was Paris. Insurrectionists captured the capital and declared the Republic on February 24—the same day Karl Marx and Friedrich Engels published *The Manifesto of the Communist Party* in London.[107] By March the revolution had spread to Bavaria, Berlin, Vienna, Hungary, and Milan. By late spring governments had fallen across much of Europe.

Eighteen months later, all of the deposed governments, with the exception of France, had been restored to power. But even in France, much of the old regime regained influence.[108] It was the only continent-wide revolution in European history. It failed in the short run but succeeded in establishing a new political dialogue and agenda that would remake Europe and much of the world to comport with an industrial way of life over the course of the next half-century.

THE ROMANTIC movement was a true revolution in the history of consciousness. What happened in Paris, Berlin, and Vienna in the spring of 1848 was a powerful expression of its yearnings. Only months later, however, the Romantic vision the young revolutionaries fought for lay decimated in the streets. The sentiment that underlaid that vision, however, would be swept up and recycled in the collective memory and passed on to successive generations.

In 1968, young revolutionaries of the baby-boom generation would take to the same streets in Paris as well as in Washington, D.C., Berlin, and cities around the world, their cries echoing the sentiments of their comrades 120 years earlier.

TEN

PSYCHOLOGICAL CONSCIOUSNESS IN A POSTMODERN EXISTENTIAL WORLD

THE REVOLUTION of 1848 was a marker, in more than one way. The First Industrial Revolution was finding its legs, and with the help of cheap print technology and steam locomotion it was spreading quickly across Europe and beginning to make its first forays on the North American continent. Ideological consciousness, which grew up alongside the new forms of inanimate power—water, wind, and coal—was maturing. The battle lines in the struggle between sense and sentiment were by now well drawn and clearly articulated, subject only to endless amplification and clarification. The Humanist Renaissance, the Age of Sentiment, and the Romantic era saw a surge in empathic consciousness, which fundamentally changed our notions about the nature of human nature and the meaning of human progress.

But even as the First Industrial Revolution and ideological consciousness continued to jolt forward together, the seeds were being sown for still another energy/communications revolution—a Second Industrial Revolution—whose impact on human consciousness and the evolution of empathic expression would be every bit as dramatic as that experienced in the previous period.

Just eleven years before the European Revolution of 1848, Samuel Morse received a patent on a fantastic new invention. He called it the telegraph. Shortly thereafter, people began to send messages to each other across vast distances and at the speed of light. The public was awestruck.

In 1859, eleven years after the European Revolution, a retired railroad conductor, Edwin Laurentine Drake, using a makeshift drill, struck oil near Titusville, Pennsylvania.[1] The flow gushed up to the surface at a rate of twenty barrels a day. In 1879, Karl Benz patented an internal combustion engine that ran on gasoline, and he began producing automobiles seven years later in 1886.[2]

The coming together of the electricity revolution with the oilpowered internal combustion engine would give birth to a new communications/energy regime and bring with it still another leap in human cognition. The world was about to enter the Age of Psychological Consciousness, a period that would stretch from the second half of the nineteenth century to the last decade of the twentieth century. While earlier forms of consciousness—mythological, theological, and ideological—were still in play all over the world and within each psyche to various degrees, the new psychological consciousness would come to dominate the twentieth century and leave its mark on every aspect of human interaction and on virtually every social convention. With psychological consciousness, people began to think about their own feelings and thoughts, as well as those of others in ways never before imaginable. They became the psychic explorers and analysts of the human mind. The new way of thinking opened the door to a great extension of empathic expression, which peaked in the 1960s and 1970s with the surge of the counterculture and social activism among the baby-boom generation.

ELECTRICITY AND THE FIRST STIRRINGS OF PSYCHOLOGICAL CONSCIOUSNESS

The new psychological consciousness began with electricity in the early 1800s. The new communications medium was to have as significant an effect on the way people think as the print revolution more than four hundred years earlier.

In 1850, a certain John Bovee Dods was asked by several "eminent members" of the United States Senate to give a lecture on the science of electrical psychology. Early experimentation with electricity had captured the public's imagination. Here was a force that required a wholesale rethinking of the nature of human nature. It was a mysterious, immaterial medium, whose power had long been regarded with awe. Dods lectured widely. His book *The Philosophy of Electrical Psychology* was a small sensation at the time.

Dods was one of the first to popularize the idea that electricity is "the connecting link between mind and inert matter" and that it is the "grand agent employed by the Creator to move and govern the universe."[3]

Scientific experiments dating back to the work of Italian anatomist Luigi Galvani in 1786 had shown that electricity played a critical role in physiology. Galvani experimented with stimulating dissected frog legs with electricity and speculated that animals moved because of the electricity in their muscles and nerves. In 1838, another Italian, Carlo Matteucci, a professor of physics at the University of Pisa, showed that "an electrical current accompanies each heart beat."[4] In 1843, the German physiologist Emil du Bois-Reymond was able to detect voltage potential in resting muscles.[5]

In this early period of electricity development, the observations of physiologists studying the electrical workings in humans and animals proved helpful to engineers constructing the first practical electrical devices. The engineers' work, in turn, provided helpful clues to the workings of the central nervous system. For example, the nervous system provided a useful model for building the telegraph, while the electric fish gave Volta ideas about how to build a battery. Du Bois-Reymond dedicated *Animal Electricity*, his 1848 book on electrical excitation in nerves and muscles, to Michael Faraday, whose "descriptions of induction in electrical circuits" provided useful analogies for describing excitation of nerves.[6]

In a public lecture delivered in 1851, du Bois-Reymond explained how the workings of the telegraph and other new electrical technology paralleled the way animals are constructed. He wrote:

> the wonder of our time, electrical telegraphy, was long ago
> modeled in the animal machine. But the similarity between

the two apparatus, the nervous system and the electric telegraph, has a much deeper foundation. It is more than similarity; it is a kinship between the two, an agreement not merely of the effects, but also perhaps of the causes.[7]

Dods picked up on the experimentation going on in the laboratories and boldly proclaimed that "[i]t is through electricity, that the mind conveys its various impressions and emotions to others, and through this same medium receives all its impressions from the external world."[8] Dods was proposing a radical hypothesis: that electricity is the medium that communicates feelings and emotions. He went even further, arguing that all diseases occur when "*the electricity of the system [is] thrown out of balance.*" That imbalance, contended Dods, could occur because of "mental impressions" or because of "physical impressions from external nature."[9]

Some of Dods's observations turned out to be right, others to be dead wrong. He anticipated the use of electrical shock treatment to treat depression. Equally important, Dods was among the very first to believe in what William James would later call mind-cure. In the introduction to Dods's work, Robert W. Rieber and Dagna K. Skoog make the observation that Dods's pioneering efforts and others in the early days of the electricity revolution "laid the groundwork for the assimilation of psychoanalysis in America."[10]

By arguing that the "eternal substance is *electricity,* [which] contains all the original properties of all things in being . . . [and that] human beings and all animated existences are subject to the same grand electrical law that pervades the universe,"[11] Dods was unintentionally offering up a new set of metaphors for describing nature, human nature, and the workings of civilization. Electrical metaphors would come to replace the hydraulic metaphors of the earlier agricultural civilizations and the mechanical metaphors that governed the medieval water- and wind-power revolutions and the First Industrial Revolution.

The new interest in electricity as an agent and metaphor found a welcome home among Romantic scholars, writers, poets, and artists, who were quick to pick up electrical language and incorporate it into their worldview. The electrical metaphors would outlive the Romantic era and provide a bridge between that period and the Age of Psychological Consciousness that rode alongside the Second Industrial Revolution for most of the twentieth century.

Nathaniel Hawthorne foresaw the late–twentieth century idea of the world as a global brain and central nervous system—the Age of Psychological Consciousness—popularized by Marshall McLuhan and the communications theorists of the Internet generation. He asked himself:

> Is it a fact—or have I dreamt it—that, by means of electricity, the world of matter has become a great nerve, vibrating thousands of miles in a breathless point of time? Rather, the round globe is a vast head, a brain, instinct with intelligence! Or, shall we say, it is itself a thought, nothing but thought, and no longer the substance which we deemed it![12]

Part of the Romantics' fascination with electricity as metaphor is the connective nature of electrical fields. Electricity creates a field of simultaneous interactivity. That is its basic nature. For Romantics, who intuited the idea of nature as an interconnected realm, electricity seemed to provide unequivocal scientific proof.

The Romantics no longer had to suffer under the yoke of mechanical metaphors with their emphasis on a static world populated by autonomous pieces of solid matter, endlessly bombarding each other in a timeless vacuum. Electricity conjured up not only connectivity but organic growth, creativity, and change over time. The notion of "fields" provided a new way of imagining a unified world. Conversely, Paul Gilmore, writing in the journal *American Literature*, observes, "romantic theories imagining the universe as a unified, organic whole provided a key theoretical model for those conducting electrical experiments."[13]

The lure of the electrical metaphor lies in the notion that electricity is perceived as neither material nor immaterial. While it can't be seen, it has the power to act forcefully on the world. Similarly, human thoughts, which are electrically induced, seem caught in the netherworld between the immaterial and material. In the new scheme, the old boundary line separating inspiration from application and thought from action disappears. Suddenly the physical world seems less materialistic, while the mental world seems less ethereal.

The new sense of a porous nature helped create a new sense of social fluidity. Bodies were no longer constrained by their corporeality. If the world is both material and immaterial at the same time, then the idea of clear-cut boundaries between people is more a social contrivance than a scientific reality. Walt Whitman used the new sense of a porous world in his exploration of sexuality, often referencing electrical metaphors to create a notion of the erotic experience. In the sexual union, one surrenders the self and becomes connected to another, and in that very loss of self and reconnection one feels part of a larger unity, "the field" of nature.

The thought that thought itself is unbounded would give rise in the early twentieth century to the notion of the collective unconscious in psychiatric literature. It would also give impetus to early work in psychiatry and psychology exploring empathic pathways and developing an understanding of how empathic feelings are generated across individual boundaries. After all, by its very nature, empathy partially dissolves the boundaries between self and other. The empathic experience is both of an immaterial and material nature. One physically experiences another's feelings by way of the immaterial medium of thought.

The dynamism of electricity—even the term itself conjures up the powerful specter of the electric dynamo—also suggests creativity. Romantics, and especially American poets, were quick to seize on this quality of electricity and attach it to popular notions of creative genius. Emerson alludes to "a power transcending all limit and privacy, and by virtue of which a man is the conductor of the whole river of electricity."[14]

The "electric spirit" became associated not only with creativity but with a heightened level of consciousness. The Romantics envisioned a future when the world would be connected by electricity, leading to a unification of mankind. In "Years of the Modern," published in 1865, Whitman reflected on how the telegraph was already connecting the commercial and social life of humanity, and he suggested that eventually it would lead to "the solidarity of races." He asked:

> Are all nations communing? [I]s there going to be but one
> heart to the globe? Is humanity forming en-masse?[15]

Not everyone was so convinced. Henry David Thoreau noted that the telegraph now allowed people in Maine to talk to people in Texas but asked, tongue and cheek, whether people in Maine had anything important to say to people in Texas.[16]

The Romantics shared the belief that electricity opened up a new metaphorical door to understanding human consciousness itself. Electricity provided a treasure trove of new words that allowed human beings to redefine themselves in psychological terms in ways not available with hydraulic and mechanistic metaphors. The latter are all based in the world of physical forces. "Lifting one's spirit," "grasping a concept," "stretching a thought," "throwing out an idea," and "balancing one's emotions" "ground" the emotions in hydraulic and mechanistic metaphors that seem too constrictive to apply to consciousness. They put "the brakes" on the free flow of thought. Electrical metaphors, by contrast, appear open-ended, connective, ethereal, and therefore unbounded.

Think of an "electrifying performance." What comes to mind is a powerful, evocative experience that spreads, connects, and fuses the performers and audience instantaneously. Everyone becomes one. Individual consciousness melds into a single throbbing, emotional experience. The awareness of passing time and physical limitations are suspended in a moment of collective transcendence, which is boundaryless. "A flash of insight," "turned on," "shock therapy," "plugged in," "energetic," "felt the electricity," "polarity," "short-circuited," "overloaded," "burned out," "a spark of imagination," "hardwired," "a short fuse," "a powerhouse," "a live wire," an "outlet" for one's feelings, and "feeling disconnected" all conjure up immaterial feelings and thoughts. They are the vocabulary of psychological consciousness. These words, derived from the world of electricity, are both ephemeral and embodied at the same time. They give people the language they need to explore the workings of their own psyche.

By its very nature, electricity seems to encompass attributes that make it feel more mental than physical. An article that appeared in the *United States Democratic Review* in 1848 captured the sense in which electricity is more akin to the world of thought. The essay drove home the comparison between communicating by electrical signaling with the telegraph and the way thought is communicated via language.

> Language is but the medium of thought—which flies as
> rapidly and acts as instantaneously as the invisible element
> which flashes along the Telegraphic wire. The more closely,
> then, that it follows the operation of thought [in a telegraphic
> manner], the more perfectly does it perform its office.[17]

Gilmore makes the interesting point that authors, like professionals in every other discipline, both consciously and unconsciously picked up on the electricity metaphors and that "reimagining literature in such terms fostered the notion of a boundaryless, yet embodied, social collective."[18]

ELECTRIFICATION, OIL, AND THE AUTOMOBILE

The electricity revolution surged forward in the last half of the nineteenth century. The telegraph was, in the words of William Orton, president of Western Union, "the nervous system of the commercial system."[19] Samuel Morse explained that the new discoveries in electrical physiology had inspired his thinking and that he had purposely set out to create a communications system that mirrored the one found in the human body. He believed that his telegraph would become the central nervous system for American society and bind together the economy and body politic in a single interdependent organism. He confided in his colleague and collaborator F. O. J. Smith that

> it [will] not be long ere the whole surface of this country [is]
> channeled for those *nerves* which are to diffuse, with the speed
> of thought, a knowledge of all that is occurring throughout
> the land.[20]

The U.S. government agreed and weighed in with a $30,000 allocation to establish the first telegraphic line from Baltimore to Washington. The line became operational in 1844. Telegraph lines were laid down quickly across North America and Europe in the 1850s and 1860s. In 1858, Queen Victoria and President Buchanan sent messages to each other on the first transatlantic cable. The new lifeline seemed to reconfirm Morse's boast that with the coming of the telegraph, "space [is] annihilated."[21]

For millions of emigrants from Europe who had braved the Atlantic waters to reach the distant shores of the Americas, the very idea that one could now send messages back to family at the speed of light seemed incomprehensible, even magical. One observer gushed that the transatlantic cable is "a living, fleshy bond between severed portions of the human family."[22]

In 1851, Paul Julius Reuter established the Reuters news service.[23] By the 1860s, "news" was being telegraphed around the world. Millions of people could pick up their morning newspaper and read of faraway events that had occurred literally overnight while eating their morning breakfast.

The railroads were the first to take advantage of the telegraph, using it to route traffic, track shipments, and coordinate rights-of-way for trains coming from both directions on single tracks. By 1866, one company, Western Union, dominated the telegraph business.[24] It would be synonymous with the term "telegraph" from that time on.

Both the economies of scale and speed dictated the terms of development of American railroads and the telegraph. Large amounts of capital were required to build and maintain the operations and highly centralized command-and-control functions were necessary to coordinate the increased pace, flow, speed, and density of commercial activity.

Economists, long used to thinking of markets as made up of small, independent sellers and buyers coming together to make rather simple exchanges of goods and services, soon began to talk instead about the merits of "natural monopoly."

The railroad and the telegraph, besides providing the new organizational model for doing business, also provided the core infrastructure for the advent of the modern factory system. Quick, dependable, year-round transportation and instantaneous communications allowed companies uninterrupted access to suppliers upstream and retail markets downstream. Industry, which had long been seasonal, could now operate 365 days of the year. Coal, and then oil, provided electricity to illuminate and heat factories and to power equipment. The capital costs of maintaining a fossil-fuel energy infrastructure favored large factories over small shops. Large factories, in turn, required centralized command-and-control mechanisms to coordinate activity. The telegraph, and later the telephone, became the indispensible communications medium to manage the business activity of an expansive, more agile, and complex economy.

The modern business bureaucracy was a creature born of the fossil fuel age. It came to maturity in the 1920s, with the shift from coal to oil and from steam-powered to electrified factories. While bureaucracies of various kinds existed in previous civilizations, the new business form of bureaucracy was in many ways unique. The great twentieth-century sociologist Max Weber set out to define its features. Among its essential characteristics were predetermined rules for governing decision making, authority exercised from the top of the structure down, well-defined and well-written job descriptions for every level of the organization, objective criteria for evaluating performance and advancement, and a division of labor into specialized tasks and functions. This kind of rationalized governing process, noted Weber, made it possible to oversee large, complex organizations, integrating multiple activities under a single roof at ever faster throughput speeds.

Many other rationalized mechanisms evolved in the transition years, leading to a fully mature industrial capitalism. Standardized time zones, for example, were introduced, by the railroads, to better regulate the flow of traffic. In 1870, a rail passenger traveling from Washington to San Francisco would have to reset his watch more than two hundred times to stay current with all the local time systems across the country.[25] The great divergency in local time zones created havoc for the railroads in scheduling passenger trains and routing freight. In 1884, standard time zones were established for the world, with Greenwich, England, selected as zero longitude.[26]

Other rationalized processes were hurried into place to support the new bureaucratic structures and help expedite the accelerated throughput of economic activity, including the standardized grading of commodities, standardized machine packaging, and standardized pricing of products at the retail level. Continuous flow production—the first automated factories—churned out cigarettes, matches, soup, and flour in exact units and unvarying composition. New marketing tools, including mail order catalogs and product branding, as well as new retail mechanisms like franchises—which were introduced by International Harvester and the Singer Sewing Machine Company and later by the auto industry—turned commercial life into an accelerated flow of standardized goods that were predictable and unwavering in quality.

Commercial telephone service followed quickly on the heels of the telegraph. In 1876, there were only three thousand telephones in service. By 1899, there were more than a million telephones in use.[27]

Unlike the telegraph, which required a professional dispatcher to send a message on behalf of the sender, the telephone made direct, instantaneous communication between millions of people possible for the first time in history. Its impact on social discourse was enormous. The telephone enlarged and strengthened the circle of human connections. People could stay in touch with faraway relatives, keep up with distant friends, and come into contact with diverse new people—especially in day-to-day business operations. Long before the Internet, the telephone broke through the walls of isolation, making everyone potentially available to everyone else.

The new invention was treated with a combination of awe and distrust. Hearing a disembodied voice from hundreds of miles away was disquieting and took some getting used to. Horace C. Duval made the observation that "[w]hen a man tells you a story face-to-face he can see by the expression on your face, if he has the least knowledge of physiognomy, how the story strikes you. . . ."[28] Initially people didn't trust what they were hearing on the telephone because they couldn't put a face to it. The word "phony" emerged at the time to describe the experience of not believing the voice at the other end of the phone line.

The telegraph and telephone networks were followed by electric streetcar systems, which connected commercial districts in urban cores with outlying residential neighborhoods. The incandescent electric light extended day into night, lighting up entire neighborhoods. The first American department store to introduce electric lighting to attract customers and extend commercial hours was Wanamaker's in Philadelphia in 1878. By 1895, electric signs illuminated large parts of New York City after dark.[29] The new lighting allowed industry to extend working hours and families to stay up long after dark to socialize and read. Longer days gave a quantum boost to economic productivity and increased economic prosperity, while longer evenings changed social discourse, from courting rituals to family interactivity. By 1896, there were about 2,500 electric light companies in the United States alone and nearly 200 municipal power plants with a total investment of $300 million—and an additional 7,500 isolated power plants with an additional $200 million in investments—a huge sum of investment capital at the time.[30]

In just forty years, the electricity revolution had made deep inroads in the American and European economies, becoming the communications infrastructure for the Second Industrial Revolution. In 1890, it was estimated that 250,000 people were employed in the electrical industry or "depended on it for their livelihood."[31]

In 1910, 10 percent of American homes had electricity. By 1929, most urban homes were on the electricity grid.[32] Electrification of factories came slightly later. While in 1900, factories consumed more than half of all the electricity generated, only 5 percent of factories were electrified.[33]

The electrified factory made assembly-line production practical, efficient, and cheap. The switchover from steam power to electrification of factories resulted in a 300 percent increase in productivity in the period between 1890 and 1940.[34]

Henry Ford's goal of putting every adult American behind the wheel of his Model T car could not have been realized prior to the electrification of the factories and the introduction of electrical motors. He wrote:

> The provision of a whole new system of electric generation emancipated industry from the leather belt and line shaft, for it eventually became possible to provide each tool with its own electric motor . . . The motor enabled machinery to be arranged according to the sequence of the work, and that alone has probably doubled the efficiency of industry . . . Without high speed tools . . . there could be nothing of what we call modern industry.[35]

Electricity became the communications medium as well as the control mechanism that propelled America and the world into the oil era and the auto age in the twentieth century—the Second Industrial Revolution.

While electrification was being introduced into factories, homes, and communities in America and Europe, and inventors like Daimler, Benz, Duryea, Ford, and Olds were fine-tuning the internal combustion engine, others were readying society for the oil era.

In 1868, a former clerk and bookkeeper from Cleveland, John D. Rockefeller, founded the Standard Oil Company of Pennsylvania. Rockefeller realized that the key to success in the oil business lay not just at the wellhead but also in owning the refineries and in controlling the transportation and marketing of the finished products. He went about the task of entering into favored arrangements with the railroads and later bought up pipelines. By 1879, the Standard Oil Company controlled nearly 95 percent of the refining capacity in the country.[36]

Meanwhile, other oil companies formed along the same lines as Rockefeller's, each a fully integrated petroleum enterprise, owning oil fields, pipelines, and refineries and controlling the transport and marketing of products all the way to the local gas station.

By the 1930s, the major oil companies that would come to define the biggest industry in the world were in place. They included Standard Oil of New Jersey, Gulf Oil, Humble, Atlantic Refining Company, Sinclair, Standard Oil of Indiana, Phillips 66, Sucony, Sun, Union 76, and Texaco. Together, twenty-six companies owned two-thirds of the capital structure of the industry, 60 percent of the drilling, 90 percent of the pipelines, 70 percent of the refinery operations, and 80 percent of the marketing.[37]

Oil, refined into gasoline, provided the fuel to put Americans and Europeans and later much of the rest of the world behind the wheel of the automobile. Oil was also used to fuel commercial trucks, buses, trains, and planes, making a modern logistics systems and supply chain possible for a globalizing economy.

The first U.S. filling station opened for business in 1911 in Detroit.[38] The dizzying speed of automobile production caught the oil business by surprise. In an effort to keep pace with the almost insatiable demand for gasoline, energy companies expanded their exploration, opening up new fields almost weekly. By 1916, 3.4 million autos were on the U.S. roads. Just fourteen years later, there were more than 23.1 million cars in the United States.[39]

Automobiles became the centerpiece of industrial capitalism for the rest of the twentieth century. Many other critical industries were tied to the fortunes of the car. Autos consumed

20 percent of the steel, 12 percent of the aluminum, 10 percent of the copper, 51 percent of the lead, 95 percent of the nickel, 35 percent of the zinc, and 60 percent of the rubber used in the U.S.[40]

Industrialists gushed over the great commercial possibilities opened up by the automobile. One analyst, writing in 1932, observed:

> Think of the results to the industrial world of putting on the
> market a product that doubles the malleable iron consumption,
> triples the plate glass consumption, and quadruples the use of
> rubber! . . . As a consumer of raw material, the automobile has
> no equal in the history of the world.[41]

The automobile put millions of people on the road. It also brought town and country together and spawned the suburban culture while undermining traditional notions of neighborhood and community. And, more than any other invention of the twentieth century, the automobile quickened the pace of life, making speed and efficiency the paramount virtues of our time.

Automobile production was responsible for much of the incredible economic growth experienced by the United States in the twentieth century, as well as Europe and Asia after World War II, but it was oil that made it all possible. The British statesman Ernest Bevin once remarked that "the kingdom of heaven may be run on righteousness, but the kingdom of earth runs on oil."[42]

If the automobile increased the speed and efficiency of transportation, it also brought people into closer contact with one another, providing more opportunities to socialize with relatives, friends, and diverse others. Before the automobile, people in rural areas in particular were limited in the number of people with whom they could visit. By shortening distances, the automobile, like the telephone, opened up the possibility of enlarging one's circle of relationships. The average life became enmeshed in far more extensive and intensive social activity than ever before.

RETHINKING TIME AND SPACE

The new communications/energy revolution, like those before it, forced a change in human consciousness, as millions of people wrestled with the reality of adjusting to a world where the temporal and spatial context had shifted dramatically in just a few short decades.

In his book *The Culture of Time and Space*, historian Stephen Kern explores the changes in temporal and spatial orientation that altered human perception between 1880 and the outbreak of World War I in 1914. Kern argues that the introduction of the new technologies of the Second Industrial Revolution—the telegraph, telephone, cinema, automobile, and airplane, to name a few—"established the material foundation for this reorientation" of consciousness.[43] He suggests that cultural changes, including stream-of-consciousness novels, Cubism, the theory of relativity, and psychoanalysis, developed independently, shaping consciousness "directly," and that "the result was a transformation of the dimensions of life and thought."[44] I would suggest, rather, that the two forces—technological changes and cultural developments—emerged in a symbiotic relationship, from the very beginning, each affecting the other and, in the process, giving rise to an embryonic psychological consciousness, which would grow and mature in the second half of the twentieth century. Psychological consciousness would bring with it an empathic surge on the scale of the earlier ones that accompanied new energy and communications revolutions.

Kern begins his analysis with the observation that the nineteenth century saw a heightened sense of history. Darwin's theory of evolution placed the biological world squarely in a historical frame. Hegel and Marx built off the notion of history as an evolutionary process with their theories of dialectics. Virtually every discipline, across the humanities and social and natural sciences, repositioned itself within a historical context. Stephen Toulmin and June Goodfield sum up the new interest in historical framing:

> Whether we consider geology, zoology, political philosophy or
> the study of ancient civilizations, the nineteenth century was
> in every case the Century of History—a period marked by the
> growth of a new, dynamic world-picture.[45]

By the end of the century, however, the interest in grand historical narratives was giving way to an emerging interest in personal history among intellectuals and artists and growing numbers of the middle class. The new attention to personal history was a reflection, in part, of the increasing development of selfhood.

The emerging Second Industrial Revolution continued the process of differentiation and integration in what was becoming an increasingly complex economic and social organism. As more people began to experience their own selfhood more forcefully and came to see their own unique talents and creativity as the stuff of personal history, they began to challenge the idea, popularized by Enlightenment thinkers, that there is but a single perspective by which to view the world and only one interpretation of history.

To be sure, the Romantics had already contested the Enlightenment meta narrative but chose to replace it with one of their own choosing. What was different in the late nineteenth and early twentieth centuries is that intellectuals and artists were beginning to question the very idea of a meta narrative, be it one that reinforces sense or sensibility. In the new era, each individual history was to be accompanied by its own unique perspective on the world—the democratization of worldviews accompanied the democratization of history. Later, as the middle class became acculturated into psychological consciousness, a multiperspective view of the world became more acceptable. In the therapeutic era, people are taught from a very early age that their reality is not necessarily someone else's and that it is important to validate another person's right to have their own reality, even if it differs from one's own.

The new emphasis on the unique nature of each individual's own personal history and the belief in a multiperspective reality fostered a new level of tolerance. A willingness to acknowledge another's point of view helped make people more mindful that we are each unique beings deserving respect. The new mindfulness of another's singularity and finiteness—their unique history—also sparked a more empathic response. The new multiperspective view also had a dark side—a risk of moral relativism. If everyone's story is equally valid, then on what basis do we make distinctions between what constitutes the morally appropriate way to behave and be in the world?

In the later nineteenth century, however, the multiperspective challenge was a breath of fresh air amidst the suffocating atmosphere that pervaded the Victorian era. Nietzsche led the charge. He attacked the Enlightenment idea that there are "objective" facts, arguing instead that there are only points of view. He urged his fellow philosophers "to employ a *variety* of perspectives and affective interpretations in the service of knowledge."[46] He called this new approach to philosophy "perspectivism" and in 1887 set forth his methodology.

Nietzsche went after both the theologians and the rationalists, saying that it was time to give up the illusion that there exists something called "absolute spirituality" or "pure reason." Rather,

> [t]here is *only* a perspective seeing, *only* a perspective
> "knowing"; and the *more* affects we allow to speak about one
> thing, the *more* eyes, different eyes, we can use to observe one
> thing, the more complete will be our "concept" of this thing,
> our "objectivity."[47]

Others followed suit. José Ortega y Gasset, echoing Nietzsche, proclaimed that "this supposed immutable and unique reality . . . does not exist: there are as many realities as points of view."[48]

Ortega looked to Einstein's new theory of relativity to support his claims about multiple realities. He pointed out that Einstein had put to rest the idea of a single, knowable, objective reality. Einstein rejected the notion of absolute time, arguing that time itself was a perspectival effect determined by the relative motion between an observer and the object being observed.

It was the artists of the period, however, who had the biggest impact on changing the perspective on perspective. Recall that the invention of perspective in art was perhaps the single most important development of the Renaissance. The artists broke with medieval renderings of the world as a great chain of being ascending—or floating—upward from the depths of earthly existence to the heavenly gates. The use of perspective took the human gaze away from the heavens toward the linear plane of an earthly world populated by subjects and objects. The gaze was no longer meant to conjure up the exultant expectation of ascending to the world above but, rather, an impartial ordering of the objective world below. Francis Bacon's scientific method and, later on, the rationalism of Enlightenment philosophers flowed inexorably and, in no small part, from the reorientation of time and space rendered by Renaissance artists on their canvases.

Paul Cézanne was the first to break ranks with the long tradition of the single perspective in art. His *Still Life with a Basket of Apples* (1890–94), depicts a table from different perspectives. The artist became obsessed with the multiperspective approach to the canvas. He wrote his son in 1906, conveying his sense of excitement.

> Here on the edge of the river, the motifs are plentiful, the same subject seen from a different angle gives a subject for study of the highest interest and so varied that I think I could be occupied for months without changing my place, simply bending more to the right or left.[49]

Pablo Picasso's *Les Demoiselles d'Avignon* introduced the new idea of Cubism in art. In the painting, two figures are shown frontally, "but with noses in sharp profile. The seated figure has her back to the viewer but her head is seen from the front."[50]

Cubism was a highbrow artistic expression that appealed far more to the avant-garde elites in Paris, London, and New York. The masses, however, Kern observes, were introduced to changes in temporal and spatial orientation by way of a lowbrow artistic medium—the cinema. Movies played with temporal and spatial orientations in ways that more resembled what occur in the unconscious during dreams. The linearity of everyday experience gave way to scenes that cut effortlessly to the past and future and to other places and times, forcing the viewer to readjust the way he or she absorbed and integrated temporal and spatial information that was out of sequence. Splitting the screen allowed one to view two events unfolding simultaneously in different places. By freezing frames, the director could give the sense of slowing time to a halt. Comedies often sped up the movement into a madcap romp or reversed movement: for example, showing a diver coming out of the water and up onto the diving board—to the howls of the audience.

The manipulation of temporal and spatial orientation took movie-goers out of their conscious reality of normal temporal and sequential order and into a fantasy world where all sorts of new realities are possible to imagine. It's no accident that Hollywood came to be known as the "dream factory." Like dreams, where temporal and spatial boundaries are nonexistent and one's mind floats in and out of the past, future, and present, so too in the cinema. By the time Freud began articulating his theory about the importance of dreams and the workings of one's unconscious, his ideas didn't seem so far-fetched to a generation that had already spent countless hours viewing movies and reprogramming their brains to think in dreamlike ways.

James Joyce played with time and space and multiple perspectives in his literary works, with similar effect, notes Kern, to what Cézanne, Picasso, and the Cubists were able to do on canvas. In *Ulysses*, Joyce's protagonist, Bloom, jumps in and out of a dizzying array of places, times, and realities as his mind wanders through the universe—musing over galaxies far away and the tiniest realm of the molecule—in the course of a very average day in Dublin. With Joyce we are introduced, for the first time, to stream of consciousness, the kind we all experience every waking and sleeping moment, as our own minds wander off into different time dimensions and distant spaces, of which we are not always in control. What Joyce is suggesting is that every individual is experiencing multiple perspectives and realities and occupying different places and times in his own mind throughout the day, just like Bloom. Our minds simply won't let us settle on a single perspective or, for that matter, allow us to accommodate a seamless objective reality. Edmund Wilson caught the brilliance of Joyce's accomplishment when he wrote:

> Joyce is indeed really the great poet of a new phase of human consciousness. Like Proust's or Whitehead's or Einstein's

world, Joyce's world is always changing as it is perceived by different observers and by them at different times."[51]

Although like the Romantics Joyce believed that consciousness is an embodied experience, and that the expression of love and compassion is a natural predisposition, his view of human vulnerability and imperfection differs in an important respect. While Romantics like Whitman celebrate human vulnerability and pay homage to the importance of erotic sexuality as a way of getting in touch with one's natural vitality, there is a tendency to romanticize human potential by creating an ideal transcendent self that no one can ever hope to live up to.

Joyce's protagonists remind us far more of ourselves. It's not that Leopold and Molly aren't desirous of ascent. But, as Martha Nussbaum reminds us, life keeps interrupting, in all of its unanticipated twists and turns. Life is messy, chaotic, and full of banality, some of it rising to comic levels of hysteria rather than cosmic levels of transcendence. We all soldier on—but in the midst of our desire for transcendence, we need to take time out for a stool or relieve our stress with five minutes of masturbation. In the real world, our lives are lived out like the puck of a yo-yo. We're up—we're down. We have moments of brilliant insight and moments of stupefying despair.

What Joyce and Nussbaum understand is that it is in the ordinariness of our individual lives—with all of its imperfections and neediness— that we find our common humanity and the emotional wherewithal to empathize with others. By putting too much emphasis on transcendence, the Romantics risked leaving the subtle impression that the imperfections of human beings are intolerable, even disgusting. Joyce put it best when he wrote, "Life we must accept as we see it before our eyes, men and women as we meet them in the real world, not as we apprehend them in the world of faery."[52]

When we empathize with each other, we are acknowledging each other's day-to-day struggle to be and celebrating each other's desire to succeed and transcend ourselves. But more than that—we recognize in others' struggles that they are human beings, like us, who are trying to ascend to new heights, even as they wrestle with imperfections, flaws, and demons that weigh them down. We don't judge them for their weaknesses but, rather, extend our generosity. We know that it's difficult overcoming all of the obstacles put in the way of our becoming what we'd like to be. Joyce's characters are like the rest of us, real people, full of contradictions, allowing readers to empathize with them, without being maudlin.

It seems as if the entire period from 1882 to World War I was but a dress rehearsal for Freud's entrance onto the world stage and the official raising of the curtain on the Age of Psychological Consciousness. Kern points out that in architecture, the stuffy Victorian sensibility, with its emphasis on walled-off, closed spaces tucked away from the outside world, gave way to the new architecture of openness and transparency. The new skyscrapers, the first to use steel girders, eliminated supporting walls. Glass was used to open up interiors and create the sense of boundless space between inside and outside. Whereas Victorian architecture accentuated the bourgeoisie's sense of privacy, featuring buildings with so many nooks and crannies that one needed a detailed map not to get lost in the maze, the new architecture knocked down walls, opened up spaces to daylight, and even exposed internal structures, which traditionally were concealed with facades.

"Brick culture is depressing," wrote the German Expressionist Paul Scheerbart.[53] Within a few years, Freud would be shining the light of psychoanalysis on the interior rooms of the subconscious in an effort to lift the veil that hung over the human psyche. Psychoanalysts, and especially humanist psychoanalysts, would admonish their patients for being closed off and for shutting out the world and would encourage them to get in touch with their feelings and to open up and share their innermost thoughts.

Frank Lloyd Wright best expressed the new sensibility, explaining that his architecture was designed with the goal of creating a seamless integration of the interior and exterior worlds—what he called "the 'inside' becoming 'outside'"—exactly what Freud and a generation of psychoanalysts hoped to do by exposing the subconscious to a rigorous open exploration with the goal of healing the patient, which meant reintegrating his inner life back into the realities of the outer world.[54]

In this snippet of time—less than a third of a century—human consciousness was irrevocably altered, concludes Kern. The new technologies and modes of perception broke through barriers that had long separated people, partially leveling traditional social hierarchies while democratizing access to and control over time and space. The telephone, cinema, radio, the motor car, and other twentieth-century technologies gave the average man and woman the same access to speed, mobility, and different spatial realities as the well-to-do. Moreover, as Swarthmore psychology professor Kenneth Gergen points out, the new technologies also

> brought people into increasingly close proximity, exposed
> them to an increasing range of others, and fostered a range of
> relationships that could never have occurred before.[55]

The leveling of social hierarchies, the introduction of multiperspectivism, the democratization of human experience, and the increasing exposure to diverse others laid the way for the Age of Psychological Consciousness and the great empathic surge that would flare up momentarily in the Roaring Twenties—with the flappers—and blow up into a full-bodied social phenomenon that would define a generation in the 1960s.

All of those changes in social relationships couldn't help but affect the status of women. Edison had prophesied that electricity would free women from the back-breaking chores of domestic life so they could devote more time to their education and eventually achieve the status of men in society. Although electricity would come to free women up, it was less because electrical appliances eased their workload—that wouldn't happen until the 1920s for upper-middle-class women and after World War II for working-class women. Even then, the amount of time given over to household duties didn't appreciably diminish. But as factories and front offices electrified and work began to shift from manufacturing to services, women found increasing opportunities as typists, secretaries, and clerks. The working woman became a new archetype in the years leading up to World War I. Their newfound economic independence emboldened them in the political arena.

The struggle for the vote intensified during this period, as women demanded an equal right alongside men in the governing of the country. It wouldn't be until 1920, however, that the Nineteenth Amendment to the Constitution would finally give women the same rights as men—130 years after the ratification of the U.S. Constitution.

Compulsory universal public schooling also played a major role in the changing status of women—not only because of receiving an equal education to men, at least through secondary school, but also because they shared with boys a new distinction, previously denied to both—adolescence.

THE NEW CONCEPT OF ADOLESCENCE

It was during the last decade of the nineteenth century and the first three decades of the twentieth century that the concept of adolescence emerged. This was a special temporal domain to which all children—boys and girls—belonged equally. Society came to think of childhood as extending beyond puberty and into the later teenage years. Previously a child graduated to adulthood and the responsibilities that go with it upon reaching sexual maturity. No longer. Now work life was put off and children remained under the nurturing care of parents for a longer period of time.

On the one hand, young people became more dependent, even infantilized, because of their extended protective status. On the other hand, they became more introspective, even worldly. This prolonged sabbatical was not meant just to be an extended playful romp. During their adolescence, youngsters were expected to take on a different type of responsibility—creating their own identity. This was a completely new idea. Adolescence was to be devoted to developing one's personality, discovering one's interests, and even, for some, asking the big questions concerning the meaning of one's life. Although it was very much a middle-class phenomenon—and remains largely so today—the effect on girls as well as boys was historically significant, with consequences that would change consciousness.

With more time to socialize freely and without the time restraints and hardships imposed on adult working life that often shut out any kind of reflection or introspection, teenagers found themselves increasingly caught up in mind games. They had time to experiment with different roles, test out identities, and think about "careers" and the kind of life they'd like to live—and even the kind of mate they would like to share their life with—emotional and mental luxuries not available to generations before that time. For a growing number of boys attending college, adolescence could last until one's twenty-first birthday and beyond. The extended socializing time also offered teenagers the opportunity to create more meaningful relationships with their peers, both within their gender and across gender with extended periods of courtship with multiple partners.

Although it wasn't until the 1940s that Erik Erikson coined the term "identity crisis," the psychological phenomenon accompanied the new period of adolescence from the very beginning. Adolescence is about identity crises as much as it is about identity formation. One is not possible in the absence of the other. So too with the idea of alienation, which became a popular literary theme around 1900 and ever since. J. D. Salinger's 1950s book *The Catcher in the Rye*, a story of post–World War II youthful alienation, is still required reading for young teens in most American school systems in the twenty-first century.

Creating one's own identity requires a certain amount of questioning of the prevailing orthodoxy and alienating oneself from parents' reality in order to find one's own unique place in and accommodation to the social order. James Dean, who portrayed the title role in *Rebel Without a Cause* in the 1950s movie, became the archetype of alienated youth for a generation of adolescent baby boomers as they readied themselves for the counterculture of the 1960s.

The prolonged emotional playground called adolescence would prepare generations of young people over the course of the twentieth century for living in a world characterized by psychological consciousness.

THE SHIFT FROM BEING OF GOOD CHARACTER TO HAVING A GOOD PERSONALITY

Closely tied to the new experimentation with identities and the corresponding sense of alienation that came with prolonged adolescence was a basic change in the way young people began to define the very concept of self. In the 1890s, at the dawn of psychological consciousness, the long-standing notion of becoming a person of "good character" began to give way to the revolutionary new idea of developing one's "personality."

The idea of good character was a Victorian holdover with deep roots in the rationalism of the Enlightenment and even deeper roots back to the Christian worldview of the medieval era.

In the age of theological consciousness, being pious was held in high esteem. One was judged by his or her fellow human beings, the Church, and God above by strict adherence to the Ten Commandments and by leading an ascetic life dedicated to being God's humble servant on Earth. The temptations of a sensual world of earthly pleasures were to be resisted.

The gradual shift from theological consciousness to ideological consciousness saw a transformation of the concept of self from being a pious person to being a person of good character. Good character was essentially a secularization of piety. The attributes—resisting earthly temptations and living in strict accordance with Abrahamic standards of morality—remained the same, although they were expressed in an increasingly secular manner. It was assumed that there was only one proper way to live in the world and being of good character was a single standard applied universally. Therefore, in society there were only two kinds of people—those of good character and those of bad character. The notion of good character went hand in hand with the Enlightenment view of a world that operated by a single, universal, mechanistic formula and in which a sole objective reality prevailed. To be of good character was to be properly aligned with the larger unifying principles that govern the universe and nature.

The emergence of personality represented a radical break in consciousness. Individuals became less concerned about their moral stature and more interested in whether they were liked by others. A premium was placed on influencing peers. To be personable was to exude charisma, to stand out in a crowd and be the center of attention. In an increasingly impersonal and bureaucratized society, where conformity to the requisites of industrial efficiency and respectable citizenship were expected, people felt an even greater need to break loose and express their own individuality. To be acknowledged and recognized became as important as being virtuous.

The new emphasis on expressing one's individuality and being liked raised the inevitable question: What is there about my personality that people don't like? The new sense of psychological alienation in an impersonal society was compounded by a sense of personal insecurity, as young people began to wonder, Am I personable?

The narcissistic element of developing one's personality became fodder for an incipient advertising industry that played off personal insecurities and the desperate need to be liked to sell products. If you buy the product, you will stand out, be admired and liked—even loved—by others.

Recall that John Watson, a pioneer in the field of psychiatry and the leading light in the new field of behavioralism, made a career move, in the 1920s, into the new field of advertising, where he used his experience in behavioral modification to sell products to the first generation of insecure Americans in search of a winning personality.[56]

The shift from being of good character to having a good personality had another, more positive impact. People began to pay more attention to how their behavior affected others. In the process, they became more mindful of other people's feelings. Because each personality is unique, it became more natural to regard others as unique and to be more sensitive to their very personal vulnerabilities and aspirations. It was more difficult to express empathy to others in a society where the only distinction was between being of good character or not. The judgmental nature of the classification mitigated against any feeling of empathic regard to another's emotional and mental weaknesses. But in a society where being liked is the criterion for measuring one's being, it is easier to identify with another's existential sense of aloneness and desire for affection and companionship.

THE AGE OF PSYCHOLOGICAL CONSCIOUSNESS

Although there is a common misconception that psychology was a derivative of philosophy, its origins are a bit more complicated. The conventional wisdom traces the roots of psychology back to the writings of Immanuel Kant and the Scottish philosopher Thomas Reid. As mentioned earlier, there was at the same time, however, a second group of mostly nonacademic scholars, influenced by electricity and new discoveries in neurophysiology, who believed that the electrical system embedded in human and animal tissue could better unlock the heretofore hidden workings of the human mind.

Kant remained convinced that the study of the human mind would forever remain outside the realm of "scientific investigation" because thought was a function of the soul, a nonmaterial medium, and therefore not subject to rigorous quantifiable standards of measurement. Recall that Dods and many of the early psychologists also believed that thought emanated from the soul and that the soul guided the human body. The nineteenth-century neurophysiologists were not yet prepared to give a wholly materialistic and secular interpretation of the workings of the mind. Dods and others, however, believed that electricity—a medium that resided somewhere in the gray realm between the immaterial world of the spirit and the corporeal world of earthly existence, was God's communications network that linked the immortal soul with the mortal body.

Swiss philosopher Edward S. Reed points out that as late as the 1890s, many psychologists were still attempting to place psychology within a spiritual setting. Some researchers thought that further discoveries of the role electricity played in physiology would bring them closer to grasping the divine plan. But their speculations on electricity's role in psychology also led to an examination of its impacts on illness—that interest would change the nature of psychology, transforming it from a spiritual quest to a medical discipline.

William Lawrence, the distinguished British surgeon and editor of the medical journal *The Lancet*, was the first to jump into the new waters of medical psychology. He argued that research into electrical physiology would reveal that insanity and other mental disorders were not the manifestations of a depraved soul but, rather, physiological disorders and amenable to medical intervention and even cure. His hypothesis was soundly denounced as blasphemous by the medical establishment, and he was forced to withdraw a book he wrote on the subject. He also had to give up his lectureship.[57]

In the 1880s, an American, George M. Beard, began to use "electrical tonics" to treat patients suffering from what was at the time described as neuraasthenia—later clinically defined as depression. While European psychologists of the period viewed such "symptoms as eruptions of dangerous instincts or degenerate traits," Beard believed the condition was caused by exhaustion and a depletion of the body's electricity.[58] He theorized that stress produced by "brain work," especially among the bourgeoisie, depleted energy, much like what occurs in an electric lightbulb. His cures relied on a combination of rest, electrical stimulation, and what we might today call motivational counseling. The idea was to "recharge" the patient's natural energy by applying electrical charges directly into the spent muscles.[59]

The first laboratory in experimental psychology was established in 1879 in Leipzig by Wilhelm Wundt, the acknowledged father of the field.[60] His work was dedicated to the task of finding a scientifically rigorous, introspective method to explore the human mind, comparable in effect to Francis Bacon's method of scientific objectivity employed in the natural sciences. By the 1890s, experimental psychology labs started appearing in the United States, France, and Great Britain.[61]

The American psychologist William James provided a systematic overview of the new science in *The Principles of Psychology*. James too focused on introspection as the proper methodology—"looking into our own minds and reporting what we there discover"—for unlocking the inner workings of consciousness.[62]

James is perhaps best known for introducing the concept of "stream of consciousness," by which he meant that consciousness occurs "without breach, crack or division."[63] Although he acknowledged that, at first glance, it would appear that unconsciousness during sleep interrupts the stream of consciousness, a closer examination shows that each stream feeds continuously into the other. Like other psychologists of the period, James relied on electrical metaphors to describe how the conscious and unconscious minds are connected.

> When Peter and Paul wake up in the same bed, and recognize
> that they have been asleep, each one of them mentally reaches
> back and makes connection with but *one* of the two streams
> of thought which were broken by the sleeping hours. As the
> current of an electrode buried in the ground unerringly finds
> its way to its own similarly buried mate, across no matter how
> much intervening earth; so Peter's present instantly finds out
> Peter's past, and never by mistake knits itself onto that of Paul.[64]

James believed that the proper use of metaphor was critical to understanding and exploring the workings of consciousness. He opposed using terms like "chain of thought" or "train of thought," which implied that consciousness was broken up into a linear sequence of isolated events, linked together.[65] The electrical metaphors, which emphasized uninterrupted connectivity, were to James's mind a far better way to explain how consciousness works.

James's views on identity mirrored the new ideas in the arts that emphasized multiple perspectives, as well as the new interest in personality, which favored playing multiple roles. He wrote that "we have as many social selves as there are people who know us."[66]

James was also among the first to define the spiritual self in psychological terms. He rejected the idea of the soul in favor of a secular interpretation that emphasized the sum total of one's conscious experiences that inform a person's sense of meaning in the world. He wrote that one's spiritual self is present "in our nodding or shaking heads as we agreed or disagreed with what someone was telling us."[67]

James was even the first to use the term "self-esteem"—which he defined as feeling positive about oneself. He said that self-esteem is measured by the following formula:

$$\text{Self Esteem} = \frac{\text{Success}}{\text{Pretention}}$$

James argued that

> [s]uch a fraction may be increased as well by diminishing the denominator as by increasing the numerator. To give up pretensions is as blessed a relief as to get them gratified. . . .[68]

Self-esteem would become an integral part of the humanist psychology movement of the 1960s and, later, become institutionalized into school curricula in the United States and around the world as a generation of students were taught how to develop their own self-esteem. Self-esteem became even more important than personal accountability and responsibility in defining one's identity. By the end of the twentieth century, having self-esteem became as important as being personable or well-liked for millions of American children.

Finally, James anticipated the object relations psychologists of the 1930s, 1940s, and 1950s and today's researchers into embodied experience by suggesting that the pure ego as a self-contained identity is a mere fiction. What we call our personal identity, says James, is really the composite of relational experiences that make up our personal history.[69]

James's introduction of an introspective methodology for exploring the mind and his keen insights about streams of consciousness, multiple role-playing in identity formation, the development of the secular, spiritual self, and the value of self-esteem helped lay the intellectual groundwork for the Age of Psychological Consciousness. As each of these ideas became embedded in the psychological thinking of the twentieth century and came to play a role in therapeutic care in treating patients, counseling students, training workers, and the like, empathic pathways became more sophisticated and extensive. Generations of Americans grew up to think more therapeutically and, as a result, became more attuned to the feelings of others and better able to read their emotions and respond appropriately to their plight.

Dods, Wundt, James, and others paved the way for the Age of Psychological Consciousness. But it took an extraordinary storyteller to transform a scholarly discipline into a new way for average people to think about their very identity as human beings. Sigmund Freud burst onto the world scene in the 1890s with his theory of the unconscious. He created a wholly new story about human nature, tying it to the dialectical relationship between libidinal drives and social constraints. The idea of the Ego and Superego became branded onto the collective psyche. His notion of a sexually charged species reined in by a repressive civilization became the defining mantra of twentieth-century man, at least until the 1960s when the countercultural revolution and women's movement let loose, with the call for sexual liberation.

Freud literally rewrote the book on the human journey. His description of how human history emerged was entirely original. No one before had ever suggested that the Oedipus complex was anything more than mythical metaphor. He took the story to new heights with his vivid account of the son's jealousy of the father's sexual control over the mother and the son's desire to kill him and take his place as the mother's lover. Freud's primal horde is a far cry from the myth of Adam and Eve in the Garden of Eden. Nor was Freud content just to rewrite the origins of human history as a tale of sexual pathology. In *Totem and Taboo*, Freud recast the tale of mythological consciousness, tracing its roots to the same sexual pathology that he believed underwrote all of human history. He followed suit in *Moses and Monotheism*, recasting the dawn of theological consciousness as a struggle between sexual desire and social constraint.

Freud's reworking of human history struck a popular nerve, unleashing a century-long passionate public debate on the sexual underpinnings of human nature. Freud was the first to historicize sexuality, giving it a new prominence in the human schema and making it the zeitgeist of the Age of Psychological Consciousness.

Like many of the other pioneers in psychological consciousness who came before him, Freud looked to the field of electricity to explain the workings of the human mind, consciousness, and sexual release. He referred to the cerebral path of conduction as analogous to a telephone line "through which there is a constant flow of galvanic current and which can no longer be excited if that current ceases."[70] Electrical metaphors, like "sexually charged," "turned on," "playing the field" and "feeling disconnected" that would become an intimate part of the psychological jargon of the therapeutic era were a direct legacy of Freud and other psychologists use of electrical terms in describing the workings of the human mind.

As we learned in Chapter 2, Freud's view of a sexually depraved human nature would come to be rebuked by a growing number of psychologists over the ensuing decades, although many continued to believe in the oral and anal stages of development, the Oedipus complex, penis envy, the death instinct, and other equally strange ideas, which appear comical if not downright ridiculous today. Yet we still use terms like oral and anal personality types in our descriptions of people's core identities and behaviors, as if they represented a scientific fact of human development.

Lest there be any doubt about how thoroughly enmeshed twentieth-century life has been in therapeutic ways of thinking, consider some of the terms that emerged from Freud's disciples and apostles. Alfred Adler introduced generations of young Americans to the idea that a feeling of inferiority, rather than repressed sexuality, is the critical factor in human development. In the 1950s and 1960s, it even became fashionable to refer to another's "inferiority complex." Freud's own daughter, Anna, introduced sophisticated new terms like defense mechanisms, rationalizations, projection, and displacement to describe types of human behavior. Carl Jung informed us that we are either extroverts or introverts and that we each have a public persona as well as a shadow self. While all of these psychological terms have been the subject of endless controversy, they have, at the same time, given us a rich vocabulary for exploring the interior dimensions of both our unconscious and conscious minds.

The psychological era, more than any other period in history, has propelled human beings to think about their own feelings and thoughts and those of others. One hundred years after Freud psychoanalyzed himself, becoming the first psychoanalyst, millions of people around the world regularly engage in some form of personal psychological counseling on a regular basis.

As is so often the case in history, those regarded as founders of a new way of thinking turn out, in hindsight, to be more reformers of the conventional wisdom they are challenging than trailblazers of a revolutionary new paradigm. Certainly in retrospect, Freud appears less of a revolutionary than a reconstructionist. Like the rational architects of the Enlightenment, he believed that sexuality, the core of corporeal existence, was "animal like"—a toxic brew of unpredictable, explosive, and aggressive drives that needed to be repressed in the service of rational human development. Yet by opening up the realm of sexuality to public scrutiny and personal introspection, he unwittingly raised the profile of sensuality, sensibility, affection, nurturing, and intimacy—all of which share a relationship with sexuality. This was the Achilles' heel that allowed the object relations and attachment theorists to kick open the door to a different interpretation of human nature—one centered on the biological predisposition for companionship, in which empathic expression, rather than pent-up sexual aggression, becomes the driving force in infant and child development.

We've already looked at the impact the object relations and attachment theorists had on redirecting the theory and practice of psychology to an embodied empathic view of human nature. There was, however, a parallel current that shared common ground with the object relations and attachment schools of thought, many of whose leading lights were either influenced by the central tenets or at least supportive of the general approach to human nature, child development, and adult therapeutic counseling.

GROUP THERAPY AND SELF-HELP GROUPS

While Freud's disciples—particularly Adler, Rank, Jung, and Reich—were battling with each other to revise his ideas and even challenge

some of his central tenets and behavioralists like Watson were challenging the Freudians with their own views, a movement of a very different kind began to emerge within the field of psychology. Its essential
assumption, like that of the attachment theorists, was that an individual's identity is a composite of the relationships that make up his or her
own unique life experiences. In other words, we each exist in relation
to the other. David W. Johnson and Roger T. Johnson put it this way
in their book *Cooperation and Competition: Theory and Research.* They
write:

> From the moment we are born to the moment we die,
> relationships are the core of our existence. We are conceived
> within relationships, are born into relationships, and live our
> lives within relationships.[71]

And because we are, at our core, deeply social animals whose primary drive is for companionship and belonging, affection, and nurturance within a community, the best way to address mental health issues
is not in isolation, on the couch, or in the laboratory, but rather in
intimate group engagement—or group therapy.

Interestingly, group therapy began not with psychologists or psychiatrists but with a chance meeting between a New York stockbroker
and a surgeon in Akron, Ohio, in 1935. Bill Wilson was a recovering
alcoholic, while Dr. Bob Smith was a drunk. Bob, like virtually all
alcoholics at the time, believed that his alcoholism reflected a moral
lapse. Bill convinced him otherwise, explaining that alcoholism is a
mental and physical disease and that it can be cured. That simple fact
helped Bob toward recovery.

The insight led to the creation of Alcoholics Anonymous, the first
self-help group. AA was based on the idea that the best way to treat
the disease is for recovering alcoholics and active alcoholics to come
together in intimate group settings, share their stories, and help each
other toward recovery. Although the recovery process eventually
evolved into a twelve-step program, the central driving force that made
recovery work was the empathic engagement between recovering and

active alcoholics. By sharing their plights openly with one another, they were able to create the social trust that allowed the members to counsel and care for one another and facilitate recovery. As word of the remarkable success rate of AA quickly spread, so too did the movement. By 1955, the movement claimed more than two million members.[72]

AA bridged the gap between the object relationship theorists and behavioralists by acknowledging the critical relational and emotional aspects of social well-being and the important role that empathic engagement plays in recovery, while at the same time creating a twelve-step program that contained elements of behavioral conditioning.

At the same time that AA was getting off the ground, psychologists were beginning to use group intervention techniques in psychotherapy. The original impetus was the large number of psychological casualties in World War II, people suffering from traumatic stress disorders that overwhelmed the limited treatment capacity of government psychologists.

A number of psychologists, including Carl Rogers, John Rawlings, and William Sargant in the United States, and Eric Trist in Britain, began to see patients in group settings. Their work built off of earlier efforts dating back to the 1920s. Alfred Adler, who was one of Freud's leading disciples, began using "collective therapy" with adults and children in his child guidance clinics. Trigant Burrow, one of the founders of the American Psychoanalytic Association, began experimenting with bringing patients and family members together in what he called "group analysis." Unlike Freud, who believed that mental illness is essentially intra-psychic in nature—although not without cultural feedback—Burrow believed that mental illness is bound up in one's social interactions and relationships and, therefore, requires a group therapeutic setting if mental health is to be restored.[73]

The most innovative of the group therapy approaches was psychodrama, the brainchild of Jacob L. Moreno. Psychodrama as a form of group therapy started with premises that were quite alien to the Freudian worldview. Nonetheless, Moreno's influence in shaping psychological consciousness in the twentieth century was considerable. Moreno, who was both a psychologist and a sociologist, believed, like the Romantics, that the nature of human beings is to be creative and that living a creative life is key to human health and well-being. But he also believed that creativity is rarely a solitary process—a work of genius—but, rather, something that is brought out by social intercourse. He relied heavily on theatrical techniques, including role-playing and improvisation, as a means to promote creativity and generate social trust. His most important theatrical tool was what he called role reversal—asking participants to take on another's persona. The act of pretending "as if" one were in another's skin was designed to help bring out the empathic impulse and to hone it to higher levels of expression.

Moreno argued that the human imagination is tapped into by empathic engagement. It is by imagining and experiencing the feelings and thoughts of others as if they were one's own that one unleashes personal creativity. But he didn't regard empathy simply as an instrumental means to advance the individual creative spirit. Rather, he believed that empathy was at the very core of what it means to be a fully aware and responsible human being. That awareness can't help but spark one's "creative faculties," which is just another way of saying one's "self-development." The more empathic one is, the more self-developed one becomes.

Moreno was so taken by the theatrical setting as a way to promote psychic health, greater tolerance of others, and a more benign society, in part, because it provided a safe play space to explore human emotions, become more introspective and reflective, and develop more sophisticated cognitive skills. In the psychodrama environment, one could create any kind of reality imaginable and test wholly new empathic pathways. Moreno called this expanded universe "surplus reality."[74]

Moreno believed that mobilizing people's awareness—their physical movements, feelings, emotions, and cognitive responses—in a dramatic encounter is likely to lead to greater insight and more successful reengagement back into the community of social relations than endless talking about one's childhood memories to a psychiatrist while reclining on the couch.

He also butted heads with the orthodox notion that controlling one's emotions was more important than expressing them. While Freudian therapists regarded emotional outbursts with alarm, referring to such behavior as "acting out," Moreno chose to harness emotional potential in a positive manner. His psychodramas put a great deal of emphasis on "emotional catharsis," believing that such moments provide a means of resolving a long-festering conflict while affording at least a temporary sense of transcendence and a feeling of connectedness.[75]

Finally, Moreno fine-tuned the role-playing experience to allow participants the opportunity to enmesh their affective and cognitive responses into higher stages of resolution. To accomplish this goal, Moreno asked participants to engage in role-playing on three levels: thinking of oneself as an actor in a play, remaining aware that one has a life separate from the one he is playing in a therapeutic setting, and taking directions from the psychotherapists and other players on how he might improve his performance in the role. By splitting his attention into three realities, the participant can continually hone his reflective capacity, get feedback, and adjust his cognitive response more accurately to his emotional state.

Moreno was convinced that psychodrama provided a pedagogy that was applicable to every kind of human setting and, if properly applied and widely employed, could not only help restore individuals to good mental health but also improve the society at large. Psychiatrist Dr. Adam Blatner observes that "skillfulness in communications, interpersonal problem-solving, and self-awareness" that psychodrama teaches are the foundation of "psychological literacy" and argues that

> competence in such skills is becoming as necessary for
> adaptation in a rapidly changing world as becoming basically
> literate—knowing how to read and write—was in the last
> century.[76]

Moreno's ideas would play an important role in the "outing" of the human psyche and the development of psychological consciousness in the twentieth century. His influence would extend even further, affecting the transformation from psychological to dramaturgical consciousness in the last two decades of the twentieth century and the opening decade of the current century. (Dramaturgical consciousness will be examined in Chapter 14.)

At the same time that Moreno was advancing his revolutionary new ideas about human nature and experimenting with the new pedagogy for psychotherapy and social psychology, Max Wertheimer, a Czech émigré to the United States, began challenging the central thesis of the two main psychological schools of thought. He took aim at introspection and behavioralism as mental tools for understanding the unconscious as well as consciousness. Wertheimer argued that both approaches to the workings of the human mind are reductionist in nature—that is, attempting to understand the whole by analyzing the sum of the parts. Recording data about elementary units like sensations and stimuli and then trying to build up a model of how the human mind functions by assembling all of the individual components that make up the physiology is doomed to failure.

The new line of argument goes like this:

> There are wholes, the behavior of which is not determined
> by that of their individual elements, but where the part[s] are
> themselves determined by the intrinsic nature of the whole.[77]

Wertheimer used the German word *Gestalt*—which roughly translates into "unifying whole"—to explain the importance of this new approach to the study of phenomena, which requires viewing from above rather than building up from below. Wertheimer argued that his methodology was equally applicable to physiology as well as psychology. He observed, for example, that the cells that make up an organism are parts of the whole and their excitations only make sense within the context of the workings of the entire organism and unified system.

Gestalt psychology reinforced the ideas of Moreno while providing a philosophical frame of reference. Wertheimer made the point that

> [w]hen a group of people work together it rarely occurs . . .
> that they constitute a mere sum of independent Egos. Instead

the common enterprise often becomes their mutual concern
and each works *as* a meaningfully functioning part of the
whole.[78]

Psychodrama is based on a similar set of assumptions about the relationships of the parts to the whole. There is an implicit recognition that
each player is part of a larger story, in which he is both affected by and
affects the unfolding narrative—much the same as notes are not music
in isolation but only become so as part of the unfolding score. After all,
a role is always a public expression, played out in relationship to others,
and takes on meaning and validation by dint of how others respond.

Moreno's ideas were picked up in the 1940s by Kurt Lewin and his
colleagues, who created the new field of sensitivity training—a group
approach to therapy that eventually would engage millions of people
around the world, lead to the encounter groups and consciousness raising groups of the 1960s and 1970s, and result in the full flowering of
psychological consciousness.

Lewin was a gestalt psychologist who received his doctorate at the
Psychological Institute in Berlin in 1910. He emigrated to the United
States in 1933. Borrowing on his gestalt background, Lewin advanced
the notion that an attempt to change an individual was futile unless it
also led to a change in the group in which that individual participated.
He reasoned that since the individual "is to the group as a part is to the
whole," then "a change in the dynamics of the group will [invariably]
change the way" individuals within that group behave and act. This
realization led Lewin into the study of group dynamics and experiments with a new model of psychosocial interaction, which he called
sensitivity training, or T-groups.[79]

He and his colleagues set up shop in Bethel, Maine, in 1947 and
established the National Training Laboratory. The T-groups brought
together a small number of strangers with the goal of teaching them
how to function better in groups. The participants spent two to three
weeks together to give them sufficient time to reorient their behavior
and solidify their new psyche before returning to their communities.

One of the critical features of T-groups is feedback—a concept that was just then being popularized by Norbert Wiener in his work in the new field of cybernetics. As part of the sensitivity training, each participant is asked to share his or her own perceptions of everyone else in the group. In doing so, the individual often reveals as much about himself—his attitudes, biases, emotional concerns, and his preconceived ideas and opinions about human nature and relationships, and so forth, all of which, in turn, become the subject of feedback from others. The individuals in the T-group are encouraged to give one another continuous feedback on how they perceive each other's behavior vis-à-vis the group and especially the effects their behavior has on others in the group as a whole.[80]

The sessions were often highly charged emotional experiences, with individuals getting negative as well as positive feedback. "Seeing yourself as others see you" can be emotionally stressful, especially in a public setting among complete strangers. When the group feedback zeros in on negative behavior, the experience can be excruciatingly painful. Yet with the appropriate professional guidance by trained counselors, these intense emotional encounters lead participants to experience life-changing insights about how their behavior affects others. The purpose of the training is to help individuals become more sensitive to the feelings and attitudes of others and better prepared to cooperate in a humane and thoughtful way in groups. T-groups are an institutionalized, therapeutic method of increasing empathic awareness and response in a short period of time.

Today millions of people regularly engage in some form of sensitivity training in schools, the workplace, or their communities. The training addresses a wide range of sensitive cultural issues and formerly taboo subjects, including gender and racial biases, multicultural sensitivity, and attitudes toward the disabled, to name just a few. The T-group experience itself has become democratized and informalized across society. It is now common to begin any group discussion around topics and concerns of every kind, with an invitation to participants to share their feelings about expectations and outcomes and their concerns about the attitudes and feelings of others in the group as well as how the group dynamic should unfold. These are called "process questions," and they deal with the emotional and behavioral dynamic of the group. Oftentimes process questions can take up more time than deliberative questions and can and do affect the very nature of the task the group came together to address and the outcome.

But in the late 1940s, the mere idea of strangers getting together and airing their feelings about how each person's behavior and attitudes affected other members of the group and the group dynamic, even in small controlled settings, was truly revolutionary.

Sensitivity training shares some common ground with group psychology, with the interest it places on individual emotions, relationships between people, and learning to become more introspective. Yet unlike group therapy, which is aimed more exclusively at helping individual participants better understand their past and their own subconscious motives, sensitivity training is more focused on better preparing people in the here and now with the insights and understandings they need to become better listeners and more sensitive to others in group settings.

Because the sessions are all about group dynamics, discussion typically gravitates toward the question of how different participants approach the group itself. Questions concerning discrimination and submission, power struggles around leadership and controlling the group agenda, scapegoating individual members, ignoring more passive or unappealing members, acting out, and aggressive behavior all get shoved onto the floor. Correcting those negative antisocial behaviors becomes the gist for discussion.

What's most interesting is that the key assumption underlying the group dynamic is that human beings are by nature sociable and affectionate and seek to cooperate and express empathy, and that behavior that undermines these natural inclinations is hurtful and ultimately counterproductive. The fact that sensitivity training works is an affirmation of the underlying empathic nature of human beings.

Sensitivity training has become an important tool in schools and in human resource management. Preparing children and employees to live and work alongside others in an increasingly diverse society has been challenging. For the most part, sensitivity training has proven to be a successful means of engagement. That isn't to say that it's not without criticism. Critics often argue that sensitivity training forces participants to comply with already preconceived social expectations and that it spurs group think and political correctness. In schools and work settings, it can lead to people taking on a false public veneer of sensitivity while continuing to harbor old biases and unhealthy attitudes; in other words, giving those in authority the proper social signals they are seeking. Worse still, critics argue, the trainings are manipulative and can result in serious emotional damage to the participants. That said, a wealth of data collected over the years shows that while the above-stated criticisms are not unfounded, the positive emotional benefits of producing more sensitive and empathic individuals has far outweighed the occasional negative and destructive effects of the experience.[81]

In the late 1950s, the sensitivity training movement began to split off into two directions—one more focused on organizational skills and the other on personal growth. The first was used by industry to reorient workers and provide them with the emotional and cognitive skills necessary to function in complex and diverse business settings. That movement has grown exponentially in recent decades as people in an increasingly multicultural global society have had to learn how to live and work together. Becoming mindful of and sensitive to racial, ethnic, religious, gender, and generational differences, sexual preferences, disabilities, physical appearance, and even lifestyle preferences can be mind-boggling and requires a reorientation of the individual and collective psyches. The sensitivity training movement represents a hands-on process for a wholesale rethinking of cultural norms and values.

Industry has come to view sensitivity training as an indispensable human resources tool to advance a multicultural perspective at the workplace. Writing in the *Human Resource Development Quarterly*, Rose M. Wentling et al. explain the high-stakes game being played out by global companies operating in a culturally diverse world.

> It is expected that the extent to which these demographic
> workforce shifts are effectively and efficiently managed will
> have an important impact on the competitive and economic
> outcome of organizations. . . . Only companies that have
> cultures that support diversity will be able to retain the talent
> necessary to remain competitive.[82]

While the motive might be expedient and instrumental to advancing corporate profits, the process itself does, nonetheless, generally sensitize millions of workers to the unique realities of their coworkers, suppliers, clients, and customers and fosters a more cosmopolitan tolerance and empathic sensibility among diverse peoples. In a 2007 survey, nearly three out of every four U.S. employers said they planned on either increasing or maintaining spending on diversity-training programs.[83]

HUMANIST PSYCHOLOGY AND THE COUNTERCULTURE REVOLUTION OF THE 1960S AND 1970S

The second direction taken by the sensitivity training movement—personal growth—was picked up by psychologists and psychiatrists who came to constitute the emerging field of humanist psychology—the so-called third force of psychology that was to become a powerful countervailing force to both the psychoanalytical tradition of the Freudians and the behavioralist orientation of the Watsons and Skinners.

Humanist psychologists transformed sensitivity training from a controlled professional exercise to a mass movement. By the early 1970s, thousands of encounter groups and consciousness-raising groups existed in the United States and around the world. The therapeutic experience had become thoroughly democratized. In living rooms, hotel conference rooms, community centers—virtually anywhere people congregated—ideological consciousness was being shunted aside to make room for psychological consciousness.

I personally remember a moment in the summer of 1970 when the shift in thinking jolted Greenwich Village, in New York City, where I was living at the time. The Village was made up largely of two distinct social-change groups: political radicals, who came out of the civil rights, free speech, and anti–Vietnam War movements, and counterculture free spirits, whose roots lay with the beatnik generation of the 1950s, and who were experimenting with unbridled sexual liberation, hallucinogenic drugs, and rock and roll, and dabbling in Eastern religions and spirituality. The two movements intersected—the Yippies, for example, were both countercultural and political, and musical groups like Peter, Paul and Mary were comfortable skirting both milieus. If there was a simple fault line that traveled across both movements, it was the budding women's consciousness movement.

The eruption occurred inside a small countercultural/political community called the Rat Collective, which published an alternative paper called *The Rat*. A seething debate raged inside the group, with the women accusing the men of behaving toward them in the same paternalistic manner as the government and business community did with the American people and the poor and disenfranchised people of the world. They demanded an end to movement paternalism and gender bias. When their demands went unmet, they staged a coup d'état, locking the men out and seizing control of the collective and the paper. News spread quickly, igniting a heated discussion within the political movement and in the counterculture.

Women claimed that all politics is personal and accused their male counterparts of hypocrisy, of spouting abstract ideological theory while practicing the worst kind of gender discrimination. Women's consciousness groups sprung up everywhere and ideological consciousness began to give way to psychological consciousness. Young counterculturalists and political radicals alike began to direct their energies inward, into the recesses of their own psyches, in search of deeper answers as to why society was the way it was and, more important, how to find personal meaning in a heartless world.

Humanist psychologists including Rollo May, Abraham Maslow, and Carl Rogers stepped into the breach, offering a psychological approach and methodology for examining the interior world of the psyche and the condition of the human spirit. Their kindred spirits were the existential philosophers of the nineteenth and twentieth centuries.

The Russian novelist Fyodor Dostoevsky best articulated the existential point of view when he observed that "[i]f God didn't exist, everything would be possible."[84] The existential philosophers start with the assumption that all human beings are alone in the universe, and therefore totally responsible for their own lives. Not beholden to a divine presence or cosmic plan, people are totally free to make of their lives what they choose.

The American psychologists were existentialists of a different kind. They rejected the rather bleak pessimism of the European existential philosophers like Nietzsche and Sartre who viewed humankind as forever condemned to an isolated abandonment in the universe. Maslow, for one, complained of the dark nature of European existential thinking, calling it "high I.Q. whimpering on a cosmic scale."[85]

American psychologists were far more upbeat, befitting of American optimism and the "can do" frame of mind. The humanist psychologists reasoned that since man is truly on his own in the universe and is free to make choices about the way he chooses to give meaning to life, then intentionality must be central to the human psyche. Charlotte Buhler describes the emerging humanist psychology in terms that are utterly different from the fatalistic psychoanalytical school with its built-in libidinal and destructive urges and the Pavlovian vision of human beings as little more than conditioned-response machines. The humanist psychologists conceived

> of man as living with intentionality, which means living with purpose. The purpose is to give meaning to life through interpreting it within a bigger context. Within this bigger context, to which the individual relates, he wants to create values.[86]

Unlike Nietzsche, who argued that the only intentional part of human nature is the will to power, Rollo May argued that at the core every individual cares deeply about the meaning of life and the nature of their own existence and, therefore, intentionally attempts to give their own lives meaning by the choices they make to embrace life. When caring is lost, one becomes apathetic and loses the will to live. May says that at the root of caring is the ability to imbue life with love. He writes: "We *will* the world, create it by our decision, our fiat, our choice; and we *love* it, give it affect, energy, power to love and change. . . ."[87]

Abraham Maslow, who studied at Harry Harlow's laboratory in the 1930s—Harlow conducted the famous macaque-monkey studies on infant attachment to surrogate mothers—was best known for creating the idea of the "hierarchy of needs," the ordering of needs from the most basic need of physical survival to the highest need of self-actualization. Once the physical survival needs are attended to, according to Maslow, human beings proceed to the more sophisticated need of affectionate relations with others, which provides each person with a sense of personal self-esteem—that they are worthy of other people's attention and affection. If one has self-esteem, it is possible to ascend to the highest level of human needs, the desire for self-actualization or self-fulfillment, which is defined as realizing the full extent of one's potential in life.[88] Maslow's hierarchy of needs is another way of articulating the process of self-development and the stages one goes through to develop a mature empathic sensitivity.

Carl Rogers, the other influential figure in the shaping of the humanist psychology movement, introduced the controversial concept of "client-centered" therapy, the idea that the therapist needs to enter the inner world of the client and be willing to experience his reality "through his eyes, and also the psychological meaning it has for him."[89] The more empathic the therapist is with the client, the more likely the patient will open up, learn to trust, and "reorganize the structure of self in accordance with reality and his own needs."[90]

Humanist psychologists saw sensitivity training as an ideal vehicle to expose millions of people to a more empathic approach to life—one centered on a deeper sense of intimate connection to and relationship with others and a commitment to self-actualization and personal growth. Sensitivity groups metamorphosed into encounter groups and consciousness-raising groups that were often less structured and more informal than traditional T-groups. In the late 1960s and throughout the 1970s, millions of people took part in some form of encounter group in what became known as the human potential movement.

Try to imagine the cultural and political impact of millions of people, for the very first time in history, openly sharing their innermost feelings, emotions, and thoughts with strangers in countless institutional and informal settings. Carl Rogers suggested that encounter groups were "perhaps the most significant social invention of the century."[91] In an increasingly complex, bureaucratic, and depersonalized post–World War II society, the baby boom generation looked to these new psychologically contrived public encounters as forums to excise their alienation, gain insight into their own psyches, and establish deeper, more empathic relationships with more diverse people.

A SELF-HELP GROUP FOR EVERYONE

Closely aligned to the burgeoning encounter-group movement was the phenomenal growth in self-help groups during this same period. The early success of the AA movement inspired a host of copycat self-help groups, primarily dealing with addictions such as gambling, drugs, and sex. These efforts were followed by self-help groups addressing other physical and mental illnesses, including breast and prostate cancer, heart attacks, obsessive-compulsive disorders, and autism. Other popular self-help groups have been organized around child custody, adoption, divorce, care giving, grief and bereavement, health, transgender issues, rape and sexual abuse, suicide, weight loss, and so on.

Self-help groups generally are small voluntary groups organized by individuals who have a common plight and provide mutual aid, usually in the form of emotional support and information sharing. Some support groups focus on personal growth, while others pursue alternative lifestyles. Many of the groups also encourage "activist" intervention on behalf of the members.[92]

Most self-help groups focus on life-coping situations. Like encounter groups, they help participants share their personal suffering and struggle to overcome or come to grips with their situations. Because they are organized around a commonly held plight or condition, they encourage an empathetic embrace among like-minded individuals and engender a sense of belonging to a compassionate community. Being able to understand another's condition and emotional state because one has also been there is a powerful means of inducing intimacy, nurturance, and social acceptance among members. Participants feel a sense of nonjudgmental and unconditional support for one another. Empathic extension lies at the very heart of most self-help groups.

It should also be emphasized that self-help groups are exactly what the title suggests—the empathic sense of community helps each member regain a sense of personal self-esteem and self-worth and with it a feeling that they can affect their situation, that they are not "helpless," and that they are not social pariahs or freaks. The mutual support helps each member transform their self-image from victim to agent.

Incredibly, in the United States alone, upward of 7 percent of all adult Americans attend a self-help group every year.[93] Tens of millions of people have participated in some kind of self-help group in their lifetime.[94] In recent years, self-help groups have become nearly as popular as Sunday school and Bible study groups in the United States. There are currently more than 500,000 such self-help groups, making them a formidable force in shaping the personal and social life of the country.[95]

Moreover, participation in self-help groups is increasing with each generation. A 1997 survey, for example, estimated that among twenty-five- to thirty-four-year-olds, more than one in four will have taken part in some kind of self-help group by their mid-thirties, whereas only one in ten Americans in the thirty-five to forty-four age group took part in such groups by their mid-thirties, and fewer than one out of twenty had taken part in these kinds of groups among older populations.[96]

Nor is the proliferation of self-help groups only an American phenomenon. For example, three million people in Germany participate in more than seventy thousand self-help groups."[97]

. . .

WHILE IN DEVELOPING countries theological consciousness is still the dominant mode of expression, and in the middle range of developed countries ideological consciousness is the most prevalent form of public expression, in the most highly developed nations of the world, psychological consciousness has gained the upper hand, even to the extent that it partially interprets and remakes the older forms of consciousness into its own image. Both religion and politics have become increasingly psychoanalyzed and made more therapeutic. Psychological metaphors, terms, and practices have penetrated deeply into the theological and ideological realms, to the point that even the language used to describe the other two forms of consciousness is more and more psychological in nature.

A survey conducted in 2006 reported that 20 percent of American adults have had some kind of therapy or counseling in their lifetime. Moreover, there are currently more than 33,000 psychiatrists, 150,000 psychotherapists, and more than 595,000 social workers practicing in the United States alone.[98] Add to this the millions of Americans who have been involved in self-help groups and we begin to grasp the enormity of the shift to psychological consciousness. To understand how thoroughly therapeutic thinking has penetrated the human psyche, consider the fact that nearly one out of every three Americans "believe[s] that an adult's psychological problems can be traced back to his or her childhood."[99] A century ago in America, such thoughts would have been held by only a tiny minority of mostly academics.

The shift to psychological consciousness resulted in the greatest single empathic surge in history—a phenomenon that swept the world in the 1960s and 1970s at the demographic peak of the post–World War II baby boom. The anticolonial struggles, the civil rights movement, the antiwar movement, the antinuclear movement, the peace movement, the feminist movement, the gay movement, the disability movement, and the ecology and animal rights movements are all testimonials (at least in part) to the new psychological emphasis on intimate relationships, introspection, multicultural perspectives, and unconditional acceptance of others.

Virtually every facet of modern life was turned inside out as the first generation weaned on psychological consciousness began to share their innermost feelings, vulnerabilities, hopes, and aspirations among relatives, friends, neighbors, and even complete strangers.

The proliferation of these social movements seems to suggest a renewed commitment to political life and a reawakening of ideological consciousness that had remained relatively dormant in the years following the end of World War II. A closer look, however, reveals something quite different at work. It was the dawn of psychological consciousness that propelled these diverse efforts forward. All of these movements—perhaps with the qualified exception of the anticolonial ones—shared a common theme: that the individual being is precious, unique, mortal, and of ultimate worth and transcends abstract ideological concerns around class consciousness and who controls the means of production. History professor Theodore Roszak, in his book *The Making of a Counter Culture*, cuts to the great generational shift that occurred in the 1960s, which separated the first generation raised on therapeutic ways of thinking from their parents and former generations reared on ideological consciousness.

> What makes the youthful disaffiliation of our time a cultural
> phenomenon, rather than merely a political movement,
> is the fact that it strikes beyond ideology to the level of
> consciousness, seeking to transform our deepest sense of the
> self, the other, the environment.[100]

CONSCIOUSNESS POLITICS

The seismic shift in consciousness was best reflected in the emergence of the New Left movement of the 1960s. A new generation of mostly college-age activists sought to disassociate themselves from what they regarded as the old left, by which they meant ideological-based political parties and movements that were far more likely to be caught up

in struggles around power relations in society and institutional transformations. The young radicals, by contrast, were far more interested
in transformations of individual human consciousness and interpersonal relations. The new radicals made clear their intentions in the Port
Huron statement, issued in 1962, by Students for a Democratic Society
(SDS). While they professed their commitment to right the wrongs of
an unjust and bureaucratic political and social order, they took pains to
explain that their beginning point lie not with the institutions or technologies of society but, rather, with the human condition itself.

> Loneliness, estrangement, isolation describe the vast distance
> between man and man today. These dominant tendencies
> cannot be overcome by better personnel management, nor by
> improved gadgets, but only when a love of man overcomes the
> idolatrous worship of things by man.[101]

The New Left activists also took a shot at their Marxist predeces-
sors, who were often as guilty as those in power of inhumane behavior
in the name of the revolution and the better society that awaits humanity in the far-off, distant future. They wrote,

> We regard *men* as infinitely precious and possessed of
> unfulfilled capacities for reason, freedom, and love. . . . We
> oppose the depersonalization that reduces human beings to the
> status of things. If anything, the brutalities of the twentieth
> century teach that means and ends are intimately related, that
> vague appeals to "posterity" cannot justify the mutilations of
> the present. . . .[102]

The French New Left put the question of means, ends, and posterity
more simply, with the slogan that read: "A revolution that expects you
to sacrifice yourself for it is one of daddy's revolutions."[103]

The SDS motto said it all. "One man, one soul"—the idea that each
person is unique and imbued with intrinsic value and responsible for

the conscious choices he makes in an existential world: Namely, that personal politics informs societal politics.[104]

While the old left ideologues held the institutions of society up for rigorous scrutiny, the New Left held themselves up first to a more personal scrutiny. Colin MacInnes observed that unlike the old left, the young radicals of the 1960s

> hold themselves more personally responsible than the young
> used to. Not in the sense of their "duties" to the state or even
> society, but to themselves. I think they examine themselves
> more closely and their motives and their own behavior.[105]

For all of his oddity and eccentric behavior, Timothy Leary captured the temper of the age, perhaps better than any of the other principal players at the time, with the pithy observation that ideological politics had given way to "the politics of the nervous system."[106]

Theodore Roszak, whose penetrating intellectual analysis of the sixties counterculture remains the best single account of the period, summarized the gestalt change this way: "Class consciousness gives way as a generative principle to . . . *consciousness* consciousness."[107] He goes on to explain that what this means is that in the 1960s

> we find sociology giving way steadily to psychology, political
> collectivities yielding to the person. . . . The "trip" is inward,
> toward deeper levels of self-examination . . . For the beauty of
> the New Left has always lain in its eagerness to give political
> dignity to the tenderer emotions, in its readiness to talk openly
> of love, and non-violence, and pity.[108]

The countercultural movement of the 1960s and early 1970s was not without its own shortcomings. More than a few observers looked into the eyes of the young free spirits and saw not a new level of empathic sensibility but only a rampant, carefree narcissism. American sociologist Philip Rieff, among the harshest critics, decried what he called the new therapeutic self—whose only overriding interest is his or her own "manipulatable sense of well-being."[109] Comparing theological consciousness with the new psychological consciousness, Rieff snorted that while "[r]eligious man was born to be saved; psychological man is born to be pleased."[110] He painted a Dionysian vision of fun and frolic in which the evocation of feelings becomes the ultimate "turn on" and being a person of good character, accountable to immutable truths is replaced by an actor playing out various identities while engaged in pleasurable mind games.[111]

It's not hard to come to such a conclusion amid the spectacle of love-ins and happenings, of young people immersing themselves in ancient tribal rituals and pantheistic orgies, of flower children placing flowers into the gun muzzles of troops ringing the Pentagon during an antiwar rally—I was a few feet away when the first flower was inserted—of hundreds of thousands of young Americans flocking to a pasture in New York State and consecrating themselves as the Woodstock Nation—I was there as well.

But despite the fact that such criticisms have merit, there is the risk that the cynicism leads us to a rush to judgment that misses the deeper shift in reality that was taking place at the time. Roszak, the chronicler of the times, sums up the historic importance of the counterculture:

> Never before had protest raised issues that went so philosophically deep, delving into the very meaning of reality, sanity, and human purpose. Out of that dissent grew the most ambitious agenda for the reappraisal of cultural values that any society has ever produced. Everything was called into question: family, work, education, success, child rearing, male-female relations, sexuality, urbanism, science, technology, progress. The meaning of wealth, the meaning of love, the meaning of life—all became issues in need of examination.[112]

Psychological consciousness allowed an increasingly individualized population, living in an ever more technologically and economically interconnected but, nonetheless, alienating global economy, to literally "out" their central nervous system across wider realms of existence. By doing so, they created a more universal empathic embrace befitting an emerging global civilization.

PART III

THE AGE OF EMPATHY

ELEVEN

THE CLIMB TO GLOBAL PEAK EMPATHY

FOR THE VERY FIRST time in history, the majority of the human race is embedded in economic, social, and political infrastructures that span the globe (a portion of the human race is still without electricity and unconnected to the globalization process but not unaffected by its workings and externalities).

Each day, 3.2 trillion dollars are exchanged at the speed of light in capital markets around the world.[1] Forty-nine thousand airplanes are in the sky on any given day, ferrying human beings and cargo to every part of the globe in journeys measured in hours. More than 2,500 satellites circle the Earth, monitoring the planet and routing information to more than four billion human beings.[2] Geopositional satellites track the continents, keep a watchful eye on weather conditions, speed video, audio, and text to billions of people, spy on terrorist activity, and help direct millions of drivers to their destinations.

The logistical infrastructure of modern commerce and trade is becoming nearly seamless. Fruits, vegetables, cereal grains, and meat products are grown and processed thousands of miles away and transported fresh to supermarkets around the world every day. The parts that go into manufactured goods of every kind are made in different countries and shipped and assembled near home markets. A typical automobile might contain thousands of parts, each made in a factory in a different country or continent. The era of the global car and the global house is here.

The energy resources we use—oil, coal, natural gas, and uranium—are increasingly processed outside our native lands and imported back into the country to run our economies. For example, the United States, which produced 100 percent of its own energy needs in 1950, produces less than 71 percent of its energy today.[3] Energy net imports have risen from zero British thermal units (BTU) in 1950 to 29.2 quadrillion BTU in 2007.[4]

Capital investments that traditionally were more local than global just a half-century ago have metamorphosed beyond national boundaries. The Abu Dhabi Investment Council bought a 75 percent share of the famed Chrysler Building in New York City in 2008 for 800 million dollars.[5] Even our port facilities are increasingly run by companies whose home offices are in other lands.[6]

Labor has spilled over national boundaries—sometimes legally, often illegally—and spread around the world. Although human migration has been a fact of history back to the very beginning of the human journey, labor migration and mobility has become a truly global phenomenon for the first time. Today millions of people hold multiple passports and shuttle back and forth between several countries to which they have both business and familial affiliations.

The world has shrunk and the human race finds itself nearly face-to-face in the world of cyberspace. Distances are becoming less relevant in the era of globalization. Our virtual addresses now overshadow our geographic addresses. Durations have compressed to near simultaneity, multitasking has become the norm, and time itself has become the scarce commodity.

Three hundred years ago, the average European peasant had access to limited local knowledge—most of which was dispensed by the parish priest or recorded in the form of stories on the stained-glass windows that adorned the local cathedral or gleaned from traditional folklore. Today billions of people can Google billions of factoids on the Internet and, soon, the collective knowledge and wisdom contained in virtually every book that exists in the libraries of the world will be accessible in a matter of seconds.

Flu viruses now cross the world with ease. A small outbreak of swine flu virus in a remote village in Mexico in 2008 set off a world health alert and led to a pandemic in weeks. With air travel, viruses enjoy the same mobility as humans.

The global economy is accompanied by global economic institutions like the World Bank, the World Trade Organization (WTO), and the International Monetary Fund (IMF), transnational political spaces like the European Union and the United Nations, global monitoring organizations like the World Health Organization (WHO) and the World Meteorological Organization (WMO), and world justice organizations like the International Criminal Court.

The vast array of economic, social, and political institutions oversee the most complex civilization ever conceived by human beings. The entire system is managed and maintained by billions of people, differentiated into thousands of professional talents and vocational skills, all working in specialized tasks in an interdependent global labyrinth.

The globalization process has been both opportunistic and disruptive. Millions of people have moved on up, enjoying immense wealth. Many others have fallen victim, as the collective central nervous system of the human race has begun to envelop the Earth.

The psychological impacts have been as important as the economic ones. Brought together in an ever closer embrace, we are increasingly exposed to each other in ways that are without precedent. While the backlash of globalization—the xenophobia, political populism, and terrorist activity—is widely reported, far less attention has been paid to the growing empathic extension, as hundreds of millions of people come in contact with diverse others. The nearly boundaryless world of the global marketplace has been accompanied by an ever more boundaryless social space. Hundreds of millions of human beings have become part of a global floating diaspora, and the world itself is becoming transformed into a universal public square.

The tragic death of Princess Diana in 1997 and the outpouring of grief and identification, as well as empathic concern for her two sons, by hundreds of millions of people around the world is a powerful example of the new reality—the planet itself has become everyone's backyard.

Two and a half billion people in more than 190 countries watched the worldwide satellite transmission of the funeral, which was broadcast in forty-four languages.[7] It was the most watched event in all of history. Millions more shared their grief and sought solace with one another in chat rooms across the global Internet.

Many people surveyed, both before and after the event, said they identified with Diana, had followed her life, and felt that she had become a familiar part of their own lives. Psychologists refer to such reactions as parasocial relationships—when people identify with celebrities or even television characters as if they were part of their own lives.[8] They had been with her—vicariously—at her wedding, the birth of her children, during her struggles with eating disorders, at the collapse of her marriage, at her ill-treatment at the hands of the British royal family, as well as during her charitable activities and when she was exploring new relationships and making a new life for herself. Although some scholars view parasocial relationships with skepticism, even disdain, suggesting that they are at best superficial and at worst merely cathartic media experiences with little value, others argue that they are a new and powerful way for people to express their feelings and extend their empathy, just as other forms of media did for past generations.

Women especially identified with Diana's struggles and said they felt a close empathic bond with her, especially in regard to her personal suffering and her struggle to recast her life in positive ways. In later follow-up surveys, women, but also men, said that they identified with her depression and suicide attempts, her often capricious and desperate behavior, and her yearning for love and companionship.[9] Her suffering became their felt pain. Respondents also said they empathized with her strength to persevere, remake her life, and transcend her situation.

Princess Diana's death and funeral brought 40 percent of the human race together at a single moment to grieve, empathize, and share their feelings with one another.[10] To paraphrase the late Canadian philosopher of communications Marshall McLuhan, the global electronic embrace has "outed" the central nervous system of billions of human beings and transformed the world into a global village—at least partially and for brief moments of time. The ability to extend individual empathy across national cultures, continents, oceans, and other traditional divides is enormous, with profound implications for the humanization of the human race.

The global electronic public square also allows millions of people not only to identify and empathize with the plight of others but also to respond with compassion. On December 26, 2004, killer tsunamis swept over Asian and East African coastlines, killing more than 225,000 people and leaving millions of others homeless and without access to basic supplies for survival.[11] The damage was estimated to be in the billions.[12] The tsunamis were among the worst natural disasters in recent memory.

Thousands of instant home videos were shot during the unfolding of events by people on the ground, who then put the contents on blogs and dispatched them, via the Internet, around the world. A single blogger in Australia, who had collected more than twenty-five amateur videos of the tidal wave on his site, recorded 682,366 unique visitors to his site in less than five days.[13]

Overnight the blog sites and Internet became a global chat room, allowing families of victims to query whether there was any news about their loved ones and others to express their grief and extend their empathy to the victims and their families.

The blogs and Internet also became a global organizing site to collect aid and organize relief missions. Children were particularly moved by the tragedy, because so many young people and babies were killed, and responded with fundraising events in thousands of schools.

The unpolished, very personal video accounts filmed by the victims and onlookers made the unfolding tragedy all the more real in the eyes of millions of people. Close-up videos and firsthand accounts of the plight of specific individuals elicited a huge emotional response. Studies show that people almost always empathize with individual tragedies and, through that identification, are then far more likely to lend a hand to overall relief efforts.

At the same time, it should also be acknowledged that continuous vicarious exposure to the plight of others can also descend into a form of voyeuristic entertainment. Overexposure can lead to desensitization, and even ennui—the "been there, seen that" syndrome. The jury is still out on this score.

THE COSMOPOLITANIZATION OF THE HUMAN RACE

If we were to take a time-lapse camera view of human migration and settlements over the course of the past 70,000 years, since our ancestors began their migrations out of the Rift Valley in Africa, what becomes so striking is the radical change that has occurred in just the past three hundred years.[14] For most of human history, small bands of 30 to 150 people traveled across the continents and established zones of occupation.[15] Forager/hunters migrated with the seasons, setting up temporary habitats, only to move on with the cyclical ebb and flow of the flora and fauna that provided them with sustenance.

Sedentary habitats and rudimentary villages emerged with the small-scale horticultural societies in Eurasia around 9000 BC.[16] The coming of the hydraulic civilizations brought on the first truly urban habitats, small cities of tens of thousands of inhabitants. The great empires in Mesopotamia, Egypt, China, and India spawned giant capital cities with populations of between 50,000 and 100,000 people.[17] Ancient Jerusalem peaked at 60,000 and the Greek city-states of Athens and Sparta housed 100,000 or so people.[18] The only ancient city with more than a million inhabitants was Rome, at the height of its influence in the first and second centuries AD.[19]

It wasn't until two centuries ago that human settlement metamorphosed into highly complex, densely populated urban centers of a million or more inhabitants. The urbanization of the human race was made possible by the discovery of stored sun, in the form of coal and later oil and natural gas, lodged deep under the earth in the burial grounds of the Jurassic Age. This vast treasure of fossils fuel, harnessed by the steam engine and later the internal-combustion engine and converted into electricity and distributed across power lines, provided a seemingly unlimited amount of energy that could be put to use expropriating the Earth's resources. The pace, speed, and flow of economic activity made possible by the harnessing of fossil fuels was astounding. Agricultural production soared. A new kind of economic activity—the mass production of manufactured goods—allowed an emerging bourgeoisie to live better than the royalty of earlier centuries. The unprecedented increase in productivity led to the massive growth of human population and the urbanization of the world. At the outset of the Industrial Revolution, the world population hovered at one billion. By 1900 it had climbed to 1.65 billion. Just sixty years later it stood at nearly three billion. Today the world population is approaching seven billion.

The Industrial Revolution required centralized production facilities and large numbers of workers. Britain, the first country in the world to industrialize, boasted the first modern industrial city of more than one million inhabitants in 1820. By 1900, there were 11 cities with populations exceeding one million people; by 1950, 75 cities; by 1976, 191 urban areas had populations of one million people. Today 414 cities have populations of a million or more people, and there's no end in sight to the urbanization process because our species is growing at an alarming rate. Every day 340,000 people are born on Earth. The human population is expected to increase to nine billion by 2042, most living in dense urban areas.[20]

The year 2007 marked a great tipping point in the history of human settlement, similar in magnitude to the agricultural era. For the first time in history, a majority of human beings live in vast urban areas, according to the United Nations—many in mega-cities with suburban extensions—some with populations of ten million people or more. We have become *"Homo urbanus."*

The urbanization of the world has been made possible by a tremendous increase in entropic flow. Urban societal structures maintain human life far away from equilibrium by pumping more and more of the Earth's available energy and material through their arteries, to support ever more sumptuous lifestyles at the core of the infrastructure, while dumping ever more entropic waste at the margins and in the external environment. To put this in perspective, the Willis Tower in Chicago (formerly the Sears Tower), one of the tallest skyscrapers in the world, uses more electricity in a single day than a town of 35,000 inhabitants.[21]

The entropic consequences of urbanization are stark. The UN estimates that of the nearly 3.5 billion people living in urban areas, one out of three live in slum conditions, plagued by air pollution, contaminated drinking water, and open sewage. Many live on contaminated land or near landfills. The slums are the entropy sinks of the cities, the places where the waste stream produced by the energy flow-through accumulates. The health impacts are staggering. Malaria, diarrheal diseases, bronchitis, pneumonia, and other respiratory illnesses, and exposure to chemical and toxic waste kill millions of urban slum dwellers each year.[22]

At the same time, the urbanization of human life, with its complex infrastructures and operations, has led to greater density of population, more differentiation and individuation, an ever more developed sense of selfhood, more exposure to diverse others, and an extension of the empathic bond.

When we think of urban, we think of *urbane*. And when we think of urbane, cosmopolitanism comes to mind. While not every urbanite is cosmopolitan, virtually every cosmopolitan has an urban affiliation. Cosmopolitanism's roots reach back to the ancient Greek city-states. The word comes from the Greek *kosmos*, which means "world," and *polis*, which means "city." To be cosmopolitan, says professor of cultural sociology John Tomlinson, is to be "a citizen of the world."[23]

Cosmopolitanism is the name we use to refer to tolerance and the celebration of human diversity and is generally found wherever urban social structures are engaged in long-distance commerce and trade and the business of building empires. The great commercial and trading cities of history—Istanbul, Alexandria, Cairo, and Rome, to name a few—have always been the places where empathy flourished. People of various cultures, thrown together in commerce and trade, experience "the other" firsthand, and the exposure deepens not only the commercial bonds but the empathic bonds as well.

The close ties between commercial and empathic bonds might seem a bit paradoxical, but the relationship is symbiotic. Sociologist Georg Simmel, in his landmark study on *The Philosophy of Money*, observed that coins are promissory notes based on the assumption of an established collective trust among anonymous parties that guarantees that at some future date the token passed in an earlier exchange will be honored by a third party in a subsequent exchange.[24]

It's instructive to note that when anthropologists study the history of exchange, they find that social exchange virtually always precedes commercial exchange. The Trobriand Islanders engaged in an elaborate social exchange of shells, often canoeing long distances between islands to pass the tokens back and forth as a way of cementing bonds of social trust. Commercial exchange in the Trobriand Islands was always preceded by social exchange, again confirming the ancient wisdom that cultural capital precedes commercial capital and that commerce is an extension of cultural relations and, therefore, not a primary institution in the affairs of humankind.

The relationship between empathic and commercial bonds is complicated and fragile. That's because, as previously mentioned, empathic extension is always a nonconditional gift, freely given, without consideration of reciprocity on behalf of the other, either in the moment or in the future. While commercial exchange would be impossible without empathic extension first establishing bonds of social trust, its utilitarian, instrumental, and exploitive nature can and often does deplete the social capital that makes its very operations possible. That's exactly what's occurring now in the United States and around the world in the aftermath of the global economic meltdown.

Cosmopolitanism is a delicate balancing act that constantly juggles the empathic and commercial sensibilities. To be cosmopolitan is to be open to "the other" and to be comfortable amid diverse cultures. A cosmopolitan generally is a person highly differentiated and individualized, of multiple identities and affiliations, and honed to a sophisticated sense of selfhood as a result of intense exposure to and empathic connection with diverse others. He or she can feel familial and at home everywhere.

Today's sprawling urban environments are like a thousand ancient Romes—gigantic public squares where the diasporas of the world meet, carry on social life, and engage in commercial activity and exchange. They are breeding grounds for empathic extension. Although it should be added that for the less fortunate with little education, few skills, and sparse social support, the urban public square often appears more Dickensian and foreboding than familial and open.

A globalizing world is creating a new cosmopolitan, one whose multiple identities and affiliations span the planet. Cosmopolitans are the early advance party, if you will, of a fledgling biosphere consciousness. The contradiction is that the more cosmopolitan the individual, the more likely he is the beneficiary of a disproportionate amount of the Earth's energy and resources. Think global business travelers making deals around the world, taking vacation jaunts and escapes to the far reaches of the globe, satisfying gourmand tastes, and dabbling in exotic experiences and adventures. Although admittedly a bit of a caricature, I'm quite sure that a survey of cosmopolitan attitudes would find that the most cosmopolitan in attitudes leave behind them the largest entropic footprint.

Still, it would be wrong to suggest that the new cosmopolitanism is only to be found among the global elite. The growing cosmopolitan sensibility is being felt and expressed in urban environments around the globe—wherever diasporic communities coexist. My own city of Washington, D.C., and the suburbs that stretch into Virginia and Maryland have become a global public square in just the past thirty years.

In 1960, the Washington metropolitan area was a small southern city, made up of a large black population and smaller white community, with very little interaction. Today tens of thousands of people from ethnic communities all over the world reside in the region. They run businesses and are employed by local companies. Their children attend public schools. Their native foods, fashions, music, and other cultural fares have permeated the region, turning much of the area into a multicultural sphere. It's not unusual to hear three or four languages being spoken at the checkout counter at a neighborhood supermarket. While first-generation newcomers tend to remain tightly wedged in their own ethnic enclaves, their children and grandchildren socialize much more freely with young people from other ethnic backgrounds, creating a kind of bottom-up neighborhood cosmopolitanism.

Sociology professor Stuart Hall calls this "vernacular cosmopolitanism."[25] It's what happens when people are exposed to each other daily at school, at play, in the workplace, and in the civic arena. The constant engagement, especially in public spaces, creates what sociologists Annick Germain and Julie E. Gagnon call "cultures of hospitality."[26] Because students, in particular, are socially engaged with one another for most of the day in public schools—both in the classroom and in extracurricular activities like sports teams—they have more one-on-one opportunities to experience one another's lives and find some emotional common ground across cultural boundaries.

Chan Kwok-bun observes that bottom-up cosmopolitanism develops in the course of

> everyday life fusion and hybridization . . . when groups share
> a neighborhood, a history and memory based on simply living
> together and solving practical problems of living that require a
> certain transcendence of group identities.[27]

Daniel Hiebert, a Canadian geographer, explains how cosmopolitanism develops on the micro-scale in his own neighborhood of Cedar Cottage, in Vancouver, Canada. The neighborhood has been an entry point for immigrants for more than one hundred years—much like the Lower East Side of Manhattan. The descendants of earlier waves of immigrants from the UK and central and Eastern Europe still reside there. The new arrivals are largely from Asia, particularly China, Hong Kong, Taiwan, Singapore, and Indonesia. In Hiebert's own neighborhood, 72 percent of the residents are immigrants and nearly 20 percent of them have arrived in the past ten years.[28]

Hiebert observes that one of the most powerful agents in cross-cultural contact is local gardening. Much of the conversation on the street and across the backyard fence deals with sharing gardening tips and discussing the different approaches to gardening in other cultures. Many immigrants sneak native seeds into the country and in a very real sense are planting their cultural roots in their new land. Hiebert says his neighborhood is a micro-cosmopolitan ecosystem made up of tomatoes from Calabria, mint from Vietnam, bok choy from China, and fava beans from Portugal. Gardeners share their seeds and the fruits of their harvests with one another. They also share recipes. In the process, they begin to share more of their cultures and personal stories with one another. The result, says Hiebert, is that "a new micro-ecology, unlike any other on earth, is being created" in his neighborhood, because of "the everyday cosmopolitan behaviour of neighbours."[29] Hiebert calls this phenomenon "a cosmopolitan ecology."[30]

Cosmopolitanism at the local level is often an unconscious process, says Bun. "One culture sort of 'slips into' another culture, half forgetting itself and half changing the other."[31]

The New Global Migrants

The countless daily examples of microcosmopolitanism take on far greater import when we weigh them alongside the unprecedented wave of global migration taking place. Contemporary human migration is nearly triple the number in the early decades of the twentieth century—the last great peak of global migration. While the percentage of the world population that is migratory has remained close to the figure in the early twentieth century, the sheer number of migrants has swollen to historic proportions because of the dramatic rise in human population. More than eighty million human beings migrated to new lands in the 1990s—many more if we count the unaccounted-for illegal immigrants.[32]

Capital and labor flows are the earmarks of the new globalization process. Each affects the other. Today's migrants, like migrants of the late nineteenth and early twentieth centuries, are following the money.

The search for new economic opportunities is forcing a massive reset-tlement of human population from south to north and from east to west.

The number of international migrants rose dramatically in the last several decades. Between 1970 and 2000, the international migrant population climbed from 82 million to 175 million, more than doubling in just thirty years.[33] Currently one out of every thirty-five human beings in the world is an international migrant.[34]

Most of the migrants are resettling in the wealthiest countries of the developed world, reversing an earlier pattern in which a greater percentage relocated in developing countries. The migration to North America has been particularly steep, more than tripling, from 13 million to 41 million between 1970 and 2000.[35] Migration into the European Union has also been sizable, rising from 19 to 33 million between 1970 and 2000.[36] The biggest concentration of international migration is in the United States, Australia, Canada, France, Germany, and the UK.[37] More than a million legal immigrants enter the United States alone each year.[38] The number of illegal immigrants in the United States in 2000 was estimated at around seven million, the majority of whom were from Mexico. Of the total immigration to the United States, more than 80 percent has been from developing countries since 1990.[39] The United States is now home to 20 percent of the international migrants of the world.[40]

The rising tide of international migration from poorer to wealthier countries—especially illegal migration—is likely going to turn into a flood in the years ahead as the global economic downturn and the real-time impacts of climate change threaten the survival of hundreds of millions of people. We are already beginning to see the early warning signs, as trickles of migrants turn into torrents of refugees heading north and west across continents and oceans, crammed together inside truck trailers and huddled in the cargo bays of boats in a desperate trek to secure their families' lives. The outlook is grim.

The injustice of their situation is particularly egregious because of the way that climate change is impacting the Earth. The prime beneficiaries of the era of fossil fuels and the Industrial Revolution were the northern and western countries. They were able to dramatically advance their standards of living by living off of the carbon capital of the planet. Now the spent energy—the CO_2—is migrating into the atmosphere and warming up the Earth. But the effects of human-induced climate change are most pronounced in the southern hemisphere, where the poorest people of the world live—those who were virtually bypassed and left out of the Industrial Age.

Real-time climate change is already having an impact on agriculture across the poorest regions of the southern hemisphere. Climate-change-induced droughts, floods, and other forms of extreme weather have crippled food production in many parts of the world.

The crisis was compounded between 2005 and 2008 by the dramatic rise in energy prices, which led to an equally steep rise in food prices. Modern agricultural production depends on oil and fossil fuel derivatives for every stage of the food production process. Petrochemicals are used in fertilizers, pesticides, and packaging, while gasoline is used to run farm equipment and to transport food to far-off markets. The result is that skyrocketing oil prices have raised the cost of growing the world's grain. Food prices were up 54 percent in 2008 and cereal prices went up by 92 percent in the same time period.[41] Rice prices rose 217 percent, while wheat prices went up 136 percent between 2006 and 2008.[42]

For the 2.6 billion people who have incomes of two dollars a day or less, price hikes of this magnitude can tip the scale from survival to starvation and even death. The Food and Agricultural Organization (FAO) of the United Nations says there are now between 800 million and one billion people on the planet who lack adequate food.[43]

With street rioting spreading to nearly thirty countries in 2007 and 2008, political leaders are now worried that further increases in food prices and mounting public anger and desperation could topple governments across the developing world.

The devolution of the developing world is quickening migration to the northern hemisphere. Despite a rising chorus of calls to lock up the borders, there is simply no way to build a wall big enough or long enough to keep out millions of destitute people.

The new international migrants are in some respects very different from those who preceded them in earlier periods of history. Until very recently, migration across continents and oceans took months, years, and even decades. Once in new lands, contact with family and friends left behind was sparse. Before the advent of electricity and the steam locomotive and the laying down of rail lines and telegraph and telephone lines, families separated by great distances had to rely on an occasional posted letter sent via stage coach or sailing ship, and before that on sporadic news brought by itinerant merchants or other migrants passing through. Separated by great distances and out of contact, the familial or cultural ties with one's land of origin soon faded to distant memories. Migrants began life anew, unencumbered by their pasts.

Today, with quick and relatively inexpensive air travel, cheap telephone and Internet service, and global television, international migrants can be in continuous touch with their birth countries. It is literally possible to divide one's attention between one's new home and one's ancestral home. These diasporic public spheres create a new dimension to culture. No longer strictly bound by geography, cultures are becoming deterritorialized and mobile. One's sense of being is less anchored to a place than to a state of mind. Cultures are becoming transnational and global, just like commercial and political activity.

Global cultural diasporas have become commonplace. The new migrants enjoy both virtual and real-time mobility and carry on business activity and social discourse in multiple environments.

The ancient idea of diaspora—which we normally associate with the Wandering Jews and Gypsies and itinerant labor, has become a global phenomenon. It is not uncommon for international migrants to sport multiple identities and cultural loyalties. Many send money back home to support family members left behind.

An immigrant can tune in to local sports and news events and other TV programs from his or her native country via satellite. Video, audio, and text can be sent within seconds between one's current and ancestral home. Discount airfares allow migrants to take occasional trips back home and their relatives to come visit. Many diasporic migrants work part of the year in their new country with the remainder spent back with their extended family and friends in the old country.

While some might find it surprising and even jarring, more than half the nations in the world now allow multiple citizenship. In fact, 90 percent of the more than one million people who immigrate to the United States each year come from countries that make room for multiple citizenship. Some forty million Americans are eligible to claim citizenship in another country.[44]

Living with hybrid identities and multiple cultural affiliations breeds a bottom-up cosmopolitanism and empathic extension. By incorporating diverse cultures, individuals become multicultural in their own identity, and therefore more tolerant and open to the diversity around them. A multicultural identity also gives an individual a richer reservoir of personal experiences and feelings to draw upon in expressing empathy to others.

National boundaries are meant to be exclusionary. Every country requires unswerving loyalty and allegiance to the national identity. Nations invariably create a wall between the familiar and the alien, which limits empathic extension. Global cultural diasporas, by contrast, undercut the "we"/"they" exclusion of national identity and open up the possibility of establishing a global public square made up of diverse cultural communities that interact both inside and across national boundaries and are no longer constrained by territory.

International migration only captures part of the new global interactivity that's begun to transform the world into a universal public square and provide new opportunities to be exposed to diverse others and extend empathic expression.

EVERYONE IS NOW A TOURIST

Global travel and tourism is now the largest single industry in the global economy, representing more than 10 percent of the world's domestic product and 8.3 percent of the world's employment. In 2007,

231 million people were employed in the travel and tourism industry. That's one out of every twelve jobs in the world.[45]

The notion of travel and tourism has ancient roots. Wealthy Roman families and government officials visited seaside resorts at Pompeii and Herculaneum to escape the hot summer of Rome.[46] But for most of history and for most people, there was little interest in travel for pure enjoyment. The very word "travel" comes from the word "travail." Travel before the modern era generally was arduous and dangerous. It wasn't until the Industrial Revolution and quick rail transport that mass travel for pleasure became commonplace in Britain and later on the European continent and in North America.

The industry grew steadily through the mid–twentieth century and took off with the advent of cheap jet air travel in the late 1950s. In 1950, international tourist arrivals numbered twenty-five million people. By 1980, the number had jumped to 286 million.[47] In 2005, 806 million people traveled internationally.[48] The European Union is the largest travel and tourism economy, accounting for 35 percent of the global market share.[49]

Global travel and tourism, like global electronic media and global immigration, has extended the central nervous system of the human race and exposed hundreds of millions of people to one another. This kind of exposure and interaction with our fellow human beings is of a magnitude and a scale never before experienced in history. The long and short of it is that people are getting to know each other—even if it's at the most superficial of levels—in a myriad of relationships and encounters made possible by tourism. The potential to extend empathic expression is increased in direct proportion to the exposure and interaction.

Postmodern critics argue, with some justification, that travel and tourism often have the exact opposite effect, transforming the experience into an exploitive commercial affair—a kind of voyeuristic form of entertainment in which the native population and their culture becomes a purchasable commodity to satisfy hedonistic pursuits. The relationship between tourist and native is reduced to a kind of neocolonial "experiential commerce," a paid-for experience in which the host culture becomes a dramatic theatrical backdrop and a small part of the population becomes the paid performers, whose task is to provide staged entertainment. The native culture becomes trivialized and degraded, prostituting itself, if you will, to entertain those who can afford to be pleasured.

In some tourist destinations, the native populations are even excluded from enjoying their own national treasures. For example, natural habitats—beaches, mountain ranges, forests—are increasingly privatized and turned into resorts for the enjoyment of wealthy visitors, leaving local populations to find more meager enjoyments in marginal spaces. Professors of tourism management Brian Archer and Chris Cooper cite the example of beachfront along large sections of the Mediterranean, where "almost half of the coastline has been acquired by hotels for the sole use of their visitors, and in consequence the local population is denied easy access."[50] The skeptics ask, quite appropriately, how much authentic interaction do tourists really ever have with the real lives of the people whose countries they visit?

Granted. But even accepting all of the very legitimate reservations proffered by the naysayers, it is still the case that even cursory contact with other cultures generally is an enlightening experience—one that exposes the visitor to diverse others and their cultural gifts. Most tourists, even the most hedonistic and jaded, can't help but be touched occasionally by their experiences and interactions in other cultures. To the extent that tourists step outside their comfort zone—enclosed hotel resorts and specially designated theme sights and tourists spaces—and mingle with local populations, new channels are opened up for communication and possible empathic extension. Or to put it another way, how likely is it that one who never travels but always remains cloistered in the realm of familiar faces and homogeneous experiences will ever be able to make new discoveries about the way others live their lives and accumulate sufficient new experiences to allow him to broaden his own empathic sensibility? A passport is a ticket to experience the unknown, become familiar with other people, and deepen one's ability to empathize with their lives.

The debate over the virtues and vices attendant to modern-day travel and tourism are as old as the industry. Thomas Cook, the father of modern tourism, established the idea of the package tour. Although his tours were a commercial venture, his vision was to expand the cultural horizon of professional and middle-class Englishmen and -women in the nineteenth century, by promoting affordable vacations abroad. Yet even the Cook tours to the continent were treated with contempt in some quarters. One Italian critic remarked that Cook charged his English countrymen for the pleasure of coming "to stare and laugh at us."[51]

The commercial criticisms notwithstanding, the human desire to travel and tour represented a passionate pent-up desire for exploration and adventure. Increasing numbers of people sought out the exotic and unfamiliar, hoping that new experiences would broaden their frame of reference. The new openness to make contact with "the other" reflected the Romantic era of the nineteenth century. The emerging bourgeois class, tiring of industrial asceticism, with its almost pathological emphasis on relentless work and productivity, sought respite in more emotional encounters. The poets and novelists of the day fed the yearning for "authenticity," by which they meant the desire to live fully and unconditionally and in communion with nature and their fellow human beings. The writing of the period spoke to the "sublime," to feelings of "rapture" and emotional outpouring that came from traveling to and exploring other places. For example, the Alps, previously regarded as a dangerous and foreboding landscape, were transformed by Wordsworth in his musings on Mount Blanc.[52] Travel advertisements of the day beckoned people to be "adventurous" and experience the bigger world to which they belonged. Experiencing the magic of Venice, the artistry of Paris, the majesty of Rome, and the agricultural pleasures of Provence gave people a sense of their connectivity to the totality of the human journey in all of its richness and diversity. Modern tourism is inspired by people's desire to commune with their fellow humans, celebrate each other's cultures, and take delight in the wonders of nature that surround. Ask anyone why they travel, and this is what they most likely will say.

Tourism is also a two-way street. For native populations, tourism is a source of employment. Beyond the pecuniary considerations, encounters with visitors provide an opportunity to observe behavior different from one's own. For example, when very traditional cultures open up their doors to foreign guests, one of the first indelible impressions is the different ways men and women relate to one another, especially married couples. The greater sense of gender equality and mutual participation in each other's lives is often an eye-opener for local populations, especially women. Such exposure can lead to friction with foreigners and domestic conflict at home—especially as local mothers and daughters openly compare their situation to the women tourists. The differences, however, can also result in opening up new channels of communication between men and women and creating a greater sense of empathic regard for one another.

Deeper exposure and interaction with visitors can also make native populations both more aware and appreciative of their own cultural identity as well as more open and understanding of their visitors' unique cultural ways. At the same time, the human desire for companionship also stimulates an effort to find common ground. This is where empathy steps to the fore. Often the most remarkable experience a tourist takes away from a trip abroad is a momentary encounter with a local person in which a chance conversation or shared experience created an empathic bond.

Although the traditional notion of travel and tourism as a leisure activity is still the dominant mode, the emergence of extended diasporic communities around the globe has added a new dimension. As mentioned earlier, diasporic communities take advantage of relatively inexpensive air, rail, and automobile travel to shuttle back and forth between their birthplace and their current residences. (The rising cost of energy and the dramatic increases in the price of all forms of commercial travel could begin to reverse this trend in the years ahead.) Diasporic travel not only involves going back and forth between one's birth country and current residence but also regular visits with extended family and friends living in the diasporic network across the globe. Unlike conventional tourism, diasporic tourists generally stay with relatives and friends and often for far longer visits—sometimes extending for weeks and months.

Routine visits across global diasporic networks allow members of a culture to continuously renew their cultural bonds. But it also serves another purpose. As each member of a diaspora becomes partially acculturated in their new land, they take on, at least in part, their new country's cultural norms and attitudes and assume multiple identities. Their lives become a potpourri of cultural accessions, which they bring with them in their visits in the global diasporic networks. They become more cosmopolitan and by sharing their multiple cultural selves with others, they open up ever richer veins of communication and more expansive empathic opportunities within the diaspora. The diasporas, therefore, potentially become less insulated and more open by the sheer nature of the cultural diversity embodied by their members.

Global communication networks connecting the majority of the human race in a speed-of-light embrace, spreading urbanization of human life that brings with it a more cosmopolitan outlook, the surge in global migration, the trend toward multiple identities and dual citizenships, the emergence of global diasporic networks, and mushrooming global travel and tourism, are bringing the human race together in innumerable ways and as never before. What we are experiencing is new in history. The global public square is fast becoming a reality, although not without the growing pains that come with the metamorphosis into a new form of social life. We are within reach of thinking of the human race as an extended family—for the very time in history—although it goes without saying that the obstacles are great and the odds of actually developing a biosphere consciousness are less than certain.

SPEAKING THE SAME LANGUAGE

The chance that we might actually achieve some form of biosphere consciousness in this century and in the lifetime of current generations is greatly increased by another powerful phenomenon unfolding across the world. The human race is beginning to speak a common language, opening up the possibility of dramatically expanding human relationships and interdependencies, establishing more complex social and economic networks, and fostering more individualization and integration of human life on a global stage.

In the past fifty years, English has become the language of global communications and is now spoken by more than 1.5 billion people— nearly one-fourth of the human race—with projections that more than half the human race might be conversant in English by mid-century. The globalization of the English language provides the context for an exponential extension of empathic consciousness.[53]

There are a number of reasons why English is becoming the universal language. To begin with, the United States has long been the media capital of the world. By the mid-1990s, the U.S. film industry controlled 85 percent of the world film market.[54] Hollywood films have entertained generations of people around the world, with the result that moviegoers have picked up English in bits and pieces at the cinema. American television—especially sitcoms, action, and drama programs—have been syndicated globally for nearly half a century. In many countries the programs are in their original English.

The United States has also dominated the popular music and recording industries for nearly half a century. Most of the world's leading recording labels originated in America.[55] David Crystal, in his book *English as a Global Language,* notes that virtually all of the great pop groups of the past half-century have come from two English-speaking countries—the United States and the UK. Many young people have learned their English listening to Bill Haley and the Comets, Elvis Presley, the Beatles, and the Rolling Stones.[56] A survey done in 1990 by the *Penguin Encyclopedia of Popular Music* found that 99 percent of pop groups' music was entirely or primarily in English, and 95 percent of the soloists' as well.[57]

Crystal points out that English is the universal language for signs in tourist destinations and is used in an increasing number of retail stores catering to the tourist trade. It's also used in instruction sheets accompanying most products. English traditionally has been used as the international language of sea and air traffic. They are referred to as "sea speak" and "airspeak," respectively. Safety instructions on international flights and on ships at sea and emergency instructions in hotels and public spaces are increasingly in English.[58] By 1980, more than 85 percent of the professional papers published in biology and physics were in English, as were 73 percent of the medical papers, 69 percent of the mathematical papers, and 67 percent of the papers in chemistry.[59]

English has also become the accepted language of instruction in universities and graduate schools in many non-English-speaking countries—especially in the sciences and business curriculum.[60]

Finally, and perhaps most important, English has become the universal language of the Internet, the core medium of the global era. Approximately "80 percent of all of the world's electronically stored information currently is in English."[61]

Language barriers have always been an impediment to the extension of empathic consciousness. Of course, it's possible to partially understand the feelings another person is expressing by the look in their eyes, by body language, and by the tone of their voice. Feelings like embarrassment, humiliation, frustration, sadness, fear, anxiety, joy, and exhilaration can be read across language walls and can set off an empathic reaction.

But the ability to deeply comprehend another's plight, both emotionally and cognitively, is greatly enhanced by language recognition. The ability to "listen" and hear another's story amplifies and clarifies their facial expressions, body language, gestures, and tone of voice, making it more likely that one will empathize with them. Language is made up of metaphors that encapsule past feelings, emotions, and experiences. When someone hears another person use certain words to describe his or her condition, the words prompt similar memories in the listener's experience and unleashes the full force of the empathic response.

Conversely, the inability to make one's condition or needs or plight understandable to another often brings out frustration in both parties. That's because the most basic need to be recognized and acknowledged is so intimately tied to the ability to be heard and understood. When people feel they are not being heard or understood by another, they often feel anger or a sense of diminishment. They feel devalued.

Knowing a person at the deepest level is knowing how they feel and think about their life and relationships to the world around them. It's knowing their unique story. To the extent that more and more human beings can communicate with one another in a universal language, the potential for empathic consciousness expands dramatically. Like the partial elimination of economic, social, and political barriers, the elimination of language barriers brings the human race closer together, in greater interdependencies and shared contexts, and makes the prospect of empathy potentially more universal and biosphere consciousness more attainable.

While the phenomena outlined above are formidable and certainly unprecedented in human history, do they correlate with evidence suggesting a qualitative leap in empathic extension? Is empathy also becoming globalized in the twenty-first century?

GLOBAL EMPATHIC TRENDS

A very curious thing happened in the primaries leading up to the presidential election in the United States in 2008. Traditionally, opinion polls ask voters who they think would make the strongest leader, be the best commander in chief, be most capable of improving the economy, and the like. In 2008, a new question was tacked on the polls. Democratic voters were asked which attribute they thought was most important in a presidential candidate, and more people chose "empathy" than chose "the best chance to win" the election.[62] The surprise was that introducing empathy as a presidential attribute didn't raise as much as a stir among the political pundits. Apparently, the politicians, pollsters, and public all regarded the question as legitimate and highly relevant in determining the best candidate to lead the most powerful nation in the world. It would be difficult to even imagine such a question being asked in the 1952 presidential contest between Dwight D. Eisenhower and Adlai Stevenson.

The empathy question in the presidential polling is reflective of a sea change in human values that has taken place over the course of the past fifty years around the world. Much of that change has been chronicled and recorded in global public opinion surveys. Among the most detailed of the studies is the World Values Survey, conducted by Ronald Inglehart et al. at the University of Michigan. The researchers began tracking opinion shifts in eighty countries representing 85 percent of the world's population in 1981. The most recent survey was conducted in 2005. Over the course of nearly a quarter-century of surveying, Inglehart and his colleagues have seen a transformation take place in human consciousness unlike at any other time in human history. Improved living conditions, brought on by industrial development, have shaken the foundation of the more traditional patriarchal worldview that characterized much of history.

The Industrial Revolution spurred public schooling and mass literacy, preparing people for professional, technical, and vocational skills required by the new economy. These new industrial skills have liberated millions of individuals from older communal bonds by allowing them to contract for their own wage-labor and become more independent. The increasing differentiation of skills and wage-labor has nurtured a new sense of individual freedom and selfhood.

As individuals in industrializing and urbanizing societies become more productive, wealthy, and independent, their values orientation shift from survival values to materialist values and eventually postmaterialist, self-expression values.

In preindustrial societies, where survival is the paramount concern, hierarchical social regimes and authoritarian governance rule. The collective will prevails and the sense of individual expression remains undeveloped or repressed. In industrial societies, contractual labor allows people to secure their individual livelihood and frees them from dependency on extended family ties and government fiat. Understandably, preoccupation is with material values and the accumulation of wealth, which is regarded as a liberating force. When industrial societies evolve from manufacturing to services, knowledge-based industries and experiential commerce, and people's basic material needs are met, they begin to shift their value orientation to nonmaterial considerations—bundled up in the notion of "quality-of-life" aspirations. Tight communal bonds increasingly give way to looser associational ties.

The three stages of progression, from traditional values to rational materialist values to quality-of-life and self-expression values, mirror the shifts in consciousness that accompany the transition from agricultural societies to First and Second Industrial-Revolution economies. The differences in values' orientations between the three stages of consciousness are extraordinary. In one of the World Values Surveys, people were asked a series of questions to ascertain whether their values correlated with traditional or secular-rational values. If they answered yes to the questions, they were classified as traditional, and if they answered the opposite, they were categorized as secular-rationalists. Respondents were asked if they agreed with the following statements:

> Expressing one's own preferences clearly is more important
>   than understanding others' preferences. . . .
> If a woman earns more money than her husband, it's almost
>   certain to cause problems. . . .
> One must always love and respect one's parents regardless of
>   their behavior. . . .
> Respondent relatively favorable to having the army rule the
>   country. . . .
> Respondent favors having a relatively large number of
>   children.[63]

A second survey contrasts survival values with self-expression values. If one answered yes, they identified with survival values. If no, they identified with self-expression values.

> Tolerance and respect for others are *not* the most important
>   things to teach a child. . . .
> Leisure is not very important in life. . . .

Friends are not very important in life. . . .

Having a strong leader who does not have to bother with
parliament and elections would be a good form of
government. . . .

Democracy is not necessarily the best form of government. . . .

Respondent opposes sending economic aid to poorer countries.[64]

As one might expect, in the poorer, agricultural societies, traditional survival values prevail and religious affiliation and family bonds play a central role in organizing social life.

More interesting is the rapid shift in values from rational and materialist to self-expression and quality-of-life that has occurred in less than forty years in the most highly developed industrial nations.

In 1971, materialists outnumbered postmaterialists by four to one in the six Western nations from which the researchers had data. By 2005, postmaterialists equaled the number of materialists in all six countries—a breathtaking shift in attitudes in less than two generations.[65]

People in survival societies emphasize economic and physical security. Life is organized in a strict authoritarian chain of command stretching from unconditional male authority over spouse and children, to unconditional state authority over all its subjects, to unswerving devotion to God's commands on high. Traditional societies, imperiled by economic hardship and insecurities, tend to be intolerant of foreigners, ethnic minorities, and gays and staunch supporters of male superiority.[66] Populations are highly religious and nationalistic, believe in the firm hand of state authority, emphasize conformity, and exhibit a low level of individual self-expression. Because self-expression is low, empathic extension is shallow and rarely reaches beyond the family bond and kinship relations. Since the family is the basic economic unit—"economy" comes from the Greek word *oikos*, which means family household—a premium is put on reproduction. More children means more hands for work and assures greater group survival. Fostering the interests of the family is essential to assure the survival of each individual family member. Personal self-expression that might be at odds with family survival is dealt with harshly. In these societies, with their emphasis on family survival, it's not surprising that abortion, homosexuality, and divorce are unacceptable.[67]

In secular-rationalist societies engaged in the takeoff stage of industrial life, hierarchies are reconfigured away from God's created order to giant corporate and government bureaucracies. The Great Chain of Being is replaced with the corporate chain of command. Individual accumulation of wealth frees people from the vicissitudes of nature, providing some degree of economic security. In the process, the individual, as a distinct self-possessed being, begins to emerge from the communal haze but is still beholden to hierarchical institutional arrangements. Nonetheless, more developed self-expression fosters some advance in empathic consciousness.

Knowledge-based societies, with high levels of individualism and self-expression, exhibit the highest levels of empathic extension. Selfhood is conducive to more trust and openness to others and greater tolerance of those who are different. If one feels secure in his own being and more free to control his own fate, the chances are he will be less fearful of others and less likely to associate anyone outside of his immediate network of relatives as a threat. In fact, the emancipation from tight communal bonds and the development of weaker but more extended associational ties exposes the individual to a much wider network of diverse people, which, in turn, both strengthens one's sense of trust and openness and provides the context for a more extended empathic consciousness.

After nearly thirty years of tracking public attitudes and values around the world, Inglehart and his cohorts make some incontrovertible conclusions. They observe that

> When survival is uncertain, cultural diversity seems
> threatening. When there isn't enough to go around, foreigners
> are perceived as dangerous outsiders, who may take away one's
> sustenance. People cling to traditional gender roles and sexual
> norms, . . . in an attempt to maximize predictability in an
> uncertain world. Conversely, when survival begins to be taken

for granted, ethnic and cultural diversity . . . becomes *positively* valued because it is interesting and stimulating.[68]

The key finding, according to the researchers, is that "individual security increases empathy."[69]

But if, as Inglehart and his colleagues claim, increasing economic security breeds empathic expression, doesn't their conclusion fly in the face of what we learned earlier about the nature of the human condition? If the need for affection, companionship, and a sense of belonging is the most basic human drive, how is it that traditional cultures emphasize material survival and seem less prepared to extend empathy to others?

The reality is that in every culture, from the most impoverished to the best off, the drive for affection, companionship, and belonging is paramount. That's why every society in history has evolved elaborate rituals to establish bonds of fraternity and used ostracism and banishment to punish wrongdoers. Empathy exists in every culture. The issue is always how extended or restricted it is. In survival societies, empathic bonds are less developed, more meager, and reserved for a narrow category of relationships. In traditional cultures, empathic extension is generally confined to parent-child relationships and relationships between siblings, other close relatives, extended kin, and members of peer groups. The communal bond and hierarchical chain of authority leave little wiggle room for extending empathic consciousness laterally.

As energy/communications revolutions establish more complex social structures and extend the human domain over time and space, new cosmologies serve like a giant overarching frame for enlarging the imaginative bonds of empathy. Theological consciousness allowed individuals to identify with non-kin and anonymous others and, by way of religious affiliation, to incorporate them into the empathic fold. Jews empathized with Jews, Christians with Christians, Muslims with Muslims, and so on. Ideological consciousness extended the empathic borders geographically to nation-states. Americans empathize with fellow Americans, Germans with fellow Germans, Japanese with fellow Japanese citizens, and so on. Empathy, then, in every culture, extends to the boundaries of its organizational domain. Inside the walls, empathy exists, if only in limited fashion. Outside the organizational boundaries is no-man's-land—a place beyond the empathic imagination.

The evidence shows that we are witnessing the greatest surge in empathic extension in all of human history. That surge, however, is largely confined to the well-heeled populations of the most highly developed nations and to middle-class enclaves in developing countries. Again, the leap in empathic consciousness is made possible by the expropriation of vast amounts of the planet's energy and other resources to attain the level of economic security necessary to allow people to shift from survival values to materialist values and finally to quality-of-life values. Increased economic well-being has provided the security necessary to allow people to be more trusting of their fellows and more caring toward the natural world. Unfortunately, the leap in empathic consciousness rides atop the growing entropic stream that's turning much of the planet into a wasteland and further impoverishing a large proportion of the human race.

The surveys show that 83 percent of the high-income countries have transitioned into a postmaterialist culture, but 74 percent of the poorest countries have sunk back into a survival-values culture. So while a minority of the world's countries and populations are becoming increasingly cosmopolitan in their values, a majority is going the other way.[70]

The question, then, is whether the minority of the human race that is undergoing an empathic surge, but at the expense of impoverishing the planet and a large portion of the human race, can translate their post-materialist values into a workable cultural, economic, and political game plan that can steer themselves and their communities to a more sustainable and equitable future in time to avoid the abyss.

NO MORE ALIENS

While religious affiliation and national loyalty have narrowed the realm of the alien and extended the empathic domain, many groups have remained, until very recently, in the category of "the other." Wherever patriarchal societies have held sway, women, homosexuals and the disabled, as well as different religious, ethnic, and racial groups, have continued to be regarded as aliens. That's now beginning to change.

The global surveys of the last forty years show a historic shift in sentiment toward all these groups. Nowhere, however, has the change in attitude been more pronounced than in regard to women. For most of history and well into the industrial era, women were regarded as property. When my own mother was a child, women still had not been granted the right to vote in the United States.

Today gender distinctions have diminished dramatically in the most affluent countries and the women's rights movement has spilled over into the developing world, where it is beginning to have an effect on traditional gender relations. Better access to education, job opportunities, improved contraceptive practices, and exposure to global media have all contributed to the shift in attitudes.

The most egalitarian societies in the world in regard to gender are among the most affluent. Finland, Sweden, Canada, and Germany all score high on gender equality. Developing industrial countries, like Brazil and Mexico, are also showing gains in gender relations. The poorest agrarian countries, including Bangladesh, Nigeria, and Morocco, with low per capita incomes, still sport traditional patriarchal cultures.[71]

But even in these countries, the women's movement is beginning to take hold, attitudes are changing, and some progress toward gender equality can be seen. In a sixteen-nation poll conducted in 2008, "an overwhelming majority of people around the world say that it is important for 'women to have full equality of rights compared to men.'" On average, 86 percent of the adult public believes that "women's equality is important" and 59 percent say it's "very important."[72] What's surprising is the strong support for gender rights in the poorer, more traditional societies—a result seemingly at odds with the World Values Survey, which shows little support for gender equality in the poorer, more traditional societies.

In the newest global survey, public support for gender equality in the developing countries, while not as high as in the most industrially advanced societies, is still notable. In Indonesia, 71 percent of the public say that gender equality is very or somewhat important; in China, 76 percent; in Turkey, 80 percent; in Mexico, 89 percent. Even in traditional Muslim nations, support for gender equality is high. Large majorities say it's important in Iran (78 percent), Azerbaijan (85 percent), Egypt (90 percent), and the Palestinian Territory (93 percent).[73]

Equally interesting, very large majorities in nearly all the countries surveyed say that "women have gained more equality of rights as compared to men" in the course of their own lifetime.[74]

An earlier Pew Survey, conducted in 2003, in forty-four countries, with interviews of 38,000 people, shows "that women are somewhat happier than men with their lives overall," and tend to be more satisfied than men with the personal progress they have made in recent years. In twenty-six of the forty-four countries surveyed, including more traditional societies like Nigeria, more women than men say "they are better off now than they were five years ago."[75]

In fourteen countries where Muslims are either the majority or are large minorities, Pew asked both women and men what their views were on democracy. The predominantly Muslim countries are Pakistan, Turkey, Jordan, Lebanon, Indonesia, Bangladesh, Mali, Senegal, Uzbekistan, the Palestinian Authority, Morocco, and Kuwait. Minority Muslim populations in Ghana, the Ivory Coast, Nigeria, Tanzania, and Uganda were also surveyed. The polling showed that "large numbers of both genders [say] that democracy could work in their country." In six countries, a majority said it's "very important to be able to live in a country where you can openly say what you think and criticize the government, have freedom of the press and open and honest elections." According to the Pew study, both men and women "have nearly identical views about these key freedoms."[76]

Where women and men differ, however, is on the question of "whether women should be permitted to work outside the home."[77] In Bangladesh, 57 percent of women completely agree, but only 36 percent of men. In Pakistan, 41 percent of women strongly agree, and only 24 percent of men.[78]

Still, in the most traditional societies, the clear trend is toward greater gender equality. The importance of this global shift in attitudes on gender can't be overstated. This represents a radical break in patriarchal beliefs and attitudes that have blocked women from being acknowledged and recognized as full human beings for thousands of years. This gender shift has occurred in less than a century in the industrialized nations and is now occurring in the poorer countries of the world. The affirmation of women as beings of equal self-worth to men extends the potential of empathic consciousness to include half of the human race, for the very first time in "recorded" history.

Attitudes toward homosexuality have also dramatically changed in recent decades. The release of the motion picture *Brokeback Mountain*, featuring two cowboys as troubled lovers, would have been inconceivable twenty-five years ago. While many people today, both in developed and developing countries, would find the film offensive and even repulsive, the fact that millions of other moviegoers around the world saw it and empathized with the plight and struggle of the two lovers is remarkable. The movie was the eighth-highest grossing romantic drama of all time.[79]

The positive portrayal of gays in film and on television has played a significant role in exposing the public to the gay community. The TV sitcom series *Will and Grace* features a homosexual as a principal character and enjoyed eight seasons as one of America's highest-rated shows.[80]

Millions of Americans were surprised to learn that one of the country's favorite comedians and talk-show hosts, Ellen DeGeneres, is a lesbian. She "came out" in an appearance on Oprah Winfrey's television show and later in her fictional role as Ellen Morgan on the TV sitcom *Ellen*. While condemned by a small number of religious fundamentalists, the vast majority of the American public applauded her decision to reveal her sexuality and remained loyal fans. Her very public revelation inspired many other ordinary people to "come out" and sparked family discussions with gay relatives around kitchen tables across the country.

A half-century ago, most American states still had sodomy laws on the books, making it a criminal offense to engage in homosexual acts. Today most Americans would find such laws appalling. Currently nearly half of all Americans (47 percent) say homosexual relations are morally acceptable.[81] Moreover, 89 percent believe gays should be afforded equal rights in terms of employment.[82] On the more controversial question of whether gays should be allowed to teach in the schools, a near two-thirds majority—62 percent—concurred.[83]

The changing attitude toward homosexuality becomes most apparent when it gets to the question of whether or not to legalize gay marriages or civil unions. Perhaps no issue is more vexing and generates more heat in the public arena, for the reason that the heterosexual family has long been the bulwark of traditional societies, grounded in theological consciousness.

Vermont became the first U.S. state to grant homosexuals the right to enter into civil unions in the year 2000. Several other states have done so since.[84] Although Americans are divided on the question, a 2009 FOX News/Opinion Dynamics Poll showed that 33 percent favor same-sex marriages and an additional 33 percent favor same-sex civil unions.[85]

Canada legalized same-sex marriage in 2005.[86] The public in the European Union tend to be the most tolerant of same-sex marriage. In the Netherlands, where same-sex marriage has been legalized, 82 percent of the public favor such unions.[87] Civil unions or same-sex marriage has also been legalized in Sweden, the UK, Belgium, and Spain. The public in Eastern and central Europe tend to be less supportive of the proposition.

Even in the more traditional Catholic countries of South America, legislation is being introduced to recognize same-sex unions. Colombia became the first country in Latin America to enact a law recognizing such unions in 2007.[88]

Globally the attitudes on homosexuality are deeply divided. A 2003 Pew Research Center Poll of attitudes in forty-four nations found that openness toward homosexuality is highest in Western European countries. By three to one, Europeans in France, Italy, Britain, and Germany say that "homosexuality should be accepted by society."[89] Attitudes toward homosexuality in the poorer nations of Africa and in Muslim countries, however, are overwhelmingly negative.

Even on the contentious question of whether gays should be allowed to serve in the military, 60 percent of Americans are in favor of the practice.[90]

The disabled have long been treated as an outcast group in every country. It was common in medieval Europe to regard the mentally ill and, to a lesser extent, physically disabled people who suffered from seizures and other uncontrollable muscle and body movements, to be possessed by demons and the devil. The disabled traditionally have been the subject of abuse and neglect, often locked up and out of sight for fear they might do harm or contaminate the public in some way. While often pitied, the disabled generally were regarded as less than human. Rarely were they acknowledged as worthy of the same regard as one might have for a "normal" human being.

The plight of the disabled remained the same in most countries until after World War II and even into the 1960s. Because they were shuttered away from the rest of society, most people had limited experience with the disabled and therefore were unable to develop relationships and create empathic bonds. Although many families had a relative who suffered from some kind of disability, the stigma attached to their condition was a source of embarrassment and something rarely talked about, especially to neighbors and cohorts at work.

Attitudes toward the disabled, like those toward women and gays, have dramatically changed in the past thirty years. A major shift in public perception began in the 1970s, as parents and disabled activists began demanding that disabled students be mainstreamed into public school classrooms. Previously, virtually all disabled children in the United States and other developed countries were educated in special education schools for "the handicapped." Parents and progressive educators argued that the separation stigmatized the children by keeping them segregated from other children and normal social life. Moreover, continuing to quarantine the disabled meant that other children were little exposed to them and therefore less able to create friendships and empathic bonds. Special education schooling, they alleged, perpetuated the traditional fears about the disabled and kept them classified as an outcast group.

Today in the United States, Europe, and elsewhere, most disabled children—except for the most seriously challenged—attend public schools, although they may also take special education classes during the school week. Early on, special education teachers worried that exposing disabled children to regular school settings would risk greater teasing, ridicule, and bullying by classmates. Subsequent studies have shown, however, that if students are prepared in advance and teachers serve as role models for appropriate behavior with both the disabled and nondisabled students, the newcomers generally are welcomed, included, and integrated into the peer group.

Like inclusive education, national legislation designed to ensure equal rights and equal access to the disabled has done a great deal to integrate them into the larger community. Once closeted away, the disabled can now be found in shopping malls, movie theaters, restaurants, and other public spaces in many countries. More important, legislation to protect the disabled against discrimination in employment has brought many more of them into the workforce.

Intermingling between disabled and able-bodied fellow workers has done much to dispel age-old myths and prejudices. When employees have an opportunity to work alongside disabled colleagues, they come to know them as human beings, with life stories and sensibilities not unlike their own and with vulnerabilities, fears, prejudices, longings, and aspirations, like everyone else. The social interaction makes possible the extension of the empathic bond to an entire group of human beings once isolated away and regarded as less than human.

This didn't just happen. As with other social movements in recent history, disabled activists and their organizations forced the public to pay attention to their plight and demands. "Outcast" groups are exactly that—out of sight and consequently out of mind. Minorities always remain partially invisible to the majority. While they may be physically present and perform useful tasks, they are not intimately seen or heard. Their lives are, at best, an abstraction, at worst invisible, and rarely thought about or made the object of reflection. I remember when disabled activists took to the streets of Washington, D.C., in wheelchairs, blocking intersections and stopping rush-hour traffic in a public protest concerning lack of access to public transportation and a dearth of wheelchair-friendly curbs and walkways in public buildings and other areas. These early demonstrations were startling to a public that had never before considered the near-total absence of the physically disabled in the public square. The disabled got our attention, then our engagement, and, finally, our affection and companionship. Their activism changed the social equation.

Again, as with the changing attitudes toward homosexuality, recasting the narrative of the disabled to reflect their shared humanity with everyone else has made the general public more informed, aware, and attuned—by breaking down the stereotypes—and more willing to imagine the plight of disabled individuals as if it were their own.

Films and TV have done much to awaken the public consciousness of the plight of the disabled. I sat in a packed movie theater more than twenty years ago watching *Mask*, a true story about a young teenager named Rocky Dennis who had a massive facial skull deformity and lived with his unconventional mother (played by Cher). The young man, who was the subject of gawking, ridicule, and prejudice, did everything in his power to overcome his adversity and let his humanity come through to others. In one scene, he becomes emotionally involved with a beautiful blind teenage girl, who "saw" only his warmth and sensitivity. Their love, however, was thwarted by her parents, who were repulsed by his disability.

The young man died from his disability, but his humanity touched the lives of many others during his short sojourn on Earth, creating deep bonds of empathy. At the end of the film, the audience too was overcome with emotion. Tears flowed as dozens of moviegoers rose for a standing ovation. The story drew an empathic response and moved everyone in the audience.

Other blockbuster films, like *Rain Man*, about an autistic man; *Forrest Gump*, the story of a slightly retarded man; *Children of a Lesser God*, a film about a school for the deaf; and *A Beautiful Mind*, the true-life story of John Forbes Nash, the Nobel laureate mathematician who suffered from paranoid schizophrenia, have been seen by millions of people around the world and have helped change people's attitudes toward the disabled.

The global media has become a powerful communications tool to reshape the narrative of formally "outcast" groups in life-affirming terms, opening up new channels of empathy for millions of people.

THE DECLINE OF RELIGION

The shift to greater tolerance toward outcast groups and the extension of the empathic bond to diverse others is bound up with the growing sense of individuation and self-expression acted out against the backdrop of an increasingly interconnected and interdependent world. A complex, globally structured civilization made up of hundreds of millions of individuals interacting in vast associational networks—social, economical, and political—requires a sense of openness, a nonjudgmental point of view, an appreciation of cultural differences, and a desire to continually find common ground among people. The extension of the empathic bond is the social glue to establishing a global network of millions of human beings.

It's probably not surprising that in the most technologically advanced countries, where self-expression is high, the older theological consciousness, with its emphasis on strict external codes, the communal bond, and a hierarchically organized command and control, is losing its hold. Religious hierarchies make less and less sense in a flat, networked world.

Global surveys over the past thirty years show a striking decline in traditional religious affiliation in the most technologically advanced industrial countries. While 44 percent of the public attend religious services at least weekly in the agrarian societies, less than one-quarter do so in the industrial countries and only one-fifth in the postindustrial nations.[91] Similarly, more than half the population prays regularly in the traditional agricultural societies, but only a third do in industrial countries and just one-quarter in postindustrial nations.[92] Most important, two-thirds of the people in poorer countries say that religion is "very important," while only one third agree in industrial nations, and only one-fifth of the population of postindustrial countries think religion is very important.[93]

The United States seems to be the only exception to the trend found in other highly industrial countries. Traditional religious values are still strong among older Americans, but they show a marked decline among the younger generations, leading some analysts to suggest that American youth are catching up to their more secular peers in other countries.

Every global opinion poll shows religion declining among the youngest generation. While traditional religious affiliation is declining in the most technologically advanced societies, spirituality is increasing. Spirituality refers to the very individual quest to find meaning in the broader cosmic scheme of things. The Global Values Survey has been tracking the shift toward spirituality since 1981. Those surveyed are asked: "How often, if at all, do you think about the meaning and purpose of life? Often, sometimes, or never?" The percentage who say "often" has increased dramatically. In Canada, 37 percent said "often" in 1981 and 52 percent in 2001. In Italy, 37 percent said "often" in 1981 and 50 percent by 2001. Even in mid-level developing countries, the numbers have risen. In Mexico, 31 percent said "often" in 1981 and 47 percent in 2001, and in South Africa, 39 percent in 1981 and 54 percent in 2001.[94] In the United States, Americans who say they are "spiritual but not religious" has increased by 10 percentage points since 1999. In 2006, 40 percent of U.S. adults described themselves as "spiritual but not religious."[95]

The growth in spirituality and the decline in religiosity shadows the shift to a greater sense of individuality and self-expression. Younger generations are increasingly uncomfortable with the idea of unquestioned allegiance to ancient religious dogma and prefer to think for themselves about their own spiritual journeys.

The transformation from religiosity to spirituality represents a tumbling of ancient barriers separating the "true believers" from the "heathens." Millions of individuals in search of the meaning of life are far less likely to be hampered by traditional religious prejudices and exclusionary biases and far more likely to empathize with other people's existential quests to find meaning in life and a purpose to existence.

But before we become too anxious to declare the Age of Aquarius, it's important to bear in mind the demographic reality that's tempering, perhaps even checking, the newly emerging cosmopolitan consciousness. There is an old saying that demographics are destiny. This may well turn out to be a deciding factor in the race to biosphere consciousness.

Although the trend toward increased self-expression, spirituality, cosmopolitanism, tolerance of others, and extension of the empathic bond is demonstrable among each new generation in the technologically advanced industrial nations, it is those same countries that are experiencing a precipitous decline in fertility rates. While birthrates are declining around the world, they are plunging in the advanced industrial countries. Women in these countries are averaging 1.8 children. In the poorer, traditional, religious countries, women average 2.8 children.[96]

Currently about 2 billion people live in secular societies, and 1.7 billion live in more traditional religious societies. But while the secular countries have only experienced a 41 percent increase in population in the past three decades, the poorer, traditional countries have witnessed an 82 percent growth in population.[97] The demographic trends suggest that unless there is a significant turnaround in the fertility rates in both secular and traditional societies in the coming years, the population of the latter will far outnumber the former by midcentury.

The key variable is whether the economic conditions of the poor countries can be improved at the same time that the wealthier countries learn to bring their economies into a more sustainable mode. If both were to happen, birth rates would likely stabilize. Improved economic conditions in the poorer countries would potentially lead to greater gender equality—although that's not yet happened in several of the rich, oil-producing countries in the Persian Gulf. The demographic statistics show clearly that the steady advance into an industrial way of life opens up greater opportunity for education for women, and, with that, improved job prospects and more independence, all of which translates into the decision to have fewer children.

The Globalization of the Family

In a globalizing world, where every kind of boundary separating people of diverse backgrounds is beginning to fall, the last remaining bulwark of exclusivity, the family, is experiencing the same tumultuous changes.

Families are beginning to mirror the sense of openness and tolerance occurring in the schools, the workplace, and the broader community. Greater exposure and interactivity in the other domains of daily life are bound to find their way into the most intimate and private realm. The new family identities are increasingly multireligious, multicultural, and multiracial—and, in a very real sense, have become mini diasporas.

In my parents' generation, it would have been considered a scandal for a Jew to marry outside the religion. Such unions were frowned upon and the couple was often shunned by both families. Today among Jews over the age of fifty-five, 20 percent of married people have non-Jewish spouses. Among those Jews between the ages of thirty-five to fifty-four, 37 percent have non-Jewish spouses, and for those under thirty-five, the percentage marrying outside the religion has reached 41 percent.[98]

Intermarriage between Protestants and Catholics has also risen dramatically. Such unions were rare before the 1960s, especially in the southern United States, where friction between Southern Baptists and Catholics ran high and discrimination against Catholics was common. Today half of all Catholics marry outside the faith.[99]

Even marriages between Muslims and non-Muslims are on the rise in industrialized countries. According to Islamic law, Muslim men can marry Jewish or Christian women because both faiths are considered "People of the Book" . . . that is, Abrahamic religions. The Islamic Society of North America reports that interfaith marriages now make up 30 percent of the wedding ceremonies performed at the center.[100]

A 2001 survey in the United States found that 22 percent of all married or domestic partners were of mixed religious affiliations.[101]

Marriages across ethnic boundaries have also grown rapidly, keeping pace with an increasingly open and globalizing world. Austria, for example, traditionally a rather insular society—with the exception of Vienna—reported that a foreign partner accounted for 24 percent of the marriages in 2002. In France, marriages with foreigners accounted for nearly 14 percent of the total in 2001. In Sweden, the number of marriages to non-nationals topped 20 percent in 2001.[102]

Germany offers a case study of the tremendous change occurring in marriage patterns. In 1960, in nearly every marriage, both spouses were German. Only one in every twenty-five marriages involved a foreign-born national. By 1994, in one out of every seven marriages, one or both of the partners were foreign born. Similarly, in 1960, only 1.3 percent of births had a foreign parent. By 1994, 18.8 percent of newborns had a foreign-born father, mother, or both.[103] Germany, traditionally a homogeneous culture, is now one of the most multicultural societies in the world. The breaking down of cultural walls and the blending of ethnic identities has brought individuals from formerly separated and even estranged cultures together, narrowing the realm of "the other," in the most intimate of all social relationships: the extended family. When that happens, empathic consciousness is afforded a much bigger playing field to express itself.

Even in Japan, long regarded as one of the most inbred and closed countries in the world, one in every fifteen marriages performed in 2004 was with a foreign spouse. Most of the marriages were between Japanese men and foreign nationals, the largest percentages being people of Chinese, Filipino, and Korean descent.[104]

In the United States, two-thirds of all Hispanics who have attended college marry non-Hispanics.[105]

Perhaps the last taboo in the United States, as far as mixed marriage is concerned, is the coupling of white and black partners. In 1967, Hollywood released the movie *Guess Who's Coming to Dinner*, a comedy about a black man invited to dinner at the family home of his white girlfriend. The catch line was she hadn't informed her parents that he was black. The movie touched off a firestorm of controversy. That same year, the U.S. Supreme Court, by a unanimous decision, outlawed miscegenation laws, which barred interracial marriages. At one time, forty-one states had such laws on the books.[106]

To understand the importance of the Court's decision, consider that just nine years earlier, in 1958 in North Carolina, two black boys, age seven and nine, were arrested, convicted, and sentenced to twelve to fourteen years in prison after a little white girl kissed one of them. President Dwight D. Eisenhower eventually intervened to secure their release.[107]

The shift in opinion on black/white relationships is dramatic. In 1987, only 48 percent of the public said they agreed with the statement, "I think it's all right for blacks and whites to date each other," and 25 percent of Americans said they "had little in common with people of other races."[108] By 2003, 77 percent of adults said it's "all right for blacks and whites to date each other."[109] On the dicier question of interracial marriage, the change in opinion has been even more pronounced. In 1958, only 4 percent of whites approved of intermarriage with blacks. By 1997, 67 percent of whites approved of intermarriage between blacks and whites.[110]

Today about four in ten Americans report they have dated someone of another race and three in ten report they have had serious relationships.[111]

The question of interracial dating becomes virtually a non-issue among young people born after 1976 (the Gen Y cohort). An overwhelming 91 percent of the Gen Ys say "interracial dating is acceptable," compared to 50 percent of the oldest generation.[112]

The change in sentiments is reflected in the change in the number of interracial marriages in the United States. In 1970, less than 1 percent of all marriages were composed of spouses of different races. By 2000, the number of interracial marriages had risen to 5 percent,[113] and by 2005, the number had risen to 7 percent of America's 59 million married couples.[114] Meanwhile, 50 percent of married Asians under the age of thirty-five have a spouse from a different race.[115]

In 2008, the prominent TV reporter and interviewer Barbara

Walters revealed in her autobiography that she had secretly had a serious affair with a black senator, Edward Brooke of Massachusetts, back in the 1970s. She said she was warned about the relationship becoming public at the time, for fear it would create a backlash and hurt both of their careers. Today few young people would give such a relationship a second thought. Many prominent Americans are in black-white marriages, including former U.S. Senator Carol Moseley Braun, civil rights leader Julian Bond, former defense secretary William Cohen, and actor Robert De Niro.

Children of interracial marriages are becoming commonplace. Barack Obama and Tiger Woods immediately come to mind. There are more than 3 million interracial children in the United States.[116]

Interracial marriages are extending the empathic bond into domains that would have been beyond the realm of possibility just thirty years ago. Stanford University sociologist Michael Rosenfeld observes that "the racial divide is a fundamental divide . . . but when you have the 'other' in your own family, it's hard to think of them as 'other' anymore."[117] More than one in five American adults—22 percent—say that one of their close relatives is married to someone of a different race.[118] When individuals of two different races or, for that matter, different ethnic groups, come together in marriage, they bring with them all of their relatives' and their relatives' friends and associates as well. The circle of "the we" is widened, exposing many more people to each other. As populations become more culturally and racially diverse, the familial sphere becomes a multicultural, multiracial space, a common ground for discovering each other's shared humanity.

EMPATHIZING WITH OUR FELLOW SPECIES

The profound change in attitudes concerning women, homosexuals, and the disabled, and the phenomenal growth in interreligious, inter-ethnic, and interracial dating and marriage patterns is impressive, by any standard, and a clear sign that the traditional boundaries separating people are beginning to give way to a more cosmopolitan sensibility and, with it, the extension of empathic consciousness to wholly new domains.

The expansion of empathic consciousness, however, doesn't stop at the last outpost of human considerations. A new movement has emerged, with the potential to extend human empathy beyond the human race, to our fellow creatures. The notion of granting recognition to other creatures is controversial and regarded as cutting edge by some and absurd by others. Stretching human imagination to regard other species as we do our own has forced open a profound debate about our relationship to the other beings that inhabit the planet.

Concern for the welfare and protection of animals came of age in the nineteenth century with the creation of the Societies for the Prevention of Cruelty to Animals in England and the United States. The modern environmental movement came in on the tail of these early reforms at the beginning of the twentieth century. Protecting natural habitats and preserving species was an integral part of the Progressive-era movement to establish more efficient and rational means to manage natural resources. The mainstream environmental movement, even today, is to a great extent guided by a utilitarian ethos dedicated to maintaining a proper store of natural resources for human purposes. Land easement and conservation practices are designed to ensure a reserve of flora and fauna for future human-development needs.

The creation of the great national parks in the United States—Yellowstone, Yosemite, Acadia, Glacier—in the late nineteenth and early twentieth centuries was justified by the government as a means of preserving the country's largesse of natural resources. The rationale, however, included an aesthetic sensibility as well—to conserve the beauty and majesty of America's great natural monuments for enjoyment and recreation.

The modern ecology movement that was spawned in the late 1960s and officially launched with the Earth Day celebration in 1970 introduced the idea of acknowledging the intrinsic value of species, along with their utilitarian value. Battles were waged from the 1970s onward over the question of preserving rare species versus economic development. The struggle to save the now-infamous northern spotted owl against the threat posed by clear-cutting in the Pacific Northwest created a national controversy over the worth of a single species versus the loss of employment of thousands of loggers. Similarly, whaling practices that threaten the extinction of the world's great sea mammals put Norwegian and Japanese whalers at odds with environmental activists and have stirred global public debate.

But generally in those debates, the environmental discussion has centered on the question of the interconnectedness of ecosystems' dynamics and the need to preserve species' habitats in order to ensure the proper functioning of the whole. Even discussions of the intrinsic values of species had less to do with their existential right to exist and more with the instrumental role they play in the ecological scheme of things. That's not to say that the love of nature has not also been a prime motivating theme. A younger generation of environmentalists feel a deep affinity to nature—what E. O. Wilson calls *biophilia*—and a passion to commune with their fellow creatures. Still, in public policy debates, the rational utilitarian arguments have figured far more prominently. What's new and revolutionary is the sudden and powerful emergence of the animal rights movement—a force that was virtually nonexistent forty years ago.

My wife, Carol Grunewald, a longtime animal rights activist, makes the telling point that unlike the conventional environmental organizations, whose frame of reference is more abstract and deals with the well-being of whole species, animal-rights advocates begin with a deep emotional commitment to alleviate the suffering of individual creatures, whom they regard as having the same right to exist and flourish as themselves. Although the animal-rights activists acknowledge that the rights of other creatures differ in degree and kind from human rights, they are steadfast in the belief that their individual journey is no less significant and meaningful than our own.

For a long time these two movements shared little common ground and were like two ships passing in the night. Even today there is very little interaction between the two, despite the fact that the animal-rights movement is becoming increasingly involved in broader environmental issues, as activists are realizing that the suffering of individual animals can't be divorced from the macroenvironmental policies that affect their well-being. For their part, the environmentalists have also begun to give some acknowledgment to the rights of individual creatures. International organizations like Greenpeace, for example, engage in antiwhaling campaigns and protest the inhumane mass slaughters of seal pups in Canada each year that speak to the suffering of individual animals.

The divide between the environmentalists and animal-rights people is illustrative of the difference between an older ideological consciousness, with its emphasis on rationality, utility, and efficiency, and an emerging biosphere consciousness grounded in personal participation, emotional identification, and empathic extension.

Emotional affiliation with animals has a long history. But it was in the twentieth century that the new medium of film brought millions of people into an intimate relationship with animals, albeit vicariously. In 1946, the novel *The Yearling*, which was published in 1938 and won the Pulitzer Prize a year later, was made into a film and released to audiences around the world.

The story revolves around the intimate friendship between a young, backwoods youth and an orphaned fawn and the cruel realities of survival in the frontier, which forced him to choose between his family's security and the fawn's life.

Millions of moviegoers wept in empathy with both the boy's plight and his animal companion's fate. Sharing such experiences en masse, in public places, helped legitimize newfound feelings of empathy for other creatures.

Walt Disney productions exploited similar themes, especially in animated films like *Bambi*, helping condition generations of youngsters to vicariously experience a bond of empathy with other creatures.

Critics argued that sentimentalizing and anthropomorphizing the human/animal bond not only painted an inaccurate picture of other creatures but also trivialized the harsh realities that separated the human and animal worlds—the Disneyfication of nature. True! But such portrayals on film also awakened the empathic imagination of millions of youngsters—and adults—to the plight of other creatures, opening up a new empathic domain for human consciousness.

As it turns out, in hindsight, Disney fared better in the portrayal of animals than many of the scientific experts of the day, with their belief that animals were little more than stimulus-response mechanisms, locked into instinctual behavioral patterns and unable to learn by doing or experience feelings.

In the 1990s, a new genre of animal films like *Babe*, as well as TV channels, like Animal Planet, and popular TV programs, like *The Crocodile Hunter,* awakened the biophilia connection for millions of people.

The media interest in animals reflects the growing real-time exposure and interaction humans enjoy with other animals as companions. In the United States alone, the pet industry has burgeoned into a $38-billion-a-year business.[119] A total of 63 percent of American families have a dog, cat, or other nonhuman companion.[120] According to a recent survey, in upward of 69 percent of American families, companion dogs and cats sleep on the bed with their human companions each night.[121]

The reconnection with other animals, both through the media and in the home, has not only made people more aware of and sensitive to the plight of other species, but also more activist in their defense of other creatures. According to a 2008 Gallup Poll concerning the treatment of animals, 64 percent of the public favor "passing strict laws concerning the treatment of farm animals," 38 percent of those polled approve of "banning sports that involve competition between animals, such as horse or dog races," and 35 percent would like to see a ban on "all medical research on laboratory animals." On the overarching question of animal rights, 25 percent of Americans believe that "animals deserve the exact same rights as people to be free from harm and exploitation," while 72 percent believe "animals deserve some protection from harm and exploitation, but that it is still appropriate to use them for the benefit of humans."[122]

Sentiment to protect the rights of animals is even higher in the EU and has led to landmark legislation. The EU has the strictest laws protecting farm animals in the world, and is the first government to issue a directive "that efforts must be undertaken to replace animal experiments with alternative methods."[123]

Nor is this just an American or European phenomenon. A survey conducted in 2005 in China, South Korea, and Vietnam, traditionally thought of as societies where animals are less well treated, found that 90 percent of the public believe "we have a moral duty to minimize suffering" of animals, and the vast majority said they favor legislation to protect animals.[124]

We have to bear in mind that just fifty years ago, these opinions about the rights of other creatures barely existed in public consciousness. While a small percentage of Americans favored a minimum standard of animal-welfare protection, the vast majority would have considered the idea that animals have feelings and rights to be sheer lunacy.

In recent years, the University of Pennsylvania, Stanford, Duke, and 88 other law schools in America have introduced law courses on animal rights. The European Union has recognized in law that animals are sentient beings, with feelings and consciousness. In 2002, Germany became the first country in the world to guarantee animal rights in its constitution. In 2008, the Spanish parliament became the first national legislature in the world to prepare legislation to grant limited legal rights to the great apes—chimpanzees, gorillas, and orangutans.[125]

A study done at Kansas State University to measure children's empathy found that children with a high pet bond and more empathy for animals also had higher scores on empathy for other children. The researchers concluded that children exposed to animals at an early age and made partially responsible for their care were more likely to develop pro-social behavior toward peers.

Companion animals are increasingly being prescribed by therapists to help awaken empathic consciousness among troubled children. Youth detention centers have initiated programs with local humane societies to allow youth offenders in prison to help train homeless dogs and prepare them for adoption. Developing a close bond with the animals allows young teenage males, in particular, to express tenderness and care and extend empathy in ways that might be considered inappropriate among their peers out on the streets. This newfound emotional expression often makes the difference in turning a young man from violent and aggressive behavior to more pro-social behavior.[126]

The extension of empathy to include all living beings is a significant milestone for the human race. While the animal rights movement is still nascent, it is a possible harbinger of the coming Age of Empathy.

SIX DEGREES OF SEPARATION TO GLOBAL EMPATHY

Is it possible that the establishment of strong empathic bonds across formerly taboo human and animal domains could ripple out across the world, picking up momentum as it goes, with the potential of transforming human consciousness within just a few decades? To even suggest such a possibility just a few years ago would have been laughed off or dismissed as fantasy. While the skeptics still vastly outnumber the optimists on this score—and I'm not sure in which camp I reside—new developments in global Internet connections suggest that it might be possible to imagine a paradigmatic shift in human thought and a tipping point into global consciousness in less than a generation.

The new possibility is being raised by IT researchers at the cutting edge of social networking theory. Social networks like MySpace and Facebook, educational networks like Wikipedia, and business networks like Linux are beginning to venture into what is known as the small world theory. What they are discovering is mind-boggling in its implications.

The small world theory posits that there are only "six degrees of separation" between any two strangers on Earth. According to the theory,

> if a person is one step away from each person they know and two steps away from each person who is known by one of the people they know, then everyone is an average of six "steps" away from each person on Earth.[127]

In other words, every person alive today—all 6.8 billion—could be connected by only six or so acquaintances.

The small world theory, which has been part of popular folklore for eighty years, began in 1929, with the musings of a Hungarian author, Frigyes Karinthy, in a book of short stories titled *Everything Is Different*. In one story, "Chain-links," he suggested that the world was shrinking because of technological advances in travel and communications that were compressing distances, shortening durations, and connecting people in denser human networks. As a result, the characters in his short story opined that any two people in the world could be connected by five or so other acquaintances. The characters in the story go on to create an experiment to test their hypothesis.

> One of us suggested performing the following experiment
> to prove that the population of the Earth is closer together
> now than they have ever been before. We should select
> any person from the 1.5 billion inhabitants of the Earth—
> anyone, anywhere at all. He bet us that, using no more than
> *five* individuals, one of whom is a personal acquaintance, he
> could contact the selected individual using nothing except the
> network of personal acquaintances.[128]

Karinthy's speculation spawned a cottage industry of research among sociologists, psychologists, and anthropologists studying social networks. Michael Gurevich, in a 1961 doctoral dissertation at MIT, did an empirical study on social networks. Gurevich's work was picked up by an Austrian mathematician, Manfred Kocher, who used the results of Gurevich's study to create a mathematical extrapolation of the small world theory. Kocher concluded that in a country with a population the size of the United States and without social restrictions, "it is practically certain that any two individuals can contact one another by means of at least two intermediaries."[129]

The American psychologist Stanley Milgram at the City University of New York, along with Jeffrey Travers at Harvard, followed up on Gurevich's work in "network" theory in the 1960s. Milgram's studies suggested that, at least in the United States, people were connected by an average of slightly more than five friendship links.[130] Then in 1978, Milgram published an article in *Psychology Today* that helped create the popular lore on the subject.

The theory of "six degrees of separation" became the subject of novels, films, and television shows. The film *Six Degrees of Separation*, released in 1993, became a box-office hit, and a more recent film, *Babel*, enjoyed similar success. A television series, *Six Degrees*, on the ABC network in the United States also used the theory as a context and plotline for the show.

The theory fell into disrepute, however, in scientific circles and was derided by some critics as an "academic urban myth."[131] The disbelief was met head-on in a 2007 study by computer scientist Jure Leskovec and Microsoft researcher Eric Horvitz. Using instant electronic messages of 30 billion conversations among 180 million people all over the world, they corroborated the small world theory that only 6.6 degrees of separation exist between any two strangers on Earth.[132] Horvitz, said: "To me, it was pretty shocking. What we're seeing suggests there may be a social-connectivity constant for humanity." The researchers concluded that "[t]o our knowledge, this is the first time a planetary-scale social network has been available to validate the well-known '6 degrees of separation' finding by Travers and Milgram."[133]

Researchers in the field of IT, communications, and social network theory are buoyed by the findings and suggest that the small world phenomenon could be harnessed to bring the human race together quickly around natural disaster relief or for political and social purposes. Horvitz envisions the possibility that with global Internet search engines and social networking spaces, "[t]hey could create large meshes of people who could be mobilized with the touch of a return key."[134]

Suddenly the potential to leap quickly to biosphere consciousness seems not quite so far-fetched or far off. The increasing inclusion of women, homosexuals, the disabled, and other formerly outcast groups, including other species, and the proliferation of multireligious, multicultural, and multiracial dating and marriages, while already extending empathic consciousness, could spread quickly to envelop a much larger swath of the human race in the years ahead. That's because the new empathic consciousness is emerging in the very societies that are the most technologically advanced and increasingly interconnected in a global complex of cultural, social, and economic associations and networks.

The new communications and IT technologies now make possible the real-time transition from small world theory to small world practice. Global communications networks allow us to imagine the possibility of an "empathic multiplier effect," whereby each new compassionate foray across traditional boundaries that have separated members of the human race from each other and from our fellow creatures, ripples out and affects the lives of countless others, quickly encompassing the whole of the human race.

The likelihood of biosphere consciousness, if not right around the corner, is now only six degrees of separation from a possibility, all of which makes the odds a bit less daunting. But will we get there in time to radically transform our lifestyles and economic way of life toward a more sustainable relationship with the Earth's biosphere? Climate change appears to be accelerating every bit as fast as biospheric consciousness, leaving in doubt whether we will be able to turn the corner early enough to ward off the more extreme impacts of global warming.

TWELVE

THE PLANETARY ENTROPIC ABYSS

WE ARE APPROACHING the sunset of the oil era in the first half of the twenty-first century. The price of oil on global markets continues to fluctuate wildly and peak global oil is within sight in the coming decades. While oil, coal, and natural gas still continue to provide a portion of the world's energy, there is a growing consensus that we are entering a twilight period where the full costs of our fossil-fuel addiction are beginning to act as a drag on the world economy. At the same time, the dramatic rise in carbon dioxide emissions from the burning of fossil fuels is raising the Earth's temperature and threatening an unprecedented change in global climate, with ominous consequences for the future of human civilization and the ecosystems of the Earth.

The rising cost of fossil fuel energy and the increasing deterioration of the Earth's climate and ecology are the driving factors that will condition and constrain all of the economic and political decisions we make in the course of the next half-century. The economic question every country and industry needs to ask is how to grow a sustainable global economy in the sunset decades of an energy regime whose rising externalities and deficiencies are beginning to outweigh what were once its vast potential benefits.

The spreading ecological destruction is already precipitating an extraordinary human migration, as environmental refugees flee vulnerable areas in search of food and water and new living arrangements. There are already an estimated twenty-five million environmental refugees, and that number is expected to turn into a human swarm of two hundred million or more displaced persons by mid-century.[1]

In January 2007, the United Nations Intergovernmental Panel on Climate Change (UN IPCC) issued its long-anticipated fourth assessment report. Twenty-five hundred scientists across a range of scientific disciplines and fields from more than 130 nations spent years conducting field surveys, collecting data, running computer simulation models, and publishing studies, all culminating in the release of the most extensive report ever conducted on the state of the Earth's biosphere. Their report concludes that human-induced global warming is now affecting the very climate and chemistry of the Earth and threatening the ecosystems and species we depend upon for our survival.

According to the UN IPCC, "the global atmospheric concentration of carbon dioxide has increased from a preindustrial value of 280 ppm [parts per million] to 379 ppm in 2005." The concentration of carbon dioxide in the Earth's atmosphere now "exceed[s] by far the natural range over the last 650,000 years (180 to 300 ppm), as determined from ice cores."[2]

The global atmospheric concentration of methane—a global warming gas that is twenty-three times more potent than carbon dioxide—"increased from a preindustrial value of about 715 ppb [parts per billion] to . . . 1,774 ppb in 2005." Like the carbon dioxide concentration, the methane concentration in the Earth's atmosphere today "exceeds by far the natural range" of methane over "the last 650,000 years."[3]

The global atmospheric concentration of nitrous oxide, the third major global-warming gas, increased from a preindustrial value of 270 ppb to 319 ppb in 2005.[4] Nitrous oxide has nearly three hundred times the global-warming effect of carbon dioxide.

Together these three global-warming gases are becoming more concentrated in the Earth's atmosphere and are trapping the heat created by solar radiation striking the Earth from escaping back into space.

The result is that the Earth's atmosphere is heating up very quickly. Eleven of the last twelve years rank among the twelve warmest years since records began to be kept in 1850.[5]

THE ENTROPY BILL FOR THE INDUSTRIAL AGE

Global warming represents the entropy bill for the Industrial Revolution. We have burned massive amounts of coal, oil, and natural gas to propel us into an industrial and urban way of life. The spent carbon dioxide—entropy—is now clogging the atmosphere, preventing heat from exiting the planet.

Buildings consume the lion's share of carbon-based fuels, primarily in the form of electricity. In the United States, approximately 36 percent of total energy and 65 percent of electricity is consumed by buildings, resulting in 30 percent of greenhouse gas emissions into the atmosphere.[6]

The fossil-fuel age also gave rise to industrial agriculture and the historic shift to a more pervasive grain-fed meat diet. Modern animal husbandry, and especially cattle production, produces large amounts of methane, as well as carbon dioxide and nitrous oxide, and is now the second leading cause of global warming after energy consumed in buildings.[7]

Understandably, Rajendra Kumar Pachauri, the chairman of the Intergovernmental Panel on Climate Change (co-recipient of the 2007 Nobel Peace Prize), has asked consumers to reduce their consumption of meat as a first step in addressing climate change.

A United Nations Food and Agricultural Organization (FAO) study reports that livestock generate 18 percent of the greenhouse gas emissions. This is more than transport. While livestock—mostly cattle—produce 9 percent of the carbon dioxide derived from human-related activity, they are responsible for a far greater share of the more potent global warming gases. Livestock account for 65 percent of human-related nitrous oxide emissions. Most of the nitrous oxide emissions come from manure. Livestock also emit 37 percent of all human-induced methane.[8]

The IPCC estimates that a doubling of carbon dioxide concentration in the Earth's atmosphere in the current century is likely to heat up the Earth's surface by 2 to 4.5 degrees Celsius, with 3 degrees Celsius being the most likely increase. However, the scientists caution that the Earth's temperature could rise "substantially higher" than 4.5 degrees Celsius, according to some of the forecasting models.[9]

Other climate change models forecast an even more devastating future. In the first ever distributed-computing project to model climate change, Myles Allen, a physicist at Oxford University, along with several British universities and the famed Hadley Centre for Climate Prediction and Research, used the computing power of ninety thousand personal computers to run more than 2,000 unique simulations of the future of global climate, in the biggest climate modeling study ever undertaken. Previous simulations using supercomputers never exceeded 128 simulations. The results of the massive study were published in the journal *Nature* in 2005. While highly controversial, what they found, according to Allen, was "very worrying." While most simulation scenarios averaged about 3.4 degrees Celsius, about the same middle forecast that the IPCC panel had predicted, the worst-case scenario way exceeded any previous forecast, with a forecast of an 11.5 degrees Celsius rise in temperature by the end of the century.[10] A temperature rise in this range would mean the virtual extinction of most of the species of life on Earth.

But even a rise in temperature of 3 degrees Celsius, which some scientists say is overly conservative given the potential positive feedback effects that have yet to be anticipated, would take us back to the temperature on Earth three million years ago during the Pliocene era. That was a very different world than the one we experience today.

Even more frightening, the panel estimates that a 1.5 to 3.5 degree Celsius or more rise in temperature in less than one hundred years threatens the potential extinction of between one-fifth and upward of 70 percent of all species assessed so far.[11] To put the magnitude of this in perspective, we need to bear in mind that there have been five waves of mass biological extinctions in the 3.8 billion years that life has existed on Earth, and every time there was a biological wipeout, it took approximately ten million years to recover the biodiversity lost.[12]

In a very real sense, the human race has yet to grasp the enormity of the changes taking place on Earth as the temperature on the planet continues to rise. Imagine central Canada having the climate of present-day central Illinois, or New York City having the climate of Miami Beach, Florida. While human populations will be able to trek north, plants and animals may not be able to migrate quickly enough to keep pace with their own temperature ranges. Many ecosystems, unable to adjust, will die out or be replaced by new regimes.

Sir John Houghton, of the IPCC panel (1988–2002) and chairman of the United Kingdom's Royal Commission on Environmental Pollution (1992–1998), points out that microorganisms, plants, and animals throughout the world have evolved and adapted to specific climatic zones. "Changes in climate," says Houghton,

> alter the suitability of a region for different species, and change
> their competitiveness within an ecosystem, so that even
> relatively small changes in climate will lead, over time, to
> large changes in the composition of an ecosystem.[13]

The temperature changes that Houghton has in mind take place over the course of thousands of years. Global warming, however, threatens to alter climatic conditions in less than a century. "Most ecosystems cannot respond or migrate that fast," says Houghton. When ecosystems and climates become increasingly mismatched, the ecosystems become more prone to disease, attacks by pests and other assaults.[14]

Because trees in particular live so long and take so long to reproduce, forests are especially vulnerable to disruption, destabilization, and dieback when the temperature changes rapidly. Since trees cover one-fourth of the land surface of the Earth and are home to many of the world's creatures, any change in global temperature would have a significant effect on the Earth's remaining species.[15]

Scientists working in Costa Rica over the past sixteen years have recorded a continuous decline in the growth rate of trees in the rain forests as surface temperatures there have steadily increased. Researcher Deborah A. Clark of the University of Missouri reports that "[t]ropical trees are being increasingly stressed through higher nighttime temperatures."[16] The higher nighttime temperatures also force the trees to respire more and release more CO_2. These findings worry scientists. Researchers studying the effects of temperature rise on declining tree growth observe that tropical rain forests absorb as much as one-third of all the CO_2 "taken out of the atmosphere by photosynthesis on land."[17] If trees continue to release more and more CO_2 as a by-product of respiration, in effect shifting the balance between intake and release of CO_2, the amount of CO_2 added to the atmosphere could significantly increase global temperature above the current forecasts.

Peter Cox of the UK Meteorological Office in Bracknell says that in the coming decades we could see massive forest dieback in the Amazon as a result of increasing heat stress and the release of billions of tons of CO_2 into the atmosphere. The virtual collapse and die-out of the Earth's largest remaining landmass sink of CO_2 and other forests around the world could push global temperatures up by an additional six to eight degrees Celsius over the course of the century, according to John Mitchell, also of the UK Meteorological Office.[18]

The most important impacts of climate change will be on the Earth's water cycle, according to the UN climate change report. The changes in the hydrologic cycle, in turn, will result in widespread destruction of the Earth's ecosystems.

More than 75 percent of the Earth's surface is covered by water. That's why the Earth is often referred to as "the watery planet." Unfortunately, only 2.5 percent of the total is fresh water, and 75 percent of it is encased in glaciers and snow cover. Less than 0.3 percent of the freshwater is available as surface water in rivers and lakes.[19]

While lack of available fresh water has often been a regional challenge in parts of the world, leading to the constriction and even collapse of local ecosystems and the human habitats embedded in them, it's always been assumed that there would be enough water to maintain our species as a whole. (Two-thirds of the body mass of human beings is made up of water.) Now we face the very real possibility of vast planetary changes in the Earth's hydrologic cycle that could imperil our very survival as a species.

Rising Earth temperatures increase evaporation, releasing more water vapor into the atmosphere. Every rise in temperature of one degree Celsius leads to a 7 percent increase in the moisture-holding capacity of the atmosphere. The change in the moisture-holding capacity of the atmosphere affects the hydrologic cycle, especially the "amount, frequency, intensity, duration, and type" of precipitation. The most important effect of increased water vapor is "more intense precipitation, but reductions in duration and/or frequency."[20] The result is more intense floods and more prolonged droughts occurring each year.

Human-induced global warming is already beginning to have "real-time" impacts on the Earth's water cycle, forcing changes in seasonal precipitation and leaving wide swaths of the Earth's surface more vulnerable to drought and desertification, increased flooding, and other more intense weather-related activity, including hurricanes, tornadoes, and wildfires.

The scientific community is increasingly alarmed by the acceleration of climate change. The fact is, each of the three previous UN assessment reports greatly underestimated the speed of the changes in the Earth's weather patterns and the ecosystem consequences from rising temperatures.

For example, the previous UN report, issued just six years earlier in 2001, noted that the great snow peaks atop the world's mountain ranges were already experiencing a melt-off. In the current report, however, the scientists note that snow and ice cover in certain regions are retreating even more rapidly than previously anticipated.[21] In some regions, the glaciers are projected to lose upward of 60 percent of their volume by the year 2050.[22]

Likewise, the earlier report raised concerns about the potential of increased hurricane intensity in the twenty-second century. The 2007 report, however, states that hurricane intensity has in fact increased over the past thirty years, with far more hurricanes labeled as category 4 and 5.[23] A 2005 study published in the journal *Science* states that the number of 4 and 5 category storms has doubled since the 1970s.[24]

Finally, while the earlier report acknowledged that Arctic ice melt is already occurring, the 2007 report projects that large portions of the Arctic Ocean could have 75 percent less summer ice cover and be open to commercial traffic by mid-century.[25]

The reason for the underprojections is that current climate change forecasting models can't anticipate every potential positive feedback loop that might trigger a tipping point in the entire biospheric system, setting off further temperature rises. For example, while the current UN report mentioned the permafrost melt in the Siberian Arctic and sub-Arctic regions and noted some potential consequences, the likelihood of setting in motion a qualitative change in the Earth's temperature regime as a consequence of permafrost melt was not comprehensively addressed. Recent field studies conducted in the Siberian sub-Arctic region and published in the journal *Nature* suggest the possibility of a dramatic positive feedback loop that could trigger the catastrophic release of carbon dioxide and methane, accelerating the rise in temperature on Earth beyond the current modeling range.[26]

Much of the Siberian sub-Arctic region, an area the size of France and Germany combined, is a vast frozen peat bog. Before the previous ice age, the area was mostly grasslands, teaming with wildlife. The coming of the glaciers entombed the organic matter below the permafrost, where it has remained ever since. While the surface of Siberia is largely barren, there is as much organic matter buried underneath the permafrost as there is in all of the world's tropical rain forests.

Now, with the Earth's temperature steadily rising because of CO_2 and other global warming gas emissions, the permafrost is melting, both on land and along the seabeds. If the thawing of the permafrost is in the presence of oxygen on land, the decomposing of organic matter leads to the production of CO_2. If the permafrost thaws along lake shelves, in the absence of oxygen, the decomposing matter releases methane into the atmosphere. As already mentioned, methane is a more potent greenhouse gas, with a greenhouse effect that is twenty-three times greater than that of CO_2.

Researchers are beginning to warn of a tipping point sometime within this century when the release of carbon dioxide and methane could create an uncontrollable feedback effect, dramatically warming the atmosphere. Once that threshold is reached, the temperature on Earth could rise dramatically in just a few decades, and if that were to happen, there would be nothing human beings could do, of a technological or political nature, to stop the runaway feedback effect.

Dr. Katey Walter, of the Institute of Arctic Biology at the University of Alaska in Fairbanks, and her research team, writing in the journal *Nature* in 2006 and in *Philosophical Transactions of the Royal Society* in May 2007, say that the permafrost melt is a giant ticking "time bomb."[27]

Scientists note that similar events have occurred in the ancient past, between glacial and interglacial periods. In a disturbing report issued by the U.S. National Academy of Sciences (NAS) in 2002, scientists cautioned that it is possible that the global warming trend projected over the course of the next one hundred years could, without warning, dramatically accelerate in just a handful of years—forcing a qualitative new climatic regime that could undermine the Earth's ecosystems and human settlements throughout the world, leaving little or no time for plants, animals, and humans to adjust. The new climate regime could result in a wholesale change in the Earth's environments, with effects that would be felt for thousands of years into the future.

The authors of the NAS study point out that abrupt changes in climate, whose effects are long lasting, have occurred repeatedly in the last 100,000 years. For example, at the end of the Younger Dryas interval about 11,500 years ago,

> global climate shifted dramatically, in many regions by about one-third to one-half the difference between ice-age and modern conditions, with much of the change occurring over a few years.[28]

According to the study, "an abrupt climate change occurs when the climate system is forced to cross some threshold, triggering a transition to a new state at a rate determined by the climate system itself and faster than the cause."[29] Moreover, the paleoclimatic record shows that "the most dramatic shifts in climate have occurred when factors controlling the climate system were changing."[30] Given the fact that human activity—especially the burning of fossil fuels—is expected to double the CO_2 content emitted into the atmosphere in the current century, the conditions could be ripe for an abrupt change in global climate, perhaps in only a few years. The authors of the NAS report write:

> Current trends along with forecasts for the next century
> indicate that the climate averages and variabilities likely
> will reach levels not seen in instrumental records or in recent
> geological history. These trends have the potential to push
> the climate system through a threshold to a new climate
> state.[31]

What is really unnerving is that it may take only a slight deviation in boundary conditions or a small random fluctuation somewhere in the system to "excite large changes . . . when the system is close to a threshold," says the NAS committee.[32]

An abrupt change in climate, like the kind that occurred during the Younger-Dryas interval, could prove catastrophic for the planet's ecosystems and species. During that particular period, for instance, spruce, fir, and paper birch trees experienced mass extinction in southern New England in less than fifty years. The "extinction of horses, mastodons, mammoths, saber-toothed tigers, and many other animals were greater at this time than at any other extinction event over millions of years."[33]

The committee lays out a potentially nightmarish scenario in which randomly occurring events take the climate across the threshold into a new regime, causing widespread havoc and destruction. Ecosystems could collapse suddenly with forests decimated in wildfires and grasslands dying out and turning into dust bowls. Wildlife could disappear and waterborne diseases like cholera and vector-borne diseases like malaria, dengue fever, and yellow fever could spread uncontrollably beyond host ranges, threatening human health.

The NAS concludes its report with a dire warning:

> On the basis of the inference from the paleoclimatic record,
> it is possible that the projected changes will occur not
> through gradual evolution proportional to greenhouse-gas
> concentrations, but through abrupt and persistent regime
> shifts affecting subcontinental or larger regions. . . . [D]enying
> the likelihood or downplaying the relevance of past abrupt
> changes could be costly.[34]

Global warming represents the dark side of the commercial ledger for the Industrial Age. For the past several hundred years, and especially in the twentieth century, human beings burned massive amounts of "stored sun," in the form of coal, oil, and natural gas, to produce the energy and materials that made an industrial way of life possible. That spent energy has accumulated in the Earth's atmosphere and has begun to adversely affect the climate of the planet and the workings of its many ecosystems.

The IPCC panel concluded its assessment with the urgent warning that human civilization has less than ten years to begin laying out a coherent, unified, and systemic long-term plan to reduce global-warming emissions.[35] If we fail to do so, the planet will be locked into an irreversible path, with catastrophic effects for human civilization, our species, and the other forms of life on Earth.

Despite the mounting concern about global-warming feedback loops and their potential impacts on the biosphere, there is one category of feedback variables that is little mentioned in the models. The increasing dislocations resulting from climate change already pose an unprecedented threat to the security of hundreds of millions of people, and soon billions of human beings. More severe weather, in the form of hurricanes, floods, droughts, and wildfires, and rising temperatures, both on land and in the oceans, are spawning regional conflicts around the world. People are fighting each other for access to water, oil, land, minerals, and countless other resources that are essential to survival. Millions of refugees are crossing borders in a scramble to keep one step ahead of the effects of energy prices and climate change, creating strife between neighboring countries.

Oil shortages and the dramatic fluctuation in the price of oil on the world market are fanning political unrest and precipitating armed conflict and civil wars on three continents. Currently, one-third of all the civil wars being fought in the world are in the oil-producing countries. As we head toward global peak oil production—the point where half of the world's available supply of oil is used up—and accelerating climate change, the real-time destructive impacts on ecosystems, economies, and social spaces are potential lightning rods for escalating violence.

A NUCLEAR ARMAGEDDON

Human desperation is likely to reach levels never before experienced in our history on Earth. Within this context, the proliferation of nuclear material and relatively easy access to deadly genetically engineered pathogens becomes all the more terrifying. Knowledge about how to make a small nuclear bomb or a souped-up genetically engineered pathogen is becoming more easy to access. Weapons of mass destruction, once the preserve of elites, are becoming more democratized with each passing day. A growing number of security experts believe that it is no longer even possible to keep weapons of mass destruction locked up and out of the hands of rogue governments, terrorist groups, or just deranged individuals. The perfect storm, say some political analysts, is the confluence and feedback between rising energy prices, accelerating climate change, and escalating conflict, as a more desperate humanity fights for survival on a more inhospitable planet. Either way, we could spell our own doom, via the impacts of climate change or by unleashing weapons of mass destruction. The current state of affairs and projected trend lines are anything but comforting.

The nuclear club has inched forward in recent years. Nine nations now have nuclear weapons. More disquieting is the fact that forty other nations have the technical expertise, and many of them have access to the material necessary to build a bomb.[36]

The danger of nuclear weapons being universally available has become more real of late with renewed interest among many nations of the world in building nuclear reactors. It is another one of the dark ironies of our time that the all but moribund nuclear industry has resurrected itself on the coattails of climate change, with an ingenious if not disingenuous twist. The global nuclear lobby argues that it alone among the existing sources of conventional power, does not emit harmful CO_2 and therefore can take up the breach and supply an increasing amount of the world's energy and help mitigate global warming. Leaving aside the fact that renewable forms of energy—wind, solar, geothermal, hydro, biomass, and ocean waves—might prove a better option, there is little likelihood that nuclear power will provide much assistance in addressing global warming, but a great deal of concern that it might careen the world into a new nuclear arms race and the inevitability of nuclear war.

To have even a "marginal impact" on climate change, it would be necessary for nuclear power to generate at least 20 percent of the world's energy. This would require replacing all 443 aging power plants currently in use and constructing an additional 1,500 plants for a total of nearly 2,000 nuclear power plants—at a cost of approximately $5 trillion.[37] To accomplish this Herculean task, we'd have to put under construction three nuclear power plants every thirty days for the next sixty years—a feat that even the power and utility companies believe is a pipe dream.

The notion of building hundreds, even thousands, of nuclear power plants in an era of spreading regional conflict seems daft. On the one hand, the United States, the European Union, and much of the world is frightened over the mere possibility that just two countries, Iran and North Korea, might get their hands on enriched uranium from their programs to build nuclear power plants, and use the material to build nuclear bombs. On the other hand, the United States, the UK, France and other governments are anxious to spread nuclear power plants around the world, placing them in every nook and cranny of the planet. This means uranium and spent nuclear waste in transit everywhere and piling up in makeshift facilities, often close to heavily populated urban areas.

Security concerns become even more contentious in light of the ability to use nuclear power to enrich uranium and to extract plutonium from spent nuclear fuel. The thought of plutonium getting into the hands of terrorist groups and rogue countries sends shivers down the spines of security analysts. Nuclear power plants are the ultimate target for terrorist attacks. On November 8, 2005, the Australian government arrested eighteen Islamic terrorists who were allegedly plotting to blow up Australia's only nuclear power plant. Had they succeeded, Australia would have experienced its own devastating version of the catastrophic 9-11 attack that crippled New York City.

Renewed interest in nuclear power has ignited a "uranium rush." A few years ago there were only a few dozen companies prospecting for uranium. Today there are hundreds of companies scouting the Earth for new deposits. More troubling, many countries, including South Africa, Australia, and Argentina, are preparing to enrich uranium and other nations are considering following suit.[38]

Concerned that the resurrection of nuclear power could lead to a new nuclear arms race prompted the International Atomic Energy Commission to host an emergency summit of government leaders in 2006 to talk about placing tighter restrictions on who would be allowed to produce nuclear fuel.

Former U.S. Senator Sam Nunn, a leading expert in nuclear proliferation, issued a stern warning, saying that "[t]hese dangers are urgent . . . We are in a race between cooperation and catastrophe and, at this moment, the outcome is unclear."[39]

The nub of the problem is that there is no failsafe firewall separating the Atoms for Peace use of nuclear material to generate electricity and using the same material and expertise to make nuclear bombs. Experts in the field point out that with the exception of the first three nuclear powers, all of the newer entrants into the nuclear bomb club got there, in part, by harnessing knowledge of civilian nuclear energy and by enriching uranium beyond the requirements needed for power plants or by extracting plutonium from spent reactor fuel.[40]

What most worries security experts is the broad diffusion of knowledge of how to assemble and detonate nuclear weapons. W. J. Broad and D. E. Sanger summed up the problem in an extensive article on the subject in the *New York Times*, with the observation that

> after decades of scholarly digging, government declassification, open research in uranium and plutonium metallurgy and the rise of the Internet, much of that information is freely available.[41]

Kofi Annan, then secretary-general of the United Nations, captured the mood of pessimism that's taken hold in nuclear disarmament circles by arguing that "the international community seems almost to be sleepwalking" down the road to nuclear proliferation without thinking through the logic and consequences attendant to a resuscitation of the nuclear power industry.[42]

THE SPREAD OF DEADLY DESIGNER PATHOGENS

The converse of living in an increasingly dense, interconnected, and complex civilization is that the entire system is more vulnerable to wholesale disruption and devastation. This reality was brought home to America in 2001 when envelopes containing deadly anthrax spores began arriving by mail to seemingly randomly selected individuals around the country. Six people died in the anthrax attacks. A frightened country began to ponder the question of whether new kinds of deadly biological agents might not pose a serious threat to national security of the same magnitude and scale posed by nuclear weapons. Much of the concern centered around the burgeoning biotechnology revolution and the coming of age of genetic engineering technologies.

Experts observe that like Atoms for Peace, whose dark side is nuclear bombs, a similar analogy holds true with biotechnology. The same database of information and knowledge about genetics that is being used for commercial purposes, ranging from modifying crops and animals to creating new kinds of vaccines and drugs, is convertible to creating souped-up genetically engineered pathogens, whose potential lethality rivals nuclear bombs.

Designer-gene weapons are often called the cheap man's nuclear bomb. All that's required is an off-the-rack laboratory, which can be installed in a basement for as little as $10,000. Many of the most dangerous pathogens in the world can be grown or are available through commercial channels. Restriction enzymes and other biotech materials can also be secured, often with little or no background security checks.

Recombinant DNA "designer" weapons can be created in many ways. New biotech processes can be used to program genes into infectious microorganisms to increase their antibiotic resistance, virulence, and environmental stability. It is possible to insert lethal genes into harmless microorganisms, resulting in biological agents that the body recognizes as friendly and does not resist. It is even possible to insert genes into organisms that affect regulatory functions that control mood, behavior, and body temperature. Scientists say they may be able to clone selective toxins to eliminate specific racial or ethnic groups whose genotypical makeup predisposes them to certain diseases. Genetic engineering can also be used to destroy specific strains or species of agricultural plants or domestic animals if the intent is to cripple the economy of a country.

Most governments claim that their biological warfare work is only defensive in nature. Yet it is widely acknowledged that it is virtually impossible to distinguish between defensive and offensive research in the field. That's because in order to develop vaccines, which are merely attenuated versions of the pathogens, it's necessary to develop the virulent pathogens themselves. Writing in the November 1983 edition of the *Bulletin of Atomic Scientists*, Robert L. Sinsheimer, a renowned biophysicist and former chancellor of the University of California at Santa Cruz, observed that because of the nature of this particular category of experimentation, there is no adequate way to properly distinguish between peaceful uses of deadly toxins and military uses.

Until the 1980s, deadly pathogens could not be successfully cultured on an industrial scale, thus limiting their potential impact. The biotech revolution changed the equation. In a 1986 report to the Committee on Appropriations of the U.S. House of Representatives, prepared by the Department of Defense, Pentagon officials pointed out that

> Potent toxins which until now were available only in minute quantities, and only upon isolation from immense amounts of biological materials, can now be prepared in industrial quantities after a relatively short developmental period. This process consists of identifying genes, encoding for the desired molecule, and transferring the sequence to a receptive microorganism which then becomes capable of producing the substance. The recombinant organisms may then be cultured and grown at any desired scale. . . . Large quantities of compounds, previously available only in minute amounts, thus become available at relatively low costs.[43]

Do deadly pathogens deserve to be ranked alongside nuclear bombs as weapons of mass destruction? A study done by the U.S. Office of Technology Assessment in 1993 found that the release of just 220 pounds of anthrax spores from an airplane over Washington, D.C., could kill upward of three million people.[44]

Worried about the possibility of future biological warfare incidents, the U.S. government committed almost $50 billion in federal funds to build new high-security laboratories, create new vaccines, and store drugs.[45]

In the United States alone, there are more than fourteen thousand people working in over four hundred laboratories who are allowed to experiment with pathogens of military interest. This doesn't include the thousands of other researchers in commercial and academic labs with knowledge of how to use genetic-engineering technologies for the possible creation of designer-gene weapons.[46] Add to that number thousands of graduate students with access to university labs, material, and equipment, and one begins to understand why critics are alarmed about what they call the "democratization of biological knowledge" and the possibility it raises for creating a new generation of biologically engineered weapons of mass destruction.

THE ABILITY of nuclear technology and biotechnology to wreak havoc in a more interdependent global society increases with each passing day. Of course, we could attempt to anticipate all the possible threats posed to our increasingly complex way of life. That's what our political leaders continue to pin their hopes on. The problem is that while the complexity of the global economy is visible, knowable, and therefore vulnerable, the threats are largely invisible and as variable in their permutations as the imagination of their perpetrators. The only real solution is to radically redirect human consciousness over the course of the coming century so that the human species can begin to learn how to live on a shared planet.

That prospect seems difficult to imagine but not entirely impossible. First the good news. There is no doubt that at least a sizable portion of the human race is beginning to take on a global cosmopolitan consciousness, with the extension of empathy to more diverse human and animal domains. Now the bad news. The new global sensibility has been made possible by the creation of more complex, dense, and interdependent social structures, which, in turn, rely on more intensive use of fossil fuels and other resources to maintain their scaffolding, supply chains, logistics, and services. The greater the energy and resource flow-through, the higher the entropy bill, in the form of global warming gas emissions and climate change. The destabilizing effect of climate change, coupled with the high price of energy as the world heads into the twilight of the fossil-fuel era, is creating social and political unrest all over the world and leading to open conflict, civil wars, and cross-border confrontations. These conflicts are escalating beyond regions and onto the global stage, intensifying the pursuit of nuclear and biological weapons of mass destruction.

But if human progress has, up to now, required a continuous increase in entropy to feed a growing empathic sensibility, is the race destined to end in the ultimate human tragedy—finally arriving at biosphere consciousness in the end days of human civilization? In other words, if advancing empathic consciousness and global cosmopolitanism are dependent on ever more intensive energy flow-through, doesn't each cancel the other, leaving us with a bittersweet worldly wisdom as we descend into the dust heap of history? If your gut feeling is yes, this feels like where we are heading, you are not alone. This could well be our final signature.

BREAKING THE PARADOX OF HUMAN HISTORY

But there is also another possibility—that we may be approaching the end of this long stage in human history and the beginning of a wholly new journey. A spate of new studies on what makes human beings really happy suggest that the dialectic of history that has characterized the human saga since the first hydraulic civilizations thousands of years ago may have played itself out.

Lest skepticism get the better of us at the very get-go, an analogy to ecosystem dynamics may be helpful in making the case that we could be entering a new biosphere phase in our evolutionary development on Earth.

Traditionally, ecologists have referred to the two phases of evolutionary succession in an ecosystem as the pioneer and near-climax stages. In the pioneer stage, a succession of flora and fauna proliferate and extend outward, consuming as much energy as is available to them. Pioneer activity changes the physicality of the habitat and produces new sources of food, which, in turn, change the kinds and numbers of species that develop at subsequent stages. Over a period of time, this succession of flora and fauna develop mutually dependent, symbiotic relationships and consumption of matter and energy come into equilibrium. As the famed ecologist Eugene Odum notes, the near-climax community is

> self perpetuating and in equilibrium with the physical
> habitat. . . . In a climax community, in contrast to a

developmental or unstable [pioneer] community, there is no
net annual accumulation of organic matter. That is, the annual
production and import is balanced by the annual community
consumption and export.[47]

The Amazon Rainforest is a good example of a near-climax ecosystem. Near-climax communities are far more stable than pioneer communities. The biota exist in an equilibrium relationship. The excess production of the pioneer community has been replaced by the sustainable production that preserves both the habitat and the biota that dwell within it. It should be emphasized, however, that even near-climax communities are not static, but rather subject to new introductions of species, feedbacks, lags and perturbations that continually affect their internal relationships, dynamics, range, and entropic flow.

The near-climax ecosystem serves as a useful guide and metaphor for exploring the deep meaning of sustainable development, a much-bandied-about term in international political dialogue. The notion of sustainable economic development—a concept popularized in the 1980s with the Brundtland Report—is patterned after the workings of mature near-climax ecosystems. The question is, has the human race finished its pioneer stage of development now that is has invaded and colonized virtually every square foot of the biosphere and, if so, is it ready to settle into a near-climax stage of development vis-à-vis the biosphere?

All of which gets us back to the question of what makes people happy. As noted in Chapter 9, Thomas Jefferson inserted the term into the Declaration of Independence, declaring that all people have an inalienable right to the pursuit of happiness. His choice of happiness, however, needs to be qualified. It was common at the time to associate happiness with the acquisition of property. For example, the Virginia Declaration of Rights proclaimed that

all men are by nature equally free and independent, and have
certain inherent rights . . . namely, the enjoyment of life and
liberty, with the means of acquiring and possessing property,
and pursuing and obtaining happiness and safety.[48]

Hegel tried to capture the relationship by arguing that property is an extension of one's personality. He noted that property enables an individual to put his will into a "thing." One expropriates parts of the external world through his labor and incorporates it into his inflated persona. The property becomes part of one's extended self, a way to project one's presence and being among one's fellows. He writes:

> Personality is that which struggles to . . . give itself reality, or, in other words, to claim that external world as its own. To claim that external world as its own personality requires the institution of property.[49]

Others come to know and recognize one's personality through the objects one owns. For Hegel, property and personality became nearly tautological. Each becomes an expression of the other. The implicit assumption is that the more property one amasses, the more developed one's personality becomes. A more developed personality, in turn, makes for a happier self.

It's hard to overstate the extent to which the notion of accumulating private property was equated with man's state of happiness. Utilitarian philosophers picked up the banner of natural law theory, arguing that "[t]he greatest possible happiness of society is attained by insuring to every man the greatest possible quantity of the produce of his labour."[50]

By tying man's happiness to the acquisition of private property and stitching private property into the sinew of man's basic nature, utilitarian philosophers set the foundations for the idea that human beings are an acquisitive animal whose very nature predisposes them to acquire more and more wealth.

Although from time to time, critics have questioned the prevailing orthodoxy that "money buys happiness," the conventional wisdom is that the road to riches and the road to happiness are one and the same. If that were in fact the case, then there would be little hope that humanity could extricate itself from the iron hand of history by which advances in human consciousness rest atop the wealth generated by ever more complex social arrangements, which, in turn, require more intense energy throughput, resulting in a more degraded entropic environment.

A flood of new sociological, psychological, and cognitive studies, however, have begun to challenge the basic proposition equating increased wealth with greater happiness. What we are beginning to discover is something relatively apparent but largely overlooked in the public dialogue. Studies show that if people are very poor and unable to muster up the bare essentials for their physical survival, they are unhappy. The interesting new twist is that the same studies show that once people have reached a minimum level of economic well-being that allows them to adequately survive and prosper, additional accumulations of wealth do not increase their happiness but, rather, make them less happy, more prone to depression, anxiety, and other mental and physical illnesses, and less content with their lot.

Professor of psychology Tim Kasser cites a long list of studies that report that

> people who strongly value the pursuit of wealth and
> possessions report lower psychological well-being than those
> who are less concerned with such aims.[51]

In his own surveys, Kasser finds that with both students and young adults, those whose primary motivation was "money, image, and fame" exhibited higher levels of depression and more physical ailments than those who were less preoccupied with those values.[52] Other studies find a high correlation between materialistic values and substance abuse.[53] Equally important, the studies show that young people with strong materialist strivings express fewer positive emotions than those with less materialistic value orientations.[54] They also exhibit more ADHD, are more obsessive-compulsive, isolate themselves from their peers, are more possessive, less generous, more envious, and less trusting, have more difficulty controlling impulses, are more avoidant or overdependent on others, and are more passive-aggressive toward others.[55] Studies done in Germany, Denmark, the UK, India, Russia, Romania, Australia, and South Korea all came up with similar findings.

In study after study, the findings clearly show that "[t]he more materialistic values are at the center of our lives, the more our quality of life is diminished."[56] The studies also show that people in the wealthier countries of the world are no happier today than they were fifty years ago, despite the fact that the average income has doubled.[57] British economist Richard Layard, in his book *Happiness: Lessons from a New Science*, points out that in countries where the average income is above $20,000 per year, additional income does not correlate with more happiness.[58]

What virtually all of the studies show is that after reaching the minimum level necessary to feel economically comfortable average happiness levels actually go down with increasing accumulation of wealth. Americans today make twice the income they enjoyed in 1957, but the percentage of "very happy" has dropped from 35 to 29 percent.[59] Similar results are recorded in other industrial countries. The social and political repercussions and, more important, the ecological implications are enormous.

If the richest people in the world are only marginally happier than people living in less-well-off societies, and even less happy as they become wealthier, then the evolution of the empathic bond does not depend solely on the continued increase in economic well-being—after a certain level of economic security is obtained—nor on an accompanying upward spiral in energy consumption and entropic waste. Quite the contrary. The same studies show that as personal wealth accumulates beyond the minimum level necessary to maintain one's basic needs, the increasing preoccupation with the pursuit of wealth makes one less likely to be empathetic to others. One's possessions end up possessing a person and the pursuit of wealth becomes a vicious cycle and an end in itself.

Since we are continually counseled that greater wealth increases our chances of being happy, people continue to pursue each additional increment in hopes of attaining more happiness, only to be disappointed. We assume that the erosion of our previous feeling of happiness is due to not yet being rich enough, so we more rigorously pursue what becomes an ever more elusive goal, only to continue to lose ground—all helped along by a commercial marketplace pouring billions of dollars into advertising, marketing, and image creation to feed our addiction and keep the profits flowing. As obsession takes over, people engage in more expedient behavior, transferring everyone and everything into a means to further their own ambition to gain wealth and secure happiness. They cease to regard others as unique and special beings. By devaluing others, we become ever more isolated from the affections and companionship of our fellows. The only thing that appreciates in value is our sense of alienation.

The devaluing of others has multiple impacts on the psyche. Because they are out for themselves, materialists assume everyone else must feel the same way—after all, it's "human nature." The higher up on the materialist value scale one is perched, the more mistrusting of others one becomes. In the United States, where rampant materialism has become a national epidemic over the course of the past twenty-five years, trust has plummeted. In the mid-1960s, 56 percent of Americans said most people can be trusted. Today less than a third do.[60] By contrast, in continental Europe, where materialism is less pronounced, levels of trust have improved in many countries and at least not fallen in others.[61]

A slew of studies also show that the more materialistic people become, the less giving and generous they are in their dealings with others.[62] Selfless gives way to selfish.

In a similar vein, studies of students find that those who are more preoccupied with materialist values are also less inclined to "get into another person's shoes" and have less regard for another person's point of view.[63] The materialist gains the world but loses touch with his or her deepest drive, the empathic bond.

The new studies in happiness also show that the increasing loss of happiness not only correlates with increasing wealth beyond the minimum necessary to secure comfort, but is also relational to how well-off people around you happen to be. Layard reports on a study conducted with students at Harvard University who were asked to choose between two alternative worlds. "In the first world, you get $50,000 a year, while other people get about $25,000. In the second world, you get $100,000 a year, while other people get about $250,000."[64] The majority of the students chose the first world.[65] Other studies have found the same results. In a society where individual wealth creation is regarded as synonymous with happiness, the pursuit itself becomes a fiercely competitive enterprise. People continue to measure their own happiness, not in absolute terms but relative to everyone else. The assumption being that a more elevated social status will bring with it more happiness. Instead, it generally brings only more envy and ill will from others, who feel passed up and left behind. We begin to regard each other solely in terms of our relative wealth, leaving little room for empathetic feelings to develop.

Finally, the studies show that the more we have, the more we come to believe that we can't possibly live on less. An experience I had as a young man was revealing. I was working at the time in an antipoverty program and was assigned to a wealthy suburb of New York City, with the task of developing cultural exchange programs with poor inner-city youth. One evening, while I was visiting a wealthy family, the breadwinner took me aside and confessed that while he was making $100,000 a year—equivalent to more than $600,000 today—he was barely able to make ends meet. I thought he was kidding. He wasn't. We continually adjust to each new income level, and what were formerly considered luxuries quickly become necessities.

Layard sums up the happiness syndrome. He writes:

> So living standards are to some extent like alcohol or drugs.
> Once you have a certain new experience, you need to keep
> on having more of it if you want to sustain your happiness.
> You are in fact on a kind of treadmill, a "hedonic" treadmill,
> where you have to keep running in order that your happiness
> stand still.[66]

The happiness syndrome locks people into a race to despair. There is no way to get ahead of the game and find true happiness. The solution, of course, is clear, but it flies in the face of the Enlightenment idea that continuous acquisition of wealth increases one's sense of autonomy and freedom, provides pleasure, and makes a person more happy.

Although some might find it counterintuitive, the happiness-syndrome studies suggest that living in a society where the essentials for a comfortable life are met but where the gap in wealth and income between people is relatively narrow is likely to produce the happiest citizens. The United States and the European Union provide a good case study in this regard.

In 1960, the United States could justifiably claim to be the most middle-class society in the world. Today the United States ranks twenty-seventh among industrial countries in income disparity—that is, the gap between the very rich and poor. Only Mexico, Turkey, and Portugal, of the OECD nations, have greater disparity of income.[67] The European Union member states by and large have a far smaller gap in relative income. Not surprisingly, surveys show that in many countries their citizens express "a slight upward trend in happiness," whereas their American peers show a slight downward trend.[68] That's in part due to a difference in philosophical outlook. The American Dream has always emphasized "individual opportunity to succeed" and generally regards success in financial terms. The European Dream, however, focuses more on quality of life and regards success in terms of social criteria like providing universal health care, quality education, leisure, safe communities, and a clean environment.

The important point, which the Europeans seem to recognize in their emphasis on the quality of life of the community, is what Layard and other scholars have found in their own studies. Layard writes:

> From this psychological reality it follows that if money is transferred from a richer person to a poorer person, the poor person gains more happiness than the rich person loses. So average happiness increases. Thus a country will have a higher level of average happiness the more equally its income is distributed—all else being equal.[69]

The income per capita for Europeans is, on average, 29.3 percent lower than American income, and Europeans have smaller houses, cars, and wardrobes and fewer electronic conveniences.[70] Moreover, a greater percentage of their income goes to taxes to pay for an array of "public" services, designed to improve the quality of life of the entire community. Their greater emphasis on the social model, as opposed to the American emphasis on the market model, narrows the gap in wealth. After all, when wealth is redistributed—via taxes—into public services that benefit the whole community, distinctions in status between people are narrowed, although by no means eliminated.[71]

Nowhere is the difference in approach between the European social model and American market model more in evidence than in the energy flow-through used to maintain their respective societies. Despite the fact that the population of the European Union's twenty-seven members states exceeds 500 million people compared with the 300 million citizens of America's fifty member states, U.S. society uses more energy per capita and more energy overall to maintain the economy and social structure. As a result, the United States emits 18 percent of the world's global-warming gases compared to 13 percent emitted by the European Union.[72]

The European Union remains the most committed, among the governments of the world, to pursuing quality of life via a social/market model. Toward this end, the EU member states have made the concept of sustainable development the centerpiece of their long-term economic vision. But even the EU has a long road to travel to break the dialectic of history.

The question is, what is the appropriate therapy for recovering from the wealth/happiness addiction? A spate of studies over the past fifteen years have shown a consistently close correlation between parental nurturance patterns and whether children grow up fixated on material success. If a parent is warm, affectionate, responsive, and able to nurture an infant and balance his or her needs for both security and self-expression, the child will likely develop trusting relationships and will have the confidence to develop his or her own sense of selfhood. If, however, the principal caretaker is cold, arbitrary in her or his affections, punitive, unresponsive, and anxious, the child will be far less likely to establish a secure emotional attachment and the self-confidence necessary to create a strong independent core identity. These children invariably show a greater tendency to fix on material success, fame, and image as a substitute mode for gaining recognition, acceptance, and a sense of belonging. Needless to say, the global advertising and marketing phalanx preys on those emotional insecurities by promising that greater wealth, more possessions, and improved status and social standing will buy the affection, warmth, and acceptance so desperately sought.

Kasser et al. conducted a series of experiments to determine whether early infant parental nurturance had an effect later in life on teenagers' materialistic values and found that young adults who strongly valued financial success had mothers who were less nurturing than those who put greater value on developing strong relationships and contributing to the larger community.[73] Other studies have corroborated Kasser's findings. A study done by psychology professors Patricia Cohen and Jacob Cohen found that teenagers with strong materialist values had parents who were either possessive or controlling with their children, favored harsh punishment if children misbehaved, or were unable to provide appropriate structure for their kids, often exhibiting inconsistent or arbitrary behavior.[74]

Kasser suggests the children of non-nurturant parents "may be especially susceptible to consumer messages that prey on their insecurities and promise happiness and security through consumption."[75] Insecure teenagers also are likely to look to other people for the approval they are denied by their parents and to associate material values like fame and wealth as ways to attract other people's attention and companionship.

Within the context of making a potential leap into biosphere consciousness, what's particularly interesting about all of these studies is the finding that people who exhibit strong materialist values are less likely to develop intimate personal relationships, are less tolerant of others, and care less about the welfare of their fellows.[76] In other words, they are far less empathetic.

Other studies show a high correlation between materialist values and lack of concern or outright contempt for the environment and nature.[77] Like their relationships with people, their relationships to other creatures and nature tend to be purely instrumental, expedient, and self-serving.

Researchers Ken Sheldon and Holly McGregor tested 150 University of Rochester students to assess their values orientation.[78] The students were ranked as either high or low on materialist values. They were then put in three groups, four materialistic; two materialistic and two nonmaterialistic; and four nonmaterialistic people, and asked to play a game where they were the president of a timber company that was competing with three other companies in logging two hundred hectares of national forest.[79] "Each company could bid to cut up to one thousand acres" per year, and "whatever remained would grow back at a rate of 10 percent a year."[80] So if the company bid to cut only a few acres per year, the profits would be low, but if they bid to harvest too much, they would exhaust the forest in a relatively short time. Materialist groups harvested far more than the non-materialist groups, resulting in a quick profit but swift depletion of the forest. The materialist-oriented students consistently placed short-term financial interests ahead of long-term conservation practices. The nonmaterialist groups actually made more profit in the long run because the forest lasted longer.[81]

While postmaterialist self-expression values are on the rise, especially among a younger generation raised in more nurturing affluent environments, the materialist drive of the commercial market is a formidable counterforce. Thus making the transition from a pioneer to a near-climax society and a truly sustainable economic era hinges on a far more self-conscious approach to parenting to prepare youngsters with deep pro-social values that will allow empathy to grow and the lure of the market to be tempered.

Although "conscious" parental nurturing dates back to the Enlightenment and early Romantic era in the eighteenth and early nineteenth centuries, a qualitative change in the approach to parenthood emerged with the baby-boomer generation of the 1960s, the repercussions of which continue to reverberate into the twenty-first century.

Baby boomers broke through the older class-based politics that had characterized the age of ideological consciousness, with its emphasis on rational approaches to achieving material success and happiness. As mentioned in Chapter 10, the 1968 student revolution was really a shift in consciousness from ideological to psychological, as a generation of activists began to focus on what they called personal politics. The emphasis no longer simply revolved around who should control the means of production and how best to assure the fair distribution of the economic rewards of society. Instead, the counterculture generation began to look inward to probe feelings and emotions and outward to establish meaningful relationships and empathetic bonds.

The 1960s saw a great surge in the empathetic bond. A younger generation began to question the rampant materialism of their parents. Radical activists took to the streets from Paris to San Francisco with banners proclaiming DOWN WITH CONSUMER SOCIETY. As the baby boomers transitioned into parenthood, they took their newfound values into the nursery, with radical parenting styles that were more nurturing than previous generations. The empathetic surge was passed on, in part, to their children, creating a more tolerant and open generation. The empathetic surge has continued to gain momentum into the millennial generation. However, its thrust has been slowed by a massive advertising and marketing effort designed to target younger children, and now even toddlers, inculcating the very young into a materialistic ethos.

Youngsters commonly referred to in the advertising business as "tweens" (kids between the ages of six and twelve) are the most heavily targeted, with the hope of turning them into lifelong, habitual consumers. Kids as young as two years old can identify brand names. In the United States, one out of every four preschool children has a television in his or her room and is bombarded by commercial messages. By the time kids reach first grade, they can identify two hundred brands and boast more than seventy new toys per year.[82]

The average youngster is in front of the television set three and a half hours per day, being continually fed a diet of 40,000 commercials a year. It is estimated that American companies spend a total of $15 billion annually on advertising and marketing to children. It works. Children make an extraordinary three thousand requests for specific products and services each year.[83]

The kiddy-consumer culture has become big business. Sales to the four-to twelve-year-old children's market totaled $6.1 billion in 1989 and are currently more than $30 billion, a 400 percent increase. Teenagers' spending is even more, a staggering $170 billion a year. That's more than $100 per person per week.[84]

No other country in the world comes close to the United States on kiddy consumption. Economist and professor of sociology Juliet Schor, in her book *Born to Buy*, points out that while the United States is only 4.5 percent of the world's population, American children consume 45 percent of global toy production.[85]

If there was any lingering doubt as to the influence the consumer culture wields over American youth, Schor puts it to rest with the telling fact that by 1997, children spent

> as much time shopping as visiting, twice as much time
> shopping as reading or going to church, and five times as much
> as playing outdoors.[86]

Schor says that the upshot of the selling of consumer culture to the young is "the upsurge in materialist values." Forty-four percent of American youngsters in fourth to eighth grade dream "a lot" about becoming rich and two out of every three parents say that "my child defines his or her self-worth in terms of the things they own and wear more than I did when I was that age." Most distressing among the findings of surveys of U.S. youngsters—from age nine to fourteen—is that more than a third of them "would rather spend time buying things than doing almost anything else," and more than half believe that "when you grow up, the more money you have, the happier you are."[87]

The advertising and marketing blitz aimed at youngsters has been far more pervasive in the United States, Japan, and the UK, and less so in continental Europe. The juxtaposition of nurturing parental guidance, on the one hand, and mass advertising and marketing to youth, on the other hand, has stymied the full potential of the parenting revolution and, in some instances, has led to enculturating children who are overloved, overcoddled, overindulged, and overempowered—the Generation Me.

Child development experts worry that the young are being sent mixed signals. Told so often that they are the most loved youngsters in the world and the most special, they become the center of their parents' universe and are "spoiled," the result of which is that they often slip over the edge from nurturance to narcissism, with consequences that can nullify the best intentions of nurturing parents. Overindulgence can result in new kinds of insecurities that are easily exploitable by marketing campaigns.

Perhaps the single biggest impediment to the creation of biosphere consciousness is commercial advertising to the very young, which continues to undermine parental nurturing by exploiting the insecurities of the youngest and most vulnerable of the population and, by so doing, keep a materialistic consumer culture alive and robust.

In wealthier societies, then, happiness levels out, and even declines as incomes push past the minimum threshold needed to assure the essentials of life. At the same time, a greater focus on relative wealth feeds the acquisition addiction at the expense of deepening relationships, establishing a sense of community, and extending empathetic consciousness.

But what about the poor—40 percent of the human race with incomes of $2 a day or less—who live in what can only be described as a squalid survival mode. Studies show that happiness, for them, increases as their incomes improve. Not surprisingly, it's quite difficult for them to extend empathy to others beyond their immediate kin, for the reason that their every waking moment is focused on pure survival. They have very little emotional reserves and even fewer temporal reserves left to be mindful of and attentive to the plight of distant others. Understandably, for the very poor in most societies, materialist values take precedence over self-expression values.

Getting to the threshold of essential comforts is the main preoccupation for nearly half of the human race. This means expropriating more resources, building more complex social structures, and increasing the entropy bill. The upside is that the process of development leads to greater individuation, an emerging sense of selfhood, an extension of empathetic consciousness, and a more open, tolerant, and cosmopolitan attitude. The downside is that more energy flow-through further depletes the Earth's remaining resources and leads to an increase in global-warming gas emissions and human-induced climate change.

A global debate is raging between half of the human race that has passed the threshold of minimum comfort and the other half that has not. With climate change threatening the whole human race, the post-materialist nations argue that every society needs to radically reduce their fossil-fuel energy use and help reduce global-warming gas emissions. The developing countries, understandably, argue that their per capita energy use is a mere fraction of the per capita energy used in wealthy countries like the United States, and to deny them the opportunity to increase their economic development is to keep them locked into poverty and despair.

Some people in the wealthier nations understand their position. Still, they point out that if every one of the nearly three billion people living on two dollars a day or less were to raise their lifestyle to the level of the wealthier half of the human race, the entropic bill would tip the biosphere into a radical new temperature regime and threaten the potential extinction of the human race.

This is the stalemate that now divides one-half of the human race from the other. It is only likely to worsen in the years ahead—creating worldwide conflict on a scale never before experienced—because we are running short on the fossil fuel reserves that are essential to maintain and expand the industrial way of life. Quite simply, there isn't enough carbon-based energy to go around.

With global oil reserves dwindling and the worldwide demand for energy increasing—especially in the emerging nations of India and China, where two billion plus inhabitants make up more than one-third of the human race—concern over global peak oil is becoming more urgently debated. Once peak oil is reached, the oil age is effectively over because the price of energy becomes virtually unaffordable on the backside of the bell curve.

While no one knows for sure when oil is likely to peak, the gap in perspective between optimists and pessimists continues to narrow. The former argue that global peak oil is likely to occur between 2030 and 2035. The latter say it will likely peak between 2010 and 2020.[88] A few of the world's leading oil experts say it's already peaked.[89] The North Sea peaked in 2000.[90] Mexico, the world's seventh-largest oil producer, is likely to peak around 2010.[91] Russia is likely to peak shortly thereafter.

What we do know for sure is that for the past three decades, we have been consuming three barrels of oil for every barrel we discover—and while a few new super oil fields will likely be discovered, most of the world's potential oil fields have already been located and put under production, and most of them are nearing either peak or exhaustion. The problem is that the entire global economy relies on fossil fuels. Our food is grown in petrochemical fertilizers and pesticides. Our plastics, packaging, and building materials, our synthetic fibers and fabrics, and most of our pharmaceutical products, as well as the power to heat and cool our buildings, light our communities, and operate our economies are primarily derived from fossil fuels. And now more than half of the human race—in the emerging, developing countries—is pushing to modernize their economies and societies and increasing their consumption of oil, coal, and gas, leaving less to go around. The situation is already dire, as nations compete with each other to secure favorable arrangements with oil- and gas-producing countries and companies to assure a steady flow of black gold to fuel their growing economies.

Rising world demand and diminishing world supply are creating unprecedented conflict, as 192 nations vie with one another to keep the oil spigot flowing to their people. If world leaders are worried about escalating geopolitical tensions—and open warfare—in the oil-producing countries of the world today, imagine the desperation in 2015, 2020, and 2025 as we enter the late-twilight period of the oil era. This emerging reality makes the very specter of a proliferation of weapons of mass destruction all the more terrifying.

Oil and the other fossil fuels are elite energies. They are not broadly distributed but exist only in certain pockets and regions of the world. They require huge military investments to secure them, rigorous geopolitical management to maintain them, and huge infusions of investment capital to mine, process, and distribute them. And even when they were still plentiful and cheap, they were beyond the reach of a good portion of the human race.

Although difficult for most of those in the wealthy countries to fathom, one out of every four human beings on the planet has never had electricity and an additional third has only marginal and infrequent access to electricity and, therefore, remains impoverished.[92] The point is, if we weren't successful at getting adequate electricity to a large portion of the human race when oil, gas, and coal were plentiful and cheap, there is no conceivable scenario in which we can imagine getting electricity to the needy as oil—and natural gas and coal—becomes more scarce and oil prices continue to hover at $50 per barrel or more.

The bottom line is this: Half of the human race is using up more of the Earth's fossil-fuel energy and natural resources than is necessary for a comfortable life and is becoming increasingly unhappy with each increment of additional wealth. The other half of the human race is digging its way out of poverty and becoming happier as it approaches a minimal level of comfort. But there isn't enough oil and other fossil fuels—or uranium for nuclear power—to keep the wealthy in a luxurious lifestyle or elevate three billion poor people to a comfortable lifestyle.

However, we also know that empathetic development accompanies economic development at least until a threshold of comfort is reached. After that, increasing increments of wealth tend to lock people into an addictive materialist lifestyle that makes them more instrumental in their behavior and less sensitive to the plight of others, all of which slows down or undermines the development of empathetic consciousness.

How, then, do we reorganize our relationships with each other and the Earth so the "haves" can tread more lightly and the "have nots" establish a more firm footing with the environment, allowing each other to come together at the threshold of human comfort? It's at the threshold that we optimize empathetic consciousness and create the conditions for a sustainable global society.

The critical business at hand is to imagine an energy regime and economic revolution in which the kinds of energy we use are found in our backyards, relatively equitably distributed everywhere on Earth, free and easily accessible, and renewable with the changing seasons and cycles of the biosphere. Such an energy regime and economic revolution would need to provide at least the possibility that every human being on Earth could achieve the threshold for a quality of life without undermining the health of the biosphere, so life on Earth can continue to flourish.

THIRTEEN

The Emerging Era
of Distributed Capitalism

In 1956, the U.S. Congress enacted the Federal-Aid Highway Act. The legislation, signed into law by President Dwight D. Eisenhower, appropriated $25 billion for the construction of 41,000 miles of interstate highways over a thirty-year period, in what was at the time the biggest single public works project in U.S. history.[1] The resulting interstate highway system joined every part of the continental United States and provided the road infrastructure for completing the Second Industrial Revolution. The oil-powered internal combustion engine was the economic engine of the twentieth-century economy and provided the stimulus for virtually every other industry, from steel production to tourism. Americans took for granted that "what's good for General Motors is good for the country." The interstate highway system created the connective infrastructure for a suburban commercial and housing construction boom that made the United States the most prosperous economy and society in the world, and Americans the wealthiest people on Earth, by the late 1980s.

The Long Sunset
of the Second Industrial Revolution

Even while America was celebrating its unprecedented commercial success, some ominous storm clouds were brewing on the horizon, but it would be another half-century before they came together to create the perfect economic storm, bringing the United States and the world economy to the brink of collapse.

At the same time that the interstate highway system was being constructed, scientists began to take note of a troubling trend in the chemical composition of the Earth's atmosphere—the buildup of CO_2 concentrations. Scientists speculated that the burning of fossil fuels and the emission of CO_2 might be warming up the Earth's atmosphere, leading to unimaginable consequences. By the 1960s, computer models were projecting a possible increase in the Earth's temperature of a few degrees within a century. In 1979, the U.S. National Academy of Sciences issued its first preliminary report on global warming, suggesting that human-induced activity might be adversely affecting the temperature of the planet.[2] The findings were tentative and highly speculative in nature, and did not so much as register a blip on the public radar screen at the time.

Although awash in oil—remember that the United States was the world's leading producer of oil in the mid–twentieth century—and confident of a prosperous future, other troubling signs began to appear. The 1973 OPEC oil embargo and the subsequent rise in oil prices in the 1970s turned public attention to the question of whether we might one day run out of oil. But, the general consensus at the time was that the oil embargo was less about supply than about oil-producing countries flexing their economic and political muscle to exact gains in the marketplace and command respect and attention in the geopolitical arena.

What no one knew was that peak available global oil per capita— not to be confused with peak global oil production—occurred in 1979. While more oil reserves have been found since then, the growing human population means that if oil were distributed equally to every person today, each individual would have less oil available to them. This fact alone would have ominous consequences in July 2008 when oil hit a record price of $147 a barrel on world markets.

The entropy bill for the Second Industrial Revolution was inexorably building up in the last half of the twentieth century but was all but ignored in a world economy that was growing by leaps and bounds.

By the late 1980s, the Second Industrial Revolution had matured in the United States. The suburban building boom, which had led to the largest economic expansion in U.S. history, began to cool off. The recession of 1989 to 1991, which was triggered by a downturn in suburban construction in the southern and western parts of the country, marked a milestone for the Second Industrial Revolution, although no one at the time recognized its importance.

There would be another major building boom in the last half of the 1990s and the first six years of the twenty-first century. However, it would be generated more by irresponsible extension of mortgage credit instruments and driven by wild speculation than by technology-driven increases in productivity and the generation of new "real" wealth. The reality is that the economic multiplier effect of establishing an interstate highway network had mostly run its course with the completion of the infrastructure and the suburban build-out.

Economic growth from the early 1990s to the crash of 2008 was led less by new technological innovations and entrepreneurial acumen, even though that was the official public explanation for the new prosperity. That's not to say that new technologies—especially the information and communication technology (ICT) revolution—didn't play some role in the restoration of economic growth, but it was far less significant than the media, business community, and politicians led the public to believe. The fact is that the great economic growth made possible by the Second Industrial Revolution had begun to slow by then.

Wages had already been stagnant in the United States for nearly a decade, and the technologies that made up the Second Industrial Revolution were now passing into their mature and even senescent stage.

What brought the United States and the world out of the economic downturn of the late 1980s and early 1990s was the issuing of massive consumer credit, first in the United States and then in other countries. The "credit card culture" boosted purchasing power and put American companies and employees back to work in the early 1990s to produce all of the goods and services being bought on credit. For the last eighteen years, American consumers have propped up the global economy, largely by their credit-driven purchases. The price for maintaining a global economy on the shoulders of increasing U.S. consumer debt, however, has been the depletion of American family savings. The average family savings in 1991 was approximately 8 percent. By 2006 family savings entered the negative category.[3] Many families were spending more than they made. The term for this is "negative income," an oxymoron that represents a failed approach to economic development.

As family savings moved into negative territory, the mortgage and banking industry created a second line of artificial credit, allowing American families to purchase homes with little or no money down, at low or nonexistent short-term interest rates—subprime mortgages—with the interest rate going up and the principle coming due pushed off into the future. Millions of Americans took the bait and bought homes beyond their ability to pay in the long run, creating a housing bubble. Strapped for money, homeowners used their homes as ATM cash machines, refinancing mortgages—sometimes two or three times—to secure needed cash. The housing bubble has now burst, with millions of Americans facing foreclosures and banks facing collapse.

The result of eighteen years of living on extended credit is that the United States is now a failed economy. The gross liabilities of the U.S. financial sector, which were 21 percent of GDP in 1980, have risen steadily over the past twenty-seven years, and were an incredible 116 percent of GDP by 2007.[4] Worse still, the accumulated household consumer debt now exceeds $13.9 trillion.[5] Because the U.S., European, and Asian banking and financial communities are intimately intertwined, the credit crisis has swept out of America and engulfed the entire global economy.

What essentially happened in the past two decades is that the global economy continued to expand by depleting the accumulated American savings reaped during the forty-year growth spurt of the Second Industrial Revolution that began at the end of World War II and ran its course by the late 1980s.

To make matters worse, the global credit crisis escalated even further over the past two years as oil prices soared, reaching $147 per barrel on world markets in July 2008. The increasing price of oil stoked inflation, dampened consumer purchasing power, slowed production, and increased unemployment, wreaking further havoc on an already debt-ridden economy.

We now face a new phenomenon. It's called "peak globalization," and it occurred at around $147 per barrel. Beyond this point, inflation creates a firewall to continued economic growth, pushing the global economy back down toward zero growth. It is only with the contraction of the global economy that the price of energy falls as a result of less energy use.

The importance of "peak globalization" can't be overemphasized. The underlying assumption of globalization has been that plentiful and cheap oil allows companies to move capital to cheap labor markets, where food and manufactured goods can be produced at minimum expense and at high profit margins and then shipped abroad. This core assumption has disintegrated.

To understand how we got to this point, we need to go back and revisit 1979, the year that global oil per capita peaked, according to a study done by the British oil company BP.[6] When China and India began their dramatic economic growth in the 1990s, their demand for oil skyrocketed. Demand began to outstrip supply and the price of oil began to climb. With less oil potentially available for every human being, efforts to bring one-third of the human race—the combined population of China and India—into an oil-based Second Industrial Revolution have come up against a limited supply of oil. In other words, demand pressure of a growing human population against finite oil reserves inevitably pushes the price up, and when oil hits $147 per barrel, inflation becomes so powerful that it acts as a drag on further economic growth and the global economy contracts.

The rising price of energy is embedded in every product we make. Therefore, the increase in the price of energy impacts every aspect of production, making long-haul transport of goods by air and cargo ship increasingly prohibitive. Whatever marginal value companies previously enjoyed by moving production to cheap labor markets is canceled by the increasing cost of energy across the entire supply chain. This represents the real turning point for the Second Industrial Revolution and occurs well before the point of peak global oil production.

At the same time, the effects of "real-time" climate change are further eroding the economy in many regions. The cost in damages just from Hurricanes Katrina, Rita, Ike, and Gustav is estimated to be in excess of $100 billion.[7] Floods, droughts, wildfires, tornadoes, and other extreme weather events have decimated ecosystems on every continent, crippling both agricultural output and infrastructures, slowing the global economy, and displacing millions of human beings.

The convergence of the global credit crisis, the energy crisis, and real-time impacts of climate change have brought the world economy to the brink of collapse.

Oil, coal, and natural gas will provide a decreasing portion of the world's energy in the twenty-first century. It has become clear to most observers that we are approaching the end of the fossil-fuel era. During this twilight era, nations are making efforts to ensure that the remaining stock of fossil fuels is used more efficiently and are experimenting with clean technologies to limit carbon dioxide emissions in the burning of conventional fuels. The European Union in particular is mandating that its member states increase energy efficiency by 20 percent by 2020 and reduce their global warming emissions by 20 percent (based on 1990 levels), again by 2020.

But greater efficiencies in the use of fossil fuels and mandated global warming gas reductions alone are not going to be enough to adequately address the unprecedented crisis of global peak oil and gas production and global warming. Looking to the future, every government will need to explore new energy paths and establish new economic models with the goal of achieving as close to zero carbon emissions as possible.

THE RISE OF THE THIRD INDUSTRIAL REVOLUTION

Even as the Second Industrial Revolution is entering into its endgame, a new Third Industrial Revolution is looming on the horizon. Whether it will come on line quickly enough to mitigate the long-term entropic impact that has built up over the two-hundred-year time span that marks the fossil-fuel era and the first two industrial revolutions is still an open question.

Recall in Chapter 1 that we mentioned that the great economic changes in history occur when new communications revolutions converge with new energy regimes to create wholly new living environments. We are on the cusp of just such a convergence—the coming together of the distributed information and communications technology (ICT) revolution of the past two decades with the distributed renewable energy regime of the twenty-first century. The use of distributed information and communications technology, as the command-and-control mechanism to organize and manage distributed energy, ushers in a powerful Third Industrial Revolution with an economic multiplier effect that should extend well into the second half of the twenty-first century and beyond.

Distributed energies are energies that are found in the backyard. The sun shines all over the world. The wind blows across the Earth every day. We all generate garbage. People living in rural areas have access to agriculture and forestry waste. People living in coastal areas have the energy generated from the incoming tides. Geothermal energy lies beneath the Earth and water provides hydropower. We call these energies distributed because unlike the conventional elite energies—coal, oil, natural gas, and uranium—that are only found in limited geographic regions, the renewable energies are found in various proportions everywhere.

Today the information and communications technologies that gave rise to the Internet are being used to reconfigure the world's power grids, enabling millions of people to collect and produce their own renewable energy in their homes, offices, retail stores, factories, and technology parks and share it peer-to-peer across smart grids, just as they now produce and share their own information in cyberspace. Companies are already beginning to establish the beginnings of an infrastructure and market for what business leaders call "distributed capitalism."

Renewable forms of energy—solar, wind, hydro, geothermal, ocean waves, and biomass—make up the first of the four pillars of the Third Industrial Revolution. While these sunrise energies still account for a small percentage of the global energy mix, they are growing rapidly as governments mandate targets and benchmarks for their widespread introduction into the market and their falling costs make them increasingly competitive. Billions of dollars of public and private capital are pouring into research, development, and market penetration, as businesses and homeowners seek to reduce their carbon footprint and become more energy efficient and independent.

Although renewable energy is found everywhere and new technologies are allowing us to harness it more cheaply and efficiently, we need infrastructure to load it. This is where the building industry steps to the fore, to lay down the second pillar of the Third Industrial Revolution.

As stated earlier, buildings are the major contributor to human-induced global warming and consume 30 to 40 percent of all the energy produced and are responsible for equal percentages of all CO_2 emissions. Now, new technological breakthroughs make it possible to convert existing buildings and design new ones that can create some, or even all, of their own energy from locally available renewable energy sources, allowing us to reconceptualize the future of buildings as "power plants." The commercial and economic implications are far-reaching for the real estate industry and, for that matter, the world.

In twenty-five years from now, millions of buildings—homes, offices, shopping malls, factories, industrial and technology parks—will be renovated or constructed to serve as "power plants" as well as habitats. These buildings will collect and generate energy locally from the sun, wind, garbage, agricultural and forestry waste, ocean waves and tides, hydropower and geothermal power sources—enough energy to provide for their own power needs as well as surplus energy that can be shared.

The GM factory in Aragon, Spain, the largest GM production facility in Europe, has just installed a 10 megawatt solar plant on its factory roof for the cost of $78 million. The power station is able to produce enough electricity for the factory or provide electricity for 4,600 homes. The initial investment will be paid back in less than ten years, after which the generation of electricity is virtually free, except for the maintenance of the solar facility.[8]

In France, the giant French construction company Bouygues is putting up a state-of-the-art commercial office complex in the Paris suburbs that collects enough solar energy to provide not only for all of its own needs but even generates surplus electricity for sale back to the main power grid.

The Walqa Technology Park in Huesca, Spain, is nestled in a valley in the Pyrenees and is among a new genre of technology parks that produce their own renewable energy on-site to power virtually all of their operations. There are currently a dozen office buildings in operations at the Walqa Park, and forty more already slated for construction. The facility is run almost entirely by renewable forms of energy, including wind power, hydropower, and solar power. The park houses leading high-tech companies, including Microsoft and other ICT and renewable energy companies.

The introduction of the first two pillars of the Third Industrial Revolution—renewable energy and "buildings as power plants"—requires the simultaneous introduction of the third pillar of the Third Industrial Revolution. To maximize renewable energy and to minimize cost, it will be necessary to develop storage methods that facilitate the conversion of intermittent supplies of these energy sources into dependable assets. Batteries, differentiated water pumping, and other media can provide limited storage capacity. There is, however, one storage medium that is widely available and relatively efficient. Hydrogen is the universal medium that "stores" all forms of renewable energy to assure that a stable and reliable supply is available for power generation and, equally important, for transport.

Hydrogen is the lightest and most abundant element in the universe, and when used as an energy source, the only by-products are pure water and heat. Our spaceships have been powered by high-tech hydrogen fuel cells for more than thirty years.

Here is how hydrogen works: Renewable sources of energy—solar, wind power, hydropower, geothermal power, and ocean waves—are used to produce electricity. That electricity, in turn, can be used, through a process called electrolysis, to split water into hydrogen and oxygen. Hydrogen can also be extracted directly from energy crops, animal and forestry waste, and organic garbage—biomass—without going through the electrolysis process.

The important point to emphasize is that a renewable energy society becomes viable to the extent that part of that energy can be stored in the form of hydrogen. That's because renewable energy is intermittent. The sun isn't always shining, the wind isn't always blowing, water isn't always flowing when there's a drought, and agricultural yields vary. When renewable energy isn't available, electricity can't be generated and economic activity grinds to a halt. But if some of the electricity being generated when renewable energy is abundant can be used to extract hydrogen from water, which can then be stored for later conversion back to electricity, society will have a continuous supply of power.

In 2008, the European Commission announced a Joint Technology Initiative (JTI), an ambitious public/private partnership to speed the commercial introduction of a hydrogen economy in the twenty-seven member states of the EU, with the primary focus on producing hydrogen from renewable sources of energy.

By benchmarking a shift to renewable energy, advancing the notion of buildings as power plants, and funding an aggressive hydrogen fuel-cell technology R&D program, the EU has erected the first three pillars of the Third Industrial Revolution. The fourth pillar, the reconfiguration of the power grid along the lines of the Internet, allowing businesses and homeowners to produce their own energy and share it with each other, is just now being tested by power companies in Europe, the United States, Japan, China, and other countries.

The smart intergrid is made up of three critical components. Mini-grids allow homeowners, small- and medium-size enterprises (SMEs), and large-scale economic enterprises to produce renewable energy locally—through solar cells, wind power, small hydropower, animal and agricultural waste, and garbage—and use it off-grid for their own electricity needs. Smart metering technology allows local producers to more effectively sell their energy back to the main power grid, as well as accept electricity from the grid, making the flow of electricity bidirectional.

The next phase in smart grid technology is embedding sensing devices and chips throughout the grid system, connecting every electrical appliance. Software allows the entire power grid to know how much energy is being used, at any time, anywhere on the grid. This interconnectivity can be used to redirect energy uses and flows during peaks and lulls, and even to adjust to the price changes of electricity from moment to moment.

In the future, intelligent utility networks will also be increasingly connected to moment-to-moment weather changes—recording wind changes, solar flux, and ambient temperature—giving the power network the ability to adjust electricity flow continuously, to both external weather conditions and consumer demand. For example, if the power grid is experiencing peak energy use and possible overload because of too much demand, the software can direct a homeowner's washing machine to go down by one cycle per load or reduce the air conditioning by one degree. Consumers who agree to slight adjustments in their electricity use receive credits on their bills. Since the true price of electricity on the grid varies during any twenty-four-hour period, moment-to-moment energy information opens the door to "dynamic pricing," allowing consumers to increase or drop their energy use automatically, depending upon the price of electricity on the grid. Up-to-the-moment pricing also allows local minigrid producers of energy to either sell energy back to the grid or go off the grid altogether. The smart intergrid will not only give end users more power over their energy choices, but it also creates new energy efficiencies in the distribution of electricity.

The intergrid makes possible a broad redistribution of power. Today's centralized, top-down flow of energy becomes increasingly obsolete. In the new era, businesses, municipalities, and homeowners become the producers as well as the consumers of their own energy—what is referred to as "distributed generation."

The distributed smart grid also provides the essential infrastructure for making the transition from the oil-powered internal combustion engine to electric and hydrogen fuel-cell plug-in vehicles. Electric plug-in and hydrogen-powered fuel-cell vehicles are also "power stations on wheels" with a generating capacity of twenty or more kilo-watts. Since the average car, bus, and truck is parked much of the time, it can be plugged in during nonuse hours to the home, office, or main interactive electricity network, providing premium electricity back to the grid.

The introduction of the internal combustion engine and the auto highway infrastructure marked the beginning of the oil era and the Second Industrial Revolution in the twentieth century, just as the introduction of the steam engine, the locomotive, and the railbed infra-structure marked the beginning of the coal era and the First Industrial Revolution in the nineteenth century.

Transport revolutions are always embedded in larger infrastructure revolutions. The coal-powered steam engine revolution required vast changes in infrastructure, including a shift in transport from water-ways to railbeds, and the ceding of public land for the development of new towns and cities along critical rail links and junctions. Similarly, the introduction of the gasoline-powered internal combustion engine required the building of a national road system, the laying down of oil pipelines, and the construction of new suburban commercial and resi-dential corridors along the interstate highway system.

The shift from the internal combustion engine to electric and hydro-gen fuel-cell plug-in vehicles requires a comparable new commitment to a Third Industrial Revolution infrastructure.

In 2008, Daimler and RWE, Germany's second-largest power and utility company, launched a project in Berlin to establish recharging points for electric Smart and Mercedes cars around the German capi-tal. Renault-Nissan is readying a similar plan to provide a network of battery-charging points in Israel, Denmark, and Portugal. The distrib-uted electric power–charging stations will be used to service Renault's all-electric Mégane car. By 2030, charging points for plug-in electric vehicles and hydrogen fuel-cell vehicles will be installed virtually everywhere—along roads and in homes, commercial buildings, facto-ries, parking lots, and garages, providing a seamless distributed infra-structure for sending electricity to the main electricity grid as well as receiving electricity from it.

IBM, General Electric, Siemens, and other global IT companies are just now entering the smart power market, working with utility companies to transform the power grid to intergrids, so that building owners can produce their own energy and share it with each other. CPS Energy in San Antonio, Texas; CenterPoint Utility in Houston, Texas; Xcel Energy in Boulder, Colorado; and Sempra Energy and Southern Cal Edison in California are beginning to lay down parts of the smart grid, connecting thousands of residential and commercial buildings.

The question is often asked as to whether renewable energy, in the long run, can provide enough power to run a national or global economy. Just as second-generation information-systems grid technologies allow businesses to connect thousands of desktop computers, creating far more distributed computing power than even the most powerful centralized supercomputers, millions of local producers of renewable energy, with access to intelligent utility networks, can potentially produce and share far more distributed power than the older centralized forms of energy—oil, coal, natural gas, and nuclear—that we currently rely on.

The transition to the Third Industrial Revolution will require a wholesale reconfiguration of the entire economic infrastructure of each country, creating millions of jobs and countless new goods and services. Nations will need to invest in renewable energy technology on a massive scale; convert millions of buildings, transforming them into power plants; embed hydrogen and other storage technology throughout the national infrastructure; transform the automobile from the internal combustion engine to electric plug-in and fuel-cell cars; and lay down an intelligent utility network.

The remaking of each nation's infrastructure and the retooling of industries is going to require a massive retraining of workers on a scale matching the vocational and professional training at the onset of the First and Second Industrial Revolutions. The new high-tech workforce of the Third Industrial Revolution will need to be skilled in renewable energy technologies, green construction, IT and embedded computing, nanotechnology, sustainable chemistry, fuel-cell development, digital power grid management, hybrid electric and hydrogen-powered transport, and hundreds of other technical fields.

Entrepreneurs and managers will need to be educated to take advantage of cutting-edge business models, including open-source and networked commerce, performance contracting, distributed and collaborative research and development strategies, and sustainable low-carbon logistics and supply-chain management. The skill levels and managerial styles of the Third Industrial Revolution workforce will be qualitatively different from those of the workforce of the Second Industrial Revolution.

A fully integrated intelligent intergrid allows each country to both produce its own energy and share any surpluses with neighboring countries in a "network" approach to assuring global energy security. When any given region enjoys a temporary surge or surplus in its renewable energy, that energy can be shared with regions that are facing a temporary lull or deficit.

The Third Industrial Revolution leads to a new social vision where power itself is broadly distributed, encouraging unprecedented new levels of collaboration among peoples and nations. Just as the distributed communications revolution of the last decade spawned network ways of thinking, open-source sharing, and the democratization of communications, the Third Industrial Revolution follows suit with the democratization of energy. We begin to envision a world where hundreds of millions of people are empowered, both literally and figuratively, with momentous implications for social and political life.

A NEW SOCIAL VISION

The democratization of energy becomes a rallying point of a new distributed social vision. Access to power becomes an inalienable social right in the Third Industrial Revolution era. The twentieth century saw the extension of the political franchise and the broadening of educational and economic opportunities to millions of people around the world. In the twenty-first century, individual access to energy also becomes a social and human right. Every human being should have the right and the opportunity to create his or her own energy locally and share it with others across regional, national, and continental inter-grids. For a younger generation that is growing up in a less hierarchical and more networked society, the ability to share and produce their own energy in an open-access intergrid will be regarded as a fundamental right and responsibility.

The half-century transition from the Second to the Third Industrial Revolution is going to change dramatically the globalization process. The most significant impact is likely to be on developing nations. Lack of access to electricity is a key factor in perpetuating poverty. Con-versely, access to energy means more economic opportunity. If millions of individuals in developing communities were to become producers of their own energy, the result would be a notable shift in the configura-tion of power. Local peoples would be less subject to the will of far-off centers of power. Communities would be able to produce goods and services locally and sell them globally. This is the essence of the politics of sustainable development and reglobalization from the bottom up. The developed nations, working with industries and civil-society orga-nizations, can help facilitate the next phase of sustainable globalization by reorienting development aid, leveraging macro- and microfinancing and credit, and providing favored-nation trade status in order to help developing nations establish a Third Industrial Revolution.

The shift from elite fossil fuels and uranium-based energies to dis-tributed renewable energies takes the world out of the "geopolitics" that characterized the twentieth century, and into the "biosphere poli-tics" of the twenty-first century. Much of the geopolitical struggles of the last century centered on gaining military and political access to coal, oil, natural gas, and uranium deposits. Wars were fought and countless lives lost, as nations vied with each other in the pursuit of fos-sil fuels and uranium security. The ushering in of the Third Industrial Revolution will go a long way toward diffusing the growing tensions over access to more limited supplies of fossil fuels and uranium and help facilitate biosphere politics based on a collective sense of responsibility for safeguarding the Earth's ecosystems.

DISTRIBUTED CAPITALISM

The peer-to-peer sharing of energy among millions, and eventually billions, of people marks the beginning of a new era that could see the steady erosion of traditional hierarchical modes of organization and management and the widespread adoption of distributed networks characterized by mass collaboration. A more distributed and collaborative global economy is beginning to radically transform the temporal and spatial orientation of the human species, leading to: greater differentiation of skills, a furthering of selfhood, greater connectivity, the extension of empathy and the expansion of consciousness—this time to the biosphere envelope that cloaks the earth.

To appreciate the potential impact of the new distributed capitalism, it is necessary to understand the power of distributed communications as a managing agent for a distributed energy society.

As mentioned earlier, distributed computing, often called grid computing, is the centerpiece of the second-generation information technology revolution that is sweeping the global business community, facilitating new global social networks and revolutionizing the educational system.

The idea of using massive distributed computing power first occurred to David Gedye, a software designer, and David Anderson, a former computer science professor. The two were interested in trying to discover whether there might be extraterrestrial life somewhere in the universe. They realized early on that scanning radio waves in the universe to try to find someone out there broadcasting interstellar communications was a massive undertaking. They used the Arecibo Observatory in Puerto Rico, the largest radio telescope in the world, to monitor the sky twenty-four hours a day, listening to millions of radio frequencies simultaneously. Analyzing the mountain of information would necessitate the use of the world's largest simulators. Since that kind of open-ended access to supercomputers was an impossibility, they hit on the idea of recruiting and connecting millions of personal computers to the Internet to crunch the data. Given the fact that personal computers are idle much of the time and even when in use are not used to capacity, they reasoned that if people could be convinced to donate their computers' time, enough distributed computer power could be created to assess the flow of incoming data. By 2001, more than a million personal computers had been recruited into the project.[9] While the Search for Extra-Terrestrial Intelligence (SETI) project has yet to hear from anyone in the galaxy, it created the prototype for the next big IT revolution—distributed computing.

Since then, distributed computing has been used to tackle some of the most complex and difficult problems facing humanity. For example, Oxford University researchers convinced 100,000 people from 150 nations to donate some of their computers' time to analyze climate change data and create forecasting models. The distributed computing power at their disposal is twice as powerful as some of the world's fastest computers.[10]

Distributed computer projects are proliferating. Millions of computers are now being connected to collect and analyze data for a range of projects, including the search for new protein structures, finding gravitational waves, studying nanosystems, searching for prime numbers, and developing new drugs, to name just a few.[11]

Why do people willingly lend their computers to these kinds of projects? While motivations run the gamut, "altruism" is the reason most given by "crunchers," as they are affectionately referred to in the distributed computer community. Millions of people are anxious to help, in any way they can, to address the big challenges facing the human race, from climate change to curing diseases.[12]

Donating computer time is just a small part of the new distributed approach to human collaboration. Millions of people are also being actively recruited by businesses and academia to share their knowledge and creativity. "Wikinomics" is the term used to describe the new mass collaborative model of collecting data, sharing knowledge, and problem-solving that has shown impressive results across entire fields of endeavor, often eclipsing knowledge gained and solutions applied by professional experts in the same fields. A "wiki workplace" refers to a collaborative venture involving scores, hundreds, and even thousands of people—some experts and others amateurs—usually across many different fields, who come together to share their ideas and problem-solve. These new flat collaborative learning environments mobilize the collective wisdom of crowds, and their track record is impressive when compared to traditional hierarchically organized corporate learning environments.

The phenomenon known as the "wisdom of crowds" is not something that just emerged with the advent of distributed computing technology. Francis Galton, a scientist best known for his championing of human eugenics—he was also Charles Darwin's half cousin—was the first to grasp the importance of collaborative wisdom. In 1906, Galton was visiting a country fair in his home town of Plymouth, England. He happened on a weight-judging competition. A huge ox was brought forward, and the fairgoers queued up to place wagers on what his weight would be after being slaughtered and processed. Eight hundred people placed a wager, including butchers and farmers as well as office clerks and others with no particular expertise. When the contest was over, Galton collected all eight hundred of the entry slips, arranged them in order from highest to lowest, placed them along a bell curve, and then added up all of the estimates and calculated the mean of the group's guesses—the number that represented the collective wisdom of the group. The crowd's mean estimate came in at 1,197 pounds, just one pound short of the ox's weight.[13] Galton subsequently published his findings in the British journal *Nature*, but it would be a hundred years before the new distributed computing technology would allow millions of people to aggregate their knowledge and creativity to collaborative learning ventures.

One of the first companies to harness the power of collective wisdom and collaborative learning was a small gold-mining firm called Goldcorp, based in Toronto. Facing higher costs of production, accumulating debt, labor unrest, and few prospects of finding new gold deposits, the company was on the brink of insolvency when its CEO, Robert McEwen, got an idea while attending a seminar at MIT. The discussion turned to Linux, the open-source code-sharing network where thousands of programmers give freely of their time to help correct problems in software code. McEwen came up with the radical idea of taking all of the company's geological data on its Red Lake property, going back to 1948, putting it up on the Web, and asking the world to tell the company where it was likely to find gold.[14] To sweeten the pot, the company offered $575,000 in prize money to the best methods of discovery and estimates of deposit locations. Over one thousand cyberspace prospectors from fifty countries began analyzing the data.[15] Geologists weighed in, as did mathematicians, military personnel, and graduate students from diverse fields.

What was so interesting, observed McEwen, was the range of expertise from so many different disciplines that was brought to bear on the search, including advanced physics, applied math and intelligent systems. "There were capabilities I had never seen before in the industry," noted McEwen. The results were startling. "When I saw the computer graphics I almost fell out of my chair," said McEwen. The contestants had pinpointed 110 locations on the company's property, half of which had never been earmarked by company geologists. Amazingly, more than 80 percent of the new targets yielded large amounts of gold—more than eight million ounces.[16]

"Peer production" or "peering" is becoming standard operating procedure in some of the world's largest companies, especially in the pharmaceutical and chemical industries. Mass collaboration has helped companies like Procter & Gamble rethink their R&D models. Procter & Gamble has reinvented its R&D program, supplementing its in-house researchers with outside collaboration. The company uses InnoCentive, a cybermarketplace venture that matches up thousands of scientists across a range of disciplines with companies like Procter & Gamble in collaborative projects. Procter & Gamble expects to get 50 percent of its new ideas for products and services from these kinds of collaborative outsourcing efforts.[17]

Cisco's CEO, John Chambers, has transformed one of the world's

leading high-tech ICT companies into a collaborative work environment and is now exporting the model to clients. Mike Mitchell, the
director of technology communications, says that at Cisco, "[w]e want
a culture where it is unacceptable not to share what you know."[18] The
company encourages social networking among all of its employees and
promotes internal blogs so that everyone can share thoughts and ideas
across departments and job descriptions. With analysts estimating that
the "collaboration marketplace" could quickly become a $34 billion
opportunity, Chambers is anxious to make Cisco a prime catalyst for
moving the new business model.[19]

Chambers is particularly interested in the emerging distributed energy side of the Third Industrial Revolution. With 75 percent of its
revenue coming from routers, switches, and advanced network technologies, Chambers is using the company's prime technologies to work
with European customers who are beginning to put smart-grid technology on line. "By handling peak loads, [and] switching to alternative
energy sources, we can dramatically reduce the cost of electricity and
cut carbon emissions. . . . It can be a one billion or ten billion business
for us," says Chambers.[20] Cyberspace ventures like MySpace, Second
Life, and InnoCentive are all collaborative spaces.

Don Tapscott and Anthony D. Williams, in their book *Wikinomics*, make the point that the collaborative human potential, when connected by way of distributed-computing technology, takes the economy
beyond business-as-usual operating assumptions into new territory
based on "openness, peering, sharing, and acting globally."[21]

Third Industrial Revolution peer-to-peer technologies give rise to
"distributed capitalism" and, in the process, make many of the central
assumptions of market capitalism outmoded and irrelevant. For example, consider Adam Smith's firm belief that human nature predisposes
each individual to pursue his own self-interest in the marketplace,
against the interests of others. Smith allowed the dubious qualification
that even though it's only his own self-interest that he has in mind, by
so doing he contributes somehow to the common good.

The distributed model begins with the exact opposite assumption
about human nature—that is, that when given a chance, it is human

nature to want to collaborate with others, often freely, for the sheer joy of contributing to the common good. Moreover, by contributing to the well-being of the group, one is better able to optimize his or her own self-interest. In other words, champions of distributed collaboration celebrate what they call the "digital commons," rather than lamenting the "tragedy of the commons." It was ecologist Garret Hardin who wrote the famous essay that proposed the idea that self-interest leads to the fall of common economic enterprises—simply because it's human nature to look out for number one.

How then do we explain Linux and Wikipedia? With Linux, thousands of programmers willingly and freely give their expertise to help correct and improve software code used by millions of others. The code itself is open-source and not the intellectual property of any particular contributor to the software. Had I taught a theoretical version of this business model at the Wharton School's executive education program, even in the early 1990s, it would have been dismissed as completely contrary to the self-interested nature of human beings to engage in such activity over a protracted period of time. Yet Linux is now a major global player and challenges more traditional companies like Microsoft in the same field.

Likewise, consider Wikipedia, a free open-source online encyclopaedia with only five full-time employees, but which is ten times the size of *Encyclopaedia Britannica*.[22] The English version boasts more than 2.8 million entries.[23] All of the contributions are provided free. Everyone is also free to add their own contributions and points of view to any article, and yet because of the collaborative nature of the process, the error rate is only slightly higher than *Encyclopaedia Britannica*, despite the latter's reliance on chosen experts in their fields.[24]

In the case of Linux and Wikipedia, by contributing to the good of an ever expanding collaborative network, individual participants experience the joy of using their creativity in the service of others and reap the benefits of free access to ever-improving networks.

Economic activity is no longer an adversarial contest between embattled sellers and buyers but, rather, a collaborative enterprise between like-minded players. The classical economic idea that another's gain is at the expense of one's own loss is replaced by the idea that enhancing the well-being of others amplifies one's own well-being. The win/lose game gives way to the win/win scenario.

Similarly, the old adage *Caveat emptor*—"Let the buyer beware"—is replaced with the idea of transparency and openness. In a traditional business setting, one never divulges internal data that might compromise one's advantage over a supplier, competitor, client, or even a colleague. In a collaborative setting, by contrast, it is only by sharing data openly with one another that the players can optimize their collaboration together and create additional value for everyone in the network. A venture like Linux, for example, only works when the software, code, and new applications are openly shared among everyone in the network.

FROM PROPERTY RIGHTS TO ACCESS RIGHTS

Nowhere is the old classical economic paradigm and the new distributed capitalism model more at odds than when it comes to the notion of holding intellectual property. Patents and copyrights are sacrosanct in the traditional business scheme. In a collaborative economy, however, open-sourcing of critical information becomes essential to collaboration. Possessing and controlling knowledge thwarts collaboration.

The struggle in the life-sciences sector over patents on genes is illustrative of the difference between traditional market-based capitalism and the new distributed capitalism. For nearly thirty years, life science companies have been patenting genetic sequences and genes and novel hybrid chimeric and cloned organisms, as well as the processes used to isolate their properties and create the organisms. In recent years, however, a younger generation of researchers who grew up in the Internet era have begun to challenge what they regard as a blatant and stifling attempt to squirrel away knowledge that, if freely and openly shared, might speed up new life-saving medical discoveries, spur advances in agriculture, lead to breakthroughs in alternative clean energies, and pave the way to a new generation of sustainable construction materials.

Worried that companies like Monsanto might hold the world's farmers and consumers hostage by locking up patents on all of the genes that comprise the world's store of germ plasm for growing crops, biologists at CAMBIA, a biotech research institute, have begun to release their own genetic discoveries publicly under an open-source licensing agent called BiOS, which is similar to the kind of licensing agent used by Linux and other open-source software ventures.[25]

Some global pharmaceutical companies are beginning to follow suit—although in a far more limited fashion—by putting some of their research online in publicly available databases to encourage more collaborative research. While these efforts are tentative, and life science companies are still wedded to protecting intellectual property, it is becoming increasingly clear that in the warp speed of the global economy, where distributed collaboration allows for continuous breakthroughs and new discoveries, patents become increasingly outmoded mechanisms for creating added value.

Patent law dates back to the early patents issued in Venice and other Italian city-states during the Renaissance to encourage invention and protect local craftsmen in the glass-blowing industry and other crafts. Today the idea of holding a patent on a process or product for twenty years, when product life cycles often run their course in a few years or even a few months, seems almost quaint.

Similarly, copyright laws have run up against file sharing, blogging, and open-source collaborative ventures whose modus operandi is "information likes to run free." On the Internet and in the blogosphere, where volumes of information are routinely made free—think Wikipedia, YouTube, MySpace, Flickr—holding on to copyrights means restricting, not expanding, one's commercial outreach.

The challenges to intellectual property rights are part of a larger challenge to the notion of property relations itself, the foundation upon which classical economic theory is built. Recall that John Locke, Adam Smith, and other Enlightenment philosophers believed that acquiring property was intrinsic to human nature and that the market provided a self-adjusting mechanism to ensure the continuous acquisition and exchange of property among sellers and buyers.

The very idea of the propertied autonomous individual is the cornerstone of Enlightenment thinking and the leitmotif for the modern notion of individual freedom. For the philosophers and jurists of the eighteenth and nineteenth centuries, freedom was defined in negative terms as the right to exclude others. Ennobling the idea of private property rights allowed the emerging bourgeoisie of Europe to create an alternative legal bulwark to counter ancient obligations to the Church and feudal estates and the limitations imposed by craft guilds, as well as the many other conventions that kept them indentured to an old order. Understandably, an emerging capitalist class came to see private property rights as a symbol of personal freedom. Property rights, protected by law, meant that no man could be bullied, oppressed, or made subject to another man's will. Greater accumulation of property and control over its use ensured increased autonomy and mobility, which, in turn, ensured personal freedom. If one were secure in one's property, then all of the other rights would be guaranteed—the right to privacy, the right to be free of coercion, and especially the right to happiness.

At a time when Great Britain and the other European countries were beginning to establish the rudimentary elements of a capitalist market, expand their colonial reach to large parts of the globe, and advance a mercantilist policy designed to secure more control over land, resources, people, and markets, the idea that man's very nature is to be acquisitive and to secure property assured them that their policies were a societal reflection of the natural order of things.

The metamorphosis in thinking about the nature of property paralleled the many other changes that were transforming a continent from a feudal economy to a market economy and from dynastic rule to nation-state governance. The new concept of property was a way for Europeans to reorder their relationship to space and time. The new technologies opened the door to vast new spaces and dramatically quickened the human tempo. Space that had for so long been conceived of as cloistered and vertical was suddenly horizontal and wide open to the vanishing point of the horizon. Time, which for eons had been experienced as cyclical and relatively closed, suddenly was experienced as linear and expansive. The old feudal institutions, with their constricted spatial and temporal boundaries, simply collapsed in the wake of what appeared to be an endless frontier running alongside an infinite future. The development of a private property perspective was the critical mental tool for domesticating the new spatial and temporal frontier.

The whole of earthly reality was reconfigured into a single formula—"mine versus thine." And with this formulation, Europeans set out to colonize the whole of space and time. In the new future being born, every person would become his or her own private god whose divinity lay in amassing property, inflating his or her being, and casting an ever larger shadow over existence and duration. More mine, less thine. Those who could, by talent and cunning, acquire the most property, could transform it into capital and use that capital to control not only nature but the lives of other people as well. They were called "capitalists."

The modern market economy and the nation-state, in turn, became the institutional mechanisms to speed along this new reorganization of the world. The market would serve as the impartial arena where each capitalist would lock in battle against his fellow warriors in the struggle to capture space and sequester time in the form of private property. The infant nation-state, in turn, was to be the protector of every person's property by establishing legal codes and enforcement mechanisms—and, by so doing, guarantee his or her freedom.

Embedding private property relations into the heart of human nature was a double-edged sword. Securing each person's right to the fruits of their own labor against the privileges of a feudal order and, later, monarchial regimes, furthered the process of differentiation, individualization, and selfhood. Each propertied white male became sovereign over his own propertied domain—an island to himself. The development of the natural law theory of private property relations has marched side by side with the emergence of the autonomous individual in Western history.

A deepening sense of individuality and selfhood helped elevate the idea of the unique importance of each individual life in the grand scheme of things while fostering a greater sense of one's existential aloneness in the world. These psychological changes hastened the empathic drive, as individuals became increasingly mindful of each other's unique being and their existential struggle to overcome their isolation, connect with their fellow human beings, and find meaning in their life and prosper.

Yet the near fanatical commitment to private property—to the point of anointing it as the primary aspect of man's nature—also had the opposite effect of establishing a boundary line between "mine and thine," walling people off from one another in wholly new ways by creating new social barriers between the privileged and the unfortunate. Ensconcing private property relations at the center of societal organization helped flatten human discourse on one level by extending the idea that every propertied man is sovereign, while establishing a new exclusionary principle of "mine versus thine" as the basis for managing economic, social, and political relations between people to the end of both advancing and thwarting empathic extension at the same time.

Now, however, the rationale that spawned private property relations is beginning to fray in the wake of new technologies that are once again altering our sense of space and time. The quickening connection of the central nervous system of every human being to every other human being on Earth, via the Internet and other new communications technologies, is propelling us into a global space and a new simultaneous field of time. The result is that property exchange in national markets in the twenty-first century is going to increasingly give way to access relationships in vast global networks.

Diminished attachment to a private property regime has great potential import both for the future of global commerce and the collective human psyche. If the commercial, psychological, and ideological attachment to private property continues to weaken, what will be the eventual fate of the marketplace? Equally important is the potential impact of such a change on consciousness and our conception of human nature.

The market economy is far too slow to take full advantage of the speed and productive potential made possible by the software and communications revolutions. The result is that we are witnessing the birth of a new economic system that is as different from market capitalism as the latter was from the feudal economy of an earlier era.

Nor is it just a matter of finding new organizational formats to upgrade the conduct of business in a market economy. It's the market exchange mechanism itself that is becoming outmoded.

Markets are linear, discrete, and discontinuous modes of operation. Sellers and buyers come together for a short moment of time to exchange goods and services, then part. The lapsed time between the completion of one exchange and the introduction of the next exchange represents the lost productivity and added cost of doing business that eventually makes markets obsolete.

The new information and communications technologies, by contrast, are cybernetic, not linear. They allow for continuous activity over extended periods of time. That means that the start and stop mechanism of market exchanges can be replaced with the idea of establishing an ongoing commercial relationship between parties over time.

For example, consider the conventional way of selling a CD versus the new music company models for marketing music. In a conventional market-exchange relationship, the buyer pays the retailer for an individual compact disc. By contrast, in the new network model used by music companies like Rhapsody, the user pays a monthly subscription fee that gives him or her unlimited access to the music company's library. In the old model, the physical CD—the property—is exchanged between seller and buyer, whereas in the new network model, the user is paying for the time for which he or she has access to the music.

In pure networks, property still exists, but it stays with the producer and is accessed in time segments by the user. Subscriptions, memberships, rentals, time-shares, retainers, leases, and licensing agreements become the new medium of exchange. The music company creates a 24/7 commodified relationship with the client, making him part of a music network. Now the user is paying for access to the music when he is asleep, awake, and working, as well as when he is listening to the music. The music company prefers commercializing an ongoing relationship with the user over a period of time rather than having to sell each CD as a separate market transaction. It's a matter of time and cost.

The music companies maintain a fast, efficient, smooth, and continuous relationship with the client, while brick-and-mortar retail stores are slogging along, having to negotiate each and every transaction as a discrete closed-end process. In a world where everyone is connected via cyberspace and information is being exchanged at the speed of light, time becomes the most scarce and valuable resource. In pure networks, providers and users replace sellers and buyers, and access to the use of goods in extended time segments substitutes for the physical exchange of the goods.

Transaction costs and margins also come into play in the shift from market-exchange models to network models. In a market exchange economy, sellers make profit on their margins, and margins are dependent on transaction costs. But in most industries, margins are continuing to go down, mainly because of the introduction of new information, communications, and production technologies and new energy-saving technologies, as well as new methods of organization that are reducing their transaction costs. When transaction costs approach zero, margins virtually disappear, and market exchanges are no longer viable ways of conducting business.

Book publishing is a case in point. In a market, I sell my book to a publisher, who then sends it to a printer. From there it is shipped to a wholesaler and then to a retailer, where the customer pays for the product. At each stage of the process, the seller is marking up the cost to the buyer to reflect his or her transaction costs. Now an increasing number of publishers—especially of textbooks and research books, which require continuous updating—are bypassing all of the intermediate steps in publishing a physical book and the transaction costs involved at each stage of the process. While *Encyclopaedia Britannica* still charges $1,395 for its thirty-two-volume set of books, the company sells far fewer physical books. Instead, the company puts the book contents on the World Wide Web, where information can be updated and accessed continuously. Users now pay a subscription fee to access the information over an extended period of time. *Encyclopaedia Britannica* eliminates virtually all of the remaining transaction costs of getting the information to its subscribers. The company has made the transition from selling a physical product to a buyer to providing the user access to a service over time. How does a physical book compete with an online book in the future when the latter has reduced the transaction costs so dramatically? The same process is at work across many industries.

Buying an automobile, for most people, represents their baptism into an adult world of property relationships. It is a signal of our willingness to accept the responsibilities that go along with being a member of the propertied class. In the modern world, where rites of passage are few, owning an automobile remains the one constant bridge from adolescence to adulthood.

The automobile, however, is going the way of so many other valued products in society as we move from an age of property exchange to an age of access. The automobile is being transformed from a good to a service and from something people own to something they lease. By 1999, noncommercial auto leasing had risen from obscurity to encompass nearly 40 percent of automobiles and trucks put on the U.S. roads.[26] In an era when the automobile has been central to our way of life, our economy, and our sense of personal identity, its metamorphosis from a possession to a service is a bellwether of the dramatic changes taking place in the restructuring of property relationships.

The shift from ownership to access is going to have a dramatic impact on the way businesses manage their relationship to energy and natural resources. Because of the nature of the market-based business model with its focus on exchanging property between sellers and buyers, there has been little incentive to reduce energy inefficiency and slow the entropic stream. Often just the reverse is prized, at least until recently, when energy costs began to rise and carbon cap-and-trade systems and recycling laws began to be put in place by governments. That's because once a product is exchanged with a buyer, the producer is no longer responsible for its impact on the environment.

Now, however, lighting companies like Philips are beginning to shift part of their operations from products to services. Philips enters into what are called performance contracts with clients. Under the new business model, Philips contracts, for example, with a city to provide a new generation of more efficient, compact fluorescent, and LED outdoor lighting for the metropolitan area. Philips finances the project, including providing the lighting and installation. The city, in turn, pays Philips back with the revenue that comes from energy savings over an agreed-upon period of time. No lightbulbs are ever sold. The property remains with Philips, who becomes a service provider rather than a supplier.

Performance contracts are becoming standard fare in the new energy-conscious marketplace. In the new business model, providers like Philips are continually finding new ways to minimize the energy they use to provide efficient and sustainable services in order to optimize profits.

As more and more companies make the transition from selling products to delivering services, energy efficiency and tighter resource management will increasingly drive the economic process. Reducing entropic flow will become an integral part of the operations of every enterprise.

FROM BELONGINGS TO BELONGING

The changing nature of how we think about our relationship to property is forcing a reappraisal of the human condition, just as it did in the early modern era. The "great transformation" from proprietary obligations on the feudal commons to property exchange in a market economy marked a watershed in thinking about the nature and purpose of human intercourse. Likewise, today the transition from property exchange in markets to access relationships in networks is again changing the assumptions about human nature.

Unfortunately, there's been scant discussion, either in academia or in public policy circles, about how to reconstruct our theories of property relations to bring them in line with the reality of network commerce operating in a distributed globalized economy.

We are so used to thinking of property as the right to exclude others from the use or benefit of something that we've lost sight of the fact that in previous times property was also defined as the right not to be excluded from the use or enjoyment of something. The late University of Toronto professor Crawford Macpherson resurrects the older sense of property, the right of access to property held in common—the right to navigate waterways, walk along commonly used country lanes, and enjoy access to the public square.

While this dual notion of property still exists, the right of public access and inclusion became increasingly marginalized and diminished by the right of private ownership and exclusion in the nineteenth and twentieth centuries as the market economy came to dominate more and more of the social domain.

Now, says Macpherson, at least for the developed countries, interest is turning to the more expansive and deeper issue of securing a "quality of life." Macpherson argues, in turn, that property needs to be redefined to include the "right to an *immaterial* revenue, a revenue of enjoyment of the quality of life." He suggests that "such a revenue can only be reckoned as a right to participate in a satisfying set of social relations."[27]

In a collaborative economy, the right of inclusion becomes more important in establishing economic and social relationships than the right of exclusion. As we've seen, traditional property rights, in the form of intellectual and real property, can act as a damper on the commercial and social possibilities opened up by the new distributed communications technologies and energies that make up the operating infrastructure of a Third Industrial Revolution economy.

In a collaborative society, immaterial values assume greater importance, especially the pursuit of self-fulfillment and personal transformation. The right not to be excluded from "a full life"—the right to access—becomes the most important property value people hold. Property in the new era, argues Macpherson, "needs to become a right to participate in a system of power relations which will enable the individual to live a fully human life."[28]

The individual and collective struggle to secure "access rights" in the twenty-first century will likely be as significant as was the struggle to secure property rights in the nineteenth and twentieth centuries.

A COLLABORATIVE AND CARING WORLD

The Third Industrial Revolution, with its emphasis on distributed information, communications and energy and peer-to-peer collaboration, continues the process of greater individualization in more integrated and complex human organizations while flattening hierarchical forms of managing economic, social, and political life.

The Internet is transforming the world into a giant global public square where literally billions of people can connect, collaborate, and create value together simultaneously and in real time. It's probably not an understatement when Tapscott and Williams claim that "the ability to pool the knowledge of millions (if not billions) of users in a self-organizing fashion demonstrates how mass collaboration is turning the new Web into something not completely unlike a global brain."[29] They note that the Net generation numbers more than two billion young people who have grown up using the Internet as a collaborative medium.[30]

Their nonhierarchical, networking way of relating to each other and the world, their collaborative nature, their interest in access and inclusion rather than autonomy and exclusion and their greater sensitivity to human diversity, predisposes the millennial generation to being the most empathic generation in history. A distributed, collaborative, nonhierarchical society can't help but be a more empathic one.

The statistical trends outlined in Chapter 11 show that the Internet generation consistently outpaces their older cohorts when it comes to acknowledging gender equality, championing ethnic diversity, respecting the rights of minorities and previously outcast groups, and being more accepting of sexual differences, more open to marriage across racial and religious lines, and more sensitive to the rights of other creatures.

The new nonhierarchical and collaborative way of thinking among the younger generation is even beginning to slowly penetrate the interior of organizations and the management styles of some of the world's global companies. Although the evidence of a change from hierarchical to networked types of management is still cursory and anecdotal, it appears that a company like Cisco is not alone in encouraging a more transparent and less hierarchical approach. A growing number of companies are abandoning the old corporate pyramids and the top-down command-and-control structures favored by twentieth-century management. In their place, they are instituting networking and collaborative arrangements, in part to accommodate the new productive potential and market opportunities afforded by distributed ICT, but also, in large measure, to accommodate a younger workforce that has grown up on and is comfortable with transparent, nonhierarchical, collaborative ways of engagement.

When I was a student at the Wharton School more than forty years ago, the hierarchical approach to decision making, with its emphasis on unconditional acceptance of commands from the top and robotic feedback of efficient results from the bottom, was taken for granted. Today that style of management has become increasingly problematic because it is slow, cumbersome, and at odds with the new distributed information and communications technologies that allow for a more flat and collaborative approach that is more efficient at collecting information, solving problems, and executing market operations.

Empathic sensibility lies at the heart of the new management style. In their book *The New Leaders*, Daniel Goleman, Richard Boyatzis, and Annie McKee examine the new empathic approach to management that is just beginning to gain traction as the global business community is forced to rethink the way it conducts business in the wake of the colossal failure and near collapse of the global capitalist economy. The simple reality is that distributed information technologies and a distributed communications and energy infrastructure are giving rise to distributed capitalism and necessitate a new type of management that is compatible with the Third Industrial Revolution.

Goleman et al. start with the importance of establishing transparency at every level of management. By transparency they have in mind not just sharing information but also expressing "an authentic openness to others about one's feelings, beliefs, and actions."[31] Emotional transparency builds trust among employees and fosters collegiality and collaboration. Being more open with one's feelings, in turn, encourages more empathic engagement.

Goleman is unequivocal in his belief that "empathy is the sine qua non of all social effectiveness in working life" and the key to the collaborative management style of a twenty-first-century distributed capitalist economy. He writes,

> Empathetic people are superb at recognizing and meeting the
> needs of clients, customers, or subordinates . . . They listen
> carefully, picking up what people are truly concerned about,
> and they respond on the mark. . . . Finally, in the growing
> global economy, empathy is a critical skill for both getting
> along with diverse workmates and doing business with people
> from other cultures.[32]

Empathic sensibility, according to Goleman, becomes indispensable to managing the emerging collaborative work environment. He notes that

> as the tasks of leadership become more complex and
> collaborative, relationship skills become increasingly
> pivotal. . . . [A]s organizations realize that the old functional
> silos—marketing over here, strategy there, compensation
> here—must be broken down, more leaders routinely work
> with their peers as part of cross-functional teams. . . . And that
> means establishing close and smooth relations so that everyone
> can share information easily and coordinate effectively.[33]

Goleman et al. refer to this new empathic style of management as "affiliative" and suggest that it "represents the collaborative competence in action."[34]

The Columbia University Business School in New York City is one of a number of business schools that has introduced social intelligence pedagogy directly into its MBA curriculum. Its Program on Social Intelligence (PSI) "is organized around the psychological capabilities involved in collaborating with, motivating, and leading others" and draws together faculty from the psychology department and the business school to provide experiential opportunities, both in the classroom and in the community, to develop empathic skills.[35]

While classical economic theory states that individuals rationalize the sale of their labor power to maximize their income and profit, it turns out that most employees put a higher value on a caring boss, adding credence to the new empathic style of management. A Gallup study of more than two million employees found that workers rank "a caring boss" higher in priority than more money and benefits.[36] Similarly, a number of studies have shown that productivity at the workplace is positively correlated with an emotionally positive feeling about one's colleagues.[37]

THE NEW DREAM OF QUALITY OF LIFE

The new empathic spirit shows up most prominently in the shift in personal dreams. For a long time, the American dream, with its emphasis on personal opportunity and material success, was the gold standard to which much of the world looked for inspiration and guidance. In the twenty-first century, the emerging European dream of quality of life is beginning to attract the Net generation. Although the American dream is still the standard for many, it has lost some of its hegemony as young people turn their attention to tackling global climate change, restoring the health of the biosphere, protecting the Earth's other species, maintaining safe communities, providing universal access to health care, ensuring a high-quality and affordable universal education, living a less materialistic and more experiential lifestyle, and creating communities rich in cultural diversity. Quality of life is a shared dream that can only be realized collaboratively. While still a minority vision, held largely by a younger middle-class generation, the dream of quality of life is gaining currency among young people around the world.

The shift in emphasis from the individual to the community's well-being can be seen in the election of Barack Obama as president of the United States. Although his personal life history epitomizes the American Dream, he made a critical decision early in life, just out of law school, to take a different path. As the first black president of the *Harvard Law Review*, Obama could have written his ticket and followed generations of individual Americans before him in pursuit of personal financial success. He chose instead to become a grassroots activist in the poorest section of Chicago's South Side—in a neighborhood just blocks away from where I grew up—to improve the lot of the community.

The older American dream and the newer European dream reflect two very different ideas about human nature. The American dream puts a premium on individual autonomy and opportunity and emphasizes material self-interest as a means to secure both personal freedom and happiness. While the European dream doesn't discount personal initiative and economic opportunity, it tends to put equal weight on advancing the quality of life of the entire society. The dream is an acknowledgment that one doesn't thrive alone in autonomous isolation but, rather, in deep relationship to others in a shared social space. Quality of life emphasizes the common good as an important means to securing the happiness of each individual member of the community.

Quality of life of late has become an important factor in rethinking many of the central assumptions of twentieth-century economic theory. At the top of the list is the near obsession with recording the gross domestic product, or GDP. It has long been the compass for judging the well-being of America and other countries.

GDP was created by the U.S. Department of Commerce in the 1930s to provide a gauge for assessing the economy's recovery from the Depression. The problem with GDP is that it only measures the value of the sum total of economic goods and services generated over a twelve-month period. It does not, however, distinguish between economic activity that actually improves the quality of life of the society and negative economic activity that takes away from it. Every type of economic activity is calculated in the GDP, including the building of more prisons, enlarging the police force, military spending, spending for cleaning up pollution, increased health-care costs resulting from cigarette smoking, alcohol, and obesity, as well as the advertising spent to convince people to smoke and drink more or eat processed and fatty fast food.

Simon Kuznets, the man who invented GDP, warned in his first report to the U.S. Congress in 1934 that "[t]he welfare of a nation can . . . scarcely be inferred from a measurement of national income."[38] Thirty years later Kuznets addressed the subject of GDP's inherent limitations even more strongly writing that "[d]istinctions must be kept in mind between quantity and quality of growth. . . . Goals for 'more' growth should specify more growth of what and for what."[39]

A number of attempts have been made over the years to come up with a suitable alternative to GDP. The Index of Sustainable Economic Welfare (ISEW), the Genuine Progress Indicator (GPI), the Fordham Index of Social Health (FISH), the UN's Human Development Index (HDI), and the Index of Economic Well-Being (IEWB) are among the more popular indicators. They each attempt to determine "real" economic improvement in human welfare.

The earliest effort at establishing an alternative index was the ISEW, created by then World Bank economist Herman Daly and theologian John Cobb in 1989. Their index begins with personal consumption spending and then adds unpaid domestic labor. Then they subtract activity that is primarily designed to mitigate losses, like money spent on crime, pollution, and accidents. The ISEW also adjusts for income disparity and depletion of natural resources.[40] The GPI includes many of the same criteria but adds the value of voluntary work in the community and subtracts the loss of leisure time.[41] The FISH measures sixteen social-economic indicators, including infant mortality, child abuse, childhood poverty, teen suicide, drug abuse, high school dropout rates, average weekly earnings, unemployment, health insurance coverage, poverty among the elderly, homicides, housing, and income inequality.[42] The IEWB takes into account such things as the family savings rate and the accumulation of tangible capital such as housing stocks, which measure one's sense of future security.[43]

Both the French government and the European Commission are working on high-level studies to create quality-of-life indexes to judge the real health and well-being of the economy and the citizenry. The fact that governments are now pursuing the idea of an alternative way of measuring economic success is a good indicator of the broader social changes taking place as quality of life becomes as important as mere production output in assessing economic performance.

THE ROLE OF SOCIAL AND PUBLIC CAPITAL

Promoting a quality-of-life society requires a collaborative commitment at two levels: civic-minded engagement in the community and a willingness to have one's tax money used to promote public initiatives and services that advance the well-being of everyone in the society. Resurrecting social capital in the civil society and revitalizing public capital in the governance sector will be essential for achieving the dream of quality-of-life in every country.

Civil society is where we establish fraternal and affectionate bonds, create culture, and contribute to the social capital of the community. It is where we engage in both light and deep play with one another for the sheer joy of companionship and with the desire to make a difference in the lives of others and the well-being of the community. We volunteer our time willingly and enthusiastically, and the reward comes in the form of strengthening affiliation and intimacy. Participation in sports clubs, pursuit of the arts, assisting others in need, preserving the natural environment, mentoring the young, caring for the old, as well as promoting public works projects and initiatives are all ways we take part in the civic and cultural life of the community.

Although traditional civic engagement in fraternal organizations like the Lions Club, Kiwanis, Ruritan, and the Elks has withered with the passing of the World War II generation, there has been a surge in civic engagement in self-help groups and in collaborative types of activity in cyberspace.

While sometimes referred to as the third sector, as if to suggest that it is of less relevance than the marketplace or government, in fact, civil society is the primary sector. It's where people create the narratives that define their lives and the life of the society. These narratives create the cultural common ground that allows people to create emotional bonds of affection and trust which are the mother's milk of empathic extension.

Without culture it would be impossible to engage in either commerce and trade or governance. The other two sectors require a continuous infusion of social trust to function. Indeed, the market and government sectors feed off social trust and weaken or collapse if it is withdrawn. That's why there are no examples in history in which either markets or governments preceded culture or exist in its absence. Markets and governments are extensions of culture and never the reverse. They have always been and will always be secondary rather than primary institutions in the affairs of humanity because culture creates the empathic cloak of sociability that allows people to confidently engage each other either in the marketplace or government sphere.

Civil society organizations (CSOs), also known as nongovernmental organizations (NGOs) or not-for-profit organizations (NPOs), are proliferating on every continent. In the developed nations, where postmaterialist self-expression values are becoming a more dominant lifestyle orientation, CSOs appeal to a younger generation committed to advancing the quality of life of the community. But even in developing countries a new generation of activists are creating CSOs to further their dream of promoting a quality-of-life society. Where once young idealistic youth flocked to political parties, they now are more likely to find their way to civil society organizations, believing that building social capital—which is another way to describe a sense of collective shared empathy—precedes building political capital.

The American public school system has leaped ahead of their counterparts in other countries by initiating a critical reform in the educational system, whose purpose is to better prepare future generations for the responsibilities attendant to creating social capital.

In the past fifteen years, American secondary schools and colleges have introduced service learning programs into the school curriculum—a revolutionary change that has altered the educational experience for millions of young people. As part of the requirement for graduation, students are expected to volunteer in neighborhood nonprofit organizations and in community initiatives designed to help those in need, and to improve the well-being of the communities in which they live.

The exposure to diverse people from various walks of life has spurred an empathic surge among many of the nation's young people. Studies indicate that many—but not all—students experience a deep maturing of empathic sensibility by being thrust into unfamiliar environments where they are called upon to reach out and assist others. These experiences are often life-changing, affecting their sense of what gives their life meaning. And because service learning is an exercise in social engagement designed to advance the well-being of others and the community, it is collaborative in nature and strengthens and reinforces the collaborative emotional and cognitive skills that young people are developing and using in other parts of their life.

Service learning, as pedagogy and practice, is just beginning to spread to other countries and promises to affect the emotional and social intelligence of millions of young people in ensuing decades.

Creating quality of life requires not only a commitment of social capital but also a commitment to invest public capital to promote the common good. Europeans have long shown a willingness to tax personal incomes—in some countries as much as 45 to 50 percent—to advance the quality of life of everyone in the community.[44] That's why in Europe, health care is a public good and, as a result, infant mortality rates are lower and life expectancy is longer than in the United States. European countries also spend more public funds on assisting the poor and have lower rates of childhood poverty than the United States. Europeans also enjoy safer communities, have far lower homicide rates, and have far fewer incarcerated people. The public transport system is among the best in the world. Europeans also have the most stringent regulations in the world regarding environmental safeguards.

Until recently, Americans have not expressed the same willingness to be taxed to promote the public good of the society. The recent economic downturn, however, has undermined public confidence in the business community and opened up a new dialogue about the government's role in creating a quality-of-life society for every American.

Barack Obama's presidential campaign emphasized the need for universal health care, more public funds to advance public education, and more rigorous protection of the environment, among other public goods.

President Obama also called on the nation's youth to make a lifetime commitment to community service, signaling a new era of collaboration between the government and civil society. Obama appears to understand that reinvigorating government starts with revitalizing civil society. It's easy to see how a more collaborative generation used to social networking might feel more at home in civil society organizations that are, by their very nature, cooperative, "grassroots" oriented, and playful, and therefore far more appealing than political parties and governing institutions, which tend to concentrate power, be more competitive in nature, and instrumental in human interaction. To the extent that future generations become more skilled in creating social capital and extending empathy into more inclusive domains, it is likely that political parties and government will be made over as well to reflect the new collaborative way of thinking that is unfolding in civil society.

A quality-of-life society promotes both the market and social models simultaneously by emphasizing personal economic opportunity along with a sense of collective commitment to create a sustainable society for every citizen. In the Third Industrial Revolution, "distributive power" becomes the technological means to greatly expand entrepreneurial initiative while establishing a collaborative approach to securing the well-being of society. Empowering hundreds of millions and eventually billions of people to produce their own energy makes everyone a potential entrepreneur in a vastly extended global marketplace, but this time reconfigured from the bottom up rather than from the top down. Millions of small- and medium-size enterprises and producer cooperatives will expand commercial opportunities on a lateral scale never before experienced.

Billions of people sharing energy will require new governing policies at the local, regional, national, and transnational levels to ensure universal access to power generation and distribution and equitable dispensation of the commercial fruits of the Third Industrial Revolution. It is only by encouraging both individual entrepreneurial initiative in the distributive energy market and seamless collaboration between neighborhoods, communities, municipalities, regions, and nations in the marshalling, storing, and delivering of energy that we can create a sustainable global economy in the coming century.

Streamlining the market and social models to accommodate a distributed and collaborative Third Industrial Revolution will be the pressing political agenda for the next half-century as governments transition to a new dream of creating a quality-of-life society in a biosphere world.

In the distributed capitalist economy, where collaboration trumps competition, access rights become as important as property rights and quality of life figures as prominently as the desire for personal financial success, empathic sensibility has room to breathe and thrive. It is no longer so constrained by hierarchies, boundaries of exclusion, and a concept of human nature that places acquisitiveness, self-interest, and utility at the center of the human experience.

FOURTEEN

The Theatrical Self in an Improvisational Society

A NEW DRAMATURGICAL consciousness is beginning to emerge among the millennial youth, the first generation to grow up on the Internet and live in the collaborative social spaces that exist all along the World Wide Web. The new consciousness goes hand in hand with the distributed communication and energy regime of the Third Industrial Revolution, just as psychological consciousness accompanied the Second Industrial Revolution and ideological consciousness attended the First Industrial Revolution.

The new dramaturgical consciousness shows early signs of propelling a younger generation to global cosmopolitanism and a universal empathic sensibility. The problem is that the same communications technology revolution that is paving the way toward global consciousness has a dark side that could derail the journey and sidetrack the Internet generation into a dead-end corridor of rampant narcissism, endless voyeurism, and overwhelming ennui.

Dramaturgical consciousness flows directly out of psychological consciousness and represents a universalization of the role-playing experimentation that began with Moreno's theory and practice of psychodrama and that found expression in the T-groups, encounter groups, and self-help groups of the last half of the twentieth century. While the baby-boom generation experimented with role-playing as a therapeutic technique, in their adult years they integrated the practice into their parenting styles, spawning the first generation in history to grow up with a dramaturgical frame of mind. Role-playing is no longer a therapeutic technique but, rather, a form of consciousness for Generation X and the Millennial Generation.

The shift in consciousness reflects the shift in communications from first-generation centralized electricity to second-generation distributed electricity. The whole world might well be a stage, but during the twentieth century most of the people were in the audience, whereas in the twenty-first century everyone is onstage and in front of the spotlights, thanks to YouTube, MySpace, Facebook, the blogosphere, et al.

The advent of the movies, radio, and television created the first mass audiences in history. Millions of people crowded into giant movie houses or huddled at home around the family radio, and later the television set, watching and listening to a select number of highly stylized and carefully choreographed stories that plumbed the depths of human emotion and sentiment from tragedy to farce. The channels of communication were centralized and the story lines flowed from the top down. Millions of people became passive audiences, in the sense that they had no way to interact directly with those on the screen or in the studio.

Still, they weren't completely passive. While they couldn't talk back and affect the actors—although in Woody Allen's spoof *The Purple Rose of Cairo*, the actors came off the screen and into the audience while members of the audience climbed up and onto the screen to engage the actors—audiences did create relationships of a sort with the actors through engagement in parasocial relationships.

The parasocial relationship was first examined in a landmark paper written by Donald Horton and Richard Wohl in the journal *Psychiatry* in 1956. They noticed that radio and television "give the illusion of face-to-face relationship with the performer" and that the more radio and television actors adjust their acting to "the supposed response of the audience, the more the audience tends to make the response anticipated."[1] Although the viewer could not carry on a dialogue in the normal sense of the term, he or she did create a shadow dialogue of sorts.

Early television talk show hosts like Dave Garroway, on NBC's *Today,* and Steve Allen, on *The Tonight Show*, engaged in small talk with their audiences, with close-up shots making it appear as if they were talking directly to the individual viewer on the other side of the screen.

Garroway later observed that when he was on air, he would often say

> whatever came into my mind. I was introspective. I tried to
> pretend that I was chatting with a friend . . . I consciously
> tried to talk to the listener as an individual, to make each
> listener feel that he knew me and I knew him. It seemed to
> work pretty well . . . I know that strangers often stop me on
> the street today, call me Dave and seem to feel that we are old
> friends who know all about each other.[2]

Radio listeners, and later television viewers, began to develop a virtual relationship with the radio and television hosts. The on-air radio and television personalities became a regular part of the listeners' and viewers' lives, often sharing intimate details of their own lives on air.

Horton and Wohl speculated that the enactment of parasocial roles by millions of radio listeners and television viewers might serve as a training ground by which people explore new relationships, if only vicariously, outside their normal everyday realms.

Soap operas, for example, were avidly watched—and still are—by millions of women with an eye toward seeing how others handle their day-to-day romantic and familial relationships. Horton and Wohl note that

> In this culture, it is evident that to be prepared to meet
> all the exigencies of a changing social situation, no matter
> how limited it may be, could—and often does—require a
> great stream of plays and stories, advice columns and social

how-to-do-it books. What, after all, is soap opera but an
interminable exploration of the contingencies to be met with
in "home life?"[3]

Today, parasocial relationships have become part of everyone's
lives—we often chat about our favorite actors, TV hosts, and other personalities as if they were intimate friends whose lives intersect with our
own. Although, in a sense, this ought to be regarded as pathological
behavior, even delusional, we have come to accept it as quite normal.
The important point to emphasize is that even more so than novels of
the eighteenth and nineteenth centuries, movies, radio, and TV allow
millions of people to suspend disbelief and slip into roles and try on
new personas. Young people, in particular, will take on the persona
of their favorite performers—hairstyles, clothes, vocabulary, and even
their swagger—and even begin to act as if they were either them or
in ways that they imagine would be acceptable and attractive to their
on-screen heroes and heroines. Taking on such roles and developing
a vicarious intimacy with on-air performers is a way for viewers to
practice passing over traditional social barriers and gaining a new sense
of social mobility. Most important, parasocial relationships allow millions of people to be exposed to the stories of diverse others in a range
of unique environments—even if they are fictional in character. The
parasocial relationships, in effect, become a classroom for exploring a
range of emotional responses to the plight or circumstance of others
and enlarging one's empathic repertoire.

The Internet revolution transformed parasocial relationships to
peer-to-peer relationships. The shift from centralized top down, one-
to-many connections to flat, open-source, many-to-many connections
allowed a new generation to be the actors in their own scripts and to
share a global stage with two billion other like-minded thespians—all
performing for and with one another. Now the world truly is a stage
and everyone is an actor. But Andy Warhol's quip that everyone will
get their fifteen minutes of fame has had to be amended. Today millions of people spend a lifetime role playing and performing for each
other on the World Wide Web. Hundreds of millions of young people,

equipped with webcams, Skype, cell phone cameras, video recorders, and the like are acting out their lives for one another—and experimenting with new roles and personas in the largest continuous performance in history.

Young people today are in front of the screen or on the screen, spending much of their waking day in virtual worlds where they are scripting multiple stories, directing their own performances, and choreographing virtually every aspect of their lives—hoping that millions of others will log on and follow along. "Mass intimacy" may no longer qualify as an oxymoron, at least for the millennial generation.

The great success of reality TV is a reflection of the new dramaturgical consciousness—ordinary people living out their lives, although with sufficient scripting to assure the audience's attention. Even here, the traditional top-down flow of communication so characteristic of the TV medium has bent to a high degree of interactivity and feedback. In popular reality TV shows like *American Idol*, the TV audience gets to weigh in by text message to help shape the direction and story line. The dramaturgical age is upon us.

Moreno could never have imagined psychodrama on a planetary scale. Nor could the early theorists of dramaturgical consciousness have guessed that one day the dramaturgical frame of mind would come to be so thoroughly internalized and externalized that a generation of young people would come to think of themselves as actors playing roles during most of their waking hours.

The dramaturgical perspective was advanced in the 1950s just as television was coming of age. Many of the early theorists, like Kenneth Burke, Erving Goffman, and Robert Perinbanayagam, came from the field of sociology. The more they observed human behavior in social settings, the more apparent it became to them that many, if not most, of the operating conventions and techniques used in theater are used both consciously and often unconsciously in day-to-day social situations. In other words, art imitates life if only in a more consciously contrived and highly scripted way.

Kenneth Burke introduced the notion of dramatism, a radical new approach to analyzing and understanding human behavior based on the principles of drama and theater.

It was Erving Goffman, however, who first applied the dramaturgical metaphor in a scientifically rigorous fashion to human behavior. In his book *The Presentation of Self in Everyday Life*, published in 1959—at the height of the TV era—Goffman suggested that everyone's life is, in reality, lived out dramaturgically, whether they are conscious of the fact or not. He cites W. F. Whyte's prescient observation about how a skilled waitress goes about winning over a customer and taking charge of the encounter. She has to establish the proper first impression when the curtain rises by taking command of the situation and assuring compliance with her script, while eliciting gratitude on the part of the customer when the final curtain comes down.[4]

Goffman calls social situations "encounters"—a term shortly thereafter taken up by humanist psychologists. He goes on to identify the key features of the dramaturgical encounter. First, there is the performance itself, which he defines as "all the activity of a given participant on a given occasion which serves to influence in any way any of the other participants."[4] The established pattern of behavior, which a performer plays out during the performance, is a role or part. By part, Goffman means conveying the impression that the performer "possesses the attributes he appears to possess, [and] that the task he performs will have the consequences that are implicitly claimed for it."[5] In other words, the performer's part needs to be believable. He needs to appear sincere.

Goffman observes that professionals of every kind—doctors, lawyers, scientists, accountants—not to mention salesman, secretaries, and clerks, take on a persona that reflects the expectations others have of how they should handle themselves. Their performance is part and parcel of their proficiency—their professional demeanor—and if they stray too far from the accepted script, they risk losing credibility and clients, bosses, and customers.

What young person hasn't experienced the embarrassing situation of running into a teacher in a social situation and been utterly taken aback by their out-of-context behavior and unsure of exactly how to relate to them? William James caught the dramaturgical nature of human behavior a good half century before the theorists of dramaturgical consciousness came on the scene. With every individual

> we may practically say that he has as many different social
> selves as there are distinct *groups* of persons about whose
> opinion he cares. He generally shows a different side of himself
> to each of these different groups. Many a youth who is demure
> enough before his parents and teachers, swears and swaggers
> like a pirate among his "tough" young friends. We do not
> show ourselves to our children as to our club companions, to
> our customers as to the laborers we employ, to our masters and
> employers as to our intimate friends.[6]

Goffman believed that all intentional social behavior is theatrical in nature. He noted that in every performance, the actors rehearse "backstage"—usually in their mind—and then perform "onstage" where they deliver their lines. When we reflect on our own social intercourse over the course of a day, we quickly begin to note how much time we devote to rehearsing what we are going to say and how we are going to deliver our lines before doing so, even if it's just for a fleeting moment when we are thinking about the next line we are going to utter and the appropriate gestures and body language that should accompany it.

Dramaturgical consciousness becomes almost a necessity in a complex, interconnected, high-speed civilization. If life is the acting out of countless personal and collective social dramas, then the more complex the economic and social networks in which one is embedded, the more diverse roles each person is called on to play.

In the dramaturgical way of looking at human behavior, the self is no longer a private possession of an individual, as John Locke would have us believe but, rather, says Goffman, "a sense given to [a person] by the very people he wishes to share it with." The self, then, is not an entity, say Dennis Brissett and Charles Edgley in their book *Life as Theatre*, but rather "a kind of fictional, constructed, consensually validated quality" that results from the interaction and communication between people.[7] If so, then one's very being in the world depends on acting out scripts onstage with other players, each of whom validates a part of one's selfhood. This view is quite different from Hegel's notion that each person's unique self is both imprinted in and manifested by the possessions he or she acquires over a lifetime.

Clearly, dramaturgists do not see their methodology as a mere metaphor for explaining the sociology of human behavior. They believe that life itself is in fact deeply dramaturgical. Robert Perinbanayagam makes the point that "it is not that reality is theatrical or dramatic; rather what is considered reality by society, or part thereof, is theatrically realized and constructed."[8] The reason why, writes Perinbanayagam, is that dramatism

> takes off from the premise that humans cannot help but communicate with symbols, on the one hand, and [we] cannot help but be aware that the others around us are interpreting the world around them. . . . The world consists of communication-worthy social facts or social objects that dramatistically develop and present a theme . . . the theatre, then, is not something apart from society . . . Rather it is a crystallization and typification of what goes on in society all the time—or more sharply, what a social relationship in fact is.[9]

Even our possessions, argues Perinbanayagam, become part of the larger dramas we act out. We surround ourselves with material objects and continually rearrange them in various ways, "converting them into symbols so as to elicit particular responses from others," says Perinbanayagam. They become what Goffman calls part of "the presentation of a self."[10]

The dramaturgical perspective places communications at the heart of human activity, redefines the self in relational terms, makes experience itself a theatrical affair, and transforms property into symbols that help people act out their many dramatic roles as they flit in and out of networks of lived experiences, each representing a different aspect of their life story. The dramaturgical perspective is, in the final analysis, a vivid description of the state of mind that accompanies a generation that is continually shifting identities, roles, scripts, and stage settings as it toggles between social and commercial networks, both in virtual and real space.

The dramaturgical view of human behavior has become so acceptable as a way of explaining human nature that when theatrical conventions and techniques are introduced into professional training practices and learning to become a skilled actor becomes an intimate part of one's career development, few express any disapproval. That has not always been the case.

Several years ago, the *British Medical Journal* published a controversial article suggesting that doctors engage in theatrical performance every time they interact with their patients and, that being the case, they ought to be as well versed in the proper theatrical conventions as they are in their medical training if they are to properly dispatch their duties. Drs. Hillel Finestone and David Conter of the University of Western Ontario observe that:

> If a physician does not possess the necessary skills to assess
> a patient's emotional needs . . . and to display clear and
> effective responses to those needs, the job is not done.
> Consequently, we believe that medical training should
> include an acting curriculum, focused on the conveying of
> appropriate, beneficial responses to those emotional needs.[11]

Today directors and actors have found a new gig preparing professionals in the appropriate theatrical techniques for improving their "performance" on the job.

The advocates of dramaturgical training argue that the traditional way of understanding behavior in organizational settings relies too heavily on mechanistic metaphors and is too wedded to an outdated notion of human nature as strictly rational, utilitarian, and self-interested. What's lost is the very social nature of human interaction. People are storytellers and act out their lives in highly dramatic ways that can best be analyzed, understood, and modified using theatrical techniques and conventions.

Leading business schools like the Kellogg Graduate School of Management at Northwestern University and the Columbia Business School have introduced dramaturgical principles into their Advanced Management programs. Professional actors and directors coach business executives in the art of theatrical presentation and engage them in intensive role-playing sessions to familiarize them with how to use drama techniques to elicit the desired response from coworkers and clients.

Nor does theatrical training stop upon graduation. Companies have introduced dramaturgical techniques into every aspect of their operations, from human resources management to marketing. Scripted performances using professional actors are often used as a device to engage employees around a certain problem, for example sexual harassment at the workplace. Employees are also encouraged to co-create their own scripts and act out various scenarios from different perspectives and vantage points. Improvisational theater is also increasingly used to help employees "experiment with successful ways of 'performing,'" especially when confronted by unpredictable circumstances and events that were never included in the training manuals or case studies.[12] Collective script writing and the improv experience are highly collaborative ventures and help hone the new collaborative way of working that is becoming the norm in a distributed network world.

Nick Nissley, executive director for The Banff Centre's Leadership Development programs, emphasizes the often unstated but important feature of all theatrical performances. Anyone who has ever acted in, directed, stage-managed, or otherwise taken part in theatrical performances knows that they are always collaborative experiences. The intimacy, camaraderie, and collective creativity that go into a theater production are what draw so many individuals to the theater experience. Nissley et al. write:

> *Thus, no one has complete control over the professional theatre performance—it is, by definition, a collaboration.* The playwright

can only exercise so much control; while the actors bring alive what they will, they do not have infinite choice, but instead, must create a reality within the script. The audience will make sense of the performance in their own way. *For organizational theatre interventions and training, this means that we must recognize that the performance's meaning is jointly constructed and will reflect a variety of interests.*[13]

The principles of theater and the theory and practice of dramaturgy are finding their way into virtually every field. Entrepreneurs who have to tell the story of something that doesn't yet exist as if it did in order to spark the imagination of investors and clients have to be able to use dramatic license to make their case. Their audience needs to "suspend disbelief"—which is what theater is all about—and actually place themselves in the fictional setting the entrepreneur has created and experience the proposed venture as if it were real.[14]

BEING AUTHENTIC

Dramaturgical consciousness raises the troublesome question of authenticity. Whenever the question of performance comes up, it inevitably leads to the related question of pretending versus believing.

In the age of mythical consciousness, being heroic was the measure of a man, while in the age of theological consciousness, one was expected to be pious, and in the age of ideological consciousness, men of goodwill were expected to be sincere and of good character. In the age of psychological consciousness, being personable became an obsession. For the generation growing up in a dramaturgical consciousness, however, being authentic becomes the test of a man or woman.

If human beings are, by their very nature, dramaturgical, then how do we establish the idea of authenticity? If everyone is always consciously, or even unconsciously, playing out multiple roles with different scripts and on different stages, how do we know who the authentic person is behind all of the masks?

The issue of authenticity is increasingly being raised in professional circles. For example, while the clergy has long been aware of the theatrical nature of pastoral care, it is only very recently that the profession has begun a spirited debate on what dramaturgical conventions can tell us about artificiality versus authenticity. Pastoral psychology professor Reinard Nauta addresses the critical question of clerical performance and authenticity by suggesting that

> [t]he dilemma of artificiality and authenticity can possibly
> be solved by pretending one believes in the performance one
> gives. In doing so, one brings about a reality that is grounded
> in faith in one's performance.[15]

Nauta observes that like many types of drama in which the aim is to achieve an emotional catharsis in the audience, the pastor's role before the congregation is often similarly construed.

> It is the kind of drama in which personal problems are acted
> out on stage in a stylized, recognizable, and substitute fashion,
> and in which, by identifying with the actors, emotions can be
> expressed that would not otherwise have found a way out.[16]

The various theatrical devices the pastors use "bear the ideals, fantasies, desires, and fears of their followers" and become "the containers of other people's feelings."[17]

To be effective at what he does, however, that is—to bring out the feelings of his parishioners and allow them to reflect on their emotions and behavior and respond appropriately to the catharsis—the pastor needs to engage in the theatrical conceit. It becomes a contrivance that makes an authentic response by members of the congregation possible. In other words the pastor's very performance, even though it is make-believe, becomes instrumental to creating authentic responses. "Make believe, to act as if, [and] performance and play are the basis of any liberating communication, even for pastors who wish to be authentic," according to Nauta.[18]

The question of authenticity is brought up whenever the dramaturgical theory of conscious behavior is used to describe how people act in social situations. Quite simply, there is the disquieting feeling that human behavior, if it is truly dramaturgical, is not very honest. After all, in one sense, theater without deceit is an impossibility. In another sense, however, taking on different masks—personas—in different situations might be an authentic expression of one aspect of a person's identity. That is, if each of us is in fact a composite of multiple personalities, then the question is if we were true to the specific role we played at the moment.

Again, the theater offers a way to distinguish between pure deceit, on the one hand, and active imagination on the other hand. While deceit is universally disparaged, active imagination is lauded as essential to creating a sense of self and world and forming mature bonds of empathy. Theater theorists like Constantin Stanislavski talk about surface acting versus deep acting. The first relies on the art of deceit, the second on the art of imagination. Surface acting is form over substance, while deep acting emanates from deep inside the performer's subconscious.

With surface acting, the performer uses grand gestures, modulated tones, and exaggerated movements to "portray" a character, but puts nothing of his own life into the part . . . it's all technique. Stanislavski says of surface acting,

> [its] form is more interesting than its content. It acts more on
> your sense of sound and sight than on your soul. Consequently
> it is more likely to delight than to move you. . . . Only what
> can be accomplished through surprising theatrical beauty
> or picturesque pathos lies within the bounds of this art. But
> delicate and deep human feelings are not subject to such
> technique. They call for natural emotions at the very moment
> in which they appear before you in the flesh. They call for the
> direct cooperation of nature itself.[19]

In other words, with surface acting, the actor is acting as if he had feeling but not really feeling as he is acting. True deep acting, by contrast, which Stanislavski terms method acting, comes about when the actor reaches into his own subconscious and semiconscious memory and searches for an analogous past emotional experience that he might draw upon that would allow him to feel as if he were experiencing the emotional state of the character he is playing.

Stanislavski cautioned actors not to simply try to evoke a feeling de novo, saying that is not the way emotions are generated in real life. He writes,

> On the stage there cannot be, under any circumstances, action which is directed immediately at the arousing of a feeling for its own sake . . . Never seek to be jealous, or to make love, or to suffer for its own sake.[20]

Stanislavski points out that all feelings have a history—they are the result of past embodied experiences. Therefore, deep acting requires the actor to induce his own subconscious and remember how he felt and the emotions he conjured up in similar situations.

> The aim of the actor's preparation is to cross the threshold of the subconscious. . . . Beforehand we have "true-seeming feeling," afterwards "sincerity of emotion."[21]

Remembering experiences emotionally is important in calling them forth in the future. Stanislavski asks his actors to train themselves to think of their feelings as an object as well as an experience, with the thought that they might be called up and used at a future time.

The memory of a past feeling, however, only becomes valuable to an actor if he can harness it with his imagination and act as if that feeling were happening again in the execution of his role. He must feel the role he is playing as if he were that person.

With deep acting, an actor becomes transformed for a brief period of time and emotionally becomes what he is portraying. But when his performance ends, the part ends as well. In real life, we all engage in deep acting as well, but with a different modus operandi—affecting the reality of our relationships with others. In real life, deep acting has real-life consequences.

A study conducted by sociologist Albert Cohen of college students training to be counselors at a camp for emotionally disturbed children shows how the deep acting method, when applied to the real world, can have empathic real-life consequences.

First, senior counselors gave the trainees a brief background on the children who would be under their care and how they should perceive them.

> They were expected to see the children as victims of
> uncontrollable impulses somehow related to their harsh and
> depriving backgrounds, and in need of enormous doses of
> kindliness and indulgence in order to break down their images
> of the adult world as hateful and hostile.[22]

After providing context, the trainees were then counseled on how to feel toward the children.

> The clinician must never respond in anger or with intent
> to punish, although he might sometimes have to restrain or
> even isolate children in order to prevent them from hurting
> themselves or one another. Above all, the staff were expected
> to be warm and loving and always to be governed by a
> "clinical attitude."[23]

In their relationship with the children, the young counselors were cautioned not to conjure up possible negative past feelings that might be analogous to the situation they might face with a particularly difficult child. For example, "Tommy reminds me of the terrible brat I had to babysit when I was thirteen, and if he's like that I'll end up hating him." Rather, the new counselors were encouraged to think of another past feeling that might put a positive emotional spin on the situation at hand. For example,

Tommy is really like the other kid I used to babysit when
I was fourteen. He was difficult but I got to like him, so I
expect I'll get to like Tommy despite the way he pushes me
away suspiciously.[24]

The exercise in deep acting was remarkably successful. Cohen
reports that

[t]o an extraordinary degree they fulfilled these expectations,
including, I am convinced, the expectation that they *feel*
sympathy and tenderness and love toward their charges, despite
their animal-like behavior. The speed with which these
college students learned to behave in this way cannot be easily
explained in terms of gradual learning through a slow process
of "internalization."[25]

In her book *The Managed Heart*, Arlie Russell Hochschild reports
on her study of Delta Airlines flight attendant training courses, where
personnel were instructed in the proper emotional engagement with
passengers. While the flight attendant training was purely instructional
and did not involve attendants in deep acting, the attendants themselves
reported that they often did so, on their own, when on the job.

A flight attendant might psych herself up before putting on the
"happy face" by conjuring up past experiences that made her feel
happy and bring those feelings to the job. One flight attendant told
Hochschild that conjuring up a happy feeling and taking on a happy
demeanor invariably has a positive feedback effect.

If I pretend I'm feeling really up, sometimes I actually get into
it. The passenger responds to me as though I were friendly,
and then more of me responds back.[26]

Another flight attendant said that when she's dealing with a passenger who's been drinking too much or getting obnoxious,

I try to remember that if he's drinking too much, he's probably scared of flying. I think to myself, "He's like a little child." Really, that's what he is. And when I see him that way, I don't get mad that he's yelling at me. He's like a child yelling at me then.[27]

Hochschild raises the very legitimate concern that acting is increasingly being used as a training technique to prepare a service-oriented workforce on how to manage their feelings to optimize commercial relationships in an experiential economy. That's true, but it is also true that deep acting provides a theory and technique to help train individuals to be more mindful of their own feelings, to keep a firm memory of them, and to improve their ability to conjure up those memories from their subconscious and to harness them to their imagination when the occasion arises, so that they might experience another's plight as if it were their own. Deep acting, when used for the appropriate pro-social ends, is a powerful mental tool to stimulate empathic feelings. And empathy, as we discussed in Chapter 5, is the means by which we participate in deeper realms of reality, for reality is the shared understandings we create about the world by dint of the relationships into which we enter.

Deep acting, then, can prepare people to extend the empathic bond and, with it, deepen one's sense of reality—a far cry from surface acting, which conjures up only facsimiles in form and deceit in execution.

Meryl Streep, arguably the world's greatest living actress and a master of deep acting, once remarked that "[t]he great gift of human beings is that we have the power of empathy."[28]

THE RELATIONAL SELF
IN AN INTERCONNECTED WORLD

What does dramaturgical consciousness tell us about the psyche of the millennial generation? Many psychologists—perhaps most—agree that in a diverse, complex, interconnected world of increasing novelty and fast-changing contexts, with children growing up in both cyberspace and real space, and in both a parallel and linear temporality, multiple role-playing and myriad identities are becoming the norm. They disagree as to whether dramaturgical consciousness is necessarily leading to an advance in consciousness or possibly a disintegration.

Kenneth J. Gergen acknowledges that in a globalizing world that is connected at the speed of light, "[w]e engage in greater numbers of relationships, in a greater variety of forms, and with greater intensities than ever before."[29] We are awash in relationships, some virtual, others real. Where privacy was the coveted value of a bourgeois generation which defined freedom in terms of autonomy and exclusivity, access is the most sought after value of the Millennial Generation, which defines freedom in terms of the depth and scope of one's relationships. Exclusivity has become less important than inclusivity, and the competitive ethos is beginning to be challenged—albeit tentatively—by an ethos of collaboration.

In the era of dramaturgical consciousness, where one's very identity is relational and exists only to the extent one is embedded in a plethora of relationships, to be denied access is to be isolated and to cease to exist. Alone time—as distinguished from being lonely—continues to shrink and is already approaching near zero in a 24/7 interconnected world. In a time-starved society, every spare nanosecond becomes an opportunity to make "another connection."

We live in a world in which getting and holding one another's attention becomes paramount, and relationships of all kinds become central to our existence. Descartes's dictum "I think, therefore I am" and the humanist psychologist dictum "I participate, therefore I am" have been replaced by a new dictum, "I am connected, therefore I exist."

The old idea of "mine versus thine," which fostered the sense of a predictable "one-dimensional self," is giving way to the new idea of inclusivity and a "multidimensional self." Gergen observes:

> The relatively coherent and unified sense of self inherent in
> a traditional culture gives way to manifold and competing
> potentials. A multiphrenic condition emerges in which

one swims in ever-shifting, concatenating, and contentious currents of being.[30]

Like improv artists caught up in ever-changing contexts and fast-moving story lines, each vying for our attention, we are forced to shift into new roles and switch back and forth between different sets and scripts so quickly that we risk slowly losing ourselves in the labyrinthine network of short-lived and ever-changing connections and experiences in which we find ourselves embedded. Gergen warns that,

> This fragmentation of self-conceptions corresponds to a multiplicity of incoherent and disconnected relationships. These relationships pull us in myriad directions, inviting us to play such a variety of roles that the very concept of an "authentic self" with knowable characteristics recedes from view. The fully saturated self becomes no self at all.[31]

Gergen worries that in the new world unfolding,

> the self vanishes fully into a stage of relatedness. . . . [O]ne ceases to believe in a self independent of the relationships in which he or she is embedded . . . thus placing relationships in the central position occupied by the individual self for the last several hundred years of Western history.[32]

Most postmodern thinkers welcome the new sense of a relational self, suggesting that by breaking down the barriers of "mine versus thine," we open up the possibility of a more tolerant, multicultural approach to socialization in the twenty-first century. Jean Baudrillard, for one, sees an unfolding globalized society in which "our private sphere has ceased to be the stage where the drama of the subject at odds with his objects . . . is played out." We no longer exist as subjects at all, argues Baudrillard, but, rather, "as terminals of multiple networks."[33]

Robert J. Lifton has another take on the shift in consciousness. Lifton believes that dramaturgical consciousness—having multiple personas— is a coping mechanism, a way for the psyche to accommodate the escalating demands being placed on it in the emerging hyper-real global society. Lifton argues that playing roles and having multiple personas, far from representing the disappearance of self, is really a more plastic and mature stage of consciousness—one in which a person is able to live with ambiguities and complex and often competing priorities. Being able to live and experience as many potential realities as possible, sometimes even at the same time, says Lifton, requires a protean consciousness.[34]

Gergen seems to share some common ground with Lifton, but with reservations. It's not that Gergen is pessimistic about where human consciousness is heading. He would agree with the philosopher Martin Buber's analysis of human nature. Buber believed that "[i]n the beginning is the relationship."[35] Gergen sees a complex globalizing world in which human beings are becoming increasingly embedded in relationships of every style and kind. His concern is that the relational demands on our attention and psyche could overwhelm our individual and collective consciousness and plunge identity into chaos.

Gergen raises an important qualification that dramaturgical theorists often ignore or skirt. That is, that the dramaturgical way of thinking is unique to the modern age. He notes that,

> The sense of "playing a role" depends for its palpability on the contrasting sense of a "real self." If there is no consciousness of what it is to be "true to self," there is no meaning to "playing a role."[36]

By the time Shakespeare wrote that "All the world's a stage, /And all the men and women merely players," the self was already developed enough to understand when it was playing a role—the mind could separate itself sufficiently from its behavior to consciously take on a persona or mask and know that it was doing so. Today the self has to take on so many new roles and continually shift from role to role so quickly that it runs the risk of withering away altogether.

As the dramaturgical self becomes even more plastic and thespian and such behavior comes to be thought of as normal, the very idea of authenticity recedes in importance. To be "authentic" presupposes an immutable core self, an autonomous psyche. In the era of dramaturgical consciousness, however,

> [t]he pastiche personality is a social chameleon, constantly borrowing bits and pieces of identity from whatever sources are available and constructing them as useful or desirable in a given situation.[37]

The dramaturgical self, then, is open to two very different interpretations. Sociologist Louis Zurcher suggests that if we abandon the idea of the self as "an object" and think of it more as "a process," then the self is open "to the widest possible experience"[38] and becomes truly cosmopolitan.

But Zurcher also warns that the mutable self can just as easily lead to a more pronounced narcissism, as individuals lose a sense of an authentic self to which they are beholden and accountable and become mired in deceit after deceit—a Machiavellian existence—where role-playing becomes instrumental to advancing endless self-gratification.

Gergen, in the final analysis, appears guardedly optimistic about the future of human consciousness. He holds out hope that in an increasingly interconnected and collaborative world, made up of ever more embedded relationships that transcend traditional boundaries that separate "mine from thine," that "we can move from a self-centered system of beliefs to consciousness of an inseparable relatedness with others"—I and thou.[39] That's possible, but only if we retain a sufficient sense of self as an "I" to allow the empathic impulse to grow.

While each of us is a composite of the relationships that makes us up, it is the unique constellation of relational experiences that separate one person from another. There is no inherent contradiction in believing that the self is made up of the sum total of experiences that an individual is embedded in over a lifetime, and the idea that those same embedded relationships and experiences make one a unique being, different from all others. It is only by keeping that distinction in mind that empathic consciousness can continue to grow and become the psychic and social glue for a global consciousness.

If the sense of self as a unique ensemble of relationships is lost, and one becomes only a "we," empathy is lost and the historical progression toward global consciousness dies. That's because empathic awareness is born out of the sense that others, like ourselves, are unique, mortal beings. When we empathize with another, it's because we recognize her fragile finite nature, her vulnerability, and her one and only life. We experience her existential aloneness and her personal plight and her struggle to be and succeed as if it were our own. Our empathic embrace is our way of rooting for her and celebrating her life.

If we fall prey to an undifferentiated global "we," we may find ourselves back to square one, when we lived in an undifferentiated mythological fog, with little sense of self and only a rudimentary sense of empathic distress built into our biology. Maintaining a dialectic balance between an ever more differentiated sense of self, embedded in an ever more integrated relational web that encompasses the world, is the critical test that might well determine the future prospects for our survival as a species.

More Attached in Social Networks

The evidence suggests that the new dramaturgical consciousness emerging in the very early stages of the shift into a Third Industrial Revolution and a new distributed capitalism is leading both to a greater sense of relatedness and empathic extension as well as a more fractured sense of self, and increased narcissism.

The first question to ask is whether the new distributed forms of communications technology do create greater social interconnectivity and relatedness? For years critics warned that increasing time spent in cyberspace in virtual reality meant less time spent in nurturing real face-to-face social relationships. The fear was that while the Internet connected more people in networks, the new social affiliations would be less intimate and more superficial than those garnered in traditional face-to-face social discourse. Accumulating data in recent years suggests that these concerns were, by and large, ill-founded. In fact, the opposite is the case.

The Pew Internet and American Life Project's 2007 report found that social relationships and the sense of community are not "fading away in America" but growing, although in nontraditional ways. Social affiliations are increasingly shifting from extended family relationships and engagement in neighborhood-based organizations to "social networks," bringing together people of like-minded interests that transcend geography.

> Because individuals—rather than households—are separately connected, the Internet and the cell phone have transformed communication from house to house to person to person.[40]

The Pew survey asked people about how their Internet involvement affected both their core ties and significant ties. Core ties are with people to whom one has close, intimate relationships, while significant ties were defined as those with people to whom one is somewhat closely connected.

What the Pew survey found is that contrary to the concerns of critics, the more contact individuals had by e-mail, the more in-person and phone contact they had, suggesting that "Americans are probably more in contact with members of their communities and social networks than before the advent of the internet."[41] A total of 31 percent of the respondents in the Pew survey reported that engagement on the Internet increased the size of their social networks while only 2 percent said it decreased them. Overall, Internet users boast "somewhat larger social networks than nonusers."[42]

Pew also wanted to know whether online network relationships created as much social capital—people helping one another—as local churches and fraternal organizations performed in the past. In other words, has civic involvement waxed or waned? Pew found that civic engagement remains high, but much of it takes place outside of geographic boundaries and up in cyberspace. Online self-help networks, support groups, chat rooms, and listservs are increasingly becoming the new public square where people connect up and come to each other's mutual aid.[43]

Increased Internet use assists users in maintaining existing social ties, often strengthening them, while helping users forge new social ties. It has not, as some critics had previously warned, been at the expense of having less time available for face-to-face interaction with core and significant ties. Rather, the additional time spent online reduced the time spent on unsocial activities like TV and sleeping.[44]

A related survey showed that more frequent communications via Internet text messaging encourages the desire to spend more time face-to-face. Researchers found that the reason lies not only in the frequency of staying in contact but also the nature of the medium and the way it is used. Text messaging requires a more careful crafting of communiqués than telephone or face-to-face communications and, therefore, encourages more intimate exchange. And because Internet messaging is often done at home, often late at night, there is a greater tendency to share more private matters than one might in more public situations.[45] "Three in ten teens say they can share more with a friend online" and 29 percent say "that they are more honest when they talk to friends online."[46]

Perhaps the most interesting finding about Internet use is that it seems to bring out a person's "true self" more than do face-to-face social encounters. Psychologists talk about actual selves, ideal selves, and true selves. The actual self is the one we show to others and the ideal self is the one we aspire to be, while the true self is who we really perceive ourselves to be. This actual self is often not revealed to others for fear of becoming more vulnerable or risking rejection.

Years ago MIT sociologist Sherry Turkle suggested, on the basis of her early pioneering work, that the relative anonymity afforded by cyberspace encouraged people to experiment with other aspects of their selves by taking on personas and roles that one might feel less comfortable exploring in real-time social encounters. This kind of disclosure via role-playing amounts to a kind of "dramaturgical outing" of one's previously undisclosed personas.

Disclosing more of the true self to others is critical to creating intimacy and bonds of empathy. It's only by being open and vulnerable, sharing our inner being, our plight, and our struggle to be that we establish empathic bonds. If then it is found that the medium of the Internet helps facilitate a disclosure of one's true self to others and fosters the establishment of empathic bonds and relationships with others, then a powerful case can be made that this new form of communications can advance empathic awareness to new heights.

Studies have revealed that the Internet does just that. Laboratory experiments have shown that "the relative anonymity of Internet interactions greatly reduces the risks" of personal disclosures, "especially about intimate aspects of the self, because one can share one's inner beliefs and emotional reactions with much less fear of disapproval and sanction."[47]

Equally important, researchers have found that initial contact on the Internet encourages "greater self-disclosure" because of the lack of gating features that often block the development of a closer relationship, especially physical appearance and stigmas like stuttering, shyness, anxiety, and other perceived social deficits.[48] On the Internet, these "first impressions" are absent, allowing the parties to reveal themselves to each other and begin creating a relationship.

Finally, the Internet helps people of like-minded interests to find one another more easily. Sharing similar interests is a comfortable entry point to get to know one another and develop a relationship. The Internet literally allows hundreds of millions of people to locate those of similar interest quickly and effortlessly, and in ways that were never before possible, giving them a door open to new relationships that might otherwise only occur by chance in normal social discourse. The Internet also allows individuals who are locked into routines—

work, single parenting, et cetera—that limit their exposure to new relationships to find them in cyberspace.

A study done by New York University psychology professor Katelyn McKenna found that

> the more people express facets of the self on the Internet that they cannot or do not express in other areas of life, the more likely they are to form strong attachments to those they meet on the Internet.[49]

Moreover, their online relationships develop faster compared to their non-Internet relationships. They also tend to bring their new online friendships into more personal contact through phone conversations, exchanging letters and photos and personal meetings. And because online disclosures about one's true self helps kindle more intimacy, those relationships tend to result in more romantic real-time relationships, including marriages.

Sixty-three percent of respondents to the McKenna survey had spoken by phone to someone they met on the Internet, "56% had exchanged pictures of themselves, 54% had written a letter," and "54% had met with an Internet friend" face-to-face, on average eight times.[50]

Online relationships also remained fairly stable over a two-year period and compared favorably to more traditional face-to-face relationships. "71% of the romantic relationships that had begun on the Internet . . . [and 75% of all reported Internet relationships] were still intact two years later—with the majority being reported as closer and stronger." Moreover, 84 percent of the respondents said that their online relationships were "as real, as important, and as close as their non-Internet relationships."[51]

Finally, when asked what effect use of the Internet had on "their feelings of loneliness," 47 percent said it had no effect, but another 47 percent said it had reduced the feelings of aloneness. A majority, 68 percent of respondents, said that the Internet had enlarged their social circle.[52]

Contrary to the idea that spending time in cyberspace further isolates individuals in a technologically mediated world, the McKenna survey, the Pew report, and countless other studies show just the opposite to be the case, at least for a majority of people. The most counterintuitive part of the findings is that individuals are more likely to reveal their true selves to others in virtual reality and form strong, intimate personal attachments that carry over into face-to-face reality.[53]

By affording the opportunity for individuals to play their "true self" role the Internet provides a unique virtual stage for the engagement of dramaturgical consciousness. While playing one's true self is a role, just like playing one's actual or ideal self, it is the role of a lifetime. Strange to imagine that playing one's authentic self is sometimes made more possible in a virtual rather than a real environment—but, then again, maybe not so strange. After all, the novel—a fictional form—allowed millions of people in the eighteenth and nineteenth centuries to find and release their innermost feelings and develop a keener empathic sensitivity. What's different this time is the overarching reach of the Internet and the ability of millions of people to be in direct intimate contact with each other on a global public stage. The potential to experience empathic sensibility and to take it to a global level is now within reach.

THE FAME FACTOR: IT'S ALL ABOUT ME

But before getting too carried away, there is a dark side to a technologically mediated global public stage that deserves equal attention—that is, the Internet's incredible power to inflate and amplify each person's desire for recognition—the fame factor. While the Internet is a tool for sharing and collaboration, it also serves as a forum for boundless exhibitionism and narcissism. The same medium that opens up the possibility of showing one's true self to others and nurturing more embedded relationships and shared intimacy can put everyone on Earth on center stage, in front of the biggest audience ever assembled in history. For the narcissistically predisposed, the opportunity to exhibit themselves is as seductive as is the inclination of the voyeuristic to watch. In a commercial world that increasingly plays off both narcissistic and voyeuristic tendencies, the Internet becomes an unmatched commercial medium to commodify every aspect and stage of life.

The rap on today's young people in the age group that stems from toddlers to young adults in their early thirties (everyone born after the mid-1970s) is that they are coddled, overexposed, overindulged, told they are special, believe that to be the case, are self-centered—"it's all about me"—and are trapped in their self-absorbed inflated self-esteem. We are also told, however, that they are more open and tolerant, less prejudiced, multicultural in their views, nonjudgmental, civic- and service-oriented, and more collaborative than any other generation in history. Certainly, any observer of the American scene can't fail to have witnessed both psychologies at play across American society—as well as across Europe, Japan, Australia, and other highly developed societies, although perhaps less pronounced.

Is it possible that today's young people are caught between both poles and that some of the parenting and schooling practices—not to mention commercial influences—have produced a generation of children that swing both ways? Yes, but with the qualification that the newest data shows a trend away from the "it's all about me" phenomenon prevalent in the 1980s and 1990s among Generation X toward the more collaborative relational mind-set of the younger Millennial Generation.

Here's a short snapshot of the two very different sensibilities that seem to be riding side by side in the psyche of the two generations that have grown up with a dramaturgical consciousness.

Back in 2004, a national survey found that about "1 out of 20 college students expects to become an actor, artist, or musician."[54] An early survey done in the 1990s asked Americans whether they would rather be famous or contented. Twenty-nine percent of young people chose being famous.[55]

Reality TV shows capture the deep yearning among the younger generation to be "discovered" and become famous, hopefully overnight. "That could be me up there on the screen" has fed the unrealistic expectations that with a little luck and not much talent everyone can be famous and adored by millions. Thousands of young people line up to audition for shows like *American Idol*, *Big Brother*, and *Survivor*. There have been more than 500 reality shows on television.[56]

Even if they are denied an audition and a "role" on reality TV, there are countless other media outlets more easily accessible on the Internet, like YouTube, MySpace, Facebook, and Flickr, to draw attention and become famous. Tens of millions of mostly young people all over the world are producing their own videos and performing for others in hopes of attracting attention and becoming a star. A Pew survey found that 76 percent of bloggers say that their prime purpose in blogging is to document their personal stories and share them with others with the assumption that their personal life is potentially meaningful enough to warrant widespread public attention and scrutiny.[57]

The desire for personal fame has become so much of an obsession among young people that it is spurring serious discussion and debate, as well as studies among a growing number of psychologists and sociologists who wonder, why now? The media is, in part, the reason. The sheer ability to use the Internet to get attention is seductive.

But researchers also sense that the drive for fame reflects a new sense of existential aloneness and a desperate need to be recognized. The desire for fame is often driven by a fear of mortality and the need to gain at least a fleeting sense of immortality or, if not that, at least to know that one's existence is duly noted, recognized, and celebrated by millions of others. Fame reinforces the idea that one's life has meaning. Some wonder whether the precarious nature of human existence itself—with the prospect of climate change and nuclear Armageddon threatening our very survival—might not play a subconscious role in generating the desire for fame and immortality.

Nor is the desire for fame a wholly American-born passion. Similar surveys carried out in cities in China and Germany report that about 30 percent of adults "regularly daydream about being famous" and, incredibly, more than 40 percent expect that limited fame will come their way someday. The percentages are even higher among teenagers.[58]

Psychologists say that much of the preoccupation with fame stems from feelings of neglect or rejection and suspect that the growing phenomenon of divorce and growing up in broken homes or being raised by single parents might play an important role in the feelings of abandonment. Again, the question seems to get back to the issue of proper attachment in early child rearing.[59]

Some psychologists and educators believe that a contributing factor to the fame fetish is the self-esteem movement that spread across the country in the 1980s and 90s and became deeply embedded in child-raising practices and, even more important, in school pedagogy and curriculum.

In her book *Generation Me*, Dr. Jean M. Twenge compiled data from twelve studies covering the generational differences in behavior among 1.5 million young Americans and found that the current generation of young people born in the 1970s, 1980s, and 1990s is the most narcissistic in history. She places much of the blame on what she refers to as the over-the-top self-esteem movement in American classrooms. She says that young people have been told, ad nauseam, that they are special, that everything they do is valuable and worthy of praise, that they should love themselves first, and that if they do, that the world will come to recognize their very special talents and contributions and praise them. While a somewhat uncompromising view of the self-esteem movement, it is true that beginning in the 1980s, teachers and parents began to celebrate children for who they were and to praise them for their unique being. A Google Web search for "elementary school mission statement self-esteem" came up with an astounding 308,000 Web pages in 2006.[60] Nine thousand books on self-esteem and children were published in the 1980s and 1990s compared to only five hundred books published on the subject in the 1970s.[61]

In a study done by Cynthia Scott of the University of North Florida, 60 percent of teachers and 69 percent of school counselors said that encouraging student self-esteem is important. Scott argues that schools should be "providing more unconditional validation to students based on who they are rather than how they perform or behave."[62]

Twenge describes a typical self-esteem curriculum for elementary school called "I'm great." The other students in the class are asked to say good things about a chosen student and later that student reviews a written list of all the praise. At the end of the session, the child being praised is asked to say something good about himself as well, in front of the class.[63]

In sporting events, every little boy and girl is expected to get equal time on the playing field, regardless of how good they are, and everyone is given a trophy for showing up and trying.

Competitive success also becomes less important than feeling good about oneself in school. Grade inflation has become a favorite means of reinforcing the changeover from competition to recognition. In 2004, 48 percent of American college freshman reported having an A average in high school compared with only 18 percent of college freshmen in 1968, despite the ironic fact that hours devoted to homework in high school had declined, as had SAT scores. When asked why so many kids were getting better grades for inferior work, Howard Everson of the College Board said, "Teachers want to raise the self-esteem and feel-good attitudes of students."[64]

A revealing CBS News poll summed up the shift in student attitudes that took place in the 1980s and 1990s when it asked high school graduates of the class of 2000: "What makes you feel positive about yourself?" Thirty-three percent answered self-esteem, while school performance only received 18 percent and popularity 13 percent.[65]

The self-esteem movement has proven to be an unqualified success. By the mid 1990s, the average college male boasted a "higher self-esteem than 86 percent of college men in 1968," while the average college female had a "higher self-esteem than 71 percent of the college women in 1968."[66]

While having high self-esteem is a positive quality, what Twenge and other educators criticize is a curriculum that overinflates one's sense of self-worth, to the point of overempowerment. Such children often have an unrealistic assessment of how great they are, which feeds narcissism and the belief that the world revolves around them. In the

1950s, only 12 percent of teenagers between the ages of fourteen and sixteen agreed with the statement, "I am an important person," but by the 1980s, 80 percent of teenagers claimed they were important.[67]

The problem is that when so many young people feel they are special and more important than other people, they become less tolerant of others and less willing to brook criticism; they also are less able to manage failures that are an inevitable part of life and less able to express empathy to others.

Narcissism and the pursuit of fame enjoy a long and entangled history. To suggest that a rising tide of narcissism might be feeding the belief that one is destined for fame—just because one is so special and important—is not so difficult to entertain.

Are our young people really that self-absorbed? Have we raised a generation of unadulterated narcissists—monsters, if you will—who care only about themselves? The evidence is more mixed than the above studies suggest. Some educators believe that the excesses of the early self-esteem rush have been moderated in the schools and in parenting practices as feedback raised the alarm and more sophisticated and appropriately contextured approaches to building self-esteem began to take hold.

Much of Twenge's research findings covered the period of the mid-1990s to 2002 and 2003. Newer survey findings, however, are beginning to tell a slightly different story. Unlike the Gen Xers, the Millennial Generation coming of age in the second decade of the twenty-first century appear to be expressing themselves in a different manner.

SIZING UP THE MILLENNIAL GENERATION

The Millennials are the first generation to have grown up entirely with the Internet and to be fully embedded in social networking, text messaging, and the like as a way of life. New surveys and studies suggest that the distributed nature of the new information and communications technology and the collaborative relationships they spawn are increasingly reflected in the collective psyche of the generation.

To begin with, unlike the baby boomers, who rebelled against parental authority, and Gen Xers, who were often neglected by their baby-boom parents, the Millennial Generation appears to be much more connected to their families and enjoy a high sense of familial attachment and trust. Millennial children—especially among the middle class—spend more time with their parents than perhaps any other generation in history. Fifty percent of Millennials see their parents daily and 45 percent talk with their parents by cell phone each day.[68]

Surveys also show that unlike Gen Xers, Millennials are "much more likely to feel empathy for others in their group and to seek to understand each person's perspective."[69] Studies also show that they are much more disposed to give the opinion of each member of a group equal weight, to work collaboratively, and to seek group consensus. Having grown up on the Internet, they are less likely to accept the word of experts and more likely to believe in the combined wisdom of crowds. They are less trusting of centralized command and control and top-down exercise of authority and more responsive to the kind of flat participatory knowledge-gathering found in open-source models like Linux and Wikipedia.

In their book *Millennial Makeover*, Morley Winograd and Michael D. Hais cite new studies that show that Millennials are more keenly engaged in the larger community and even the global community. They are far more concerned about the planetary environment and especially climate change, and more eager to support sustainable as opposed to unregulated growth. In a 2007 survey, "18- to 24-year-olds ranked global warming and other environmental issues among the five most important issues that the nation needed to address."[70] Forty-three percent of Millennials, as opposed to 40 percent of Gen Xers and only 38 percent of baby boomers "favor environmental protection even at the cost of economic growth."[71]

They are also more supportive of a larger role by government than older generations. Seventy-three percent of Millennials believe that government has a responsibility to "take care of people who can't care for themselves," compared to 68 percent of the rest of the adult population. Moreover, 73 percent favor federally guaranteed health insurance, whereas only 66 percent of the rest of the adult population does. Overall, the Millennial Generation is far more supportive of a bigger role of government when it comes to providing services than are older Americans—69 percent of Millennials favor more government services, as compared to only 39 percent of the rest of the adult population.[72]

The Millennials' more empathic approach to the environment, the needs of the poor, and the larger community is also manifest in their more active civic involvement. A PBS program in 2007 on the Millennial Generation reported "that 80 percent of Millennials had participated in some kind of community or societal improvement program" in the past year.[73]

The Millennial Generation is also the most cosmopolitan in U.S. history. Seventy percent of Millennial college students and 59 percent of all eighteen- to twenty-four-year-olds have traveled outside the United States. This might account for the fact that they are also the most enthusiastic supporters of globalization, with 37 percent favorably disposed, measured against only 20 percent of the adult population.[74] Their cosmopolitan attitudes spill over into the question of immigration. A 52 percent majority favor immigration—as opposed to 39 percent of the adult population—saying that "immigrants today strengthen our country because of their hard work and talents." Their views are in sharp contrast to the prevailing view of anti-immigrant Americans who believe that immigrants are "a burden because of their impact on jobs, housing, and health care."[75]

The more empathic consciousness of Millennials is due, in large part, to their own makeup. The Millennials are the most racially diverse generation in U.S. history. Forty percent are black, Latino, Asian, or from racially mixed backgrounds, in contrast to only 25 percent of the older generations.[76]

Statistics show that the Millennial Generation, not only in the United States, but around the world, at least in developed nations, is the most tolerant of any generation in history in its support for gender equality and the most willing to champion the rights of the disabled, gays and our fellow creatures.

While the new data is encouraging, it comes with a disconcerting caveat that could seriously undermine the strong gains in global consciousness thus far registered by the Millennial Generation. Although, the connectivity made possible by the Internet is bringing the millennial generation together in what might be thought of as a global cosmopolitan embrace, new research findings suggest that the same technology may be seriously eroding the ability of the current generation to communicate intelligently among themselves. It is ironic to consider the possibility that a technology touted for facilitating an exponential increase in the collection, storage, and exchange of communication among people, may be dumbing down articulate speech and the wherewithal of people to understand others' feelings and thoughts.

Yet surveys over the past ten years show an alarming trend among the young growing up in front of the screen. Vocabulary is plummeting and, along with it, reading proficiency and the ability to communicate effectively, all of which has far-reaching implications for the ability of people to empathize with one another. The findings of the 2003 National Assessment of Adult Literacy are troubling. The study showed a plunge in literacy among college graduates. In 1992, 40 percent of college graduates achieved what is defined as "proficiency" in literacy, whereas less than 31 percent of college graduates in 2003 were proficient in literacy, despite greater access to information via the Internet.[77]

Worse still, research suggests that the Internet and television may be, in large part, the source of the decline in literacy. Emory University English professor Mark Bauerlein, formerly a director of research and analysis at the National Endowment for the Arts, explains that electronic media differ from conventional print media like newspapers and adult books in the number of "rare" words commonly encountered. Rare words are those "words that do not rank in the top 10,000 in terms of frequency of usage."[78]

For example, the average newspaper contains 68.3 rare words per

1,000 and adult books contain 52.7 rare words per 1,000. By contrast, prime-time adult television shows contain only 22.7 rare words per thousand words uttered. The Internet, with its emphasis on speed, browsing, multitasking, and quick referrals, favors simple words and more simple sentence constructions. Text messaging and new communication vehicles like Twitter further simplify language construction, significantly reducing the use of rare words and, in the process, narrowing the pool of commonly available words and terms used.[79]

The trends are disquieting, with studies showing that greater Internet use has led to a dramatic decline in the reading of newspapers, magazines, and books, the very media that expose people to more rare words.

In every previous communication revolution in history, from oral to script to print, vocabulary increased, giving people a richer reservoir of metaphors and language constructions to build on. More extensive vocabulary allows people to create more complex thoughts and, by so doing, expand the empathic domain, for the obvious reason that people can better express their innermost feelings, intentions, and expectations to one another.

We face yet another paradox of the present moment in history: the new Internet connectivity provides the human race with boundless knowledge and channels of communication, but because of the nature of the medium and how it is used, it might be dramatically lessening the ability of human beings to express themselves in deep and meaningful ways that advance common understandings, shared meanings, and empathic connections. What, then, might we make of the millennial generation?

The situation at present is anything but clear. While there are some among the younger generation who dream of personal fame, there are as many others just as devoted to community service and assisting those less fortunate. The likely reality is that a younger generation is growing up torn between both a narcissistic and empathic mind-set, with some attracted to one and some to the other.

The long-term economic downturn facing the global economy as the Second Industrial Revolution moves toward a sunset will probably weaken the narcissist impulse, as personal and collective survival looms ever larger and individual illusions of grandeur amid global chaos come to be regarded as delusionary, even comic. A collective narcissism could, however, just as easily be transformed into a virulent xenophobia, with political diatribes aimed at characterizing minorities and other cultures and nationalities as inferior and less than human. It's happened before.

Troubled times could also lead to an extension of empathic consciousness—"we're all in this together"—as we heighten our sensitivity to each other's common plight. The Great Depression of the 1930s led to just such an awakening, at least in the United States, with neighbors pitching in and aiding each other in dire times.

Much will depend on the ability to speed along a new Third Industrial Revolution—i.e., a distributed form of capitalism that brings out our collaborative nature, is motivated by a sense of the common good, and is expressed through a new dream of quality of life and planetary sustainability.

UNTIL NOW, we've had to live with the terrible, although unconscious reality that our growing empathic sensibility has been made possible by an ever-quickening flow of energy and materials through increasingly more complex and expansive social structures, with an increasingly large entropic bill shadowing every advance.

The economic downturn is already leading to a decrease in the standard of living all over the world. The well-off are learning to live on less, while the poor are being thrown to the very margins of survival.

The readjustment of lifestyles among the well-off could be a blessing in disguise—that is, if it leads to a reassessment of what constitutes the good life. Even before the current economic crisis, millions of well-off people made conscious choices to simplify their lifestyles and find meaning in the quality of their relationships rather than in the number of their possessions. They grasped, in their own lives, what the psychologists and sociologists are discovering in their research and studies—that after a minimum of income is secured to provide for the basics and a reasonably comfortable way of life, that increasing increments of wealth actually make societies less happy.

Now that hundreds of millions of people find themselves having to involuntarily downsize because of economic circumstances, the opportunity exists to shift the pursuit of happiness from emphasis on riches to a focus on meaningful relationships and from market capital to social capital. Bad times—as long as they don't become so bad that they threaten everyone's survival—could allow for a great renewal of civil society and an empathic surge as millions of people become sensitized to their common plight and actively engaged in mutual support and aid.

The shift from emphasis on the quantity and worth of one's possessions to the quality and meaning of one's relationships—or quality of life—requires a change in both spatial and temporal orientation. The exclusive-autonomous self, embedded in private property relations, gives way to the inclusive-relational self, participating in both the virtual and brick-and-mortar global public square. The efficient use of time to maximize individual material self-interest makes room for the empathic use of time to deepen civic relationships and steward the environment.

If a quality-of-life society were to become both the dream and norm around the world in the twenty-first century, we finally might be able to break the dialectic of history by which increasing empathy inevitably leads to increasing entropy.

A more equitable distribution of nature's wealth could allow the formerly overindulged to ease into a more sustainable lifestyle, while those less well-off can improve their lot. A more sustainable quality of life in the developed countries combined with a greater share of responsibility toward advancing the standard of living and well-being of people in the less-developed countries would bring human civilization into balance while aligning our species' consumption habits to nature's ability to recycle and replenish the stock.

It's a tall order, which just a few years ago might have seemed idealistic and naïve. But, times have changed as have human needs, priorities, and perhaps aspirations—especially when it comes to pondering the particulars of what constitutes a good and decent life.

The great value of the new distributed Third Industrial Revolution is that it allows us to connect the human race in a universal embrace, while using only the renewable energies that bathe the Earth and in a way that allows everyone their fair access to locally available energy sources.

This means that we are at the point where we can entertain the idea of establishing a complex global human civilization in a locally distributed way and, in so doing, extend the empathic embrace while lowering the entropic bill. This would bring the human race to the cusp of biosphere consciousness in a climax global economy.

FIFTEEN

BIOSPHERE CONSCIOUSNESS IN A CLIMAX ECONOMY

ALL THE STAGES of consciousness that human beings have entertained through history still exist and are very much alive, in various shades and degrees. Most of us are a composite, in some measure, of our deep historical past, and keep alive bits and pieces of ancestral consciousness, in the form of mythological, theological, ideological, psychological, and dramaturgical frames of reference.

The challenge before us is how to bring forward all of these historical stages of consciousness that still exist across the human spectrum to a new level of biosphere consciousness in time to break the lock that shackles increasing empathy to increasing entropy.

The question, then, is what does every human being share in common at his critical juncture that can unite the human race as a species? The answer is obvious, from a biological point of view, but far from fully acknowledged. We all share a common biosphere to which we are wholly dependent, along with all other forms of life, and the biosphere is now threatened with a change in temperature that potentially imperils our species and threatens our survival.

In a world characterized by increasing individuation and made up of human beings at different stages of consciousness, the biosphere itself may be the only context encompassing enough to unite the human race as a species.

While the new distributed communications technologies—and,

soon, distributed renewable energies—are connecting the human race, what is so shocking is that no one has offered much of a reason as to why we ought to be connected. We talk breathlessly about access and inclusion in a global communications network but speak little of exactly why we want to communicate with one another on such a planetary scale. What's sorely missing is an overarching reason for why billions of human beings should be increasingly connected. Toward what end? The only feeble explanations thus far offered are to share information, be entertained, advance commercial exchange, and speed the globalization of the economy. All the above, while relevant, nonetheless seem insufficient to justify why nearly seven billion human beings should be connected and mutually embedded in a globalized society. Seven billion individual connections, absent any overall unifying purpose, seem a colossal waste of human energy. More important, global connections without any real transcendent purpose risk a narrowing rather than an expanding of human consciousness.

The financier Bernard Baruch once remarked that, "If all you have is a hammer, the whole world begins to look like a nail." Today we might just as well say, "If all we have is a personal computer connected to the Internet, the whole world begins to look like networks of relationships."

The point is that the increasing connectivity of the human race is advancing personal awareness of all the relationships that make up a complex and diverse world. A younger generation is beginning to view the world less as a storehouse of objects to expropriate and possess and more as a labyrinth of relationships to access.

How, then, will we choose to use our newfound relational consciousness? Interestingly, just as we are beginning to develop a relational sense of consciousness, we are beginning to understand the relational nature of the forces that govern life on this planet.

A BIOSPHERE WORLD

Enlightenment science is wedded to the notion that the behavior of the whole is best understood by analyzing the individual parts that make it up. The analytical method reduces all phenomena to their most fundamental building blocks and then examines the individual properties of each element in the hope of better understanding the construction of the whole. As mentioned in Chapter 5, this mechanistic approach to science borrowed heavily from popular mechanical metaphors of the day. Machines can be understood by taking them apart, analyzing their individual components, and then reassembling them back into the whole. But in the real world of nature, behavior is not mechanistic and fixed but conditional, open-ended, affected by other phenomena, and continually metamorphosing and mutating in response to the patterns of activity around it.

As long as science and technology were more narrowly engaged in questions of acceleration and location, Newton's mechanistic laws served well. Only phenomena that could be isolated, timed, and measured, and made subject to rigorous quantification were considered to be real. By the twentieth century, however, the reductionist and mechanistic idea was too limited a concept to capture the embeddedness of nature. It became more apparent to scientists that understanding society or nature required understanding the relationships between phenomena and not just the properties of the component parts.

Social scientists began to ask, how do we know a man except in relationship to the world around him? Taking the measure of a man— knowing his place of birth, age, height, weight, physical, and emotional characteristics—tells us little of value about who he really is. It is only by understanding his relationship to the larger environment in which he is embedded and the many relationships he shares that we get a sense of him. In the old scheme, man was the sum total of his individual properties. In the new scheme, he is a snapshot of the pattern of activities in which he is engaged.

If each human being is a pattern of interactivity, why wouldn't all of nature be so as well? Scientists in the twentieth century began to reexamine many of their most basic operating assumptions, only to see them overthrown. The old idea that phenomena could be known by analyzing the individual parts gave way to the opposite conception—that the individual parts can be understood only by knowing something about their relationships to the whole within which they are embedded. In a word, nothing exists in isolation, as an autonomous object. Rather, everything exists in relation to "the other." The new science was called systems theory, and it put in doubt the older thinking about the nature of nature. Systems theory also cast a shadow on the rest of the Enlightenment project, including the idea of the autonomous being functioning in a detached, self-optimizing world, populated by other autonomous beings, each maximizing his or her own individual utility.

Systems theory holds that the nature of the whole is greater than the sum of its parts. That's because it is the relationship between the parts that creates something qualitatively different at the level of the whole. For example, we know from personal experience that a living being is qualitatively different from a corpse. At the moment of death, all of the relationships that made that living being a whole disappear, leaving just a body of inert matter.

The new systems thinking owes much to the emerging field of ecology. Ecology challenged the Darwinian model, with its emphasis on the competitive struggle between individual creatures for scarce resources. In the newer ecological model, nature is made up of a multitude of symbiotic and synergistic relationships, where each organism's fate is determined as much by reciprocal engagement as by any competitive advantage. Where Darwin's biology concentrated more on the individual organism and species and relegated the environment to a backdrop of resources, ecology views the environment as all the relationships that make up what we call nature and existence.

The early ecologists concentrated their efforts on local ecosystems. In 1911, however, a Russian scientist, Vladimir Vernadsky, published a paper that would expand the notion of ecological relationships to include the entire planet. He described what he called "the biosphere," which he defined "as the area of the Earth's crust occupied by transformers which convert cosmic radiation into effective terrestrial energy: electrical, chemical, mechanical, thermal, etc."[1]

In a book published in 1926, which he titled *Biospheria*, Vernadsky broke with the scientific orthodoxy of the day, arguing that geochemical and biological processes on Earth evolved together, each aiding the other. His radical idea was at odds with orthodox Darwinian theory, which hypothesized that geochemical processes evolved separately, creating the atmospheric environment in which living organisms emerged, adapted, and evolved—the notion of the environment as a storehouse of resources. Vernadsky suggested that the cycling of inert chemicals on Earth is influenced by the quality and quantity of living matter, and the living matter, in turn, influences the quality and quantity of inert chemicals being cycled through the planet. Today scientists define the biosphere as

> an integrated living and life-supporting system comprising the peripheral envelope of Planet Earth together with its surrounding atmosphere, so far down, and up, as any form of life exists naturally.[2]

The biosphere is very thin, extending only from the ocean depths, where the most primitive forms of life exist, to the upper stratosphere. The entire reach of the biosphere envelope is less than forty miles from ocean floor to outer space. Within this narrow band, living creatures and the Earth's geochemical processes interact to sustain each other.

In the 1970s, an English scientist, James Lovelock, and an American biologist, Lynn Margulis, expanded on Vernadsky's theory with the publication of the Gaia hypothesis. They argued that the Earth functions like a self-regulating living organism. The flora and fauna and the geochemical composition of the atmosphere work in a synergistic relationship to maintain the Earth's climate in a relatively steady state that is conducive to life.

Lovelock and Margulis use the example of the regulation of oxygen and methane to demonstrate how the cybernetic process between life and the geochemical cycle works to maintain a homeostatic climate regime. They remind us that oxygen levels on the planet must be confined within a very narrow range or the entire planet could erupt into flames, destroying all living matter, at least on the land surface. The two scientists believe that when the oxygen in the atmosphere rises above a tolerable level, a warning signal of some kind triggers an increase in methane production by microscopic bacteria. The increased methane migrates into the atmosphere, dampening the oxygen content until a steady state is reached again. (Methane acts as a regulator, both adding and taking away oxygen from the air.)

The constant interaction and feedback between living creatures and the geochemical content and cycles act as a unified system, maintaining the Earth's climate and environment and preserving life. The planet, then, is more like a living creature, a self-regulating entity that maintains itself in a steady state conducive to the continuance of life. According to the Gaian way of thinking, the adaptation and evolution of individual creatures become part of the larger process: the adaptation and evolution of the planet itself. It is the continuous symbiotic relationships between every living creature and between living creatures and the geochemical processes that ensure the survival of both the planetary organism and the individual species that live within its biospheric envelope.

Many other scientists have since weighed in on the Gaia thesis, moderating, qualifying, and expanding on Lovelock and Margulis's work. For more than two decades, the idea that the Earth functions like a living organism has become a critical avenue of exploration for rethinking the relationship between biology, chemistry, and geology.

If, in fact, the Earth does function like a living organism, then human activity that disrupts the biochemistry of the biosphere can lead to grave consequences, both for human life and the planet as a whole. The massive burning of fossil-fuel energy is the first example of "human activity," on a global scale, that now threatens a radical shift in the climate of the Earth and the undermining of the biosphere that sustains all living creatures.

Our dawning awareness that the Earth functions like an indivisible organism requires us to rethink our notions of global risks, vulnerability, and security. If every human life, the species as a whole, and all other life-forms are entwined with one another and with the geochemistry of the planet in a rich and complex choreography that sustains life itself, then we are all dependent on and responsible for the health of the whole organism. Carrying out that responsibility means living out our individual lives in our neighborhoods and communities in ways that promote the general well-being of the larger biosphere within which we dwell.

Perhaps the most interesting aspect of the new science, with its emphasis on relationships and feedback, is how closely it mirrors the network way of thinking that is beginning to permeate the social and commercial realms and governance. The science of ecology and the notion of a self-regulating biosphere are all about relationships, feedbacks, and networks. Ecologist Bernard Patten has observed that "ecology *is* networks. . . . To understand ecosystems ultimately will be to understand networks."[3] Physicist and philosopher Fritjof Capra points out:

> As the network concept became more and more prominent
> in ecology, systemic thinkers began to use network models
> at all systems levels, viewing organisms as networks of cells,
> organs, and organ systems, just as ecosystems are understood as
> networks of individual organisms.[4]

In other words, every organism is made up of smaller networks of organs and cells while it is also part of larger networks that comprise biotic communities, whole ecosystems, and the biosphere itself. Each network is nested in networks above it while also made up of networks below it, in a complex choreography—what Capra calls "the web of life." Over eons of evolutionary history, says Capra, "many species have formed such tightly knit communities that the whole system resembles a large, multicreatured organism."[5]

A new science is emerging whose operating principles and assumptions are more compatible with network ways of thinking. The old science views nature as objects; the new science views nature as relationships. The old science is characterized by detachment, expropriation, dissection, and reduction; the new science is characterized by engagement, replenishment, integration, and holism. The old science is committed to making nature productive; the new science to making nature sustainable. The old science seeks power over nature; the new science seeks partnership with nature. The old science puts a premium on autonomy from nature; the new science on reparticipation with nature.

The new science takes us from a colonial vision of nature as an enemy to pillage and enslave, to a new vision of nature as a community to nurture. The right to exploit, harness, and own nature in the form of property is tempered by the obligation to steward nature and treat it with dignity and respect. The utility value of nature is slowly giving way to the intrinsic value of nature.

Our growing involvement in networks, our newfound ability to multitask and operate simultaneously on parallel tracks, our increasing awareness of economic, social, and environmental interdependencies, our search for relatedness and embeddedness, our willingness to accept contradictory realities and multicultural perspectives, and our process-oriented behavior all predispose us to systems thinking. If we can harness holistic thinking to a new global ethics that recognizes and acts to harmonize the many relationships that make up the life-sustaining forces of the planet, we will have crossed the divide into a near-climax world economy and biosphere consciousness.

BIOSPHERE EDUCATION

The American classroom is fast becoming a laboratory for preparing young people for biosphere awareness. In schools across the country, students are being instructed in the intricacies of ecosystem dynamics. They are being taught about the need to be more energy efficient and to recycle wastes as well as to nurture wildlife and safeguard biomes. Equally important, classroom pedagogy is beginning to emphasize the impacts that personal consumption habits have on the Earth's ecosystems. Children are learning, for example, that the wasteful use of energy in the family automobile or home results in the increase of emissions of carbon dioxide into the atmosphere. The heating up of the Earth's temperature that follows can lead to less rainfall and more drought in other parts of the world, adversely affecting food production and putting more of the world's poor at risk of malnutrition and even starvation. Children are becoming aware that everything they do—the very way they live—affects the lives of every other human being, our fellow creatures, and the biosphere we cohabit. They come to understand that we are as deeply connected with one another in the ecosystems that make up the biosphere as we are in the social networks of the blogosphere.

Now the newly emerging biosphere awareness is being accompanied by cutting-edge curriculum designed to help young people develop an even deeper sense of interconnectivity and social responsibility at the level of their personal psyches.

While the self-esteem movement swept into American classrooms and, to a lesser extent, classrooms in other developed countries in the 1980s and 1990s, with mixed results as mentioned earlier, the new pedagogical revolution is emphasizing empathic development. In April 2009, *The New York Times* ran a front-page article reporting on the empathy revolution occurring in American classrooms. Empathy workshops and curriculums now exist in eighteen states, and the early evaluations of these pioneer educational reform programs are encouraging. Schools report a marked reduction in aggression, violence, and other antisocial behavior, a decrease in disciplinary actions, greater cooperation among students, more pro-social behavior, more focused attention in the classrooms, a greater desire to learn, and improvement in critical thinking skills.[6]

The empathy curriculum helps students draw global emotional connections in the same way that the environmental curriculum helps youngsters draw global ecological connections. Michael McDermott, a middle school principal in Scarsdale, New York, put it this way: "As a school we've done a lot of work with human rights. . . . But you can't have kids saving Darfur and isolating a peer in the lunchroom. It all has to go together."[7]

In many schools the empathy curriculum starts as early as first grade with five- and six-year-olds. One of the most interesting innovations is the Roots of Empathy Project, begun by a Canadian educator, Mary Gordon, which has been successfully introduced into classrooms across Canada and more recently in the United States. A mother and her baby visit the classroom once a month for an entire school year. (The baby is five months old at the beginning of the school year.) Before the visits, the students are prepped on what to expect, what to look for, and how to interact with the baby and mother. They will be asked to closely watch the interaction between mother and infant, especially how they communicate and respond to each other. They will observe temperament, mood, and intentionality with an eye to relating back to the group their impressions and feelings in the post-visit debriefing, with particular emphasis on their emotional reactions. The students are encouraged to dig into their own memories and life experiences as a way of understanding what the baby might be feeling or thinking or intending. For example, if the baby is experiencing frustration in attempting to sit up, the children will be asked how it must feel for him and relate it to their own feelings when frustrated in a new learning experience—like riding a bike.

As the monthly visits proceed, the students will take notice of the baby's emotional, mental, and psychological development, his evolving attachment to and relationship with his mother, his emerging curiosity and exploratory behavior and his improved coordination and communications skills. They will watch how the mother responds to her baby's distress, joy, and curiosity and the effect her responses have on him. Over the course of the year, the children come to experience the baby and his mother as unique individuals with needs and desires for affiliation and affection, not unlike their own. They become attuned to reading the baby's feelings and develop an empathic relationship with both the infant and the mother.

The learning experience often has a life-changing impact on the students' own emotional and cognitive development. Gordon tells the story of a young teenager who had been held back in eighth grade for two years. He was a deeply troubled youth who had watched his own mother murdered in front of him when he was four years old and had been subsequently shuffled into a succession of foster homes. He was a loner and was a menacing presence in the classroom.

One day during a mother–infant visit, the mother confided in the class that her baby was not much of a cuddler, much to her chagrin. Even when in his snuggly, the baby preferred to face outward rather than cuddle.

At the end of one session, much to everyone's surprise, the young teen, Darren, asked if he could try on the snuggly with the infant inside. What happened next shocked the teacher and mother and the entire class. Darren put the baby in the snuggly facing toward his chest. The baby snuggled in and cuddled while the youth took him to a quiet corner and rocked back and forth. When he returned to the mother and teacher with the infant a few minutes later, he asked, "If nobody has ever loved you, do you think you could still be a good father?"[8] In a single moment, an unloved youth experienced the unconditional affection of a tiny infant, giving him the very first sense of being loved and giving one's love. He had experienced an empathic breakthrough that would change his own life. Gordon has chronicled thousands of such experiences. Although not always as dramatic, children come to learn about emotional literacy—which Gordon defines as "[t]he ability to find our humanity in one another."[9]

The Roots of Empathy curriculum is geared to three age groups— grades 1 to 3, grades 4 to 6, and grades 7 to 8. Each grade group is brought into a more mature empathic relationship with the infant, commensurate with their stage of development. For example, while the youngest cohort group is encouraged to learn "the language of their feelings" and to share their own experiences, the ten-year-olds will learn to navigate more complex emotional experiences like the "contagion of feelings" and holding many often conflicting feelings at the same time.[10]

The program weaves the experience with the baby and mother into the curriculum. Students express and apply what they learn in writing, social studies, art, music, math, and other assorted subjects. For example, the teacher might use popular children's literature to examine emotions that come up in the sessions with the mother and baby, like feelings of loneliness, frustration, sadness, or joy. The stories are designed to encourage perspective taking.

Tens of thousands of students have gone through the Roots of Empathy program. What educators find is that the development of empathic skills leads to greater academic success in the classroom. Gordon points to a plethora of data that connects empathic development with emotional development and pro-social behavior. A troubled child is less likely to be an attentive and engaged learner than a happy child. Empathic maturity is particularly correlated with critical thinking. The ability to entertain conflicting feelings and thoughts, be comfortable with ambiguity, approach problems from a number of perspectives, and listen to another's point of view are essential emotional building blocks to engage in critical thinking. Gordon makes the telling observation that "love grows brains."[11]

Gordon argues that putting students into direct emotional contact with the parent/infant attachment process and empathic bond is a key step in producing adults whose emotional commitment extends to the entirety of the biosphere. She writes:

> The Roots of Empathy classroom is creating citizens of the world—children who are developing empathic ethics and a sense of social responsibility that takes the position that we all share the same lifeboat. These are the children who will build a more caring, peaceful and civil society, child by child.[12]

The Roots of Empathy program provides a distributed and collaborative learning environment in which children share their feelings and thoughts with one another and, by so doing, come to think of the educational process as a shared experience.

Because empathic engagement is the most deeply collaborative experience one can ever have, bringing out children's empathic nature in the classroom requires collaborative learning models. Unfortunately, the traditional classroom curriculum continues to emphasize learning as a highly personal experience designed to acquire and control knowledge by dint of competition with others. The shift into the distributed ICT revolution, however, and the proliferation of social networks and collaborative forms of engagement on the Internet are creating deep fissures in the orthodox approach to education. The result is that a growing number of educators are beginning to revise curricula by introducing distributed and collaborative learning models into the classroom. Intelligence, in the new way of thinking, is not something that is divided up among people but, rather, the field of experience that is shared between people.

We mentioned in Chapter 5 that truths are the levels of meaning we attach to our shared experiences with one another and the world around us. In this context, the new classroom emphasizes cooperation over competition and the sharing of minds. Education becomes a collaborative venture rather than an individual pursuit. The aim of all knowledge is existential: that is, to come ever closer to understanding the meaning of existence as well as our place in its evolution through our shared experiences and the meanings we glean from them. Technical or vocational knowledge becomes merely instrumental to the pursuit of this larger goal.

Collaborative education begins with the premise that the combined wisdom of the group, more often than not, is greater than the expertise of any given member and that by learning together the group advances its collective knowledge, as well as the knowledge of each member of the cohort. Collaborative education, at its core, is "concerned with shifting the center of educational concern from the individual mind, to forms of relationship."[13]

The value of collaborative education first came to light in the 1950s in research conducted by L. J. Abercrombie at the University Hospital, University of London. Dr. Abercrombie observed that when medical students worked together collaboratively in small groups to diagnose patients, they were able to more quickly and accurately assess a patient's medical condition than when they diagnosed alone. The collaborative context allowed students the opportunity to challenge each other's assumptions, build on each other's ideas and insights, and come to a negotiated consensus regarding the patient's situation.[14]

Other anecdotal evidence of the superiority of collaborative learning began to filter through the academic community in subsequent years. Uri Treisman, a mathematician at the University of California's Berkeley campus, noted with puzzlement that his Asian-American students tended to perform much better on exams than his African-American and Hispanic students. To try to understand why, Treisman followed all three groups of students around campus to see if there was something about the way they socialized that might account for the difference. He found that the Asian-American students traveled in packs, ate and socialized together, and were continually engaged in conversation about their classwork, testing hypotheses, challenging one another's ideas, sharing insights, and, like Abercrombie's medical students, negotiating a collective understanding and consensus about how to approach their assignments. By contrast, the African-American and Hispanic students were more likely to travel alone and less likely to talk about their classwork together.

To see if this was the key factor in the difference in performance levels in the classroom, Treisman brought together the African-American and Hispanic students, gave each group a place to study, and helped them learn how to work collectively and collaboratively. The results were impressive. Many of his "remedial" students went on to become A and B students.[15]

Collaborative work environments have long been standard fare in commercial fields and in the civil society. Scientists, attorneys, contractors, people in the performing arts, not-for-profit organizations, and self-help groups traditionally engage in collaborative work environments. School systems, however, have been slower to catch up. That's now beginning to change. Although not yet the norm, an increasing number of classrooms at the university and secondary school level, and even in the lower grade levels, are being transformed into collaborative work environments, at least for small periods of time. It's not uncommon for large class groups to be divided up into smaller work groups, who are then given an assignment to work on collaboratively. They then reconvene in plenary sessions where they share their findings, generally in the form of group reports. The teacher's new role becomes less that of a lecturer and more of a facilitator, charged with the responsibility of establishing the context, explaining the nature of the assignment, recording the various groups' reports, and serving as a referee of sorts in an effort to reach a class consensus. While the teacher is expected to share his own academic expertise and to point out the similarities and differences in points of view between the academic discipline to which he is a part and the students own insights and beliefs, his input is seen as an important contribution to the dialogue but not the definitive last word on the subject matter under discussion.

In collaborative learning environments, the process becomes as important as the product. The old hierarchical model of learning gives way to network ways of organizing knowledge. Learning becomes less about drilling expert knowledge into individual students' brains and more about how to think collaboratively and critically. To be effective, collaborative learning requires mutual respect among all the players in the cohort, a willingness to listen to other perspectives and points of view, being open to criticism, and a desire to share knowledge and be responsible for and accountable to the group as a whole.

The role of the teacher in collaborative learning environments is transformed. Kenneth A. Bruffee, the author of *Collaborative Learning*, says that the new teachers "think of teaching as helping students converse with increasing facility in the language of the communities they want to join. . . ."[16] It goes without saying that collaborative learning, with its emphasis on mindfulness, attunement to others, nonjudgmental interactions, acknowledgment of each person's unique contributions, and recognition of the importance of deep participation and a shared sense of meaning coming out of embedded relationships, can't help but foster greater empathic engagement. In this sense, collaborative learning transforms the classroom into a laboratory for empathic expression which, in turn, enriches the educational process.

TEACHING EMPATHIC SCIENCE

If we were going to look for ground zero in the teaching of the conventional Enlightenment model of classroom education, it would be the inculcation of the scientific method—an approach to learning that has been nearly deified in the centuries that have followed the European Enlightenment. Children are introduced to the scientific method in middle school and informed that it is the only accurate process by which to gather knowledge and learn about the real world around us.

Students are instructed that the best way to investigate phenomena and discover truths is by objective observation. A premium is put on dispassionate neutrality. The objective approach to analyzing phenomena assumes that the world is made up of objects that can be analyzed in isolation, independent of the larger wholes of which they are a part. The scientific observer is never a participant in the reality he or she observes, but only a voyeur. As for the world he or she observes, it is a cold, uncaring place, devoid of awe, compassion, or sense of purpose. Even life itself is made lifeless to better dissect its component parts. We are left with a purely material world, which is quantifiable but without quality.

It's no wonder that generations of schoolchildren have found the learning experience to be dispiriting and alienating. They are expected to give up a sense of awe, eliminate passion, become disinterested, and assume the role of a bystander to existence. How would anyone expect to find personal meaning or be engaged in such a world?

The scientific method is at odds with virtually everything we know about our own nature and the nature of the world. It denies the relational aspect of reality, prohibits participation, and makes no room for empathic imagination. Students in effect are asked to become aliens in the world.

It should be noted that even at the beginning of the Age of Reason, not everyone agreed with Francis Bacon's approach to ferreting out the truths of nature. Goethe, for one, took exception. He argued that nature is best approached as a participant rather than as a disinterested bystander. For example, when studying the morphology of a plant, the botanist must enter in the life of plant. Goethe called his scientific approach "a delicate empiricism which in a most inward way makes itself identical with the object and thereby becomes the actual theory."[17]

Goethe's scientific method is the near mirror opposite of Bacon's. Goethe believed that his "power of thought is active while *united with the objects*" and that his "thinking does not separate itself from the objects."[18] Goethe argued that true insights come not from detached observation but from deep participation with the phenomena under investigation.

Goethe's musings on appropriate scientific methodology lay dormant for more than 130 years but were picked up again by a number of psychologists in the last half of the twentieth century. Heinz Kohut was the first to revise the idea of a participatory approach to scientific investigation. He argued that the existing scientific methodology was "experience-distant" and therefore removed from actual observation, and suggested an alternative experimental theory, which he called "experience-near" because the data gathered flowed directly from empathy and introspection.[19]

Kohut believed that the most significant contribution of psychoanalysis to scientific thought "is that it has combined empathy and traditional scientific method. . . ." Introducing empathy into the field of science "as a tool of observation" would, according to Kohut, "increase the depth and breadth of the investigations conducted by a number of scientific disciplines."[20] Moreover, embedding empathy into the heart of a rigorous scientific methodology was essential, argued Kohut, lest scientific pursuits "become increasingly isolated from human life."[21] Kohut reminded his colleagues how a cold, disinterested, and rational approach to science had been instrumental in the twentieth century in fostering the aims of brutal totalitarian regimes and had led to "some of the most inhuman goals the world has ever known."[22]

Kohut did not intend to throw out the abstract nature of traditional scientific inquiry, but only to deepen the investigation process upon which such abstractions are made. Kohut concluded that, "[t]his combination of empathic-introspective data-gathering with abstract formulation and theoretical explanation . . . constitutes a revolutionary step in the history of science."[23] The new ideal in science, said Kohut, "can be condensed into a single evocative phrase: we must strive not only for scientific empathy but also for an empathic science."[24]

Abraham Maslow, among others, concurred with Kohut's vision of a new science and attempted to calm the rising fury within the scientific establishment by clarifying what was perhaps the most dangerous challenge to science in its modern incarnation. He wrote,

> I certainly wish to be understood as trying to *enlarge*
> science, not destroy it. It is not necessary to choose between
> experiencing and abstracting. Our task is to integrate them.[25]

Maslow heaped scorn on the idea that a neutral observer, uninvolved and removed from reality and existence, could bring much insight to the workings or meaning of either reality or existence. Like Goethe and Kohut, Maslow reasoned that "[m]ore sensitive observers are able to incorporate more of the world into the self, i.e., they are able to identify and empathize with wider and more inclusive circles of living and nonliving things."[26]

Maslow used the case of Alcoholics Anonymous to make his point. Certainly a recovering alcoholic knows far more of the reality of an alcoholic than a disinterested neutral observer.[27] Maslow called for what he called a "receptive strategy" of knowing, by which he meant "a receptive openness, a non-interfering willingness for things to be themselves, an ability to wait patiently for the inner structure of percepts to reveal themselves to us, a finding of order rather than an ordering."[28] He noted that in certain fields—ethnology, ethology, clinical psychology, and ecology—such an approach yielded better scientific results.

Maslow goes even further than Kohut, suggesting that the scientific community use two scientific methods, depending on the nature of the phenomena being investigated. He writes,

> But I wish to raise the more radical question: can *all* the
> sciences, *all* knowledge be conceptualized as a resultant
> of loving or caring interrelationship between knower and
> known? What would be the advantages to us of setting this
> epistemology alongside the one that now reigns in "objective
> science"? Can we simultaneously use both?

> My own feeling is that we can and should use both
> epistemologies as the situation demands. I do not see them as
> contradictory but as enriching each other.[29]

Maslow's notion of "caring objectivity" has taken hold in the more than half century since he first reflected on the need for a second scientific method. A new generation of empathic researchers, like Jane Goodall in primatology, have used the "experience-near," empathic approach to scientific investigation, to elicit new discoveries and insights about the nature of nature that would have been impossible to imagine using the traditional disinterested, value-neutral, scientific method.

Educational systems in many countries are in the very early stages of transforming their curricula to help prepare young people to participate with the biosphere. The key to a successful journey into a biosphere world will depend on how deep the reparticipation becomes. The decision to reparticipate with nature is quite different from the kind of original participation that marks the early development of the human species. In the past, participation was not willed but, rather, fated. The self was not developed sufficiently to make self-aware choices. In the case of our Paleolithic forebears, fear of nature's wrath, as much as dependency, conditioned the relationship. To reparticipate with nature willingly, by exercising free will, is what separates biosphere consciousness from everything that has gone before.

Preparing students to reparticipate with the biosphere will require active engagement outside the classroom in natural environments. The biosphere learning experience needs to be as fully engaged in local ecosystems as in the classroom if succeeding generations are to recapture the biophelia connection. Schools across the United States are already beginning to extend the classroom into the outdoors through their service learning programs, internship programs, and extended field trips. Reaffiliating with the biosphere is an empathic experience that has to be felt as well as intellectualized to be meaningful. It also has to be practiced.

In some communities, school buildings are being transformed into renewable energy power plants and Third Industrial Revolution infrastructures to provide an on-site learning environment for a generation that will be producing and sharing its own energy on the intergrid, just as they now produce and share their own information on the Internet. Students will need to be as technologically proficient in the new distributed energy technologies as they now are in the information and communications technologies if we are to develop the high-tech workforce of the twenty-first century. In 2009, the Los Angeles community college system became the first school system in the world to begin the process of converting their campus buildings into a dynamic Third Industrial Revolution four-pillar infrastructure and learning environment for students. Thousands of other schools and colleges will likely follow suit in the years ahead.

The new biosphere learning environments provide a new type of open classroom to prepare succeeding generations for the next phase of human consciousness—the extension of the central nervous system of the human race from the geosphere to the biosphere.

THE ENDGAME OF HISTORICAL CONSCIOUSNESS

The unfolding global crisis that is beginning to envelop civilization forces us to ask whether we have reached a turning point in the history of the human race—at least as it has been defined from the advent of the great hydraulic civilizations that marked the very beginning of "historical awareness." Our quest for universal belonging has catapulted us into ever more complex social and economic arrangements, each of which has pushed out and filled up more of the globe upon which we live. We now have colonized virtually every square inch of the planet and established the scaffolding for a truly global civilization that is connecting the human race in a single embrace, but at the expense of an entropic bill that is threatening our extinction.

Through all of the great stages of human history—forager/hunter, hydraulic agriculture, and the First, Second, and emerging Third Industrial Revolutions—human consciousness, expanded to encompass the complex energy/communications structures we created. Mythological consciousness, theological consciousness, ideological consciousness, psychological consciousness, and now dramaturgical consciousness mark the evolutionary passages of the human psyche. And with each successive reorientation of consciousness, empathic sensibility reached new heights. But the increasing complexity of human social arrangements also came with greater stresses, and more terrifying implosions, especially when the strains produced by increasing differentiation and individuation came up against the demands for increasing integration into the new complex systems we created.

Human beings have not always been successful at readjusting their own spatial and temporal orientations to accommodate the many new societal demands made on their physiology and psyche. Even though we are a deeply social animal that seeks inclusion and yearns for a universal embrace, our biology predisposes us to intimate units of 30 to 150 individuals. And herein lies still another of the enigmas that makes us the only creature to exhibit a true sense of awe and angst. The search for intimacy and universality at the same time continually forces the human mind to stretch itself in both directions. Although the two realms often appear at odds, the reality is that human beings are forever searching for "universal intimacy"—a sense of total belonging. What appears to be a strange confluence of opposites is really a deeply embedded human aspiration. It is our empathic nature that allows us to experience the seeming paradox of greater intimacy in more expansive domains. The quest for universal intimacy is the very essence of what we mean by transcendence.

Occasionally, the pull between individuation and integration and the related drive for both intimacy and universality becomes too strained. Either the new connection fails or the existing connection snaps. It is in these moments of pure terror and dread, when the society stumbles, losing a firm grip on its own sense of intimacy and universality, that the wholesale fears of humanity are let loose, in the form of uncontrollable oppression and violence. Every great civilization has had its fair share of holocausts.

The empathic predisposition that is built into our biology is not a fail-safe mechanism that allows us to perfect our humanity. Rather, it is an opportunity to increasingly bond the human race into a single extended family, but it needs to be continually exercised. Lamentably, the empathic drive is often shunted aside in the heat of the moment when social forces teeter on disintegration.

We may be approaching such a moment now. The Third Industrial Revolution and the new era of distributed capitalism allow us to sculpt a new approach to globalization, this time emphasizing continentalization from the bottom up. Because renewable energies are more or less equally distributed around the world, every region is potentially amply endowed with the power it needs to be relatively self-sufficient and sustainable in its lifestyle, while at the same time interconnected via smart grids to other regions across countries and continents.

While some level of globalization will continue to exsist in the Third Industrial Revolution, it is likely that continentalization will play a more dominant role in the extension of commerce and trade, because the Third Industrial Revolution intergrids and the logistical systems that accompany them favor sharing renewable energy across contiguous land masses.

When every community is locally empowered, both figuratively and literally, it can engage directly in regional, transnational, continental, and limited global trade without the severe restrictions that are imposed by the geopolitics that oversee elite fossil fuels and uranium energy distribution.

Continentalization is already bringing with it a new form of governance. The nation-state, which grew up alongside the First and Second Industrial Revolutions, and provided the regulatory mechanism for managing an energy regime whose reach was the geosphere, is ill suited for a Third Industrial Revolution whose swath is the biosphere. Distributed renewable energies generated locally and regionally and shared openly—peer to peer—across vast continental land masses connected by intelligent utility networks and smart logistics and supply chains favor continental governing institutions.

The European Union is the first continental governing institution of the Third Industrial Revolution era. The EU is already beginning to put in place the four-pillar infrastructure for a European-wide energy regime, along with the codes, regulations, and standards to effectively operate a seamless transport, communications, and energy grid that will stretch from the Irish Sea to the doorsteps of Russia by midcentury. Asian, African, and Latin American continental political unions are also in the making and will likely be the premier governing institutions on their respective continents by 2050.

In this new era of distributed energy, governing institutions will more resemble the workings of the ecosystems they manage. Just as habitats function within ecosystems, and ecosystems within the biosphere in a web of interrelationships, governing institutions will similarly function in a collaborative network of relationships with each integrated into the other and the whole. This new complex political organism operates like the biosphere it attends, synergistically and reciprocally. This is biosphere politics.

Geopolitics has always been based on the assumption that the environment is a giant battleground—a war of all against all—where we fight with one another to secure resources to ensure our individual survival. Biosphere politics, by contrast, is based on the idea that the Earth is like a living organism made up of interdependent relationships and that we each survive by stewarding the larger communities of which we are a part.

The new bottom-up continentalization and globalization allow us to complete the task of connecting the human race and opens up the possibility of extending the empathic sensibility to our species as a whole, as well as to the many other species that make up the life of the planet.

The era of economic entrenchment that we now find ourselves in, during the twilight of the Second Industrial Revolution and the dawn of the Third Industrial Revolution, is likely to last for a generation. That period should be used both to rethink the conventional wisdom that has brought us to this dangerous impasse in human history and to prepare a powerful new narrative for the generations that will follow and in whose hands will rest the awesome responsibility of rehealing the Earth and creating a sustainable planet.

Ironically, climate change is forcing us, as never before, to recognize our shared humanity and our common plight, in an essential way, rather than a superficial way. We are truly all in this life and on this planet together, and there is simply nowhere any longer for any of us to escape or to hide, because the entropic bill our species has created has now enveloped the Earth and threatens our mass extinction.

My sense is that while the initial response to climate change, which has teetered somewhere between disinterest, denial, and, at best, weak acceptance—that is, without commensurate emotional and political commitment—is fast changing. We are entering a new phase in which the "real-time" impacts of climate change are beginning to impinge on whole regions of the world, affecting large segments of humanity. The first reactions coming in are fear and anger on the part of the early victims and feigned interest among those not yet affected. That is going to change rapidly in the coming decades as the effects of climate change ripple out and impinge on larger pools of humanity.

At some critical point, the realization will set in that we share a common planet, that we are all affected, and that our neighbors' suffering is not unlike our own. At that juncture recriminations and retributions will be of little avail in addressing the enormity of the crisis at hand. Only by concerted action that establishes a collective sense of affiliation with the entire biosphere will we have a chance to ensure our future. This will require a biosphere consciousness.

The Empathic Civilization is emerging. We are fast extending our empathic embrace to the whole of humanity and the vast project of life that envelops the planet. But our rush to universal empathic connectivity is running up against a rapidly accelerating entropic juggernaut in the form of climate change and the proliferation of weapons of mass destruction. Can we reach biosphere consciousness and global empathy in time to avert planetary collapse?

NOTES

CHAPTER 1: THE HIDDEN PARADOX
OF HUMAN HISTORY
1. Weintraub, Stanley. *Silent Night: The Story of the World War I Christmas Truce*. New York: Simon and Schuster, 2001.
2. Brown, D. "Remembering a Victory for Human Kindness." *Washington Post*. December 25, 2004.
3. White, Matthew. *Twentieth Century Atlas: Death Tolls*. http://users.erols.com/mwhite28/warstat1.htm
4. Hobbes, Thomas. *Leviathan*. Oxford, UK: Oxford University Press, 1998 [1651]. p. 84.
5. Locke, John. *Two Treatises of Government*. Whitefish, MT: Kessinger Publishing, 2004 (1690). Sec. 42, p. 16.
6. Ibid. Sec. 40, p. 16.
7. Locke, John. *John Locke: Critical Assessments*. Richard Ashcraft, contrib. London: Routledge, 1991. p. 178.
8. Sagi, A., and M. L. Hoffman. "Empathic Distress in Newborns." *Developmental Psychology*. Vol. 12. No. 2. 1976. pp. 175–176. Simner, M. L. "Newborn's Response to the Cry of Another Infant." *Developmental Psychology* Vol. 5. No. 1. 1971. pp. 136–150. Davis, Mark H. *Empathy: A Social Psychological Approach*. Boulder, CO: Westview, 1996.
9. Kagan, Jerome. Introduction to *The Emergence of Morality in Young Children*. Jerome Kagan and Sharon Lamb, eds. Chicago: University of Chicago Press, 1990.
10. Dean, Carolyn. *The Fragility of Empathy After the Holocaust*. Ithaca, NY: Cornell University Press, 2004. p. 6.
11. Davis, Mark H. *Empathy: A Social Psychological Approach*. Boulder, Co: Westview Press, 1996. p. 5.
12. Hoffman, Martin L. *Empathy and Moral Development: Implications for Caring and Justice*. Cambridge, UK: Cambridge University Press, 2000. p. 30.
13. Rogers, Carl R. "Reinhold Niebuhr's *The Self and the Dramas of History*: A Criticism," *Pastoral Psychology* 9, 1958. pp. 15–17.
14. Gay, Peter. *The Enlightenment: The Science of Freedom*. New York: W. W. Norton, 1996. p. 150.
15. Wilson, Edward O. *Biophilia*. Cambridge, MA: Harvard University Press, 1984.

16. Smith, Adam. *An Inquiry into the Nature and Causes of the Wealth of Nations*. Edwin Cannan, ed. London: Methuen & Co., 1961. Vol. 1. p. 475.
17. Harlow, Harry F. "The Nature of Love." *American Psychologist*. Vol. 13. No. 12. 1958. p. 676.
18. Ibid. p. 677.
19. Canetti, Elias. *Crowds and Power*. Carol Stewart, trans. London: Gollancz, 1962. p. 448.
20. Gimbutas, Marija. *The Civilization of the Goddess: The World of Old Europe*. Joan Marler, ed. San Francisco: HarperSanFrancisco, 1991. p. 48.
21. Ibid. p. 352.
22. Partridge, Eric. *Origins: A Short Etymological Dictionary of Modern English*. New York: Greenwich House, 1983. p. 84.
23. "North Pole May Have No Ice This Summer." *Cosmos: The Science of Everything*. June 30, 2008. www.cosmosmagazine.com/news/2062/north-pole-may-have-no-ice-summer
24. Hansen, James, Makiko Sato, Pushker Kharecha, David Beerling, Robert Berner, Valerie Masson-Delmotte, Mark Pagani, Maureen Raymo, Dana L. Royer, and James Zachos. "Target Atmospheric CO_2: Where Should Humanity Aim?" *The Open Atmospheric Science Journal*. Vol. 2. 2008. p. 217.
25. Miller, G. Tyler, and Scott Spoolman. *Sustaining the Earth*. Florence, KY: Cengage Learning, 2008.
26. Haberl, H., K. H. Erb, F. Krausmann, V. Gaube, A. Bondeau, C. Plutzar, S. Gingrich, W. Lucht, and M. Fischer-Kowalski. "Quantifying and Mapping the Human Appropriation of Net Primary Production in Earth's Terrestrial Ecosystems." *Proceedings of the National Academy of Science USA*. Vol. 104. No. 31. 2007. p. 12,942.
27. Miller, G. Tyler. *Energetics, Kinetics and Life: An Ecological Approach*. Belmont, CA: Wadsworth, 1971. p. 46. Quotation by Albert Einstein.
28. Asimov, Isaac. "In the Game of Energy and Thermodynamics You Can't Even Break Even." *Smithsonian*. August 1970. p. 9.
29. Soddy, Frederick. *Matter and Energy*. New York: H. Holt and Company, 1911. pp. 10–11.
30. Blum, Harold F. *Time's Arrow and Evolution*. Princeton, NJ: Princeton University Press. 1968. p. 94.
31. Schrödinger, Erwin. *What Is Life?* New York: Macmillan, 1947. pp. 72, 75.

32. Russell, Bertrand. *An Outline of Philosophy.* New York: Meridian, 1974 [1927/1960]. p. 30.

33. Miller, G. Tyler. *Energetics, Kinetics, and Life.* p. 291.

34. Ibid.

35. Lotka, Alfred. *Elements of Physical Biology.* Internet archive. "Full Text of *Elements of Physical Biology.*" www.archive .org/stream/elementsofphysic017171mbp/ elementsofphysic017171mbp_djvu.txt

36. Lotka, Alfred J. "Contribution to the Energetics of Evolution." *Proceedings of the National Academy of Science,* 1922. 8:149.

37. Lotka, Alfred J. "The Law of Evolution as a Marxian Principle." *Human Biology* 17. September 1945. p. 186.

38. White, Leslie A. *The Science of Culture: A Study of Man and Civilization.* New York: Farrar, Straus, and Company, 1949. p. 371.

39. MacCurdy, George Grant. *Human Origins: A Manual of Prehistory.* New York: Johnson Reprint, 1965 [1924]. p. 134.

40. White. *The Science of Culture.* p. 376.

41. Odum, Howard T. *Environment, Power, and Society.* New York: Wiley-Interscience, 1971. p. 27.

42. White. *The Science of Culture.* p. 368.

43. Ibid. pp. 368–369.

44. Ibid. p. 374.

45. Mays, Larry W. "Irrigation Systems, Ancient." *The Water Encyclopedia.* www.waterencyclopedia .com/Hy-La/Irrigation-Systems-Ancient.html

46. "Information Processing." *Encyclopaedia Britannica.* 2009. Encyclopaedia Britannica Online. www.britannica.com/EBchecked/topic/249878/ Johannes-Gutenberg

47. Farr, Jason. "Point: The Westphalia Legacy and the Modern Nation-State." *International Social Science Review.* Fall–Winter 2005. http:// findarticles.com/p/articles/mi_m0IMR /is_3-4_80/ai_n27864045/

48. "Watt, James." Encyclopaedia Britannica. 2009. Encyclopaedia Britannica Online. www.britannica .com/EBchecked/topic/637673/James-Watt

49. Howells, John, and Marion Dearman. *Tramp Printers.* Pacific Grove, CA: Discovery Press, 1996. www.discoverypress.com/trampweb/hist4.html

50. Prigogine, Ilya, and Isabelle Stengers. *Order out of Chaos: Man's New Dialogue with Nature.* New York: Bantam Books, 1984.

51. "Timeline: The Evolution of Life." *New Scientist.* www.newscientist.com

52. Polanyi, Michael. *Personal Knowledge: Toward a Post-Critical Philosophy.* London: Routledge, 1998. p. 352.

53. Cobb, Edith. *The Ecology of Imagination in Childhood.* Putnam, CT: Spring Publications, 1977. p. 44.

54. Ibid. p. 38.

55. Kwok-bun, Chan. "Both Sides, Now: Culture Contact, Hybridization, and Cosmopolitanism." In Vertovec, Steven, and Robin Cohen, eds. *Conceiving Cosmopolitanism: Theory, Context, and Practice.* Oxford, UK: Oxford University Press, 2002. p. 204.

CHAPTER 2: THE NEW VIEW OF HUMAN NATURE

1. Freud, Sigmund. *Civilization and Its Discontents.* James Strachey, trans. New York: W.W. Norton, 1961. p. 23.

2. Ibid. p. 41.

3. Ibid. p. 48.

4. Ibid. p. 58.

5. Ibid. p. 59.

6. Ibid.

7. Ibid. p. 62.

8. Ibid. pp. 65–66.

9. Ibid. p. 66.

10. Ibid.

11. Róheim quoted in Ian D. Suttie. *The Origins of Love and Hate.* New York: Julian Press, 1952. p. 227.

12. Suttie; *The Origins of Love and Hate.* pp. 227–228.

13. Ibid. p. 231.

14. Freud. *Civilization and Its Discontents,* 2nd ed. Introduction by Peter Gay. James Strachey, trans. New York: W. W. Norton, 1989. p. 11.

15. Freud quoted in Suttie, *The Origins of Love and Hate.* p. 236. (Suttie's emphasis)

16. Suttie. *The Origins of Love and Hate.* p. 236. (Suttie's emphasis)

17. Freud. *Civilization and Its Discontents.* p. 19.

18. Montagu, Ashley. Introduction to Suttie, *The Origins of Love and Hate.* p. i.

19. Freud, Sigmund. *Three Essays on the Theory of Sexuality.* James Strachey, trans. and ed. New York: Basic Books, 2000. pp. 1–2.

20. Ibid. p. 83.

21. Gerson, G. "Object Relations Psychoanalysis as Political Theory." *Political Psychology.* Vol. 25. No. 5. 2004. p. 773.

22. Buckley, P. "Instincts Versus Relationships: The Emergence of Two Opposing Theories." In Peter Buckley, ed. *Essential Papers on Object Relations.* New York: New York University Press, 1986. p. 2.

23. Fairbairn, W. R. D. *Psychoanalytic Studies of the Personality.* Hove, UK: Brunner-Routledge, 2003 [1952]. p. 33.

24. Ibid.

25. Ibid. p. 34.

26. Ibid. pp. 39–40.

27. Ibid. p. 39.

28. Ibid. p. 60.

29. Ibid. p. 88.
30. Ibid. p. 89.
31. Kohut, Heinz. *The Restoration of the Self.* New York: International University Press, 1977. p. 116.
32. Vetlesen, Arne Johan. *Perception, Empathy, and Judgment:* An Inquiry into the Preconditions of Moral Performance. University Park, PA: Pennsylvania State University Press, 1994. p. 262.
33. Kohut. *The Restoration of the Self.* p. 123.
34. Ibid. p. 122.
35. Kohut, Heinz. *Self Psychology and the Humanities: Reflections on a New Psychoanalytical Approach.* Charles B. Strozier, ed. New York: W. W. Norton, 1985. p. 166.
36. Ibid. p. 167.
37. Winnicott, D. W. *Human* Nature. Philadelphia: Brunner/Mazel, 1988. p. 131.
38. Winnicott, D. W. *Through Paediatrics to Psychoanalysis.* London: Karnac, 1984. p. 99.
39. Winnicott. *Human Nature.* p. 103.
40. Ibid. p. 102.
41. Ibid. p. 106.
42. Ibid. p. 108.
43. Ibid. p. 104.
44. Suttie. *The Origins of Love and Hate.* p. 4. (Suttie's emphasis)
45. Ibid. p. 6.
46. Ibid. p. 16. (Suttie's emphasis)
47. Ibid. p. 18.
48. Ibid. p. 22.
49. Ibid. p. 49.
50. Ibid. p. 50.
51. Ibid. p. 53.
52. Levy, David. "Primary Affect Hunger." *American Journal of Psychiatry* 94. 1937. p. 644.
53. Bender, L., and H. Yarnell. "An Observation Nursery: A Study of 250 Children on the Psychiatric Division of Bellevue Hospital." *American Journal of Psychiatry* 97. 1941. pp. 1, 169.
54. Karen, Robert. *Becoming Attached: First Relationships and How They Shape Our Capacity to Love.* New York: Oxford University Press. p. 19.
55. Bakwin, Harry. "Loneliness in Infants." *American Journal of Diseases of Children* 63. 1941. p. 31.
56. Karen. *Becoming Attached.* p. 20.
57. Ibid. pp. 20–21.
58. Ibid. p. 21.
59. Ibid. p. 24.
60. Bowlby, John. Foreword to M.D.S. Ainsworth. *Infancy in Uganda: Infant Care and the Growth of Love.* Baltimore: Johns Hopkins University Press. 1967. p. v.
61. Bowlby, John. *The Making and Breaking of Affectional Bonds.* London: Tavistock Publications, 1979. p. 128.
62. Ibid.
63. Karen. *Becoming Attached.* Interview with Bowlby, January 14–15, 1989. p. 90.
64. Bowlby. *The Making and Breaking of Affectional Bonds.* pp. 128–129.
65. Ibid. p. 131.
66. Ibid. p. 133.
67. Ibid. p. 136.
68. Ibid.
69. Ibid.
70. Ibid. p. 137.
71. Ibid. p. 141.
72. Watson, John B. *Psychological Care of Infant and Child.* New York: W. W. Norton, 1928. pp. 81–82.
73. Karen. *Becoming Attached.* p. 147. Interview with Ainsworth, 1988.
74. Karen. *Becoming Attached.* p. 172.
75. Sroufe, L. Alan. Talk at City University of New York, Graduate Center. February 10, 1989. Quoted in Karen. *Becoming Attached.* p. 195.
76. Bowlby, John. *Attachment and Loss.* Vol. 1: *Attachment.* New York: Basic Books. 1982. p. 368.
77. Karen. *Becoming Attached.* p. 304.
78. Ibid. p. 312.

CHAPTER 3: A SENTIENT INTERPRETATION OF BIOLOGICAL EVOLUTION

1. Miller, Greg. "Neuroscience: Reflecting on Another's Mind." *Science.* Vol. 308. No. 5724. May 13, 2005. pp. 945–947.
2. Blakeslee, Sandra. "Cells That Read Minds." *The New York Times.* Jan. 10, 2006.
3. Glenberg, Arthur M. "Naturalizing Cognition: The Integration of Cognitive Science and Biology." *Current Biology.* Vol. 16. No. 18. Sept. 19, 2006. pp. R802–804.
4. Siegel, Daniel J. *The Mindful Brain: Reflection and Attunement in the Cultivation of Well-Being.* New York: W.W. Norton, 2007. p. 165.
5. Ibid. pp. 165–166.
6. Blakeslee. "Cells That Read Minds."
7. Keysers, C., B. Wicker, V. Gazzola, J. L. Anton, L. Fogassi, and V. Gallese. "A Touching Sight: SII/PV Activation During the Observation and Experience of Touch." *Neuron.* Vol. 42. No. 2. Apr. 22, 2004. p. 336.
8. Ibid. p. 342.
9. Holden, Constance. "Neuroscience: Imaging Studies Show How Brain Thinks About Pain." *Science.* Vol. 303. No. 5661. February 20, 2004. p. 1121.
10. Blakeslee. "Cells That Read Minds."
11. "Why Autistic Children Do Not Imitate or Empathize: It Could Be a Dysfunctional Mirror-Neuron System." University of California–Los Angeles. *ScienceDaily.* May 4, 2007.
12. Ibid.

13. Blakeslee. "Cells That Read Minds."

14. Stein, Rob. "Science Notebook: Chimps Show Desire to Fit In." *The Washington Post*. Aug. 22, 2005. p. A5.

15. Bradshaw, G. A., Allan N. Schore, Janine L. Brown, Joyce H. Poole, and Cynthia J. Moss. "Elephant Breakdown." *Nature*. Vol. 433. February 24, 2005. p. 807.

16. Miller. "Neuroscience: Reflecting on Another's Mind." pp. 945–946.

17. Plotnik, Joshua M., Frans B. M. de Waal, and Diana Reiss. "Self-Recognition in an Asian Elephant." *Proceedings of the National Academy of Sciences*. Vol. 103. No. 45. Nov. 7, 2006. pp. 17,053–17,057.

18. Masson, Jeffrey. *When Elephants Weep: The Emotional Lives of Animals*. New York: Delta, 1995. p. 155.

19. Berreby, David. "Deceit of the Raven." *The New York Times Magazine*. Sept. 4, 2005. pp. 20–22.

20. Ibid.

21. Ibid.

22. Begley, Sharon. "Animals Seem to Have an Inherent Sense of Fairness and Justice." *The Wall Street Journal*. Nov. 10, 2006. p. B1.

23. Darwin, Charles. *The Descent of Man*. New York: Appleton and Co. 1879. p. 74.

24. Ibid.

25. Ibid. p. 72.

26. Ibid. p. 40.

27. Ibid. p. 104.

28. Darwin, Charles. *The Descent of Man, and Selection in Relation to Sex*. Princeton, NJ: Princeton University Press, 1982 [1871]. p. 77.

29. Darwin, Charles. *The Descent of Man*. Encyclopaedia Britannica, Great Books. Vol. 49. 1952. p. 316.

30. Ibid.

31. Darwin, Charles. *The Descent of Man*. Princeton, NJ: Princeton University Press, 1981 [1871]. p. 101.

32. Overton, Rebecca. "Lonely Only." *Horse and Rider*. Vol. 45. No. 3. March 2006.

33. Panksepp, Jaak. *Affective Neuroscience: The Foundation of Emotions*. New York: Oxford University Press, 1998.

34. MacLean, Paul. *The Triune Brain in Evolution: Role in Paleocerebral Functions*. New York: Plenum Press, 1990. p. 380.

35. Ibid. p. 520.

36. Huizinga, Johan. *Homo Ludens: A Study of the Play Element in Culture*. Boston: Beacon Press, 1955. p. 46.

37. Vygotsky, Lev S. "The Role of Play in Development." *Mind in Society*. M. Cole, trans. Cambridge, MA: Harvard University Press, 1978. p. 103.

38. Ibid. p. 102.

39. Schiller, Friedrich. *On the Aesthetic Education of Man, In a Series of Letters*. Elizabeth M. Wilkinson and L. A. Willoughby, eds. and trans. Oxford: Clarendon Press, 1967.

40. Sartre, Jean-Paul. *The Writings of Jean-Paul Sartre*, Vol. 2. Evanston, IL: Northwestern University Press, 1974.

41. Arbib, Michael A. "The Mirror System Hypothesis on the Linkage of Action and Languages." In Michael A. Arbib, ed. *Action to Language via the Mirror Neuron System*. Cambridge, UK: Cambridge University Press, 2006. p. 25.

42. Ibid. p. 26.

43. de Waal, Frans. *Primates and Philosophers: How Morality Evolved*. Stephen Macedo and Josiah Ober, eds. Princeton, NJ: Princeton University Press, 2006. p. 24.

44. Ibid. p. 25.

45. Ibid. p. 27.

46. Ibid. p. 28.

47. Ibid. p. 29.

48. Ibid. p. 31.

49. Ibid. p. 36.

50. Ibid. p. 43.

51. Dunbar, Robin. *Grooming, Gossip, and the Evolution of Language*. Cambridge, MA: Harvard University Press, 1996. p. 35.

52. Ibid. p. 36.

53. Ibid. p. 62.

54. Ibid. p. 70.

55. Ibid. p. 116.

56. Ibid. p. 78.

57. Arbib, Michael A. "The Mirror System Hypothesis." In Arbib. *Action to Language via the Mirror Neuron System*. p. 42.

58. McNeill, David. *Hand and Mind: What Gestures Reveal About Thought*. Chicago: University of Chicago Press, 1992. p.2.

CHAPTER 4: BECOMING HUMAN

1. James, William. *The Principles of Psychology*. Vol. 1. New York: Henry Holt, 1918. p. 488.

2. Greenspan, Stanley (with Beryl Lieff Benderly). *The Growth of the Mind: And the Endangered Origins of Intelligence*. Reading, MA: Addison Wesley, 1997. p 50.

3. Ibid. p. 54.

4. Ibid. p. 58.

5. Ibid. p. 64.

6. Ibid. p. 72.

7. Ibid. p. 75.

8. Ibid. p. 78.

9. Ibid. p. 82.

10. Ibid. p. 85.

11. Ibid. p. 88.

12. Ibid. p. 113.

13. Ibid. p. 116.

14. Ibid. p. 120.

15. Ibid. p. 193.

16. Hoffman, Martin L. *Empathy and Moral Development: Implications for Caring and Justice.* Cambridge, UK: Cambridge University Press, 2000. p. 5.

17. Ibid.

18. Smith, Adam. *Theory of Moral Development; or, An Essay Towards an Analysis of the Principles by Which Men Naturally Judge Concerning the Conduct and Character, First of Their Neighbours, and Afterwards of Themselves.* London: H. G. Bohn, 1853. pp. 4, 10.

19. Chartrand, Tanya L., William W. Maddux, and Jessica L. Lakin. "Beyond the Perception-Behavior Link: The Ubiquitous Utility and Motivational Moderators of Nonconscious Mimicry." In Hassin, Ran R., James S. Uleman, and John A. Bargh, eds. *The New Unconscious.* Oxford: Oxford University Press, 2005. p. 337.

20. Hoffman. *Empathy and Moral Development.* p. 38.

21. Ibid. pp. 38–39.

22. Chartrand, Maddux, and Lakin. "Beyond the Perception-Behavior Link: The Ubiquitous Utility and Motivational Moderators of Nonconscious Mimicry." p. 339.

23. Ibid. p. 344.

24. Ibid. p. 336.

25. Ibid. p. 340.

26. Ibid. p. 344.

27. Bargh, John A. "Bypassing the Will: Toward Demystifying the Nonconscious Control of Social Behavior." In Hassin, Uleman, and Bargh, eds. *The New Unconscious.* p. 45.

28. Levenson, Robert W., and Anna M. Ruef. "Physiological Aspects of Emotional Knowledge and Rapport." In William Ickes, ed. *Empathic Accuracy.* New York: Guilford Press, 1997. pp. 68–69.

29. James, William. Quoted in Martin L. Hoffman. *Empathy and Moral Development: Implications for Caring and Justice.* p. 40.

30. Laird, J. D., J. J. Wagener, M. Halal, and M. Szedga. "Remembering What You Feel: Effects of Emotion and Memory." *Journal of Personality and Social Psychology.* Vol. 42. 1982. p. 480.

31. Laird, J. D. "The Real Role of Facial Response in the Experience of Emotion." *Journal of Personality and Social Psychology.* Vol. 47. 1984. pp. 909–917.

32. Ekman, Paul E., Richard Sorenson, and Wallace V. Friesen. "Pan-Cultural Elements in Facial Displays of Emotion." *Science.* Vol. 164. 1969. pp. 86–88.

33. Hoffman, *Empathy and Moral Development.* p. 42.

34. Ibid. p. 44.

35. Bavelas et al. "Form and Function in Motor Mimicry." *Human Communications Research.* Vol. 14. 1988. pp. 275–299. Bavelas et al. "Motor Mimicry as Primitive Empathy. In N. Eisenberg and J. Strayer, eds. *Empathy and Its Development.* Cambridge, UK: Cambridge University Press, 1987. pp. 317–338.

36. Wingert, Pat, and Martha Brant. "Reading Your Baby's Mind." *Newsweek.* August 15, 2005. pp. 32–39.

37. Hoffman. *Empathy and Moral Development.* p. 47.

38. Ibid. p. 48.

39. Ibid. pp. 56–57.

40. Ibid. p. 140.

41. Ibid. p. 141.

42. Ibid.

43. Ibid. p. 142.

44. Ibid. p. 143.

45. Ibid. pp. 158.

46. Ibid. p. 152.

47. Lewis, Michael, Jeannette M. Haviland-Jones, and Lisa Feldman Barrett. *Handbook of Emotions.* New York: Guilford Press, 2008. p. 445.

48. Nussbaum, Martha C. *Upheavals of Thought: The Intelligence of Emotions.* Cambridge, UK: Cambridge University Press, 2003. pp. 216–217.

49. Freud, Sigmund. *Civilization and Its Discontents.* James Strachey, trans. New York: W. W. Norton, 1961. p. 74.

50. Freud, Sigmund. *Group Psychology and the Analysis of the Ego.* James Strachey, trans. James Strachey and Peter Gay, contribs. New York: W. W. Norton, 1975. p. 68.

51. Hoffman. *Empathy and Moral Development.* p. 198.

52. Bretherton, Inge, Janet Fritz, Carolyn Zahn-Waxler, and Doreen Ridgeway. "Learning to Talk About Emotions: A Functionalist Perspective." *Child Development.* Vol. 57. No. 3. 1986. pp. 529–548.

53. Astington, J. W., and A. Gopnik. "Theoretical Explanations of Children's Understanding of the Mind. *British Journal of Developmental Psychology.* Vol. 9. 1991. pp. 7–31.

54. Mascolo, M. F., and K. W. Fischer. "Developmental Transformations in Appraisals for Pride, Shame, and Guilt. In J. P. Tangney and K. M. Fischer, eds. *Self-Conscious Emotions.* New York: Guilford Press, 1995. pp. 64–113.

55. Strayer, Janet. "Children's Concordant Emotions and Cognitions in Response to Observed Emotions." *Child Development.* No. 64. 1993. pp. 188–201.

56. Mascolo and Fischer. "Developmental Transformations in Appraisals for Pride, Shame, and Guilt. In Tangney and Fischer, eds. *Self-Conscious Emotions.* pp. 64–113.

57. Weiner, B., S. Graham, P. Stern, and M. E. Lawson. "Using Affective Cues to Infer Causal Thoughts." *Developmental Psychology* 18. 1982. pp. 278–286.

58. Pazer, S., E. Slackman, and M. L. Hoffman. "Age and Sex Differences in the Effect of Information on Anger." Unpublished manuscript. City University of New York, 1981. Cited in Hoffman. *Empathy and Moral Development.* p. 76.

59. Mascolo and Fischer. "Developmental Transformations in Appraisals for Pride, Shame, and Guilt." In Tangney and Fischer, eds. *Self-Conscious Emotions.* pp. 64–113.

60. Donaldson and Westerman. "Development of Children's Understanding of Ambivalence and Casual Theories of Emotions." In William Ickes, ed. *Empathic Accuracy.* p. 95.

61. Ibid.

62. Rotenberg, K. J., and N. Eisenberg. "Developmental Differences in the Understanding of and Reaction to Others' Inhibition of Emotional Expression." *Developmental Psychology.* Vol. 33. 1997. pp. 526–537.

63. Hoffman L. *Empathy and Moral Development.* p. 82.

64. Ibid. p. 85.

65. Hamlin, J. Kiley, Karen Wynn, and Paul Bloom. "Social Evaluation by Preverbal Infants." *Nature.* Vol. 450. No. 2. November 22, 2007. p. 557.

66. Ibid.

67. Ibid.

68. Ibid. pp. 558–559.

69. "Roots of Altruism Show in Babies' Helping Hands." *Associated Press.* March 2, 2006. www.msnbc.com/id/11641621/

70. Hoffman. *Empathy and Moral Development.* p. 33.

71. Batson, C. D. "How Social an Animal? The Human Capacity for Caring." *American Psychologist.* Vol. 45. No. 3. March 1990. p. 342.

72. Batson, C. D., Judy G. Batson, Jacqueline K. Slingsby, Kevin L. Harrell et al. "Empathic Joy and the Empathy-Altruism Hypothesis." *Journal of Personality and Social Psychology.* Vol. 61. No. 3. September 1991. pp. 413–426.

73. Ibid.

74. Ibid.

75. Batson. "How Social an Animal?" p. 344.

76. Kitayama, S., H. Matsumoto, H. R. Markus, and V. Norasakkunkit. "Individual and Collective Processes in Construction of the Self: Self-Enhancement in the United States and Self-Criticism in Japan. *Journal of Personality and Social Psychology.* Vol. 72. No. 6. 1997. pp. 1,244–1,267.

77. Ibid. p. 1254.

78. Ibid. pp. 1254–1255.

CHAPTER 5: RETHINKING THE MEANING OF THE HUMAN JOURNEY

1. Jenkins, J. I., and T. Burish. "Reason and Faith at Harvard." *The Washington Post.* October 23, 2006. p. A21.

2. Ibid.

3. Bombardieri, M. "Harvard Panel Sets Aside Plan on Religion." *The Boston Globe.* December 13, 2006.

4. Hoyt, R. S. *Europe in the Middle Ages,* 2nd ed. New York: Harcourt, Brace, and World. 1966. pp. 382–383.

5. Ibid. p. 383.

6. Randall, J. H. *The Making of the Modern Mind.* Cambridge, MA: Houghton Mifflin, 1940. p. 241. Quotation by Descartes.

7. Ibid. pp. 241–242.

8. Descartes, René. "Meditations on First Philosophy: Second Meditation." In John Cottingham et al., eds. *The Philosophical Writings of Descartes.* Vol. 1 Cambridge, UK: Cambridge University Press. 1986. p. 21. (Descartes's emphasis)

9. Descartes, René. *The Philosophical Works of Descartes.* Vol. 1. Elizabeth S. Haldane and G.R.T. Ross, trans. New York: Cambridge University Press, 1970. p. 101.

10. Damasio, Antonio. *Descartes' Error: Emotion, Reason, and the Human Brain.* New York: Quill, 2000. p. 252.

11. Ibid. p. xii.

12. Ibid. p. xiii.

13. Ibid. p. 64.

14. Ibid. p. 71.

15. Ibid. p. 72.

16. Ibid. p. xvii.

17. Ibid.

18. Bakhtin, M. M. *Problems of Dostoevsky's Poetics.* Caryl Emerson, ed. and trans. Minneapolis, MN: University of Minnesota Press, 1984. p. 287. (Bakhtin's emphasis)

19. John Rowan and Mick Cooper. *The Plural Self: Multiplicity in Everyday Life.* London: Sage, 1999. p. 83.

20. Ibid. p. 87.

21. Kant, Immanuel. *Critique of Pure Reason.* Norton Kemp Smith, trans. New York: St. Martin's Press, 1963. p. 257.

22. Valera, Francisco, Evan T. Thompson, and Eleanor Rosch. *The Embodied Mind: Cognitive Science and Human Experience.* Cambridge, MA: MIT Press, 1991. p. 66.

23. Lakoff, George, and Mark Johnson. *Philosophy in the Flesh: The Embodied Mind and Its Challenge to Western Thought.* New York: Basic Books, 1999. p. 37.

24. Ibid.

25. "A Bald Eagle's Eyesight and Hearing." American Bald Eagle Information. www.baldeagleinfo.com

26. Lakoff and Johnson. *Philosophy in the Flesh.* p. 4.

27. Freud, Sigmund. *Collected Papers.* Joan Reviere and James Strachey, eds. New York: International Psycho-Analytical Press, Vol. 4, 1924–1950. p. 215.

28. Skolimowski, Henryk. *The Participatory Mind.* London: Penguin, 1994. p. 373. (Skolimowski's emphasis)

29. Francis Bacon, as quoted in Randall, John Herman. *The Making of the Modern Mind*. Cambridge, MA: Houghton Mifflin, 1940. p. 233.

30. Bacon, Francis. "Novum Organum." In *The Works of Francis Bacon*. Vol. 4. London: W. Pickering, 1850. p. 114.

31. Brandon, S. G. F. *History, Time and Deity*. Manchester, UK: Manchester University Press, 1965. p. 206.

32. Condorcet, Marquis de. "Outline of an Historical View of Progress of the Human Mind." Quoted in John Hallowell, *Main Currents in Modern Political Thought*. New York: Holt, Rinehart, and Winston, 1950. p. 132.

33. Rilke quoted in Norman O. Brown. *Life Against Death: The Psychoanalytical Meaning of History*, 2nd ed. Middletown, CT: Wesleyan University Press, 1985. p. 108.

34. Hegel, G.W.F. *The Science of Logic*. London: G. Allen and Unwin, 1929. p. 142.

35. Ciaramicoli, Arthur P., and Katherine Ketcham. *The Power of Empathy*. New York: Dutton, 2000. p. 213.

36. Leo Tolstoy, as quoted in Ibid. p. 212.

37. Ibid.

38. Borg, M. J. *The God We Never Knew: Beyond Dogmatic Religion to a More Authentic Contemporary Faith*. San Francisco: HarperSanFrancisco, 1997.

39. "Luke, Chapter 10." United States Conference of Catholic Bishops. http://usccb.org/nab/bible/luke/luke10.htm

40. Kant, Immanuel. *Grounding for the Metaphysics of Morals*; with *On a Supposed Right to Lie Because of Philanthropic Concerns*, 3rd ed. James W. Ellington, trans. Indianapolis: Hackett Publishing, 1993. p. vi.

41. Ibid. p. 36.

CHAPTER 6: THE ANCIENT THEOLOGICAL BRAIN AND PATRIARCHAL ECONOMY

1. Goethe, Johann Wolfgang von. *Goethe's Fairy Tale of the Green Snake and the Beautiful Lily*. Donald Maclean, trans. Grand Rapids, MI: Phanes Press, 1993. p. 16.

2. Dupré, Louis. *The Enlightenment and the Intellectual Foundations of Modern Culture*. New Haven, CT: Yale University Press, 2004. p. 76.

3. Miller, Peggy, and Barbara Byhouwer Moore. "Narrative Conjunctions of Care-Giver and Child: A Comparative Perspective on Socialization Through Stories." *Ethos*. Vol. 17. No. 4. 1989. pp. 428–449.

4. Nelson, Katherine. "Narrative and the Emergence of a Consciousness of Self." pp. 17–36. In Fireman, Gary D, Ted E. McVay, Jr., and Owen J. Flanagan, eds. *Narrative and Consciousness: Literature, Psychology, and the Brain*. Oxford, UK: Oxford University Press, 2003. p. 22.

5. Bruner, Jerome. *Acts of Meaning*. Cambridge, MA: Harvard University Press, 1990. p. 95.

6. Hardcastle, Valerie Gray. "The Development of the Self." pp. 37–50. In Fireman and Flanagan. *Narrative and Consciousness*. pp. 46–47.

7. Mumford, Lewis. *Technics and Human Development*. New York: Harcourt Brace Jovanovich/Harvest Books, 1966. p. 101.

8. Kahler, Erich. *Man the Measure: A New Approach to History*. Cleveland: Meridian Books, 1967. p. 35.

9. Lucien Lévy-Bruhl, as quoted in Ibid. p. 34.

10. Kahler, *Man the Measure*. p. 36.

11. Mumford. *Technics and Human Development*. p. 127.

12. Ibid. p. 130.

13. Ibid. p. 142.

14. Ibid. p. 146.

15. Ibid. p. 157.

16. Debeir, Jean-Claude, Jean-Paul Deléage, and Daniel Hémery. *In the Servitude of Power: Energy and Civilization Through the Ages*. John Barzman, trans. London: Zed Books, 1991. p. 21.

17. Logan, Robert K. *The Alphabet Effect: The Impact of the Phonetic Alphabet on the Development of Western Civilization*. New York: William Morrow, 1986. p. 60.

18. Diringer, David. *The Alphabet: A Key to the History of Mankind*, 2nd ed. New York: Philosophical Library, 1953. Gelb, Ignace. *A Study of Writing*, rev. ed. Chicago: University of Chicago Press, 1963.

19. Logan. *The Alphabet Effect*. pp. 67–69.

20. White, L. A. *The Evolution of Culture: The Development of Civilization to the Fall of Rome*. Walnut Creek, CA: Left Coast Press, 2007. p. 356.

21. Logan. *The Alphabet Effect*. p. 70

22. Ibid. p. 32.

23. Ibid. p. 78.

24. Debeir, Deléage, and Hémery. *In the Servitude of Power*. pp. 22–23.

25. Mumford, Lewis. *The Transformations of Man*. Gloucester, MA: Peter Smith, 1978. p. 40.

26. Wittfogel, Karl A. *Oriental Despotism: A Comparative Study of Total Power*. New York: Vintage Books, 1981. pp. 254–255.

27. Ibid. p. 37.

28. Mitchell, Stephen. *Gilgamesh*. New York: Free Press, 2004. pp. 1–4.

29. Rainer Maria Rilke, as quoted in Ibid. p. 3.

30. Ibid. p. 8.

31. Ibid. p. 47

32. Mumford. *Technics and Human Development*. p. 167.

33. Ibid. p. 173.

34. Wittfogel. *Oriental Despotism*. p. 93.

35. Labat, René. *Le Caractère Religieux de la Royauté Assyro-Babylonienne*. Paris, 1939. p. 63.

36. White. *The Evolution of Culture.* p. 361.

37. Ibid. pp. 361–362.

38. Breasted, James H. *The Development of Religion and Thought in Ancient Egypt.* New York: Charles Scribner's Sons, 1912. pp. 312, 315.

39. Wittfogel. *Oriental Despotism.* p. 95.

40. Logan. *The Alphabet Effect.* p. 81.

41. Ong, Walter. *Orality and Literacy: The Technologizing of the Word.* New York: Routledge, 2000. p. 71.

42. Duby, Georges. "Solitude: Eleventh to Thirteenth Century." In Georges Duby, ed. *A History of Private Life: Revelations in the Medieval World.* Vol. 2. Cambridge, MA: Harvard University Press, 1988. p. 510. Tuan, Yi-Fu. *Segmented Worlds and Self: Group Life and Individual Consciousness.* Minneapolis: University of Minnesota Press, 1982. p. 58.

43. Ambrose of Milan, as quoted in Ong. *Orality and Literacy.* p. 117.

44. Edmonson, Munro S. *Lore: An Introduction to the Science of Folklore and Literature.* New York: Holt, Rinehart and Winston, 1971. pp. 323, 332.

45. Ong. *Orality and Literacy.* p. 8.

46. Ibid. p. 54.

47. Luria, Aleksandr Romanovich. *Cognitive Development: Its Cultural and Social Foundations.* Michael Cole, ed. Martin Lopez-Morillas and Lynn Solotaroff, trans. Cambridge, MA, and London: Harvard University Press, 1976. p. 15.

48. Ibid. pp. 32–39.

49. Ibid. p. 56.

50. Ong. *Orality and Literacy.* p. 55.

51. Ibid. p. 104.

52. Ibid.

53. Exodus 31:18 (King James Version)

54. Logan. *The Alphabet Effect.* p. 80.

55. Kahler. *Man the Measure.* p. 68.

56. Leviticus 19:18 (King James Version)

57. Armstrong, Karen. *The Great Transformation: The Beginning of Our Religious Traditions.* New York: Alfred A. Knopf, 2006. p. 379.

58. Leviticus 19:34 (King James Version)

59. Deuteronomy 15, 16, 23, 24.

60. Armstrong. *The Great Transformation.* p. 367.

61. Ibid. p. 205.

62. Confucius, Analects 6:28. *The Analects of Confucius.* Arthur Waley, trans. and ed. New York, 1992. p. 68.

63. Ibid. Analects 15:23.

64. Mencius. *The Works of Mencius.* Gu Lu, trans. Shanghai: Shangwu, n.d. [372–289 BC]. p. 78.

65. Armstrong. *The Great Transformation.* p. 242.

66. Ibid. p. 277.

67. Ibid.

68. Ibid. p. 279.

69. Jacobsen, Thorkild, and Robert M. Adams. "Salt and Silt in Ancient Mesopotamian Agriculture: Progressive Changes in Soil Salinity and Sedimentation Contributed to the Breakup of Past Civilizations." *Science.* Vol. 128. No. 3334. November 21, 1958. pp. 1251–1252.

70. Ibid. p. 1252.

71. Ibid. p. 1252.

72. Pearce, Fred. *Keepers of the Spring: Reclaiming Our Water in an Age of Globalization.* Washington, DC: Island Press, 2004.

73. Kotzer, Eli. "Artificial Kidneys for the Soil—Solving the Problem of Salinization of the Soil and Underground Water." *Desalination.* Vol. 185. 2005. pp. 71–77.

74. Krech, Shepard, John Robert McNeill, and Carolyn Merchant. *Encyclopedia of World Environmental History.* New York: Routledge, 2004. pp. 1089–1090.

CHAPTER 7: COSMOPOLITAN ROME AND THE RISE OF URBAN CHRISTIANITY

1. Kessler, David, and Peter Temin. "The Organization of the Grain Trade in the Early Roman Empire." *Economic History Review.* Vol. 60. No. 2. 2006. pp. 313–332.

2. Wittfogel, Karl A. *Oriental Despotism: A Comparative Study of Total Power.* New York: Vintage Books, 1981. p. 211.

3. Chevallier, Raymond. *Roman Roads.* N. H. Field, trans. London: B.T. Batsford Ltd, 1976. p. 203.

4. Meeks, Wayne A. *The First Urban Christians: The Social World of the Apostle Paul.* New Haven: Yale University Press, 1983. p.18.

5. Debeir, Jean-Claude, Jean-Paul Deléage, and Daniel Hémery. *In the Servitude of Power: Energy and Civilization Through the Ages.* John Barzman, trans. London: Zed Books, 1991. p. 35.

6. Meeks. *The First Urban Christians.* p. 16.

7. La Piana, George. "Foreign Groups in Rome During the First Centuries of the Empire." *Harvard Theological Review.* Vol. 20. No. 4. Oct 1927. p. 188.

8. Peterson, Daniel C., and William J. Hamblin. "Ancient Rome: A Merging of Religious Ideas." *Meridian Magazine,* 2005. www.meridianmagazine .com/ideas/050110rome.html

9. Cato. *De Agricultura* XVI. Quoted in Debeir, Deléage, and Hémery. *In the Servitude of Power.* p. 36.

10. Debeir, Deléage, and Hémery. *In the Servitude of Power.* p. 37.

11. Apuleius. *Metamorphoses* IX. Quoted in Debeir et al. *In the Servitude of Power.* pp. 37–38.

12. La Piana, G. "Foreign Groups in Rome During the First Centuries of the Empire." p. 191.

13. Ibid. p. 197.

14. Ibid. p. 201.

15. Moatti, Claudia. "Translation, Migration, and Communication in the Roman Empire: Three Aspects of Movement in History." *Classical Antiquity*. Vol. 25. No. 1. 2006. p. 116.

16. Aristides, Aelius. *Orations* 37 "Regarding the Emperor." In C. A. Behr, trans. *P. Aelius Aristides: The Complete Works.* Vol. 2. Leiden, 1981.

17. La Piana. "Foreign Groups in Rome During the First Centuries of the Empire." p. 323.

18. Ibid. p. 328.

19. Ibid. p. 346. Meeks. *The First Urban Christians.* p. 34.

20. Kahler, Erich. *Man the Measure: A New Approach to History.* Cleveland: Meridian Books, 1967. pp. 174–175.

21. Meeks. *The First Urban Christians.* pp. 21–22.

22. Ibid. p. 23.

23. Ibid. p. 28.

24. Ibid. p. 73.

25. Ibid. p. 86.

26. Ibid. p. 88.

27. Acts 17:26. (The Holy Bible, King James Version)

28. Galatians 3:28. (The Holy Bible, King James Version)

29. Matthew 5:38, 5:39. (The Holy Bible, King James Version)

30. Ibid. Matthew 5:43, 5:44.

31. Ibid. Luke 23:34.

32. Sennett, Richard. *Flesh and Stone: The Body and The City in Western Civilization.* New York: W. W. Norton, 1994. p. 132.

33. Pagels, Elaine. *The Origin of Satan: How Christians Demonized Jews, Pagans, and Heretics.* New York: Vintage Books, 1995. p. xix.

34. Pagels, Elaine. *The Gnostic Gospels.* New York: Vintage Books, 1989. p. xv.

35. Ibid. xvi.

36. Koester, Helmut. "Introduction to the *Gospel of Thomas.*" In *The Nag Hammadi Library.* James M. Robinson, ed. San Francisco: Harper & Row, 1988. p. 124.

37. Pagels. *The Gnostic Gospels.* p. xix.

38. Ibid. p. xx.

39. Conze, Edward. "Buddhism and Gnosis." In *Le Origini dello Gnosticismo: Colloquio di Messina.* 13–18 April 1966. Leiden, 1967. p. 665.

40. Pagels. *The Gnostic Gospels.* p. xxi.

41. Ibid.

42. Jonas, Hans. *The Gnostic Religion,* 2nd ed. Boston: Beacon Press, 1963.

43. Quispel, G. *Gnosis als Weltreligion.* Zurich: Origo, 1951.

44. "Gospel of Thomas." *The Complete Gospels: Annotated Scholar's Version.* Robert J. Miller, ed. www.westarinstitute.org/Polebridge/Excerpts/thomas.html.

45. Ibid.

46. Ibid.

47. Mark 8:29. (The Holy Bible, New International Version)

48. Ibid. pp. 72–73. (Pagel's emphasis)

49. Pagels. *The Gnostic Gospels.* p. 129.

50. Irenaeus. *Libros Quinque Adversus Haereses* 1.5.4.

51. Pagels. *The Gnostic Gospels.* p. 144.

52. Deuteronomy 8:5. (King James Version)

53. Deuteronomy 21:18–21. (King James Version)

54. Saint Augustine. *On Christian Doctrine.* D. W. Robertson, Jr., trans. Indianapolis: Bobbs-Merrill, 1958. pp. 55–56.

55. The Holy Bible. Matthew 18:3, 18:10, 18:14. New York: Thomas Nelson and Sons, 1903.

56. Greven, Philip. *Spare the Child: The Religious Roots of Punishment and the Psychological Impact of Physical Abuse.* p. 51.

57. Colossians 3:20–21. (King James Version)

58. Lyman, Richard B., Jr. "Barbarism and Religion: Late Roman and Early Medieval Childhood." In Lloyd deMause, ed. *The History of Childhood: The Untold Story of Child Abuse.* p. 95.

59. Ibid.

60. Ibid. p. 90.

61. deMause, Lloyd. "The Evolution of Childhood." In Lloyd deMause, ed. *The History of Childhood: The Untold Story of Child Abuse.* p. 27.

62. Ibid. p. 28.

63. Lyman, Richard. B., Jr. "Barbarism and Religion: Late Roman and Early Medieval Childhood." In deMause. *The History of Childhood.* p. 76.

64. Krautheimer, Richard. *Early Christian and Byzantine Architecture.* 4th ed. New York: Viking-Penguin, 1986. p. 24–25.

65. Sennett. *Flesh and Stone.* p. 142.

66. La Piana, G. "Foreign Groups in Rome During the First Centuries of the Empire." p. 395.

67. Krautheimer. *Christian and Byzantine Architecture,* p. 40.

68. Kahler. *Man the Measure.* p. 166.

69. Ibid.

70. Weintraub, Karl J. *The Value of the Individual: Self and Circumstance in Autobiography.* Chicago: University of Chicago Press, 1978. p. 21.

71. Saint Augustine. *Confessions,* 6th ed. R. S. Pine-Coffin, trans. and contrib. London: Penguin Classics, 1961. p. 169.

72. Lévy, Jean-Philippe. *The Economic Life of the Ancient World.* John G. Biram, trans. Chicago: University of Chicago Press, 1967. pp. 62–65.

73. Jones, A.H.M. *The Later Roman Empire, 284–602: A Social, Economic and Administrative Survey.* Norman, OK: University of Oklahoma Press,

1964. pp. 114–115. Frank Tenney. *An Economic Survey of Ancient Rome.* Vol. V: *Rome and Italy of the Empire.* Baltimore: John Hopkins Press, 1940. pp. 7–9.

74. Gibbon, Edward. *The Decline and Fall of the Roman Empire.* New York: Modern Library, 1776–88. p. 142.

75. Levy. *The Economic Life of the Ancient World.* pp. 69, 77.

76. Jones. *The Roman Economy: Studies in Ancient Economic and Administrative History.* Oxford: Basil Blackwell, 1974. pp. 116, 127. Hammond, Mason. "Economic Stagnation in the Early Roman Empire." *Journal of Economic History*, Supplement. Vol. 6. pp. 75–76.

77. Tainter, Joseph A. *The Collapse of Complex Societies.* Cambridge, UK: Cambridge University Press, 1988. p. 133.

78. La Piana, G. "Foreign Groups in Rome During the First Centuries of the Empire." p. 199.

79. Ibid.

80. Tainter. *The Collapse of Complex Societies.* p. 142.

81. Ibid. p. 145.

82. Simkhovitch, Vladimir G. "Rome's Fall Reconsidered." *Political Science Quarterly.* Vol. 23, No. 2, June 1916. p. 226.

83. McNeill, William H. *Plagues and Peoples.* Garden City, NY: Anchor/Doubleday, 1976. p. 116. Hughes, Donald J. *Ecology in Ancient Civilizations.* Albuquerque, NM: University of New Mexico Press, 1975. p. 131.

84. Tainter. *The Collapse of Complex Societies.* p. 144.

85. Simkhovitch. "Rome's Fall Reconsidered." p. 237.

86. Debeir, Deléage, and Hémery. *In the Servitude of Power.* p. 40.

87. Tainter. *The Collapse of Complex Societies.* p. 150.

88. "Ancient Rome." *Encarta Online Encyclopedia*, 2001. Harl, Kenneth. "Early Medieval and Byzantine Civilization: Constantine to Crusades." www.tulane.edu/~august/H303/Byzantine.html

CHAPTER 8: THE SOFT INDUSTRIAL REVOLUTION OF THE LATE MEDIEVAL ERA AND THE BIRTH OF HUMANISM

1. Randall, John Herman, Jr. *The Making of the Modern Mind: A Survey of the Intellectual Background of the Present Age.* New York: Columbia University Press, 1976. p. 89.

2. Debeir, Jean-Claude, Jean-Paul Deléage, and Daniel Hémery. *In the Servitude of Power: Energy and Civilization Through the Ages.* London: Zed Books, 1991. p. 71.

3. White, Lynn, Jr. *Medieval Technology and Social Change.* London: Oxford University Press, 1964. p. 76.

4. Gimpel, Jean. *La Révolution Industrielle du Moyen-Age*, Paris: Le Seuil, 1975.

5. Carneiro, Robert L. "The Measurement of Cultural Development in the Ancient Near East in Anglo-Saxon England." *Transactions of the New York Academy of Sciences.* 2nd ser. Vol. 31. No. 8. p. 1020.

6. Hogden, M. T. "Domesday Water Mills." *Antiquity.* Vol. xiii. 1939. p. 266.

7. White. *Medieval Technology and Social Change.* p. 84.

8. Ibid. p. 89.

9. Debeir, Deléage, and Hémery. *In the Servitude of Power.* p. 75.

10. Ibid. p. 76.

11. *Records of the Templars in England in the Twelfth Century: The Inquest of 1185.* B. A. Lees, ed. London, 1935. p. 131.

12. Debeir, Deléage, Hémery. *In the Servitude of Power.* p. 79.

13. Ibid. p. 90.

14. White. *Medieval Technology and Social Change.* p. 129.

15. Ibid. pp. 128–129.

16. Clapham, Michael. "Printing." *A History of Technology, Vol. 3, From the Renaissance to the Industrial Revolution.* Charles Singer, E. G. Holmyard, A. R. Hall, and Trevor Williams, eds. Oxford, 1957. p. 37.

17. Cipolla, Carlo M. *Literacy and Development in the West.* London, 1969. p. 60.

18. Dickens, Arthur Geoffrey. *Reformation and Society in Sixteenth Century Europe.* New York, 1968. p. 51.

19. Wright, Louis B. *Middle-Class Culture in Elizabethan England.* Chapel Hill, NC, 1935. pp. 239–241.

20. Ong, Walter. *Orality and Literacy: The Technologizing of the Word.* London: Routledge, 2002. p. 129.

21. Ibid. p. 130.

22. Eisenstein, Elizabeth L. *The Printing Revolution in Early Modern Europe.* Cambridge, UK: Cambridge University Press, 1983. p. 95.

23. Toulmin, Stephen. *Cosmopolis: The Hidden Agenda of Modernity.* Chicago: University of Chicago Press, 1992. p. 28.

24. Montaigne, Michel de. *The Complete Essays of Montaigne.* Donald M. Frame, ed. Stanford, CA: Stanford University Press, 1958. p. 641.

25. Ibid. p. 855.

26. Trilling, Lionel. *Sincerity and Authenticity.* Cambridge, MA: Harvard University Press, 1972. p. 2.

27. Shakespeare, William. *Hamlet.* Act I, Scene III.

28. Trilling. *Sincerity and Authenticity.* p. 20.

29. Ibid. p.13.

30. Baumeister, Roy F. *Identity: Cultural Change and the Struggle for Self.* New York: Oxford University

Press. 1986. p. 40. Quotation from *Oxford English Dictionary*, c. 1400.

31. Barley, M. W. *The House and Home: A Review of 900 Years of House Planning and Furnishing in Britain.* Greenwich, CT: New York Graphic Society, 1971. pp. 40–41. Aries, Philippe. "The Family and the City." In Alice Rossi, ed. *Family.* New York: W. W. Norton, 1965. pp. 227–235. Holmes, U. T., Jr. *Daily Living in the Twelfth Century: Based on the Observations of Alexander Neckham in London and Paris.* Madison: University of Wisconsin Press, 1952. p. 231.

32. Tuan, Yi-Fu. *Segmented Worlds and Self: Group Life and Individual Consciousness.* Minneapolis: University of Minnesota Press, 1982. pp. 59–60. Everett, Alan. "Farm Labourers." In Joan Thirsk, ed. *The Agrarian History of England and Wales: 1500– 1640.* Cambridge, UK: Cambridge University Press, 1967. pp. 442–443.

33. Giedion, Siegfried. *Mechanization Takes Command: A Contribution to Anonymous History.* New York: W. W. Norton, 1969. pp. 268–269.

34. Lukacs, John. "The Bourgeois Interior." *American Scholar* 39. Fall 1970, Vol. 623. Tuan. *Segmented Worlds and Self.* p. 83.

35. Elias, Norbert. *The Civilizing Process: The Development of Manners.* Oxford, UK: Blackwell, 1944. pp. 100–127.

36. Archbishop Cranmer, *Prayer Book,* as quoted in Stone, Lawrence. *The Family, Sex, and Marriage in England 1500–1800.* New York: Harper Torchbooks. p. 101.

37. Ibid. p. 138. Quotation from Matthew's Bible of 1537.

38. Ibid. p. 183.

39. Ibid. p. 110.

40. Locke, John. *Two Treatises of Government.* Chapter II. "Of Paternal and Regal Power," and "Of Government." London: C. Baldwin, 1824. pp. 7–8.

41. Bishop Fleetwood, as quoted in Stone. *The Family, Sex, and Marriage in England 1500–1800.* p. 165.

42. Ibid.

43. Duc de La Rochefoucauld, as quoted in Ibid. p. 214.

44. Wetenhall Wilkes, as quoted in Ibid. pp. 218–219.

45. Stone, *The Family, Sex, and Marriage, England, 1500–1800.*

46. Ibid. p. 232.

47. Sir Thomas More, as quoted in Ibid. p. 119.

48. Ibid. p. 117.

49. Ibid. p. 125.

50. Ibid.

51. Ibid. p. 259.

52. Ibid. p. 260.

53. Rousseau, Jean-Jacques. *Émile.* Barbara Foxley, trans. Whitefish, MT: Kessinger Publishing, 2004. p. 8.

54. Stone. *The Family, Sex, and Marriage in England 1500–1800.* pp. 268–269.

55. Ibid. p. 272–273.

56. James Nelson, as quoted in Ibid. p. 274.

57. Thomas Sheridan, Sr., as quoted in Ibid. p. 280.

58. Heilbroner, Robert L. *The Making of Economic Society.* Englewood Cliffs, NJ: Prentice-Hall, 1962. pp. 36–38, 50.

59. Jones, E. L. *The European Miracle: Environments, Economies and Geopolitics in the History of Europe and Asia.* pp. 98–100.

60. Dobb, Maurice M. *Studies in the Development of Capitalism.* New York: International Publishers, 1947. pp. 140–141.

61. Ibid. p. 143.

62. Polanyi, Karl. *The Great Transformation: The Political and Economic Origins of Our Time.* p. 65.

63. Hobsbawm, E. J. *Nations and Nationalism Since 1780: Programme, Myth, Reality.* Cambridge, UK: Cambridge University Press, 1990. p. 45. Said at the first meeting of the parliament of the newly united Italian Kingdom (1861). (E. Latham, *Famous Sayings and Their Authors.* London: Swan Sonnenschem, 1906.) Refers to "We have made Italy, now we have to make Italians."

64. Brunot, Ferdinand, ed. *Histoire de la Langue Française.* 13 vols. Paris: 1927–43. de Mauro, Tullio. *Storia Linguistica dell'Italia Unita.* Bari. 1963, p. 41. Wehler, H. U. *Deutsche Gesellschaftgeschichte 1700– 1815.* Munich, Germany: 1987. p. 305.

65. Hobsbawm, E. J. *Nations and Nationalism Since 1780.* p. 54.

66. Wright, Lawrence. *Clockwork Man.* New York: Horizon Press, 1969. p. 121.

67. Hindess, Barry. "Neo-Liberalism and the National Economy." In M. Dean and B. Hindess, eds. *Governing Australia: Studies in Contemporary Rationalities of Government.* Cambridge, UK: Cambridge University Press, 1988. pp. 210–226. Held, David, Anthony McGrew, David Goldblatt, and Jonathan Perraton. *Global Transformations: Politics, Economics and Culture.* Chichester: Blackwell, 2006. p. 37.

68. Held, McGrew, Goldblatt, and Perraton. *Global Transformations: Politics, Economics and Culture.* pp. 37–38.

69. Dobb. *Studies in the Development of Capitalism.* p. 193. "Mercantilism." *The Columbia Encyclopedia.* Sixth Edition, 2001.

70. Shapiro, Michael J., and Hayward R. Alker. *Challenging Boundaries: Global Flows, Territorial Identities.* Minneapolis: University of Minnesota Press, 1996. p. 238. "French Revolution." *The Columbia Encyclopedia.* Sixth Edition, 2001.

"Declaration of the Rights of Man and the Citizen." Article 3. Adopted by the National Assembly August 27, 1789.

71. Smith, Anthony D. *Nationalism: Theory, Ideology, History*. Cambridge, UK: Polity Press, 2001. p. 45. For further information, see Rogers Brubaker. *Citizenship and Nationhood in France and Germany*. Cambridge, MA: Harvard University Press, 1992. Sluga, Glenda. "Identity, Gender, and the History of European Nations and Nationalism." In Hobsbawm, *Nations and Nationalism*. Vol. 4. No. 1. 1998. pp. 87–111.

72. Hobsbawm. *Nations and Nationalism Since 1780*. pp. 82–83.

73. "Human Evolution." *Encyclopaedia Britannica*. www.britannica.com/EBchacked/topic/275670/human-evolut

74. Weintraub. *The Value of the Individual*. Chicago: University of Chicago Press, 1978. p. 49.

75. Ibid. pp. 278–279.

76. Ibid. p. 289.

77. Rousseau, Jean-Jacques. *Oeuvres Complètes. Vol. 1. Les Confessions et Autre Textes Autobiographiques*. Bernard Gagnebin and Raymond, et al., eds. Paris: Bibliothèque de la Pleiade, 1959. p. 517.

78. Weintraub. *The Value of the Individual*. p. 325.

79. Rousseau. *Oeuvres Complètes*. Vol. 1. pp. 516–517.

80. Weintraub. *The Value of the Individual*. p. 300.

81. Rousseau, Jean-Jacques. *The Confessions of Jean-Jacques Rousseau*. J. M. Cohen, trans. Baltimore: Penguin Classics, 1953. p. 17.

82. Rousseau, Jean-Jacques. *Oeuvres Complètes*. Vol. 1. p. 1123.

83. Weintraub. *The Value of the Individual*. p. 308. Quotation by Jean-Jacques Rousseau.

84. Rousseau. *The Confessions of Jean-Jacques Rousseau*. p. 25.

85. Ibid. p. 88.

86. Ibid.

87. Ibid. p. 89.

88. Ibid. p. 322.

89. Weintraub. *The Value of the Individual*. p. 324.

90. Rousseau. *The Confessions of Jean-Jacques Rousseau*. p. 333.

91. Weintraub. *The Value of the Individual*. pp. 320–321.

92. Goethe, Johann Wolfgang von. *Werke, Briefe und Gespräche. Gedenkausgabe*. 24 vols. *Naturwissneschaftliche Schriften*. Vols. 16–17. Ernst Beutler, ed. Zurich: Artemis, 1948–53. pp. 921–23.

93. Ibid.

94. Ibid.

95. Weintraub. *The Value of the Individual*. pp. 364–369.

96. Goethe. *Werke, Briefe und Gespräche. Naturwissneschaftliche Schriften*. Vols. 16–17. p. 880.

97. Goethe. *Werke, Briefe und Gespräche. Dichtung und Wahrheit*. Vol. 10. p. 168.

98. Ibid. p. 664.

99. Ibid. p. 425.

100. Kahler, Erich. *The Inward Turn of Narrative*. Richard and Clara Winston, trans. Princeton: Princeton University Press, 1973. p. 9.

101. Ibid. p. 49. (Kahler's emphasis)

102. Ibid.

103. Armstrong, Nancy. *How Novels Think: The Limits of Individualism from 1719–1900*. New York: Columbia University Press, 2005. p. 10.

104. Kahler. *The Inward Turn of Narrative*. p. 139. Quotation from Pierre Carlet de Marivaux, Chamblain. *La Vie de Marianne*. Jean-Marie Goulemot, contrib. Paris: LGF/Le Livre de Poche, 1756.

CHAPTER 9: IDEOLOGICAL THINKING IN A MODERN MARKET ECONOMY

1. Armstrong, Nancy. *How Novels Think: The Limits of Individualism from 1719–1900*. New York: Columbia University Press, 2005. p. 12.

2. Bredvold, Louis I. *The Natural History of Sensibility*. Detroit, MI: Wayne State University Press, 1962. p. 5.

3. Barfield, Owen. *History in English Words*, new ed. London: Faber and Faber, 1954. p. 177.

4. Campbell, Colin. *The Romanic Ethic and the Spirit of Modern Consumerism*. Oxford, UK: Basil Blackwell, 1987. p. 138.

5. Sickels, Eleanor. *The Gloomy Egoist: Moods and Themes of Melancholy from Gray to Keats*. New York: Octagon Books, 1969. p. 195.

6. Campbell. *The Romanic Ethic and the Spirit of Modern Consumerism*. p. 138. Quotation by Sebastien Mercier.

7. Sickels. *The Gloomy Egoist*. p. 195.

8. Vickers, Brian. Introduction to Henry Mackenzie. *The Man of Feeling*. London: Oxford University Press, 1967. p. ix.

9. Ibid. p. viii.

10. Campbell. *The Romanic Ethic and the Spirit of Modern Consumerism*. p. 141.

11. Zerubavel, Eviatar. *Hidden Rhythms: Schedules and Calendars in Social Life*. Chicago: University of Chicago Press, 1981. p. 85.

12. Ibid. pp. 89–90.

13. Ibid. pp. 90–91.

14. Ibid. p. 92.

15. de Grazia, Sebastian. *Of Time, Work, and Leisure*. New York: Twentieth Century Fund, 1962. p. 119.

16. McNeill, William. *Plagues and Peoples*. New York: Doubleday/Anchor Books, 1976. p. 147.

17. Mumford, Lewis. *Technics and Civilization*. New York: Harcourt, Brace, 1934. pp. 119–120.

18. Ibid. p. 120.

19. Wilkinson, Richard G. *Poverty and Progress: An Ecological Perspective on Economic Development*. New York: Praeger, 1973. p. 114–115.

20. Sperber, Jonathan. *The European Revolutions, 1848–1851*, 2nd ed. Cambridge, UK: Cambridge University Press, 2005. p. 42

21. Debeir, Jean-Claude, Jean-Paul Deléage, and Daniel Hémery. *In the Servitude of Power: Energy and Civilization Through the Ages*. London: Zed Books, 1991. p. 90.

22. Ibid.

23. Armytage, W.H.G. *A Social History of Engineering*. London, 1961. Quotation by Edmund Howes, ed. *Stow's Annals*. London, 1631.

24. Debeir, Deléage, and Hémery. *In the Servitude of Power*. p. 100.

25. Ibid. p. 102.

26. Hobsbawm, Eric. *The Age of Revolution: 1789–1848*. New York: The World Publishing Company, 1962. p. 207.

27. Ibid. p. 208.

28. Debeir, Deléage, and Hémery. *In the Servitude of Power*. pp. 104–105.

29. Hobsbawm, Eric. *The Age of Capital 1848–1875*. London: Cardinal, 1975. p. 55.

30. Debeir, J. C., J. P. Deléage, and D. Hémery. *In the Servitude of Power*. p. 106.

31. Holden, Andrew. *Tourism Studies and the Social Sciences*. New York: Routledge, 2005. p. 26.

32. Debeir, Deléage, and Hémery. *In the Servitude of Power*. p. 104.

33. Hobsbawm. *The Age of Revolution: 1789–1848*. p. 350.

34. Chandler, Alfred, Jr. *The Visible Hand: The Managerial Revolution in American Business*. Cambridge, MA: Belknap Press of Harvard University Press, 1977. p. 83.

35. Ibid. p. 86.

36. Debeir, Deléage, and Hémery. *In the Servitude of Power*. p. 109.

37. Redford, Arthur, and William Henry Chaloner. *Labour Migration in England, 1800–1850*. Manchester, UK: Manchester University Press, 1976. p. 14.

38. Hobsbawm. *The Age of Capital 1848–1875*. p. 205.

39. Ibid. p. 248.

40. Hobsbawm. *The Age of Revolution: 1789–1848*. p. 204.

41. Hobsbawm. *The Age of Capital 1848–1875*. p. 49.

42. Davis, Angela E. *Art and Work: A Social History of Labour in the Canadian Graphic Arts Industry to the 1940s*. Montreal: McGill-Queen's University Press, 1995. p. 21.

43. Consuegra, David. *American Type Design and Designers*. Allworth Communications, 2004. pp. 19, 263.

44. Curtis, Bruce. "Patterns of Resistance to Public Education: England, Ireland, and Canada West, 1830–1890. *Comparative Education Review*. Vol. 32. No. 3. 1988. p. 318; MSN Encarta. "Public Education in the United States." www.Encarta .msn.com; Sperber. *The European Revolutions, 1848–1851*. p. 33

45. Sperber, J. *The European Revolutions, 1848–1851*, 2nd ed. p. 33.

46. Hobsbawm, E. *The Age of Capital 1848–1875*. p. 118.

47. Sperber. *The European Revolutions, 1848–1851*, 2nd ed. p. 33

48. Sennett, Richard. *Flesh and Stone: The Body and the City in Western Civilization*. New York: W. W. Norton, 1994. p. 285.

49. Ibid. pp. 286–287.

50. Ibid. p. 288.

51. Sennett. *Flesh and Stone*. pp. 312–313.

52. Ibid. p. 312.

53. Hobsbawm. *The Age of Revolution: 1789–1848*. p. 263.

54. Randall, J. H., Jr. *The Making of the Modern Mind*. pp. 419–420.

55. Shelley, Percy Bysshe. "A Defence of Poetry." In Harold Bloom and Lionel Trilling, eds. *Romantic Poetry and Prose*. New York: Oxford University Press, 1973. p. 750.

56. *Selections from the Writings of John Ruskin, Second Series 1860–1888*. Orpington, UK: George Allen, 1899. p. 231. (Ruskin's emphasis)

57. Hobsbawm. *The Age of Revolution: 1789–1848*. p. 305.

58. Marx, Karl, and Friedrich Engels. *The Communist Manifesto*. Gareth Stedman Jones, contrib. New York: Penguin Classics, 2002. p. 222.

59. Tennyson, Alfred. "Flower in the Crannied Wall." In Edmund Clarence Stedman, ed. *A Victorian Anthology, 1837–1895*. Cambridge, MA: Riverside Press, 1895.

60. Randall. *The Making of the Modern Mind*. p. 425.

61. Taylor, Charles. *Sources of the Self: The Making of the Modern Identity*. Cambridge, MA: Harvard University Press, 1989. p. 430.

62. Nussbaum, Martha C. *Upheavals of Thought: The Intelligence of Emotions*. Cambridge, MA: Harvard University Press, 2001. p. 674.

63. Whitman, Walt. *The Wisdom of Walt Whitman: Selected and Edited, with Introduction by Laurens Maynard*. Laurens Maynard, ed. New York: Brentano's, 1917.

64. Nussbaum. *Upheavals of Thought*. p. 674.

65. Cartwright, David E. Introduction to Arthur Schopenhauer. *On the Basis of Morality*. Providence, RI: Berghahn Books, 1995. p. ix.

66. Ibid.

67. Kant, Immanuel. Grounding for the Metaphysics of Morals; with *On a Supposed Right to Lie Because of Philanthropic Concerns*, 3rd ed. James W. Ellington, trans. Indianapolis: Hackett Publishing, 1993. p. vi.

68. Schopenhauer. *On the Basis of Morality*. p. 61. The quotation within Schopenhauer's quotation is by Immanuel Kant. *Critique of Practical Reason*. (Schopenhauer's emphasis)

69. Ibid. Quotation by Immanuel Kant. *Foundation of the Metaphysics of Morals*. (Schopenhauer's emphasis)

70. Ibid. p. 62.

71. Ibid. p. 66. Quotation by Immanuel Kant. *Critique of Practical Reason*.

72. Ibid. pp. 143, 147. (Schopenhauer's emphasis)

73. Ibid. p. 144. (Schopenhauer's emphasis)

74. Ibid. p. xxvii.

75. Ibid. p. 210–211.

76. Giddens, Anthony. *The Transformation of Intimacy: Sexuality, Love and Eroticism in Modern Societies.* Cambridge, UK: Polity Press, 1993. p. 26.

77. Ibid. p. 43.

78. Cancian, Francesca M. *Love in America*. Cambridge, UK. Cambridge University Press, 1987. p. 21.

79. Giddens. *The Transformation of Intimacy*. p. 46.

80. Ibid. p. 41.

81. Ryan, Mary. *The Cradle of the Middle Class.* Cambridge, UK: Cambridge University Press, 1982. p. 102.

82. Juge, J. J. *Changemens Survenus dans les Moeurs des Habitans de Limoges Depuis une Cinquantaine d'Années*, 2nd ed. Limoges, 1817. pp. 34, 84.

83. Ibid.

84. Shorter, Edward. *The Making of the Modern Family*. New York: Basic Books, 1977. p. 191.

85. Rousseau, Jean-Jacques. *Émile*. P. D. Jimack, ed. London, 1974. pp. 53–54.

86. Ibid. p. 43.

87. Wordsworth, William. "My Heart Leaps when I Behold." *The Complete Poetical Works*. London: Macmillan, 1888.

88. Wordsworth, William. "Intimations of Immortality from Recollections of Early Childhood." *The Complete Poetical Works*. London: Macmillan, 1888.

89. Cunningham, Hugh. *Children and Childhood in Western Society Since* 1500, 2nd ed. Harlow, UK: Pearson, 2005. p. 69.

90. Ibid. p. 70.

91. Wordsworth, William. "Intimations of Immortality from Recollections of Early Childhood." *The Complete Poetical Works*.

92. Cunningham. *Children and Childhood in Western Society Since* 1500. pp. 142–146.

93. Ibid. p. 146.

94. Browning, Elizabeth Barrett. "The Cry of the Children." In Edmund Clarence Stedman, ed. *A Victorian Anthology*, 1837–1895. Cambridge, UK: Riverside Press, 1895.

95. *Encyclopaedia Britannica's Guide to Black History*. Online, "Slavery." www.britannica.com/blackhistory/article-24156

96. Katz, Alfred H., and Eugene Bender. "Self Help Groups in Western Society: History and Prospects." *Journal of Applied Behavioral Science*. Vol. 12. No. 265. 1976. p. 270.

97. Hunt, Lynn. *Inventing Human Rights: A History*. New York: W.W. Norton, 2007. p. 76.

98. Ibid. p. 77.

99. Bentham, Jeremy. *An Introduction to the Principles of Morals and Legislation*. New York: Hafner Publishing, 1948.

100. Finsen, Lawrence, and Susan Finsen. *The Animal Rights Movement in America: From Compassion to Respect*. New York: Twayne, 1994. p. 25.

101. Ibid. p. 29.

102. Ibid. p. 31.

103. Sartre, Jean-Paul. Introduction to Nathalie Sarraute. *Portrait of a Man Unknown*. M. Jolas, trans. New York: Braziller, 1958, p. ix.

104. Marx, Karl. *Early Writings*. T. B. Bottomore, ed. and trans. New York: McGraw-Hill, 1964. pp. 171–172. (Marx's emphasis)

105. Rousseau, Jean-Jacques. *Rousseau's Émile, or Treatise on Education*. William H. Payne, trans. New York: D. Appleton, 1899, p. 1.

106. Hobsbawm. *The Age of Capital 1848–1875*. p. 21.

107. Ibid.

108. Ibid. p. 22.

CHAPTER 10: PSYCHOLOGICAL CONSCIOUSNESS IN A POSTMODERN EXISTENTIAL WORLD

1. "Edwin Laurentine Drake." *Encyclopaedia Britannica*. 2009. Encyclopaedia Britannica Online. www.britannica.com/EBchecked/topic/170909/Edwin-Laurentine-Drake

2. "Karl (Friedrich) Benz—Early life, Benz's Factory and his first inventions (1871 to 1882)." Cambridge Encyclopedia: Cambridge Encyclopedia Vol. 43. http://encyclopedia.stateuniversity.com/pages/12682/Karl-Friedrich-Benz.html

3. Dods, John B. *The Philosophy of Electrical Psychology*. New York: Da Capo Press, 1982. pp. 18–19.

4. "A (Not So) Brief History of Electrocardiography." ECG Library. www.ecglibrary.com/ecghist.html

5. Ibid.

6. Otis, Laura. "The Metaphoric Circuit: Organic and Technological Communication in the

Nineteenth Century." *Journal of the History of Ideas.*
Vol. 63. No. 1. January 2002. p. 105.

7. Ibid. p. 105.

8. Dods. *The Philosophy of Electrical Psychology.*
p. 54.

9. Ibid. p. 71. (Dods's emphasis)

10. Rieber, R.W. Introduction to the Da Capo
edition. In Dods. *The Philosophy of Electrical
Psychology.* n. p.

11. Dods. *The Philosophy of Electrical Psychology.*
pp. 51, 54. (Dods's emphasis)

12. Hawthorne, Nathaniel. *The House of Seven
Gables: A Romance.* New York: Macmillan, 1910.
p. 223.

13. Gilmore, Paul. "Romantic Electricity, or the
Materiality of Aesthetics." *American Literature.* Vol.
76. No. 3. September 2004. p. 474.

14. Emerson, Ralph Waldo. *Essays and
English Traits.* The Harvard Classics. Charles W.
Eliot, ed. New York: P. F. Collier & Son, 1909.
p. 181.

15. Whitman, Walt. *The Complete Poems.* Francis
Murphy, contrib. New York: Penguin Classics,
1986. pp. 498–499.

16. Carlyon, David. *Dan Rice: The Most
Famous Man You've Never Heard Of.* New York:
PublicAffairs, 2004. p. xii. Quotation by Thoreau.

17. "Influence of the Telegraph upon Literature."
United States Democratic Review, May 1848. p. 411.

18. Gilmore. "Romantic Electricity, or the
Materiality of Aesthetics." p. 479.

19. Otis. "The Metaphoric Circuit." p. 121.

20. Morse, Samuel F. B. *Samuel F. B. Morse: His
Letters and Journals.* Vol 2. Edward Lind,
ed. Boston: Morse, 1914. p. 85.

21. Otis. "The Metaphoric Circuit." p. 121.

22. Field, Henry. *History of the Atlantic Telegraph.* 3rd
Ed. New York: Charles Scribner & Co., 1869. p. 421.

23. Hobsbawm, Eric. *The Age of Capital 1848–1875.*
London: Cardinal, 1975. p. 77.

24. Chandler, Alfred D., Jr. *The Visible Hand.*
Cambridge, MA: Belknap Press of Harvard
University Press, 1977. p. 89.

25. Kern, Stephen. *The Culture of Time and Space
1880–1918.* Cambridge, MA: Harvard University
Press, 1983. p. 12.

26. Landes, David S. *Revolution in Time.*
Cambridge, MA: Harvard University Press, 1983.
pp. 285–286.

27. Marvin, Carolyn. *When Old Technologies Were
New: Thinking About Electric Communication in
the Late Nineteenth Century.* New York: Oxford
University Press, 1988. p. 64.

28. Ibid. p. 87.

29. Ibid. p. 163.

30. Ibid. p. 164.

31. Ibid. p. 11.

32. Nye, David E. *Electrifying America: Social
Meanings of a New Technology, 1880–1940.*
Cambridge, MA: MIT Press, 1991. p. 239.

33. Ibid. p. 186.

34. Ibid.

35. Ford, Henry, and Samuel Crowther. *Edison
as I Know Him.* New York: Cosmopolitan Books,
1930. p. 30.

36. Anderson, Robert. *Fundamentals of the Petroleum
Industry.* Norman, OK: University of Oklahoma
Press, 1984. p. 20.

37. Ibid. pp. 20–22, 29–30. Yergin, Daniel. *The
Prize: The Epic Quest for Oil, Money and Power.*
New York: Simon and Schuster, 1992. p. 210.

38. Ibid.

39. Yergin, Daniel. *The Prize.* p. 208.

40. Mowbray, A. Q. *Road to Ruin.* Philadelphia:
Lippincott, 1969. p. 15.

41. Schneider, Kenneth R. *Autokind vs. Mankind.*
New York: Schocken, 1972. p. 123.

42. "The Dramatic Story of Oil's Influence on the
World." *Oregon Focus.* January 1993. pp. 10–11.

43. Kern, Stephen. *The Culture of Time and Space
1880–1918.* p. 1.

44. Ibid. pp. 1–2.

45. Toulmin, Stephen, and June Goodfield. *The
Discovery of Time.* New York, 1965. p. 232.

46. Nietzsche, Friedrich. *On the Genealogy of Morals*
and *Ecce Homo.* W. Kaufman and R. J. Hollingdale,
trans. New York: Vintage. 1967. p. 119.

47. Ibid.

48. Ortega y Gasset, José. "Adam en el Paraíso."
In José Ortega y Gasset. *Obras Completas.* Madrid,
1946. Vol. I. p. 471.

49. Cézanne, Paul. *Paul Cézanne Letters.* John
Rewald, ed. Oxford, 1946. p. 262.

50. Kern. *The Culture of Time and Space 1880–1918.*
p. 143.

51. Wilson, Edmund. *Axel's Castle.* New York,
1931. p. 221.

52. Nussbaum, Martha C. *Upheavals of Thought:
The Intelligence of Emotions.* Cambridge, UK:
Cambridge University Press, 2001. pp. 682–683.
Quotation by James Joyce.

53. Scheerbart, Paul. *Glasarchitektur.* Berlin: Mann,
2000.

54. Wright, Frank Lloyd. "An Autobiography." In
Frank Lloyd Wright: Writings and Buildings. Edgar
Kaufmann and Ben Raeburn, eds. New York,
1960. p. 82.

55. Gergen, Kenneth J. *The Saturated Self.* New
York: Basic Books, 1991. pp. 52–53.

56. Cushman, Philip. "Psychotherapy to 1992: A
Historically Situated Interpretation." In Donald
K. Freedheim et al., eds. *History of Psychotherapy: A
Century of Change.* Washington, D.C.: American
Psychological Association. pp. 40–41.

57. Reed, Edward S. *From Soul to Mind: The Emergence of Psychology, from Erasmus Darwin to William James.* New Haven, CT: Yale University Press, 1997. p. 44.

58. Cushman, Philip. "Psychotherapy to 1992: A Historically Situated Interpretation." In Freedheim et al., eds. *History of Psychotherapy.* p. 32.

59. Ibid. p. 33.

60. Benjafield, John G. *A History of Psychology,* 2nd ed. Ontario, Canada: Oxford University Press, 2005. p. 71.

61. Reed, Edward S. *From Soul to Mind: The Emergence of Psychology from Erasmus Darwin to William James.* New Haven, CT: Yale University Press; 1997. p. 184.

62. James, William. *The Principles of Psychology,* 2 vols. New York: Dover, 1950. Vol. 1. p. 185.

63. Ibid. p. 237.

64. Ibid. p. 238.

65. Benjafield. *A History of Psychology.* p. 87.

66. James, William. *Psychology: Briefer Course.* New York: Collier, 1962 [1892]. p. 294.

67. Coon, D. J. "Salvaging the Self in a World Without Soul: William James' "The Principles of Psychology." *History of Psychology.* Vol. 3. 2000. p. 91.

68. James, William. *The Principles of Psychology.* 1950. p. 310–311.

69. Benjafield. *A History of Psychology.* pp. 89–90.

70. Freud, Sigmund. *Studies on Hysteria.* James Strachey, trans. Anna Freud Bernays, contrib. New York: Basic Books, 1957. p. 193.

71. Johnson, David W., and Roger T. Johnson. *Cooperation and Competition: Theory and Research.* Edina, MN: Interaction Books, 1989. p. 105.

72. General Service Office of Alcoholics Anonymous. *A.A. Fact File.* New York: A. A. Publishing. 1956.

73. Scheidlinger, S. "The Small Healing Group—A Historical Overview." *Psychotherapy.* Vol. 32. No. 4. 1995. p. 658.

74. Blatner, Adam. "Theoretical Foundations of Psychodrama." 2006. Presented at the Annual Meeting of American Society for Group Psychotherapy and Psychodrama. April 9, 1999. www.blatner.com/adam/pdntbk/pdtheory .htm

75. Ibid.

76. Ibid.

77. Wertheimer, Max. "Gestalt Theory." In Willis D. Ellis. *A Source Book of Gestalt Psychology.* New York: Humanities Press, 1967. p. 2.

78. Ibid. p. 6.

79. Benjafield. *A History of Psychology.* p. 185.

80. Ibid. p. 280.

81. *Task Force Report 1: Encounter Groups and Psychiatry.* American Psychiatric Association. Washington, D.C. 1970.

82. Wentling, Rose M., and N. Palma-Rivas. "Current Status of Diversity Initiatives in Selected Multinational Corporations." *Human Resource Development Quarterly.* Vol. 11. No. 1. p. 35.

83. "Global Work Drives Diversity Training." *The Houston Chronicle.* Jan. 22, 2007. p. 3.

84. Fyodor Dostoevsky, as quoted in Benjafield. *A History of Psychology.* p. 267.

85. Maslow, Abraham H. "Existential Psychology: What's in It for Us?" In *Existential Psychology.* New York: Random House. p. 60.

86. Buhler, Charlotte. "Some Observations on the Psychology of the Third Force." *Journal of Humanistic Psychology.* Vol. 5. p. 55.

87. May, Rollo. *Love and Will.* New York: Norton, 1969. p. 324.

88. Maslow, Abraham H. *Motivation and Personality.* New York: Harper & Row, 1954. pp. 91–92.

89. Rogers, Carl R. "Some Observations on the Organization of Personality." In Hilgard, E. R. *American Psychology in Historical Perspective.* Washington: American Psychological Association, 1978. p. 419.

90. Rogers, Carl R. " 'Client-Centered' Psychology." *Scientific American.* Vol. 187. 1952. p. 67.

91. Rogers, Carl R. "Interpersonal Relationships." *Journal of Applied Behavioral Science.* Vol. 4. No. 3. 1968. p. 16.

92. Katz, Alfred H., and Eugene I. Bender. "Self Help Groups in Western Society: History and Prospects." *Journal of Applied Behavioral Science.* Vol. 12. No. 3. 1976. p. 278.

93. Norcross, John C. "Integrating Self-Help into Psychotherapy: 16 Practical Suggestions." *Professional Psychology: Research and Practice.* Vol. 37. No. 6. 2006. p. 685.

94. Kessler, Ronald C., Kristin D. Mickelson, and Shanyang Zhao. "Patterns and Correlates of Self-Help Group Membership in the United States." *Social Policy.* Vol. 27. No. 3. March 2, 1997. pp. 27–47.

95. Ibid.

96. Ibid.

97. Steinke, Bernd. "Rehabilitation Initiatives by Disability Self-Help Groups: A Comparative Study." *International Social Security Review.* Vol. 51. No. 1. December 19, 2002. p. 97.

98. Adler, Jerry. "Freud in Our Midst." *Newsweek.* March 27, 2006. pp. 35–41; Bureau of Labor Statistics. *Occupational Outlook Handbook, 2008–09 Edition: Social Workers.* U.S. Department of Labor. www.bls.gov/oco/ocos060.htm

99. Adler. "Freud in Our Midst." pp. 35–41.

100. Roszak, Theodore. *The Making of a Counter Culture: Reflections on the Technocratic Society and Its Youthful Opposition.* Berkeley, CA: University of California Press, 1995. p. 49.

101. Ibid. pp. 58–59.
102. Ibid. p. 58.
103. Ibid.
104. Ibid. p. 61.
105. MacInnes, Colin. "Old Youth and Young." *Encounter.* September 1967.
106. Roszak. *The Making of a Counter Culture.* p. 62.
107. Ibid.
108. Ibid. pp. 60, 63, 64.
109. Rieff, Philip. *The Triumph of the Therapeutic.* Chicago: University of Chicago Press, 1966. p. 13.
110. Ibid. pp. 24–25.
111. Ibid. pp. x–xi.
112. Roszak. *The Making of a Counter Culture.* p. xxvi.

CHAPTER 11: THE CLIMB TO GLOBAL PEAK EMPATHY

1. "Foreign Exchange and Derivatives Market Activity in 2007." Bank for International Settlements. 2007. www.bis.org/publ/ rpfxf07t.pdf
2. "Satellite Tracking." Science@NASA. www .science.nasa.gov/realtime
3. "Annual Energy Review 2006: Energy Perspectives." Energy Information Administration. www.eia.doe.gov/emeu/aer/ep/ep_frame.html
4. "Figure 1.4: Primary Energy Trade by Source, 1949–2007." Energy Information Administration. www.eia.doe.gov/emeu/aer/pdf/pages/sec1_10.pdf
5. Thomas, Landon. "Abu Dhabi Buys 75% of Chrysler Building in Latest Trophy Purchase." *New York Times,* July 9, 2008.
6. Kaplan, Eben. "The UAE Purchase of American Port Facilities." Council on Foreign Relations. February 21, 2006. www.cfr.org
7. Brown, W. J., M. D. Basil, and M. C. Bocarnea. "Social Influence of an International Celebrity: Responses to the Death of Princess Diana." *Journal of Communication.* Vol. 53. No. 4. December 2003. p. 588.
8. Ibid. pp. 589–590.
9. Watson, C. W. "Born a Lady, Became a Princess, Died a Saint: The Reaction to the Death of Diana, Princess of Wales." *Anthropology Today,* Vol. 13. No. 6. December 1997. pp. 6–7.
10. Brown, Basil, and Bocarnea. "Social Influence of an International Celebrity: Responses to the Death of Princess Diana." p. 588.
11. U.S. Geological Survey, National Earthquake Information Center. "Magnitude 9.1—Off the West Coast of Northern Sumatra." http:// earthquake.usgs.gov/eqcenter/eqinthenews/2004/ usslav/#summary
12. Musil, Steven. "Tech Community Joins Tsunami Relief Effort." cnet news.com. January 3, 2005.
13. MacMillan, Robert. "Tsunami Prompts Online Outpouring." *Washington Post.* January 3, 2005.

14. Owen, James. "Modern Humans Came out of Africa, 'Definitive' Study Says." *National Geographic News.* July 18, 2007. www.nationalgeographic .com/news; "Effects of Ecology and Climate on Human Physical Variations." CultureChange.org. www.culturechange.org
15. Steele, James, and Stephen Shennan. *The Archaeology of Human Ancestry: Power, Sex, and Tradition.* New York: Routledge, 1996. p. 385.
16. Gimbutas, Marija. *The Civilization of the Goddess: The World of Old Europe.* New York: HarperCollins, 1994. p. 2.
17. Chandler, Tertius, and Gerald Fox. *3000 Years of Urban Growth.* New York: Academic Press, 1974.
18. "Jerusalem: From Town to Metropolis." University of Southern Maine. www.usm.maine .edu; Cartledge, Paul. "The Democratic Experiment: Greek Democracy and Modern Democracy." BBC Ancient History. www.bbc .co.uk/history
19. Modelski, George. *World Cities: −3000 to 2000.* Washington, DC: Faros 2000, 2003.
20. Brown, Lester. *Plan B 3.0: Mobilizing to Save Civilization.* New York: W. W. Norton, 2008. www.earthpolicy.org; "World Population Clock—Worldometers. www.worldometers.info/ population; "How Many Births per Day Globally?" www.wiki.answers.com; Rifkin, Jeremy. "The Risks of Too Much City." *Washington Post.* December 17, 2006. p. B07.
21. Craats, Rennay. *USA Past Present Future— Science and Technology.* New York: Weigl, 2001.
22. Harvey, Fiona. "An Inhuman Race? How the Lure of the City Is Rapidly Swelling the World's Slums." *Financial Times.* August 7, 2006. p. 8.
23. Tomlinson, John. *Globalization and Culture.* Chicago: University of Chicago Press, 1999. p. 184.
24. Simmel, Georg. *The Philosophy of Money.* Tom Bottomore and David Frisby, trans. London: Routledge, 1990.
25. Hiebert, Daniel. "Cosmopolitanism at the Local Level: The Development of Transnational Neighbourhoods." In Steven Vertovec and Robin Cohen, eds. *Conceiving Cosmopolitanism: Theory, Context, and Practice.* Oxford, UK: Oxford University Press, 2002. p. 212.
26. Ibid. p. 217.
27. Kwok-bun, Chan. "Both Sides Now; Culture, Contact, Hybridization, and Cosmopolitanism." In Vertovec and Cohen, eds. *Conceiving Cosmopolitanism.* p. 206.
28. Hiebert. "Cosmopolitanism at the Local Level." In Vertovec and Cohen, eds. *Conceiving Cosmopolitanism.* p. 209.
29. Ibid. p. 210.
30. Ibid. p. 209.

31. Kwok-bun. "Both Sides Now." In Vertovec and Cohen, eds. *Conceiving Cosmopolitanism.* p. 206.
32. Mckeown, A. "Global Migration, 1846–1940." *Journal of World History.* Vol. 15. No. 2. June 2004. pp. 155–189.
33. International Organization for Migration. "World Migration 2005: Costs and Benefits of International Migration, Volume 3—IOM World Migration Report Series." Geneva, Switzerland. 2005. www.iom.int.
34. Ibid. p. 379.
35. Ibid. p. 380.
36. Ibid. p. 381.
37. Ibid. p. 382.
38. Ibid. p. 387.
39. Ibid. p. 388.
40. Ibid. p. 394.
41. "Virtual Press Room: High Food Prices." United Nations World Food Programme. June 2, 2008. www.wfp.org/node/7906
42. Steinberg, Stefan. "Financial Speculators Reap Profits from Global Hunger." GlobalResearch. ca: The Centre for Research on Globalization. April 24, 2008. http://globalresearch.ca/index. php?context=va&aid=8794
43. "The World Only Needs 30 Billion Dollars a Year to Eradicate the Scourge of Hunger. Time for Talk Over—Action Needed." FAO Newsroom. Food and Agricultural Organization of the United Nations. June 3, 2008. www.fao.org/newsroom/ EN/news/2008/1000853/index.html
44. Sellers, Frances Stead. "A Citizen on Paper Has No Weight." *Washington Post.* January 19, 2003. p. B01.
45. World Travel & Tourism Council. "Progress and Priorities 2007/2008." 2007.
46. Theobald, William F. "The Meaning, Scope, and Measurement of Travel and Tourism." In *Global Tourism,* 3rd ed. William F. Theobald, ed. Amsterdam: Elsevier, 2005. p. 5.
47. Ibid. p. 6.
48. World Travel and Tourism Council. "Facts and Figures: Historical Perspective of World Tourism." 2006.
49. World Travel and Tourism Council. "Progress and Priorities 2007/2008." 2007.
50. Archer, Brian, Chris Cooper, and Lisa Ruhanen. "The Positive and Negative Impacts of Tourism." In *Global Tourism,* 3rd ed. p. 90.
51. Berghoff, Hartmut. "From Privilege to Commodity? Modern Tourism and the Rise of the Consumer Society." In *The Making of Modern Tourism: The Cultural History of the British Experience, 1600–2000.* Berghoff, Hartmut, Barbara Korte, Ralf Schneider, and Christopher Harvie, eds. Houndmills, Basingstoke, Hampshire, UK: Palgrave, 2002. p. 168.

52. Stilz, Gerhard. "Heroic Travellers—Romantic Landscapes: The Colonial Sublime in Indian, Australian and American Art and Literature. In Berghoff et al., ed. *The Making of Modern Tourism.* p. 86.
53. Crystal, David. *English as a Global Language,* 2nd ed. Cambridge, UK: Cambridge University Press, 2003. p. 69.
54. Robinson, David. "The Hollywood Conquest." In *Encyclopaedia Britannica Book of the Year.* Chicago: Encyclopaedia Britannica, 1995. p. 245.
55. Crystal. *English as a Global Language.* p. 101.
56. Ibid. p. 102.
57. Ibid. p. 103.
58. Ibid. p. 105.
59. Ibid. p. 111.
60. Ibid. p. 112.
61. Ibid. p. 115.
62. Langer, Gary, and Brian Hartman. "Economy Casts Shadow Over Super Tuesday." *ABC News.* February 6, 2008.
63. Inglehart, Ronald, and Christian Welzel. *Modernization, Cultural Change, and Democracy: The Human Development Sequence.* Cambridge, UK: Cambridge University Press, 2005. p. 53.
64. Ibid. p. 56.
65. Ibid. pp. ix–x.
66. Ibid. p. 52.
67. Ibid. p. 7.
68. Ibid. p. 54.
69. Ibid. p. 33.
70. Ibid. pp. 106–107.
71. Inglehart, R. and P. Norris. *Rising Tide: Gender Equality and Cultural Change Around the World.* Cambridge, UK: Cambridge University Press, 2003. pp. 32–34.
72. "International Poll Finds Large Majorities in All Countries Favor Equal Rights for Women." World PublicOpinion.org. 2008
73. Ibid.
74. Ibid.
75. "Global Gender Gaps; Women Like Their Lives Better." Pew Research Center for the People and the Press. October 29, 2003. http://people-press .org/commentary/?analysisid=71
76. Speulda, Nicole, and Mary McIntosh. "Global Gender Gaps." Pew Global Attitudes Project. May 13, 2004. http://pewglobal.org/commentary/ display.php?AnalysisID=90
77. Ibid.
78. Ibid.
79. *Brokeback Mountain.* Wikipedia. http:// en.wikipedia.org/wiki/Brokeback_Mountain.
80. *Will and Grace.* Wikipedia. http://en.wikipedia .org/wiki/Will_&_Grace
81. Saad, L. "The Gallup Poll: Tolerance for Gay Rights at High-Water Mark." Gallup Poll News Service. May 29, 2007. www.galluppoll.com

82. Ibid.

83. "Religious Beliefs Underpin Opposition to Homosexuality: Republicans Unified, Democrats Split on Gay Marriage." The Pew Research Center for the People and the Press. November 18, 2003.

84. "Gay Marriage Around the Globe." BBC News. December 22, 2005.

85. FOX News/Opinion Dynamics Poll. Polling Report. Law and Civil Rights. "Same-Sex Marriage, Gay Rights." May 12–13, 2009. http://www.pollingreport.com/civil.htm

86. "Gay Marriage Around the Globe." BBC News.

87. "Same-Sex Marriage: Redefining Legal Unions Around the World." Pew Research Center Publications. July 11, 2007.

88. Forero, J. "Colombia to Recognize Gay Unions With Extension of Health, Other Benefits." *Washington Post.* June 16, 2007.

89. "Religious Beliefs Underpin Opposition to Homosexuality." Pew Research Center.

90. "Less Opposition to Gay Marriage, Adoption and Military Service." The Pew Research Center for the People and the Press. March 22, 2006.

91. Norris, Pippa, and Ronald Inglehart. *Sacred and Secular: Religion and Politics Worldwide.* Cambridge, UK: Cambridge University Press, 2004. p. 57–58.

92. Ibid. p. 58.

93. Ibid. p. 58–59.

94. Norris and Inglehart. *Sacred and Secular.* p. 75.

95. "The Spiritual State of the Union: The Role of Spiritual Commitment in the United States. Executive Summary." Princeton, NJ: The Gallup Organization, 2006.

96. Norris and Inglehart. *Sacred and Secular.* p. 233.

97. Ibid. p. 234.

98. "NJPS Report. Intermarriage: Variations in Intermarriage." United Jewish Communities. 2000–2001.

99. Kulczycki, A., and A. P. Lobo. "Patterns, Determinants, and Implications of Intermarriage Among Arab Americans." *Journal of Marriage and Family,* Vol. 64. February 2002. pp. 202–210.

100. Mastony, C. "Muslims Discover Risks, Rewards in Interfaith Unions." *Chicago Tribune.* August 16, 2002.

101. Kosmin, B. A., and E. Mayer. "American Religious Identification Survey." City University of New York, the Graduate Center. December 19, 2001. http://www.gc.cuny.edu/faculty/research_studies/aris.pdf

102. "SOPEMI: Trends in International Migration. Annual Report." Organization for Economic Cooperation and Development. 2004.

103. Beck, Ulrich. *What Is Globalization?* Cambridge, UK: Polity Press, 2000. p. 48.

104. "Mixed Marriages More Popular Now Than Ever." *The Asahi Shimbun.* December 31, 2005.

105. Suro, R. "Mixed Doubles—Interethnic Marriages and Marketing Strategy—Statistical Data Included." *American Demographics.* November 1999.

106. Kristof, N. D. "Blacks, Whites, and Love." *New York Times.* April 24, 2005.

107. Ibid.

108. "The 2004 Political Landscape: Evenly Divided and Increasingly Polarized. Social and Political Attitudes about Race (Part 5)." Pew Research Center for the People and the Press. November 5, 2003.

109. "Guess Who's Coming to Dinner: 22% of Americans Have a Relative in a Mixed-Race Marriage." The Pew Research Center for the People and the Press. March 16, 2006.

110. Qian, Zhenchao. "Breaking the Last Taboo: Interracial Marriage in America." *Contexts.* Vol. 4. No. 4. Fall 2005. pp. 33–37.

111. Fears, D., and C. Dean. "Biracial Couples Report Tolerance." *Washington Post.* July 5, 2001.

112. "Guess Who's Coming to Dinner." Pew Research Center for the People and the Press.

113. Ibid.

114. "Interracial Marriage Flourishes in U.S." The Associated Press. April 13, 2007.

115. Suro, R. "Mixed Doubles—Interethnic Marriages and Marketing Strategy—Statistical Data Included." *American Demographics.* November 1999.

116. "Interracial Marriages Increasing in U.S.; Report: New Marriages, New Families: U.S. Racial and Hispanic Intermarriage." *U.S. Newswire.* July 1, 2005.

117. "Interracial Marriage Flourishes in U.S." The Associated Press.

118. "Guess Who's Coming to Dinner." Pew Research Center for the People and the Press.

119. Bennett, Laura. "Pet Trends in 2007." *Small Business Trends.* January 16, 2007. www.smallbiztrends.com

120. Davi, Robert. "Our Pets Are Family, Too." *Washington Times.* April 21, 2009.

121. "Pets Are 'Members of the Family' and Two-Thirds of Pet Owners Buy Their Pets Holiday Presents." The Harris Poll #120. December 4, 2007.

122. Newport, Frank. "Post-Derby Tragedy, 38% Support Banning Animal Racing." Gallup Poll, May 8–11, 2008.

123. "The Welfare of Non-Human Primates Used in Research: Report of the Committee on Animal Health and Animal Welfare." The European Commission. December 17, 2002. p. 72.

124. "Asia 'Wakes Up' to Animal Welfare: Caring for Animals Is Not Just a Western

Whim—Millions of People in Asian Countries Think Animal Welfare Is Important, a Mori Poll Has Discovered." *BBC News.* March 17, 2005.

125. McNeil, Donald G., Jr. "When Human Rights Extend to Nonhumans." *Dallas Morning News.* July 31, 2008.

126. Kitching, C. "Agassiz Has Gone to the Dogs." *Daily Graphic.* August 2003.

127. "Six Degrees of Separation." Wikipedia. http://en.wikipedia.org/wiki/Six _ degrees _ of _ separation

128. Karinthy, F. "Chain-links." Translated from Hungarian and annotated by Adam Makkai and Eniko Janko. Cited in "Six Degrees of Separation." Wikipedia.

129. de Sola Pool, Ithiel, and Manfred Kochen. "Contacts and Influence." *Social Networks.* Vol. 1. No. 1. 1978–1979. p. 42.

130. Travers, Jeffrey, and Milgram Stanley. "An Experimental Study of the Small World Problem." *Sociometry.* Vol. 32. No. 4. December 1969. pp. 425–443.

131. Kleinfeld, Judith. "Could It Be a Big World After All?" University of Alaska at Fairbanks. *Society* 2002. www.uaf.edu/northern/big_world .html

132. Lescovec, Jure, and Horvitz, Eric. "Worldwide Buzz: Planetary-Scale Views on a Large Instant-Messaging Network" *Microsoft Technical Report* MSR-TR-2006-186. June 2007. p. 1.

133. Whoriskey, Peter. "Instant-Messagers Really Are About Six Degrees from Kevin Bacon." *Washington Post.* Aug. 2, 2008. p. A6.

134. Ibid.

CHAPTER 12: THE PLANETARY
ENTROPIC ABYSS

1. McCarthy, M. "Climate Change 'Will Cause Refugee Crisis.' " *Independent Online.* October 20, 2006.

2. United Nations Intergovernmental Panel on Climate Change. *Climate Change 2007: The Physical Science Basis: Summary for Policy Makers: Contribution of Working Group I to the Fourth Assessment Report of the Intergovernmental Panel on Climate Change.* p. 2.

3. Ibid. p. 3.

4. Ibid.

5. Ibid. p. 5.

6. "Why Build Green?" U.S. Building Council. 2008.

7. Food and Agriculture Organization of the United Nations. *Livestock's Long Shadow—Environmental Issues and Options,* 2006. p. 272. ftp://ftp.fao.org/docrep/fao/010/a0701e/A0701E07.pdf

8. Ibid.

9. United Nations Intergovernmental Panel on Climate Change. February 2 2007. *Climate Change 2007: The Physical Science Basis.* p. 12 www.ipcc.ch/

10. Stainforth, D. A., T. Alna, C. Christensen, M. Collins, N. Fauli, D. J. Frame, J. A. Kettleborough, S. Knight, A. Martin, J. M. Murphy, C. Piani, D. Sexton, L. A. Smith, R. A. Spicer, A. J. Thorpe, and M. R. Allen. "Uncertainty in Predictions of the Climate Response to Rising Levels of Greenhouse Gases." *Nature.* Vol. 433. No. 27. 2005.

11. Bemstein, Lenny, et al. *Climate Change 2007: Synthesis Report.* Intergovernmental Panel on Climate Change. www.ipcc.ch/pdf/assessment-report/ar4/syr/ar4_syr.pdf

12. Whitty, Julia. "By the End of the Century Half of All Species Will Be Gone. Who Will Survive?" *Mother Jones* 32. No. 3. p. 36–90.

13. Houghton, John. *Global Warming: The Complete Briefing,* 2nd ed. Cambridge, UK: Cambridge University Press, 1997, p. 127.

14. Ibid.

15. Ibid.

16. Beardsley, Tim. "In the Heat of the Night." *Scientific American.* Vol. 279. No. 4. October 1998. p. 20.

17. Ibid.

18. Pearce, Fred. "Violent Future." *New Scientist.* July 21, 2001. p. 4.

19. Mayell, H. "UN Highlights World Water Crisis." *National Geographic News.* June 5, 2003.

20. United Nations Intergovernmental Panel on Climate Change. *Climate Change 2007: The Physical Science Basis.* Chapter 3: Observations: Surface and Atmospheric Change. Contribution of Working Group I to the Fourth Assessment Report of the Intergovernmental Panel on Climate Change, p. 254.

21. United Nations Intergovernmental Panel on Climate Change. *Climate Change 2007: The Physical Science Basis.* Chapter 4: Observations: Changes in Snow, Ice and Frozen Ground. Contribution of Working Group I to the Fourth Assessment Report of the Intergovernmental Panel on Climate Change, p. 376. United Nations Intergovernmental Panel on Climate Change. *Climate Change 2007: Climate Change Impacts, Adaptation and Vulnerability:* Chapter 15: Polar Regions (Arctic and Antarctic). Contribution of Working Group II to the Fourth Assessment Report of the Intergovernmental Panel on Climate Change, p. 655.

22. Schneeberger, C., H. Blatter, A. Abe-Ouchi, and M. Wild. "Modelling Changes in the Mass Balance of Glaciers of the Northern Hemisphere for a Transient $2 \times CO_2$ Scenario." *Journal of Hydrology* 282. 2003. pp. 145–163.

23. United Nations Intergovernmental Panel on Climate Change. February 2 2007. *Climate Change 2007: The Physical Science Basis:* Chapter 10: Global Climate Projections. Contribution of Working Group I to the Fourth Assessment Report of the

Intergovernmental Panel on Climate Change, p. 783.

24. Webster, P. J., G. J. Holland, J. A. Curry, H. R. Chang. "Changes in Tropical Cyclone Number, Duration, and Intensity in Warming Environment." *Science*. Vol. 309. No. 5742. pp. 1844–1846. Sept. 16, 2005.

25. United Nations Intergovernmental Panel on Climate Change. *Climate Change 2007: Climate Change Impacts, Adaptation and Vulnerability*. Chapter 15: Polar Regions (Arctic and Antarctic). Contribution of Working Group II to the Fourth Assessment Report of the Intergovernmental Panel on Climate Change, p. 676. Instanes, A., O. Anisimov, L. Brigham, D. Goering, B. Ladanyi, et al. "Infrastructure: Buildings, Support Systems, and Industrial Facilities." In C. Symon, L. Arris, and B. Heal, eds. *Arctic Climate Impact Assessment, ACIA*. Cambridge, UK: Cambridge University Press, 2005, 907–944.

26. Walter, K. M., S. A. Zimov, J. P. Chanton, D. Verbyla, and F. S. Chapin. "Methane Bubbling from Siberian Thaw Lakes as a Positive Feedback to Climate Warming." *Nature*. Vol. 443, No. 7. 2006. 71–75.

27. Ibid. Walter, K. M., L. C. Smith, and F. S. Chapin (2007). Methane Bubbling From Northern Lakes: Present and Future Contributions to the Global Methane Budget. Philosophical Transactions of the Royal Society. 365. pp. 1657–1676. 2007. "A Sleeping Giant?" *Nature Reports Climate Change*. March 5, 2009.

28. Committee on Abrupt Climate Change. "Abrupt Climate Change: Inevitable Surprises." National Research Council of the National Academy of Sciences. 2002. Washington, D.C.: National Academy Press, p. 14.

29. Ibid.

30. Ibid. pp. 153–154.

31. Ibid. pp. 119–120.

32. Ibid. p. 111.

33. Ibid. p. 128.

34. Ibid. pp. 114, 154.

35. Walsh, Bryan. "A Last Warning on Global Warming." Nov. 17, 2007. www.time.com/time/health/article/0,8599,1685199,00.html

36. Broad, William J., and David E. Sanger. "Restraints Fray and Risks Grow as Nuclear Club Gains Members." *New York Times*. October 16, 2006. www.nytimes.com/2006/10/15/world/asia/15nuke.html?_r=1&ref=todayspaper

37. "IEA Energy Technology Essentials: Nuclear Power." International Energy Agency. www.iea.org/Textbase/techno/essentials.pdf; Ansolabehere, Stephen, et al. *The Future of Nuclear Power: An Interdisciplinary MIT Study*. Cambridge, MA: MIT Press. 2003. p. 3; Lipták, Béla. "If Global Carbon Emissions Were Cut by 15% by 2050 by

the Increased Use of Nuclear Power, 1,070 Plants Would Need to Be Built at a Cost of $5 Trillion." ControlGlobal.com. www.controlglobal.com; Birol, Fatih. "Nuclear Power: How Competitive Down the Line?" International Atomic Energy Agency. *IAEA Bulletin*. Vol. 48. No. 2. March 2007. p. 19. "Nuclear Power Can't Stop Climate Change." Nuclear Information and Resource Service. www.nirs.org/factsheets/climatenukes.pdf

38. Broad and Sanger. "Restraints Fray."

39. Ibid.

40. Ibid.

41. Ibid.

42. Ibid.

43. U.S. Department of Defense, Biological Defense Program, *Report to the Committee on Appropriations, House of Representatives*, May 1986, p. 4. A brief but informative survey of the development and use of biological and chemical weapons is found in Frank Barnaby, *The Gaia Peace Atlas: Survival into the Third Millennium*. New York: Doubleday, 1988. pp. 134–38.

44. Horrock, Nicholas, "The New Terror Fear—Biological Weapons: Detecting an Attack Is Just the First Problem," *U.S. News & World Report*. May 12, 1997. p. 36.

45. Lipton, Eric, and Scott Shane. "Anthrax Case Renews Questions on Bioterror Effort and Safety." *New York Times*. Aug. 3, 2008, p. 1.

46. Ibid. p. 17.

47. Odum, Eugene P. *Fundamentals of Ecology*. Philadelphia: Saunders, 1971, p. 266.

48. Virginia Declaration of Rights. http://www.history.org/almanack/life/politics/varights.cfm

49. Reeve, Andrew. *Property*. London: Macmillan, 1986. pp. 137–138.

50. Mill, James. "Essay on Government." In James Mill. *Political Writings*. Terrence Ball, ed. Cambridge, UK: Cambridge University Press, 1992. p. 5.

51. Kasser, Tim. *The High Price of Materialism*. Cambridge, MA: MIT Press, 2002. p. 5.

52. Ibid. p. 11.

53. Kasser, Tim, and R. M. Ryan. "Be Careful What You Wish For: Optimal Functioning and the Relative Attainment of Intrinsic and Extrinsic Goals." In P. Schmuck and K. M. Sheldon, eds. *Life Goals and Well-Being: Towards a Positive Psychology of Human Striving*. Goettingen, Germany: Hogrefe & Huber, 2001. pp. 116–131.

54. Sheldon, K. M., and T. Kasser. " 'Getting Older, Getting Better': Personal Strivings and Psychological Maturity Across the Life Span." *Developmental Psychology* 37, 2001, pp. 491–501.

55. Cohen, Patricia, and Jacob Cohen. *Life Values and Adolescent Mental Health*. Mahwah, NJ: Erlbaum. 1996.

56. Kasser. *The High Price of Materialism*. p. 14.

57. Layard, Richard. *Happiness: Lessons from a New Science*. New York: Penguin Press. p. 29–30.

58. Ibid. p. 33.

59. Myers, David G., and Edward Diener. "The Pursuit of Happiness." *Scientific American*. May 1996. pp. 70–72.

60. Putnam, Robert D. *Bowling Alone: The Collapse and Revival of American Community*. New York: Simon and Schuster. p. 140.

61. Layard. *Happiness*. p. 82.

62. Kasser. *The High Price of Materialism*. p. 69.

63. Sheldon, K. M., and T. Kasser. "Coherence and Congruence: Two Aspects of Personality Integration." *Journal of Personality and Social Psychology* 68. 1995. pp. 531–543. The empathy survey was from M. H. Davis. "A Multidimensional Approach to Individual Differences in Empathy." *JSAS Catalog of Selected Documents in Psychology* 10. No. 85. 1980.

64. Layard. *Happiness*. p. 41–42.

65. Solnick, S., and D. Hemenway. "Is More Always Better? A Survey on Positional Concerns." *Journal of Economic Behaviour and Organisation* 37. 1998. pp. 373–383.

66. Layard. *Happiness*. p. 48.

67. "Growing Unequal? Income Distribution and Poverty in OECD Countries." Organisation for Economic Co-operation and Development. www.oecd.org/els/social/inequality

68. Ibid. p. 30.

69. Ibid. p. 52.

70. Ibid. pp. 106–107.

71. Layard, p. 52.

72. "International Poll Finds Large Majorities in All Countries Favor Equal Rights for Woman." World Public Opinion.org. 2008. www.worldpublicopinion.org

73. Kasser, T., R. M. Ryan, M. Zax, and A. J. Sameroff. "The Relations of Maternal and Social Environments to Late Adolescents' Materialistic and Prosocial Values. *Developmental Psychology* 31, 1995. pp. 907–914.

74. Cohen, Patricia, and Jacob Cohen. *Life Values and Adolescent Mental Health*. Mahwah, NJ: Erlbaum. 1996.

75. Kasser. *The High Price of Materialism*. p. 32.

76. Ibid. p. 65.

77. Ibid. pp. 92–93.

78. Sheldon, K. M., and H. McGregor. "Extrinsic Value Orientation and the Tragedy of the Commons." *Journal of Personality* 68, 2000. pp. 383–411.

79. In an endnote, Kasser explains that "one hectare actually equals 100 ares [sic] or 2.47 acres, but subjects in this study were mistakenly told that 1 hectare equals 100 acres."

80. Kasser. *The High Price of Materialism*. p. 93.

81. Ibid. 93–95.

82. Schor, Juliet B. *Born to Buy: The Commercialized Child and the New Consumer Culture*. New York: Scribner, 2004. p. 19.

83. Ibid. p. 20.

84. Ibid. p. 23.

85. Ibid. p. 27.

86. Ibid. p. 31.

87. Ibid. p. 37.

88. Cooperman, Gene. "Beyond Peak Oil: A Survey Based on Primary Statistics." www.ccs.neu.edu/home/gene/peakoil/

89. Zittel, Werner, and Jorg Schindler. "Crude Oil: The Supply Outlook." *Report to the Energy Watch Group*. 2007. p. 12.

90. Ibid. p. 43.

91. "Mexico." Energy Information Administration, Official Energy Statistics from the U.S. Government Country Analysis Briefs. March 2009.

92. "Developing the World and the Electricity Challenge." International Energy Agency. January 2005. www.iea.org/Textbase/work/2005/poverty/blurb.pdf. Zhongmao Gu. "Securing Nuclear Fuel Cycle When Embracing Global Nuclear Renaissance." http://www.pub.iaea.org/mtcd/meetings/PDFplus/2009/cn169/Beijing_TS/TS4/1%20GUzhongmao.pdf

CHAPTER 13: THE EMERGING ERA OF DISTRIBUTED CAPITALISM

1. "National Interstate and Defense Highways Act (1956)." U.S. National Archives and Records Administration. www.ourdocuments.gov/doc.php?doc=88

2. Mooney, Chris C. *Storm World: Hurricanes, Politics, and the Battle over Global Warming*. Boston: Houghton Mifflin Harcourt, 2007. pp. 56–57.

3. Federal Reserve Bank of San Francisco: Educational Resources. "Ask Dr. Econ: What Steps Can Be Taken to Increase Savings in the United States Economy?" www.frbsf.org; Crutsinger, Martin. "Consumer Spending, Incomes Up in December; Savings Rate Worst Since 1933." *USA Today*. February 1, 2007.

4. Wolf, Martin. "Paulson's Plan Was Not a True Solution to the Crisis." *Financial Times*. September 23, 2008. http://us.ft.com/ftgateway/superpage.ft?news_id=ft0092320081447402080

5. Board of Governors of the Federal Reserve System. *Flow of Funds Accounts of the United States: Flows and Outstandings, Third Quarter* 2008. Federal Reserve Statistical Release. December 11, 2008. www.federalreserve.gov/releases/Z1/20081211/z1.pdf

6. BP Amoco Statistic Review of World Energy, London: BP Amoco, 2000. pp.11, 40. www.bpamoco.com/worldenergy

7. *Progress Report October Two Thousand Eight:* Baton Rouge, LA: Louisiana Recovery Authority. www .tra.louisiana.gov

8. Keeley, Graham. "GM Installs World's Biggest Rooftop Solar Panels." *The Guardian.* July 9, 2008. www.guardian.co.uk

9. Bohannon, J. "Distributed Computing: Grassroots Supercomputing." *Science.* Vol. 308. No. 5723. May 6, 2005. pp. 810–813.

10. Ibid.

11. "List of Distributed Computing Projects." Wikipedia. http://en.wikipedia.org/wiki/ List_of_distributed_computing_projects

12. Bohannon. "Distributed Computing: Grassroots Supercomputing."

13. Surowiecki, James. *The Wisdom of Crowds: Why the Many Are Smarter Than the Few and How Collective Wisdom Shapes Business, Economies, Societies, and Nations.* New York: Doubleday, 2004. p. xiii.

14. Tapscott, Don, and Anthony D. Williams. *Wikinomics: How Mass Collaboration Changes Everything.* New York: Penguin, 2006. p. 8.

15. Ibid. p. 9.

16. Ibid.

17. Ibid. p. 13.

18. McGirt, Ellen. "How Cisco's CEO John Chambers Is Turning the Tech Giant Socialist." (Also published as "Revolution in San Jose.") *Fast Company: Where Ideas and People Meet.* Vol. 131. December 2008/January 2009. p. 94. www .fastcompany.com/magazine/131/revolution-in-san-jose.html

19. Ibid. p. 93.

20. Ibid. p. 135.

21. Tapscott and Williams. *Wikinomics.* p. 3.

22. Ibid. p. 13.

23. "Wikipedia." Wikipedia: The Free Encyclopedia. May 14, 2009. http://en.wikipedia .org/wiki/Wikipedia

24. Giles, Jim. "Internet Encyclopedias Go Head to Head." *Nature.* Vol. 438. No. 531. December 15, 2005.

25. Tapscott and Williams. *Wikinomics.* p. 24.

26. "The Basics: Auto Leasing Is Back—and Better." Bankrate.com. www.moneycentral.msn.com

27. Macpherson, Crawford. *Democratic Theory: Essays in Retrieval.* Oxford, UK: Oxford University Press, 1973. p. 139.

28. Ibid. p. 140.

29. Tapscott and Williams. *Wikinomics.* p. 41.

30. Ibid. p. 47.

31. Goleman, Daniel, Richard E. Boyatzis, and Annie McKee. *The New Leaders: Transforming the Art of Leadership into the Science of Results.* London: Sphere, 2002. p. 59.

32. Ibid. p. 63.

33. Ibid. pp. 65–66.

34. Ibid. p. 82.

35. "PSI: Program on Social Intelligence." Columbia Business School. www0.gsb.columbia .edu/psi/about/faqs

36. Moriarty, Maureen. "Workplace Coach: Don't Underestimate Emotional Intelligence." *Seattle Post-Intelligencer.* June 3, 2007.

37. Lyubomirsky, Sonja, Laura King, and Edward Diener. "The Benefits of Frequent Positive Affect: Does Happiness Lead to Success?" *Psychological Bulletin.* Vol. 131. No. 6. 2005. pp. 803–855. Staw, Barry, Robert I. Sutton, and Lisa H. Pelled. "Employee Positive Emotion and Favorable Outcomes at the Workplace." *Organization Science.* Vol. 5. No. 1. February 1994. pp. 51–71. Judge, Timothy A., Amir Erez, and Joyce E. Bono. "The Power of Being Positive: The Relation Between Positive Self-Concept and Job Performance." *Human Performance.* Vol. 11. Nos. 2 & 3. June 1998. pp. 167–187.

38. *National Income 1929–32, Senate Report.* Division of Economic Research, Bureau of Foreign and Domestic Commerce. January 4, 1934. p. 7.

39. Kuznets, Simon. "How to Judge Quality." *The New Republic.* October 20, 1962.

40. Tomkins, Richard. "How to Be Happy." *Financial Times Weekend.* March 8–9, 2003.

41. Ibid.; "Economic Value of Civic Voluntary Work." GPI Atlantic. www.gpiatlantic.org/ clippings/voluntaryclips.htm; "Genuine Progress Indicator." Redefining Progress. www .rprogress.org/sustainability _ indicators/ genuine _ progress _ indicator.htm.

42. "Alternatives to the GDP." McGregor Consulting Group. March 25, 2003.

43. Osberg, Larry, and Andrew Sharpe. "Human Well-Being and Economic Well-Being: What Values Are Implicit in Current Indices?" Center for the Study of Living Standards. July 2003.

44. "The Basics: Think Your Taxes Are Bad?" MSN Money. www.moneycentral.msn.com

CHAPTER 14: THE THEATRICAL SELF IN AN IMPROVISATIONAL SOCIETY

1. Horton, Donald, and R. Richard Wohl. "Mass Communication and Para-Social Interaction: Observations on Intimacy at a Distance." *Psychiatry,* Vol. 19. 1956. p. 215.

2. Ibid. p. 217.

3. Ibid. p. 222.

4. Goffman, Erving. *The Presentation of Self in Everyday Life.* New York: Anchor Books, 1959. p. 15.

5. Ibid. p. 17.

6. James, William. *The Philosophy of William James.* Modern Library Edition. New York: Random House, n.d. pp. 128–129.

7. Brissett, Dennis, and Charles Edgley. "The Dramaturgical Perspective." In Dennis Brissett and Charles Edgley, eds. *Life as Theater: A Dramaturgical Sourcebook*, 2nd ed. New York: Aldine de Gruyter, 1990. pp. 15–16.

8. Perinbanayagam, Robert S. *Signifying Acts: Structure and Meaning in Everyday Life.* Carbondale, IL: Southern Illinois University Press, 1985. p. 63.

9. Ibid. p. 62–63.

10. Perinbanayagam, Robert S. "Dramas, Metaphors, and Structures." *Symbolic Interaction.* Vol. 5. No. 2. 1982. p. 266.

11. Finestone, Hillel M., and David B. Conter. "Acting in Medical Practice." *The Lancet.* Vol. 344. No. 8925. Sept. 1994. p. 801.

12. Nissley, Nick, Steven S. Taylor, and Linda Houden. "The Politics of Performance in Organizational Theatre-Based Training and Interventions." *Organizational Studies.* Vol. 25. No. 5. June 2004. p. 825.

13. Ibid. p. 832. (Nissley's emphasis)

14. Anderson, Alistair. "Enacted Metaphor: The Theatricality of the Entrepreneurial Process." *International Small Business Journal.* Vol. 23. No. 6. December 2005. p. 597.

15. Nauta, Reinard. "The Performance of Authenticity: Ordination and Profession in Pastoral Care." *Pastoral Psychology.* Vol. 51. No. 5. May 2003. p. 428.

16. Ibid. p. 428. See also: Scheff, T. J. *Catharsis in Healing, Ritual and Drama.* Berkeley, CA: University of California Press, 1979. p. 60.

17. Nauta, Reinard. "The Performance of Authenticity: Ordination and Profession in Pastoral Care." *Pastoral Psychology.* p. 430. See also: W. R. Bion. *Experience in Groups.* London: Tavistock, 1959.

18. Nauta, Reinard. "The Performance of Authenticity: Ordination and Profession in Pastoral Care." *Pastoral Psychology.* p. 431.

19. Stanislavski, Constantin. *An Actor Prepares.* Elizabeth Reynolds Hapgood, trans. New York: Theatre Arts Books, 1965. p. 22.

20. Ibid. p. 57.

21. Ibid. p. 267.

22. Cohen, Albert. *Deviance and Control.* Englewood Cliffs, NJ: Prentice-Hall, 1966. p. 105.

23. Ibid.

24. Hochschild, Arlie Russell. *The Managed Heart: Commercialization of Human Feeling.* Berkeley, CA: University of California Press, 1983. p. 53.

25. Cohen. *Deviance and Control.* p. 105.

26. Hochschild. *The Managed Heart.* p. 55.

27. Ibid.

28. Thinkexist.com. Quotation by Meryl Streep.

29. Gergen, Kenneth J. *The Saturated Self: Dilemmas of Identity in Contemporary Life.* New York: Basic Books, 1991. p. 79.

30. Ibid. p. 80.

31. Ibid. p. 7.

32. Ibid. pp. 17, 146–147.

33. Baudrillard, Jean. *The Ecstasy of Communication.* Sylvére Lotringer, ed. Bernard and Caroline Schutze, trans. New York: Semiotext, 1988. p. 16.

34. Lifton, Robert Jay. *The Protean Self: Human Resilience in an Age of Fragmentation.* New York: Basic Books, 1993. p. 17.

35. Buber, Martin. *I and Thou.* Walter Kaufman, trans. New York: Scribner, 1970. p. 69.

36. Gergen. *The Saturated Self.* p. 150.

37. Ibid.

38. Zurcher, Louis A., Jr. *The Mutable Self.* Beverly Hills, CA: Sage, 1977. n.p.

39. Gergen, Kenneth J. "The Decline and Fall of Personality." *Psychology Today.* Vol. 25. No. 6. November 1992. p. 63.

40. Boase, Jeffrey, John Horrigan, Barry Wellman, and Lee Rainie. *The Strength of Internet Ties.* Pew Internet and American Life Project. Jan 25, 2006.

41. Ibid.

42. Ibid.

43. Ibid.

44. Ibid.

45. Hu, Yifeng, Jacqueline F. Wood, Vivian Smith, and Nalova Westbrook. "Friendships Through IM: Examining the Relationship Between Instant Messaging and Intimacy." *Journal of Computer Mediated Communication.* Vol. 10. No. 1. Nov. 2004. n.p.

46. Markow, Dana. "Friendships in the Age of Social Networking Websites." *Trends & Tudes.* Vol. 5. No. 9. Oct. 2006. p. 4.

47. McKenna, Katelyn Y. A, Amie S. Green, and Marci E. J. Gleason. "Relationship Formation on the Internet: What's the Big Attraction?" *Journal of Social Issues.* Vol. 58. No. 1. 2002. p. 10.

48. Ibid.

49. Ibid. p. 16.

50. Ibid. p. 17.

51. Ibid. p. 22.

52. Ibid. p. 23.

53. Ibid. p. 17.

54. Twenge, Jean M. *Generation Me: Why Today's Young Americans Are More Confident, Assertive, Entitled—and More Miserable Than Ever Before.* New York: Free Press, 2006. p. 82.

55. Ibid. p. 87.

56. "All Reality TV Shows Index, Reality TV World—News." Reality TV World. www.realitytvworld.com/realitytvworld/allshows.shtml

57. "Blogging Is Bringing New Voices to the Online World." Pew Internet and American Life Project. Press Release. July 19, 2006.

58. Carey, Benedict. "The Fame Motive." *New York Times*. August 22, 2006. pp. D1, D6.

59. Ibid.

60. Twenge. *Generation Me*. p. 56.

61. Manning, T., B. Fields, and C. Roberts. "The Millennial Generation: The Next Generation in College Enrollment." Charlotte, NC: Central Piedmont Community College Center for Applied Research. n.d. http://www.cpcc.edu/planning/studies-and-reports/Wyoming percent20Seminary percent20Millennials.ppt

62. Scott, Cynthia G., Gerald C. Murray, Carol Mertens, and E. Richard Dustin. "Student Self-Esteem and the School System: Perceptions and Implications. *Journal of Education Research* Vol. 89. No. 5. 1996. pp. 289–290.

63. Twenge. *Generation Me*. p. 55.

64. Ibid. p. 63.

65. CBS News. *The Class of 2000*. Simon and Schuster eBook, 2001. p. 64.

66. Twenge, Jean M., and W. Keith Campbell. "Age and Birth Cohort Differences in Self-Esteem: A Cross-Temporal Meta-Analysis. *Personality and Social Psychology Review*. Vol. 5. pp. 321–344.

67. Newsom, C. R., et al. "Changes in Adolescent Response Patterns on the MMPI/MMPI-A Across Four Decades. *Journal of Personality Assessment*. Vol. 81. 2003. pp. 74–84.

68. Pew Research Center. "A Portrait of Generation Next: How Young People View Their Lives, Futures and Politics." January 9, 2007. http://pewresearch.org/pubs/278/a-portrait-of-generation-next

69. Winograd, Morley, and Michael D. Hais. *Millennial Makeover: MySpace, YouTube, and the Future of American Politics*. Piscataway, NJ: Rutgers University Press, 2008. p. 5.

70. Ibid. p. 263; See also Harvard University Institute of Politics. "The 12th Biannual Youth Survey on Politics and Public Service." April 17, 2007. www.iop.harvard.edu/var/ezp_site/storage/fckeditor/file/pdfs/Research-Publications/survey_s2007_topline.pdf

71. Winograd and Hais. *Millennial Makeover*. pp. 263–264.

72. Pew Research Center. "Trends in Political Values and Core Attitudes: 1987–2007." March 22, 2007. http://pewresearch.org/pubs/434/trends-in-political-values-and-core-attitudes-1987-2007

73. "Generation Next." PBS Broadcast. January 7, 2007.

74. Harvard University Institute of Politics. "The 12th Biannual Youth Survey on Politics and Public Service."

75. Pew Research Center. "Trends in Political Values and Core Attitudes: 1987–2007." March 22, 2007.

76. Winograd and Hais. *Millennial Makeover*. pp. 66–67.

77. "A First Look at the Literacy of America's Adults in the 21st Century." *National Assessment of Adult Literacy*. National Center for Education Statistics. U.S. Department of Education. P.15. www.nces.ed.gov/NAAL/PDF/2006470_1.PDF

78. Bauerlein, Mark. *The Dumbest Generation: How the Digital Age Stupefies Young Americans and Jeopardizes Our Future*. New York: Tarcher/Penguin, 2009. p. 128.

79. Ibid. p. 128–129.

CHAPTER 15: BIOSPHERE CONSCIOUSNESS IN A CLIMAX ECONOMY

1. Lovelock, James. *The Ages of Gaia: A Biography of Our Living Earth*. New York: Norton, 1988. p. 312. Quotation by Vladimir Vernadsky.

2. Polunin, N. "Our Use of 'Biosphere,' 'Ecosystem,' and Now 'Ecobiome.' " *Environmental Conservation*. Vol. 11. 1984. p. 198. Serafin, Rafal. "Noosphere, Gaia, and the Science of the Biosphere." *Environmental Ethics*. Vol. 10. Summer 1988. p. 125.

3. Patten, Bernard C. "Network Ecology." In M. Higashi and T. P. Burns, eds. *Theoretical Studies of Ecosystems: The Network Perspective*. New York: Cambridge University Press, 1991.

4. Capra, Fritjof. *The Web of Life: A New Scientific Understanding of Living Systems*. New York: Anchor Books, 1996. pp. 34–35.

5. Ibid. p. 34. Thomas, Lewis. *The Lives of a Cell*. New York: Bantam, 1975. pp. 26ff, 102ff.

6. Hu, Winnie. "Gossip Girls and Boys Get Lessons in Empathy." *New York Times*. April 4, 2009.

7. Ibid.

8. Gordon, Mary. *Roots of Empathy*. Toronto: Thomas Allen Publishers. 2005. p. 6.

9. Ibid. p. 8.

10. Ibid. p. 11.

11. Ibid. p. 78.

12. Ibid. p. xvii.

13. Gergen, Kenneth J. "Theory Under Threat: Social Construction and Identity Politics." In Charles W Tolman, Frances Cherry, Rene Van Hezewijk, and Ian Lubek, eds. *Problems of Theoretical Psychology*. North York, Ontario, Canada: Captus University Publications, 1996. p. 21.

14. Bruffee, Kenneth A. *Collaborative Learning: Higher Education, Interdependence, and the Authority of Knowledge*, 2nd ed. Baltimore, MD: Johns Hopkins University Press. 1999. p. 15.

15. Ibid. p. 14.

16. Ibid. p. 73.

17. Goethe, Johann Wolfgang von. *Maximen und Reflexionen*. No. 509, HA XII, p. 435.

18. Goethe, as quoted in Cottrell, Alan P. *Goethe's View of Evil and the Search for a New Image of Man in Our Time*. Edinburgh: Floris Books, 1982. p. 227.

19. MacIsaac, David S. "Empathy: Heinz Kohut's Contribution." In A. C. Bohart and L. S. Greenberg, eds. *Empathy Reconsidered: New Directions in Psychotherapy*. Washington: American Psychological Association, 1997. p. 248.

20. Kohut, Heinz. "The Psychoanalyst in the Community of Scholars." In Paul H. Ornstein, ed. *The Search for the Self: Selected Writings of Heinz Kohut: 1950–1978*. Vol. 2. New York: International Universities Press. 1978. p. 702.

21. Ornstein ed. *The Search for the Self: Selected Writings of Heinz Kohut: 1950–1978*. Vol. 1. New York: International Universities Press. 1991. p. 82.

22. Kohut, Heinz. "The Psychoanalyst in the Community of Scholars." In Ornstein, Paul H., ed. *The Search for the Self: Selected Writings of Heinz Kohut: 1950–1978*. Vol. 2. New York: International Universities Press. 1978. p. 714.

23. Ornstein. *The Search for the Self: Selected Writings of Heinz Kohut: 1950–1978*. Vol. 1. p. 529.

24. Ibid. p. 707.

25. Maslow, Abraham H. *The Psychology of Science: A Renaissance*. South Bend: Gateway Editions, Ltd. 1966. p. xvi. (Maslow's emphasis)

26. Ibid. p. 50.

27. Ibid. p. 58.

28. Ibid. pp. 97–98.

29. Ibid. pp. 108–109.

BIBLIOGRAPHY

Abrams, Dominic, Michael A. Hogg, and José M. Marques, eds. *The Social Psychology of Inclusion and Exclusion*. New York: Psychology Press, 2005.

Adam, Barry D. *The Rise of a Gay and Lesbian Movement*. New York: Twayne Publishers, 1995.

Adams, Richard N. *Energy and Structure: A Theory of Social Power*. Austin: University of Texas Press, 1975.

Agnew, Jean-Christophe. *Worlds Apart: The Market and the Theater in Anglo-American Thought, 1550–1750*. Cambridge, UK: Cambridge University Press, 1986.

Almond, Gabriel A., R. Scott Appleby, and Emmanuel Sivan. *Strong Religion: The Rise of Fundamentalisms Around the World*. Chicago: University of Chicago Press, 2003.

Andresen, Jensine, ed. *Religion in Mind: Cognitive Perspectives on Religious Belief, Ritual, and Experience*. Cambridge, UK: Cambridge University Press, 2001.

Arbib, Michael A., ed. *Action to Language via the Mirror Neuron System*. Cambridge, UK: Cambridge University Press, 2006.

Archard, David. *Children: Rights and Childhood*. London: Routledge, 1993.

Ariès, Philippe. *The Hour of Our Death*. Trans. H. Weaver. New York: Oxford University Press, 1981.

Armstrong, Alison, and Charles Casement. *The Child and the Machine: How Computers Put Our Children's Education at Risk*. Beltsville, MD: Robins Lane Press, 2000.

Armstrong, Karen. *Islam: A Short History*. New York: Modern Library, 2000.

———. *The Great Transformation: The Beginning of Our Religious Traditions*. New York: Knopf, 2006.

Armstrong, Nancy. *How Novels Think: The Limits of Individualism from 1719–1900*. New York: Columbia University Press, 2005.

Arnett, Jeffrey J. *Emerging Adulthood: The Winding Road from the Late Teens Through the Twenties*. Oxford, UK: Oxford University Press, 2004.

Bales, Kevin. *Disposable People: New Slavery in the Global Economy*. Berkeley: University of California Press, 2004.

Banks, James A., and Cherry A. McGee Banks. *Multicultural Education: Issues and Perspectives*. 6th ed. Hoboken, NJ: Wiley, 2007.

Baron-Cohen, Simon. *The Essential Difference: The Truth About the Male and Female Brain*. New York: Basic Books, 2003.

Batson, C. Daniel, Patricia Schoenrade, and W. Larry Ventis. *Religion and the Individual: A Social-Psychological Perspective*. New York: Oxford University Press, 1993.

Bauerlein, Mark. *The Dumbest Generation: How the Digital Age Stupefies Young Americans and Jeopardizes Our Future (Or, Don't Trust Anyone Under 30)*. New York: Tarcher/ Penguin, 2009.

Bauman, Zygmunt. *Mortality, Immortality and Other Life Strategies*. Stanford, CA: Stanford University Press, 1992.

Baumeister, Roy F. *Identity: Cultural Change and the Struggle for Self.* New York: Oxford University Press, 1986.

Beck, Ulrich, and Elisabeth Beck-Gernsheim. *Individualization: Institutionalized Individualism and Its Social and Political Consequences.* London: Sage Publications, 2005.

Becker, Ernest. *Escape from Evil.* New York: Free Press, 1985.

———. *The Denial of Death.* New York: Free Press, 1997.

Benamou, Michel, and Charles Caramello, eds. *Performance in Postmodern Culture.* Madison, WI: Coda Press Inc., 1977.

Beniger, James R. *The Control Revolution: Technological and Economic Origins of the Information Society.* Cambridge, MA: Harvard University Press, 1986.

Benjafield, John G. *A History of Psychology.* 2nd ed. Ontario: Oxford University Press, 2005.

Bentley, Jerry H. *Old World Encounters: Cross-Cultural Contacts and Exchanges in Pre-Modern Times.* New York: Oxford University Press, 1993.

Berghoff, Hartmut, Barbara Korte, Ralf Schneider, and Christopher Harvie, eds. *The Making of Modern Tourism: The Cultural History of the British Experience, 1600–2000.* Hampshire, UK: Palgrave, 2002.

Bohart, Arthur C., and Leslie S. Greenberg, eds. *Empathy Reconsidered: New Directions in Psychotherapy.* Washington, DC: American Psychological Association, 1997.

Boltanski, Luc. *Distant Suffering: Morality, Media and Politics.* Trans. Graham Burchell. New York: Cambridge University Press, 1999.

Boswell, John. *The Kindness of Strangers: The Abandonment of Children in Western Europe from Late Antiquity to the Renaissance.* Chicago: University of Chicago Press, 1998.

Bowlby, John. *The Making and Breaking of Affectional Bonds.* London: Tavistock Publications, 1979.

Brissett, Dennis, and Charles Edgley. *Life as Theater: A Dramaturgical Sourcebook.* 2nd ed. New York: Aldine de Gruyter, 1990.

Brizendine, Louann. *The Female Brain.* New York: Morgan Road Books, 2006.

Brown, Norman O. *Life Against Death: The Psychoanalytical Meaning of History.* 2nd ed. Middletown, CT: Wesleyan University Press, 1985.

Brubaker, Rogers. *The Limits of Rationality: An Essay on the Social and Moral Thought of Max Weber.* London: George Allen and Unwin, 1984.

Bruffee, Kenneth A. *Collaborative Learning: Higher Education, Interdependence, and the Authority of Knowledge.* 2nd ed. Baltimore: Johns Hopkins University Press, 1999.

Bruner, Jerome S. *Acts of Meaning.* Cambridge, MA: Harvard University Press, 1990.

Buckley, Peter, ed. *Essential Papers on Object Relations.* New York: New York University Press, 1986.

Bugeja, Michael. *Interpersonal Divide: The Search for Community in a Technological Age.* New York: Oxford University Press, 2005.

Callahan, Raymond E. *Education and the Cult of Efficiency.* Chicago: University of Chicago Press, 1964.

Campbell, Colin. *The Romantic Ethic and the Spirit of Modern Consumerism.* Oxford, UK: Blackwell, 1987.

Canetti, Elias. *Crowds and Power.* Trans. Carol Stewart. London: Gollancz, 1962.

Capra, Fritjof. *The Web of Life: A New Scientific Understanding of Living Systems.* New York: Anchor Books, 1996.

Casey, Edward S. *The Fate of Place: A Philosophical History*. Berkeley: University of California Press, 1997.

Chandler, Alfred D. *The Visible Hand: The Managerial Revolution in American Business*. Cambridge, MA: Belknap Press, 1977.

Chevallier, Raymond. *Roman Roads*. Trans. N. H. Field. London: B. T. Batsford, 1989.

Chodorow, Nancy J. *The Reproduction of Mothering: Psychoanalysis and the Sociology of Gender*. Berkeley: University of California Press, 1999.

Ciaramicoli, Arthur P., and Katherine Ketcham. *The Power of Empathy: A Practical Guide to Creating Intimacy, Self-Understanding, and Lasting Love*. New York: Dutton, 2000.

Cobb, Edith. *The Ecology of Imagination in Childhood*. Putnam, CT: Spring Publications, 1977.

Cohen, Robin. *Global Diasporas: An Introduction*. Seattle: University of Washington Press, 1997.

Cohn, Norman. *Cosmos, Chaos, and the World to Come: The Ancient Roots of Apocalyptic Faith*. New Haven: Yale Nota Bene, 1999.

Collingwood, R. G. *The Idea of Nature*. New York: Oxford University Press, 1960.

Combs, James E., and Michael W. Mansfield, eds. *Drama in Life: The Uses of Communication in Society*. New York: Hastings House, 1976.

Cottrell, Alan P. *Goethe's View of Evil and the Search for a New Image of Man in Our Time*. Edinburgh: Floris Books, 1982.

Cunningham, Hugh. *Children and Childhood in Western Society Since 1500*. 2nd ed. Harlow: Pearson, 2005.

Crystal, David. *English as a Global Language*. 2nd ed. Cambridge: Cambridge University Press, 2003.

———. *Language and the Internet*. 2nd ed. Cambridge: Cambridge University Press, 2006.

Csikszentmihalyi, Mihaly. *Flow: The Psychology of Optimal Experience*. New York: Harper and Row, 1990.

Damasio, Antonio R. *Descartes' Error: Emotion, Reason, and the Human Brain*. New York: Quill, 2000.

Darwin, Charles. *The Descent of Man*. Princeton, NJ: Princeton University Press, 1981 [1871].

Davis, Lennard J. *Enforcing Normalcy: Disability, Deafness, and the Body*. London: Verso, 1995.

Davis, Mark H. *Empathy: A Social Psychological Approach*. Boulder, CO: Westview Press, 1996.

Dean, Carolyn. *The Fragility of Empathy After the Holocaust*. Ithaca, NY: Cornell University Press, 2004.

Debeir, Jean-Claude, Jean-Paul Deléage, and Daniel Hémery. *In the Servitude of Power: Energy and Civilisation Through the Ages*. Trans. John Barzman. London: Zed Books, 1991.

de Grazia, Sebastian. *Of Time, Work, and Leisure*. Garden City, NY: Anchor Books, 1964.

de Mause, Lloyd, ed. *The History of Childhood: The Untold Story of Child Abuse*. New York: Peter Bedrick Books, 1988.

de Waal, Frans. *Primates and Philosophers: How Morality Evolved*. Ed. Stephen Macedo and Josiah Ober. Princeton, NJ: Princeton University Press, 2006.

Dods, John B. *The Philosophy of Electrical Psychology*. New York: Da Capo Press, 1982.

Donald, Merlin. *A Mind So Rare: The Evolution of Human Consciousness*. New York: Norton, 2002.

Douglas, Mary. *Purity and Danger: An Analysis of Concept of Pollution and Taboo*. New York: Routledge, 2002.

Dunbar, Robin. *Grooming, Gossip, and the Evolution of Language*. Cambridge, MA: Harvard University Press, 2002.

Dupré, Louis. *The Enlightenment and the Intellectual Foundations of Modern Culture*. New Haven: Yale University Press, 2004.

Edsall, Nicholas C. *Toward Stonewall: Homosexuality and Society in the Modern Western World*. Charlottesville: University of Virginia Press, 2003.

Ehrenfeld, David. *The Arrogance of Humanism*. Oxford: Oxford University Press, 1981.

Eisenberg, Nancy, and Paul H. Mussen. *The Roots of Prosocial Behavior in Children*. Cambridge, MA: Cambridge University Press, 1989.

Eisenstein, Elizabeth L. *The Printing Revolution in Early Modern Europe*. Cambridge, UK: Cambridge University Press, 2000.

Elgin, Duane. *Awakening Earth: Exploring the Evolution of Human Culture and Consciousness*. New York: William Morrow, 1993.

Eliade, Mircea. *The Myth of the Eternal Return: Or, Cosmos and History*. Trans. Willard R. Trask. Princeton, NJ: Princeton University Press, 1971.

Eliade, Mircea. *The Forge and the Crucible*. Trans. Stephen Corrin. 2nd ed. Chicago: University of Chicago Press, 1978.

Elias, Norbert. *The Civilizing Process: The History of Manners and State Formation and Civilization*. Trans. Edmund Jephcott. Oxford, UK: Blackwell, 1994.

Elkind, David. *The Hurried Child: Growing Up Too Fast Too Soon*. Reading, MA: Addison-Wesley, 1981.

———. *Ties That Stress: The New Family Imbalance*. Cambridge, MA: Harvard University Press, 1994.

Erdoes, Richard. *AD 1000: Living on the Brink of Apocalypse*. San Francisco: Harper and Row, 1988.

Evreinoff, Nicolas. *The Theatre in Life*. Trans. and ed. Alexander Nazaroff. New York: Benjamin Bloom, 1970.

Fairbairn, W. R. D. *Psychoanalytic Studies of the Personality*. London: Routledge, 1999.

Finsen, Lawrence, and Susan Finsen. *The Animal Rights Movement in America: From Compassion to Respect*. New York: Twayne Publishers, 1994.

Fireman, Gary D., Ted E. McVay, Jr., and Owen J. Flanagan, eds. *Narrative and Consciousness: Literature, Psychology, and the Brain*. New York: Oxford University Press, 2003.

Frank, Arthur W. *The Wounded Storyteller: Body, Illness, and Ethics*. Chicago: University of Chicago Press, 1995.

French, Marilyn. *From Eve to Dawn: A History of Women*. Vol. 1, *Origins*. Toronto: McArthur and Co., 2002.

———. *From Eve to Dawn: A History of Women*. Vol. 2, *The Masculine Mystique*. Toronto: McArthur and Co., 2002.

———. *From Eve to Dawn: A History of Women.* Vol. 3, *Infernos and Paradises.* Toronto: McArthur, 2003.

Freud, Sigmund. *Civilization and Its Discontents.* Trans. James Strachey. New York: Norton, 1961.

———. *Moses and Monotheism.* New York: Vintage Books, 1939.

———. *Three Essays on the Theory of Sexuality.* Trans. James Strachey. New York: Basic Books, 2000.

Fromm, Erich. *To Have or To Be?* New York: Continuum, 2002.

Gay, Peter. *The Enlightenment: The Science of Freedom.* New York: Norton, 1996.

Gebser, Jean. *The Ever-Present Origin.* Trans. Noel Barstad and Algis Mickunas. Athens, OH: Ohio University Press, 1985.

Gergen, Kenneth. *The Saturated Self: Dilemmas of Identity in Contemporary Life.* New York: Basic Books, 1991.

Giddens, Anthony. *The Transformation of Intimacy: Sexuality, Love and Eroticism in Modern Societies.* Cambridge, UK: Polity, 1993.

Giedion, Sigfried. *Mechanization Takes Command: A Contribution to Anonymous History.* New York: Norton, 1969.

Gilligan, Carol. *In a Different Voice: Psychological Theory and Women's Development.* Cambridge, MA: Harvard University Press, 1982.

Gimbutas, Marija. *The Civilization of the Goddess: The World of Old Europe.* Ed. Joan Marler. San Francisco: HarperSanFrancisco, 1991.

Gimpel, Jean. *The Medieval Machine: The Industrial Revolution of the Middle Ages.* New York: Penguin Books, 1976.

Gleick, James. *Faster: The Acceleration of Just About Everything.* New York: Pantheon Books, 1999.

Goffman, Erving. *The Presentation of Self in Everyday Life.* New York: Anchor Books, 1959.

Goleman, Daniel. *Social Intelligence: The New Science of Human Relationships.* New York: Bantam Books, 2006.

Goleman, Daniel, Richard Boyatzis, and Annie McKee. *The New Leaders: Transforming the Art of Leadership into the Science of Results.* London: Sphere, 2008.

Gordon, Mary. *Roots of Empathy: Changing the World Child by Child.* Toronto: Thomas Allen, 2005.

Greenspan, Stanley I., and Beryl Lieff Benderly. *The Growth of the Mind: And the Endangered Origins of Intelligence.* Reading, MA: Addison-Wesley, 1997.

Greenspan, Stanley I., and Stuart Shanker. *The First Idea: How Symbols, Language, and Intelligence Evolved from Our Primate Ancestors to Modern Humans.* Cambridge, MA: De Capo Press, 2004.

Greven, Philip. *Spare the Child: The Religious Roots of Punishment and the Psychological Impact of Physical Abuse.* New York: Vintage Books, 1992.

Groebel, Jo, and Robert A. Hinde, eds. *Aggression and War: Their Biological and Social Bases.* Cambridge, UK: Cambridge University Press, 1989.

Haber, Samuel. *Efficiency and Uplift: Scientific Management in the Progressive Era 1890–1920.* Chicago: University of Chicago Press, 1964.

Halpern, Jodi. *From Detached Concern to Empathy: Humanizing Medical Practice.* New York: Oxford University Press, 2001.

Harman, Willis. *Global Mind Change: The Promise of the* 21st *Century.* 2nd ed. Sausalito, CA: Institute of Noetic Sciences, 1998.

Harris, Sam. *The End of Faith: Religion, Terror, and the Future of Reason.* New York: Norton, 2004.

Hartigan, Richard Shelly. *The Forgotten Victim: A History of the Civilian.* Chicago: Precedent, 1982.

Hassin, Ran R., James S. Uleman, and John A. Bargh, eds. *The New Unconscious.* Oxford, UK: Oxford University Press, 2005.

Haugh, Sheila, and Tony Merry, eds. *Rogers' Therapeutic Conditions: Evolution, Theory and Practice.* Vol 2, *Empathy.* Ross-on-Wye, UK: PCCS Books, 2001.

Hauser, Marc D. *Moral Minds: How Nature Designed Our Universal Sense of Right and Wrong.* New York: HarperCollins, 2006.

Havelock, Eric A. *Preface to Plato.* Cambridge, MA: Belknap Press, 1963.

Hawken, Paul, Amory Lovins, and Hunter Lovins. *Natural Capitalism: Creating the Next Industrial Revolution.* Boston: Little Brown, 1999.

Healy, Jane M. *Failure to Connect: How Computers Affect Our Children's Minds—and What We Can Do About It.* New York: Touchstone, 1999.

Heilbroner, Robert L. *The Making of Economic Society.* Englewood Cliffs, NJ: Prentice-Hall, 1962.

Herlihy, David. *The Black Death and the Transformation of the West.* Ed. Samuel K. Cohn, Jr. Cambridge, MA: Harvard University Press, 1997.

Heywood, Colin. *A History of Childhood: Children and Childhood in the West from Medieval to Modern Times.* Cambridge, UK: Polity Press, 2001.

Hill, Annette. *Reality TV: Audiences and Popular Factual Television.* London: Routledge, 2005.

Hobbes, Thomas. *Leviathan.* Oxford, UK: Oxford University Press, 1998 [1651].

———. *The Age of Revolution: 1789–1848.* New York: Mentor, 1962.

Hobsbawm, Eric J. *The Age of Capital 1848–1875.* London: Cardinal, 1975.

———. *The Age of Empire: 1875–1914.* New York: Vintage Books, 1987.

Hochschild, Arlie R. *The Managed Heart: Commercialization of Human Feeling.* Berkeley: University of California Press, 1983.

Hoffman, Martin L. *Empathy and Moral Development: Implications for Caring and Justice.* New York: Cambridge University Press, 2000.

Holmes, Su, and Deborah Jermyn, eds. *Understanding Reality Television.* London: Routledge, 2004.

Horkheimer, Max. *Eclipse of Reason.* New York: Continuum, 1974.

Howe, Neil, and William Strauss. *Millenials Rising: The Next Great Generation.* New York: Vintage Books, 2000.

Hoyt, Robert S. *Europe in the Middle Ages.* 2nd ed. New York: Harcourt Brace and World, 1966.

Huizinga, Johan. *Homo Ludens: A Study of the Play Element in Culture.* Boston: Beacon Press, 1950.

Humphrey, Nicholas. *A History of the Mind: Evolution and the Birth of Consciousness.* New York: Simon and Schuster, 1992.

Hunt, Lynn. *Inventing Human Rights: A History.* New York: Norton, 2007.

Huntington, Samuel P. *The Clash of Civilizations and the Remaking of World Order.* New York: Simon and Schuster, 1996.

Ickes, William, ed. *Empathic Accuracy.* New York: Guilford Press, 1997.

Inglehart, Ronald, and Pippa Norris. *Rising Tide: Gender Equality and Cultural Change Around the World.* New York: Cambridge University Press, 2003.

Inglehart, Ronald, and Christian Welzel. *Modernization, Cultural Change, and Democracy: The Human Development Sequence.* New York: Cambridge University Press, 2005.

Innis, Harold A. *Empire and Communications.* Victoria, BC: Press Porcépic, 1986.

Jenkins, Philip. *The Next Christendom: The Coming of Global Christianity.* New York: Oxford University Press, 2002.

Kahler, Erich. *The Inward Turn of Narrative.* Trans. Richard Winston and Clara Winston. Princeton, NJ: Princeton University Press, 1973.

———. *Man the Measure: A New Approach to History.* Cleveland, OH: Meridian Books, 1967.

Kahn, Peter H., and Stephen R. Kellert, eds. *Children and Nature: Psychological, Sociocultural, and Evolutionary Investigations.* Cambridge, MA: MIT Press, 2002.

Kant, Immanuel. *Critique of Pure Reason.* Trans. Norton Kemp. New York: St. Martin's Press, 1963.

Karen, Robert. *Becoming Attached: First Relationships and How They Shape Our Capacity to Love.* New York: Oxford University Press, 1998.

Kasser, Tim. *The High Price of Materialism.* Cambridge, MA: MIT Press, 2002.

Kellert, Stephen R., and Edward O. Wilson, eds. *The Biophilia Hypothesis.* Washington, DC: Island Press, Shearwater Books, 1993.

Kelly, John. *The Great Mortality: An Intimate History of the Black Death, the Most Devastating Plague of All Time.* New York: HarperCollins, 2005.

Kern, Stephen. *The Culture of Time and Space: 1880–1918.* Cambridge, MA: Harvard University Press, 1983.

Khalil, Elias L., and Kenneth E. Boulding, eds. *Evolution, Order and Complexity.* London: Routledge, 1996.

Kindlon, Dan, and Michael Thompson. *Raising Cain: Protecting the Emotional Life of Boys.* New York: Ballantine Books, 2000.

Klapp, Orrin E. *Overload and Boredom: Essays on the Quality of Life in the Information Society.* New York: Greenwood Press, 1986.

Kohut, Heinz. *The Restoration of the Self.* New York: International Universities Press, 1977.

———. *The Search for the Self: Selected Writings of Heinz Kohut: 1950–1978.* Vol. 2. Ed. Paul H. Ornstein. New York: International Universities Press, 1978.

———. *Self Psychology and the Humanities: Reflections on a New Psychoanalytic Approach.* Ed. Charles B. Strozier. New York: Norton, 1985.

Kubey, Robert, and Mihaly Csikszentmihalyi. *Television and the Quality of Life: How Viewing Shapes Everyday Experience.* New York: Lawrence Erlbaum Associates, 1990.

Kurtz, Ernest, and Katherine Ketcham. *The Spirituality of Imperfection: Storytelling and the Journey to Wholeness.* New York: Bantam Books, 1994.

Kurzweil, Ray. *The Age of Spiritual Machines: When Computers Exceed Human Intelligence.* New York: Penguin Books, 2000.

———. *The Singularity Is Near: When Humans Transcend Biology.* New York: Viking, 2005.

Kyvig, David E. *Daily Life in the United States, 1920–1940: How Americans Lived Through the "Roaring Twenties" and the Great Depression*. Chicago: Ivan R. Dee, 2002.

Lakoff, George. *The Political Mind: Why You Can't Understand 21st-Century American Politics with an 18th-Century Brain*. New York: Viking, 2008.

————. *Whose Freedom? The Battle over America's Most Important Idea*. New York: Farrar, Straus and Giroux, 2006.

Lakoff, George, and Mark Johnson. *Metaphors We Live By*. Chicago: University of Chicago Press, 1980.

————. *Philosophy in the Flesh: The Embodied Mind and Its Challenge to Western Thought*. New York: Basic Books, 1999.

La Piana, George. "Foreign Groups in Rome During the First Centuries of the Empire." *Harvard Theological Review* 20, no. 4 (1927): 183–403.

Lasch, Christopher. *The Culture of Narcissim: American Life in an Age of Diminished Expectations*. New York: Warner Books, 1979.

Laszlo, Ervin. *The Systems View of the World: A Holistic Vision for Our Time*. Cresskill, NJ: Hampton Press, 1996.

Layard, Richard. *Happiness: Lessons from a New Science*. New York: Penguin Press, 2005.

Lazarus, Richard S., and Bernice N. Lazarus. *Passion and Reason: Making Sense of Our Emotions*. New York: Oxford University Press, 1994.

Lerner, Daniel. *The Passing of Traditional Society: Modernizing the Middle East*. New York: Free Press, 1958.

Lerner, Gerda. *The Creation of Patriarchy*. New York: Oxford University Press, 1986.

Lifton, Robert Jay. *Protean Self: Human Resilience in an Age of Fragmentation*. New York: Basic Books, 1993.

Linton, Simi. *Claiming Disability: Knowledge and Identity*. New York: New York University Press, 1998.

Locke, John. *Two Treatises of Government*. Whitefish, MT: Kessinger Publishing, 2004 [1690].

Locke, John L. *Why We Don't Talk to Each Other Anymore: The De-Voicing of Society*. New York: Touchstone, 1998.

Logan, Robert K. *The Alphabet Effect: The Impact of the Phonetic Alphabet on the Development of Western Civilization*. New York: William Morrow, 1986.

Longmore, Paul K. *Why I Burned My Book and Other Essays on Disability*. Philadelphia: Temple University Press, 2003.

Louv, Richard. *Last Child in the Woods: Saving Our Children from Nature-Deficit Disorder*. Chapel Hill, NC: Algonquin Books, 2005.

Lovelock, James. *The Ages of Gaia: A Biography of Our Living Earth*. New York: Norton, 1988.

————. *The Revenge of Gaia: Earth's Climate Crisis and the Fate of Humanity*. New York: Basic Books, 2006.

Lowe, Donald M. *History of Bourgeois Perception*. Chicago: University of Chicago Press, 1982.

Loye, David. *Darwin's Lost Theory of Love: A Healing Vision for the New Century*. Lincoln, NE: toExcel Press, 2000.

Lukacs, John. *Historical Consciousness: The Remembered Past*. New Brunswick, NJ: Transaction Publishers, 1994.

Macfarlane, Alan, and Gerry Martin. *Glass: A World History*. Chicago: University of Chicago Press, 2002.

Mahler, Margaret S., Fred Pine, and Anni Bergman. *The Psychological Birth of the Human Infant: Symbiosis and Individuation*. New York: Basic Books, 1975.

Mannheim, Karl. *Ideology and Utopia*. San Diego, CA: Harvest Books, 1936.

Manuel, Frank E., and Fritzie P. Manuel. *Utopian Thought in the Western World*. Cambridge, MA: Belknap Press, 1979.

———. *One-Dimensional Man*. Boston: Beacon Press, 1964.

Marcuse, Herbert. *Eros and Civilization*. Boston: Beacon Press, 1966.

———. *An Essay on Liberation*. Boston: Beacon Press, 1969.

Marris, Peter. *The Politics of Uncertainty: Attachment in Private and Public Life*. London: Routledge, 1996.

Marvin, Carolyn. *When Old Technologies Were New: Thinking About Electric Communication in the Late Nineteenth Century*. New York: Oxford University Press, 1988.

Marx, Leo. *The Machine in the Garden: Technology and the Pastoral Ideal in America*. New York: Oxford University Press, 1964.

Maslow, Abraham H. *The Psychology of Science: A Reconaissance*. South Bend, IN: Gateway Editions, 1966.

Mason, Jim. *An Unnatural Order: Why We Are Destroying the Planet and Each Other*. New York: Continuum, 1997.

Masson, Jeffrey, and Susan McCarthy. *When Elephants Weep: The Emotional Lives of Animals*. New York: Delta, 1995.

Mauss, Marcel. *The Gift: The Form and Reason for Exchange in Archaic Societies*. Trans. W. D. Halls. New York: Norton, 1990.

McLuhan, Marshall. *Understanding Media: The Extensions of Man*. New York: Signet Books, 1964.

Meeks, Wayne A. *The First Urban Christians: The Social World of the Apostle Paul*. New Haven, CT: Yale University Press, 1983.

Meyer, Marvin. *The Gospel of Thomas: The Hidden Sayings of Jesus*. San Francisco: Harper San Francisco, 1992.

Midgley, Mary. *Science as Salvation: A Modern Myth and Its Meaning*. London: Routledge, 1992.

Miller, Alice. Trans. *For Your Own Good: Hidden Cruelty in Child-Rearing and the Roots of Violence*. Hildegarde Hannum and Hunter Hannum. New York: Farrar, Straus and Giroux, 2002.

Mitchell, David T., and Sharon L. Snyder, eds. *The Body and Physical Difference: Discourses of Disability*. Ann Arbor: University of Michigan Press, 1997.

Mitchell, Stephen. *Gilgamesh*. New York: Free Press, 2004.

Montagu, Ashley. *Learning Non-Aggression: The Experience of Non-Literate Societies*. New York: Oxford University Press, 1978.

Morris, David B. *Illness and Culture in the Postmodern Age*. London: University of California Press, Ltd, 1998.

Mumford, Lewis. *The Pentagon of Power*. New York: Harvest/HBJ Book, 1964.

———. *The Pentagon of Power*, Vol. 2. New York: Harcourt Brace Jovanovich, 1970.

———. *Technics and Civilization*. New York: Harcourt Brace and World, 1962.

———. *Technics and Human Development: The Myth of the Machine*. Vol. 1. New York: Harcourt Brace Jovanovich, 1966.

———. *The Transformations of Man.* Gloucester, MA: Peter Smith, 1978.

Newberg, Andrew, Eugene D'Aquilli, and Vince Rause. *Why God Won't Go Away: Brain Science and the Biology of Belief.* New York: Ballantine Books, 2001.

Nisbett, Richard. *The Geography of Thought: How Asians and Westerners Think Differently . . . and Why.* New York: Free Press, 2003.

Noble, David F. *Forces of Production: A Social History of Industrial Automation.* New York: Oxford University Press, 1984.

———. *The Religion of Technology: The Divinity of Man and the Spirit of Invention.* New York: Knopf, 1997.

———. *A World Without Women: The Christian Clerical Culture of Western Science.* New York: Oxford University Press, 1992.

Norris, Pippa, and Ronald Inglehart. *Sacred and Secular: Religion and Politics Worldwide.* Cambridge, UK: Cambridge University Press, 2004.

Nowotny, Helga. *Time: The Modern and Postmodern Experience.* London: Polity Press, 1994.

Nussbaum, Martha C. *Hiding from Humanity: Disgust, Shame, and the Law.* Princeton, NJ: Princeton University Press, 2004.

———. *Upheavals of Thought: The Intelligence of Emotions.* Cambridge, UK: Cambridge University Press, 2001.

Nye, David E. *Electrifying America: Social Meanings of a New Technology, 1880–1940.* Cambridge, MA: MIT Press, 1991.

Odum, Howard T. *Environment, Power, and Society.* New York: Wiley-Interscience, 1971.

Oliner, Samuel P., and Pearl M. Oliner. *The Altruistic Personality: Rescuers of Jews in Nazi Europe.* New York: Free Press, 1988.

Ong, Walter J. *Orality and Literacy: The Technologizing of the Word.* London: Routledge, 2002.

Ornstein, Paul H., ed. *The Search for the Self: Selected Writings of Heinz Kohut: 1950–1978.* Vol. 2. New York: International Universities Press, 1978.

Ornstein, Robert. *The Right Mind: Making Sense of the Hemispheres.* New York: Harcourt Brace and Co., 1997.

Ornstein, Robert E., and Paul R. Ehrlich. *New World, New Mind.* New York: Doubleday, 1989.

Otto, Rudolf. *The Idea of the Holy.* London: Oxford University Press, 1923.

Pagels, Elaine H. *The Gnostic Gospels.* New York: Vintage Books, 1989.

———. *The Origins of Satan.* New York: Vintage Books, 1995.

Panksepp, Jaak. *Affective Neuroscience: The Foundations of Human and Animal Emotions.* New York: Oxford University Press, 2004.

Passmore, John A. *The Perfectability of Man.* 3rd ed. Indianapolis: Liberty Fund, 2000.

Patterson, Orlando. *Slavery and Social Death: A Comparative Study.* Cambridge, MA: Harvard University Press, 1982.

Perinbanayagam, R. S. *Signifying Acts: Structure and Meaning in Everyday Life.* Carbondale, IL: Southern Illinois Press, 1985.

Persinger, Michael A. *Neuropsychological Bases of God Beliefs.* New York: Praeger, 1987.

Polanyi, Karl. *The Great Transformation.* Boston: Beacon Press, 1944.

Polyani, Michael. *Personal Knowledge: Towards a Post-Critical Philosophy.* London: Routledge, 1998.

Postman, Neil. *The Disappearance of Childhood*. New York: Vintage Books, 1994.

Randall, John H., Jr. *The Making of the Modern Mind: A Survey of the Intellectual Background of the Present Age*. Cambridge, MA: Houghton Mifflin Company, 1940.

Rank, Otto. *Beyond Psychology*. New York: Dover Publications, 1941.

Reed, Edward S. *The Necessity of Experience*. New Haven, CT: Yale University Press, 1996.

——. *From Soul to Mind: The Emergence of Psychology from Erasmus Darwin to William James*. New Haven, CT: Yale University Press, 1997.

Regan, Tom. *The Case for Animal Rights*. Berkeley: University of California Press, 2004.

Restak, Richard. *The Naked Brain: How the Emerging Neurosociety Is Changing How We Live, Work, and Love*. New York: Harmony Books, 2006.

Rheingold, Howard. *Smart Mobs: The Next Social Revolution*. Cambridge, MA: Basic Books, 2002.

Richardson, Angélique, and Chris Willis, eds. *The New Woman in Fiction and in Fact: Fin-de-Siècle Feminisms*. New York: Palgrave MacMillan, 2002.

Rieff, Philip. *Triumph of the Therapeutic: Uses of Faith After Freud*. Chicago: University of Chicago Press, 1966.

Rifkin, Jeremy. *The Age of Access*. New York: Tarcher/Putnam, 2000.

——. *Biosphere Politics*. New York: Crown Publishers, 1991.

——. *The Biotech Century: Harnessing the Gene and Remaking the World*. New York: Tarcher/Putnam, 1998.

——. *The End of Work*. New York: Tarcher/Putnam, 1995.

——. *Entropy*. New York: Bantam Books, 1981.

——. *The European Dream*. New York: Tarcher/Penguin, 2004.

——. *The Hydrogen Economy*. New York: Tarcher/Putnam, 2002.

——. *Time Wars: The Primary Conflict in Human History*. New York: Henry Holt and Co., 1987.

Roszak, Theodore. *The Voice of the Earth: An Exploration of Ecopsychology*. Grand Rapids, MI: Phanes Press, 2001.

——. *The Making of a Counter Culture: Reflections on the Technocratic Society and Its Youthful Opposition*. Berkeley: University of California Press, 1995.

Rowan, John. *Ordinary Ecstasy: The Dialectics of Humanistic Psychology*. 3rd ed. Hove, UK: Brunner Routledge, 2001.

Rowan, John, and Mick Cooper, eds. *The Plural Self: Multiplicity in Everyday Life*. London: Sage Publications, 1999.

Salomon, Gavriel, ed. *Distributed Cognitions: Psychological and Educational Considerations*. Cambridge, UK: Cambridge University Press, 1993.

Sanderson, Stephen K., ed. *Civilizations and World Systems: Studying World-Historical Change*. Walnut Creek, CA: AltaMira Press, 1995.

Santillana, Giorgio de. *The Age of Adventure: The Renaissance Philosophers*. New York: Mentor Books, 1956.

Sartre, Jean-Paul. *The Writings of Jean-Paul Sartre*. Vol. 2. Evanston, IL: Northwestern University Press, 1974.

Saul, John R. *Voltaire's Bastards: The Dictatorship of Reason in the West*. New York: Vintage Books, 1992.

Scholes, Robert E., James Phelan, and Robert L. Kellogg. *The Nature of Narrative.* Oxford, UK: Oxford University Press, 2006.

Schopenhauer, Arthur. *On the Basis of Morality.* Providence, RI: Berghahn Books, 1995.

Schor, Juliet B. *Born to Buy: The Commercialized Child and the New Consumer Culture.* New York: Scribner, 2004.

Schumann, John H. *The Neurobiology of Affect in Language.* Malden, MA: Blackwell, 1997.

Schütze, Alfred. *The Enigma of Evil.* Edinburgh: Floris Books, 1978.

Schwartz, Jeffrey M., and Sharon Begley. *The Mind and the Brain: Neuroplasticity and the Power of Mental Force.* New York: ReganBooks, 2002.

Selye, Hans. *The Stress of Life.* New York: McGraw-Hill, 1976.

Sennett, Richard. *Flesh and Stone: The Body and the City in Western Civilization.* New York: Norton, 1994.

Serpell, James. *In the Company of Animals: A Study of Human-Animal Relationships.* Cambridge, UK: Cambridge University Press, 1996.

Shepard, Paul. *Nature and Madness.* Athens: University of Georgia Press, 1998.

———. *The Others: How Animals Made Us Human.* Washington, DC: Island Press, 1996.

Shorter, Edward. *The Making of the Modern Family.* New York: Basic Books, 1977.

Siegel, Daniel J. *The Developing Mind: How Relationships and the Brain Interact to Shape Who We Are.* New York: Guilford Press, 1999.

———. *The Mindful Brain: Reflection and Attunement in the Cultivation of Well-Being.* New York: Norton, 2007.

Simmel, Georg. *The Philosophy of Money.* Trans. Tom Bottomore and David Frisby. London: Routledge, 1990.

Singer, Peter. *Animal Liberation.* New York: Avon Books, 1990.

———. *A Darwinian Left: Politics, Evolution and Cooperation.* New Haven, CT: Yale University Press, 1999.

Skolimowski, Henryk. *The Participatory Mind: A New Theory of Knowledge and of the Universe.* London: Penguin, 1994.

Smith, Adam. *An Inquiry into the Nature and Causes of the Wealth of Nations.* Ed. Edwin Cannan, London: Methuen, 1961.

Sober, Elliott, and David S. Wilson. *Unto Others: The Evolution and Psychology of Unselfish Behavior.* Cambridge, MA: Harvard University Press, 1998.

Soddy, Frederick. *Matter and Energy.* New York: Holt, 1912.

Sperber, Jonathan. *The European Revolutions, 1848–1851.* 2nd ed. Cambridge, UK: Cambridge University Press, 2005.

Steiner, George. *In Bluebeard's Castle: Some Notes Towards the Re-definition of Culture.* London: Faber and Faber, 1971.

Stern, Daniel N. *The Present Moment in Psychotherapy and Everyday Life.* New York: Norton, 2004.

Stiker, Henri-Jacques. *A History of Disability.* Trans. William Sayers. Ann Arbor, MI: University of Michigan Press, 1999.

Stone, Lawrence. *The Family, Sex and Marriage in England 1500–1800.* New York: Harper Torchbooks, 1977.

Strang, Heather. *Repair or Revenge: Victims and Restorative Justice.* Oxford: Clarendon Press, 2002.

Surowiecki, James. *The Wisdom of Crowds: Why the Many Are Smarter Than the Few and How Collective Wisdom Shapes Business, Economies, Societies, and Nations.* New York: Doubleday, 2004.

Suttie, Ian D. *The Origins of Love and Hate.* New York: Julian Press, 1952.

Svenson, Ola, and A. J. Maule, eds. *Time Pressure and Stress in Human Judgment and Decision Making.* New York: Plenum Press, 1993.

Tainter, Joseph A. *The Collapse of Complex Societies.* Cambridge, UK: Cambridge University Press, 1988.

Tapscott, Don, and Anthony D. Williams. *Wikinomics: How Mass Collaboration Changes Everything.* New York: Penguin, 2006.

Taylor, Charles. *Sources of the Self: The Making of the Modern Identity.* Cambridge, MA: Harvard University Press, 1989.

Theobald, William F., ed. *Global Tourism.* 3rd ed. Amsterdam: Elsevier, 2005.

Thomas, Keith. *Religion and the Decline of Magic.* London: Penguin, 1971.

Thomas, William L., ed. *Man's Role in Changing the Face of the Earth.* Chicago: University of Chicago Press, 1956.

Thomson, Rosemarie, ed. *Freakery: Cultural Spectacles of the Extraordinary Body.* New York: New York University Press, 1996.

Tichi, Cecelia. *Shifting Gears: Technology, Literature, Culture in Modernist America.* Chapel Hill: University of North Carolina Press, 1987.

Tolman, Charles W., Frances Cherry, René van Hezewijk, and Ian Lubek, eds. *Problems of Theoretical Psychology.* Toronto: Captus University Publications, 1996.

Toulmin, Stephen. *Cosmopolis: The Hidden Agenda of Modernity.* Chicago: University of Chicago Press, 1992.

Trilling, Lionel. *Sincerity and Authenticity.* Cambridge, MA: Harvard University Press, 1972.

Tuan, Yi-Fu. *Dominance and Affection: The Making of Pets.* New Haven, CT: Yale University Press, 1984.

———. *Passing Strange and Wonderful.* Washington, DC: Island Press, 1993.

Turner, Jonathan H., and Jan E. Stets. *The Sociology of Emotions.* Cambridge, UK: Cambridge University Press, 2005.

Turner, Victor. *From Ritual to Theater: The Human Seriousness of Play.* New York: Performing Arts Journal Publications, 1982.

———. *The Anthropology of Performance.* New York: Performing Arts Journal Publications, 1986.

Twenge, Jean M. *Generation Me: Why Today's Young Americans Are More Confident, Assertive, Entitled—and More Miserable Than Ever Before.* New York: Free Press, 2006.

Urgo, Jospeh R. *In the Age of Distraction.* Jackson, MS: University Press of Mississippi, 2000.

Varela, Francisco J., Evan Thompson, and Eleanor Rosch. *The Embodied Mind: Cognitive Science and Human Experience.* Cambridge, MA: MIT Press, 1991.

Vertovec, Steven, and Robin Cohen, eds. *Conceiving Cosmopolitanism: Theory, Context, and Practice.* Oxford, UK: Oxford University Press, 2002.

Vetlesen, Arne J. *Perception, Empathy, and Judgment: An Inquiry into the Preconditions of Moral Performance.* University Park: Pennsylvania State University Press, 1994.

Volf, Miroslav. *Exclusion and Embrace: A Theological Exploration of Identity, Otherness, and Reconciliation.* Nashville, TN: Abingdon Press, 1996.

Watson, Lyall. *Dark Nature: A Natural History of Evil*. New York: HarperCollins, 1995.

Weber, Max. *The Protestant Ethic and the Spirit of Capitalism*. New York: Charles Scribner's Sons, 1958.

Weber, Steve. *The Success of Open Source*. Cambridge, MA: Harvard University Press, 2004.

Weintraub, Karl J. *The Value of the Individual: Self and Circumstance in Autobiography*. Chicago: University of Chicago Press, 1978.

Weintraub, Stanley. *Silent Night: The Story of the World War I Christmas Truce*. New York: Simon and Schuster, 2001.

White, Leslie A. *The Evolution of Culture: The Development of Civilization to the Fall of Rome*. Walnut Creek, CA: Left Coast Press, 2007.

White, Lynn, Jr. *Medieval Technology and Social Change*. London: Oxford University Press, 1962.

Wiener, Norbert. *The Human Use of Human Beings: Cybernetics and Society*. New York: Da Capo Press, 1950.

Wilber, Ken. *Up from Eden: A Transpersonal View of Human Evolution*. Wheaton, IL: Quest Books, 1996.

Williams, Kipling D. *Ostracism: The Power of Silence*. New York: Guilford Press, 2001.

Wilson, Edward O. *Biophilia*. Cambridge, MA: Harvard University Press, 1984.

Wilson, Frank R. *The Hand: How Its Use Shapes the Brain, Language, and Human Culture*. New York: Vintage Books, 1998.

Winn, Marie. *The Plug-In Drug: Television, Computers, and Family Life*. New York: Penguin, 2002.

Winnicott, D. W. *Human Nature*. London: Routledge, 1988.

——. *Playing and Reality*. London: Routledge, 2005.

Winograd, Morley, and Michael D. Hais. *Millennial Makeover: MySpace, YouTube, and The Future of American Politics*. Piscataway, NJ: Rutgers University Press, 2008.

Wise, Steven M., and Jane Goodall. *Rattling the Cage: Toward Legal Rights for Animals*. Cambridge, MA: Perseus Publishing, 2000.

Wittfogel, Karl A. *Oriental Despotism: A Comparative Study of Total Power*. New York: Vintage Books, 1981.

Wright, Robert. *Nonzero: The Logic of Human Destiny*. New York: Vintage Books, 2000.

Zajonc, Arthur. *Catching the Light: The Entwined History of Light and Mind*. New York: Bantam Books, 1993.

Zeitz, Joshua. *Flapper: A Madcap Story of Sex, Style, Celebrity, and the Women Who Made America Modern*. New York: Three Rivers Press, 2006.

INDEX

ABOUT THE AUTHOR

One of the most popular social thinkers of our time, JEREMY RIFKIN is the bestselling author of books including *The European Dream, The Hydrogen Economy, The End of Work, The Biotech Century,* and *The Age of Access.* His books have been translated into more than thirty languages. Rifkin is an adviser to the European Union and heads of state around the world. He is a senior lecturer at the Wharton School's Executive Education Program at the University of Pennsylvania, where he instructs CEOs and corporate management on new trends in science, technology, the economy, and society. Rifkin is the president of the Foundation on Economic Trends in Washington, D.C.